THE BEST OF

AMERICA'S TEST KITCHEN

THE YEAR'S BEST RECIPES,
EQUIPMENT REVIEWS, AND TASTINGS

2016

BY THE EDITORS AT
AMERICA'S TEST KITCHEN

AMERICA'S TEST KITCHEN
17 Station Street, Brookline, MA 02445

THE BEST OF AMERICA'S TEST KITCHEN 2016
The Year's Best Recipes, Equipment Reviews, and Tastings

1st Edition

Hardcover: US $35.00 / $40.00 CAN
ISBN: 978-1-940352-34-3
ISSN: 1940-3925

Manufactured in the United States of America

10 9 8 7 6 5 4 3 2 1

Distributed by Penguin Random House Publisher Services
Tel: 800-733-3000

EDITORIAL DIRECTOR: Jack Bishop
EDITORIAL DIRECTOR, BOOKS: Elizabeth Carduff
EXECUTIVE EDITOR: Lori Galvin
ASSISTANT EDITOR: Rachel Greenhaus
EDITORIAL ASSISTANTS: Kate Ander and Samantha Ronan
DESIGN DIRECTOR: Greg Galvan
ART DIRECTOR: Carole Goodman
DEPUTY ART DIRECTOR: Taylor Argenzio
DESIGNERS: Allison Boales and Jen Kanavos Hoffman
PHOTOGRAPHY DIRECTOR: Julie Cote
FRONT COVER PHOTOGRAPH: Keller + Keller
ASSOCIATE ART DIRECTOR, PHOTOGRAPHY: Steve Klise
STAFF PHOTOGRAPHER: Daniel J. van Ackere
ADDITIONAL PHOTOGRAPHY: Carl Tremblay
FOOD STYLING: Catrine Kelty and Marie Piraino
PHOTOSHOOT KITCHEN TEAM:
    ASSOCIATE EDITOR: Chris O'Connor
    TEST COOK: Daniel Cellucci
    ASSISTANT TEST COOK: Matthew Fairman
ILLUSTRATIONS: John Burgoyne and Jay Layman
PRODUCTION DIRECTOR: Guy Rochford
SENIOR PRODUCTION MANAGER: Jessica Quirk
PRODUCTION MANAGER: Christine Walsh
PROJECT MANAGER: Britt Dresser
IMAGING MANAGER: Lauren Robbins
PRODUCTION AND IMAGING SPECIALISTS: Heather Dube, Sean MacDonald, Dennis Noble, and Jessica Voas
COPYEDITOR: Cheryl Redmond
PROOFREADER: Amanda Poulsen Dix
INDEXER: Elizabeth Parson

PICTURED ON FRONT COVER: Raspberry Charlotte (page 247)

CONTENTS

STARTERS AND SALADS

PIMENTO CHEESE

PIMENTO CHEESE

✓ **WHY THIS RECIPE WORKS:** Equally at home with a sleeve of saltines or melted on a burger or a grilled cheese sandwich, pimento cheese is a flavorful spread of cheddar cheese, mayonnaise, and chopped pimentos. For our version, we used sharp cheddar for its moderately intense flavor and creamy consistency (extra-sharp cheddar tends to be more crumbly) and shredded it with both the large and small holes of a box grater to give the cheese a cohesive yet chunky consistency. A couple tablespoons of cream cheese kept the mixture spreadable, even right out of the fridge, and a ratio of ⅔ cup mayo to 1 pound cheese added a tangy punch and creamy texture. Some Worcestershire and lemon juice added brightness and depth without overpowering the cheese.

As Southern comfort foods go, pimento cheese is right up there with fried green tomatoes and ham biscuits. Except it's not really Southern at all, according to food historian Robert Moss. Pimento cheese, he says, has roots in New York. In the late 19th century, cream cheese (produced in New York state) and pimentos (imported from Spain) were new to the American marketplace. Before long, consumers were combining them to spread on sandwiches. In 1908, the first published recipe for pimento cheese appeared in *Good Housekeeping*. By 1910, prepared pimento cheese was on store shelves.

So why is pimento cheese so closely associated with the South? "I've never been fully able to answer this," Moss told me. "A lot of it has to do with the Southern tradition of bringing dips and spreads to community gatherings. People would compete with each other to have the best."

Devotees have strongly held beliefs about what belongs in pimento cheese, but most will agree on cheddar cheese, mayonnaise, drained and diced pimentos, and cayenne or a splash of hot sauce. Other often-used components include cream cheese, pickles, olive juice, and grated onion.

Today, the most iconic version of pimento cheese may be the one served at the Augusta National Golf Club in Georgia. I mail-ordered a tub from the local WifeSaver restaurant that used to supply it to the golf club and whipped up a few more recipes claiming to be "the best pimento cheese ever" for a five-way taste test. (The WifeSaver version was passable but not great.)

The more popular versions had a chunky, homespun quality, so I quickly determined that the food processor, which many recipes employ, wasn't the way to go—the processed ingredients had the consistency of whipped cream cheese. Instead, I'd mix by hand to get the pebbly spread I was looking for.

After settling on the type of cheese to pair with the cream cheese (combinations of Colby and Monterey Jack paled in comparison with 100 percent sharp yellow cheddar), I found that ⅔ cup mayonnaise to 1 pound grated cheese was a balanced ratio for flavor and the best spreadable texture.

To round out the flavor, I added just a teaspoon each of lemon juice and Worcestershire sauce and ¼ teaspoon of cayenne for some gentle heat. I spread some on a cracker for a final test . . . and experienced a sudden rise in popularity in the test kitchen. If the true test of pimento cheese is how it brings people together, then I think I have a winner on my hands.

—CHRISTIE MORRISON, *Cook's Country*

Pimento Cheese

MAKES ABOUT 3 CUPS

You will need one 4-ounce jar of pimentos for this recipe. Yellow cheddar cheese is traditional, but you can substitute white cheddar cheese. Use the pimento cheese as a sandwich spread or serve it with crackers or crudités.

- ⅔ cup mayonnaise
- 2 tablespoons cream cheese, softened
- 1 teaspoon lemon juice
- 1 teaspoon Worcestershire sauce
- ¼ teaspoon cayenne pepper
- 1 pound yellow sharp cheddar cheese
- ⅓ cup pimentos, patted dry and minced

1. Whisk mayonnaise, cream cheese, lemon juice, Worcestershire, and cayenne together in large bowl.

2. Shred 8 ounces cheddar on large holes of box grater. Shred remaining 8 ounces cheddar on small holes of box grater. Stir pimentos and all cheddar into mayonnaise mixture until thoroughly combined. Serve. (Pimento cheese will keep refrigerated for at least 1 week.)

VARIATION

Smoked Pimento Cheese

Substitute 8 ounces smoked cheddar cheese, shredded on small holes of box grater, for finely shredded sharp cheddar.

PUMPKIN SEED DIP

✔ **WHY THIS RECIPE WORKS:** This sweet and spicy hummus-like dip doesn't hail from the Middle East, but from Mexico. It's made from toasted pumpkin seeds, tomatoes, and habanero chiles. We used unhulled pumpkin seeds, which are still encased in their white shells (or hulls), for best flavor. However, unhulled pumpkin seeds are almost always sold roasted and salted; to avoid an inedibly salty dip, we rinsed off the salt before we processed the seeds in the blender, which broke down the hulls more thoroughly than a food processor. And to bring out their nutty flavor further, we roasted the seeds before processing them with roasted tomatoes, onions, habanero, and lime juice.

Every year as the leaves change, pumpkin-flavored recipes pop up in almost every kitchen. The flesh of the pumpkin gets a lot of attention, but I was determined to give the underappreciated seeds a place on the table. Turns out, the Mayans were already about 500 years ahead of me.

Pumpkin seed dip is native to Mayan cuisine in the Yucatán peninsula, where it's known as *sikil pak*. Unhulled pumpkin seeds, tomatoes, and habanero chiles are ground by hand using a mortar and pestle, giving the dip a hummus-like texture and slightly spicy taste just as delicious as better-known options like guacamole and salsa.

Because pepitas, hulled pumpkin seeds, are readily available at most grocery stores, I used them in my first round of testing. The flat, dark green seeds were subtly sweet and nutty, but the resulting mixture was rich and fatty, completely masking the bright heat of the habanero chile. I went back to the more traditional unhulled seeds. The fibrous shell helped to break up the fattiness and gave the dip a surprisingly spicy taste—the mild hull allowing the additional spices to come through. But the salted seeds made the dip too salty to eat. I seriously needed to fix the sodium level before breaking out the chips.

Unsalted seeds were hard to find, so I decided to make the recipe work with the salted variety. The solution was surprisingly simple: By rinsing the seeds before roasting, I was able to control the amount of salt in the recipe. I dried the seeds and toasted them in a hot oven until they turned a rich, golden color. Perfectly seasoned, the seeds were ready to be processed into the dip.

Next, I moved on to the other ingredients. Habanero chile is a traditional choice, and its fruity taste went a long way in this dip. It stayed. Tomatoes, though, needed an extra boost to achieve the rich flavor I wanted and avoid a watery mess. The oven was already warm from roasting the pumpkin seeds, so I fired up the broiler and roasted the tomatoes to concentrate their savory aspect. The resulting flavor was deep and a little smoky—the ideal complement to the spicy pepper.

With the flavor right where I wanted it, I turned to the texture. I wanted something smooth and creamy, but so far in the testing the consistency had been chunky and rough. I didn't want to spend the time it takes to crush everything by hand, so I pulled out the food processor. The resulting texture was OK, but nothing to write home about. It wasn't until I tried out the blender that things started to come together.

The dip from the blender had the smooth consistency I had wanted, but the richness still had a ways to go. Although not traditional to the Yucatán region, olive oil was the final addition to the ingredient list. By emulsifying the olive oil with the rest of the mixture, I finally had a dip that could bring pumpkin season all year round.

—DANIELLE DESIATO, *America's Test Kitchen Books*

Pumpkin Seed Dip

MAKES ABOUT 3 CUPS

If using unsalted pumpkin seeds, you can skip the rinsing and drying in step 1 and go directly to toasting. Serve with Homemade Fried Tortilla Chips or Homemade Baked Tortilla Chips (recipes follow).

1½ cups roasted, unhulled pumpkin seeds

1 pound tomatoes, cored and halved

¼ cup extra-virgin olive oil

1 onion, chopped

2 tablespoons lime juice

1 habanero chile, stemmed, seeded, and chopped

Salt and pepper

2 ounces queso fresco, crumbled (½ cup)

2 tablespoons chopped fresh cilantro

1. Adjust 1 oven rack to middle position and second rack 6 inches from broiler element. Heat oven to 400 degrees. Rinse pumpkin seeds under warm water and dry thoroughly. Spread seeds on rimmed baking sheet, place sheet on lower rack, and toast seeds until golden brown, stirring occasionally, 12 to 15 minutes. Set aside to cool slightly and heat broiler.

2. Line second rimmed baking sheet with aluminum foil. Toss tomatoes with 1 tablespoon oil and arrange cut side down on prepared sheet. Place sheet on upper rack and broil until tomatoes are spotty brown, 7 to 10 minutes. Transfer tomatoes to blender and let cool completely.

3. Add onion, lime juice, habanero, pumpkin seeds, and remaining 3 tablespoons oil to blender and process until smooth, about 1 minute, scraping down sides of blender as needed. Transfer dip to serving bowl and refrigerate until completely chilled, at least 2 hours or up to 24 hours. Season with salt and pepper to taste. Sprinkle with queso fresco and cilantro before serving.

Homemade Fried Tortilla Chips
MAKES 4 OUNCES; SERVES 4

We prefer the flavor of peanut oil when deep frying, but vegetable or corn oil will also work. We like the larger crystal size of kosher salt here because it's easy to sprinkle evenly over the chips and its small crunch is a nice addition. The recipe can be doubled; be sure to fry the chips in four batches.

8 (6-inch) corn tortillas

5 cups peanut oil

Kosher salt

1. Cut each tortilla into 6 wedges. Line 2 baking sheets with several layers of paper towels. Heat oil in Dutch oven over medium-high heat to 350 degrees.

2. Add half of tortillas and fry until golden and crisp around edges, 2 to 4 minutes. Transfer fried chips to prepared sheet, sprinkle lightly with salt, and let cool. Repeat with remaining tortillas. Serve. (Cooled chips can be stored at room temperature for up to 4 days.)

Homemade Baked Tortilla Chips
MAKES 2½ OUNCES; SERVES 2 TO 3

You can substitute flour tortillas for the corn tortillas if desired. Flour tortillas come in a variety of sizes; if using tortillas larger than 6 inches, you will need fewer of them and will be able to cut more wedges out of each.

5 (6-inch) corn tortillas

Vegetable oil spray

Kosher salt

1. Adjust oven rack to middle position and heat oven to 350 degrees. Spray both sides of tortillas liberally with oil spray, then cut each tortilla into 6 wedges. Season with salt and spread into single layer on baking sheet.

2. Bake tortillas, stirring occasionally, until golden and crisp, 15 to 20 minutes. Remove chips from oven and let cool before serving. (Cooled chips can be stored at room temperature for up to 4 days.)

NOTES FROM THE TEST KITCHEN

TOASTING PUMPKIN SEEDS

1. If salted, rinse pumpkin seeds, dry thoroughly, and spread on rimmed baking sheet.

2. Toast seeds in 400-degree oven until golden brown, 12 to 15 minutes.

TOMATILLO SALSA

✓ WHY THIS RECIPE WORKS: Most tomatillo salsa recipes call for cooking the tomatillos to soften the fruit's acidic flavor. But we found that charring just half under the broiler and leaving the other half raw produced a fresh, moderately tangy flavor and slightly chunky texture. Fresh chiles, cilantro, garlic, onion, and lime juice rounded out the flavors. This salsa comes together easily in the food processor and can be served with chips or as an accompaniment to simply prepared chicken or fish.

In Mexico and the Southwest, the tomatillo—a small, green, tomato-like fruit with a thin, papery husk and tangy, juicy flesh—is widely used, particularly in salsa. The bright-tasting sauce is scooped up with tortilla chips or served as an accompaniment to everything from chicken to fish to pork. It shares many of the ingredients of its raw-tomato sibling, salsa cruda—fresh green chiles, onion, garlic, lime juice, and cilantro—but the tomatillos are often cooked to soften their crunch. Cooking also mellows the abundant citric acid in the fruit.

I jotted down a wish list for my ideal version of tomatillo salsa. Fire-roasted tomatillo salsas are commonplace, but I had in mind a superquick indoor recipe. I also wanted to highlight the unique lemony-herbal flavor of tomatillos. Finally, the salsa would have to have enough body to hold up nicely on a tortilla chip.

After husking several pounds of tomatillos and rinsing off the sticky material that coats their skin, I got to work. Before investigating cooking techniques, I tried an oddball approach, buzzing raw tomatillos in the food processor with some placeholder aromatics and seasonings. Unsurprisingly, this uncooked salsa left a lot to be desired; it was crunchy, with an astringent, mouth-puckeringly sour taste.

The fruit would have to be cooked, but by what method? I had high hopes for pan-roasting the tomatillos on the stovetop, but by the time the fruit was tender, the skin had turned leathery and tough. Another approach, processing all the ingredients (for now I was using just tomatillos, onion, and chiles) and then simmering the concoction, produced a sludge that could have come from a jar. Boiling the fruit prior to processing offered clean flavor but also a drawback: Whole tomatillos cooked unevenly as they bobbed in the bubbling water, and halving the fruit before boiling only exacerbated their already watery consistency.

Broiling, on the other hand, was a real winner. All it required was tossing the whole husked and rinsed tomatillos in vegetable oil and placing them under the broiler (I arranged them on a foil-lined baking sheet for easy cleanup) until they turned spotty brown. The blazing heat drove off some of the watery liquid in the tomatillos, producing a salsa with a thicker texture and a more concentrated taste.

This was good progress, but the flavor of the salsa was still lackluster. I tried broiling the onions and chiles along with the tomatillos, but this contributed an overcooked taste. Left raw, the aromatics had a fresh, pungent bite. Still, something was missing. I recalled how I'd salvaged some of the less desirable salsas left over from my initial tests by mixing them with the tastier versions. One particular pairing came to mind. The raw salsa that wasn't very palatable on its own actually tasted pretty good when blended with one of the cooked salsas.

That sparked an idea: What if I left some of the tomatillos raw? I broiled half of the tomatillos and left the other half uncooked and then gave them a few quick pulses together in the food processor along with the other ingredients. It turned out to be a good move: The cooked tomatillos broke down into a thick, juicy base, while the uncooked tomatillos, onion, and chile provided a refreshingly crunchy, chunky foil.

With the base of the recipe solidified, I adjusted the remaining ingredients. White onion contributed a relatively mellow flavor that melded well with the tomatillos whereas yellow and red onion were a little too sharp; scallions were too grassy. A single clove of garlic was enough to add depth without imparting sting; ½ cup of chopped cilantro provided fresh, herbal notes; and 2 tablespoons of lime juice provided a measure of acidity to complement the tart tomatillos.

As for the chile component, I compared two of the most commonly available fresh green chiles: jalapeño and serrano. Side by side, it was difficult to tell a difference between salsas containing either one, so in the end, I elected to go with the slightly more widely available jalapeño, seeding it and giving the option to add the seeds (most of the heat resides in the ribs and seeds) back to the finished salsa to reach a desired level of spiciness.

Finally, because tomatillos vary in tartness, I seasoned the salsa to taste with a sprinkle of sugar in addition to the usual salt. I also stirred in a couple of

TOMATILLO SALSA

teaspoons of extra-virgin olive oil to round out all the flavors and give the dip a little more body.

With a big bowl of tortilla chips at the ready, I dug in. A condiment this fresh-tasting and herbaceous meant there was no reason that tomatillo salsa would ever have to take a back seat to red salsa again.

—SANDRA WU, *Cook's Illustrated*

Tomatillo Salsa

MAKES 2 CUPS

This salsa can be served with chips (see our homemade recipes on page 5) or as an accompaniment for pork, chicken, or fish. For a spicier salsa, reserve and add the jalapeño seeds.

1 pound tomatillos, husks and stems removed, rinsed well, and dried

1 teaspoon vegetable oil

1 small white onion, chopped

1 jalapeño chile, stemmed, halved, and seeded

½ cup fresh cilantro leaves

2 tablespoons lime juice

1 garlic clove, minced

Salt

2 teaspoons extra-virgin olive oil

Sugar

1. Adjust oven rack 6 inches from broiler element and heat broiler. Line rimmed baking sheet with aluminum foil. Toss half of tomatillos with vegetable oil and transfer to prepared sheet. Broil until tomatillos are spotty brown and skins begin to burst, 7 to 10 minutes. Transfer tomatillos to food processor and let cool completely.

2. Halve remaining tomatillos and add to food processor with broiled tomatillos. Add onion, jalapeño, cilantro, lime juice, garlic, and ¼ teaspoon salt. Pulse until slightly chunky, 16 to 18 pulses. Transfer to salsa bowl and let stand at room temperature for 15 minutes. Stir in olive oil and season with salt and sugar to taste. Serve.

NOTES FROM THE TEST KITCHEN

TOMATILLO PRIMER

When shopping for tomatillos, choose those of a similar size so they will cook evenly. Look for firm specimens that boast bright green skin—a yellow color indicates that the flesh is overripe and will taste sweet, not tangy. A light green, flexible, unblemished husk is also desirable; a brown hue and a dry, papery texture indicate overripeness. Finally, the tomatillo should completely fill out its husk (the husk should not balloon away from the fruit). Remove the inedible husk just before cooking the tomatillo and then use cool water to rinse off the sticky, resinous material covering the skin (it serves to protect the fruit from bugs).

PREPARING TOMATILLOS FOR SALSA

1. Pull papery husks and stems off of tomatillos; discard.

2. Rinse tomatillos in colander to rid them of sticky residue from husks and dry.

3. Broil half of tomatillos until skins are spotty brown, leaving other half raw to add to salsa later.

TOMATO AND BURRATA SALAD WITH PANGRATTATO

🗸 **WHY THIS RECIPE WORKS:** For a decadent take on traditional Caprese salad, we turned to burrata, a fresh, ultra-rich mozzarella in a subtle brine. This rich cheese, however, overwhelmed the other flavors, while the juice from the fresh tomatoes diluted the burrata's creamy liquid. To concentrate the bright, summery flavor of the tomatoes and extract some of their liquid, we salted the tomato slices and halved cherry tomatoes and let them sit for 30 minutes to draw out their watery juices. Next we tossed the tomatoes and some basil in a dressing made from shallot, olive oil, and white balsamic vinegar, which tastes crisper than standard balsamic vinegar. Finally, to marry the flavors of the tomatoes and burrata, we sprinkled the salad with garlicky bread crumbs to soak up the remaining liquids and add some crunch.

Italy is famous for *insalata caprese*, a simple dish highlighting fresh mozzarella, ripe tomatoes, and fragrant basil. But I wondered if I could amp up this standard salad by getting creative with the ingredients. Enter burrata.

Burrata is a deluxe version of fresh mozzarella in which the supple cheese is bound around a filling of cream and bits of more cheese. It comes packed in a light brine. When burrata is sliced, its flavorful filling spills out, which means that it is best served fresh. With this in mind, I wanted to create a salad in which the cheese could star alongside summer's freshest tomatoes for a dish that would be served immediately after it was assembled.

I quickly realized that tomatoes, basil, and good extra-virgin olive oil, the traditional ingredients of a Caprese salad, weren't quite enough to bring out the best in the burrata. The richness of the burrata easily overwhelmed the other components. And there was another vexing issue: The tomatoes exuded a great deal of bland liquid that diluted the cheese's luxurious flavor and creamy liquid.

The first problem I decided to tackle was the excess of liquid. The test kitchen has found that salting tomatoes destined for salads can extract the water and concentrate the tomatoes' flavor. In this case, it worked perfectly. I roughly chopped ripe tomatoes (the type is inconsequential as long as they're perfectly ripe) and

halved a handful of sweet cherry tomatoes for variety, spread them onto a thick layer of paper towels, dusted them with salt, and allowed them to sit for 30 minutes before preparing the salad. After that period, the towels were soaked and the tomatoes were firmer and more flavorful.

Blending the olive oil with a little minced shallot and mild sweet-tart white balsamic vinegar went far in improving things, bringing a bright, tangy element to the salad. But the tomatoes and burrata weren't harmonizing yet—their flavors remained too distinct—and the highly flavored combination of tomato juices and cream from the cheese pooled at the bottom of the serving bowl.

Looking for an option to both unify and absorb those juices, I thought of Italian *pangrattato* (garlicky bread crumbs). I ground fresh slices of hearty rustic bread into crumbs and then sautéed them in olive oil seasoned with salt and pepper. For a zippy punch, I added garlic to the crumbs once they had finished cooking. Sprinkled on top of the assembled salad, the crisp bread crumbs greedily absorbed all the juices, marrying tomatoes to cheese and providing a welcome textural contrast. Finally, I had a deluxe version of one of my favorite summer salads.

—MATTHEW CARD, *America's Test Kitchen Books*

Tomato and Burrata Salad with Pangrattato and Basil

SERVES 4 TO 6

The success of this dish depends on using ripe, flavorful tomatoes and fresh, high-quality burrata. Be ready to serve this dish immediately after it is assembled.

3	ounces rustic white bread, torn into rough pieces (1½ cups)
6	tablespoons extra-virgin olive oil
	Salt and pepper
1	garlic clove, minced
1½	pounds very ripe tomatoes, cored and cut into 1-inch pieces
½	pound cherry or grape tomatoes, halved
1	shallot, halved and sliced thin
1½	tablespoons white balsamic vinegar
½	cup chopped fresh basil
8–10	ounces burrata cheese, room temperature

1. Pulse bread in food processor into large crumbs measuring between ⅛ and ¼ inch, about 10 pulses. Combine crumbs, 2 tablespoons oil, pinch salt, and pinch pepper in 12-inch nonstick skillet. Cook over medium heat, stirring often, until crumbs are crisp and golden, about 10 minutes. Clear center of skillet, add garlic, and cook, mashing it into skillet, until fragrant, about 30 seconds. Stir garlic into crumbs. Transfer to plate and let cool.

2. Meanwhile, spread tomatoes out over baking sheet lined with several layers of paper towels. Sprinkle with ¼ teaspoon salt and let sit for 30 minutes.

NOTES FROM THE TEST KITCHEN

PICKING THE TOP TOMATO
When tomatoes are central to your salad, you need to choose your fruit wisely.

CHOOSE LOCAL: If at all possible, buying local produce is the best way to ensure a flavorful tomato. The shorter the distance a tomato has to travel, the riper it can be when it's picked. And commercial tomatoes are engineered to be sturdier, with thicker walls and less of the flavorful jelly and seeds.

LOOK CLOSELY: When selecting tomatoes, oddly shaped tomatoes are fine, and even cracked skin is OK. Avoid tomatoes that are overly soft or leaking juice. Choose tomatoes that smell fruity and feel heavy.

SHOP ON VINE: If supermarket tomatoes are the only option, look for those sold on the vine. They are better than regular supermarket tomatoes, which are picked when still green and blasted with ethylene gas to develop texture and color.

STORING TOMATOES
Once you've brought your tomatoes home, proper storage is important to preserve their fresh flavor and texture. Here are the rules we follow in the test kitchen:
- Never refrigerate tomatoes; cold damages enzymes that produce flavor compounds, and it ruins their texture, turning the flesh mealy. Even when cut, tomatoes should be kept at room temperature (wrap them tightly in plastic wrap).
- If the vine is still attached, leave it on and store the tomatoes stem end up. Tomatoes off the vine should be stored stem side down. We have found that this prevents moisture from escaping and bacteria from entering.
- To quickly ripen hard tomatoes, store them in a paper bag with a banana or apple, both of which emit ethylene gas, which hastens ripening.

3. Combine shallot, vinegar, and ¼ teaspoon salt in large bowl. Whisking constantly, drizzle in remaining 4 tablespoons oil. Add tomatoes and basil, toss gently to combine, then arrange on platter. Place burrata on clean plate and cut into 1-inch pieces, collecting creamy liquid. Sprinkle burrata evenly over tomatoes and drizzle with creamy liquid. Sprinkle with bread crumbs and serve immediately.

ROASTED BUTTERNUT SQUASH SALAD

✓ **WHY THIS RECIPE WORKS:** The sweet, nutty flavor of roasted butternut squash in salad? When paired with flavors that are bold enough to balance the vegetable's sweetness, this vegetable is a salad star. To fill this role, we chose the traditional Middle Eastern spice blend *za'atar* (a pungent combination of toasted sesame seeds, thyme, marjoram, and sumac). We found that using high heat and placing the rack in the lowest position produced perfectly browned squash with a firm center in about 30 minutes. Dusting the za'atar over the hot squash worked much like toasting the spice, boosting its flavor. For a foil to the bites of tender squash, we considered a host of nuts before landing on toasted pumpkin seeds. They provided a textural accent and reinforced the squash's sweet, nutty flavor. Pomegranate seeds added a burst of tartness and color.

Salads are easy in the summer. With markets overflowing with fresh corn, berries, and greens, tossing together a simple starter or a satisfying entrée with your farmers' market haul makes the lazy days of summer that much sweeter. Come winter, however, we're not as inclined to use heartier vegetables in salad, which is too bad, given the promise so many hold. Take butternut squash—its hearty, nutty sweetness is a proven winner. Why not build a salad around it? After all, like heirloom tomatoes in August, there's no shortage of this oblong squash in the produce section once the cold weather sets in.

I started by considering various cooking methods. Baking, steaming, and boiling yielded disappointing results: The squash emerged overly soft, bland, and ill-suited to the flavor-packed salad I had in mind. Roasting peeled and seeded squash on the bottom rack of a hot oven is a go-to test kitchen technique for bringing out

ROASTED BUTTERNUT SQUASH SALAD WITH ZA'ATAR AND PARSLEY

CUTTING UP BUTTERNUT SQUASH

1. After peeling squash, use chef's knife to trim off top and bottom and then cut squash in half where narrow neck and wide curved bottom meet.

2. Cut neck of squash into evenly sized planks. Then cut planks into evenly sized pieces according to recipe.

3. Cut base in half lengthwise and scoop out and discard seeds and fibers. Slice each base half into evenly sized lengths according to recipe.

4. Cut lengths into evenly sized pieces according to recipe.

ZA'ATAR

In Arabic, *za'atar* can refer to a specific herb *Thymbra spicata*; to several herbs that are related to thyme, savory, and oregano; or to a blend of spices that contain these herbs, along with sesame seeds, salt, and (tart, sour) sumac. Za'atar (the blend) is traditionally sprinkled on kebabs and vegetables. To get to know its earthy, pungent, floral flavors, dunk bread in olive oil and then dip it in za'atar.

the best in butternut squash, so that was my next move. Heating the oven to 450 degrees and roasting the slices caramelized the squash, giving it a tender, fork-ready texture and sweet, pronounced flavor. With my salad's base at the ready, I set my sights on the right seasoning and dressing to bring the butternut squash to life.

I started thinking about warm Middle Eastern spices as a way of bringing some bold, unexpected contrast to my star ingredient. Of all the options in my spice rack, the earthy, pungent, floral notes of za'atar proved the perfect complement to squash's sweetness. This ubiquitous Middle Eastern blend of dried thyme, sesame seeds, sumac, and salt is traditionally mixed with olive oil and spread on bread or simply sprinkled over kebabs and vegetables. I followed suit, sprinkling the slices with za'atar before roasting, but I found that the oven diminished its impact. Just as spices come to life when briefly toasted, I discovered that the heat of the roasted squash proved just enough to bloom the za'atar's flavor. With a blend this potent, scaling my generous spoonfuls down to just a teaspoon gave the squash a complex, herbaceous kick.

Like the za'atar, I wanted the dressing to both reinforce and contrast the squash's sweetness. In keeping with the Middle Eastern flavor profile I'd established, I first looked to pomegranate molasses—a common ingredient in Lebanese and Syrian cooking—to add a fruity, sweet-sour punch to the dressing. Off the bat, its robust flavor overwhelmed the squash, so I tried to temper its impact with granulated sugar and later with honey. The result was a round, rich flavor, but it needed some acidity to clarify it. However, even with the addition of fresh lemon juice, the molasses still overwhelmed the salad, so I put the bottle aside and tried a simple, zesty blend of lemon juice, honey, and shallot. This was just the ticket, contributing a sweet-tart dimension to the salad without dimming any of the squash's bold, perfectly seasoned flavors.

To finish off this winter salad, I looked for a way to add extra color, texture, and complementary fresh flavors. I wanted the squash to remain the focus, so I tossed in peppery fresh parsley leaves instead of a more dominant herb or green. Pepitas, or pumpkin seeds, were an easy way to add crunch to the salad while keeping it seasonal. To enhance their nutty flavor,

I spread the pepitas in a dry skillet and quickly browned them over medium heat. Once toasted, the pepitas reinforced the roasted squash flavor and contributed great crunch to contrast its tender texture. Tossed together, this vibrant salad was a showstopper, bursting with warm Middle Eastern flavors, but before serving, one more winter staple sprang to mind: pomegranate.

I removed the small kernels from the membrane and sprinkled them over the salad. Now studded with vivid crimson seeds, my roasted squash salad was brimming with complex flavors and contrasting textures, and its striking jewel-toned appearance brightened the dinner table instantly.

—MATTHEW CARD, *America's Test Kitchen Books*

Roasted Butternut Squash Salad with Za'atar and Parsley

SERVES 4 TO 6

Pepitas, or pumpkin seeds, are available at most supermarkets and natural foods stores. You can substitute chopped red grapes or small blueberries for the pomegranate seeds.

3–3½	pounds butternut squash, peeled, seeded, and cut into ½-inch pieces (8–10 cups)
¼	cup extra-virgin olive oil
	Salt and pepper
1	teaspoon za'atar spice blend
1	small shallot, minced
2	tablespoons lemon juice
2	tablespoons honey
¾	cup fresh parsley leaves
⅓	cup unsalted pepitas, toasted
½	cup pomegranate seeds

1. Adjust oven rack to lowest position and heat oven to 450 degrees. Toss squash with 1 tablespoon oil in bowl and season with salt and pepper. Lay squash in single layer on rimmed baking sheet and roast until well browned and tender, 30 to 35 minutes, stirring halfway through roasting time. Remove squash from oven, sprinkle with za'atar, and let cool for 15 minutes.

2. Whisk shallot, lemon juice, honey, and ¼ teaspoon salt together in large bowl. Whisking constantly, drizzle in remaining 3 tablespoons oil. Add squash, parsley, and pepitas and toss gently to combine. Arrange on platter, sprinkle with pomegranate seeds, and serve.

KALE CAESAR SALAD

✓ **WHY THIS RECIPE WORKS:** We had a hunch that kale and Caesar dressing could make a happy match, but kale is notorious for being fibrous and tough—and recipes where the leaves are massaged with oil to soften them seem overly fussy. In order to break down the leaves and make them more palatable, we soaked them in a warm water bath. Marinating them in the Caesar dressing in the refrigerator gave the salad time to cool back down and the flavors time to meld. To balance the strong flavor of kale, we made the dressing extra-potent, with a stronger dose of lemon juice and anchovies than is typical.

Kale, for all its popularity, is not a leaf I think of when I think of salad. But on a recent trip to the farmers' market, I couldn't help noticing the massive piles of emerald green kale beckoning to me.

One of the farmers told me how his wife has started using kale in her Caesar salads. Say what? Both kale, with its bitter earthiness, and Caesar dressing, with its savory tang, have powerful flavors. Could the two really work in a way that would allow the strong flavors to complement each other without knocking each other out?

To find out, I pulled a test kitchen Caesar salad recipe that I knew to be well seasoned and flavorful. Doubtful but hopeful, I swapped curly kale, stemmed and cut, ounce for ounce for romaine. No dice. Without being cooked, fibrous kale can be, as one taster commented, like "trying to chew on tree branches." Plus, the bitterness of the green did not allow the signature garlic, lemon, Parmesan, and anchovy flavors of the Caesar to shine through.

Simply cutting the tough kale leaves into smaller pieces didn't solve the chewability problem. I tried a variety of cooking methods—sautéing, steaming, and boiling—to soften it, but these took away any sense of freshness. I tried salting it, soaking it in a brine, and even, skeptically, massaging it (a technique that is enjoying a vogue among kale fans). Each of these methods helped with texture, but the first two made my salad too salty and massaging the kale was just too much work.

Beleaguered, I reached out to our science editor. He explained to me that these methods were all causing the cell walls of the kale leaves to break down, making for a tender, easy-to-chew leaf. Surely, I said, there's an easier way. He suggested a softer approach: soaking

KALE CAESAR SALAD

the kale in a warm water bath. Not scalding hot, just warm. He suspected that it would have the same effect.

He was right. Soaking the kale in warm tap water (110 to 115 degrees) for just 10 minutes relaxed the leaves just enough for a salad. No extra heat (or massaging) necessary. And there was a bonus: This warm water bath could double as my washing step. I wouldn't need to prerinse the leaves.

The temperature of the water, however, created a new problem. When I went to serve my salad, the kale was still warm. I needed to refrigerate the kale to cool it back down and restore some fresh crispness. A colleague suggested that I toss the kale in the dressing before cooling it to allow the flavors to meld. Twenty minutes in the fridge worked like a charm. About that dressing: The test kitchen's Caesar dressing recipe is delicious with romaine, but kale has a more powerful flavor that requires a more intense match. After a couple of tests fiddling with different ingredients and amounts, I decided to increase the number of anchovies and the volume of lemon juice to add to the dressing's pungency. An extra sprinkle of Parmesan and a few crunchy croutons (made while my salad was chilling), and I had a balanced, satisfying salad that changed my mind about kale.

—MORGAN BOLLING, *Cook's Country*

Kale Caesar Salad

SERVES 4

The kale leaves must be dressed at least 20 minutes (or up to 6 hours) before serving.

SALAD

- 12 **ounces curly kale, stemmed and cut into 1-inch pieces (16 cups)**
- 1 **ounce Parmesan cheese, grated (½ cup)**

CROUTONS

- 3 **ounces baguette, cut into ¾-inch cubes (3 cups)**
- 2 **tablespoons extra-virgin olive oil**
- ¼ **teaspoon pepper**
- ⅛ **teaspoon salt**

DRESSING

- ½ **cup mayonnaise**
- ¼ **cup grated Parmesan cheese**

- 2 **tablespoons lemon juice**
- 1 **tablespoon white wine vinegar**
- 1 **tablespoon Worcestershire sauce**
- 1 **tablespoon Dijon mustard**
- 3 **anchovy fillets, rinsed**
- 1 **garlic clove, minced**
- ½ **teaspoon salt**
- ½ **teaspoon pepper**
- ¼ **cup extra-virgin olive oil**

1. FOR THE SALAD: Place kale in large bowl and cover with warm tap water (110 to 115 degrees). Swish kale around to remove grit. Let kale sit in warm water bath for 10 minutes. Remove kale from water and spin dry in salad spinner in multiple batches. Pat leaves dry with paper towels if still wet.

2. FOR THE CROUTONS: Adjust oven rack to middle position and heat oven to 350 degrees. Toss all ingredients together in bowl. Bake on rimmed baking sheet until golden and crisp, about 15 minutes. Let croutons cool completely on sheet. (Cooled croutons can be stored in airtight container at room temperature for up to 24 hours.)

3. FOR THE DRESSING: Process mayonnaise, Parmesan, lemon juice, vinegar, Worcestershire, mustard, anchovies, garlic, salt, and pepper in blender until pureed, about 30 seconds. With blender running, slowly add oil until emulsified.

4. Toss kale with ¾ cup dressing in large bowl. Refrigerate dressed kale for at least 20 minutes or up to 6 hours. Toss Parmesan and croutons with dressed kale. Serve, passing remaining ¼ cup dressing at table.

NOTES FROM THE TEST KITCHEN

SOFTENING KALE

To soften raw kale enough for it to be enjoyed in a salad, first soak stemmed, cut leaves in warm tap water for 10 minutes. Then, after drying the leaves, dress them and refrigerate the salad for at least 20 minutes (or up to 6 hours); during the refrigerating phase, the oil in the dressing "wets" the waxy, water-repelling surface of the kale leaves, which causes them to soften further.

SOUPS AND STEWS

VEGETABLE BROTH BASE

✔ **WHY THIS RECIPE WORKS:** A good vegetable stock is an important ingredient to have on hand, but supermarket offerings don't taste like vegetables, and traditional homemade versions are expensive and time-consuming to make. For our recipe, we ground together a paste using fresh vegetables (carrots and celery root) and salt that we could store in the freezer and reconstitute as needed. Leeks provided good allium flavor and a small amount of freeze-dried onions supported the fresh flavor of the leeks. Tomato paste and soy sauce delivered an umami boost.

I wanted to make a broth that would boost my vegetarian meals the same way that chicken or beef stock boosts my meat-based cooking. But since vegetarian dishes can be more nuanced and subtle in their flavor, I would need a broth that wouldn't overpower the other ingredients or call too much attention to any one vegetable. If possible, I also wanted my recipe to generate minimal waste and be economical and simple to produce, so I could consider it a staple rather than a luxury.

To begin, I worked my way through several recipes using various vegetables and methods, but the results were anything from overly earthy and time consuming to murky orange-brown with an off-tasting tang. I had almost given up when I happened upon a recipe that ground a mixture of vegetables, herbs, and salt in a food processor. Stir a spoonful of this paste into boiling water and there you have it: vegetable broth.

The potential was clear. Grinding vegetables was quick, with no cooking required. And even better, this base was undiluted and kept all the flavorful ingredients in the final product—those flavors would be extracted by the hot water to make an infusion. There was little waste, along with an unexpected advantage: more compact storage. Instead of ending up with several quarts of broth, I'd just have one tidy container.

I loaded chopped leeks, fennel, carrots, celery root, sun-dried tomatoes, garlic, cilantro, parsley, and more than ¾ cup of salt into the food processor, as the recipe directed. The reasoning behind all that salt was persuasive: It would discourage spoilage so the base could be stored for weeks in the refrigerator. There was also an additional benefit: The salt prevents the base from solidifying in the freezer, so it's easy to scoop out only what is required.

A welcome change from the previous versions, this broth was fresh-tasting. The leeks, carrots, and celery root gave it a balanced flavor, and the sun-dried tomatoes, rich in savory amino acids, contributed depth.

But there were problems. The vegetable flavor was weak, and the 7 ounces of herbs (a huge amount) dominated the broth and turned swampy during storage. The garlic didn't fare well either. Its flavor continued to develop and became too hot. With their sweet-sour undertone, the sun-dried tomatoes were too identifiable to be an anonymous umami booster. Although fennel added a pleasant licorice-like flavor, it wouldn't be welcome in every application. And, yes, ¾ cup of salt was too much. Still, I was intrigued by the possibilities.

I pureed chopped onion, chopped carrots, and celery stalks, and used less than half the amount of salt in the previous batch. Since cilantro has a more prominent flavor than parsley, I stuck with the latter and added only ½ ounce of it.

I quickly realized that celery root, rather than my substitution of celery, was in the original recipe for a reason. The regular celery added bitterness and a slightly sour flavor. It turns out that celery root is not just milder than celery; it also has a more complex, creamy flavor. Celery root was back in. It was a similar story with the leek/onion swap. The higher moisture content of the onions made the base watery, so it solidified in the freezer. Worse, it was simultaneously sweeter and more sulfurous than the base made with leeks. So leeks went back in as well.

My broth was better now, but it still tasted a bit lightweight, so I went in search of an extra boost. When thinking about concentrated sources of flavor, I began to consider an option I've been quite snooty about in the past: those dried minced onions found in bottles in the spice aisle.

Dried minced onions aren't simply dehydrated; they're freeze-dried. Frozen food is placed in a vacuum-sealed chamber where the ice transitions into vapor and is pulled out of the food. Whereas the heat of a conventional oven pulls out flavor compounds along with the water, freeze-drying leaves many more of those compounds in place, just waiting to be reactivated by water.

The distinct flavor of the sun-dried tomatoes in the first batch had been problematic, but I appreciated their umami quality, so I considered other options. Canned and fresh tomatoes took my base back to a slurry, so next I tried tomato paste. Just 1½ tablespoons contributed an appealing savoriness.

That hint of umami left me wanting more. I went to the pantry and pulled out savory non-meat powerhouses. Shiitake mushrooms were too earthy, and miso paste was too subtle in small amounts and too identifiable in larger. Three tablespoons of soy sauce gave my broth the muscle it had lacked. To compensate for the added sodium, I cut the salt back to 2 tablespoons, which was still enough to prevent the mixture from freezing solid.

This broth had it all: easy preparation, minimal waste, convenient storage, and, best of all, fresh, balanced vegetable flavor that worked well in everything from soups and sauces to pastas and risottos.

—ANDREA GEARY, *Cook's Illustrated*

Vegetable Broth Base

MAKES ABOUT 1¾ CUPS BASE; ENOUGH FOR 7 QUARTS BROTH

For the best balance of flavors, measure the prepped vegetables by weight. Kosher salt aids in grinding the vegetables. The broth base contains enough salt to keep it from freezing solid, making it easy to remove 1 tablespoon at a time. To make 1 cup of broth, stir 1 tablespoon of fresh or frozen broth base into 1 cup of boiling water. If particle-free broth is desired, let the broth steep for 5 minutes and then strain it through a fine-mesh strainer.

  2 **leeks, white and light green parts only, chopped and washed thoroughly (2½ cups or 5 ounces)**

  2 **carrots, peeled and cut into ½-inch pieces (⅔ cup or 3 ounces)**

  ½ **small celery root, peeled and cut into ½-inch pieces (¾ cup or 3 ounces)**

  ½ **cup (½ ounce) parsley leaves and thin stems**

  3 **tablespoons dried minced onions**

  2 **tablespoons kosher salt**

1½ **tablespoons tomato paste**

  3 **tablespoons soy sauce**

Process leeks, carrots, celery root, parsley, minced onion, and salt in food processor, scraping down sides of bowl frequently, until paste is as fine as possible, 3 to 4 minutes. Add tomato paste and process for 1 minute, scraping down sides of bowl every 20 seconds. Add soy sauce and continue to process 1 minute longer.

Transfer mixture to airtight container and tap firmly on counter to remove air bubbles. Press small piece of parchment paper flush against surface of mixture and cover. Freeze for up to 6 months.

MATZO BALL SOUP

✓ **WHY THIS RECIPE WORKS:** A perfect matzo ball is substantial enough to hold its shape but not so dense that it sinks to the bottom of the soup. To achieve this delicate balance, we combined matzo meal, eggs, and water and then let the mixture sit in the refrigerator for 1 hour to allow the matzo meal to fully absorb the liquid before forming the balls. Cooking matzo balls in boiling salted water—separately from the soup—kept the soup itself from getting cloudy. To build a flavorful soup, we added subtly sweet parsnips to the classic combination of chicken broth, celery, onion, and carrot and then fortified it with two whole chicken legs for depth. (We later removed the legs, which we shredded and then added back to the soup.)

Matzo ball soup is not complicated—it's simply chicken broth with vegetables and tender boiled dumplings made from matzo meal. But ask one lifelong fan what makes a perfect version and then ask another, and you'll find yourself with completely different answers.

MATZO BALL SOUP

Matzo balls—made from matzo meal (ground matzoh), eggs, and water or broth—should be substantial but not too heavy. Also, they must be poached in water and then added to the soup later; if you cook the balls directly in the soup, they leave it starchy and sludgy.

I tried five different existing recipes for matzo balls to get my bearings. Some were heavy, dense sinkers. Others were too delicate and fell apart.

The difference was in the ratio of the ingredients. After trial and error, I settled on 1 cup of matzo meal, 4 large eggs, and 5 tablespoons of water plus a bit of chopped, cooked onion and minced dill. After an hour's rest in the fridge, the dough was delicate but strong enough to hold together.

I added 12 matzo balls to boiling, salted water. After 10, 20, 30, 40, and 50 minutes, I pulled a few of the balls out and set them aside to cool. I then cut them in half to compare their interiors. Thirty minutes yielded the most consistent texture from edge to center.

Other ingredients in the soup vary by family tradition. Chicken broth, celery, onion, and carrot are common, but from there on it's a free-for-all; rutabaga, parsnip, parsley, dill, and thyme are all options. I was sold on parsnip after a side-by-side test revealed that even committed parsnip haters loved its subtle sweetness. To deepen the chicken flavor, I added two whole chicken legs, which I removed after they cooked through. (If you're making a meal of the soup, a bit of chicken torn from the legs may be added back in.)

—DIANE UNGER, *Cook's Country*

Matzo Ball Soup

SERVES 6

Chicken fat, or schmaltz, is available in the refrigerator or freezer section of most supermarkets. Note that the matzo batter needs to be refrigerated for at least 1 hour before shaping. You can add meat from the chicken legs back to the soup.

MATZO BALLS

¼ cup chicken fat (schmaltz) or vegetable oil
1 onion, chopped fine
4 large eggs
1 teaspoon minced fresh dill
  Salt and pepper
1 cup (4 ounces) matzo meal

SOUP

1 tablespoon chicken fat (schmaltz) or vegetable oil
1 onion, chopped
2 carrots, peeled and cut into ½-inch chunks
2 celery ribs, chopped
1 parsnip, peeled and cut into ½-inch chunks
  Salt and pepper
8 cups chicken broth
1½ pounds chicken leg quarters, trimmed
1 teaspoon minced fresh dill

1. FOR THE MATZO BALLS: Heat chicken fat in Dutch oven over medium heat until shimmering. Add onion and cook until light golden brown and softened, about 5 minutes. Transfer onion to large bowl and let cool for 10 minutes. (Do not clean pot.)

2. Whisk eggs, 5 tablespoons water, dill, ¾ teaspoon salt, and ½ teaspoon pepper into cooled onion mixture. Fold in matzo meal until well combined. Cover with plastic wrap and refrigerate for at least 1 hour or up to 2 hours. (Batter will thicken as it sits.)

3. Bring 4 quarts water and 2 tablespoons salt to boil in now-empty Dutch oven. Divide batter into 12 portions (about 1 heaping tablespoon each) and place on greased plate. Roll portions into smooth balls between your wet hands and return to plate. Transfer matzo balls to boiling water, cover, reduce heat to medium-low and simmer until tender and cooked through, about 30 minutes.

4. Using slotted spoon, transfer matzo balls to colander and drain briefly. Transfer balls to clean plate and let cool to firm up, about 10 minutes. Discard cooking water. (Do not clean pot.)

5. FOR THE SOUP: Meanwhile, heat chicken fat in large saucepan over medium heat until shimmering. Add onion, carrots, celery, parsnip, and ½ teaspoon salt and cook, covered, until vegetables begin to soften, about 5 minutes. Add broth, chicken, and dill and bring to

---

NOTES FROM THE TEST KITCHEN

FULL-FLAVORED MATZO BALLS

For maximum flavor, we recommend making the matzo balls with chicken fat. When you make the chicken broth for this recipe, skim off some chicken fat and set it aside to cool. If you choose not to use chicken fat, vegetable oil will work fine, though the matzo balls won't be as flavorful.

boil. Cover, reduce heat to low, and cook until chicken is tender, 35 to 45 minutes. Remove from heat and transfer chicken to plate. Season soup with salt and pepper to taste.

6. Using 2 forks, shred chicken into bite-size pieces, discarding skin and bones. (Chicken can be used for soup or reserved for another use.) Transfer soup to now-empty Dutch oven and bring to simmer over medium heat. Carefully transfer matzo balls to hot soup (along with shredded chicken, if using). Cover and cook until matzo balls are heated through, about 5 minutes. Serve.

TO MAKE AHEAD: Matzo balls and soup can be fully cooked, cooled, and refrigerated separately in covered containers for up to 2 days. To serve, return soup to simmer over medium heat, add matzo balls, and cook until heated through, about 7 minutes.

NOTES FROM THE TEST KITCHEN

CLEANING LEEKS

Leeks grow in sandy soil, where their many layers capture and hold the dirt and grit. The classic technique for cleaning them is to split them lengthwise (not through the root), rinse under running water to remove trapped dirt, and pat dry before slicing. This technique works, but ours is much quicker:

SWISH AND SPIN: Swish cut leek in a salad spinner, drain, and spin dry.

BIENVENUE, HARICOTS VERTS

Haricots verts are the thinner, more delicate cousin of the standard American green bean and are a staple vegetable in French cooking. Look for dark green, slender beans with taut skin and intact stems.

Prepping haricots verts could not be simpler:

GIVE THEM A TRIM: Line the beans up in a row on a cutting board and trim off the inedible stem ends with one slice.

PROVENÇAL VEGETABLE SOUP

✔ WHY THIS RECIPE WORKS: Provençal Vegetable Soup is a classic French summer soup with a delicate broth that is intensified by a dollop of pistou, the French equivalent of Italy's pesto. We wanted a simple version that focused on fresh seasonal vegetables. Leeks, green beans, and zucchini all made the cut; we like their summery flavors, different shapes, and varying shades of green. We added canned white beans (which were far more convenient than dried in this quick-cooking soup) and orecchiette for its easy-to-spoon shape. For the best flavor, we make our own vegetable broth (a quick paste that's stirred into boiling water). Incorporating the cooking liquid from the canned beans adds much-needed body to the broth. For the pistou, we just whirred basil, Parmesan, olive oil, and garlic together in our food processor.

Just about every Western cuisine lays claim to a vegetable soup, but my favorite is the version native to the south of France called *soupe au pistou*. The French equivalent of minestrone, this broth is chock-full of vegetables, beans, and herbs—a celebration of the fresh produce that returns to the markets in early summer. Virtually any vegetables can and do go into the pot, but aromatics like carrots, celery, and leeks are typical, along with zucchini and the thin French green beans called *haricots verts*. Pasta often makes an appearance, along with a white bean known as *coco de Mollans*. The only component that's an absolute constant is the pesto-like condiment for which the soup is named; stirring a spoonful into each bowl lends the broth a jolt of fresh basil and garlic, along with salty Parmesan.

But when I've made the soup with the supermarket produce that is my main option most of the year, what should be a flavorful, satisfying soup often lacks character and body. I also find that when I don't have time to soak and simmer dried white beans (cannellini or navy are a typical substitute for hard-to-find coco de Mollans) and instead shortcut with canned ones, the soup suffers. But what if there was a way to have both—that is, a hearty, full-flavored soupe au pistou that I could throw together anytime?

Most classic versions use water for the soup base, but for more flavor I would make a vegetable broth.

Ordinarily, that's a labor-intensive process, but our homemade Vegetable Broth Base (page 18) takes minutes to make—just a handful of vegetables and pantry seasonings buzzed to a paste in the food processor and stirred into boiling water, 1 tablespoon per cup. I made 3 cups of broth and added an equal amount of water, which would produce a base that was flavorful but delicate enough to let other ingredients come forward.

I wanted the mixture of vegetables to be abundant but not cluttered. I softened a leek with celery and carrot, added minced garlic, poured in the broth and water, and brought it all to a simmer. I added 8 ounces of haricots verts that I had cut into short lengths. When they were bright green but still crisp, I added a can of drained cannellini beans and some chopped zucchini and tomato, which added fresh flavor and color and a touch of fruity brightness.

Within minutes, the soup's flavors seemed balanced and on target and the vegetables were tender. But there was the thin broth to address. Adding pasta to the soup helped: Not only did it make the soup heartier, but the pieces sloughed off starch as they boiled, giving the broth more body—though not enough.

But there was an ingredient already at my disposal that I hadn't yet employed: the starchy liquid from the canned cannellini beans. As we've discovered, this viscous, seasoned "broth" can be invaluable in dishes that call for canned beans, lending a body and flavor similar to that which you get from cooking dried beans and using their liquid. Adding it to the pot with the beans made all the difference in my recipe, producing a soup that was still brothy but also had some body.

As for the namesake pistou, this mixture is even simpler to make, and brighter-tasting, than Italian pesto because it lacks toasted nuts. Pureeing a generous handful of fresh basil with Parmesan, a clove of garlic, and plenty of extra-virgin olive oil yielded a bold, grass-green sauce that was sharp and rich—the perfect accompaniment for the fresh, clean soup.

And with that, I had soupe au pistou that was both fast and flavorful, not to mention satisfying enough to stand on its own.

—KEITH DRESSER, *Cook's Illustrated*

Provençal Vegetable Soup (Soupe au Pistou)
SERVES 6

We prefer broth prepared from our Vegetable Broth Base (page 18), but store-bought vegetable broth can be used.

PISTOU

- ¾ cup fresh basil leaves
- 1 ounce Parmesan cheese, grated (½ cup)
- ⅓ cup extra-virgin olive oil
- 1 garlic clove, minced

SOUP

- 1 tablespoon extra-virgin olive oil
- 1 leek, white and light green parts only, halved lengthwise, sliced ½ inch thick, and washed thoroughly
- 1 celery rib, cut into ½-inch pieces
- 1 carrot, peeled and sliced ¼ inch thick
  Salt and pepper
- 2 garlic cloves, minced
- 3 cups vegetable broth
- 3 cups water
- ½ cup orecchiette or other short pasta
- 8 ounces haricots verts or green beans, trimmed and cut into ½-inch lengths
- 1 (15-ounce) can cannellini or navy beans
- 1 small zucchini, halved lengthwise, seeded, and cut into ¼-inch pieces
- 1 large tomato, cored, seeded, and cut into ¼-inch pieces

1. FOR THE PISTOU: Process all ingredients in food processor until smooth, scraping down sides of bowl as needed, about 15 seconds. (Pistou can be refrigerated for up to 4 hours.)

2. FOR THE SOUP: Heat oil in large Dutch oven over medium heat until shimmering. Add leek, celery, carrot, and ½ teaspoon salt and cook until vegetables are softened, 8 to 10 minutes. Stir in garlic and cook until fragrant, about 30 seconds. Stir in broth and water and bring to simmer.

3. Stir in pasta and simmer until slightly softened, about 5 minutes. Stir in haricots verts and simmer until bright green but still crunchy, 3 to 5 minutes. Stir in cannellini beans and their liquid, zucchini, and tomato and simmer until pasta and vegetables are tender, about 3 minutes. Season with salt and pepper to taste. Serve, topping individual portions with generous tablespoon pistou.

Garlic Toasts
MAKES 8 SLICES

Be sure to use a high-quality crusty bread, such as a baguette; do not use sliced sandwich bread.

8   (1-inch-thick) slices rustic bread
1   large garlic clove, peeled
3   tablespoons extra-virgin olive oil
    Salt and pepper

Adjust oven rack 6 inches from broiler element and heat broiler. Spread bread out evenly over rimmed baking sheet and broil, flipping as needed, until well toasted on both sides, about 4 minutes. Briefly rub 1 side of each toast with garlic, drizzle with oil, and season with salt and pepper to taste. Serve

SLOW-COOKER MOROCCAN LENTIL SOUP

✓ **WHY THIS RECIPE WORKS:** To make a slow-cooker version of lentil soup, we needed to rethink each step of the process for tender, but not mushy, lentils. We used French green lentils (also called lentilles du Puy), which turned tender while retaining their shape. To give this soup a Moroccan flavor profile, we used traditional spices like ground coriander and cayenne for a warm, deep flavor and bloomed them in the microwave. Dates, another common Moroccan ingredient, imparted a nutty, sweet flavor to our store-bought broth. Mustard greens complemented the soup's warm spices. For richness and tang, we topped the soup with a mixture of Greek yogurt, parsley, and lemon juice.

Lentil soup is cheap to make, comes together quickly, and tastes great—at least in theory. All too often it turns into a hodgepodge of lentils and whatever vegetable happens to be available. I wanted to break this trend and create a cohesive recipe with a compelling flavor profile. Even better, I wanted to do it in the slow cooker, where it could (ideally) cook for hours without supervision.

My first round of testing left a lot to be desired. Most of the recipes I had tried called for a laundry list of ingredients and spices, and many didn't specify what kind of lentils to use (a vital piece of information I would need for a successful soup). After hours of cooking in the slow cooker, most of the recipes had a consistency that was as thick as oatmeal, with a muted and bland flavor.

After making a few more failed recipes, I started noticing a trend. The soups with the worst texture were those that used red or yellow lentils. Traditionally used in Indian cooking, these varieties broke down and lost their shape quickly. The soups with the best texture and flavor used *lentilles du Puy*. These lentils are smaller than the more common brown and green kinds. Dark olive green, almost black, in color, with mottling, these lentils were praised by tasters for their "rich, earthy, complex flavor" and "firm yet tender texture." With the main ingredient decided, I moved on to the spices.

Lentils are common in Moroccan cuisine, so I had a good feeling about the interplay between classic Moroccan flavors and the ease of this slow-cooked lentil soup. I decided on a combination of citrusy coriander, cayenne pepper for a little heat, and garam masala, a warm and complex spice blend (while not Moroccan, it fit well here). Now the issue was getting those flavors to deliver in the slow cooker. In all of the stovetop recipes I tried, the spices were first bloomed (or heated) in oil to create a flavorful base for the soup. However, this was impractical in the slow cooker, where one of my main goals was ease. To save time, I microwaved the aromatics and spices with a little oil to develop their flavors. This took just 5 minutes and was much easier than getting out a skillet.

With the lentils and spices squared away, I turned to the soup's other elements. Store-bought broth was easy to find and, thanks to the spices, tasted just as complex as the homemade variety. Chicken broth dominated the subtle flavors in the soup, so I used vegetable broth for its light and slightly sweet flavor. To give the soup more color and a deeper taste, I added a few more ingredients before the soup had finished cooking. Mustard greens, with their medium-hot flavor and a fairly strong bite, made a terrific addition. Adding them toward the end of cooking allowed them to retain their color and subtle, peppery bitterness. Another key addition was dates, widely found in Moroccan cooking. The caramel sweetness of the dates gave the soup a richer overall flavor and countered the spicier elements.

Once the soup was out of the slow cooker, I had one more step to take—creating a creamy, cooling garnish. I grabbed some Greek yogurt, squeezed in lemon juice, and stirred in fresh parsley and black pepper. Spooned onto each bowl, my yogurt topping countered the soup's spiciness and added welcome richness.

Finally, I had a lively spicy soup that delivered rich, spicy flavor, color, and aroma, straight out of the slow cooker.

—MEAGHEN WALSH, *America's Test Kitchen Books*

Slow-Cooker Moroccan Lentil Soup with Mustard Greens

SERVES 6

We prefer French green lentils for this recipe, but it will work with any type of lentil except red or yellow. If you can't find mustard greens, you can substitute kale.

- 1 onion, chopped fine
- 2 garlic cloves, minced
- 1 teaspoon canola oil
- 1 teaspoon garam masala
- ¾ teaspoon ground coriander
- ⅛ teaspoon cayenne pepper
- 8 cups vegetable broth
- 1 cup French green lentils, picked over and rinsed
  Salt and pepper
- 12 ounces mustard greens, stemmed and sliced ½ inch thick
- 4 ounces pitted dates, chopped (¾ cup)
- ½ cup 2 percent Greek yogurt
- ¼ cup chopped fresh parsley
- 1 tablespoon lemon juice

1. Microwave onion, garlic, oil, garam masala, coriander, and cayenne in bowl, stirring occasionally, until onion is softened, about 5 minutes; transfer to slow cooker. Stir in broth, lentils, and ¼ teaspoon salt. Cover and cook until lentils are tender, 7 to 9 hours on low or 4 to 6 hours on high.

2. Stir mustard greens and dates into soup, cover, and cook on high until greens are tender, 20 to 30 minutes. Season with salt and pepper to taste.

3. Combine yogurt, parsley, lemon juice, and ⅛ teaspoon pepper in bowl. Season with salt and pepper to taste. Top individual portions of soup with yogurt mixture before serving.

SLOW-COOKER BUTTERNUT SQUASH AND APPLE SOUP

☑ **WHY THIS RECIPE WORKS:** Roasting, the typical method for a flavorful butternut squash soup, produces delicious results, but between roasting, moving the squash to the stovetop to sauté the aromatics, and adding the broth and seasonings (not to mention pureeing it all), we wanted an easier method. Enter the slow cooker. Microwaving the aromatics with cayenne and cinnamon intensified the flavors just as well as sautéing—but far more conveniently. Apples are a natural pairing with squash, and we found that 1 pound of apples complemented, but didn't dominate, the squash's flavor. A combination of vegetable broth and water kept the focus on the vegetables—chicken broth was too overpowering. Slow-cooking the chunks of squash and apple in the broth with seasonings infused the vegetables and cooking liquid with lots of flavor. After pureeing, a modest amount of half-and-half bumped up the creaminess of this soup with just enough richness.

Butternut squash soup is a fall-time classic, but why not combine it with another autumn favorite to deepen the appeal? I knew that the sweet taste of apples would pair perfectly with the savory richness of butternut squash, so I gathered my ingredients and prepared for the ultimate fall soup.

The traditional cooking method behind butternut soup is to roast the squash in the oven and then move the operation to the stovetop, but the addition of the apples made the roasting step soggier and produced a taste more akin to a sweet squash pie. Plus, I wasn't willing to go through the multiple cooking steps: from oven to many steps of stovetop cooking, to blender and back to the stove. The dirty dishes alone were enough to convince me to find another way to create this soup. Luckily, I had just the tool: the slow cooker. Not only would this reduce the time I would spend monitoring the soup, it would also cut down on dishes. But first I would need to find a way to make the flavors just as rich in the moist heat of the slow cooker as they were from the oven.

My ideal recipe would have a deep flavor from the squash and a sweetness from the apples, along with a velvety texture. An uncomplicated preparation was important for this soup, so the first test I conducted focused on the ease of cooking. I combined chicken

SLOW-COOKER BUTTERNUT SQUASH AND APPLE SOUP

broth, equal amounts of squash and apples, and a little cinnamon and cayenne in the slow cooker, turned it on, and waited. Unsurprisingly, this left me with an overly sweet soup with harsh spice flavor. The apples had completely overpowered the squash. Even worse, the texture was watery and disappointing.

I couldn't perfect the texture until I'd mastered the ingredients, so I started playing with the ratio of apples to squash. I cut the amount of apples in half and tried again. This time, the fruity sweetness had taken a back-seat, although my tasters missed a little of its complexity. The texture, on the other hand, was almost perfect. Apples contain a large amount of water, and because the slow cooker is a closed environment, the apples release their liquid readily. Fewer apples meant a richer, more concentrated soup.

I wanted to gain back some of the fruitiness I had lost without increasing the amount of apples, so I turned to changing up the variety of apple. I moved from the classic Granny Smith and went for Golden Delicious, an apple that is known in the test kitchen for its sweet, but not cloying, taste. This time, the savory flavor of the squash was subtly complemented by a deep sweetness that had almost a caramel taste.

Next up, the spices. I knew that sautéing the aromatics would give me the complex taste I wanted, but I wasn't willing to use up the necessary time it would take. Luckily, microwaving the aromatics with just a little butter gave me the same intense flavor in a much faster and more convenient manner.

The deep flavor of the soup won approval from the tasters, but they also noticed a sharp onion flavor that stole a little thunder from the main ingredients. Switching to shallots, which have a milder flavor than onions, fixed this problem. Microwaving the shallots with the spices softened their texture and helped to coax out their sweetness. To bring the flavor of the vegetables forward, I switched to vegetable broth instead of chicken, which had overwhelmed the other ingredients. What really put this soup over the top was steeping a sprig of fresh sage in the slow cooker while everything cooked.

As is true with many creamed soups, texture is almost as important as flavor. I found that blending the squash and apples in batches worked best, making it easier for the blender to smooth out any lumps or remaining fibers and avoiding overflowing blender jars. Once the soup was pureed to a velvety texture, I transferred it back

to the slow cooker, stirred in half-and-half, and heated it until warmed through. With less than 15 minutes hands-on time, this soup offered all the rich, creamy, sweet squash and apple flavor I was craving.

—MEAGHEN WALSH, *America's Test Kitchen Books*

Slow-Cooker Butternut Squash and Apple Soup

SERVES 4

Serve with Spiced Croutons (page 28).

4	shallots, minced
1	tablespoon unsalted butter
½	teaspoon ground cinnamon
	Pinch cayenne pepper
3	cups vegetable broth, plus extra as needed
1	cup water
2	pounds butternut squash, peeled, seeded, and cut into 1-inch pieces (5 cups)
1	pound Golden Delicious apples, peeled, cored, and cut into 1-inch pieces (about 3 cups)
1	sprig fresh sage
	Salt and pepper
½	cup half-and-half

1. Microwave shallots, butter, cinnamon, and cayenne in bowl, stirring occasionally, until shallots are softened, about 2 minutes; transfer to slow cooker. Stir in broth, water, squash, apples, sage sprig, and ½ teaspoon salt. Cover and cook until squash is tender, 6 to 8 hours on low or 4 to 6 hours on high.

2. Discard sage sprig. Working in batches, process soup in blender until smooth, 1 to 2 minutes. Return soup to slow cooker, stir in half-and-half, and let sit

NOTES FROM THE TEST KITCHEN

PUREEING SOUPS SAFELY

To prevent an exploding blender when pureeing hot soup, make sure the blender is never more than two-thirds full. Hold the lid in place with a folded dish towel and pulse rapidly a few times before blending continuously.

until heated through, about 5 minutes. (Adjust soup consistency with extra hot broth as needed.) Season with salt and pepper to taste. Serve.

Spiced Croutons
MAKES 2 CUPS

- **4 slices hearty sandwich bread**
  Vegetable oil spray
- **¼ teaspoon ground cumin**
- **¼ teaspoon ground coriander**
- **⅛ teaspoon paprika**
- **⅛ teaspoon salt**
  Pinch cayenne pepper

Adjust oven rack to middle position and heat oven to 350 degrees. Remove crusts from bread and cut into ½-inch cubes (about 2 cups). Spray bread cubes with vegetable oil spray and toss with cumin, coriander, paprika, salt, and cayenne. Spread bread cubes in rimmed baking sheet and bake until golden brown, 20 to 25 minutes, stirring halfway through baking. Let croutons cool to room temperature before serving.

MUSHROOM BISQUE

WHY THIS RECIPE WORKS: Too often the abundance of dairy that gives a mushroom bisque its trademark richness obscures the flavor of the mushrooms. We wanted a silky texture, but we wanted deep, earthy flavor, too. To achieve these goals, we used three kinds of mushrooms—white, cremini, and shiitake. Because mushrooms will exude moisture even without being cut, we cooked them whole in the microwave until they had released most of their liquid. The dehydrated mushrooms browned more efficiently in the pot, which we then deglazed with the reserved mushroom liquid. We kept additional ingredients to a minimum so as not to distract from the mushrooms' flavor. A liaison of egg yolks and cream whisked in at the end gave the soup a texture that was luxurious without being cloying.

Mushroom bisque should be a far more sophisticated version of cream of mushroom soup: smoother, more luxurious, and with greater savory depth. And yet the abundance of dairy that gives a bisque its signature velvety texture can also mute its flavor. Decreasing the cream makes the soup more flavorful, but then it's too austere to merit the name "bisque." My goal was to reconcile an indulgent texture with robust mushroom flavor.

All the soups I tried, even those with an abundance of fungi, were surprisingly short on mushroom flavor. However, one of the recipes I'd tested boasted an ultra-satiny texture that managed not to completely obscure what mushroom flavor there was. Instead of relying entirely on cream, this soup's velvety texture came from a combination of cream and egg yolks, an old-school French thickener known as a *liaison*. With less cream in the mix, more mushroom flavor could come to the fore. I'd keep the liaison in mind when I was closer to finishing my soup, but for now I had to focus on seriously concentrating the mushroom flavor.

Mushrooms are 80 to 90 percent water, and I wanted to get rid of as much as I could for two reasons: First, the more moisture I removed, the more mushrooms (and therefore mushroom flavor) I could add to my bisque. Second, browning is an avenue to flavor, but mushrooms won't brown if they're wet. Most of the recipes I'd tried took as long as 25 minutes to brown on the stove. I knew it would be quicker to move this part of the operation to the microwave.

I tossed 2 pounds of whole button mushrooms (I'd test other varieties once I established my method) with a tablespoon of kosher salt to help draw out the liquid and microwaved them until they shrank down to about one-third of their original volume. This took 12 minutes, less than half the time that sautéing took. I was gratified to find that the whole mushrooms required exactly the same amount of time in the microwave as sliced mushrooms to shrink to one-third of their original volume. A mushroom-savvy colleague explained that fungi lack the thicker protective skin found on most vegetables that prevents evaporation, so they give up their moisture readily even when intact.

I drained the accumulated mushroom-liquid and transferred the mushrooms to the pot with some oil, where they began to brown in just 3 minutes. I added only a single finely chopped onion and a sprig of thyme to the browned mushrooms and cooked everything just a few minutes longer, after which I added chicken broth and simmered the soup for 20 minutes. I gave the soup a quick spin in the blender along with 1¼ cups of cream (the average amount in the recipes I had tested) and a sprinkle of salt and pepper, and then I was ready to taste.

I had been hoping for elegant minimalism, but this soup was just plain bland. Despite having removed all that moisture in the microwave, I found the mushroom flavor faint, one-dimensional, and partially hidden by the chicken broth. Plus, the fatty texture was as cloying as it had been in my early tests.

The next time around, I paused to sip the murky-looking liquid I had drained from the microwaved mushrooms. It had a pleasant, earthy flavor, so I set it aside instead of discarding it. After adding the onion and thyme, I let the mushrooms and the bottom of the pot get good and brown and then I added a small amount of sherry. Not only is sherry a classic partner for mushrooms, but recent test kitchen experiments have shown that sherry contains compounds that subtly boost the complexity and savoriness of meaty-tasting foods without stealing the show.

When it was time to add liquid to loosen the flavorful browned bits on the bottom of the pot, I reached for the mushrooms' own juices. Yes, it was ugly, but flavor was my main concern. For the remaining liquid I used about 4 cups each of water and chicken broth.

I pureed the soup in batches in the blender to make the soup as smooth as possible (and to avoid the tiresome step of straining it). Then I mixed up the emulsifying liaison from the earlier recipe: cream whisked with two egg yolks. I tempered the liaison with some hot broth and then added it to the soup and heated the mixture to ensure that the egg yolks were sufficiently cooked. I stirred in just a bit of lemon juice to sharpen all the flavors.

This soup was a big improvement on the prior batch. It had a rich yet clean texture, and the mushroom flavor was right up front, with just a subtle hint

NOTES FROM THE TEST KITCHEN

WHAT IS BISQUE?

Consult a tome on classic French cookery and you'll learn that "bisque" traditionally refers to a rich, creamy soup made with shellfish. Nowadays, the word is used to describe any creamy soup, shellfish-based or not, that's a step up in flavor and refinement from plainer creamed soups.

of sherry, a bit of woodsy thyme providing support, and the lemon bringing everything into focus. And happily, the flavorful mushroom juice had not muddied the appearance of the soup. Now it was time to play with mushroom varieties.

Readily available white mushrooms are inexpensive and worked well in the soup, so I decided to keep them, but I decreased the amount to just 1 pound so I could bring in other fresh varieties. Oyster mushrooms contributed little, but cremini mushrooms provided earthiness, so they were in. The last addition: shiitakes, which elevated the bisque without making it too rich.

This luxurious soup now had a deep, woodsy flavor worthy of a special occasion. A sprinkle of chives and a little cream and my work was done.

—ANDREA GEARY, *Cook's Illustrated*

Mushroom Bisque

SERVES 6 TO 10

Tying the thyme sprig with twine makes it easier to remove from the pot. For the smoothest result, use a conventional blender rather than an immersion blender.

- 1 **pound white mushrooms, trimmed**
- 8 **ounces cremini mushrooms, trimmed**
- 8 **ounces shiitake mushrooms, stemmed**
  Kosher salt and pepper
- 2 **tablespoons vegetable oil**
- 1 **small onion, chopped fine**
- 1 **sprig fresh thyme, tied with kitchen twine**
- 2 **tablespoons dry sherry**
- 4 **cups water**
- 3½ **cups chicken broth**
- ⅔ **cup heavy cream, plus extra for serving**
- 2 **large egg yolks**
- 1 **teaspoon lemon juice**
  Chopped fresh chives

1. Toss white mushrooms, cremini mushrooms, shiitake mushrooms, and 1 tablespoon salt together in large bowl. Cover with large plate and microwave, stirring every 4 minutes, until mushrooms have released their liquid and reduced to one-third their original volume, about 12 minutes. Transfer mushrooms to colander set in second large bowl and drain well. Reserve liquid.

2. Heat oil in Dutch oven over medium heat until shimmering. Add mushrooms and cook, stirring occasionally, until mushrooms are browned and fond has formed on bottom of pot, about 8 minutes. Add onion, thyme sprig, and ¼ teaspoon pepper and cook, stirring occasionally, until onion is just softened, about 2 minutes. Add sherry and cook until evaporated. Stir in reserved mushroom liquid and cook, scraping up any browned bits. Stir in water and broth and bring to simmer. Reduce heat to low and simmer for 20 minutes.

3. Discard thyme sprig. Working in batches, process soup in blender until very smooth, 1½ to 2 minutes per batch. Return soup to now-empty pot. (Soup can be refrigerated for up to 2 days. Warm to 150 degrees before proceeding with recipe.)

4. Whisk cream and egg yolks together in medium bowl. Stirring slowly and constantly, add 2 cups soup to cream mixture. Stirring constantly, slowly pour cream mixture into simmering soup. Heat gently, stirring constantly, until soup registers 165 degrees (do not overheat). Stir in lemon juice and season with salt and pepper to taste. Serve immediately, garnishing each serving with 1 teaspoon extra cream and sprinkle of chives.

SUPER GREENS SOUP WITH LEMON-TARRAGON CREAM

✓ WHY THIS RECIPE WORKS: We wanted a version of this popular, health-conscious soup that was uncompromisingly delicious. The key was to pack in all the essential nutrients of hearty greens without making any concessions on texture or flavor. For great flavor, we built a rich foundation of sweet caramelized onions and earthy sautéed mushrooms. We added broth, water, and lots of leafy greens and simmered the greens until tender before blending them until smooth. Arborio rice, blended right into the mix, thickened the soup without making it heavy or masking the vegetal flavor. For a vibrant finish, we added a drizzle of tangy lemon-tarragon cream.

Super greens such as kale, chard, and arugula are packed with fiber, digestive enzymes, vitamins, minerals, and countless antioxidants. Making soup out of these power foods is a great way to incorporate them into your diet, but if you simply boil a pile of greens,

you end up with a watery, bland pot of soup. My goal was to deliver a healthy dose of greens with a deceptively delicious, silky-smooth soup.

One of the first questions I faced was the choice of greens for the soup. I wanted a mix; some greens boast a heartier presence while others are more delicate and herbal. For my first attempt, I started with an entire pound of kale and another pound of Swiss chard, two of the darkest, heartiest greens I could get my hands on, plus spinach, watercress, and parsley. I simmered all the greens together and then blended them, which gave me a soup with plenty of heft but a less-than-ideal flavor. The kale was coming through too strong, and the spinach imparted a soapy consistency in conjunction with the other greens. To address these issues, I dialed back on the kale (and Swiss chard) and swapped the spinach for a green that added a new aspect to the mix—arugula. The arugula provided a bitter, peppery taste that complemented the fuller flavor of the heavier greens.

Now that I'd improved the mix of greens, I turned my attention to the base of the soup. I had started with mushrooms and caramelized onions, which I sautéed together before adding the liquid and greens. After the first test, I definitely knew I wanted to add garlic. I thought that maybe replacing the onions with roasted garlic would help deepen the flavor of the soup and bring more complexity to the mix. Unfortunately, making that swap threw off the balance of flavors; the roasted garlic flavor simply overwhelmed the whole pot. I knew I still wanted garlic, but as just an accent flavor, so I doubled back to the caramelized onions and added the garlic to them with the mushrooms and a pinch of cayenne pepper. This gave me a rich base for the soup that had both a touch of sweetness and savory depth (from the caramelized onions), and a bit of a bite (from the garlic and cayenne pepper). To this base I added 6 cups of liquid—half water and half vegetable broth for the right balance. Too much broth distracted from the flavors of the greens and too much water made the soup, well, watery. I steered clear of chicken broth because I wanted to keep the soup vegetarian-friendly. Next I added the greens and once they were tender, I moved to the blender, where I hit another bump, this time with the soup's texture.

One of the other main issues with a soup like this is thickening it; once I blended the cooked vegetables and greens, the consistency was too watery and thin.

SUPER GREENS SOUP WITH LEMON-TARRAGON CREAM

Many of the recipes I found were thickened with potatoes that were simmered in the pot along with the soup and then blended in. I tried this, but the potatoes tended to give the soup a muddy, earthy flavor that didn't go well with the clean taste of the greens. Instead, I opted for an unusual solution: Arborio rice. The rice—just ⅓ cup—could be boiled right in the pot with the broth and then blended in. The high starch content of the rice thickened the soup to a velvety, lush consistency without clouding the fresh, vegetal greens or the underlying complexity of the mushrooms and caramelized onions.

With such verdant flavors, this soup was in need of a vibrant finish to lighten things up a bit. Simply stirring lemon juice into the soup didn't work; the acid browned the beautiful green soup. Instead, I whisked together heavy cream, sour cream, lemon zest and juice, and bright, aromatic tarragon. Drizzled on top, the tangy cream provided the perfect pop to my deceivingly tasty, nourishing soup.

—ANNE WOLF, *America's Test Kitchen Books*

Super Greens Soup with Lemon-Tarragon Cream

SERVES 4 TO 6

- ¼ cup heavy cream
- 3 tablespoons sour cream
- 2 tablespoons plus ½ teaspoon extra-virgin olive oil
- ¼ teaspoon finely grated lemon zest plus
  ½ teaspoon juice
- ½ teaspoon minced fresh tarragon
  Salt and pepper
- 1 onion, halved through root end and sliced thin
- ¾ teaspoon light brown sugar
- 3 ounces white mushrooms, trimmed and sliced thin
- 2 garlic cloves, minced
  Pinch cayenne pepper
- 3 cups water
- 3 cups vegetable broth
- ⅓ cup Arborio rice
- 12 ounces Swiss chard, stemmed and chopped coarse
- 9 ounces kale, stemmed and chopped coarse
- ¼ cup fresh parsley leaves
- 2 ounces (2 cups) baby arugula

1. Combine cream, sour cream, ½ teaspoon oil, lemon zest and juice, tarragon, and ¼ teaspoon salt in bowl. Cover and refrigerate until ready to serve.

2. Heat remaining 2 tablespoons oil in Dutch oven over medium-high heat. Stir in onion, sugar, and 1 teaspoon salt and cook, stirring occasionally, until onion releases some moisture, about 5 minutes. Reduce heat to low and cook, stirring often and scraping up any browned bits, until onion is deeply browned and slightly sticky, about 30 minutes. (If onion is sizzling or scorching, reduce heat. If onion is not browning after 15 to 20 minutes, increase heat.)

3. Stir in mushrooms and cook until they have released their moisture, about 5 minutes. Stir in garlic and cayenne and cook until fragrant, about 30 seconds. Stir in water, broth, and rice, scraping up any browned bits, and bring to boil. Reduce heat to low, cover, and simmer for 15 minutes.

4. Stir in chard, kale, and parsley, 1 handful at a time, until wilted and submerged in liquid. Return to simmer, cover, and cook until greens are tender, about 10 minutes.

5. Off heat, stir in arugula until wilted. Working in batches, process soup in blender until smooth, about 1 minute. Return pureed soup to clean pot and season with salt and pepper to taste. Drizzle individual portions with lemon-tarragon cream, and serve.

NOTES FROM THE TEST KITCHEN

PREPARING HEARTY GREENS

1. To prepare kale, Swiss chard, and collard greens, cut away leafy green portion from either side of stalk or stem using chef's knife.

2. Stack several leaves on top of one another and either slice leaves crosswise or cut them into pieces as directed in recipe. After they are cut, wash leaves and dry using salad spinner.

EASY OVERNIGHT BEEF STEW

✔ **WHY THIS RECIPE WORKS:** We set out to reengineer our classic beef stew recipe so that we could do the bulk of the work on day one and simply finish it the next day. We usually start by cutting up a big chuck-eye roast, but this time we reached for boneless beef short ribs, which deliver big beefy flavor, require less prep, and turn tender faster than chuck roast—big advantages for this make-ahead stew. And rather than browning the meat in several batches, we saved time by throwing all the meat plus the onions into the pot at once. We used chilled broth to speed up the cooling time, and stored the stew overnight in the fridge. Holding back the vegetables until day two ensured that they were bright and fresh in the finished stew. Bringing the stew to a simmer and finishing it in the oven made for hands-free, gentle cooking.

Beef stew, with its tender meat, chunks of vegetables, and rich layers of flavor, is not a quick-cooking dish and typically, once you start cooking, you're in it for the long haul—meaning several hours of your day. I wanted to reengineer the test kitchen's classic beef stew to break down the work so I could start the stew ahead and finish it the next day—when I wanted to sit down and dig in. This would also entail streamlining our recipe—no hours-long cooking time and no staying up late waiting for a stew to cool down before I could turn in. I would also have to deal with the issue of reheating, which can result in overcooked and soggy vegetables.

The first challenge to overcome was the long cooking time, a previously necessary step when using tough, fat-marbled cuts of beef. In my first test, I had relied on a chuck roast (the test kitchen's favorite cut of beef for soups and stews). When simmered for hours, this cut breaks down to rich, meltingly tender pieces. But I didn't want to spend hours waiting for the beef to cook, so I turned to boneless beef short ribs, which deliver the same big beefy flavor with less prep and less cooking time.

Looking to streamline the recipe even more, I rethought the initial step of browning the beef. Browning meat helps to develop a deeper, more complex flavor, but the process can be tedious, requiring multiple batches to properly brown the individual pieces. For my next batch of stew, I threw all of the meat into the Dutch oven at once. For an added flavor boost, I cooked onions alongside the beef, in hopes they would soak up some of the beef's heartiness. After about 20 minutes, the pieces of beef had just begun to brown while the onions had softened. And the fond left over on the bottom of the pot was all I needed to build a satisfying base for the stew.

Deglazing the pot with red wine, I also added 2 cups of chicken broth to the pot and simmered the stew for just 30 minutes before taking it off the heat to cool. After 45 minutes of cooling time (during which the meat continued to cook), I added another 3 cups of broth that I had chilled ahead to quickly finish cooling the stew enough to store safely in the fridge, a process that can otherwise take upwards of 2 hours.

While I had been focusing on the beef, the vegetables still left a lot to be desired. Potatoes and carrots take time to cook, but between the initial stovetop work and the reheating, both vegetables became mushy and soft with very little flavor. I switched gears and decided to add the vegetables on the second day, so they could cook through just once and emerge fresh-tasting. I found that the fastest strategy was to add the vegetables and jump-start the stew by bringing it to a simmer on the stovetop and then transferring it to a preheated oven, where it cooked through gently in less than an hour. A final burst of fresh flavor came from frozen peas, which I mixed in at the end, allowing the residual heat of the stew to cook them through.

With my completed recipe, I was able to serve up bowls of hearty beef stew, a make-ahead version as good as the classic.

—SARA MAYER, *America's Test Kitchen Books*

Easy Overnight Beef Stew
SERVES 4 TO 6

- 5 **cups chicken broth, plus extra as needed**
- 3 **pounds boneless beef short ribs, trimmed and cut into ¾-inch pieces**
- 2 **onions, chopped**
- 1 **tablespoon vegetable oil**
  Salt and pepper
- 2 **garlic cloves, minced**
- 2 **teaspoons minced fresh thyme or ½ teaspoon dried**
- 3 **tablespoons all-purpose flour**

2 teaspoons tomato paste

¾ cup dry red wine

1 pound Yukon Gold potatoes, unpeeled, cut into 1-inch pieces

1 pound carrots, peeled and cut into 1-inch pieces

1 cup frozen peas

2 tablespoons minced fresh parsley

1. Refrigerate 3 cups broth. Combine beef, onions, oil, ¼ teaspoon salt, and ⅛ teaspoon pepper in Dutch oven over medium-high heat. Cook, stirring often, until released beef juices nearly evaporate and meat begins to brown, 20 to 25 minutes, reducing heat if necessary to prevent scorching.

2. Stir in garlic and thyme and cook until fragrant, about 30 seconds. Stir in flour and tomato paste and cook for 1 minute. Slowly stir in wine, smoothing out any lumps, and cook until slightly reduced, about 2 minutes. Stir in remaining 2 cups broth, scraping up any browned bits, and bring to simmer. Cover, reduce heat to low, and simmer for 30 minutes.

3. Remove pot from heat and let sit, covered, for 45 minutes. Stir in chilled broth to finish cooling.

4. Leave stew in pot or transfer to storage container. Cover and refrigerate for up to 3 days.

5. Adjust oven rack to lower-middle position and heat oven to 400 degrees. Skim excess fat from surface of stew and transfer to Dutch oven, if necessary. Add potatoes and carrots and bring to simmer over medium heat, stirring often. Cover pot, transfer to oven, and cook until beef and vegetables are tender, 45 to 50 minutes. Remove pot from oven, stir in peas, and let sit until heated through, about 5 minutes. Adjust stew consistency with extra hot broth as needed. Stir in parsley and season with salt and pepper to taste. Serve.

NOTES FROM THE TEST KITCHEN

COOL BEFORE STORING

Putting hot food in the refrigerator raises the temperature of the fridge, potentially making it hospitable to bacteria. To avoid this, make sure to cool food to room temperature before moving it to the fridge.

TUSCAN-STYLE BEEF STEW

✔ **WHY THIS RECIPE WORKS:** Tuscan beef stew (*peposo*) is a simple stew of beef braised in wine, with loads of peppercorns and a head of garlic cloves. To improve the texture and flavor of ours without veering too far from the original, we added tomato paste and anchovies for meatiness, powdered gelatin for body, and shallots, carrots, and herbs for complexity. To ensure a full-bodied wine flavor, we added some wine at the beginning of the long braise, more before reducing the sauce, and a small amount at the end. And we did the same with the peppercorns: cracked pepper at the start, ground pepper toward the end, and more cracked pepper on serving.

Peposo was supposedly created in the 15th century by Tuscan fornaciai, the furnace workers responsible for producing the terra-cotta tiles that line the dome of Florence's Basilica di Santa Maria del Fiore. As the story goes, the tilemakers would lay cheap cuts of beef into clay pots along with a head's worth of garlic cloves, a handful of peppercorns, and at least a liter of Chianti wine. The pots were said to be left uncovered near the kilns, where they would cook slowly while the tilemakers worked, until the meat was tender and the sauce reduced to a rich nap. True or not, it makes for a vivid story, just the sort of thing to get me into the kitchen, eager to experiment.

Modern interpretations of peposo incorporate tomatoes or tomato paste, along with other ingredients the tilemakers didn't have on hand: onions, carrots, celery, herbs, pancetta, and even things like frozen peas or butternut squash. I tested a fair number of these recipes, along with more purportedly traditional versions, and learned a few important things. I was drawn to the pared-down "classic" versions for their simplicity, but they were just a little too simple. On the other hand, recipes that took the dish too far from the basics were even more flawed. Some called for an excessive amount of tomatoes, and others were just overcomplicated. I wanted a version of peposo that hewed to its roots but which also boasted balance and depth. To achieve that goal, I'd need to make use of at least a few additional ingredients beyond the basics, as well as some modern techniques.

With that in mind, I got down to refining a recipe. Using what I already knew about beef cuts, I went with boneless short ribs. They have little collagen but

TUSCAN-STYLE BEEF STEW

are marbled with fat, which serves to keep the meat moist in a similar way. Salting them briefly helps them further retain moisture after long cooking (salt helps meat proteins retain water), and adding powdered gelatin gives the sauce a silky texture in lieu of the collagen.

I cut 4 pounds of short ribs into 2-inch chunks and placed them in a Dutch oven along with a head of garlic separated into cloves and lightly crushed, a few teaspoons of coarsely cracked peppercorns, and a bottle of Chianti. I covered the pot and placed it in the oven, set to a gentle 300 degrees, for about 2 hours.

The meat came out perfectly tender as I'd expected, but otherwise the dish was overall flat. To shore up its underlying flavor, I seared half of the short ribs to give the sauce a bit more meaty complexity. A tablespoon of tomato paste lent depth without calling attention to itself. Similarly, I added a teaspoon of anchovy paste, a common test kitchen practice that boosts meatiness without adding any noticeable fishiness. To help balance the wine's tartness, I added a few shallots and carrots. I left both in large pieces so that they'd be easy to discard before finishing the sauce. Finally, bay leaves and fresh rosemary brought just the right herbal notes.

Now for the key players: wine and pepper. I wondered whether a two-stage approach might work better: 2 cups of wine to give the stable flavors time to infuse the meat, and then a second hit of wine toward the end so some of the delicate volatile and unstable flavor components would still be in the pot when cooking finished. This did improve the flavor considerably, but the sauce ended up rather loose and thin. For a sauce with the proper consistency, I was better off adding a second portion of wine after straining the cooking liquid and then reducing the mixture for about 15 minutes. During this brief cooking time, most of the wine's flavor remained intact. To give the sauce a bit more body without boiling it down any further, I also added a few teaspoons of cornstarch. Saving a small amount of wine to add at the very end gave the finished sauce brightness.

At this point, there was little obvious pepper flavor to speak of, and without it, the dish wouldn't be worthy of its name. I tried simply adding more cracked pepper at the start, but the dish lacked the familiar floral pungency pepper is known for. However, adding pepper at the very end of cooking wasn't the answer either. While it brought that missing floral flavor to the dish, now the dish was lacking depth. I dug a little deeper into my science books and realized that pepper, like wine, needed to be added in stages to bring out the different flavor compounds.

To confirm my hunch, I steeped peppercorns in water for 2½ hours to mimic the stew's cooking time. Sure enough, I found that though the infusion lacked the pungency contributed by volatile and unstable compounds, it still had a uniquely earthy layer of flavor due to its stable compounds. So having some cracked peppercorns in the stew from the start made sense. I also began adding ground pepper along with the second addition of wine. Finally, a sprinkle of cracked peppercorns at serving ensured a heady aroma.

With tender, succulent meat; a rich, silky wine sauce; and a deep, peppery bite, there was nothing more this peposo needed, beyond a second bottle of Chianti to serve alongside and a hunk of crusty bread or a bowl of polenta to soak up the stew.

—ANDREW JANJIGIAN, *Cook's Illustrated*

Tuscan-Style Beef Stew

SERVES 6 TO 8

We prefer boneless short ribs in this recipe because they require very little trimming. If you cannot find them, substitute a 5-pound chuck roast. Trim the roast of large pieces of fat and sinew, and cut it into 2-inch pieces. If Chianti is unavailable, a medium-bodied wine such as Côtes du Rhône or Pinot Noir makes a nice substitute. Serve with polenta or crusty bread.

4   pounds boneless beef short ribs, trimmed and cut into 2-inch pieces
    Salt
1   tablespoon vegetable oil
1   (750-ml) bottle Chianti
1   cup water
4   shallots, peeled and halved lengthwise
2   carrots, peeled and halved lengthwise
1   garlic head, cloves separated, unpeeled, and crushed
4   sprigs fresh rosemary
2   bay leaves
1   tablespoon cracked black peppercorns, plus extra for serving

1 tablespoon unflavored gelatin

1 tablespoon tomato paste

1 teaspoon anchovy paste

2 teaspoons ground black pepper

2 teaspoons cornstarch

1. Toss beef and 1½ teaspoons salt together in bowl and let stand at room temperature for 30 minutes. Adjust oven rack to lower-middle position and heat oven to 300 degrees.

2. Heat oil in large Dutch oven over medium-high heat until just smoking. Add half of beef in single layer and cook until well browned on all sides, about 8 minutes total, reducing heat if fond begins to burn. Stir in 2 cups wine, water, shallots, carrots, garlic, rosemary, bay leaves, cracked peppercorns, gelatin, tomato paste, anchovy paste, and remaining beef. Bring to simmer and cover tightly with sheet of heavy-duty aluminum foil, then lid. Transfer to oven and cook until beef is tender, 2 to 2¼ hours, stirring halfway through cooking time.

3. Using slotted spoon, transfer beef to bowl; cover tightly with foil and set aside. Strain sauce through fine-mesh strainer into fat separator. Wipe out pot with paper towels. Let liquid settle for 5 minutes, then return defatted liquid to pot.

4. Add 1 cup wine and ground black pepper and bring mixture to boil over medium-high heat. Simmer briskly, stirring occasionally, until sauce is thickened to consistency of heavy cream, 12 to 15 minutes.

NOTES FROM THE TEST KITCHEN

CHEAP WINE IS FINE

Early recipes for *peposo* relied on inexpensive Chianti, while modern versions call for a midpriced bottle (whether Chianti or a similar Tuscan wine such as Montepulciano or Brunello). We made batches using cheap ($5), midpriced ($12), and pricey ($20) Chianti, along with other varieties we often use in the kitchen: Cabernet Sauvignon, Pinot Noir, and Côtes du Rhône.

We were surprised that the stew made with the cheapest Chianti went over well with most tasters. While the midpriced wine was agreeable to everyone, there was no advantage to cooking with the expensive bottle. Highly oaked, tannic wines like Cabernet became harsh when cooked, but cheap bottles of fruitier Pinot and Côtes du Rhône made good stand-ins for the Chianti.

5. Combine remaining wine and cornstarch in small bowl. Reduce heat to medium-low, return beef to pot, and stir in cornstarch-wine mixture. Cover and simmer until just heated through, 5 to 8 minutes. Season with salt to taste. Serve, passing extra cracked peppercorns separately. (Stew can be made up to 3 days in advance.)

SIMPLE POT-AU-FEU

✔ **WHY THIS RECIPE WORKS:** To simplify and streamline our recipe for this famous French dish of tender meat and vegetables in a savory broth, we used easy-to-find, affordable chuck-eye roast in place of hard-to-find cuts of beef and veal. To capture a savory, buttery taste, we cooked inexpensive marrow bones (often labeled soup bones) with the beef and then used the marrow in a finishing sauce of minced herbs, mustard, and minced cornichons. Turning this traditional stew into a braise created a more-concentrated broth. For a clear broth without the fuss, we skipped the skimming step most recipes require and simply kept the pot at a gentle simmer, which we guaranteed by transferring the pot to a low oven.

By many accounts, *pot-au-feu*—which translates literally to "pot on fire"—has been France's most celebrated dish since the French Revolution, extolled for providing sustenance to rich, poor, and everyone in between. Typically several cuts of meat are simmered in a pot of water with potatoes and other root vegetables until tender, at which point the meat is carved and portioned into bowls with the vegetables and the clear, complex-tasting broth is ladled over the top. To give the dish kick, pungent condiments like mustard and the tiny French pickles known as cornichons are served alongside.

In search of a hearty, satisfying meal for spring, I decided it was time to try making the dish myself. But when I gathered recipes, I was in for a surprise. I was expecting modest ingredient lists in keeping with pot-au-feu's reputation as a food of the people, but most were anything but. Instead of two or three meats, they called for practically an entire butcher's case: beef and veal shanks, oxtail, short ribs, veal breast, sausages, chicken livers—some even threw in an entire bird. Still, I wasn't ready to give up on the idea of this one-pot meal. What could I do to make it more approachable?

My first step was putting aside the massive stockpot employed by most recipes in favor of a more manageable Dutch oven. Next, I looked to whittle down the meat on the shopping list. Since beef was common to all the recipes I found, I made the bold decision to limit myself to it—and to just one cut. Whatever I chose would also have to be widely available, so I rounded up three good contenders: short ribs, brisket, and chuck-eye roast. Short ribs cooked relatively quickly and stayed juicy, but I ultimately decided that their price tag eliminated them. Brisket performed reasonably well, but it was bested in both flavor and texture by chuck roast, long one of our favorite braising cuts for its compact and uniform shape, deep flavor, and relative tenderness. Gently stewing a 4-pound roast (cut into two smaller roasts for faster cooking) for roughly 3½ hours in about 3 quarts of water until tender yielded plenty of juicy, sliceable meat. But while the broth was reasonably beefy, there was too much of it, and it tasted a bit weak.

I'd already cut the amount of water back at the start when I swapped the stockpot for the Dutch oven. Why not cut it back further and turn what was basically a soup into a braise for even more concentrated, flavorful results? I gave it a try, covering the meat only halfway with water and flipping the meat partway through cooking. Sure enough, I ended up with a quart of deeply flavored broth. I also took this opportunity to move the cooking to a low oven so I wouldn't have to worry about fiddling with the burner to keep the broth at a consistent gentle simmer.

Still, the broth was missing something. It occurred to me that in my haste to pare down the recipe, I'd overlooked a critical component: bones. Every single recipe I'd come across specified bone-in cuts, particularly beef shank. I knew from making plenty of stock that bones lend body to broth since their collagen breaks down into gelatin during cooking. But they also lend something else: marrow.

Marrow, the soft, flexible tissue found inside bones, is rich in glutamic acid, the primary compound responsible for the meaty taste called umami. It also contains diacetyl, the buttery-tasting compound often used to flavor microwave popcorn. Marrow is present in bones from many parts of the cow, but the femur, where the shank is cut from, contains an especially high ratio.

Often called soup bones, marrow bones are not only readily available in most supermarkets, but they are also inexpensive. After running a few tests, I settled on using 1½ pounds of marrow bones. Combined with the chuck, they gave me a broth with the beguiling mix of beefiness and butteriness that helps make traditional pot-au-feu such a standout.

A proper pot-au-feu broth should be clear, not cloudy. To this end, most recipes called for constant skimming the foam of the proteins and fats that rise to the top of the pot, lest they get suspended or emulsified into the broth during cooking. I tried omitting the skimming step and found that as long as the stock didn't boil, (the physical action of boiling churns fat and particles into the broth and makes it cloudy) any foam that formed settled to the bottom of the pot during cooking and was caught and discarded when I strained the liquid.

The range of vegetables found in pot-au-feu varies as much as the meat. In the name of simplicity, I narrowed it down to my tasters' top picks: potatoes and carrots. But I also found that whole stalks of asparagus added brightness and appealing color. Because I had switched from stewing the meat to braising, I didn't have enough liquid in the pot to add the vegetables while the meat was in there. So I transferred the finished chuck to a serving platter and popped it back in the oven (which I had turned off) to keep warm; I then defatted and strained the broth and returned it to the pot. In went the vegetables for a quick simmer, and that was it.

I loved the dish with its traditional accompaniments, but then I came up with something I liked even more: a simple stir-together sauce featuring parsley and chives, mustard, white wine vinegar, minced cornichons, and pepper. This bright sauce needed some fat for balance, and I knew exactly where to get it. I used the back of a spoon to harvest the soft marrow from the center of the bones, minced the marrow, and added it to the sauce. That beefy, buttery stuff elevated the sauce just as it had the broth. I not only dolloped it over the meat, but I also tossed a few tablespoons with the vegetables.

Here was a "pot on fire" that was not only simple but as satisfying as any dish I could imagine.

—DAN SOUZA, *Cook's Illustrated*

SIMPLE POT-AU-FEU

Simple Pot-Au-Feu

SERVES 6 TO 8

Marrow bones (also called soup bones) can be found in the freezer section or at the meat counter. Use small red potatoes measuring 1 to 2 inches in diameter.

MEAT

- 1 (3½- to 4-pound) boneless beef chuck-eye roast, pulled into two pieces at natural seam and trimmed Kosher salt
- 1½ pounds marrow bones
- 1 onion, quartered
- 1 celery rib, sliced thin
- 3 bay leaves
- 1 teaspoon black peppercorns
- 4–6 cups water

PARSLEY SAUCE

- ⅔ cup minced fresh parsley
- ¼ cup Dijon mustard
- ¼ cup minced fresh chives
- 3 tablespoons white wine vinegar
- 10 cornichons, minced
- 1½ teaspoons pepper

VEGETABLES

- 1 pound small red potatoes, halved
- 6 carrots, halved crosswise, thick half quartered lengthwise, thin half halved lengthwise
- 1 pound asparagus, trimmed

Flake sea salt

1. FOR THE MEAT: Adjust oven rack to lower-middle position and heat oven to 300 degrees. Season beef with 1 tablespoon salt. Using 3 pieces of kitchen twine per piece, tie each into loaf shape for even cooking. Place beef, bones, onion, celery, bay leaves, and peppercorns in Dutch oven. Add water (water should come halfway up roasts), and bring to simmer over high heat. Partially cover pot and transfer to oven. Cook until beef is fully tender and sharp knife easily slips in and out of meat (meat will not be shreddable), 3¼ to 3¾ hours, flipping beef over halfway through cooking.

2. FOR THE PARSLEY SAUCE: While beef cooks, combine all ingredients in bowl. Cover and set aside.

3. Remove pot from oven and turn off oven. Transfer beef to large platter, cover tightly with aluminum foil, and return to oven to keep warm. Transfer bones to cutting board and use end of spoon to extract marrow. Mince marrow into paste and add 2 tablespoons to parsley sauce (reserve any remaining marrow for other applications). Using ladle or large spoon, skim fat from surface of broth and discard fat. Strain broth through fine-mesh strainer into large liquid measuring cup; add water to make 6 cups. Return broth to pot. (Meat can be returned to broth, cooled, and refrigerated for up to 2 days. Skim fat from cold broth, then gently reheat and proceed with recipe.)

4. FOR THE VEGETABLES: Add potatoes to broth and bring to simmer over high heat. Reduce heat to medium and simmer for 6 minutes. Add carrots and cook 10 minutes longer. Add asparagus and continue to cook until all vegetables are tender, 3 to 5 minutes longer.

5. Using slotted spoon, transfer vegetables to large bowl. Toss with 3 tablespoons parsley sauce and season with salt and pepper to taste. Season broth with salt to taste.

6. Transfer beef to cutting board, remove twine, and slice against grain ½ inch thick. Arrange servings of beef and vegetables in large, shallow bowls. Dollop beef with parsley sauce, drizzle with ⅓ cup broth, and sprinkle with flake sea salt. Serve, passing remaining parsley sauce and flake sea salt separately.

NOTES FROM THE TEST KITCHEN

BONE UP FOR BETTER BROTH

One thing our chuck-eye roast didn't deliver was the silky body and almost buttery flavor of a broth made from bone-in cuts. The solution was simple: Add marrow bones. The soft tissue found inside the bones is packed with the amino acids responsible for meaty, umami flavors. It also contains the volatile compound diacetyl, a component of natural butter flavor, and brings a subtle buttery taste to the broth. As an added bonus, at the end of cooking, we scrape the marrow from the bones and stir it into our sauce to give it a beefy, rich boost.

CARNE GUISADA

✔ **WHY THIS RECIPE WORKS:** The hearty, warming Mexican beef stew known as *carne guisada* (literally meaning "stewed meat") is chock-full of beef and vegetables napped with an aromatic tomato sauce. We found that toasting 2 dried ancho chiles and adding them to the pot as the beef simmered, then discarding them just before serving provided seasoning without adding too much heat. Adding the traditional potatoes and bell peppers halfway through cooking allowed them to soak up the flavor of the stew without becoming too soft. We also added briny green olives at the end of cooking so they would retain their firm texture. Cutting our meat and vegetables into large pieces gave the stew an appealingly rustic texture.

During long, cold New England winters, few things provide comfort and warmth like a great beef stew. But by the time February rolls around, I find that I'm tired of the classic American standby. With weeks of cold weather still ahead of me, I went on the hunt for a beef stew with flair—and found carne guisada.

Popular throughout Mexico and Texas, this hearty dish (which literally translates as "stewed meat") is the Mexican answer to beef stew. As with its all-American cousin, versions vary widely—in the vegetables and spices they include, in the thickness of the gravy, and in the cut of meat used—though fresh chiles, bell peppers, potatoes, and canned tomatoes are all common additions. I knew I wanted my stew to taste distinctly Mexican so that it would stand apart from my traditional beef stew recipes. I wanted serious beefy flavor, a bit of spicy heat, and a thick, aromatic gravy that would carry the stew when served on its own or when served over rice. I started by choosing the best cut of meat for the job. Since the meat would be stewing for several hours, I turned to the test kitchen's favorite cut for beef stew: chuck-eye roast. Its big, beefy flavor was ideal; plus, its plentiful flavorful marbling and connective tissue converted into gelatin over the course of cooking, creating a silky, rich gravy. Cutting the roast into 1½-inch cubes made for a perfect, rustic consistency in the stew. Browning the beef before building the stew base created plenty of flavorful fond, which contributed lots of savory depth to the stew.

With the meat settled, I moved on to the traditional bell peppers and potatoes. I cut russet potatoes and red peppers into 1-inch chunks, tossed them into the pot, and let them cook with the beef, hoping that the potatoes would become infused with meaty flavor. But by the time the meat was fully tender, the vegetables were mushy beyond recognition. To fix this, I switched from starchy russet potatoes, which break down easily, to waxy red potatoes, which hold their shape nicely even with long cooking. I also decided to cut the veggies into larger pieces—1½ inches, to complement the hearty chunks of meat—and added the potatoes and the peppers halfway through cooking. This time, the potatoes came out perfectly, but tasters weren't happy with the distractingly "al dente" peppers. Luckily, this was easy to resolve: I simply cut the peppers into smaller, 1-inch pieces so that they would soften fully. For an extra flavor boost, I stirred in some chopped green olives at the end of cooking; I had seen them added in other recipes and they brightened up the dish nicely.

Next, I moved on to building a flavorful base. Most recipes I came across included some type of fresh chile for heat. I chose to use a jalapeño, which had good spice and a clean, vegetal flavor. Garlic and onion provided balanced, aromatic notes. As for the spices, the recipes I found were all over the map, ranging from simple ground cumin to premade spice blends like chili powder and Sazón. I wasn't thrilled about the idea of using packaged spice blends, which can be dusty and inconsistent from brand to brand, so I decided on a combination of dried oregano, cumin, and cinnamon, which brought warmth and an earthy sweetness to the stew. Beef broth and a can of diced tomatoes made a simple, flavorful liquid component.

At this point, the stew was tasting great—even though it looked similar to my classic American beef stew, the flavors were vivid and distinct. But tasters wanted even more Mexican flair.

I immediately thought of dried chiles; few things signify Mexican cuisine better than dried chiles and I hoped that I could use them to bring my stew to the next level. I decided on anchos, since their subtle smoky, fruity notes would underscore the other warm flavors in the stew. The trick would be to achieve deep chile flavor in the stew without overpowering all the

CARNE GUISADA

subtle nuances I had just created. I tried first grinding the toasted chiles to a powder and adding it with the other spices, but by the time I had added enough to be noticeable, the gravy was overly spicy. Instead, I decided to toast the chiles whole and drop them into the stew as it cooked. Just before serving, I pulled the anchos out and discarded them. This worked perfectly; the gravy was infused with chile flavor but maintained its multidimensional flavor profile.

Finally, I had created an intensely aromatic stew with incredible depth of flavor. This was worlds away from my classic American beef stew, and I knew I would happily eat this all winter long.

—SEBASTIAN NAVA, *America's Test Kitchen Books*

Carne Guisada
SERVES 6 TO 8

- 2 **dried ancho chiles, stemmed and seeded**
- 4 **pounds boneless beef chuck-eye roast, pulled apart at seams, trimmed, and cut into 1½-inch pieces**
  Salt and pepper
- 2 **tablespoons vegetable oil**
- 2 **onions, chopped fine**
- 3 **garlic cloves, minced**
- 1 **jalapeño chile, stemmed, seeded, and minced**
- 1 **tablespoon dried oregano**
- 1½ **teaspoons ground cumin**
- ¼ **teaspoon ground cinnamon**
- 2 **tablespoons all-purpose flour**
- 3 **cups beef broth**
- 1 **(14.5-ounce) can diced tomatoes**
- 1½ **pounds red potatoes, unpeeled, cut into 1½-inch pieces**
- 2 **red or green bell peppers, stemmed, seeded, and cut into 1-inch pieces**
- 1 **cup pitted green olives, chopped coarse**
- ¼ **cup minced fresh cilantro**

NOTES FROM THE TEST KITCHEN

TOASTING DRIED CHILES
Dried chiles can have dirt or dust on the outside, so be sure to clean them gently with a damp towel before using. Toasting deepens their flavor significantly. To make a dish spicier, include the seeds.

1. Adjust oven rack to lower-middle position and heat oven to 325 degrees. Toast anchos in Dutch oven over medium-high heat, stirring frequently, until fragrant, 2 to 6 minutes; transfer to bowl.

2. Pat beef dry with paper towels and season with salt and pepper. Heat 1 tablespoon oil in now-empty pot over medium-high heat until just smoking. Brown half of beef on all sides, 7 to 10 minutes; transfer to plate. Repeat with remaining 1 tablespoon oil and remaining beef.

3. Add onions and ¼ teaspoon salt to fat left in pot and cook over medium heat until softened, about 5 minutes. Stir in garlic, jalapeño, oregano, cumin, and cinnamon and cook until fragrant, about 30 seconds. Stir in flour and cook for 1 minute. Slowly whisk in broth, scraping up any browned bits. Stir in tomatoes and their juice and toasted anchos and bring to a simmer. Stir in browned beef and any accumulated juices, cover, transfer pot to oven, and cook for 1 hour.

4. Stir in potatoes and bell peppers, cover, and cook in oven until beef and potatoes are tender, 1 to 1½ hours.

5. Remove pot from oven and discard anchos. Stir in olives and let sit until heated through, 2 minutes. Adjust stew consistency with hot water as needed. Stir in cilantro and season with salt and pepper to taste. Serve.

CHAPTER 3

VEGETABLES, GRAINS, AND BEANS

RICE AND LENTILS WITH CRISPY ONIONS

RICE AND LENTILS WITH CRISPY ONIONS

✓ **WHY THIS RECIPE WORKS:** *Mujaddara*, the rice and beans of the Middle East, is a hearty one-dish vegetarian rice and lentil pilaf topped with crispy fried onion strings. For the pilaf, we found that precooking the lentils and soaking the rice in hot water before combining them ensured that both components cooked evenly. We pared down the typically fussy process of batch-frying onions in several cups of oil to a single batch of onions fried in just 1½ cups of oil. The trick: removing a good bit of the onions' water before frying by tossing them with salt, microwaving them for 5 minutes, and drying them thoroughly. A drizzle of rich yogurt sauce is the perfect final touch.

The Levantine rice and lentil pilaf known as mujaddara (pronounced "MOO-ha-druh") might be the most spectacular example of how a few humble ingredients can add up to a dish that's satisfying, complex, and deeply savory. Though every household and restaurant differs in its approach, it's simple to throw together. Basically: Boil basmati rice and lentils together until each component is tender but intact, then work in warm spices such as coriander, cumin, cinnamon, allspice, and pepper, as well as a good measure of minced garlic. But the real showpiece of the dish is the onions, which get stirred into and sprinkled over the pilaf just before serving. Their flavor is as deep as their mahogany color suggests, and they break up the starchy components. Finished with a bracing garlicky yogurt sauce, this pilaf is comfort food at its best.

I had every intention of making this dish a regular weeknight main course in my house but, frankly, had been disappointed with the recipes I'd tried. They all could do a better job cooking the lentils and rice, which I've found either too firm or overcooked and mushy. And while the onions should be the best part, the ones I made were either leathery, cloyingly sweet, or too crunchy. I could—and would—do better.

For any other lentil recipe, my first test might be to figure out which variety was best for the job, but in this case I knew that ordinary brown or green lentils were the way to go. When cooked properly, they become tender while just holding their shape—a consistency that ensures that they meld well with the tender-chewy rice. The other option, French *lentilles du Puy*, would remain too firm and distinct.

So I moved on to the cooking method. Lentil cookery is simple, but cooking lentils with rice was another matter, since I needed both components, which cook at different rates, to emerge evenly tender and also form a cohesive pilaf. After a battery of tests, it was clear that a combination of staggered and pilaf-style cooking was the way to go. Giving the lentils a 15-minute head start ensured that they finished cooking on pace with the rice. This step also allowed me to drain away their muddy cooking liquid before combining them with the rice, which made for a cleaner-looking dish. Toasting the rice in oil brought out the grain's nutty flavor and let me deepen the flavor of the spices and garlic by cooking them in the fat, too.

The one snag: Even after I parcooked the lentils, they still absorbed quite a bit of water, robbing the rice of the liquid it needed to cook through. Adding more water didn't help; the lentils simply soaked it up faster than the rice and turned mushy. Fortunately, I had a quick fix in mind—I soaked the raw rice in hot water for 15 minutes (while the lentils simmered), which softened the grains' exteriors so that they could absorb water more easily. Plus, this step loosened and washed away some of the excess starches, helping the rice cook up fluffy, not sticky.

On to those onions. Given that I'd be both stirring the fried onions into the dish and using them as a garnish (and, let's be honest, snacking on a few here and there), I'd start with a generous 2 pounds. That way, I'd have plenty even after the onions shrank way down during cooking.

The downsides of frying are the time it takes (multiple batches cooked for upwards of 30 minutes apiece) and the large amount of oil, so I made it my goal to cut down on both. Most of the cooking time is spent waiting for the water in the onions to boil away, so I thought about ways to rid the onions of some liquid before they hit the oil. The obvious answer: salt, the thirsty mineral we regularly use to pull water from vegetables.

So after cutting the onions into thin half-moons, I coated them with a couple of teaspoons of salt and let them sit. After 10 minutes, they'd shed a few tablespoons of water—encouraging results. I rinsed them to remove excess salt, dried them thoroughly, and piled all the onions into the Dutch oven at once, and turned the burner to high.

Most of the onion slices started out well above the surface of the oil, but sure enough, they collapsed quickly and everything was soon fully submerged.

About 25 minutes later, every last morsel was deeply golden and crispy with just a hint of chew. Not only that, but they were so far below the oil's surface that I felt bold and made another batch with just 1½ cups of oil—half the amount I'd been using. Happily, these were every bit as crispy and golden as the onions cooked in 3 cups of oil. I strained them and packed the onion-infused oil into a container to save, as it adds savory depth to salad dressings, sautés, and sauces.

In fact, why not swap the 3 tablespoons of oil that I was using for the pilaf for an equal amount of the reserved onion oil, boosting the savory flavor of the pilaf right from the start? I also added a touch of sugar to the rice and lentils to complement the warmth of the spices—a tweak I'd seen in a few mujaddara recipes. Many versions also suggested stirring in fresh herbs; I chose cilantro for its fresh, faintly citrusy flavor and bright color.

As I scooped myself a bowl of the fragrant pilaf; scattered a handful of crispy, supersavory onions on top; and dolloped on a quick-to-make garlicky yogurt sauce, I couldn't help thinking that this was in fact food fit for a king.

—ANDREW JANJIGIAN, *Cook's Illustrated*

NOTES FROM THE TEST KITCHEN

THE GARNISH THAT MAKES THE MEAL—AND MANY OTHERS

Crispy onions, stirred into the pilaf and sprinkled over the top as a garnish, add concentrated, sweet-savory depth and textural contrast, making *mujaddara* an incredibly satisfying meatless meal. But the onions are also great on salads and sandwiches and as a garnish for soups for a savory boost.

FRENCH LENTILS? NON MERCI.

Many lentil dishes benefit from the firm, distinct texture of the French variety known as lentilles du Puy. But in this dish, the softer (but still intact) texture of green or brown lentils is best because it pairs well with the tender grains of rice. A bonus: Green and brown lentils are also easier to find and cheaper than the French kind.

FIRM AND DISTINCT
Save small, firm French lentils for soups and salads.

SOFT AND CREAMY
Tender brown and green lentils work best for pilaf.

Rice and Lentils with Crispy Onions (Mujaddara)

SERVES 4 TO 6

Do not substitute smaller French lentils for the green or brown lentils. When preparing the Crispy Onions, be sure to reserve 3 tablespoons of the onion cooking oil for cooking the rice and lentils.

YOGURT SAUCE
- 1 cup plain whole-milk yogurt
- 2 tablespoons lemon juice
- ½ teaspoon minced garlic
- ½ teaspoon salt

RICE AND LENTILS
- 8½ ounces (1¼ cups) green or brown lentils, picked over and rinsed
  Salt and pepper
- 1¼ cups basmati rice
- 1 recipe Crispy Onions, plus 3 tablespoons reserved oil (recipe follows)
- 3 garlic cloves, minced
- 1 teaspoon ground coriander
- 1 teaspoon ground cumin
- ½ teaspoon ground cinnamon
- ½ teaspoon ground allspice
- ⅛ teaspoon cayenne pepper
- 1 teaspoon sugar
- 3 tablespoons minced fresh cilantro

1. FOR THE YOGURT SAUCE: Whisk all ingredients together in bowl. Refrigerate while preparing rice and lentils.

2. FOR THE RICE AND LENTILS: Bring lentils, 4 cups water, and 1 teaspoon salt to boil in medium saucepan over high heat. Reduce heat to low and cook until lentils are tender, 15 to 17 minutes. Drain and set aside. While lentils cook, place rice in medium bowl and cover by 2 inches with hot tap water; let stand for 15 minutes.

3. Using your hands, gently swish rice grains to release excess starch. Carefully pour off water, leaving rice in bowl. Add cold tap water to rice and pour off water. Repeat adding and pouring off cold tap water 4 to 5 times, until water runs almost clear. Drain rice in fine-mesh strainer.

4. Heat reserved onion oil, garlic, coriander, cumin, cinnamon, allspice, ¼ teaspoon pepper, and cayenne in Dutch oven over medium heat until fragrant, about 2 minutes. Add rice and cook, stirring occasionally, until edges of rice begin to turn translucent, about 3 minutes. Add 2¼ cups water, sugar, and 1 teaspoon salt and bring to boil. Stir in lentils, reduce heat to low, cover, and cook until all liquid is absorbed, about 12 minutes.

5. Off heat, remove lid, fold dish towel in half, and place over pot; replace lid. Let stand for 10 minutes. Fluff rice and lentils with fork and stir in cilantro and half of crispy onions. Transfer to serving platter, top with remaining crispy onions, and serve, passing yogurt sauce separately.

Crispy Onions

MAKES 1½ CUPS

It is crucial to thoroughly dry the microwaved onions after rinsing. The best way to accomplish this is to use a salad spinner. Reserve 3 tablespoons of oil when draining the onions to use in Rice and Lentils with Crispy Onions. Remaining oil may be stored in an airtight container and refrigerated up to 4 weeks.

 2 **pounds onions, halved and sliced crosswise into ¼-inch-thick pieces**
 2 **teaspoons salt**
 1½ **cups vegetable oil**

1. Toss onions and salt together in large bowl. Microwave for 5 minutes. Rinse thoroughly, transfer to paper towel–lined baking sheet, and dry well.

2. Heat onions and oil in Dutch oven over high heat, stirring frequently, until onions are golden brown, 25 to 30 minutes. Drain onions in colander set in large bowl. Transfer onions to paper towel–lined baking sheet to drain. Serve.

SLOW-COOKER FARRO RISOTTO

✔ **WHY THIS RECIPE WORKS:** Moving risotto from the stovetop to the slow cooker makes this usually finicky dish a breeze, with no laborious stirring required. Swapping out the usual Arborio rice for farro adds nutrients, including calcium and iron, and a complex, nutty taste to the dish. We had to make some small changes to our recipe to accommodate the way this grain cooks, including adding extra water toward the end of the cooking, but otherwise the farro substitution added almost no work at all to the process. For the other flavors in our slow-cooker farro risotto, we went with finely grated carrots, tangy goat cheese, and wilted baby spinach. The end result was a healthy, hearty dish with all the creaminess of traditional risotto but none of the fuss.

Making risotto usually demands a cook's attention from start to finish, which is one of the main reasons that so many home cooks avoid it. Accepted wisdom dictates that there must be near-constant stirring for as long as 30 minutes to achieve perfectly tender grains with a slight bite in the center. But most of us have neither the time nor the patience to invest this amount of work in a simple rice dish. By moving risotto to the slow cooker, I hoped to avoid all the pitfalls that plague this dish and turn it into a no-fuss exercise. In addition, I wanted to take the basics of the classic recipe and make them fresher and healthier for an alternative take on risotto, which is often enriched with an excess of high-fat cheese. My goal was to create a creamy, rich-tasting risotto with healthy ingredients and a hands-off technique for an easy slow-cooker dinner or side dish.

My first question was whether there was another grain that I could use. Arborio rice is traditional in risotto because of its high starch content. As Arborio cooks, its starches break down and gelatinize, giving traditional risotto a desirable creaminess. I wanted something with a bit more nutritional value, though, so first I turned to brown rice. I tried just replacing the Arborio with brown rice, since the whole grains and a higher nutrient content would bring the healthiness of my dish up a notch or two. I swapped in the brown rice in an adapted slow-cooker risotto recipe that we'd developed in the past, which includes microwaving the broth and adding liquid at the beginning and end of cooking, but it turns out that the starches in brown rice do not break down in the same way that the starches in Arborio do. The risotto turned out mushy instead of creamy and the grains of rice were completely lacking the firm, toothy center, or "bite" characteristic of Arborio risotto.

If I couldn't make brown rice work, what if I abandoned rice altogether? Farro is a mild, earthy grain made from hulled whole-wheat kernels. It has a sweet, nutty flavor and a chewy bite when cooked that actually makes it a good textural substitute for Arborio rice. When I substituted in the farro I did end up adding some extra water near the end of cooking in order to keep it from becoming too dry and sticky, but I didn't need to make any other dramatic changes to our usual slow-cooker risotto method. This whole-grain alternative would definitely amp up the healthiness of the dish and farro seemed like a great replacement for the rice. In fact, it turns out that Italians, who have enjoyed farro for centuries, have their own version of a risotto-style farro called *farrotto*.

Next, I turned to the question of what I would put in my risotto. This versatile dish frequently features some mix of vegetables, herbs, and cheese and can even be bulked up with fancier additions like truffles, seafood, and chicken. I wanted to keep my flavors simple and hearty to match the nutty taste of the farro, and I knew that I needed ingredients that could hold up in the slow cooker. As with our traditional Arborio slow-cooker risotto, I began with a base of onion and garlic that I microwaved along with the farro and a little bit of butter to give everything a flavor jump start before starting up the slow cooker. (Yes, you could sauté the aromatics and farro, but why dirty a pan when this hands-off microwave method works so well?) From there, carrots added a nice spot of color and finely grating them allowed them to actually overcook just slightly, which meant that the carrot "melted" into the farro to help create a creamy base. Then, at the end of cooking, once the farro was tender, I stirred in handfuls of bright, fresh baby spinach. The spinach quickly wilted in the hot farro but didn't overcook or turn into mush as it would have if added at the beginning of cooking.

The creaminess of traditional risotto usually comes not just from the Arborio rice but also from the addition of a hefty amount of rich cheeses and even heavy cream. Naturally, I wanted to skip these additions in my healthier version, but my farro risotto still needed a little extra creaminess to round it out, especially since it didn't have quite the same starchiness as Arborio risotto. Goat cheese turned out to be the perfect solution—just

4 ounces, stirred in at the end of cooking, was enough to give the dish a great creaminess and tang that were the ideal complements to the earthy sweetness of the farro, carrots, and spinach. I had a fresh, healthy, and largely hands-off dish that had all the rich creaminess of risotto, all the flavor and nutrients of farro, and all the convenience of the slow cooker.

—DANIELLE DESIATO, *America's Test Kitchen Books*

Farro Risotto with Carrots and Goat Cheese
SERVES 4

Do not substitute pearl, quick-cooking, or presteamed farro for the whole farro in this recipe; you may need to read the ingredient list on the package carefully to determine if the farro is presteamed. Use the small holes of a box grater to grate the carrots. For an accurate measurement of boiling water, bring a full kettle of water to a boil and then measure out the desired amount.

2	cups vegetable broth
1	cup whole farro
1	onion, chopped fine
1	tablespoon unsalted butter
2	garlic cloves, minced
¼	cup dry white wine
3	carrots, peeled and finely grated
	Salt and pepper
4	ounces goat cheese, crumbled (1 cup)
¼–¾	cup boiling water, plus extra as needed
4	ounces (4 cups) baby spinach

1. Lightly spray inside of slow cooker with vegetable oil spray. Microwave broth in bowl until steaming, about 3 minutes. In separate bowl, microwave farro, onion, butter, and garlic, stirring occasionally, until onion is softened, about 5 minutes; transfer to slow cooker. Stir in hot broth, wine, carrots, and ½ teaspoon salt. Cover and cook until farro is tender, 3 to 4 hours on low or 2 to 3 hours on high.

2. Stir goat cheese and ¼ cup boiling water into farro until mixture is creamy but still somewhat thin. If farro is stiff and thick, add remaining water as needed, ¼ cup at a time, until mixture is thinned. Stir in spinach, 1 handful at a time, until slightly wilted. Cover and cook on high until spinach is softened, about 15 minutes. (Adjust risotto consistency with extra boiling water as needed.) Season with salt and pepper to taste. Serve.

DRUNKEN BEANS

✔ **WHY THIS RECIPE WORKS:** To give our Drunken Beans a rich, complex flavor without imparting booziness or bitterness, we used a mixture of beer and tequila. To ensure creamy, intact beans, we brined them overnight, cooked them gently in the oven, and held back the acidic beer and tomatoes until they were tender. We used bacon for its smoky, meaty flavor, but to preserve that flavor, we removed the bacon from the pot after crisping it (to use as a garnish). Sautéing onion, garlic, and poblano chiles in bacon fat created a flavorful base.

Soupy beans, or *frijoles de la olla*, are a staple at most Mexican tables and for good reason. The humble preparation typically consists of beans, a bit of pork or lard, and just a few herbs and aromatics like onions, chiles, and maybe tomatoes. Once the flavors meld and the cooking liquid thickens slightly from the beans' starches, the dish is as satisfying as a rich stew. Add a side of rice and you've got a meal.

There are numerous iterations, but my favorite might be *frijoles borrachos*, or drunken beans, in which pinto beans are cooked with beer or tequila. The alcohol should be subtle, lending the pot brighter, more complex flavor than beans cooked in water alone. And yet, when I've made the dish at home, the alcohol tastes either overwhelmingly bitter, raw, and boozy or so faint that I can't tell it's there. I've also never gotten the consistency of the liquid quite right—that is, thickened just enough that it's brothy, not watery.

I set my sights on a pot that featured creamy, intact beans and a cooking-liquid-turned-broth that wasn't awash in alcohol but that offered more depth than a batch of plain old pintos.

My first step was to nail down the basics of Mexican pot beans. Step one was to soak the dried beans overnight in salty water—an adjustment we make to the usual plain-water soak because we've learned that sodium weakens the pectin in the beans' skins and, thus, helps them soften more quickly. For the pork element, I chose bacon; its smoky depth would ratchet up the flavor of the dish. I browned a few sliced strips in a Dutch oven. Setting aside the meat, I left the rendered fat to sauté the aromatics: a chopped onion and a couple of poblano chiles, plus minced garlic. Once they had softened, I added the drained beans, a few cups of water, bay leaves, and salt and slid the vessel into a low oven, where the beans would

simmer gently for the better part of an hour—no need to stir them or take the risk that they'd burst.

I gave the beans an hour head start before adding the beer. Though some recipes call for incorporating it from the start of cooking, we've learned that cooking dried beans with acidic ingredients (and beer is definitely acidic) strengthens the pectin in the beans' skins and prevents them from fully softening. As for what type of beer to use, recipes were divided between dark and light Mexican lagers, but I reached for the former, figuring that a full-flavored pot of beans would surely require a full-flavored brew. I mixed in 1 cup of lager and slid the pot back into the oven to meld the flavors

DRUNKEN BEANS

and thicken the liquid. But the results I returned to half an hour later weren't what I was hoping for. Most noticeable was the beer's bitter flavor. The extra liquid had also thinned out the broth so that it lacked body.

I figured that reducing the amount of beer would thereby reduce the bitterness and the volume of liquid, too. But when I used just ½ cup, the "drunken" flavor was lost. Next, I tried cooking a full cup by itself before adding it to the pot when the beans were done cooking, hoping to increase its flavor and drive off some bitterness. Wrong again. The reduced beer tasted more bitter than ever, and some research explained why: The compounds responsible for the complex aroma and flavor of beer are highly volatile and dissipate quickly when boiled, while those that contribute bitterness are more stable and, in the absence of other flavors, become more pronounced. Given that, I tried adding the beer to the pot just before serving. This did help the beer retain a more complex flavor, but it also retained more of its raw-tasting alcohol.

I decided to switch gears and try tequila instead, since I'd seen it used in a number of recipes. Further research told me that the flavor compounds in tequila are very stable and thus wouldn't be affected by a long simmer, so I added the tequila at the beginning of cooking to allow more time for some of the alcohol to evaporate.

In small amounts, the tequila's smoky-sweetness was very subtle, so I went with ½ cup, which added noticeable complexity. That said, my tasters and I all missed the beer's malty flavor, so I decided to use both types of alcohol. But this time I'd try a lighter (read: less bitter-tasting) lager.

Working up another batch, I poured in the tequila at the outset of cooking, but waited an hour to add the beer, as I had in my first test. This time I got the booze flavor just right: faint bitterness and maltiness from the beer, with a deeper underpinning of flavor from the tequila. To underscore the pot's fresh and sweet flavors, I took a cue from other Mexican dishes and added a bundle of cilantro stems (I'd use the leaves from the bunch as a garnish) along with the bay leaves and a generous ¼ cup of tomato paste with the beer.

The only lingering issue: the too-thin broth. The low oven wasn't reducing the liquid enough, so when I pulled out the pot to add the beer, I simply moved it to the stove where it would simmer more rapidly. The beans held their shape, releasing just enough starch to turn the cooking liquid into a satisfying broth.

—ANDREW JANJIGIAN, *Cook's Illustrated*

Drunken Beans

SERVES 6 AS A MAIN DISH

You'll get fewer blowouts if you soak the beans overnight, but if you are pressed for time, they can be quick-brined. In step 1, combine the salt, water, and beans in a large Dutch oven and bring to a boil over high heat. Remove from the heat, cover, and let stand for 1 hour. Drain and rinse the beans and proceed with the recipe. Serve with rice. Feta cheese can be used in place of the Cotija.

    Salt
1 pound (2½ cups) dried pinto beans, picked over and rinsed
30 sprigs fresh cilantro (1 bunch)
4 slices bacon, cut into ¼-inch pieces
1 onion, chopped fine
2 poblano chiles, stemmed, seeded, and chopped fine
3 garlic cloves, minced
½ cup tequila
2 bay leaves
1 cup Mexican lager
¼ cup tomato paste
2 limes, quartered
2 ounces Cotija cheese, crumbled (½ cup)

1. Dissolve 3 tablespoons salt in 4 quarts cold water in large bowl or container. Add beans and soak at room temperature for at least 8 hours or up to 24 hours. Drain and rinse well.

2. Adjust oven rack to lower-middle position and heat oven to 275 degrees. Pick leaves from 20 cilantro sprigs (reserve stems), chop fine, and refrigerate until needed. Using kitchen twine, tie remaining 10 cilantro sprigs and reserved stems into bundle.

3. Cook bacon in Dutch oven over medium heat, stirring occasionally, until crisp, 5 to 8 minutes. Using slotted spoon, transfer bacon to paper towel–lined bowl and set aside. Add onion, poblanos, and garlic to fat in pot and cook, stirring frequently, until vegetables are softened, 6 to 7 minutes. Remove from heat. Add tequila and cook until evaporated, 3 to 4 minutes. Return to heat. Increase heat to high; stir in 3½ cups water, bay leaves, 1 teaspoon salt, beans, and cilantro bundle; and bring to boil. Cover, transfer to oven, and cook until beans are just soft, 45 to 60 minutes.

4. Remove pot from oven. Discard bay leaves and cilantro bundle. Stir in beer and tomato paste and bring to simmer over medium-low heat. Simmer vigorously, stirring frequently, until liquid is thick and beans are fully tender, about 30 minutes. Season with salt to taste. Serve, passing chopped cilantro, lime wedges, Cotija, and reserved bacon separately.

TO MAKE AHEAD: The finished beans can be refrigerated for up to 2 days. Before reheating, thin beans slightly with water.

MILLET AND VEGGIE CAKES

WHY THIS RECIPE WORKS: Millet makes a terrific base for a savory fritter-like cake. It has a mellow taste, a bit like corn, that is easily adaptable to many different spices, and its nutty flavor stands up particularly well to bold seasonings like curry. Along with curry, we incorporated fresh spinach, sweet carrots, shallot, and garlic to create a highly flavorful, balanced mixture. Millet holds together well on its own because as it cooks the seeds burst and release starches, which become sticky and assist in binding. That said, we found that the additions of an egg and plain yogurt were helpful to further bind the cakes during cooking—plus, these ingredients gave the cakes richness and moisture. Chilling the formed cakes for 30 minutes further ensured that they were sturdy and easy to handle when cooked in a skillet until golden brown and crisp.

In the past few years, the variety of grains available at the local grocery store has skyrocketed. In addition to classics like rice, bulgur, and oats, you can now find more exotic options. With so many new grains on the market, I was excited to find one that I could add to my dinner repertoire.

The nutty, mild sweetness of millet won me over. Technically a seed rather than a grain, millet can be cooked pilaf-style or slightly overcooked so that the seeds burst and release starch. This sticky texture is an advantage when preparing a fritter-like cake. Risotto cakes are the most common grain patty in the test kitchen, and their main ingredient, Arborio rice, shares enough characteristics with millet that I felt confident in the success of millet cakes. Both Arborio and millet contain a lot of starch and are thus sticky, helping

pan-fried cakes to hold together. Served along with a salad, pan-fried millet cakes could make a hearty and satisfying vegetarian meal.

Hoping to capitalize on the natural clumping of the seeds, I made my first batch of cakes along with a little yogurt to ensure the cakes cooked up in one piece. Unfortunately, the cakes didn't hold up as well as I'd hoped. Although the millet had become sticky, it couldn't support the patties as I maneuvered them in the pan.

Millet and yogurt alone failed me on the first test, so for the next try I added an egg—and still kept the yogurt for its flavor and richness. The slightly beaten egg did the trick, binding the patties together perfectly.

Now that I had cakes that formed easily and didn't fall apart in the pan, I moved on to the flavors. Millet has a mellow corn taste that works well in both savory and sweet applications and is especially well suited for flavors from Asia and Africa, where millet is a staple. Curry powder, with its balance between sweet and spicy seemed like a good fit. Inspired by the curry's complex and warm, earthy taste, I turned to the vegetable element and chose fresh spinach and slightly sweet carrots.

But with the vegetables, the texture I had worked so hard for fell apart—literally. The spinach was full of moisture that seeped into the cakes while they cooked and made everything soggy. I removed the spinach and tried again. While the cakes did a better job of sticking together, my tasters missed the flavor and color of the leafy green. If I could find a way to include the spinach without the moisture, I reasoned, the cakes would be complex enough for my tasters without leaving a pile of mush in my frying pan.

Since I was already using a skillet to sauté a shallot with the curry powder (a technique called blooming), I tried wilting the spinach (and adding the carrots) at the same time. After 2 minutes in the pan with the aromatics, the spinach had lost most of its moisture and the carrots had taken on the flavors of the curry.

I formed some more cakes and got to work frying them in the pan, which I had wiped clean. This time the spinach-packed patties stuck together, but still not quite as well as I wanted. I had one final trick up my sleeve: Before putting them into the pan, I refrigerated the cakes for 30 minutes. The chilled cakes flipped easily in the skillet and stayed together once plated.

Looking to give the dish an extra kick and moisture, I whipped together a brightly flavored topping. A quick cilantro-mint chutney boasted the flavors of fresh herbs and warm cumin, the ideal complement to the slightly sweet and spicy millet cakes.

—STEPHANIE PIXLEY, *America's Test Kitchen Books*

Millet and Veggie Cakes

SERVES 4

Serve with Cilantro-Mint Chutney (recipe follows).

- 1 **cup millet, rinsed**
- 2 **cups water**
- **Salt and pepper**
- 3 **tablespoons vegetable oil**
- 1 **shallot, minced**
- 6 **ounces (6 cups) baby spinach, chopped**
- 2 **carrots, peeled and shredded**
- 2 **garlic cloves, minced**
- 2 **teaspoons curry powder**
- ¼ **cup plain yogurt**
- 1 **large egg, lightly beaten**
- 2 **tablespoons minced fresh cilantro**

1. Line rimmed baking sheet with parchment paper. Combine millet, water, and ½ teaspoon salt in medium saucepan and bring to simmer over medium heat. Reduce heat to low, cover, and simmer until grains are tender and liquid is absorbed, 15 to 20 minutes. Off heat, let millet sit, covered, for 10 minutes; transfer to large bowl.

2. Heat 1 tablespoon oil in 12-inch nonstick skillet over medium heat until shimmering. Add shallot and cook until softened, about 3 minutes. Stir in spinach and carrots and cook until spinach is wilted, about 2 minutes. Stir in garlic, curry powder, ½ teaspoon salt, and ¼ teaspoon pepper and cook until fragrant, about 30 seconds. Transfer to bowl with millet and wipe out now-empty skillet with paper towels.

3. Stir yogurt, egg, and cilantro into millet mixture until well combined. Divide mixture into 8 equal portions, pack firmly into 3½-inch-wide cakes, and place on prepared sheet. Refrigerate cakes until chilled and firm, about 30 minutes.

4. Adjust oven rack to middle position and heat oven to 200 degrees. Set wire rack in rimmed baking

sheet. Heat 1 tablespoon oil in now-empty skillet over medium heat until shimmering. Gently lay 4 cakes in skillet and cook until deep golden brown and crisp on both sides, 10 to 14 minutes, turning gently halfway through cooking. Transfer cakes to prepared sheet and keep warm in oven. Repeat with remaining cakes and oil. Serve.

Cilantro-Mint Chutney

MAKES 1 CUP

Any type of yogurt will work in this recipe.

- 2 **cups packed fresh cilantro leaves**
- 1 **cup packed fresh mint leaves**
- ⅓ **cup plain yogurt**
- ¼ **cup minced onion**
- 1 **tablespoon lime juice**
- 1½ **teaspoons sugar**
- ½ **teaspoon ground cumin**
- ¼ **teaspoon salt**

Process all ingredients in food processor until smooth, about 20 seconds, stopping to scrape down bowl as needed. Serve. (Chutney can be refrigerated for up to 1 day.)

CHILLED MARINATED TOFU

WHY THIS RECIPE WORKS: In the best renditions of this Japanese dish, a flavorful marinade and a few choice contrasting garnishes amplify the tofu's delicate sweet-soy flavor. We followed tradition and started with a soy sauce-enhanced dashi, the ubiquitous Japanese broth prepared from kombu seaweed and bonito flakes. This mixture produced a well-rounded marinade—sweet, salty, and robust—almost meaty in its intensity. A splash of rice wine vinegar, added off heat after the broth had steeped, provided a bit of balance. For garnishes, we liked a sprinkle of crumbled nori, sliced scallions, and a drizzle of sesame oil.

We love tofu in the test kitchen because it is an ideal canvas for bold or aromatic sauces. It also takes to a wide variety of preparations. But until a recent trip to a Japanese restaurant, I had never considered serving a plate of uncooked, marinated tofu.

Marinated raw tofu is served throughout Japan during the sticky summer months as a cool and refreshing appetizer or snack. When the heat outside is sweltering, a recipe that doesn't require a hot stove or oven is the kind I want to make. As an added bonus, this dish is significantly healthier than other tofu dishes I was used to making: I had cooked with tofu in the past but mostly by frying it and drenching it in a heavy dip. For my first time serving it raw, I decided to work from the ground up, refamiliarizing myself with the varieties of tofu, and then move on to a savory, fresh marinade.

So what is tofu, exactly? Tofu is the result of a process that is similar to cheese making: Curds, made by coagulating soy milk, are set in a mold and pressed to extract as much, or as little, of the liquid whey as desired. Depending on how long the tofu is pressed, and how much coagulant is used, the amount of whey released will vary, creating a range of textures from soft to firm. In general, firmer varieties are denser and hold their shape when cooking, while softer varieties have a creamier texture.

Hoping to strike a balance between moisture and firmness, I made my first batch of raw tofu using the medium variety. However, I needed a marinade for my dish before I could get started, so I looked to a traditional Japanese option: dashi. Dashi is a broth essential to Japanese cuisine, traditionally made with glutamate-rich kombu seaweed and shaved bonito (skipjack tuna) flakes. I wanted to keep my dish vegetarian, so I would need to find a way to replicate the bonito's fishy flavor.

After a good deal of trial and error, I found that adding a second variety of seaweed (wakame) helped to add depth to the broth, and Bragg Liquid Aminos acted as a substitute for fish sauce. Bragg Liquid Aminos is made from 16 amino acids derived from soybeans and has the meaty, savory, fermented flavor of traditional fish sauce. I then included some rice wine and sugar in the marinade to round out the flavors and stirred everything together with water. After allowing the flavors to meld, I strained out the solids and marinated the tofu for 2 hours.

The result of my first try was soggy tofu that hadn't soaked up the marinade. The choice of tofu seemed to be the problem. I had hoped that the creamy medium tofu would keep the dish from drying out, but it actually created the opposite problem: too much moisture. When I had cooked tofu in other recipes, the heat had driven away the extra water in the tofu. But now that I wasn't using heat, I needed a denser, less moist variation of tofu. Firm tofu was the answer. More whey is extracted from firm tofu when it is pressed, so it is denser and keeps its shape better than softer varieties. To get rid of even more moisture, I cut the tofu and drained the slices on a paper towel for 20 minutes and patted them dry.

I tried the recipe again with firm tofu and immediately knew I was on the right track. The tofu was moist but held together well. And as an added bonus, it had absorbed the marinade better than the medium tofu since the firmer tofu had less liquid to begin with.

Although the tofu had the texture that I wanted, the marinade still wasn't meeting my expectations. The flavors were good, but they lacked the bright kick I wanted for this summery dish. The fix was surprisingly simple: I added a few teaspoons of rice vinegar to the marinade after I had strained out the solids. The rice vinegar punched up the sweet, slightly fermented flavors of the marinade, finally giving me the ideal taste for the light dish I was envisioning. Hoping to help the tofu soak up even more of the now flavor-packed marinade, I used boiling water instead of room temperature, which aided in the absorption. Within 2 hours of refrigeration, the tofu was fully flavored and ready to serve.

The final touch was a sprinkling of garnishes, which added both a more appealing presentation and another layer of flavors. I turned to the sharp bite of thin-sliced scallions and the richness provided by a drizzle of sesame oil.

Without needing to turn on my oven, I had a fresh, healthy summer dish and a brand new way to use one of my favorite ingredients.

—MATTHEW CARD, *America's Test Kitchen Books*

CHILLED MARINATED TOFU

SERVES 4 TO 6

For an accurate measurement of boiling water, bring a full kettle of water to a boil and then measure out the desired amount.

14 ounces firm tofu, halved lengthwise,
   then cut crosswise into ½-inch-thick squares
   Salt and pepper
2 cups boiling water
¼ cup fish sauce substitute
¼ cup mirin
4 teaspoons sugar
¼ ounce wakame seaweed
¼ ounce kombu seaweed
4 teaspoons rice vinegar
2 sheets toasted nori seaweed, crumbled
2 scallions, sliced thin on bias
   Toasted sesame oil

1. Spread tofu over paper towel–lined baking sheet, let drain for 20 minutes, then gently press dry with paper towels. Season with salt and pepper.

2. Meanwhile, combine boiling water, fish sauce substitute, mirin, sugar, wakame, and kombu in bowl. Cover and let sit for 15 minutes. Strain liquid through fine-mesh strainer, discarding solids, then return broth to now-empty bowl.

3. Add tofu and vinegar, cover, and refrigerate until cool, at least 2 hours or up to 2 days. To serve, use slotted spoon to transfer tofu to platter, top with nori and scallions, and drizzle with sesame oil to taste.

NOTES FROM THE TEST KITCHEN

STORING TOFU

Tofu is highly perishable and has the best flavor and texture when it is fresh, so look for a package with the latest expiration date possible. To store an opened package, cover the tofu with water and store, refrigerated, in a covered container, changing the water daily. Any hint of sourness means the tofu is past its prime.

EGGPLANT INVOLTINI

WHY THIS RECIPE WORKS: Eggplant *involtini* recipes are often just eggplant Parmesan in a more complicated form: fried eggplant, milky cheese filling, and lots of sauce, with a blanket of mozzarella. We wanted a lighter, more summery dish that focused on the eggplant. Baking the eggplant instead of frying it allowed us to skip the salting and draining step, since the eggplant's excess moisture evaporated in the oven, and it meant that the eggplant's flavor and meaty texture weren't obscured by oil and breading. Swapping the usual ricotta-heavy filling for one that was boosted with a generous dose of Pecorino Romano meant we could use less filling without sacrificing flavor. Lastly, we made a simple but complementary tomato sauce in a skillet, added the eggplant bundles to it, and finished it under the broiler, which decreased the number of dishes required.

The first recipe I made for eggplant involtini ("little bundles" in Italian) started innocently enough with a homemade tomato sauce. While that simmered, I cut two eggplants lengthwise into ½-inch-thick planks and fried them. Frying sounds like one step, but in this case it was actually several: Before frying, I had to salt the planks for 45 minutes to remove excess moisture, pat them dry, and coat them in flour, eggs, and bread crumbs. After doing that with four batches, I was still only halfway done.

I mixed up a ricotta filling, spread a dollop of it on each slice, rolled up the slices, and arranged them in a baking dish. I poured the sauce over the bundles, topped the assembly with mozzarella and Parmesan, and baked it for 30 minutes—barely enough time to clear up the devastation my project had left in its wake.

The resulting dish was rich and hefty, similar to classic eggplant Parmesan, though the process had been even more arduous. But I was charmed by those tidy little involtini. My goal: Come up with a version of involtini that would emphasize the eggplant and minimize the fuss.

Many eggplant recipes begin by treating the cut fruit with a heavy dose of salt to draw out excess moisture. The flesh of an eggplant is made up of millions of tiny air-filled compartments enclosed by water-fortified walls. If you fry eggplant without removing some of that water beforehand, two things happen: First, those air sacs flood with oil. Second, when heat turns the water to steam, some of it will forcibly try to escape the flesh, damaging the structure of the fruit. The result? Mushy, oily, and entirely unappetizing eggplant.

When you salt eggplant, some of that potentially destructive water is removed, so the walls of the air sacs weaken and collapse. The end result is eggplant with a more compact, meatier consistency. And a denser texture means that there are fewer places for oil to get trapped.

But I didn't want to devote 45 minutes to drying out the eggplant if I didn't have to. And using a test kitchen shortcut where I microwaved the planks required almost half an hour of intermittent engagement.

By this time there was a rebellious thought lurking in the back of my mind: Maybe I wouldn't fry the eggplant. True, most recipes I found required frying the planks, but I was after a simpler, lighter, cleaner-tasting dish. And if I didn't fry, maybe I wouldn't have to salt.

Recipes for grilled eggplant rarely call for preliminary salting. That's because there's little oil on the grill for the flesh to soak up, and the eggplant's excess water quickly evaporates. I wasn't about to fire up the grill, but I wondered if other dry-heat cooking methods might offer the same benefits.

I peeled two eggplants and cut them into planks. Broiling the plain slices on a wire rack set in a rimmed baking sheet worked pretty well but demanded near-constant vigilance and flipping halfway through to prevent burning. It also required working in two batches. Hoping for a hands-off method, I tried baking instead.

I brushed the planks with oil, seasoned them with salt and pepper, and then baked them on two greased parchment-lined baking sheets in a 375-degree oven for about 30 minutes. Happily, they emerged light brown and tender, with a compact texture that was neither mushy nor sodden. I let the planks cool and firm up on the baking sheet for 5 minutes and then flipped them to allow the remaining steam to escape. These slices were meaty and tender, but not at all squishy, and I didn't miss frying. It was time to move on to the filling.

Ricotta, which forms the base for most involtini fillings, is subtle, so you have to use a lot of it if you want it to stand up to the tomato sauce. But for these lighter involtini, I wanted to decrease the overall amount of cheese. Swapping some of the ricotta for a lesser amount of a more assertive cheese seemed like the way to go.

I limited myself to 1 cup of ricotta, which was half the amount required by that initial recipe. Adding ½ cup of grated Parmesan and a handful of chopped basil to bump up its flavor didn't cut it, though, and the texture of the filling was unexpectedly tight and bouncy. In my next batch, I used bolder Pecorino Romano instead of the Parmesan, and I stirred in a tablespoon of lemon juice. Things started looking (and tasting) brighter—but that resilient texture remained.

It was clear that the dry, aged cheese was the source of that tight, granular texture. Just a small handful was fine, but when I added a full ½ cup, the texture of the filling deteriorated. In fact, it reminded me of ground meat that had been overcooked, and I wondered if it was indeed the same problem: an excessive linking of proteins. And that thought led me to the solution: bread crumbs.

When you add a paste of bread crumbs and milk (called a panade) to ground meat, it interferes with the linking of the meat proteins so that the cooked meat stays loose and soft. Bingo. When I incorporated just one slice of bread, whizzed to crumbs in the food processor, into the ricotta-Pecorino combo (no milk required), the filling remained creamy.

It was time to circle back to the beginning: the tomato sauce. The placeholder recipe I had been working with called for sautéing onions and garlic, adding canned diced tomatoes and seasonings, and simmering the sauce for at least an hour. It wasn't all that onerous, but my success with the eggplant and the filling had raised the bar, and now I demanded a sauce that could be made from start to finish while the eggplant had its 30-minute stint in the oven.

I swapped the diced tomatoes for more-tender canned whole tomatoes that I chopped roughly, and the sauce came together in about half the time. To trim a few more minutes, I stripped the sauce down to the bare bones: just garlic, oregano, tomatoes, and a pinch of red pepper flakes. I made the sauce in a 12-inch skillet instead of a saucepan, and I nestled the filled eggplant rolls directly in the simmering sauce. When the rolls had begun to warm through, I moved the whole skillet to the broiler instead of the oven.

After about 5 minutes, the eggplant was nicely browned and the sauce was bubbly and hot.

No one would mistake this light, fresh skillet supper for rich and heavy eggplant Parmesan. The eggplant truly shines, and the cheese and sauce complement it rather than weigh it down.

—ANDREA GEARY, *Cook's Illustrated*

SERVES 4 TO 6

Select shorter, wider eggplants for this recipe. Part-skim ricotta may be used, but do not use fat-free ricotta. Serve the eggplant with crusty bread and a salad.

2 large eggplants (1½ pounds each), peeled
6 tablespoons vegetable oil
  Kosher salt and pepper
2 garlic cloves, minced
¼ teaspoon dried oregano
  Pinch red pepper flakes
1 (28-ounce) can whole peeled tomatoes, drained with juice reserved, chopped coarse
1 slice hearty white sandwich bread, torn into 1-inch pieces
8 ounces (1 cup) whole-milk ricotta cheese
1½ ounces grated Pecorino Romano cheese (¾ cup)
¼ cup plus 1 tablespoon chopped fresh basil
1 tablespoon lemon juice

1. Slice each eggplant lengthwise into ½-inch-thick planks (you should have 12 planks). Trim rounded surface from each end piece so it lies flat.

2. Adjust 1 oven rack to lower-middle position and second rack 8 inches from broiler element. Heat oven to 375 degrees. Line 2 rimmed baking sheets with parchment paper and spray generously with vegetable oil spray. Arrange eggplant slices in single layer on prepared sheets. Brush 1 side of eggplant slices with 2½ tablespoons oil and sprinkle with ½ teaspoon salt and ¼ teaspoon pepper. Flip and repeat. Bake until tender and lightly browned, 30 to 35 minutes, switching and rotating sheets halfway through baking. Let cool for 5 minutes. Using thin spatula, flip each slice over. Heat broiler.

3. While eggplant cooks, heat remaining 1 tablespoon oil in 12-inch broiler-safe skillet over medium-low heat until just shimmering. Add garlic, oregano, pepper flakes, and ½ teaspoon salt and cook, stirring occasionally, until fragrant, about 30 seconds. Stir in tomatoes and their juice. Increase heat to high and bring to simmer. Reduce heat to medium-low and simmer until thickened, about 15 minutes. Cover and set aside.

4. Pulse bread in food processor until finely ground, 10 to 15 pulses. Combine bread crumbs, ricotta, ½ cup Pecorino, ¼ cup basil, lemon juice, and ½ teaspoon salt in medium bowl.

5. With widest ends of eggplant slices facing you, evenly distribute ricotta mixture on bottom third of each slice. Gently roll up each eggplant slice and place seam side down in tomato sauce.

6. Bring sauce to simmer over medium heat. Simmer for 5 minutes. Transfer skillet to oven and broil until eggplant is well browned and cheese is heated through, 5 to 10 minutes. Sprinkle with remaining ¼ cup Pecorino and let stand for 5 minutes. Sprinkle with remaining 1 tablespoon basil and serve.

VEGETABLE BIBIMBAP

✅ **WHY THIS RECIPE WORKS:** This one-bowl dish, a staple of Korean cuisine, features short-grain rice topped with sautéed vegetables, beef, and a fried egg. To make a vegetarian version of *bibimbap*, we swapped the beef for meaty shiitake mushrooms in a savory sauce made of soy sauce, garlic, and toasted sesame oil. As a topping for the mushrooms, we made a quick pickle of grated carrot, bean sprouts, and cucumber steeped in rice vinegar. This lent bright flavor and crunch to the dish. The final step was topping each bowl with a perfectly fried egg. As is traditional, we left the yolk runny so it could be broken and stirred throughout the rice and vegetables to add a silky richness to the finished dish.

Rice is all but guaranteed to be featured at every Korean meal. Perhaps the most popular way to enjoy rice is in bibimbap—a dish composed of tender-chewy short-grain rice heaped into bowls and topped with an array of sautéed vegetables, meat, and a fried egg. Just before serving, the steaming contents are traditionally drizzled with sesame oil, and the egg yolk is broken and stirred throughout the bowl, giving credence to bibimbap's literal translation of "mixed rice." Recipes for bibimbap can vary dramatically. Some rely on leftovers while others use all freshly made components, and toppings vary widely based on personal taste and opinions. I set out to develop my own version of this comforting dish that could still be savory and satisfying while skipping the beef and using the traditional aspects of bibimbap to my advantage.

First, there's the base of bibimbap: the rice. While cooking a pot of rice seems like a simple task, there is

VEGETABLE BIBIMBAP

more to it than meets the eye. We had already figured out how to deal with the more temperamental aspects of short-grain rice when we developed our traditional beef version of this dish, so I knew that I had to start with a different approach. Short-grain rice requires a completely different cooking technique than the long-grain rice that we most commonly use in the test kitchen. It must be cooked in enough water that it softens correctly; however, if you add too much liquid to short-grain rice, it takes on a creamy, risotto-like texture. A 1:1 ratio of water to rice is ideal. Rather than adding the rice to already boiling water, I brought the rice and water to a boil together and then reduced the heat and simmered the rice briefly. I then let the rice finish cooking, covered, off the heat. This very gentle, three-step cooking technique yielded delicately textured, fluffy grains that were perfect for a rice bowl; no more gummy, wet rice or scorched bottom layers. A small amount of rice vinegar added to the boiling liquid brightened the overall taste of the dish from the bottom up.

Meaty shiitake mushrooms were a natural option to replace the thinly sliced beef that usually appears in this dish, but I found that without any additional flavorings the dish tasted flat once I made this vegetarian swap. Since I wasn't relying on the complex umami notes of the beef, I had to add flavor in other ways through the seasonings and toppings I chose. Sautéed spinach with garlic is a favorite traditional topping choice for bibimbap, not only for its emerald green color and mineral flavor but also for its contrasting texture. Instead of cooking the spinach separately, I combined it right in the pan with the mushrooms and garlic to meld the flavors and give the shiitakes greater complexity. I added soy sauce and additional rice vinegar directly to the mixture to deepen and brighten the flavors. I also opted to add the toasted sesame oil to the mushroom-spinach mixture at this point to concentrate that oil's strong flavors on the mushrooms rather than drizzling it over the finished rice bowls as is more traditional.

For my other toppings, I went with carrot, cucumber, and bean sprouts, which I quick-pickled in rice vinegar—just half an hour was enough to get a great tang and crunch, although the vegetables can also be left to sit overnight. Pickling the vegetables instead of trying to sauté them not only cut down on cooking for that step in the recipe, but it also added a crisp,

bright flavor to the bibimbap. It was also a completely authentic choice, since bibimbap is often served with kimchi (a spicy-sour fermented Korean vegetable condiment). I then turned my attention to cooking the final component—the eggs. Fried eggs are an essential topper for bibimbap. The runny yolk adds richness and texture to this otherwise lean dish. Reusing my skillet, I added four eggs and cooked them covered until the whites were cooked through and tender and the yolks were hot but still runny. I easily slid the eggs out and topped each bowl of rice with one. The final touch was adding my quick-pickled vegetable topping and I had a perfectly balanced, complex, and satisfying vegetarian version of this classic rice bowl.

—STEPHANIE PIXLEY, *America's Test Kitchen Books*

Vegetable Bibimbap

SERVES 4

Grate the carrots on a coarse grater. You can use either seasoned or unseasoned rice vinegar in this recipe. You can substitute sushi rice for the short-grain rice; if using medium- or long-grain rice, increase the amount of water to 3 cups and simmer until the grains are tender, 18 to 20 minutes, in step 2.

PICKLED VEGETABLES

    4   ounces (2 cups) bean sprouts
    1   carrot, peeled and shredded
    1   cucumber, peeled, halved lengthwise, seeded,
        and sliced ¼ inch thick
    1   cup rice vinegar

RICE

    2   cups short-grain white rice
    2   cups water
    2   teaspoons rice vinegar
    1   teaspoon salt

VEGETABLES AND EGGS

    2   tablespoons vegetable oil
   12   ounces shiitake mushrooms, stemmed and
        sliced ½ inch thick
    3   garlic cloves, minced
   10   ounces (10 cups) baby spinach
    2   tablespoons soy sauce

2 tablespoons toasted sesame oil

1 tablespoon rice vinegar

Salt and pepper

4 large eggs

1. FOR THE PICKLED VEGETABLES: Combine all ingredients in bowl, pressing to submerge vegetables in vinegar. Cover and refrigerate for at least 30 minutes or up to 24 hours. Before serving, strain vegetables, discarding liquid.

2. FOR THE RICE: Bring rice, water, vinegar, and salt to boil in medium saucepan over high heat. Cover, reduce heat to low, and cook until liquid has been absorbed, 7 to 9 minutes. Remove rice from heat and let sit, covered, until tender, about 15 minutes.

3. FOR THE VEGETABLES AND EGGS: Heat 1 tablespoon vegetable oil in 12-inch nonstick skillet over medium-high heat until just smoking. Add mushrooms and cook, stirring occasionally, until they release their liquid, 5 to 7 minutes. Stir in garlic and cook until fragrant, about 30 seconds. Stir in spinach, 1 handful at a time, and cook until wilted, about 3 minutes. Off heat, stir in soy sauce, toasted sesame oil, and vinegar, and season with salt and pepper to taste. Transfer to platter and tent loosely with aluminum foil.

4. Crack eggs into 2 small bowls (2 eggs per bowl) and season with salt and pepper. Wipe out now-empty skillet with paper towels, add remaining 1 tablespoon oil, and heat over medium heat until shimmering. Working quickly, pour 1 bowl of eggs in 1 side of pan and second bowl of eggs in other side. Cover and cook until whites are set but yolks are still runny, 2 to 3 minutes.

5. To serve, portion rice into bowls, top with vegetables and fried egg, and serve with pickled vegetables.

NOTES FROM THE TEST KITCHEN

RICE VINEGAR

Rice vinegar is made from glutinous rice that is broken down into sugars, blended with yeast to ferment into alcohol, and aerated to form vinegar. It has a sweet-tart flavor that is used to accentuate many Asian dishes. It comes in an unseasoned version and a seasoned version with added sake, sugar, and salt.

VEGETABLE MOUSSAKA

✔ WHY THIS RECIPE WORKS: Traditional recipes for this Greek dish combine ground meat (typically lamb) with cinnamon, nutmeg, and tomatoes, then top that with eggplant and a thick béchamel sauce to make a layered casserole. For our vegetarian interpretation of *moussaka*, we built a hearty foundation with spiced bulgur and potatoes in place of meat. Blooming the cinnamon with sautéed onion and garlic produced warm savory flavor, and precooking the potatoes before adding them to the tomatoes and baking them in the casserole ensured they would come out tender. Bulgur requires just a brief soak to tenderize it, so we simply stirred it into the potato-tomato mixture and let it sit off the heat until it had absorbed all the excess liquid (and plenty of flavor). For our eggplant layer, we sliced it into small cubes, tossed it with olive oil, salt, and pepper and stuck it in the oven to roast while we created our potato-bulgur base. Finally, we made a thick, rich béchamel to spread over the top and baked the dish until it was hot and bubbling.

Moussaka is a familiar dish and a staple of fine Greek restaurants and informal diners alike. Traditionally, the recipe calls for a rich layered casserole of roasted eggplant, tomato sauce enriched with meat (usually ground lamb), and creamy béchamel, similar to a lasagna or shepherd's pie. The problem is that often the eggplant is soaked in oil and the filling and sauce are cloyingly rich yet disappointingly bland—nothing like the delicate, nuanced casserole that I was looking for. In addition, I knew that if I was going to remove the ground meat I would need to find something hearty and flavorful to replace it. I wanted to make a vegetarian version of moussaka that was as close to authentic as I could get, and worth all of the effort of this fairly involved dish.

I started out working with our traditional moussaka recipe, which includes ground lamb. While developing that recipe, we had discovered that eggplant is the Achilles' heel of moussaka. Most recipes either pan-fried or roasted the eggplant before assembling the casserole. Fried eggplant was, across the board, greasy. The porous vegetable greedily soaked up oil from the pan, and then leached it into the moussaka once baked. Roasted eggplant wasn't nearly as greasy, required a minimum amount of oil to brown, and had a superior texture and flavor. The high heat of the oven effectively caramelized the eggplant, magnifying its sweetness and tempering its bitterness, so roasting seemed like the best option for the eggplant component of this dish. But finding the perfect temperature and timing for the eggplant was tricky. Roasted too hot, the edges of the eggplant burned before the center cooked. Too low, and the eggplant took an eternity to brown and consequently turned mushy. The best solution was cutting the eggplant into smaller pieces, tossing them with a small amount of oil, and baking at 450 degrees for 40 to 50 minutes so the eggplant browned evenly without turning too soft. While the eggplant was cooking, I set out to prepare the filling and the béchamel.

The usual ground-meat-and-tomato filling for moussaka is rich, slightly sweet, and perfumed with cinnamon and oregano. To replace the meat I looked to bulgur—it has a similar coarseness to ground meat and makes a good base for the tomato sauce, since its mild character soaks up any flavors you add to the sauce. I started by using diced tomatoes in the sauce but found that they caused flavor and texture problems. In order to keep the sauce from being too watery and bland I switched to crushed tomatoes, which integrated with the bulgur more smoothly. To bulk up the filling a little I added potatoes to the base as well and simmered them first to ensure they would be cooked through. A good quantity of onions and garlic was a given, as their sweetness and piquancy lent the filling a solid base of flavor. I let the whole mixture sit until the filling's excess moisture soaked into the bulgur (and tenderized it) and the flavors blended together.

When it comes to seasoning the filling, Greeks tend to include a fairly substantial amount of cinnamon in traditional versions of the dish, but I found that too much cinnamon easily overpowered the moussaka's other interesting flavors, so I settled on a modest 1 teaspoon. For herbs, a small amount of oregano lent the right amount of freshness. I bloomed the herbs in the pan along with the onion and garlic to build complex flavor in the base of the dish.

The béchamel that covers a dish of moussaka needs to form a thick blanket over the top, sealing in the filling. I realized my béchamel would need to be a bit thicker than typical versions in order to seal in the bubbling filling and brown attractively in the oven, so I added extra flour. In traditional moussaka recipes, the béchamel is often enriched with a crumbly aged cheese

called *myzithra*. Since myzithra can be hard to find at the local supermarket, I looked into possible substitutions. Myzithra is saltier, drier, and richer-tasting than Greece's more common feta cheese, but it can be pretty closely approximated with a healthy dose of Parmesan, which is more common and widely available.

Baking the moussaka was a simple matter of watching the filling percolate beneath the béchamel. A moderately hot oven—400 degrees—quickly brought the moussaka up to temperature without burning the béchamel. Finally, a sprinkle of fresh chopped basil on the finished dish added a little brightness to my hearty vegetarian take on this classic Greek casserole.

—STEPHANIE PIXLEY, *America's Test Kitchen Books*

Vegetable Moussaka

SERVES 6 TO 8

When buying eggplant, look for those that are glossy, feel firm, and are heavy for their size. You can swap fine-grind bulgur for the medium-grind in this recipe. Do not substitute low-fat or skim milk in the sauce.

- 4 pounds eggplant, peeled and cut into ¾-inch pieces
- ¼ cup extra-virgin olive oil
  Salt and pepper
- 1 onion, chopped fine
- 4 garlic cloves, minced
- 1 tablespoon minced fresh oregano or 1 teaspoon dried
- 1 teaspoon ground cinnamon
- ½ cup dry white wine
- 1 pound russet potatoes, peeled and cut into ½-inch pieces
- 2 cups vegetable broth
- 1 (28-ounce) can crushed tomatoes
- 1 cup medium-grind bulgur, rinsed
- 3 tablespoons unsalted butter
- ¼ cup (1¼ ounces) all-purpose flour
- 2 cups whole milk
- 2 ounces Parmesan cheese, grated (1 cup)
  Pinch ground nutmeg
- 2 tablespoons chopped fresh basil

1. Adjust oven racks to upper-middle and lower-middle positions and heat oven to 450 degrees. Line 2 rimmed baking sheets with aluminum foil and spray with vegetable oil spray. Toss eggplant with 3 tablespoons oil, 1 teaspoon salt, and ¼ teaspoon pepper and spread evenly over prepared sheets. Bake until eggplant is light golden brown and tender, 40 to 50 minutes, switching and rotating sheets halfway through roasting. Set eggplant aside to cool. Reduce oven temperature to 400 degrees and adjust oven rack to middle position.

2. Meanwhile, heat remaining 1 tablespoon oil in Dutch oven over medium heat until shimmering. Add onion and ½ teaspoon salt and cook until onion is softened, about 5 minutes. Stir in garlic, oregano, and cinnamon and cook until fragrant, about 30 seconds. Stir in wine, scraping up any browned bits, until nearly all liquid is evaporated, about 2 minutes. Stir in potatoes and broth and bring to simmer. Cover, reduce heat to low, and cook until potatoes are nearly tender, about 15 minutes.

3. Stir in tomatoes and their juice and cook, uncovered, until flavors meld, about 5 minutes. Off heat, stir in bulgur and let sit until grains are tender and most of liquid is absorbed, about 15 minutes. Transfer to 13 by 9-inch baking dish and top evenly with roasted eggplant to form compact layer.

4. Melt butter in now-empty pot over medium heat. Stir in flour and cook for 1 minute. Gradually whisk in milk, bring to simmer, and cook, whisking often, until sauce thickens and no longer tastes of flour, about 5 minutes. Off heat, whisk in Parmesan and nutmeg and season with salt and pepper to taste. Pour sauce over eggplant and smooth into even layer.

NOTES FROM THE TEST KITCHEN

BULGUR

Bulgur is a grain made from parboiled or steamed wheat kernels/berries that are then dried and partially stripped of their outer bran layer, and coarsely ground. The result of this process is a relatively fast-cooking, highly nutritious grain that can be used in a variety of applications. Bulgur is sold in grind sizes from fine (#1) to extra-coarse (#4). Most recipes using bulgur call for medium grind (#2). To prepare bulgur, regardless of grain size, we rinse it to remove any detritus and excess starches that can turn the grain gluey. Then we simply soak the bulgur in water or another liquid, such as lemon or lime juice, until tender. Bulgur requires little more than a soak to become tender and flavorful, so it's perfect for salads and other no-cook recipes. Coarse-grind bulgur, which requires simmering, is our top choice for making pilaf. Don't confuse bulgur with cracked wheat, which is not parcooked. Cracked wheat cannot be substituted for bulgur.

5. Cover with foil and bake until bubbling around edges, about 15 minutes. Uncover and continue to bake until top is light golden brown around edges, about 15 minutes. Let cool for 10 minutes. Sprinkle with basil and serve.

SLOW-COOKER STUFFED SPICED EGGPLANTS

✓ **WHY THIS RECIPE WORKS:** When cooked, eggplants turn rich and creamy, losing the bitterness they have when raw. Italian eggplants, which are slightly smaller than common globe eggplants, are the ideal size and shape for stuffing when halved, and two of them fit easily in a slow cooker. We created a simple stuffing with canned diced tomatoes, Pecorino Romano, pine nuts, and aromatics including onion, garlic, oregano, and cinnamon. We simply nestled the halved eggplants cut side down in this fragrant mixture and let them cook until tender. After removing the eggplants from the slow cooker, we gently pushed the soft flesh to the sides to create a cavity, which we filled with the aromatic tomato mixture left behind in the slow cooker. Topped with extra cheese, pine nuts, and chopped parsley, these eggplants looked beautiful and were far easier to make than most traditional versions.

Whether grilled, roasted, or fried, eggplant's flesh is transformed from mildly bitter to rich and complex when cooked, making it a versatile, satisfying vegetable. Each preparation has its merits, but I thought the idea of marrying the creamy, rich eggplant with a texturally contrasting filling in the closed environment of the slow cooker offered great potential as a hearty meal. The slow cooker would help the flavors meld together and would make it easy to create a dish that's not only filling but also healthy. Unfortunately, many recipes for slow-cooked stuffed eggplant that I tried featured poorly cooked eggplant and bland, watery fillings. I wanted stuffed eggplant with a perfectly tender and creamy shell and a hearty, flavorful filling straight from the slow cooker.

I began my testing by picking the variety of eggplant best suited for this recipe. I quickly found that Japanese or Asian eggplants, with their long, slender shape, were not suitable to stuffing, nor were they large enough to make a substantial entrée. Large (sometimes called globe) eggplants, on the other hand, could barely fit

SLOW-COOKER STUFFED SPICED EGGPLANTS WITH TOMATOES AND PINE NUTS

into my 6-quart slow cooker. The smaller variety of eggplant—sometimes labeled Italian—was just right. Smaller than the globes but not as thin as the Japanese eggplants, these were ideal for stuffing.

Now that I had my eggplant selection squared away, I could turn my attention to the filling. I needed a filling that would transform the eggplant into a hearty meal, and one that could be easily cooked along with the eggplant in the slow cooker. To start, I tested fillings made with a tomato base, turning to canned diced tomatoes for consistent flavor and ease.

While I liked the flavor of the tomatoes, which lent a nice bright flavor and a bit of moisture without dissolving into mush, my filling needed enriching. The addition of onion was a good start, as was a touch of Pecorino cheese. Looking to add even more depth, as well as texture, I turned to other vegetables I thought might add complexity. I tried batches made with green and red bell peppers and others with zucchini. Tasters thought the green bell peppers were too bitter while the red peppers were too sweet, and the zucchini was too mild to make enough of an impact. The vegetables weren't helping the filling as I had hoped, so I started experimenting with spices to round out the flavor.

I seasoned the filling with oregano for an herbal note, cinnamon for warmth, and a little cayenne for heat. To further boost the filling's flavor, just ¼ cup of pine nuts divided among the filling for four eggplant halves imparted richness, flavor, and a little crunch. After stirring in some red wine vinegar to brighten the overall flavor and balance the sweetness of the onions, I was ready to combine the two elements of my recipe.

The test kitchen's basic method for stuffed eggplant recipes calls for precooking the vegetable, stuffing it with a prepared filling, and finally heating it through. Streamlining this process for the slow cooker would take some test kitchen innovation, and I was ready to get creative. I immediately ruled out cooking my eggplants on the stovetop because they were too big to fit in the skillet all at once, and I didn't want to deal with cooking in batches, not to mention the extra hands-on time it would take. Instead, I was hoping that the slow cooker might allow the two pieces of the recipe—the filling and the eggplant—to cook side by side from beginning to end.

With this in mind, I first tried stuffing the raw eggplants with the tomato filling before cooking them in the slow cooker. But the eggplant flesh was too firm to create a cavity; plus, maneuvering the filled eggplant halves

in and out of the slow cooker left me with a mess. The eggplants needed to be cooked before I could fill them, so I had to come up with a new way to make this recipe without too much extra work. I added the ingredients for the filling to the slow cooker and nestled the eggplant halves in the filling, cut side down. The steam from the cooking vegetables would, I hoped, cook the eggplant and meld the flavor of the filling with the roasted eggplant. Because I wanted to keep the heat mild and avoid drying out the eggplant and filling, I set the heat on low and gave the recipe some time to cook and become tender.

I returned to the slow cooker a little more than 5 hours later, took the lid off, and was enveloped in a savory steam that revealed perfectly cooked vegetables. The moist environment of the slow cooker had softened my eggplants until they were tender. I took the halves from on top of the filling and simply made a pocket in each eggplant half by pushing the soft flesh to the sides using two forks. I then mounded about ½ cup of filling into each opening and sprinkled a small amount of remaining Pecorino over the top of each eggplant half for a nice finishing touch. A bit of minced parsley on top for color and freshness was all it took to finish things off.

—SEBASTIAN NAVA, *America's Test Kitchen Books*

Slow-Cooker Stuffed Spiced Eggplants with Tomatoes and Pine Nuts

SERVES 4

Be sure to buy eggplants that are no more than 10 ounces; larger eggplants will not fit properly in your slow cooker. You may need to trim off the eggplant stems to help them fit. You will need a 5½- to 7-quart oval slow cooker for this recipe.

- 1 onion, chopped fine
- 1 tablespoon extra-virgin olive oil
- 3 garlic cloves, minced
- 2 teaspoons minced fresh oregano or ½ teaspoon dried
- ¼ teaspoon ground cinnamon
- ⅛ teaspoon cayenne pepper
- 1 (14.5-ounce) can diced tomatoes, drained
- 2 ounces Pecorino Romano cheese, grated (1 cup)
- ¼ cup pine nuts, toasted
- 1 tablespoon red wine vinegar
  Salt and pepper
- 2 (10-ounce) Italian eggplants, halved lengthwise
- 2 tablespoons minced fresh parsley

1. Microwave onion, 1 teaspoon oil, garlic, oregano, cinnamon, and cayenne in bowl, stirring occasionally, until onion is softened, about 5 minutes; transfer to slow cooker. Stir in tomatoes, ¾ cup Pecorino, pine nuts, vinegar, and ¼ teaspoon salt. Season eggplant halves with salt and pepper and nestle cut side down into slow cooker (eggplants may overlap slightly). Cover and cook until eggplants are tender, 5 to 6 hours on low.

2. Transfer eggplant halves cut side up to serving platter. Using 2 forks, gently push eggplant flesh to sides of each half to make room for filling. Stir remaining 2 teaspoons oil into tomato mixture and season with salt and pepper to taste. Mound tomato mixture evenly into eggplants and sprinkle with parsley and remaining ¼ cup Pecorino. Serve.

ROASTED MUSHROOMS WITH PARMESAN AND PINE NUTS

✓ **WHY THIS RECIPE WORKS:** For a rich, woodsy side dish, we combined straightforward cremini with meaty, smoky shiitakes. To ensure that the mushrooms were evenly seasoned and stayed moist during roasting, we started by brining them in a saltwater solution. We then roasted them in the oven for about an hour until they were deeply browned. Finally, we coated the mushrooms in melted butter and lemon juice before adding flavorful mix-ins: Parmesan, parsley, and pine nuts.

Even when I'm not in the mood for beef, I'll go to a steakhouse just for the side dishes: wedge salad, potatoes au gratin, and creamed spinach. But there's an exception—the mushroom sides, which are often uninspired. Awful? No. Dull? You bet. Still, rich, meaty-tasting mushrooms are an ideal side dish since they partner well with almost any protein. Outdoing the restaurants? It ought to be a cinch.

Right away I knew that sautéing was out since I didn't want to labor with multiple batches (crowding the pan would cause them to steam, not brown). That left roasting—the best way to develop flavorful browning without requiring my constant attention.

I wanted to avoid relatively bland white buttons, so I cut four full-flavored types—cremini, portobellos, oysters, and shiitakes—into chunks, tossed them in olive oil and salt, and roasted them both alone and in combination. Each batch emerged nicely browned, and a duo of cremini and shiitakes took top honors, the former providing pronounced earthiness and the latter a meaty, smoky taste.

But while I was testing oven temperatures—I settled on 450 degrees—a problem popped up. No matter how carefully I sprinkled on the salt, the mushrooms emerged unevenly seasoned: Some were oversalted (usually in the gills, the ribbed area underneath the mushroom cap), while others tasted flat. Plus, the shiitakes were cooking up somewhat dry.

I started brainstorming ways to make the shiitakes juicy: Use more oil, arrange them gill side down (to trap moisture), microwave them prior to roasting, add liquid to the pan, or cover them with foil. One by one, I ticked each test off my list, and one by one, each idea failed. I began to feel for the restaurants whose mushrooms I had once maligned.

It was then that a colleague offered an unconventional suggestion: brining. I was intrigued. While working on a recipe for stuffed mushrooms, we learned that the cap of any fungi is covered with a layer of hydrophobic (water-repellent) proteins that prevent water from seeping in. But could saltwater soak through the gills? I dissolved 3 tablespoons of salt in 2 quarts of water, dumped in the mushrooms, and left them to soak for 10 minutes. After blotting the mushrooms dry, I proceeded with oiling and roasting. Now they were too salty, but, encouragingly, they were all too salty: The brine had delivered consistent seasoning. I tinkered with the salt amount, finally reducing it to 5 teaspoons. After about an hour of roasting, this batch was darkly browned and evenly seasoned. And the shiitakes were as juicy as could be.

Why did brining work? Relatively dry shiitakes contain roughly 70 percent water (cremini, about 90 percent). The shiitakes sponged up the water from the brine (through the gills and any cut surfaces) via osmotic pressure, and because of this, they also retained moisture in the oven. The already succulent cremini didn't absorb enough water to noticeably alter their texture, yet—like the shiitakes—they held on to enough salt from the brine to be well seasoned.

Jazzing up the roasted mushrooms was as simple as glossing them with melted butter and mixing in a few fresh herbs and spices. Maybe I'd still hit up a steakhouse for the creamed spinach, but from now on I'd be enjoying mushrooms at home.

—ADAM REID, *Cook's Illustrated*

Roasted Mushrooms with Parmesan and Pine Nuts

SERVES 4

Quarter large (more than 2 inches) cremini mushrooms, halve medium (1 to 2 inches) ones, and leave small (under 1 inch) ones whole.

Salt and pepper

1½ pounds cremini mushrooms, trimmed and left whole if small, halved if medium, or quartered if large

1 pound shiitake mushrooms, stemmed, caps larger than 3 inches halved

2 tablespoons extra-virgin olive oil

2 tablespoons unsalted butter, melted

1 teaspoon lemon juice

1 ounce Parmesan cheese, grated (½ cup)

2 tablespoons pine nuts, toasted

2 tablespoons chopped fresh parsley

1. Adjust oven rack to lowest position and heat oven to 450 degrees. Dissolve 5 teaspoons salt in 2 quarts room-temperature water in large container. Add cremini mushrooms and shiitake mushrooms to brine, cover with plate or bowl to submerge, and let stand for 10 minutes.

2. Drain mushrooms in colander and pat dry with paper towels. Spread mushrooms evenly on rimmed baking sheet, drizzle with oil, and toss to coat. Roast until liquid from mushrooms has completely evaporated, 35 to 45 minutes.

3. Remove sheet from oven (be careful of escaping steam when opening oven) and, using thin metal spatula, carefully stir mushrooms. Return to oven and continue to roast until mushrooms are deeply browned, 5 to 10 minutes longer.

4. Combine melted butter and lemon juice in large bowl. Add mushrooms and toss to coat. Add Parmesan, pine nuts, and parsley and toss. Season with salt and pepper to taste; serve immediately.

VARIATIONS

Roasted Mushrooms with Harissa and Mint

Substitute 1 tablespoon extra-virgin olive oil for butter and increase lemon juice to 2 teaspoons. Whisk 1 garlic clove, minced to paste; 2 teaspoons harissa; ¼ teaspoon ground cumin; and ¼ teaspoon salt into oil mixture in step 4. Omit Parmesan and pine nuts and substitute mint for parsley.

Roasted Mushrooms with Sesame and Scallions

Substitute 2 teaspoons toasted sesame oil for butter and ½ teaspoon rice vinegar for lemon juice. Omit Parmesan and substitute 2 teaspoons toasted sesame seeds for nuts and 2 thinly sliced scallions for parsley.

NOTES FROM THE TEST KITCHEN

COLOR TASTE-OFF: WHITE VS. BROWN MUSHROOMS
Despite their differing appearance, white button and cremini mushrooms (and portobellos) actually belong to the same mushroom species, Agaricus bisporus. Creminis are a brown-hued variety, and portobellos are creminis that have been allowed to grow large. We think of creminis as a recent introduction to the marketplace, but all button mushrooms were actually brown until 1926, when a mushroom farmer in Pennsylvania found a cluster of white buttons growing in his beds, which he cloned and began selling as a new variety. But does the loss of color mean a loss of flavor? To find out, we sautéed white button and cremini mushrooms and tasted them side-by-side in risotto and atop pizza. The flavor of the creminis was noticeably deeper and more complex. This difference in taste was also apparent, though less obvious, when we compared both types of mushroom sprinkled raw over salads. The lesson? If bolder mushroom flavor is what you're after, it's worth shelling out a little extra for creminis.

CREMINI
Brown-hued cremini boast rich, complex flavor.

WHITE BUTTON
White button mushrooms are comparatively mild in flavor.

SLOW-COOKED WHOLE CARROTS

✔ **WHY THIS RECIPE WORKS:** We wanted a technique for cooking whole carrots (currently a popular restaurant dish) that would yield a sweet and meltingly tender vegetable from one end to the other without the carrots becoming mushy or waterlogged. Gently "steeping" the carrots in warm water before cooking them firmed up the vegetable's cell walls so that they could be cooked for a long time without falling apart. We also topped the carrots with a *cartouche* (a circle of parchment that sits directly on the food) during cooking to ensure that they were evenly cooked from end to end.

As a chef, I get particular enjoyment from dining out: It's my chance to keep up with the ever-changing culinary landscape by experiencing cutting-edge techniques and trendy ingredients. But at home I rarely have the desire to re-create restaurant food. (Who has the time to whip up a frothy bacon emulsion or labor over a batch of green apple taffy?) Still, every so often I come across a dish or approach that I absolutely have to try in my own kitchen. The most recent was a gorgeous platter of slow-cooked whole carrots. Fork-tender and without a hint of mushiness, they had a dense, almost meaty quality to them. And the carrot flavor was super concentrated: sweet and pure, but still earthy. I pictured these carrots as an accompaniment to everything from a holiday beef tenderloin to a basic roast chicken.

A search for recipes that would produce similar results generated a lot of slow-roasted and braised carrots, but none came close to what I had been served. The roasted carrots boasted plenty of sweetness because of their significant browning, but this obscured their true flavor. On the other hand, braised carrots inevitably took on the flavor of whatever liquid they were cooked in—I wanted carrots that tasted like carrots, not like chicken broth or white wine. It was obvious that I would need to use another cooking method to spotlight the carrots in the best possible way.

I got my bearings by slowly simmering 12 whole peeled carrots (I chose similarly sized specimens so that they would cook as evenly as possible) in a full saucepan of salted water (about 6 cups) until they were tender. This test shed light on two issues. The first was inconsistent cooking: By the time the thick end of the carrot was tender, the thinner tapered end was mushy and waterlogged. The second was that the carrots had been robbed of their inherent sweetness. Simmering had drawn out the soluble sugar in the vegetable and, unfortunately, all of that flavorful sugar flowed down the drain when I poured off the cooking water.

The latter problem would be solved by coming up with an approach that didn't call for discarding the sweet cooking water. Switching from a saucepan to a skillet (whose shallow sides would facilitate evaporation) and reducing the amount of water to just 3 cups were my first moves. I arranged the carrots in a single layer and simmered them uncovered until all the water evaporated and the carrots were fully tender when I pierced them with a paring knife, which took about 45 minutes. I also added a tablespoon of butter to the water at the beginning of simmering, which, in combination with the sugar released from the carrots, reduced to a light glaze that coated the carrots with a handsome sheen.

Unfortunately, even with this specialized method, the inconsistent doneness from the thick end of the carrot to the narrow end remained. I experimented with squirting some lemon juice into the water, hoping that its acid would firm up the pectin in the carrots and balance out the textural inconsistencies. The good news: It worked. The bad: In order for the lemon juice to have an effect, I needed to squeeze in so much of it that it buried the carrots' sweetness.

Looking for a better solution, I was reminded of a phenomenon called "persistent firmness." Here's how it works: Precooking certain fruits or vegetables at a low temperature sparks an enzymatic reaction that helps the produce remain tender-firm during a second cooking phase at a higher temperature. If I could use persistent firmness to my advantage in this recipe, it would mean that the thin ends of the carrots wouldn't turn mushy while the thicker ends fully cooked through.

To put the science to the test, I outfitted my skillet with a probe thermometer, brought 3 cups of salted water (along with the pat of butter) to a boil, removed the skillet from the heat, arranged the carrots in a single

SLOW-COOKED WHOLE CARROTS

layer in the water, covered the skillet, and let the carrots stand for 20 minutes. During this time, the water temperature clocked in at 135 to 150 degrees, right in the ideal range for the enzymatic reaction to work its magic. After 20 minutes, I removed the lid and switched over to my newly developed cooking method, returning the carrots to the heat and simmering them until the water evaporated. These carrots were tender from end to end, yet they still boasted a firm, meaty texture.

The carrots were now just about perfect, but I did notice that the top sides of some of them were occasionally a little underdone. I suspected that because I was using a relatively small amount of water, the level was falling below the tops of the carrots before they had time to become tender. Using a lid wasn't the answer since covering the pan only slowed evaporation. Partially covering the skillet was a no-go since finding the sweet spot would take trial and error and might not be the same for every pot. Finally, rolling the carrots during cooking to promote even cooking was a pain in the neck and imperfect at best: Some of the carrots inevitably rolled back into their initial positions, thwarting my efforts.

That's when I thought of a trick I'd learned in restaurant kitchens: using a cartouche—a piece of parchment paper that sits directly on the food as it cooks, regulating the reduction of moisture in cooking. I topped my next batch of carrots with a cartouche and was happy to find that it solved the problem. The paper allowed the perfect rate of evaporation but also trapped more of the escaping steam and kept it concentrated on top of the carrots, ensuring perfectly tender, evenly cooked results.

I was happy to eat these carrots, with their firm, tender texture and pure carrot flavor, without any embellishment. But to make them real showstoppers, I dressed them up a bit. I settled on easy relishes that could be whipped up while the carrots cooked. These toppings, made with bold ingredients like sherry vinegar, olives, fresh herbs, and nuts, packed an acidic punch that complemented the carrots' sweet, earthy flavor. Garnishing with just a small amount of relish kept the focus on the carrots. I may not be a restaurant chef any more, but no one will know that from eating these carrots.

—KEITH DRESSER, *Cook's Illustrated*

NOTES FROM THE TEST KITCHEN

MAKING A PARCHMENT LID (CARTOUCHE)

Going to the trouble of making a parchment paper lid with a small hole in the middle, or a cartouche, is worth it. It works better than a metal lid to keep steam concentrated on the top of the carrots, so they cook at the same rate as the underside of the vegetables.

1. Fold a 12-inch square of parchment into quarters to create a 6-inch square.

2. With openings at the top and right sides, fold the bottom right corner of the square to the top left corner.

3. Fold the triangle again, right side over left, to create a narrow triangle.

4. Cut ¼ inch off of the tip to create a hole. Then cut the base of the triangle straight across where it measures 5 inches from hole.

Slow-Cooked Whole Carrots
SERVES 4 TO 6

Use carrots that measure ¾ to 1¼ inches across at the thickest end. The carrots can be served plain, but we recommend topping them with one of our relishes (recipes follow).

3 cups water

1 tablespoon unsalted butter

½ teaspoon salt

12 carrots (1½ to 1¾ pounds), peeled

1. Fold 12-inch square of parchment paper into quarters to create 6-inch square. Fold bottom right corner of square to top left corner to create triangle. Fold triangle again, right side over left, to create narrow triangle. Cut off ¼ inch of tip of triangle to create small hole. Cut base of triangle straight across where it measures 5 inches from hole. Open paper round.

2. Bring water, butter, and salt to simmer in 12-inch skillet over high heat. Remove pan from heat, add carrots in single layer, and place parchment round on top of carrots. Cover skillet and let stand for 20 minutes.

3. Remove lid from skillet, leaving parchment round in place, and bring to simmer over high heat. Reduce heat to medium-low and simmer until almost all water has evaporated and carrots are very tender, about 45 minutes. Discard parchment round, increase heat to medium-high, and continue to cook carrots, shaking pan frequently, until they are lightly glazed and no water remains in skillet, 2 to 4 minutes longer. Transfer carrots to platter and serve.

Green Olive and Golden Raisin Relish

MAKES ABOUT 1 CUP

⅓ cup golden raisins

1 tablespoon water

⅔ cup pitted green olives, chopped

1 shallot, minced

2 tablespoons extra-virgin olive oil

1 tablespoon red wine vinegar

½ teaspoon ground fennel

¼ teaspoon salt

Microwave raisins and water in bowl until steaming, about 1 minute. Cover and let stand until raisins are plump, about 5 minutes. Add olives, shallot, oil, vinegar, fennel, and salt to plumped raisins and stir to combine. Serve.

Pine Nut Relish

MAKES ABOUT ¾ CUP

Pine nuts burn easily, so be sure to shake the pan frequently while toasting them.

⅓ cup pine nuts, toasted

1 shallot, minced

1 tablespoon sherry vinegar

1 tablespoon minced fresh parsley

1 teaspoon honey

½ teaspoon minced fresh rosemary

¼ teaspoon smoked paprika

¼ teaspoon salt

Pinch cayenne pepper

Combine all ingredients in bowl. Serve.

ROASTED GREEN BEANS WITH PECORINO AND PINE NUTS

✓ **WHY THIS RECIPE WORKS:** Roasted green beans are often dry and leathery; we wanted earthy, sweet beans with moist interiors and just the right amount of browning. We started by roasting the beans, covered with foil, with a mixture of oil, salt, pepper, and sugar to let them gently steam for 10 minutes. The sugar promoted browning when we removed the foil to let the beans blister in the oven's high heat. To add a lively bite to the flavorful beans, we tossed them with a lemon vinaigrette and topped them with salty, sharp Pecorino and crunchy pine nuts.

Regarding roasted green beans: I had always assumed that tossing them in olive oil, salt, and pepper and then sending them on a short swing through a hot oven would net me a rustic, fresh-tasting side dish of bright, perfectly cooked green beans with rich brown blisters. Imagine my disappointment when the beans I pulled out of the oven were limp, pale, and leathery. Where did I go wrong?

In search of an easy soultion, I collected an array of recipes, all suggesting variations on the same concept. Some recommended higher temperatures (up to 500 degrees) and shorter cook times; others promised good results with gentler oven temperatures and longer cook times. I tried several of these recipes with fresh

ROASTED GREEN BEANS WITH PECORINO AND PINE NUTS

batches of beans. No luck. Higher oven temperatures produced nicely colored but dry and leathery beans, while lower temps resulted in wilted, stringy, olive-green beans. It was clear that this simple dish needed a fresh approach.

I considered blanching the beans in salted water before roasting them, but this seemed like too much work (and too much dirty cookware) for a dish of beans. Ditto a preroast visit to the microwave.

Was the answer right under my nose in the test kitchen? In the past, my coworkers have used a hybrid roasting technique with other vegetables like cauliflower, first cooking them on a sheet pan under an aluminum foil cover, essentially steaming them during the first few minutes in the oven, and then removing the foil to expose the beans to dry heat and achieve a light browning. Could the two-fold process work on green beans, too? I gave it a shot, roasting 1½ pounds of beans covered for 10 minutes at 475 degrees and then uncovered for another 15 minutes, until they had adequate browning. Much to my dismay, the beans were overcooked.

Down but not out, I tried it again with just 10 minutes of uncovered roasting. These beans had better texture but lacked the deep brown blisters and caramelized flavor that define the best roasted vegetables.

Sugar is usually the first ingredient we turn to when we need a browning boost, and my next test confirmed its worth: When I tossed a bit of sugar into the beans, they emerged speckled with brown.

While they were in the oven, I had just enough time to whisk together a light dressing of olive oil, garlic, Dijon mustard, and lemon juice and zest. I drizzled the beans and then tossed them with a bit of minced basil, toasted pine nuts, and salty grated Pecorino Romano. The add-ons elevated the dish and brought everything into balance. Inspired, I created two variations, one with almonds and mint and one with goat cheese and hazelnuts.

—CRISTIN WALSH, *Cook's Country*

Roasted Green Beans with Pecorino and Pine Nuts

SERVES 4 TO 6

High-quality olive oil makes a difference here. Shred the Pecorino Romano on the large holes of a box grater.

1½ pounds green beans, trimmed
5½ tablespoons extra-virgin olive oil
¾ teaspoon sugar
   Kosher salt and pepper
2 garlic cloves, minced
1 teaspoon grated lemon zest plus
   4 teaspoons juice
1 teaspoon Dijon mustard
2 tablespoons chopped fresh basil
1½ ounces Pecorino Romano cheese, shredded (½ cup)
¼ cup pine nuts, toasted

1. Adjust oven rack to lowest position and heat oven to 475 degrees. Combine green beans, 1½ tablespoons oil, sugar, ¾ teaspoon salt, and ½ teaspoon pepper in bowl. Evenly distribute green beans on rimmed baking sheet.

2. Cover sheet tightly with aluminum foil and roast for 10 minutes. Remove foil and continue to roast until green beans are spotty brown, about 10 minutes longer, stirring halfway through roasting.

3. Meanwhile, combine garlic, lemon zest, and remaining ¼ cup oil in medium bowl and microwave until bubbling, about 1 minute; let mixture steep for 1 minute. Whisk lemon juice, mustard, ¼ teaspoon salt, and ¼ teaspoon pepper into garlic mixture.

4. Transfer green beans to bowl with dressing, add basil, and toss to combine. Transfer to serving platter and sprinkle with Pecorino and pine nuts. Serve.

VARIATIONS

Roasted Green Beans with Almonds and Mint
Substitute lime zest and juice for lemon zest and juice; ¼ cup torn fresh mint leaves for basil; and whole blanched almonds, toasted and chopped, for pine nuts. Omit Pecorino.

Roasted Green Beans with Goat Cheese and Hazelnuts
Substitute orange zest for lemon zest; 2 teaspoons orange juice for 2 teaspoons lemon juice; minced fresh chives for basil; ½ cup crumbled goat cheese for Pecorino; and hazelnuts, toasted, skinned, and chopped, for pine nuts.

DUCK FAT–ROASTED POTATOES

✔ **WHY THIS RECIPE WORKS:** For roasted potatoes with the best balance of creamy interior and crisp exterior, we went with Yukon Golds, which we peeled for maximum surface area. Before roasting the spuds, we boiled them briefly in a mild baking soda bath to degrade the pectin on the surface, and then roughed them up in the pot to create a starchy paste that transformed into a crispy shell in the heat of the oven. Duck fat provided unmatched flavor and richness. We spread the potatoes out on a preheated sheet pan and set them on the top rack of a hot oven to cook them from all sides at once. And rather than turn them one at a time we used an easy but effective scrape-and-toss approach.

When I'm craving roast potatoes that are a step up from the norm, I dip into the stash of leftover bacon fat that I keep tucked away in my fridge. The meaty grease bolsters the dish with a flavor and richness that plain olive oil can't match. Normally, I simply cut up whatever potatoes I have on hand, toss them with a few tablespoons of the grease, and roast them in a hot oven until tender. While the results are always good, I wanted to pull out all the stops and create an ultimate version: perfectly seasoned potatoes with supercrisp, golden-brown exteriors and moist interiors. It would also be fun, I decided, to experiment with duck fat instead of bacon fat. Once a rarity, this fat has become so popular during the past few years that it's now sold by the pint in many supermarkets.

I rounded up a bushel of Yukon Gold potatoes, which boast an ideal balance of starchiness and waxiness that would yield crisp-on-the-outside, moist-on-the-inside results. I peeled 3½ pounds of potatoes, cut them into

NOTES FROM THE TEST KITCHEN

SAVING FAT FOR COOKING

Saving the leftover fat from bacon, roasts, or poultry is easy to do. Pour the warm fat through a fine-mesh strainer into a Mason jar and discard any solids. (Alternatively, let the fat cool and harden and then scoop it into the jar, leaving any solids behind.) Put the lid on the jar, label it, and refrigerate it for up to one month or freeze it for up to six months, adding more fat as desired.

chunks, and tossed them with 3 tablespoons of duck fat and some chopped fresh rosemary (its piney taste is a natural match for potatoes) before roasting them on a baking sheet in a 450-degree oven. Instead of painstakingly turning each individual piece, I used a scrape-and-toss approach, letting the potatoes brown on one side for 15 minutes and then using a sharp, thin spatula to shuffle them around. Repeating this twice during roasting ensured that any unbrowned sides got a shot at receiving direct heat from the bottom of the sheet. Finally, I sprinkled the chunks with kosher salt as they came out of the oven.

This first-round sample wasn't nearly as good as I'd hoped that it would be. For one, the potatoes were underseasoned, despite my generous hand with salt. They also lacked sufficient meaty flavor from the fat, and some of the rosemary had burned. What's more, the chunks shed moisture as they cooked, causing them to end up somewhat shriveled and parched on the interior. And their exteriors weren't sufficiently crisp.

I focused on the textural downfalls first. Covering the baking sheet with foil at the start of roasting trapped moisture, but once the foil was removed, the chunks were so wet that they took a long time to brown. By the time the outsides finally took on color, the insides were once again dried out.

I needed potatoes with a quick-browning, starchy exterior layer surrounding an interior that would stay moist during roasting. The solution? Boil the potatoes for just 1 minute in water laced with baking soda. The soda rapidly degrades the pectin in the cells at the exterior of the potato, causing them to release a wet starch that rapidly browns. After draining the chunks, I further roughed up their exteriors by stirring them vigorously with 5 tablespoons of the duck fat—enough to boost meaty flavor without causing greasiness—and more salt. This left them coated in a thick paste that I hoped would transform in the oven into an ultracrisp shell.

To prevent the rosemary from burning, I mixed it with an extra tablespoon of fat and stirred this mixture into the potatoes toward the end of cooking. When this batch came out of the oven, I seasoned it with ground black pepper and a little more salt. These were some seriously good spuds: richly flavored with spot-on seasoning, golden brown and crisp on the outside, and moist and fluffy on the inside.

Lastly, I experimented with other types of animal fat. Unsurprisingly, chicken fat and lard produced outstanding results. Bacon fat worked better when cut with olive oil so that its salty and smoky flavors didn't take over. With a little know-how (and a little fat), I'd produced crispy roasted potatoes that taste just as good as they sound.

—ANDREW JANJIGIAN, *Cook's Illustrated*

Duck Fat–Roasted Potatoes

SERVES 6

Duck fat is available in the meat department in many supermarkets. Alternatively, substitute chicken fat, lard, or a mixture of 3 tablespoons of bacon fat and 3 tablespoons of extra-virgin olive oil.

3½	**pounds Yukon Gold potatoes, peeled and cut into 1½-inch pieces**
	Kosher salt and pepper
½	**teaspoon baking soda**
6	**tablespoons duck fat**
1	**tablespoon chopped fresh rosemary**

1. Adjust oven rack to top position, place rimmed baking sheet on rack, and heat oven to 475 degrees.

2. Bring 10 cups water to boil in Dutch oven over high heat. Add potatoes, ⅓ cup salt, and baking soda. Return to boil and cook for 1 minute. Drain potatoes. Return potatoes to pot and place over low heat. Cook, shaking pot occasionally, until surface moisture has evaporated, about 2 minutes. Remove from heat. Add 5 tablespoons fat and 1 teaspoon salt; mix with rubber spatula until potatoes are coated with thick paste, about 30 seconds.

3. Remove sheet from oven, transfer potatoes to sheet, and spread into even layer. Roast for 15 minutes.

4. Remove sheet from oven. Using thin, sharp, metal spatula, turn potatoes. Roast until golden brown, 12 to 15 minutes. While potatoes roast, combine rosemary and remaining 1 tablespoon fat in bowl.

5. Remove sheet from oven. Spoon rosemary-fat mixture over potatoes and turn again. Continue to roast until potatoes are well browned and rosemary is fragrant, 3 to 5 minutes. Season with salt and pepper to taste. Serve immediately.

GARLIC-PARMESAN MASHED POTATOES

✓ WHY THIS RECIPE WORKS: For optimal garlic mashed potatoes, we started with potatoes, butter, and whole milk and opted for Yukon Golds for their buttery flavor and super-smooth texture. To get truly complex garlic flavor, we added it in three ways: a garlic paste sautéed in butter for clean, mellow flavor; a very small amount of raw garlic paste for assertiveness; and a small amount of rehydrated garlic powder also sautéed in butter for complex, lightly roasted flavor. In order to maximize the garlic powder's flavor, we first bloomed it in water to reactivate the enzyme that produces the compound allicin, which is responsible for garlic's characteristic flavor. Warm, nutty Parmesan was the perfect complement to this triple-garlic treatment without overwhelming the dish.

Whenever I want something more inspired than plain old mashed potatoes, I turn to potent additions like garlic and Parmesan. Achieving good cheese flavor is as simple as mixing in a handful of the freshly grated stuff, but the garlic is a different story. If it isn't too subtle, it's often overpowering—whether too sharp, too sweet, or even unpleasantly bitter. I envisioned moderately rich potatoes with complex, balanced garlic flavor accented by nutty Parmesan.

We've developed a lot of mashed potato recipes over the years. Dipping into our expansive archive, it didn't take me long to settle on a potato plan. I started with one of our favorite varieties for mashing: buttery-tasting, moderately starchy Yukon Golds (peeled and cut into ½-inch-thick slices for even cooking) simmered for about 20 minutes until tender. I drained the slices and then riced the potatoes back into the pot set over low heat. This move helped evaporate excess water, avoiding a soggy mash. Next I stirred in a modest amount of melted butter (4 tablespoons for 2 pounds of potatoes), salt and pepper, and, finally, ⅔ cup of warm whole milk.

Time for the garlic. The question is never as simple as how much to add, but what kind of flavor to develop. Here's why: Garlic cells do not develop the flavorful, aromatic compound called allicin until they are ruptured by cutting or smashing. What's more, the intensity of flavor depends on the size of the cut: The finer the cut (more broken cells and thus greater allicin production), the sharper the taste—slices or slivers will pack less of a punch than minced. You also have to pay attention to how (or if) the garlic is cooked. The fiery punch of raw garlic is tamed by heat, which converts allicin into mellower-tasting compounds. And what happens if you cook whole, uncut cloves? Allicin is never produced and only a sweet, mild taste emerges.

To get a handle on how the many faces of garlic play out in potatoes, I made four separate mashes. I added several whole roasted garlic cloves to one, a few cloves of minced sautéed garlic to another, and a touch of raw garlic paste to another. For the last batch I simmered a couple of whole cloves with the potatoes. Raw garlic boasted its signature assertive taste. The roasted cloves added a pronounced sweetness; the simmered ones only a faint sweetness. Finally, the sautéed minced garlic offered middle-of-the-road flavor. I would need to mix and match multiple preparations of garlic to develop my ideal blend.

I started by using a rasp-style grater to transform two garlic cloves into 1¼ teaspoons of a flavor-packed, ultrafine paste. I sautéed 1 teaspoon of the paste in the butter from my recipe and then added the remaining ¼ teaspoon raw to the mash. This fresh-cooked combo satisfied some, but the roasted devotees also wanted sweet, mellow notes. And yet I wasn't about to run my oven for an hour in pursuit of roasted garlic flavor. I wondered about another option that might provide the same taste with a lot less hassle: garlic powder. It's made by grinding and then drying garlic cloves to remove moisture, a process via which a mild roasted flavor develops. We don't use it much in the test kitchen aside from in spice rubs, but I thought it was worth a shot in my potatoes.

Eager to give it a try, I sprinkled a bit of the powder straight from the jar into the mash. When the results were harsh-tasting, I experimented with sautéing varying amounts in the butter along with the fresh stuff. No dice: Now the garlic flavor was wan. I did a little more research, and it turns out that although garlic powder still contains alliinase, the enzyme responsible for producing flavorful allicin, the dehydration process deactivates it. But alliinase can be reactivated via rehydration. Armed with this information, I simply stirred water into the powder and let it sit for a minute before sautéing. Sure enough, the powder came to life, expressing the full garlic flavor I expected.

All that was left to do was to grab a hunk of Parmesan and grate until my tasters said stop. A savory depth that stood up to, and complemented, the sweet, sharp, and roasted garlic flavors was achieved using ¾ cup.

These garlicky, cheesy spuds are good enough for a special-occasion meal, but they're also so easy to make that I have a feeling I'll be serving them all the time.
—DAN SOUZA, *Cook's Illustrated*

Garlic-Parmesan Mashed Potatoes

SERVES 4 TO 6

Our favorite brand of garlic powder is Spice Islands.

- 2 **pounds Yukon Gold potatoes, peeled and sliced ½ inch thick**
- ½ **teaspoon garlic powder**
- 4 **tablespoons unsalted butter, cut into 4 pieces**
- 1¼ **teaspoons garlic, minced to paste**
- 1½ **ounces Parmesan cheese, grated (¾ cup)**
  Salt and pepper
- ⅔ **cup warm whole milk**

1. Place potatoes in large saucepan and add cold water to cover by 1 inch. Bring water to simmer over medium-high heat. Adjust heat to maintain gentle simmer until paring knife can be slipped into and out of center of potatoes with no resistance, 18 to 22 minutes. Drain potatoes.

2. While potatoes cook, combine garlic powder and ½ teaspoon water in small bowl. Melt butter in 8-inch skillet over medium-low heat. Stir in 1 teaspoon garlic paste and garlic powder mixture; cook, stirring constantly, until fragrant and golden, about 1 minute. Transfer butter mixture to medium bowl and thoroughly stir in Parmesan, 1¼ teaspoons salt, ½ teaspoon pepper, and remaining ¼ teaspoon garlic paste.

3. Place now-empty saucepan over low heat; set ricer or food mill over saucepan. Working in batches, transfer potatoes to hopper and process. Using rubber spatula, stir in butter-Parmesan mixture until incorporated. Stir in warm milk until incorporated. Season with salt and pepper to taste; serve immediately.

ROOT VEGETABLE GRATIN

✔️ **WHY THIS RECIPE WORKS:** Our root vegetable gratin pairs the earthy flavor of potatoes with thinly sliced sweet rutabaga, savory celery root, and just a few aromatics. We added white wine to the gratin that brightened the flavor of the vegetables. The wine's acidity strengthened the pectin in the potatoes so that they remained intact while the denser, less-starchy rutabaga and celery root cooked through. To help the top layers of the gratin cook through at the same rate, we covered the dish for the first portion of the cooking time. A layer of Parmesan-enhanced panko bread crumbs added after removing the foil created a crispy, nutty crust.

It's hard to beat the earthy flavor, lush creaminess, and golden-brown crust of classic potato gratin, but it's also hard to eat an entire helping of a dish that rich. A good alternative, I've often thought, would be a gratin that features the cleaner, more dynamic flavors of other root vegetables and a lighter, brighter sauce.

But when I tried a few, not one nailed the even cooking, cohesive structure, and crisp crust that define any good potato casserole. Instead, the recipes delivered myriad failures: slices that slid apart, sauces that were either sticky or soupy, and vegetable flavor that was often dull. Surely I could make a root vegetable gratin that offered as much flavor and textural appeal as the all-potato kind, but without its heft.

I knocked out a few basic cooking tests that I hoped would further narrow my vegetable choices. In greased baking dishes, I layered 2 pounds of thinly sliced Yukon Gold potatoes—a test kitchen favorite for their buttery flavor and moderate amount of starch, which I hoped would keep the gratin layers intact but not sticky—with combinations of rutabaga and celery root. In each dish, I made sure to sandwich these other root vegetables between layers of potatoes, both to break up the starchier spuds and to ensure that each bite would contain a variety of flavors. Then I poured in a placeholder cooking liquid (a combination of water and some heavy cream that I hoped would not be too rich) until the top layer was barely submerged. I covered the baking dishes with aluminum foil to trap the heat, hoping that would help the vegetables cook evenly from top to bottom, and baked the casserole in a moderately hot oven until the denser root vegetables

were mostly cooked through. Then I removed the foil and put the dish back in the oven to allow most of the liquid to evaporate.

The flavor of the rutabagas and celery root complemented the potatoes nicely, the former adding pungent sweetness, the latter some savory complexity.

Of course, the problem with pairing potatoes and denser rutabaga and celery root is that the spuds cook faster. That was certainly the case with my gratin—particularly the bottom layer of potatoes, which saw the most heat and were so soft that they were breaking apart. In addition, because the rutabaga and celery root contain less starch than the potatoes, they weren't sticky enough to hold the gratin layers together when I cut a slice.

I recalled that in the past we added a pinch of baking soda to potatoes as they boiled for a recipe in which we deliberately wanted to turn them mushy; the alkali raised their pH, which caused the pectin holding their cell walls together to become more soluble and break down rapidly, allowing the potatoes' starches to leach out. So it stood to reason that if I wanted to keep potatoes more firm, I should try adding acid to the cooking liquid, which would lower the pH, making the pectin less soluble and thus slower to break down. Because rutabaga and celery root have less starch than potatoes, the firming effect of the acid would be less noticeable on their texture.

White wine had potential to add acidity with subtler flavor, so I prepared another gratin, replacing a generous ⅔ cup of the water with wine. As I'd hoped, the bottom layer of potatoes now held their shape nicely.

As for keeping the slices bound together, I made up for the lack of starch in the other root vegetables by making a slurry of flour and a splash of water (plus some salt for seasoning) and whisking that with the cooking liquid so that it evenly coated the vegetables. I also stirred in a spoonful of Dijon mustard to kick up the flavor a notch.

With wine and mustard, the gratin tasted bright and clean but still needed a savory boost. Adding aromatics seemed like an obvious answer, so I scattered chopped onion, minced garlic, and fresh minced thyme—classic au gratin flavors—between the layers of vegetables. At least, I tried to scatter them, but the tiny pieces of garlic and thyme were clingy and difficult to evenly disperse, leaving some bites overwhelmingly garlicky and others bland. I was much better off tossing the garlic and thyme (plus some black pepper) with the chopped

ROOT VEGETABLE GRATIN

onion, which was easier to distribute evenly between the layers of vegetables.

The other savory component in most potato gratins is that golden crust. Thus far, I'd held off on adding cheese between the layers so that the flavors of the vegetables could dominate, but a cheese crust seemed like a subtler way to get at that rich savory flavor; I also hoped it would crisp up nicely. My first attempt was to sprinkle the casserole with a handful of grated Parmesan when I removed the foil cover and then put the dish back in the oven to bake until the cheese turned golden brown. That it did, but the results weren't nearly as crisp as I'd hoped, so for the next batch I reached for the ingredient we turn to when we want an ultracrisp crust: panko bread crumbs. When mixed with the Parmesan and a few tablespoons of melted butter, the bread crumbs formed a topping that was crisp, attractively brown, and rich and savory enough to contrast with the earthy, sweet flavors of the potatoes, celery root, and rutabaga.

Finally, my gratin had just enough richness to harken back to the classic version. And the gratin was also so light and flavorful that my dinner guests not only would have room for more but wouldn't be able to resist a second helping.

—LAN LAM, *Cook's Illustrated*

Root Vegetable Gratin

SERVES 6 TO 8

Uniformly thin slices are necessary for a cohesive gratin. We recommend a mandoline for quick and even slicing, but a sharp chef's knife will also work. Because the vegetables in the gratin are tightly packed into the casserole dish, it will still be plenty hot after a 25-minute rest.

- 1 tablespoon plus 1½ cups water
- 1½ teaspoons Dijon mustard
- 2 teaspoons all-purpose flour
  Salt and pepper
- ⅔ cup dry white wine
- ½ cup heavy cream
- ½ onion, chopped fine
- 1¼ teaspoons minced fresh thyme
- 1 garlic clove, minced
- 2 pounds large Yukon Gold potatoes, peeled and sliced lengthwise ⅛ inch thick

- 1 large celery root (1 pound), peeled, quartered, and sliced ⅛ inch thick
- 1 pound rutabaga, peeled, quartered, and sliced ⅛ inch thick
- ¾ cup panko bread crumbs
- 1½ ounces Parmesan cheese, grated (¾ cup)
- 4 tablespoons unsalted butter, melted and cooled

1. Adjust oven rack to middle position and heat oven to 375 degrees. Grease 13 by 9-inch baking dish. Whisk 1 tablespoon water, mustard, flour, and 1½ teaspoons salt in medium bowl until smooth. Add wine, cream, and remaining 1½ cups water; whisk to combine. Combine onion, thyme, garlic, and ¼ teaspoon pepper in second bowl.

2. Layer half of potatoes in prepared dish, arranging so they form even thickness. Sprinkle half of onion mixture evenly over potatoes. Arrange celery root and rutabaga slices in even layer over onions. Sprinkle remaining onion mixture over celery root and rutabaga. Layer remaining potatoes over onions. Slowly pour water mixture over vegetables. Using rubber spatula, gently press down on vegetables to create even, compact layer. Cover tightly with aluminum foil and bake for 50 minutes. Remove foil and continue to bake until knife inserted into center of gratin meets no resistance, 20 to 25 minutes longer.

3. While gratin bakes, combine panko, Parmesan, and butter in bowl and season with salt and pepper to taste. Remove gratin from oven and sprinkle evenly with panko mixture. Continue to bake until panko is golden brown, 15 to 20 minutes longer. Remove gratin from oven and let stand for 25 minutes. Serve.

NOTES FROM THE TEST KITCHEN

SCIENCE: FIRMING UP POTATOES WITH WINE

The wine in our root vegetable gratin brightens the flavor of this typically starchy-tasting dish, but more important, it also prevents the potatoes from breaking down and turning mushy while the denser celery root and rutabaga cook. Here's how it works: Potato cells have an abundance of starch granules; when these granules swell with water during cooking, they press against the cell walls, eventually causing them to burst and release starch. But when potatoes cook in water with wine, the wine lowers the pH, which strengthens the pectin in and around the cell walls, helping them resist bursting. The upshot is a pliable, not mushy, potato.

CHAPTER 4

PASTA, PIZZA, AND SANDWICHES

PASTA WITH RAW TOMATO SAUCE

PASTA WITH RAW TOMATO SAUCE

✓ **WHY THIS RECIPE WORKS:** Tomatoes are at their premium state in the peak of summertime, and we were looking for another way to enjoy them besides in their usual form: sliced or in a BLT. For the ultimate fresh tomato sauce, we let the tomatoes sit in an aromatic solution of oregano, good-quality olive oil, garlic, salt, and sugar until they broke down and released some of their juices. Rather than discard the extracted tomato liquid, we cooked the pasta in it, resulting in infused tomato flavor in every bite.

In the heart of summer when perfectly ripe tomatoes taste so unbelievably good, it almost seems like a crime to cook them. But there's a limit to the number of sliced tomatoes one person can eat. That's where pasta with raw tomato sauce comes in.

I found plenty of recipes for this summer sauce, all of which called for very different approaches. One recipe called for heating oil on the stovetop and pouring it over seasoned tomatoes to quickly wilt them. The result was a fragrant tomato mixture with absolutely no ability to cling to the pasta as a sauce should. Another recipe called for marinating tomatoes in sugar, vinegar, oil, and aromatics for a few hours before processing them through a food mill. This resulted in a sweet-and-sour tomato soup that had my tasters wondering if I had tricked them by making gazpacho. I wanted the mixture thick enough to cling nicely to the pasta, but not so thin that it would seem like a soup.

I first concentrated on figuring out how to avoid a thin, watery sauce. For this, I turned to a trick that the test kitchen often uses when faced with this challenge: salting the tomatoes. This technique extracts liquid from the tomatoes and softens their flesh. After many tests, I figured out that an hour was the optimal time to let seasoned tomatoes sit. It was shocking to see that 2 pounds of tomatoes released a full cup of liquid. Along the way, I also figured out that if I added garlic and fresh oregano to the mix along with the salt, their flavors would mellow nicely and also be somewhat absorbed by the tomatoes.

It was time to focus on how to transform my drained tomatoes into a sauce. I tried mashing them. This gave them a pretty good texture, but they were too mealy. What would it be like if I mashed half of the mixture? Good idea. Now the sauce was the ideal combination of crushed tomatoes surrounded by newly released tomato liquid, with just the right amount of chunkiness.

But I found myself wondering what to do with the drained tomato liquid. I was not about to toss it out because I knew it had a ton of flavor. One of my test kitchen colleagues had a thought: What if I used this liquid to cook the pasta? Diluted by the amount of water used to cook pasta in the traditional method, it wouldn't have much of an effect. But we have a skillet method of cooking pasta that requires much less liquid; the pasta absorbs the water as it cooks and is never drained. Using this as my guide, I combined the tomato liquid with enough water to bring the total amount to 4 cups in a 12-inch skillet. I stirred in 1 pound of pasta and cooked it until the pasta was al dente and most of the liquid was gone.

After stirring the mashed and reserved tomatoes into the now-cooked pasta, I was relieved to see a sauce—but it needed to be just a little thicker. I knew that stirring the pasta as it cooked would release its natural starches, which would in turn thicken the sauce. There wasn't room enough to do this in the skillet, though, so I switched to a Dutch oven and stirred the pasta frequently as it cooked. When the liquid was all gone, the

---

NOTES FROM THE TEST KITCHEN

COOK THE PASTA IN TOMATO WATER

After macerating the chopped tomatoes in salt, sugar, garlic, oregano, and olive oil, we drain out a cup of the flavorful juice. This juice is combined with water to cook the pasta, which infuses the noodles with subtle tomato flavor.

AVOID ADVANCE PREP FOR GARLIC

We're always looking for ways to make our kitchen work more efficiently and will often prep recipes a day in advance if we know we're going to be busy. But we noticed that garlic can develop a particularly strong odor if minced too far in advance.

Turns out, garlic flavor comes from a compound called allicin, which is not formed until after the garlic's cells are ruptured. As soon as you cut into garlic, the allicin will start to build and build until its flavor becomes overwhelmingly strong. So if you're going to prep a recipe in advance, make sure to leave the garlic cloves whole until the last minute.

pasta was cooked well, infused with tomato flavor, and coated with a light rose–colored tomato sheen. Once again I stirred in the tomatoes. There was a strong tomato presence now, created by not only the chunks and mashed tomatoes but also the subtly flavored pasta. I stirred in some basil, Parmesan cheese, and extra-virgin olive oil and finally had what I had dreamed of: a sauce with all the fresh, bright flavor of raw tomatoes.

—ASHLEY MOORE, *Cook's Country*

Pasta with Raw Tomato Sauce

SERVES 4

Use the ripest tomatoes you can find.

- 2 **pounds very ripe tomatoes, cored and cut into ½-inch pieces**
- 1½ **tablespoons chopped fresh oregano**
- 2 **teaspoons plus 2 tablespoons extra-virgin olive oil, plus extra for serving**
- 2 **garlic cloves, minced**
- **Salt and pepper**
- ¼ **teaspoon sugar**
- 3 **cups water**
- 1 **pound short pasta, such as campanelle, penne, or fusilli**
- ½ **cup fresh basil leaves, torn**
- 1 **ounce Parmesan cheese, grated (½ cup), plus extra for serving**

1. Combine tomatoes, oregano, 2 teaspoons oil, garlic, 1½ teaspoons salt, and sugar in large bowl. Let sit until tomatoes soften and release their juice, at least 1 hour or up to 3 hours.

2. Drain tomato mixture in fine-mesh strainer set over bowl and reserve juice. (You should have 1 cup tomato juice; if not, add water as needed to equal 1 cup.) Divide drained tomato mixture evenly between 2 bowls. Using potato masher, mash 1 bowl of tomato mixture to pulp.

3. Combine water, pasta, and reserved tomato juice in Dutch oven. Cover, place over medium-high heat, and cook at vigorous simmer, stirring often, until pasta is al dente and liquid has nearly evaporated, 12 to 15 minutes. Off heat, stir in basil, Parmesan, mashed and unmashed tomato mixtures, and remaining 2 tablespoons oil. Season with salt and pepper to taste. Serve with extra oil and extra Parmesan.

PASTA WITH BEANS, CHARD, AND ROSEMARY

☑ WHY THIS RECIPE WORKS: Pasta, beans, and greens provide a great combination of flavors and textures for this one-dish meal. In addition to the usual creamy cannellini beans, we added pinto beans for meatiness, while Swiss chard made an appealing twofer for the greens component. We sautéed the chopped chard stems at the outset of cooking but waited until the end to sprinkle the tender leaves on top, and then we covered the pot and let the leaves steam gently off heat. A small amount of pancetta provided a meaty background, and two additions of rosemary gave the dish a subtle but pervasive herbal flavor. Instead of draining and rinsing the canned beans, we mixed the starchy liquid with water and a handful of grated Parmesan to produce a creamy, stew-like sauce to bring it all together. We cooked the pasta separately until just shy of al dente and then finished cooking it in the broth so it would soak up some of the broth's meaty flavor.

Recipes for pasta with beans and greens abound—and are generally unremarkable. Most feature cannellini beans, plus sausage for heft, while everything from kale to spinach is fair game for the greens. And the sauce? There really aren't guidelines, but it's typically bare-bones. Yet even with numerous variations on the theme, the results are the same: a bland mix of thrown-together ingredients. It's no surprise, then, that I've never given the dish a second thought, at least not until I went to Italy. There I had a robust, flavorful bowl of pasta, beans, and greens that was a revelation.

One key to its success was its choice of beans. It featured borlotti, a staple in Italian cooking, which are creamy like cannellini but also wonderfully meaty. Despite a lack of sausage (which let the beans stay center stage), the sauce had a meaty depth, and it possessed a stew-like consistency that brought it all together. This was an exceptional, simple meal—one I'd prepare back home if I could re-create it.

Red-speckled borlotti beans (part of the cranberry bean family) aren't readily available at the average American supermarket, so I needed a substitute. Cannellini would be fine for simulating borlotti creaminess, and to provide the right meaty flavor, I'd also use an equal amount of pintos.

As for canned versus dried beans, we recently discovered that canned cannellini are often a good alternative, and not just because they are convenient. The best have a uniform tenderness that dried beans can lack. And because canned beans are simply dried beans sealed in cans with salted water (along with a few benign additives) and cooked under pressure, the canning liquid is pretty much the same mixture of bean starch and water that you get when you cook dried beans. While nearly every recipe using canned beans calls for draining and rinsing said beans, I would do no such thing. That starchy canning liquid would lend richness and body to my sauce.

For the greens, I settled on Swiss chard: I finely chopped its hearty stems to cook at the outset, and I chopped the tender leaves and set them aside to add toward the end. I sautéed an onion and the chard stems with garlic, red pepper flakes, and rosemary, and then I added 1½ cups of water and one can each of cannellini and pinto beans, scraping all their liquid and starch into the pot. Knowing that the Swiss chard leaves would turn mushy if overcooked, I took a more gentle approach. After simmering the mixture for 10 minutes to let the flavors meld, I spread the chard leaves over the surface, covered the pot, and allowed them to steam off heat for about 5 minutes. I then stirred in

some penne, which I'd cooked separately, and sprinkled Parmesan on top.

I was on the right track, but the flavor was somewhat blah. The next time I started by sautéing 3 ounces of pancetta, not enough to become a primary ingredient but I hoped sufficient to provide a meaty backbone. I also tossed in the rind from my Parmesan when I added the beans. For the pasta, I switched to fusilli since the deep grooves of its spiral shape would better capture what I hoped would be a delicious broth. I also decided to cook the pasta less this time, to just shy of al dente, so that I could finish cooking it through in the broth, allowing it to soak up flavor. When the short simmer was done, I stirred in the pasta, sprinkled the chard on top as before, and left it to finish, covered and off heat.

The sauce was wonderfully flavorful, and the pasta had absorbed its meaty depth. The sauce also had the right creamy consistency, especially after I stirred in some Parmesan. The rosemary had faded a bit, so I stirred in some more after cooking to bolster its flavor, and then seasoned with vinegar. Simple, hearty, and flavorful, this was a dinner that I would savor.

—ANDREA GEARY, *Cook's Illustrated*

NOTES FROM THE TEST KITCHEN

DON'T DRAIN THE BEANS
Most recipes call for draining and rinsing canned beans. That starchy liquid is the key to a great sauce consistency; be sure to add the bean liquid to the pot.

SODIUM IN THE WATER, NOT THE PASTA
Adding salt to pasta's cooking water ensures that the pasta is flavorful. Throughout the years we've zeroed in on a preferred ration of 1 tablespoon of table salt to 4 quarts of cooking water per pound of pasta for the most well-seasoned pasta of any shape or size.

We were curious to find out exactly how much sodium actually makes it into the pasta, so we sent samples of six different shapes—spaghetti, linguine, penne, rigatoni, campanelle, and orzo—all cooked al dente according to our method, to an independent lab for analysis.

The results? Give or take a few milligrams of sodium, all the shapes absorbed about the same amount of salt: ¹⁄₁₆ teaspoon per 4-ounce serving or a total of ¼ teaspoon per pound of pasta. The Dietary Guidelines for Americans recommend less than 2,300 milligrams daily for people under 51 and less than 1,500 milligrams for those 51 and older, so even if you are watching your sodium intake, the amount pasta actually absorbs is so small that it's probably not an issue.

Pasta with Beans, Chard, and Rosemary
SERVES 6

The sauce will thicken as it cools.

- 2 tablespoons vegetable oil
- 3 ounces pancetta, diced
- 1 onion, chopped fine
- 10 ounces Swiss chard, stems chopped fine, leaves chopped coarse
- 2 teaspoons minced fresh rosemary
- 1 garlic clove, minced to paste
- ¼ teaspoon red pepper flakes
- 1 (15-ounce) can cannellini beans (do not drain)
- 1 (15-ounce) can pinto beans (do not drain)
- 1 Parmesan cheese rind (optional), plus 1 ounce Parmesan, grated (½ cup), plus extra for serving
- 8 ounces (2½ cups) fusilli
  Salt
- 1 tablespoon red wine vinegar

1. Heat oil in Dutch oven over medium-high heat until smoking. Add pancetta and cook, stirring occasionally, until pancetta begins to brown, 2 to 3 minutes.

Stir in onion and chard stems and cook, stirring occasionally, until slightly softened, about 3 minutes. Add 1 teaspoon rosemary, garlic, and pepper flakes and cook until fragrant, about 1 minute. Stir in beans and their liquid, 1½ cups water, and Parmesan rind, if using, and bring to boil. Reduce heat to medium-low and simmer for 10 minutes.

2. Meanwhile, bring 2 quarts water to boil in large saucepan. Add pasta and 1½ teaspoons salt and cook until pasta is just shy of al dente. Drain. Stir pasta into beans and spread chard leaves on top. Cover, remove from heat, and let sit until pasta is fully cooked and chard leaves are wilted, 5 to 7 minutes. Discard Parmesan rind, if using. Stir in remaining 1 teaspoon rosemary, ½ cup Parmesan, and vinegar. Season with salt to taste, and serve, passing extra Parmesan separately.

TAGLIATELLE WITH ARTICHOKES AND OLIVE OIL

✔ **WHY THIS RECIPE WORKS:** Jarred artichoke hearts and tagliatelle make a quick and easy pantry dinner with style. We sliced the leaves from jarred artichoke hearts and then gave them a quick soak to temper the harsh flavors they pick up from the brine. We cut the hearts in half and dried them well so that they could be easily browned to bring out their natural nuttiness. Anchovies gave the sauce savory depth, and cream tied together the aromatics, wine, and artichoke flavor. A simple Parmesan bread-crumb topping gave the dish some rich, nutty crunch.

Artichokes have been cultivated in Italy since Roman times, and Italians have learned to cook them in almost every conceivable way. One of my favorite preparations is *pasta con carciofi*, a delicate pairing of herbal, nutty artichoke hearts with tender pasta. Unfortunately, to prepare the dish, you must trim, cook, and dismantle the artichokes to get to the fleshy hearts before you can even think about turning them into a sauce. I've always considered processed artichokes a poor substitute for the fresh kind, but if I could somehow transform their uninspired flavor, I knew I'd have the makings of a great weeknight dish.

To get my bearings, I made a handful of pasta sauce recipes calling for jarred or canned artichoke hearts. One required simmering the hearts in a pot with fresh tomato, onion, and dried herbs for almost 2 hours. A second called for tossing the hearts with broiled cherry tomatoes, olive oil, and oregano. Another required coating the hearts in a rich cream sauce laced with lemon and Parmesan. I even found a recipe that called for pureeing hearts into a slightly chunky, gray concoction that was then used to dress ravioli. While the recipes were easy to prepare, the artichoke flavor was lost in all of them. To succeed, my dish would need to highlight the unique subtleties of the artichoke—not force them to compete with lots of butter and cream or acidic ingredients like tomato.

Before examining the artichokes further, I decided to piece together a bare-bones sauce recipe. I brought a few quarts of water to a boil in a Dutch oven and dumped in 12 ounces of tagliatelle. (In preliminary tests, tasters expressed a strong preference for this egg pasta, whose richness was a nice counterpoint to the lean artichokes.) Meanwhile, I sautéed minced garlic, dried oregano, and red pepper flakes in extra-virgin olive oil in a skillet and then poured in a splash of dry white wine and reduced the mixture. The tagliatelle was al dente by the time I had drained a couple of jars of water-packed baby artichokes and added them to the sauce. I drained the pasta and combined it with the chunky sauce along with just enough starchy pasta water to pull the sauce together.

The good news: The artichoke flavor was no longer obscured by the other ingredients. The bad: The artichoke flavor that was present was compromised, tasting strongly of the citric and ascorbic acids that are added to the packing water during processing.

To enhance the positive flavor traits of the artichokes, I tried to brown them before building the sauce. But their irregular shape made browning difficult, plus the leaves had turned tough and leathery by the time they finally picked up color. That said, the parts of the heart that had browned tasted fantastic. For the next go-round, I cut the leaves from the hearts and set them aside. I then halved each heart to create a flat side that would make good contact with the hot pan. I blotted off the excess brine and put the hearts into a hot skillet shimmering with olive oil. Sure enough, the hearts browned beautifully and took on a deep, rich taste that disguised the off-flavor from the additives.

I dealt with the leaves next, swirling them in a bowl of water before draining them and adding them to the sauce. I was hoping that the water bath would eliminate their less-than-appealing flavor, but tasters reported that it had endured.

I wondered if I could use baking soda to neutralize the acidity from the additives. In the test kitchen, we use soda to neutralize odors on cutting boards, so maybe it could block unwanted flavors in my artichokes. I briefly soaked some leaves in a mild baking soda solution and then drained and rinsed them. They definitely tasted less acidic, but alas, the soda dip had left behind a chemical flavor.

Instead of trying to neutralize the acid, maybe I just needed to try harder to wash it away. I prepped more artichoke leaves and left them to soak in water for various amounts of time. Five- and 10-minute samples still hinted of brine. But 15 minutes was the ideal amount of time, after which only the subtle flavor of artichoke remained.

Happy with the state of my artichokes, I was ready to perfect the rest of the dish. The aromatics, wine, olive oil, and artichokes needed just a splash of something rich to bring them together into a unified sauce. Stirring in a mere 2 tablespoons of cream with the wine did just that. I also tried adding small amounts of bacon and prosciutto for depth of flavor, but even two slices overwhelmed the artichokes with porkiness. Using a mere half of a slice of bacon was a possibility but seemed impractical, so I rooted through the test kitchen pantry for other options. I quickly landed on anchovies: Two fillets, added along with the aromatics, contributed a hint of savoriness, and none of my tasters picked out any fishiness.

When finished with chopped parsley, lemon zest, Parmesan, and a generous drizzle of extra-virgin olive oil, the pasta boasted a range of clear flavors—richness from touches of cream and cheese, brightness from the lemon and artichokes, and grassy notes from the herbs and olive oil.

The flavor of the dish was spot-on, but it was lacking a little textural contrast. That was nothing that some toasted bread crumbs couldn't fix. I pulsed two slices of sandwich bread in a food processor and then toasted the crumbs in a skillet. Just as they began to brown, I added a sprinkling of Parmesan and continued to cook the mixture until it was nicely toasted. Sprinkled on top of my pasta, the cheesy crumbs added pops of crunchiness.

With its tangy, creamy, cheesy, and crunchy elements—and genuine artichoke flavor—this dish is far more than something to turn to for a quick dinner. In fact, it's so good that I'd even make it for company.

—LAN LAM, *Cook's Illustrated*

IMPROVING JARRED ARTICHOKE HEARTS

Jarred artichokes have a sharp taste from the acids they are packed in. Here's how we tempered that quality.

CUT AWAY LEAVES: Separating the leaves from the hearts allows us to treat each component independently.

SOAK: Soaking the leaves in water for 15 minutes takes away the sour taste while still leaving them well seasoned.

BROWN HEARTS IN OIL: Browning adds rich depth to the hearts (we skipped this step with the leaves, which turned tough).

Tagliatelle with Artichokes and Olive Oil

SERVES 4 TO 6

We prefer jarred artichoke hearts labeled "baby" or "cocktail" that are 1½ inches or shorter in length. Larger artichoke hearts tend to have fibrous leaves. If you are using larger hearts, trim the top ¼ to ½ inch from the leaves. Do not use marinated or oil-packed artichoke hearts. You'll need three 9.9-ounce jars of artichokes for this recipe. The anchovies add depth without imparting a fishy taste; don't omit them. Tagliatelle is a long, flat, dry egg pasta that is about ¼ inch wide. Pappardelle can be substituted for the tagliatelle.

- **3 cups jarred whole artichoke hearts packed in water, preferably baby or cocktail size**
- **2 slices hearty white sandwich bread, torn into 1-inch pieces**
- **3 tablespoons plus ¼ cup extra-virgin olive oil**

1 ounce Parmesan cheese, grated (½ cup), plus extra for serving

Salt and pepper

3 garlic cloves, minced

2 anchovy fillets, rinsed, patted dry, and minced

½ teaspoon dried oregano

⅛ teaspoon red pepper flakes

⅓ cup dry white wine

2 tablespoons heavy cream

12 ounces tagliatelle

¼ cup minced fresh parsley

1 teaspoon grated lemon zest

1. Cut leaves from artichoke hearts. Cut hearts in half and dry with paper towels. Place leaves in bowl and cover with water. Let leaves stand for 15 minutes. Drain well.

2. Pulse bread in food processor until finely ground, 10 to 15 pulses. Heat 2 tablespoons oil in 10-inch nonstick skillet over medium heat until shimmering. Add bread crumbs and cook, stirring constantly, until crumbs begin to brown, 3 to 5 minutes. Add ¼ cup Parmesan and continue to cook, stirring constantly, until crumbs are golden brown, 1 to 2 minutes. Transfer crumbs to bowl and season with salt and pepper to taste. Wipe out skillet.

3. Heat 1 tablespoon oil in now-empty skillet over medium-high heat until shimmering. Add artichoke hearts and ⅛ teaspoon salt; cook, stirring frequently, until hearts are spotty brown, 7 to 9 minutes. Add garlic, anchovies, oregano, and pepper flakes; cook, stirring constantly, until fragrant, about 30 seconds. Stir in wine and cream and bring to simmer. Remove skillet from heat and stir in artichoke leaves. Set aside.

4. Meanwhile, bring 4 quarts water to boil in large pot. Add pasta and 1 tablespoon salt and cook, stirring often, until al dente. Reserve 1 cup cooking water, then drain pasta and return it to pot. Stir in artichoke sauce, remaining ¼ cup Parmesan, ⅔ cup reserved cooking water, remaining ¼ cup oil, parsley, and lemon zest. Adjust consistency with remaining reserved cooking water as needed. Season with salt and pepper to taste. Serve, passing bread-crumb mixture and extra Parmesan separately.

MUSHROOM BOLOGNESE

✓ **WHY THIS RECIPE WORKS:** Traditional Bolognese sauce gets its rich, complex flavor from a combination of several types of meat, which makes creating a vegetarian version a particular challenge. Mushrooms possess a meaty flavor and texture, so we turned to two types to replicate that complexity: Dried porcini delivered depth of flavor while 2 pounds of fresh cremini gave the sauce a satisfying, substantial texture. To further round out the sauce's savory flavor, we added two more umami-rich ingredients: soy sauce and tomato paste. Red wine contributed further definition to our sauce. To make prep easy, we used the food processor both to roughly chop the cremini and to finely chop the onion and carrot. Pulsing whole canned tomatoes in the food processor allowed us to get just the right texture, and a dash of heavy cream made it extra smooth.

There's so much to love about classic Bolognese sauce—tomatoes, meat, and red wine are slowly simmered and then finished with cream to produce a thick, ultrarich, undeniably complex pasta sauce. But what if you're vegetarian? Is meatless Bolognese—one as satisfying as the original—a fantasy? Some of my test kitchen colleagues certainly thought so. Undeterred by their snickers, I set out to prove them wrong.

Following our standard recipe sans meat, I softened carrot, onion, and porcini mushrooms, adding garlic and sugar for balance. Instead of using meatloaf mix (a combination of ground beef, ground veal, and ground pork) I swapped in veggie protein crumbles. Made of seasoned, textured soy protein, veggie protein crumbles can be a great vegetarian stand-in for ground meat. Soy sauce is an unusual ingredient in classic Bolognese, but it added some much-needed umami undertones traditionally supplied by the meat. I mixed in the soy sauce, reduced wine, and a little tomato paste to round out the flavors, and let the sauce simmer for 15 minutes.

The sauce didn't deliver my ideal, but it had potential. The two biggest issues here were the off-putting texture and the one-dimensional flavor. The sauce also lacked complexity. The first step in creating this vegetarian sauce would be to fill the gap that meat left behind, in terms of both bite and flavor.

MUSHROOM BOLOGNESE

I kicked soy crumbles to the curb and reached for another meat substitute: tempeh. Tempeh, made from fermented soybeans, has a strong nutty flavor and holds together well during cooking. After another batch of sauce with tempeh, I was no closer to my goal. During the 15 minutes of simmering, the tempeh had become bitter and crumbly.

At this point, I washed my hands of meat substitutes and took another look at the sauce to see what was working. Porcini mushrooms, which are full of umami, enhance the meaty flavor of classic Bolognese, as they were doing with our vegetarian version. Thus, it made sense to add more of these mushrooms to the mix. But I started thinking maybe even more mushrooms, with their meaty flavor and resilient texture, would fill out the sauce. Creminis are another mushroom with an especially rich, savory flavor, so into the mix they went.

I made another batch of the Bolognese with the cremini mushrooms chopped until the pieces were small enough to resemble the texture of ground meat. The small pieces of mushroom were exactly what the sauce needed.

With so many mushrooms in the mix, I made further adjustments to bring the other ingredients forward. The extra mushrooms masked the tomato paste, which had added complexity. I decided to use some canned whole tomatoes that I had chopped in the food processor, and the acidity and fresh tomato flavor I wanted shone through.

Now that I had the ingredients squared away, I had only a few more adjustments to make. I was using the food processor for both the cremini and the tomatoes, so instead of taking the time to cut up the carrot and onion, I simply processed them until chopped fine. I had stayed away from dairy in my sauce, afraid that it would mute the flavors in the vegetables, but found that a mere 3 tablespoons of heavy cream at the end of the cooking time was all I needed to round out the sauce and give it a decadent silkiness.

I tossed my Bolognese together with thick strands of fettuccine and dished out samples to my skeptical colleagues. Won over, they quickly finished off the pasta and sauce. Making no sacrifices in flavor or texture, I had created a sauce that was remarkably rich and complex—no meat required.

—SARA MAYER, *America's Test Kitchen Books*

NOTES FROM THE TEST KITCHEN

PAIRING PASTA SHAPES AND SAUCES

Pairing a pasta shape with the right sauce might be an art form in Italy, but we think there's only one basic rule to follow: Thick, chunky sauces go with short pastas, and thin, smooth, or light sauces with strand pasta.

SHORT PASTAS

Short tubular or molded pasta shapes do an excellent job of trapping chunky sauces. Sauces with very large chunks are best with large tubes. Sauces with small chunks pair better with fusilli or penne.

STRAND PASTAS

Long strands are best with smooth sauces or thinner sauces. In general, wider noodles, such as pappardelle and fettuccine, can support slightly chunkier sauces like our Mushroom Bolognese.

Mushroom Bolognese

SERVES 4 TO 8

Serve with grated Parmesan.

- 2 pounds cremini mushrooms, trimmed and quartered
- 1 carrot, peeled and chopped
- 1 small onion, chopped
- 1 (28-ounce) can whole peeled tomatoes
- 3 tablespoons unsalted butter
- ½ ounce dried porcini mushrooms, rinsed and minced
- 3 garlic cloves, minced
- 1 teaspoon sugar
- 2 tablespoons tomato paste
- 1 cup dry red wine
- ½ cup vegetable broth
- 1 tablespoon soy sauce
  Salt and pepper
- 3 tablespoons heavy cream
- 1 pound fettuccine or linguine

1. Working in batches, pulse cremini mushrooms in food processor until pieces are no larger than ½ inch, 5 to 7 pulses; transfer to large bowl. Pulse carrot and onion in now-empty processor until chopped fine, 5 to 7 pulses; transfer to bowl with mushrooms. Pulse tomatoes and their juice in now-empty processor until chopped fine, 6 to 8 pulses; set aside separately.

2. Melt butter in Dutch oven over medium heat. Add processed vegetables and porcini mushrooms, cover, and cook, stirring occasionally, until they release their liquid, about 5 minutes. Uncover, increase heat to medium-high, and cook until liquid has evaporated and vegetables begin to brown, 12 to 15 minutes.

3. Stir in garlic and sugar and cook until fragrant, about 30 seconds. Stir in tomato paste and cook for 1 minute. Stir in wine and simmer until nearly evaporated, about 5 minutes.

4. Stir in processed tomatoes, vegetable broth, soy sauce, ½ teaspoon salt, and ¼ teaspoon pepper, and bring to simmer. Reduce heat to medium-low and simmer until sauce has thickened but is still moist, 8 to 10 minutes. Off heat, stir in cream.

5. Meanwhile, bring 4 quarts water to boil in large pot. Add pasta and 1 tablespoon salt and cook, stirring often, until al dente. Reserve ½ cup cooking water, then drain pasta and return it to pot. Add sauce and toss to combine. Season with salt and pepper to taste, and adjust consistency with reserved cooking water as needed.

MAKE-AHEAD STUFFED SHELLS

✓ **WHY THIS RECIPE WORKS:** A satisfying pasta dish prepared ahead of time is a lifesaver for time-crunched cooks. We wanted a stuffed shells recipe that could be assembled in advance and go from refrigerator to oven without sacrificing flavor or texture. But when we reheated some basic stuffed shells in marinara sauce, we found the ricotta had turned watery and the sauce's flavor was washed out. A little Parmesan cheese and two eggs helped bind the filling and prevent it from getting watery, and mozzarella cheese gave the filling a rich, creamy texture. To amp up the sauce, we were inspired by the bold flavors of Italian Amatriciana sauce, with its smoky pancetta and spicy red pepper flakes. Those few simple ingredients ensured that the sauce was rich and flavorful. Crushed tomatoes provided a smooth sauce base with just the right amount of texture.

Cheese-stuffed pasta shells are simple weeknight family fare. But because it takes so long to cook the pasta, make the filling, prepare the sauce, and stuff the shells, the recipe can seem like a daunting prospect for a busy home cook. An ideal solution would be to prepare the dish ahead of time and then just finish it in the oven right before dinner. Unfortunately, a long chill in the refrigerator is tough on this dish. When I tried the shells from a handful of classic recipes in my make-ahead version, the results were especially bad—gummy pasta, grainy filling, pasty sauce, and rubbery mozzarella. It was clear that a make-ahead recipe would have to compensate for the moisture loss that occurred during the chilling and heating process.

I started with the shells. First, I tried cooking the pasta until it was tender, but then when I finished the dish in the oven, it baked up mushy. So I switched to cooking the pasta just short of completely soft, then drained and separated the shells to get them ready for stuffing. The filled al dente pasta shells finished cooking to just the right texture in the oven.

Once I'd figured out the pasta, I moved on to the filling. Traditional recipes stuff the shells with a mixture of ricotta cheese and seasonings. Ricotta is great for straight-to-the-oven recipes but it loses moisture when refrigerated and reheated, making for a separated, grainy texture. My solution was to add two whole eggs to the cheese as a binder. The fat and emulsifiers in the eggs helped the ricotta filling stay creamy and sturdy throughout the whole process. Adding plenty of mozzarella, Parmesan, garlic, and fresh basil ramped up the richness of the filling enough that it could withstand a long sit in the refrigerator without losing its flavor. I used a makeshift pastry bag made from a zipper-lock bag with a corner snipped off to pipe the filling into the shells with less mess and waste.

Next, I tackled the sauce. I tried topping the shells with the test kitchen's simple marinara sauce; but sitting in the refrigerator washed out its flavor and the refrigerated sauce dried to a thick, pasty texture in the oven. To boost the flavor, I tried making a version of Amatriciana sauce instead, which is a bold and brash traditional Italian sauce that contains tomato, bacon, onion, and dried chile. I started by browning bacon on the stove. I kept the rest of the sauce simple, with onion, salt, pepper, and dried red pepper flakes for a nice bite, all sautéed in rendered fat from the bacon. Crushed tomatoes made a perfect base once I cooked them down to remove as much excess moisture as possible. When I tasted this sauce, however, regular bacon turned out to be a weak link; by the time the dish was cooked, the flavor of the sauce had become bland and lost the distinct elements of bacon, onion, and spice. To solve this problem, I tried replacing the bacon with Italian pancetta (bacon made from pork belly), which is actually more traditional in Amatriciana recipes. Unlike American bacon, pancetta is not smoked and the cure does not contain sugar—just salt, pepper, and cloves. The pure, straightforward pork and salt flavors of the pancetta lasted even through the chilling and reheating process and made for a superior sauce. I layered this thick, flavorful sauce both underneath and on top of my stuffed shells in the baking dish and wrapped the whole thing up. This casserole can chill out in the refrigerator as long as 24 hours for make-ahead convenience. The next day, I came back to put the finishing touches on my recipe.

Stuffed shells wouldn't be complete without a melty layer of mozzarella on top. However, refrigerating the mozzarella along with the shells led to a rubbery mess. To remedy this, I reserved the cheese separately to add toward the end of baking. I put the dish of shells into the oven covered with foil and baked it until the sauce started to bubble, then removed the foil and sprinkled the mozzarella over the top along with some Parmesan for extra flavor. I then finished baking the dish uncovered until the cheese was melted into a gooey, golden crust. Altogether, it took only about an hour to finish the dish, which made it a much more approachable option for a weeknight dinner. A light sprinkling of basil was the perfect fresh accent on top of this great make-ahead dish.

—DANIELLE DESIATO, *America's Test Kitchen Books*

NOTES FROM THE TEST KITCHEN

MAKING A STURDY FILLING

To keep the filling creamy through storing and reheating, we added Parmesan to thicken it, plus two eggs to bind the cheeses. A zipper-lock bag made it easy to pipe the filling into the shells.

WRAP TIGHTLY AND HEAT GENTLY

To ensure that make-ahead casseroles emerge from the oven moist and saucy, it is important to cover them tightly with aluminum foil to trap steam and prevent moisture loss. Heating casseroles gently in a moderate oven prevents uneven cooking.

Make-Ahead Stuffed Shells with Amatriciana Sauce

SERVES 6 TO 8

When buying pancetta, ask to have it sliced ¼ inch thick. If you can't find pancetta, you can substitute 6 ounces of thick-cut, or slab, bacon.

- 1 tablespoon extra-virgin olive oil
- 6 ounces pancetta, cut into 1 by ¼-inch pieces
- 1 onion, chopped fine
  Salt and pepper
- ¼ teaspoon red pepper flakes
- 2 (28-ounce) cans crushed tomatoes
- 12 ounces jumbo pasta shells
- 12 ounces (1½ cups) whole-milk or part-skim ricotta cheese
- 10 ounces mozzarella cheese, shredded (2½ cups)
- 3 ounces Parmesan cheese, grated (1½ cup)
- 2 large eggs, lightly beaten
- ¼ cup chopped fresh basil
- 2 garlic cloves, minced
- 2 tablespoons chopped fresh basil

1. Heat oil in large saucepan over medium heat until shimmering. Add pancetta and cook until lightly browned and crisp, about 8 minutes. Using slotted spoon, transfer pancetta to paper towel–lined plate.

2. Pour off all but 3 tablespoons fat from saucepan, add onion and ¼ teaspoon salt, and cook until softened, about 5 minutes. Stir in pepper flakes and cook until fragrant, about 30 seconds. Stir in tomatoes, bring to simmer, and cook until slightly thickened, about 10 minutes. Let cool to room temperature, about 45 minutes. Stir in pancetta and season with salt and pepper to taste.

3. Meanwhile, line rimmed baking sheet with clean dish towel. Bring 4 quarts water to boil in large pot. Add pasta and 1 tablespoon salt and cook, stirring occasionally, until just beginning to soften, about 8 minutes. Drain pasta and transfer to prepared baking sheet. Using dinner fork, pry apart any shells that have clung together, discarding any that are badly torn (you should have 30 to 33 good shells).

4. Combine ricotta, 1½ cups mozzarella, 1 cup Parmesan, eggs, basil, garlic, and ½ teaspoon salt in bowl; transfer to zipper-lock bag. Using scissors, cut off 1 corner of bag and pipe 1 tablespoon filling into each shell.

5. Spread 2 cups cooled sauce on bottom of 13 by 9-inch baking dish. Arrange filled shells seam side down in dish. Spread remaining sauce over shells.

6. Wrap dish tightly with plastic wrap and refrigerate for at least 8 hours or up to 24 hours.

7. Adjust oven rack to middle position and heat oven to 400 degrees. Unwrap dish and cover tightly with greased aluminum foil. Bake shells until sauce begins to bubble around edges, 25 to 30 minutes. Remove foil, sprinkle with 1 cup mozzarella and ½ cup Parmesan, and bake, uncovered, until shells are hot throughout and cheese is melted and begins to brown, about 10 minutes. Let cool for 10 minutes. Sprinkle with basil and serve.

SEMOLINA GNOCCHI

✔ WHY THIS RECIPE WORKS: Most recipes for these Roman-style dumplings call for stirring semolina flour into hot milk and cooking it much like polenta to make dough. This mixture is then spread out into a thin layer and allowed to cool before being cut into rounds, which are shingled in a baking dish, topped with cheese, and baked. We found that the key was getting the ratio of liquid to semolina right: too loose and the mixture took a long time to set up, and the gnocchi fused together in the heat of the oven. A mixture made with 2½ cups of milk and 1 cup of semolina was stiff enough that we could shape the dumplings immediately—no need to cool. And instead of stamping out rounds, which wasted much of the semolina mixture, we simply portioned dumplings straight from the pot. Refrigerating them before baking ensured that they held their shape and could be lifted out of the dish cleanly to be served individually. An egg provided binding power and, along with a little baking powder, lift.

Gnocchi to me has always meant pillowy, thimble-size dumplings shaped from a dough of riced potato, flour, and egg, and so that's what I was expecting when I ordered so-called Roman gnocchi at a recent dinner out. But instead of the familiar little boiled pouches, these gnocchi turned out to be plump 2-inch rounds that arrived at the table shingled in a baking dish. One bite and I was sold: Made from semolina flour, egg, and cheese, with a creamy, slightly dense texture more like that of polenta than potato dumplings, they were

pure comfort food. I would definitely be making these at home the first chance I got.

When I gathered recipes, I found that all followed the same basic approach. Each began with semolina, a deep yellow flour made from durum wheat that has a richer flavor and coarser texture than regular wheat flour. The semolina is whisked into a heated liquid (milk contributes the best flavor) and stirred over the heat until it comes together to make a pourable batter or dough. Eggs, butter, and cheese are then stirred in to enrich the mixture and help it set. At that point, most recipes call for spreading the dough out on a flat surface into a thick slab and letting it cool until stiff enough to cut into rounds with a biscuit cutter. The disks are then shingled (which helps keep them moist), topped with additional butter and cheese, and reheated in a baking dish.

When I took these recipes into the kitchen, I found that the process was indeed straightforward, but the results presented a host of issues. The cooked mixture took an awfully long time to firm up to a stiff enough consistency to allow for stamping out the dumplings, and even then it was problematic, with a wet consistency that made cleanly cutting out circles and transferring them to a baking dish difficult at best. I also didn't like that much of the semolina mixture was wasted in the cutting-out process. And because the dough was fairly soft, the dumplings tended to fuse together in the heat of the oven, which made it impossible to lift them out individually for neat, attractive portions. And finally, there was the flavor—or lack thereof. Most versions tasted bland or starchy. I wanted a recipe that gave me individual dumplings with enough flavor to stand alone with a salad or be served with a simple sauce.

Finding the proper ratio of milk to semolina flour seemed like the most promising way to address the consistency problems. Recipes that called for significantly more milk than flour took too long to cook, barely set up once cooled, and formed a unified and hardly distinguishable mass once baked. Those that relied on a ratio on the lower end of that spectrum resulted in gnocchi that took much less time to cook to the desired thick consistency and set up much more firmly. Unfortunately, they also tasted floury and had a pasty texture because the semolina wasn't able to fully hydrate. Several tests later, I found the happy medium: 2½ cups milk to 1 cup semolina gave me a dough with the right consistency but without that raw-flour flavor.

Now that I had the texture right, I was ready to address the butter, egg, and cheese, which are added to the dough after it comes off the heat. Three tablespoons of butter (plus one more to grease the pan) lent adequate flavor and richness without tipping my gnocchi over into greasy territory. And I found that one lightly beaten whole egg provided sufficient binding power and lightness as well as some richness.

As for the cheese, softer varieties like mozzarella and fontina resulted in gnocchi that were too tender and inclined to fuse together. I eventually settled on firmer Gruyère since it added flavor without having any negative effect on texture. A bit of grated Parmesan sprinkled over the gnocchi before baking provided another savory hit and gave the dumplings a nicely browned top. My final flavor tweak was to incorporate some minced rosemary and some nutmeg to add complexity and woodsy notes and a hint of warm spice.

Now the flavor was spot on and the texture was really close, but the dumplings were a little denser than I would have liked. Adding more egg would only loosen the mixture and put me back where I started. The answer? Stirring in ½ teaspoon of baking powder when I added the cheese. As it does in many doughs and batters, baking powder gave the dumplings lift.

Up to this point, I had been cooling the dough by spreading it out in a baking dish and leaving it in the refrigerator for about an hour. But now that I had a very thick dough right off the stove, I didn't really need to let it cool; the dumplings would hold their shape even if warm. Was there a more efficient way to shape them?

I liked the idea of simply using a ¼-cup dry measuring cup, dipped in water between scoops to avoid sticking, to portion out each dumpling. When I tried this, I ended up with perfectly shaped disks. But there was one issue remaining: My dumplings still fused together in the oven more than I would have liked.

To ensure easy-to-portion individual dumplings, I found that I could simply let the shaped dumplings cool in the refrigerator before baking them. (While a 30-minute stint in the fridge was the minimum, I discovered that the longer the dumplings sat in there—up to 24 hours—the better, so they turned out to be a great make-ahead dish.)

These dumplings were just the savory, simple comfort food I was after, but they also lent themselves to some flavorful variations. A combination featuring prosciutto and chives and another with sun-dried tomatoes and basil nicely complemented semolina's nutty, buttery flavor. Whether I went with my simple version or a variation, my semolina gnocchi were as easy to prepare as they were satisfying to eat.

—DAVID PAZMIÑO, *Cook's Illustrated*

Semolina Gnocchi (Gnocchi alla Romana)
SERVES 4 TO 6

Serve as a side dish or as a light entrée topped with Quick Tomato Sauce (recipe follows).

2½	cups whole milk
¾	teaspoon salt
	Pinch ground nutmeg
1	cup (6 ounces) fine semolina flour
4	tablespoons unsalted butter
1	large egg, lightly beaten
1½	ounces Gruyère cheese, shredded (⅓ cup)
1	teaspoon minced fresh rosemary
½	teaspoon baking powder
2	tablespoons grated Parmesan cheese

NOTES FROM THE TEST KITCHEN

FORMING SEMOLINA GNOCCHI
By making a very stiff dough and then refrigerating the shaped dumplings before shingling them in the pan, we ensure that they don't fuse together in the oven.

SHAPE GNOCCHI: Use moistened ¼ cup measure to portion gnocchi, inverting onto tray.

CHILL: Refrigerate gnocchi, uncovered for at least 30 minutes and up to 24 hours.

1. Adjust oven rack to middle position and heat oven to 400 degrees. Heat milk, salt, and nutmeg in medium saucepan over medium-low heat until bubbles form around edges of saucepan. Whisking constantly, slowly add semolina to milk mixture. Reduce heat to low and cook, stirring often with rubber spatula, until mixture forms stiff mass that pulls away from sides when stirring, 3 to 5 minutes. Remove from heat and let cool for 5 minutes.

2. Stir 3 tablespoons butter and egg into semolina mixture until incorporated. (Mixture will appear separated at first but will become smooth and bit shiny.) Stir in Gruyère, rosemary, and baking powder until incorporated.

3. Fill small bowl with water. Moisten ¼-cup dry measuring cup with water and scoop even portion of semolina mixture. Invert gnocchi onto tray or large plate. Repeat, moistening measuring cup between scoops to prevent sticking. Place tray of gnocchi, uncovered, in refrigerator for 30 minutes. (Gnocchi can be refrigerated, covered, for up to 24 hours.)

4. Rub interior of 8-inch square baking dish with remaining 1 tablespoon butter. Shingle gnocchi in pan, creating 3 rows of 4 gnocchi each. Sprinkle gnocchi with Parmesan. Bake until tops of gnocchi are golden brown, 35 to 40 minutes. Let cool for 15 minutes before serving.

Quick Tomato Sauce

MAKES ABOUT 3 CUPS

Our favorite crushed tomatoes are Tuttorosso Crushed Tomatoes in Thick Puree with Basil.

- 2 tablespoons unsalted butter
- ¼ cup grated onion
- 1 teaspoon minced fresh oregano or ¼ teaspoon dried
  Salt and pepper
- 2 garlic cloves, minced
- 1 (28-ounce) can crushed tomatoes
- ¼ teaspoon sugar
- 2 tablespoons chopped fresh basil
- 1 tablespoon extra-virgin olive oil

Melt butter in medium saucepan over medium heat. Add onion, oregano, and ½ teaspoon salt and cook, stirring occasionally, until onion is softened and lightly browned, 5 to 7 minutes. Stir in garlic and cook until

fragrant, about 30 seconds. Stir in tomatoes and sugar, bring to simmer, and cook until slightly thickened, about 10 minutes. Off heat, stir in basil and oil and season with salt and pepper to taste.

VARIATIONS

Semolina Gnocchi with Prosciutto and Chives
Stir 1½ ounces finely chopped thinly sliced prosciutto into semolina mixture with Gruyère. Substitute 1 tablespoon minced fresh chives for rosemary.

Semolina Gnocchi with Sun-Dried Tomatoes and Basil
Stir ⅓ cup rinsed and patted dry oil-packed sun-dried tomatoes into semolina mixture with Gruyère. Substitute 1 tablespoon minced fresh basil for rosemary.

PASTA FRITTATA WITH SAUSAGE AND HOT PEPPERS

✓ WHY THIS RECIPE WORKS: For a pasta frittata that showcased egg and pasta in equal measure, we opted for superthin angel hair pasta. We started with dried pasta instead of leftover cooked pasta so that we could make this dish any night of the week. For convenience's sake we skipped the traditional pasta cooking method, which requires a large pot of boiling water, and instead cooked the angel hair in just 3 cups of water in the same 10-inch nonstick skillet we then used for cooking the frittata. We kept the eggs tender by using a generous amount of extra-virgin olive oil, and we created a crispy pasta crust by letting it fry in the skillet before adding the eggs. Finally, for flavor and textural contrast, we incorporated bold add-ins.

Leftovers get a bad rap. It's too bad, because they're the foundation of some of the best dishes out there. For me, one of the most underrated made-from-leftovers preparations is pasta frittata, in which leftover pasta is transformed into a thick, creamy, golden-brown omelet laced with noodles. The dish got its start in Naples, Italy. The classic Neapolitan pasta frittata starts with leftover cooked and sauced pasta (most often a long noodle shape) and half a dozen or so eggs beaten with salt, pepper, melted lard or butter, and grated Parmigiano-Reggiano cheese. The best versions I've

PASTA FRITTATA WITH SAUSAGE AND HOT PEPPERS

eaten also featured small bites of meat or vegetables that contributed flavor without overly disrupting the creamy texture of the dish.

The only barrier I encounter in whipping up a quick pasta frittata for dinner is that I rarely find myself with leftover pasta. But why should that stand in the way? Cooking dried pasta would add a little more effort, but maybe I could streamline the process.

Since I wasn't dealing with leftovers, I had the whole world of pasta open to me. To see which particular type might work best, I boiled up a variety of shapes and sizes and tested them in a bare-bones recipe. It was clear right off the bat that long noodles were superior to short and tubular types, which created gaps and led to frittatas that broke apart during slicing. Among the long noodles, angel hair pasta was the winner, ensuring a more balanced ratio of pasta to egg in each bite compared with the wider linguine and fettuccine. These delicate strands proved ideal, bringing a satisfying web of pasta to every bite without marring the tender egg texture.

While most Italians will claim that there is only one way to cook pasta—in a large quantity of boiling water—we've actually found that the process works equally well with just a little water. Perhaps even more surprising is that you can start pasta directly in cold water that is then brought to a boil and get results identical to those you'd get from throwing it into already boiling water. I decided to put these discoveries into practice in the name of convenience. I tossed 6 ounces of halved angel hair pasta into a 10-inch nonstick skillet along with 3 cups of water and some salt. I placed the skillet over high heat and stirred occasionally as it came to a boil. Then I let it simmer, stirring occasionally, until the pasta was tender and the water had evaporated. All told it took about 15 minutes, and by cooking off the water, I could even skip dirtying a strainer. On to the egg mixture.

Beating together eight eggs (a number that provided the right balance and structure for 6 ounces of dried pasta) with salt, pepper, and Parmesan and tossing in cooked angel hair is about as easy as it gets—but ensuring that this mixture cooks up creamy and tender takes a bit more thought. Gently cooking any egg preparation ensures that the exterior portions don't overcook and turn rubbery while the interior comes up to temperature. Turning my stove dial to medium,

covering the frittata during cooking, and flipping it halfway through proved a winning formula. The top and bottom took on a burnished appearance while the inside stayed moist and relatively tender.

But I wanted it to be even more tender, so I turned my attention to fat. Fat keeps eggs tender by coating their proteins and preventing them from bonding together too firmly. My tasters preferred extra-virgin olive oil since it produced a frittata that tasted more of egg and less of rich dairy.

I was feeling pretty pleased and nearly ready to close the file on the recipe but for one thing: All along, tasters had raved when they encountered the inevitable few strands of angel hair that had settled at the bottom or sides of the hot pan, turning brown and crispy. The contrast between the creamy eggs and these crispy strands was actually one of the best parts. Was there any way to get even more of these browned strands?

I started fiddling with how I layered the egg and the noodles, thinking that I could purposely leave some of the pasta on the bottom of the frittata to ensure contact with the pan. I got mixed results—sometimes the pasta would stay put and other times the egg would just seep under it and foil my plans. Up to this point I'd been boiling the pasta in the skillet and then pouring in the egg mixture. What I really needed to do was fry the pasta before incorporating the eggs. Why not just add a little oil to the skillet with the pasta and water and let it start frying once the water evaporated? This is the same technique that is used with potstickers and, to my delight, it worked just as well here. As soon as the last bit of water evaporated, the pasta started sizzling. I cooked it, swirling and shaking the pan to prevent sticking, until the strands at the bottom of the pan turned lightly crispy. Then I simply poured my egg mixture over the pasta and used tongs to mix the egg throughout the uncrisped strands, leaving the bottom layer as undisturbed as possible. Sure enough, the time that it took to cook the egg through resulted in a substantial, lacy layer of crispy, browned pasta that almost served as a crust, delivering satisfying crunch in every bite. Meanwhile, the rest of the pasta stayed tender, melding into the creamy eggs.

The frittata was ready to be flavored with some bold ingredients. I knew that the key to adding vegetables and meat was cutting everything into small pieces (which wouldn't disturb the interior texture). The add-ins also needed to precook in the skillet since they would just warm through in the frittata. My favorite combination was a mix of savory sweet Italian sausage and chopped hot cherry peppers. It offered richness and plenty of acidity and heat to balance. I also whipped up a version featuring broccoli rabe and a pinch of pepper flakes. Finally, I made one with thinly sliced cremini mushrooms, sage, and pungent Gorgonzola. No matter the flavor, my pasta frittata never lasted long in the kitchen. A shame—I like leftovers.

—DAN SOUZA, *Cook's Illustrated*

Pasta Frittata with Sausage and Hot Peppers
SERVES 4 TO 6

To ensure the proper texture, it's important to use angel hair pasta. We like to serve the frittata warm or at room temperature, with a green salad.

- 8 large eggs
- 1 ounce Parmesan cheese, grated (½ cup)
- 3 tablespoons extra-virgin olive oil
- 3 tablespoons coarsely chopped jarred hot cherry peppers
- 2 tablespoons chopped fresh parsley
  Salt and pepper
- 8 ounces sweet Italian sausage, casings removed, crumbled
- 2 garlic cloves, sliced thin
- 3 cups water
- 6 ounces angel hair pasta, broken in half
- 3 tablespoons vegetable oil

1. Whisk eggs, Parmesan, olive oil, cherry peppers, parsley, ½ teaspoon salt, and ½ teaspoon pepper in large bowl until egg is even yellow color; set aside.

2. Cook sausage in 10-inch nonstick skillet over medium heat, breaking up sausage with wooden spoon, until fat renders and sausage is about half cooked, 3 to 5 minutes. Stir in garlic and cook for 30 seconds. Remove skillet from heat. Transfer sausage mixture (some sausage will still be raw) to bowl with egg mixture and wipe out skillet.

3. Bring water, pasta, vegetable oil, and ¾ teaspoon salt to boil in now-empty skillet over high heat. Cook, stirring occasionally, until pasta is tender, water has evaporated, and pasta starts to sizzle in oil, 8 to 12 minutes.

Reduce heat to medium and continue to cook pasta, swirling pan and scraping under edge of pasta with rubber spatula frequently to prevent sticking (do not stir), until bottom turns golden and starts to crisp, 5 to 7 minutes (lift up edge of pasta to check progress).

4. Using spatula, push some pasta up sides of skillet so entire pan surface is covered with pasta. Pour egg mixture over pasta. Using tongs, lift up loose strands of pasta to allow egg to flow toward pan, being careful not to pull up crispy bottom crust. Cover skillet and continue to cook over medium heat until bottom crust turns golden brown and top of frittata is just set (egg below very top will still be raw), 5 to 8 minutes. Slide frittata onto large plate. Invert frittata onto second large plate and slide it browned side up back into skillet. Tuck edges of frittata into skillet with rubber spatula. Continue to cook second side of frittata until light brown, 2 to 4 minutes longer.

5. Remove skillet from heat and let stand for 5 minutes. Using your hand or pan lid, invert frittata onto cutting board. Cut into wedges and serve.

VARIATION

Pasta Frittata with Broccoli Rabe
Omit cherry peppers, parsley, and sausage. Heat 2 teaspoons vegetable oil in 10-inch nonstick skillet over medium heat until shimmering. Add garlic and ⅛ teaspoon red pepper flakes and cook for 1 minute. Stir in 8 ounces broccoli rabe, trimmed and cut into ½-inch pieces, 1 tablespoon water, and ¼ teaspoon salt; cover skillet and cook until broccoli rabe is crisp-tender, 2 to 3 minutes. Remove skillet from heat and add 1 tablespoon white wine vinegar. Transfer broccoli rabe to bowl with egg mixture. Proceed with recipe from step 3, cooking pasta with remaining 7 teaspoons vegetable oil.

NOTES FROM THE TEST KITCHEN

A TOASTY BOTTOM

A layer of crispy golden pasta on the bottom of the frittata (shown here before we flipped it to brown the top) distinguishes our version.

JAPANESE-STYLE STIR-FRIED NOODLES WITH BEEF

✓ **WHY THIS RECIPE WORKS:** For a home-cook–friendly version of this classic Japanese noodle stir-fry, we started by isolating the best possible supermarket alternatives to hard-to-find Japanese ingredients. In place of chewy *yakisoba* noodles, we used lo mein noodles (which, like yakisoba, contain an alkaline ingredient that gives them some elasticity) and undercooked them to enhance their chew. We also rinsed them very well with cold water, which removed surface starches and made them appropriately slick. We treated thinly sliced flank steak with baking soda to ensure that each piece was tender and juicy. Soy sauce, Worcestershire, ketchup, and rice wine vinegar made up the savory-sweet sauce—a facsimile of the traditional version made with Japanese Worcestershire sauce.

Lo mein has long been my go-to noodle stir-fry to make at home because it's quick to prepare and contains meat and vegetables that add up to a satisfying one-dish meal. But when I want those qualities and also a bit more character, the Japanese equivalent called *yakisoba* comes to mind. This dish shares the same hearty combination of springy noodles, meat (often beef), and vegetables, but instead of the typical soy-garlic profile of Chinese American stir-fries, it boasts a bright, sweet-savory-tangy sauce. Its bold garnishes—namely, pickled ginger and a spice blend with sesame seeds and orange peel known as *shichimi togarashi*—make the dish even more distinctive. Then there's the noodles themselves. Like many Asian wheat noodles (including lo mein), yakisoba strands have a springy quality; they also have an ultraslick surface that takes up just a thin coating of sauce and makes the strands fun to slurp.

Wanting to add a homemade version to my repertoire, I paged through some cookbooks and found that recipes all followed a basic approach: Brown the vegetables and beef in a skillet and set them aside, boil up the noodles and then add them to the skillet, stir in the sauce and cook until it thickens, toss the sauced noodles with the beef and vegetables, and serve with the garnishes.

The problem: Springy, slippery yakisoba noodles and the distinctive spice blend were impossible to find outside an Asian market, as was the key ingredient to the sauce—a Japanese condiment modeled after British Worcestershire sauce that bears the same name.

I was certain I could fine-tune the cooking approach by using the foolproof techniques that the test kitchen has developed over the years for stir-fries. But could I make yakisoba taste the way it's meant to without all the hard-to-find ingredients? I set out to try.

Of the three beef cuts we tend to use in the test kitchen for stir-frying—blade steak, flap meat, or flank steak—I chose flank. It's a chewier cut, but its wide availability and easy preparation won me over. I sliced a 12-ounce portion into strips, cut each strip crosswise, and then seared the strips in two batches in a large nonstick skillet—a vessel that we've found makes better contact with flat Western burners than a round-bottomed wok does. The meat tasted great, and to soften its chew, I briefly soaked it in a solution of baking soda and water before searing. This treatment, we've discovered, raises the meat's pH, preventing its proteins from bonding excessively so that the meat is more tender and juicy.

As for the vegetables, thinly sliced carrots, shiitake mushrooms, cabbage, and onions are yakisoba standards; I had been adding these directly to the skillet, and my tasters and I were more or less happy with the results. The only changes I made were to swap conventional green cabbage for faster-cooking napa leaves, and grassy, more colorful scallions for the onion. The carrots and mushrooms also needed a bit more help softening. I browned them together and, once they'd developed color, added a splash of chicken broth to the pan, which generated a puff of steam that helped them turn tender.

Now for that complex sauce. While many recipes use sake or mirin as their base, the best always featured a generous amount of that Japanese Worcestershire sauce. The British original was a common substitute, but on its own this stand-in missed some of the fruity, savory notes of the Japanese kind; plus, it lacked body. Comparing the ingredient lists clarified their differences: Both contain vinegar and sweeteners, but instead of British Worcestershire's tamarind extract and anchovies, the Japanese sauce boasted tomato paste and pureed fruit, as well as dried sardines and yeast extract.

To doctor the British kind, I measured 2 tablespoons into a bowl and added ¼ cup of ketchup. That got me closer to the fruitiness of the Japanese sauce, but I didn't nail the sweet-tangy flavor until I whisked in rice vinegar and brown sugar. Meanwhile, ¼ cup of soy sauce took me partway to the savory flavor, and a few cloves of minced garlic helped, too. Dried sardines were out of the question, but a few finely minced anchovies added nice umami depth.

It was time to figure out a suitably slick and snappy substitute for the yakisoba strands. As a longtime fan of the dish, I knew that chewy noodles like these are called "alkaline" noodles because they contain a pair of salts, sodium carbonate and potassium carbonate. These salts raise the pH of the dough, strengthening the network of protein strands, or gluten, that give the noodles structure so that they develop elasticity. Because lo mein has a similar texture, I wasn't surprised to discover that these noodles also include the alkalizing salts. But before I settled on them as my easier-to-find alternative to the yakisoba strands, I rounded up other widely available Asian noodles that also contained sodium and potassium carbonates. Besides fresh and dried lo mein, these included dried Chinese-style egg noodles, dried ramen, and even dried instant ramen. I boiled them all and then staged a taste test against proper yakisoba noodles.

All the alkaline noodles delivered elasticity, but ultimately the lo mein strands were the closest match, as they were roughly the same width as yakisoba. But when I worked them into the stir-fry, they weren't slick like the yakisoba noodles I'd eaten in Japanese restaurants—and, frankly, neither were the actual yakisoba

NOTES FROM THE TEST KITCHEN

HOW ASIAN NOODLES GET THEIR SPRING

Asian noodles come in countless varieties, but many, including yakisoba, ramen, and lo mein, are characterized by a satisfying chew. These springy noodles contain the same core ingredients as Italian pastas—wheat flour and water—along with two salts, sodium and potassium carbonates, that raise the pH of the dough. A little research confirmed that the alkaline environment increases the bonding between gluten strands, making the gluten network stronger and more elastic, for noodles that stretch and spring back. The effect of the alkalizing salts is clearly visible if you compare cooked Italian spaghetti strands with the alkaline noodles: The former swell more and have less give, while the latter stay firm and chewy.

noodles I'd used in my earlier tests. In fact, the lo mein was sticky and soaked up so much of the sauce that the stir-fry was a bit dry. Adding ½ cup of chicken broth to the skillet along with the sauce helped hydrate the dish.

As for the stickiness, I looked back through my test recipes and discovered that a few called for rinsing the noodles under cool running water after boiling. When I did the same, the lo mein's exterior became pleasantly slippery. Why? Rinsing with cold water removes the surface starches from the noodles. Less starch means that less sauce will cling, mitigating that sticky texture.

Back to the chile spice blend. The commercial togarashi that we sampled was both spicy and faintly sweet, so I mixed a spoonful of black pepper with a dash of cayenne and then incorporated sweetness with paprika. In lieu of dried orange peel, I stripped ¾ teaspoon of zest off the fruit and dried it in the microwave. Ground ginger and powdered garlic rounded out the sweet and savory notes, respectively.

This blend, along with a few slivers of pickled ginger, topped off a version of yakisoba that was as satisfying as any I'd eaten in a Japanese restaurant.

—LAN LAM, *Cook's Illustrated*

Japanese-Style Stir-Fried Noodles with Beef (Yaki Udon)

SERVES 4 TO 6

This recipe calls for lo mein noodles, but use yakisoba noodles if you can find them and follow the same cooking directions. Garnish the noodles with pickled ginger (often found in the refrigerated section of the grocery store near tofu) and our Sesame-Orange Spice Blend (recipe follows) or, if you can find it, commercial shichimi togarashi.

⅛ teaspoon baking soda

12 ounces flank steak, trimmed, sliced lengthwise into 2- to 2½-inch strips, each strip sliced crosswise ¼ inch thick

¼ cup ketchup

¼ cup soy sauce

2 tablespoons Worcestershire sauce

1½ tablespoons packed brown sugar

3 garlic cloves, minced

3 anchovy fillets, rinsed, patted dry, and minced

1 teaspoon rice vinegar

1 pound fresh or 8 ounces dried lo mein noodles

1 tablespoon vegetable oil

6 ounces shiitake mushrooms, stemmed and sliced ¼ inch thick

1 carrot, peeled and sliced ⅛ inch thick on bias

¾ cup chicken broth

6 cups napa cabbage, sliced crosswise into ½-inch strips

7 scallions, cut on bias into 1-inch lengths

Salt

1. Combine 1 tablespoon water and baking soda in medium bowl. Add beef and toss to coat. Let sit at room temperature for 5 minutes.

2. Whisk ketchup, soy sauce, Worcestershire, sugar, garlic, anchovies, and vinegar together in second bowl. Stir 2 tablespoons sauce into beef mixture and set aside remaining sauce.

3. Bring 4 quarts water to boil in large pot. Add noodles and cook, stirring often, until almost tender (center should still be firm with slightly opaque dot), 3 to 10 minutes (cooking times will vary depending on whether you are using fresh or dry noodles). Drain noodles and rinse under cold running water until water runs clear. Drain well and set aside.

4. Heat ½ teaspoon oil in 12-inch nonstick skillet over high heat until just smoking. Add mushrooms and carrot and cook, stirring occasionally, until vegetables are spotty brown, 2 to 3 minutes. Add ¼ cup broth and cook until all liquid has evaporated and vegetables are tender, about 30 seconds. Transfer vegetables to bowl.

5. Return skillet to high heat, add ½ teaspoon oil, and heat until beginning to smoke. Add cabbage and scallions and cook, without stirring, for 30 seconds. Cook, stirring occasionally, until cabbage and scallions are spotty brown and crisp-tender, 2 to 3 minutes. Transfer to bowl with mushrooms and carrot.

6. Return skillet to high heat, add 1 teaspoon oil, and heat until beginning to smoke. Add half of beef in single layer. Cook, without stirring, for 30 seconds. Cook, stirring occasionally, until beef is spotty brown, 1 to 2 minutes. Transfer to bowl with vegetables. Repeat with remaining beef and remaining 1 teaspoon oil.

7. Return skillet to high heat; add reserved sauce, remaining ½ cup broth, and noodles. Cook, scraping up any browned bits, until noodles are warmed through, about 1 minute. Transfer noodles to bowl with vegetables and beef and toss to combine. Season with salt to taste, and serve immediately.

Sesame-Orange Spice Blend

MAKES ¼ CUP

In addition to garnishing our stir-fry, this blend makes a great seasoning for eggs, rice, and fish. Store it in an airtight container for up to one week.

¾ teaspoon grated orange zest

2 teaspoons sesame seeds

1½ teaspoons paprika

1 teaspoon pepper

¼ teaspoon garlic powder

¼ teaspoon ground ginger

⅛ teaspoon cayenne pepper

Place orange zest in small bowl and microwave, stirring every 20 seconds, until zest is dry and no longer clumping together, 1½ minutes to 2½ minutes. Stir in sesame seeds, paprika, pepper, garlic powder, ginger, and cayenne.

SINGAPORE NOODLES

✓ WHY THIS RECIPE WORKS: Singapore noodles, a traditional Hong Kong favorite, are often so heavily seasoned with curry powder that they can feel unpleasantly dusty and gritty. To fix this problem, we bloomed the curry powder in oil, which smoothed out the texture and intensified the flavor. Though the noodles are the main feature in the traditional dish, we tweaked the amounts of starch, vegetables, and protein for a balanced one-dish meal. Cutting the noodles to slightly shorter lengths, though unconventional, made the components easier to incorporate and the dish easier to eat.

Nomenclature aside, Singapore noodles have nothing to do with Singapore. In fact, this light, almost fluffy stir-fry of thin, resilient rice noodles, vegetables, and shrimp is native to Hong Kong, and nobody seems to know for sure how it came to be named for a city that's more than 1,500 miles away.

What makes Singapore noodles truly a Hong Kong invention isn't just that the dish includes typical Chinese ingredients like garlic, ginger, and soy. It's that it prominently features curry powder, a spice blend invented by the Brits that probably trickled into Hong

Kong's cuisine when it was under British rule. The heady spice blend lends the dish a pervasive aroma of cumin and coriander and a pleasant chile burn.

But the curry powder can also be the most problematic element of Singapore noodles. Because this dish is not saucy, the dry powder doesn't distribute evenly, leading to patchy curry flavor (and color), not to mention gritty texture.

This was the core problem I set out to solve when I created my own version of Singapore noodles. And given that I wanted this dish to function as a light yet satisfying one-dish meal, I also vowed to revise the typical ratio of ingredients, which tends to be about 80 percent noodles, with the vegetables and protein acting almost as garnishes.

The ingredient list for Singapore noodles is simple—just dried rice noodles (usually thin vermicelli), ordinary vegetables, shrimp, a handful of seasonings, and maybe some eggs—and once the ingredients are prepped, the cooking takes all of 15 minutes.

The universal first step is to soak the rice noodles; you want them to be just pliable, but not fully softened since they'll continue to absorb liquid during cooking. Covering 6 ounces of noodles with boiling water, letting them soak for 2½ minutes, stirring them occasionally, and draining them produced exactly the texture I was hoping for.

From there, I broke out my large nonstick skillet for stir-frying. We've found that this vessel's wide, level surface makes more contact with flat domestic burners than the bowl shape of a wok does, allowing for quicker evaporation, so foods don't steam.

Over a medium-high flame, I heated a couple of teaspoons of vegetable oil and sautéed 12 ounces of large shrimp in a single layer until they'd browned on the bottom. Then I slid the cooked shrimp onto a plate, lowered the heat, added another spoonful of oil, and stir-fried some grated ginger and minced garlic until fragrant. In went some thin-sliced red bell pepper and shallots, which I cooked until tender but still verging on crisp, followed by the drained noodles, ⅔ cup of chicken broth, a couple of splashes of soy sauce, and 2 tablespoons of mild (or "sweet") curry powder—a generous amount that's about par for the course in this dish. Then I added back the shrimp, cranked the heat

to high, and briefly tossed everything together until the mixture was relatively dry and the noodles were al dente.

At least, I tried to toss everything together. What actually happened was that the long noodles tangled, forming a tight ball that forced most of the vegetables and shrimp to the sides of the skillet. The dish was also still much too noodle-heavy, not to mention lean with just a few teaspoons of oil. And then there was the curry powder: It had given the whole ensemble a predictably gritty texture and a slightly bitter edge.

I tried switching from mild curry powder to the spicier Madras variety. But it turns out that brands of Madras curry vary widely in their heat output. I was better off using the mild variety and adding heat with a touch of cayenne and balancing the bitterness with a spoonful of sugar. As for enhancing the curry flavor, I'd gotten nowhere.

Then it occurred to me to try changing not the amount or type of curry powder, but how I was treating it. It's possible to increase the flavor of a given amount of spice by heating it in oil or butter—a technique called "blooming." That's because the flavor compounds in most spices are fat-soluble, so they infuse readily into oil, and like most chemical interactions, this happens more quickly in a warm environment. As the compounds are drawn from the spice granules into the warm oil, they mix, producing stronger and more complex flavors. I also thought that making a curry-infused oil could provide the missing fat to the dish.

I heated 3 tablespoons of oil in the skillet and stirred in the 2 tablespoons of curry powder I had been using originally. Then I heated the spice oil for 4 minutes over medium-low heat. By that point I could smell that I was on the right track from the rich curry aroma, and my tasters confirmed as much when they tasted the curry oil–dressed noodles, noting the richer, more complex flavor. Even better, blooming the curry powder had caused the spice granules to disperse evenly in the oil, so their grittiness was no longer noticeable. On to tackling that ball of noodles.

In Chinese tradition long noodles symbolize a long life, but in wrestling with them I'd grown short-tempered, so I made a drastic move. After soaking and draining the vermicelli, I cut across them twice to make them shorter and less tangle-prone.

SINGAPORE NOODLES

I also cut the shrimp into ½-inch pieces that dispersed nicely throughout the noodles, and I bulked up the protein and vegetables by adding 4 eggs (scrambled with a little salt), 4 scallions cut into ½-inch pieces, and a couple of cups of bean sprouts.

Of course, adding more elements to the dish made it that much harder to toss everything together neatly in the confines of a skillet, so I moved the operation to a larger mixing bowl. Tossing the cut noodles with the curry oil, soy sauce, and sugar in the deeper vessel made it easier to distribute the dressing evenly throughout the noodles; the lubricating effect of the oil also helped the noodles combine with the rest of the ingredients.

Then, as each pair of components—shrimp and eggs, aromatics and vegetables—finished cooking, I collected them in a second large bowl. To finish softening the dressed noodles, I simmered them in the skillet with the chicken broth, tossing them for about 2 minutes until the broth had been absorbed. Finally, I slid the hot noodles into the bowl with the shrimp and vegetables and squeezed fresh lime juice over the bowl to brighten the flavor.

With a bold, complex curry flavor and a more evenly balanced ratio of noodles, protein, and vegetables, my version of Singapore noodles was as satisfying as any I'd had and would slip easily into my weeknight lineup.

—ANDREA GEARY, *Cook's Illustrated*

Singapore Noodles

SERVES 4 TO 6

For spicier Singapore noodles, add the optional cayenne pepper. Look for dried rice vermicelli in the Asian section of your supermarket. A rasp-style grater makes quick work of turning the garlic into a paste.

- 4 tablespoons plus 1 teaspoon vegetable oil
- 2 tablespoons curry powder
- ⅛ teaspoon cayenne pepper (optional)
- 6 ounces rice vermicelli
- 2 tablespoons soy sauce
- 1 teaspoon sugar
- 12 ounces large shrimp (26 to 30 per pound), peeled, deveined, tails removed, and cut into ½-inch pieces
- 4 large eggs, lightly beaten
  Salt
- 3 garlic cloves, minced to paste
- 1 teaspoon grated fresh ginger

- 1 red bell pepper, stemmed, seeded, and cut into 2-inch-long matchsticks
- 2 large shallots, sliced thin
- ⅔ cup chicken broth
- 4 ounces (2 cups) bean sprouts
- 4 scallions, cut into ½-inch pieces
- 2 teaspoons lime juice, plus lime wedges for serving

1. Heat 3 tablespoons oil, curry powder, and cayenne, if using, in 12-inch nonstick skillet over medium-low heat, stirring occasionally, until fragrant, about 4 minutes. Remove skillet from heat and set aside.

2. Bring 1½ quarts water to boil. Place noodles in large bowl. Pour boiling water over noodles and stir briefly. Soak noodles until flexible, but not soft, about 2½ minutes, stirring once halfway through soaking. Drain noodles briefly. Transfer noodles to cutting board. Using chef's knife, cut pile of noodles roughly into thirds. Return noodles to bowl, add curry mixture, soy sauce, and sugar; using tongs, toss until well combined. Set aside.

3. Wipe out skillet with paper towels. Heat 2 teaspoons oil in skillet over medium-high heat until shimmering. Add shrimp in even layer and cook without moving them until bottoms are browned, about 90 seconds. Stir and continue to cook until just cooked through, about 90 seconds longer. Push shrimp to 1 side of skillet. Add 1 teaspoon oil to cleared side of skillet. Add eggs to clearing and sprinkle with ¼ teaspoon salt. Using rubber spatula, stir eggs gently until set but still wet, about 1 minute. Stir eggs into shrimp and continue to cook, breaking up large pieces of egg, until eggs are fully cooked, about 30 seconds longer. Transfer shrimp-egg mixture to second large bowl.

4. Reduce heat to medium. Heat remaining 1 teaspoon oil in now-empty skillet until shimmering. Add garlic and ginger and cook, stirring constantly, until fragrant, about 15 seconds. Add bell pepper and shallots. Cook, stirring frequently, until vegetables are crisp-tender, about 2 minutes. Transfer to bowl with shrimp.

5. Return skillet to medium-high heat, add broth to skillet, and bring to simmer. Add noodles and cook, stirring frequently, until liquid is absorbed, about 2 minutes. Add noodles to bowl with shrimp and vegetable mixture and toss to combine. Add bean sprouts, scallions, and lime juice and toss to combine. Transfer to warmed platter and serve immediately, passing lime wedges separately.

SICILIAN-STYLE PIZZA

✓ **WHY THIS RECIPE WORKS:** In order to create a Sicilian pie with a creamy, golden interior and a delicate, crisp bottom, we used a mixture of semolina and all-purpose flours. To give it a fine-textured, almost cake-like crumb, we took a three-pronged approach: We used a generous amount of olive oil in the dough to tenderize it, cold-fermented the dough overnight to let flavors develop without large bubbles forming, and then rolled it out and weighed it down with another baking sheet during the final proof to keep the crumb even and tight. Finally, we topped it with a concentrated and complex long-cooked tomato sauce and a mixture of cheeses—a combination that stood up to the thickness of the crust below.

As pizza goes, the category commonly known as "Sicilian" gets a bad rap. At most American pizzerias, these thick, rectangular slabs baked in sheet pans are often just larger masses of the same dough that's used for round thin-crust pies—a halfhearted concession to customers who prefer a thick crust to a thin one. Usually, that crust is bready and dense, lacks textural contrast between the interior crumb and the bottom, and offers little in the way of interesting flavor.

The few worthy exceptions I've had came from Sicilian shops in New York City, where the pies featured a tight, even, cake-like crumb that was pale yellow and almost creamy. The underside of the crust was delicately crisp. Spread over the top was a layer of tomato sauce that was concentrated and complex and, following that, a blanket of cheese. The combined effect was terrific, and exactly what I wanted for my own version.

Most Sicilian pizza recipes that I found called for a combination of white and semolina flours. The latter, a variety made from durum wheat, is the same type used to make many Italian pastas, couscous, and many Sicilian breads and is the source of a Sicilian pizza crumb's creamy yellow color. I started with a ratio test. In a stand mixer, I combined all-purpose flour with increasing amounts of semolina (from 20 to 100 percent semolina), plus yeast, salt, a touch of sugar, a couple of tablespoons of olive oil for richness and tenderness, and 2 cups of ice water; the water's cold temperature would keep the dough from overheating during kneading. I mixed each batch for about 6 minutes, by which time the dough was smooth, and then I kneaded it for another minute by hand. I let it ferment for a few hours

at room temperature to allow flavor to develop and the dough to rise. I then stretched it and placed it into a rimmed baking sheet coated with both nonstick spray and extra-virgin olive oil (the spray would prevent sticking on the sides of the pan, while the oil would "fry" the crust during baking). Because Sicilian-style pies should rise tall, I let the dough proof for another hour to double in thickness, topped it with (for now) a simple cooked tomato sauce and a mixture of grated mozzarella and Parmesan cheeses, and baked it in a 450-degree oven for 20 minutes or so, until the underside was golden and the cheese brown and bubbly.

The clear takeaway from that first test: More semolina made the crust more cake-like, but only up to a point. Once I got above about 50 percent, the crumb became dense and the exterior tough. Some further semolina research helped explain why. This flour is very high in protein, but unlike other high-protein flours, it doesn't form gluten that is strong enough to hold air and allow the dough to expand and produce a chewy texture. As a result, doughs made with semolina were more cakey— that is, finer, with fewer bubbles and less chew—but too much semolina made the crust dense and tough. So I settled on using slightly less than a 1:1 ratio of semolina to all-purpose flour, which gave me a relatively cakey crumb and crisp exterior. Increasing the amount of oil in the dough to 3 tablespoons also increased tenderness.

To create an even finer crumb with yet-smaller bubbles, I chilled the dough as it rested. When dough ferments at room temperature, its sugars, alcohol, and acids rapidly convert to carbon dioxide, which causes bubbles in the dough to expand. At colder temperatures, less carbon dioxide forms, and bubbles in the dough stay small.

The cold rest certainly got me closer to that tight crumb, but I'd have to figure out another way to make it even finer. At least the 24-hour rest in the fridge had boosted the flavor of the crust, since a longer fermentation produces a more complex-tasting array of flavor compounds. The day-long rest also gave it make-ahead convenience.

The reason the crumb wasn't as tight and fine as I'd hoped was that the dough was puffing up unevenly during the second rise. But what if I compromised by tempering the rise? My thought was to roll instead of stretch the dough, since a rolling pin would surely make it evenly flat. I removed the dough from the fridge, lightly floured its surface, pressed the dough into a rough rectangle, rolled it to fit the rimmed baking sheet, and baked it as I had before. When I cut a slice, I was pleased to see that the crumb was tighter and more even, though still not quite as fine as I wanted.

Thinking about other fine-textured breads, I had another idea, this one inspired by Pullman-style sandwich breads. These loaves are proofed and baked in metal pans with tight-fitting lids that limit the expansion of the dough. I couldn't bake my pizza in an enclosed pan, but I could limit its expansion as it proofed by compressing the dough.

NOTES FROM THE TEST KITCHEN

WHY IS THAT FLOUR YELLOW?

If you've ever seen cellophane bags of semolina flour at the supermarket, its yellow color and coarse texture might have led you to think that it was cornmeal. However, this flour is made from wheat. Specifically, it's the coarsely ground endosperm of durum wheat, the same variety used to make most dried Italian pasta and Moroccan couscous. Semolina's deep yellow color comes from high concentrations of carotenoids (the same compounds responsible for the brilliant colors of carrots, mangos, and apricots). We use semolina flour in our Sicilian-Style Pizza to give the dough a slightly sweet, rich flavor; a finer, more cake-like crumb; and an appealing buttery color. You can find durum semolina flour in many supermarkets near the flour or specialty grains and in Italian and Indian markets.

TOPPING TIPS FOR SICILIAN PIZZA

Our pizza gets a topping of mozzarella and Parmesan cheeses, but if you want to embellish a bit, here are a few guidelines for how to handle different types of toppings.

HEARTY VEGETABLES

Aim for a maximum of 12 ounces spread out in a single layer. Vegetables such as onions, peppers, and mushrooms should be thinly sliced and lightly sautéed (or microwaved for a minute or two along with a little olive oil) until wilted before using.

DELICATE VEGETABLES AND HERBS

Leafy greens and herbs like spinach and basil are best placed beneath the cheese to protect them or added raw to the fully cooked pizza.

MEATS

Raw proteins (no more than 8 ounces per pizza) should be precooked and then drained to remove excess fat. We like to poach meats like sausage (broken up into ½-inch chunks) or ground beef for 4 to 5 minutes in a wide skillet along with ¼ cup of water, which helps render the fat while keeping the meat moist. Cured meats such as pepperoni or salami can be placed directly on top of the cheese in a single layer.

After fitting the next batch of dough into the baking sheet, I covered it with plastic wrap and then placed a second baking sheet over it as it proofed. After an hour, the dough had visibly risen, but its surface was perfectly flat. It was exactly as I wanted: tender, fine, and even.

All that remained was to perfect the toppings, starting with the sauce. For concentrated flavor and body that would stand up to the thicker crust, I slowly cooked tomatoes with a touch of sugar and bold seasonings: sautéed garlic, dried oregano, minced anchovies (for savory, not fishy, depth), tomato paste, and a dash of hot pepper flakes. Tangy and savory-sweet, this sauce was the perfect match for the combination of rich, gooey mozzarella and salty, sharp Parmesan.

—ANDREW JANJIGIAN, *Cook's Illustrated*

Sicilian-Style Pizza

SERVES 6 TO 8

This recipe requires refrigerating the dough for 24 to 48 hours before shaping it. King Arthur all-purpose flour and Bob's Red Mill semolina flour work best in this recipe. It is important to use ice water in the dough to prevent overheating during mixing. Anchovies give the sauce depth without a discernible fishy taste; if you decide not to use them, add an additional ¼ teaspoon of salt.

DOUGH

2¼ cups (11¼ ounces) all-purpose flour

2 cups (12 ounces) semolina flour

1 teaspoon sugar

1 teaspoon instant or rapid-rise yeast

1⅔ cups (13⅓ ounces) ice water

3 tablespoons extra-virgin olive oil

2¼ teaspoons salt

SAUCE

1 (28-ounce) can whole peeled tomatoes, drained

2 teaspoons sugar

¼ teaspoon salt

¼ cup extra-virgin olive oil

3 garlic cloves, minced

1 tablespoon tomato paste

3 anchovy fillets, rinsed, patted dry, and minced

1 teaspoon dried oregano

¼ teaspoon red pepper flakes

PIZZA

¼ cup extra-virgin olive oil

2 ounces Parmesan cheese, grated (1 cup)

12 ounces whole-milk mozzarella, shredded (3 cups)

1. FOR THE DOUGH: Using stand mixer fitted with dough hook, mix all-purpose flour, semolina flour, sugar, and yeast on low speed until combined, about 10 seconds. With machine running, slowly add water and oil until dough forms and no dry flour remains, 1 to 2 minutes. Cover with plastic wrap and let dough stand for 10 minutes.

2. Add salt to dough and mix on medium speed until dough forms satiny, sticky ball that clears sides of bowl, 6 to 8 minutes. Remove dough from bowl and knead briefly on lightly floured counter until smooth, about 1 minute. Shape dough into tight ball and place in large, lightly oiled bowl. Cover tightly with plastic wrap and refrigerate for at least 24 hours or up to 48 hours.

3. FOR THE SAUCE: Process tomatoes, sugar, and salt in food processor until smooth, about 30 seconds. Heat oil and garlic in medium saucepan over medium-low heat, stirring occasionally, until garlic is fragrant and just beginning to brown, about 2 minutes. Add tomato paste, anchovies, oregano, and pepper flakes and cook until fragrant, about 30 seconds. Add tomato mixture and cook, stirring occasionally, until sauce measures 2 cups, 25 to 30 minutes. Transfer to bowl, let cool, and refrigerate until needed.

4. FOR THE PIZZA: One hour before baking pizza, place baking stone on upper-middle rack and heat oven to 500 degrees. Spray rimmed baking sheet (including rim) with vegetable oil spray, then coat bottom of a second baking sheet with oil. Remove dough from refrigerator and transfer to lightly floured counter. Lightly flour top of dough and gently press into 12 by 9-inch rectangle. Using rolling pin, roll dough into 18 by 13-inch rectangle. Transfer dough to first baking sheet, fitting dough into corners. Spray top of dough with vegetable oil spray and lay sheet of plastic wrap over dough. Place second baking sheet on dough and let stand for 1 hour.

5. Remove top baking sheet and plastic wrap. Gently stretch and lift dough to fill pan. Using back of spoon or ladle, spread sauce in even layer over surface of dough, leaving ½-inch border. Sprinkle Parmesan evenly over entire surface of dough to edges followed by mozzarella.

6. Place pizza on stone; reduce oven temperature to 450 degrees and bake until bottom crust is evenly browned and cheese is bubbly and browned, 20 to 25 minutes, rotating pizza halfway through baking. Remove pan from oven and let cool on wire rack for 5 minutes. Run knife around rim of pan to loosen pizza. Transfer pizza to cutting board, cut into squares, and serve.

(FREEZER) CHEESE PIZZA

WHY THIS RECIPE WORKS: The appeal of store-bought frozen pizza is undeniable, but it always pales in comparison to freshly made pizza. Freezing our favorite homemade recipe seemed like an easy solution, but our first tests resulted in a flat, tough crust. The reason was that as the dough froze, ice crystals formed, inhibiting the yeast's ability to rise the dough. Drawing on some test kitchen tricks to solve this problem, we added baking powder, which gave the dough extra lift, creating air pockets during baking that resulted in a lighter crust with more rise. To ensure tenderness, we swapped out a little of the all-purpose flour for cornstarch, which has less protein, translating to less gluten production and a more tender dough. Using half-and-half in place of some of the water further tenderized the dough and added richness. To prevent the cheeses from drying out in the freezer, we tossed them with more half-and-half. To make the pizzas easy to shape and store, we simply patted the dough out into 12-inch disposable aluminum pizza pans. Finally, this pizza offered the best of both worlds: great homemade flavor with the convenience of coming straight from the freezer.

I love the idea of brightening my workweek with homemade pizza for dinner. But on an average weeknight, who has time for a big cooking project? No problem; I could make my usual homemade pie over a leisurely weekend and pop it in the freezer for later. I was looking for the ease of commercial frozen pizza with the flavor and texture—cheesy, crisp, and gooey—of fresh-baked.

I set to work making the test kitchen's pizza dough (flour, salt, sugar, yeast, olive oil, and water), which I moved into the freezer until stiff. I topped the chilled crust with sauce and cheese, wrapped it in plastic, and back into the freezer it went. A few days later, I baked it on a pizza stone—the test kitchen's preferred method.

(FREEZER) CHEESE PIZZA

To my dismay, this homemade pizza was as ghastly as a commercial frozen pie. The cheese had dried out. The sauce had lost its vibrancy. The crust was tough and brittle on the outside, and gummy and dense on the inside. Freezing, I found out, equals loss of moisture and flavor. Manufacturers use gums, protein film formers, extra leaveners, and surfactants (wetting agents) to address those problems—not very successfully, judging by the way the stuff tastes—but what's a home cook to do?

I started with the crust. None among the slew of recipes I tried had a crust that even approached my ideal of soft and light on the inside, crispy and chewy on the outside. Tackling the gummy interior first, it was obvious that the yeast was being weakened by its time in the freezer. A quick review of science explained why: Ice crystals that form in dough in the freezer puncture the yeast cells, inhibiting their ability to form carbon dioxide, which is what causes the dough to rise. I decided to try to bolster the dough's rising power by adding baking powder, and was pleased to find that this also eliminated the problem of a wet interior.

But the crust was still a bit tough. For this problem I turned to a test kitchen pizza dough recipe that uses milk. The dairy acts as a tenderizer, making for rich, soft dough—think of the difference between rustic bread made with water and tender sandwich bread made with milk. Half-and-half turned out to be even better than milk, adding extra richness that my tasters appreciated. At the same time I replaced some of the flour with cornstarch to further tenderize the dough. (Cornstarch has less protein than flour does: the weaker the protein, the softer the dough.)

I was happy with the inside of the crust, but a crisp and chewy exterior eluded me. It remained tough and leathery. Most pizza dough recipes have a 60 percent water-to-flour ratio. Would wetter dough that took into account the inevitable moisture loss that occurs in the freezer produce the crisp-chewy crust I was seeking? I mixed up dough with a higher proportion of liquid to flour (4 cups flour, ¼ cup cornstarch, and 2 cups half-and-half for two pizzas). Unfortunately, the extra half-and-half made the crust taste like a biscuit. Next, I substituted water for ½ cup of the half-and-half. I gave the pizza a few days in the freezer and then baked it.

The good news? The floppy, wet dough produced a lovely crust with a crisp shell and tender interior. The bad? The dough had been so sticky, it was a major hassle to handle. A colleague suggested I pat it out into disposable aluminum pizza pans (which I would remove before baking) instead of rolling it. Unruly Dough Syndrome solved.

With relief, I turned my attention to toppings. I started with the test kitchen's favorite pizza sauce recipe, but it too became bland and muted when frozen. Ultimately, switching from fresh to dried herbs and doubling the amounts normally called for compensated for the dulling capacity of the freezer. After the pies baked, the cheese (mozzarella and Parmesan) peeled off in tough, rubbery sheets. They, too, were drying out in the freezer. I tried test after test to moisten them, mixing the cheese with oil, water, milk, half-and-half, and ricotta. In the end, as with the crust, half-and-half worked best.

To bake the pizza, a preheated baking stone was a must for crispness, and baking the pizza on the upper-middle rack (the hottest part) of the oven browned the cheese and further ensured a crisp crust.

Even to me, the final recipe looked downright weird. Who'd ever heard of a pizza crust calling for half-and-half, cornstarch, and baking powder? Who would think to stir half-and-half into cheese? But the proof was in the pizza, which had freezer-to-oven ease without freezer taste.

—LYNN CLARK, *America's Test Kitchen Books*

NOTES FROM THE TEST KITCHEN

HOW LONG CAN I FREEZE IT?

From a safety standpoint, food that is frozen properly and kept at a constant temperature of 0 degrees or lower will be safe to eat for a very long time. In our experience, however, "safe to eat" is not the same as "at its best." Moisture loss and the activity of enzymes and other chemical processes that are slowed, but not stopped, by freezing cause the quality of frozen food to diminish over time, usually a matter of months. Exactly how much time depends on the freshness of the food when frozen; the age, efficiency, and type of freezer; how full the freezer is; the frequency with which the freezer door is opened; and various other factors. To avoid storing dishes past their prime, label and date them clearly with a permanent marker. For the best results, we recommend eating them within a month of storing.

(Freezer) Cheese Pizza

SERVES 4

If you do not have a baking stone, you can use an inverted rimmed baking sheet. You will need two 12-inch disposable aluminum pizza pans for this recipe.

DOUGH

1½   cups warm half-and-half (110 degrees)
½   cup warm water (110 degrees)
2   tablespoons extra-virgin olive oil
4   cups (20 ounces) all-purpose flour
¼   cup cornstarch
2¼   teaspoons instant or rapid-rise yeast
1½   teaspoons salt
½   teaspoon baking powder
½   teaspoon sugar

SAUCE AND TOPPINGS

1   (14.5-ounce) can diced tomatoes, drained with
    ½ cup juice reserved
1   tablespoon extra-virgin olive oil
1   tablespoon tomato paste
2   garlic cloves, minced
1   tablespoon minced fresh oregano or
    1 teaspoon dried
¼   teaspoon red pepper flakes
    Salt and pepper
8   ounces mozzarella cheese, shredded (2 cups)
1   ounce Parmesan cheese, grated (½ cup)
¼   cup half-and-half

4   tablespoons extra-virgin olive oil

1. FOR THE DOUGH: Spray large bowl with vegetable oil spray and set aside. Combine half-and-half, water, and oil in 4-cup liquid measuring cup. Using stand mixer fitted with dough hook, mix flour, cornstarch, yeast, salt, baking powder, and sugar together on medium-low speed until combined. Slowly add half-and-half mixture and mix until dough comes together, about 1 minute. Continue mixing until sticky strands form around exterior but center of dough is uniform in texture, about 5 minutes. (Dough will be wet and cling to sides of bowl.) Transfer dough to prepared bowl, cover with plastic wrap, and let rise at room temperature until doubled in size, about 1 hour.

2. FOR THE SAUCE AND TOPPINGS: Meanwhile, pulse drained tomatoes and reserved juice in food processor until coarsely ground, about 5 pulses. Heat oil in large saucepan over medium heat until shimmering. Add tomato paste and cook, stirring frequently, until just beginning to brown, about 2 minutes. Stir in garlic, oregano, and pepper flakes and cook until fragrant, about 30 seconds. Add pulsed tomatoes, bring to simmer, and cook until reduced to 1 cup, about 10 minutes. Season with salt and pepper to taste and let cool to room temperature, about 30 minutes.

3. Mix mozzarella, Parmesan, and half-and-half together in separate bowl until well combined.

4. Divide dough equally between two 12-inch disposable aluminum pizza pans. Using well-oiled hands, press dough out evenly toward edges of pans. Spread ½ cup sauce over each dough round, leaving ½-inch border around edge, then sprinkle cheese mixture evenly over sauce.

5. Wrap each pizza tightly with plastic and cover with aluminum foil. Freeze pizzas for up to 1 month. (Do not thaw before reheating.)

6. Thirty minutes before baking, adjust oven rack to upper-middle position (rack should be 4 to 5 inches from broiler), set baking stone on rack, and heat oven to 500 degrees. Unwrap 1 pizza and remove from aluminum pan. Transfer pizza to pizza peel or cutting board and brush edges of dough with oil. Carefully slide pizza onto baking stone and bake until crust is well browned and cheese is bubbling and beginning to brown, 15 to 25 minutes, rotating pizza halfway through baking. Transfer pizza to wire rack and let cool for 5 minutes before slicing and serving.

NEW ENGLAND BAR PIZZA

WHY THIS RECIPE WORKS: Bar pizza, a New England favorite, is baked in well-seasoned rimmed pans, with the dough forming a thin lip up the sides. The crust is tender yet crispy. Replicating this style of pizza required us to use all-purpose flour rather than the usual bread flour for the dough. We created the distinctive edges by rolling the pizza dough thin and baking the pies in 9-inch cake pans, pressing the dough ¼ inch up the sides of the pan. Brushing the edges with tomato sauce and cheese also gave us the "laced" edges that bar pizzas are known for. Finishing the pies with a mixture of cheddar and mozzarella best imitated the classic version's distinct tangy flavors.

Situated between Boston and the shoulder of Cape Cod is a stretch of mostly suburban towns collectively known as the South Shore. While this region has a rich cultural history dating back to Colonial times, pizza fanatics know it as the spiritual home of New England bar pizza.

Truthfully, I had never heard of this pizza—despite living just 20 miles away—until a colleague who grew up on the South Shore lovingly described the pies at her favorite pizza place, the family-owned and -operated Lynwood Café in Randolph, Massachusetts. She described their pizza as having a tender, thin crust with a crisp underside, a fresh and potent sauce, and plenty of browned, bubbly cheese on top. When I mentioned that I was contemplating a visit, her expression turned very serious: "You have to get a pie with laced edges," she said. A secret, off-menu option, a "laced" pizza has sauce and cheese spread beyond the dough's lip, where it sinks between the dough and this pizza's signature lipped pan, resulting in a well-charred edge where the cheese and sauce crisp and caramelize into a delicious, crackly lace.

With my mouth practically watering, I wasted no time in driving down to the Lynwood Café. I ordered a cheese pizza and their signature pie, the baked bean special, which is loaded with Boston baked beans, onions, and salami. While I waited, I had a chance to speak with Steve, the fourth generation of his family to work there. I tried my best to squeeze some trade secrets out of Steve, but he preferred to let the pizza speak for itself. It spoke loud and clear; it was love

at first bite. And the baked bean version, odd as it sounded, was delicious.

I headed to the test kitchen determined to replicate New England bar pizza with the few clues I had. I tried the handful of copycat recipes I found online, but they were poor imitations, with crusts that were too chewy or too thick and that lacked the defining crisp bottom. Sauces were ho-hum. The best cheese toppings used equal amounts of cheddar (for robust flavor) and mozzarella (for easy melting).

Getting the dough right was paramount. It had to be tender yet crisp—not chewy like most pizza crusts. I decided to start by baking the test kitchen's thin-crust pizza dough recipe in cake pans (since most home cooks don't have rimmed pizza pans). The recipe calls for mixing bread flour, sugar, instant yeast, and water in the food processor to form a ball. The dough rests until the flour is hydrated and then oil and salt are processed in; the dough rises at room temperature for about 2 hours before shaping. Once it had risen, I divided the dough in half, rolled each piece out, and pressed the dough into two 9-inch round cake pans, making a ¼-inch lip up the sides. I spooned on a quick tomato sauce and sprinkled a mix of mozzarella and cheddar over the top. Following the original recipe, I baked the pizzas on a pizza stone on the top rack of a 500-degree oven.

The resulting pizzas were promising, if not quite right. The dough was a little too chewy on the edges, and the bottom wasn't perfectly crisp all over, although the cake pans seemed to work well as baking vessels. For a more tender dough, I switched to all-purpose flour instead of the bread flour; the all-purpose flour is lower in protein and thus creates less gluten and chew. But how could I get the bottom appropriately crisp?

I tried adding lots of olive oil to the pans, which helped a bit. But the real solution was placing the oven rack at the lowest position, closest to the heating element. Moving the pizzas away from the reflected heat at the top of the oven meant that the cheese took longer to brown, which allowed extra time for the pizza's bottom to crisp. The extra baking time also meant that I no longer needed the pizza stone, another plus. Now the pizzas were tender and nicely browned with crisp bottom crusts—just as they are at the Lynwood.

I turned to the sauce. Simplicity was the key here, and that meant an uncooked sauce. Working to replicate the Lynwood's straightforward yet flavorful version, I processed one can of diced tomatoes together with a touch of olive oil, dried oregano, sugar, salt, pepper, and pepper flakes and ladled ⅓ cup of the sauce over each pan of dough. Equal parts sharp cheddar and mozzarella made for the perfect cheesy topping. To get that authentic "lacing" on the crust, I brushed the sauce and sprinkled the cheese over the edge where the dough met the pans. These pizzas, finally, tasted a lot like what had made me swoon in Randolph.

Is the world ready to fall in love with New England bar pizza? With this recipe, I think it just might be.

—CRISTIN WALSH, *Cook's Country*

New England Bar Pizza

SERVES 4

Clean the food processor in between making the dough and the pizza sauce. You will have some sauce left over; reserve it for another use. Use sharp cheddar cheese, not extra-sharp (which makes the pizzas too greasy).

DOUGH

1⅔ cups (8⅓ ounces) all-purpose flour
1 tablespoon sugar
1 teaspoon instant or rapid-rise yeast
⅔ cup water
1½ teaspoons extra-virgin olive oil
¾ teaspoon salt

SAUCE

1 (14.5-ounce) can diced tomatoes
1 teaspoon extra-virgin olive oil
½ teaspoon dried oregano
½ teaspoon sugar
¼ teaspoon salt
⅛ teaspoon pepper
⅛ teaspoon red pepper flakes

TOPPING

4 ounces sharp cheddar cheese, shredded (1 cup)
4 ounces whole-milk mozzarella, shredded (1 cup)
1 tablespoon extra-virgin olive oil

1. FOR THE DOUGH: Process flour, sugar, and yeast in food processor until combined, about 3 seconds. With processor running, slowly add water; process dough until

just combined and no dry flour remains, about 10 seconds. Let dough stand for 10 minutes. Add oil and salt to dough and process until dough forms satiny, sticky ball that clears sides of workbowl, 30 to 60 seconds.

2. Transfer dough to lightly oiled counter and knead until smooth, about 1 minute. Shape dough into tight ball and place in greased bowl. Cover with plastic wrap and let rise at room temperature until almost doubled in size, 2 to 2½ hours.

3. FOR THE SAUCE: Process all ingredients in clean, dry food processor until smooth, about 30 seconds; set sauce aside. (Sauce can be refrigerated for up to 2 days or frozen for up to 1 month.)

4. FOR THE TOPPING: Adjust oven rack to lowest position and heat oven to 500 degrees. Combine cheddar and mozzarella in bowl. Using pastry brush, grease bottom and sides of 2 dark-colored 9-inch round cake pans with 1½ teaspoons oil each.

5. Transfer dough to lightly floured counter, divide in half, and shape into balls. Gently flatten 1 dough ball into 6-inch disk using your fingertips. Using rolling pin, roll disk into 10-inch round. Transfer dough to prepared pan and press into corners, forcing ¼-inch lip of dough up sides of pan. Repeat with remaining dough ball.

6. Spread ⅓ cup sauce in thin layer over entire surface of 1 dough. Using pastry brush, brush sauce over lip of dough. Sprinkle 1 cup cheese mixture evenly over pizza, including lip. Repeat with remaining dough, ⅓ cup sauce, and remaining 1 cup cheese mixture.

7. Bake until crust is browned and cheese is bubbly and beginning to brown, about 12 minutes, switching and rotating pans halfway through baking. To remove pizzas from pans, run offset spatula along top edge of pizza crust. Once loosened, slide spatula underneath pizza and slide pizza onto wire rack. Let cool for 5 minutes. Slice and serve.

NEW ORLEANS MUFFULETTAS

✅ WHY THIS RECIPE WORKS: We wanted to do this iconic Southern sandwich justice, so we started with (semi) homemade bread. Store-bought pizza dough baked up into puffy rounds of bread, and we topped it with sesame seeds just like at Central Grocery in New Orleans. We layered the traditional meats and cheeses—mortadella, salami, hot capicola for kick, and provolone cheese—into the split loaves along with the signature ingredient: olive salad. Ours was a briny, bright combination of olives, capers, giardiniera, garlic, herbs and spices, and just a splash of vinegar for extra tang.

Looking for a quick lunch in the French Quarter of New Orleans? Check out Central Grocery on Decatur Street. The signature—and only—sandwich served there is the muffuletta, a hefty round of seeded bread stuffed with Italian meats, cheeses, and olive spread. And just like every signature sandwich, it's got an origin story to match. In 1906, Salvatore Lupo, the owner of Central Grocery, noticed Sicilian immigrants on their lunch breaks eating meals of meats, cheeses, olives, and bread. The enterprising grocer decided to save the workers some trouble by putting all the components together in a convenient, handheld sandwich. Thus was born the muffuletta, named after the round Sicilian bread it's made on and served at Central Grocery—and elsewhere all over the city—ever since.

On my last trip to New Orleans, I stopped in at Central Grocery to sample a muffuletta at its place of origin. The sandwich was salty and spicy, with the tangy olive salad balancing the generous swath of meat and cheese in the middle and savory oil seeping into the bread. The bread itself was sturdy but soft, chewy but not crusty, and topped with plenty of sesame seeds. I decided right then that I would try to replicate this sandwich in the test kitchen.

The muffuletta recipes I found were fairly similar. The meats and cheeses varied only slightly—I ended up using a pretty standard grouping of salami, mortadella, and capicola with provolone cheese—but the bread selection was all over the place (muffuletta bread is hard to find outside New Orleans), as were the recipes for the olive salad that is the heart and soul of this sandwich. Since none of the salads seemed spot on, I went to the source, ordering a jar from Central Grocery. When it arrived, I perused the ingredient list and got to work. Olives, both black and green, were key, and opting for the pimento-stuffed variety added more flavor. Capers, vinegar, oil, and garlic followed. The next six items—celery, cauliflower, carrots, sweet peppers, onions, and pepperoncini—brought to mind bottled giardiniera, a spicy Italian-style mixed vegetable pickle, which conveniently combines all those ingredients in one jar. My first round of tests showed that if the olive salad was too coarse, it wouldn't hold the sandwich together properly, so I reached for the food processor and pulsed olives (I used twice as many green as kalamata, since the latter are far saltier and the sandwich tends to be on the oversalty side), giardiniera, capers (rinsed to control the salt), red wine vinegar, and fresh garlic. Judging by the flavor of the Central Grocery version, the "spices" included oregano and thyme, so I threw in both. To flavor and bind the salad, I stirred in plenty of olive oil. After assembling a sandwich (with store-bought Italian bread for now) and tasting, I knew I'd nailed it.

It was time to figure out what bread to use. Through the course of my testing, I had tried every iteration of supermarket bread, but none was working. A boule was too crusty and turned into a soggy mess, focaccia was too fluffy and not nearly thick enough, and sourdough bread just had the wrong flavor. I finally had a breakthrough when one of my coworkers commented that the giant sandwich reminded her of a calzone—what about store-bought pizza dough? After a trip to the supermarket and some experimentation, I learned that a 1-pound ball of dough was the perfect size for a sandwich cut in quarters, but if I was going to the trouble, I figured I might as well serve a crowd—two balls of dough meant that I could feed eight or more with about the same amount of work. One hour of

NEW ORLEANS MUFFULETTAS

rising on the counter was plenty, and a brushing of egg wash followed by a sprinkling of sesame seeds before baking gave the finished loaves an extra touch of authenticity.

After the loaves cooled, it was time to assemble. The flavor and texture of my ersatz homemade bread were spot on, and after plenty of tumbling olive salad and wayward cold cuts, I found the best method of construction: After splitting the loaves horizontally, I spread olive salad on the cut sides of both the tops and the bottoms, which effectively "glued" everything together. Alternating layers of cheeses and meats created more stability, and finally, weighting the sandwiches for an hour rendered them compact and sliceable as well as helped the oil soak into the bread. I had assembled, pressed, and sliced my muffulettas and was rewarded by salty meats, briny olives, creamy cheese, and fresh, chewy bread, all in a convenient, handheld package. Mr. Lupo would be proud.

—REBECCA MARSTERS, *Cook's Country*

New Orleans Muffulettas

SERVES 8

You will need one 16-ounce jar of giardiniera to yield 2 cups drained; our favorite brand is Pastene. If you like a spicier sandwich, increase the amount of pepper flakes to ½ teaspoon.

- 2 (1-pound) balls pizza dough
- 2 cups drained jarred giardiniera
- 1 cup pimento-stuffed green olives
- ½ cup pitted kalamata olives
- 2 tablespoons capers, rinsed
- 1 tablespoon red wine vinegar
- 1 garlic clove, minced
- ½ teaspoon dried oregano
- ¼ teaspoon red pepper flakes
- ¼ teaspoon dried thyme
- ½ cup extra-virgin olive oil
- ¼ cup chopped fresh parsley
- 1 large egg, lightly beaten
- 5 teaspoons sesame seeds
- 4 ounces thinly sliced Genoa salami
- 6 ounces thinly sliced aged provolone cheese
- 6 ounces thinly sliced mortadella
- 4 ounces thinly sliced hot capicola

1. Form dough balls into 2 tight round balls on oiled baking sheet, cover loosely with greased plastic wrap, and let sit at room temperature for 1 hour.

2. Meanwhile, pulse giardiniera, green olives, kalamata olives, capers, vinegar, garlic, oregano, pepper flakes, and thyme in food processor until coarsely chopped, about 6 pulses, scraping down sides of bowl as needed. Transfer to bowl and stir in oil and parsley. Let sit at room temperature for 30 minutes. (Olive salad can be refrigerated for up to 1 week.)

3. Adjust oven rack to middle position and heat oven to 425 degrees. Keeping dough balls on sheet, flatten each into 7-inch disk. Brush tops of disks with egg and sprinkle with sesame seeds. Bake until golden brown and loaves sound hollow when tapped, 18 to 20 minutes, rotating sheet halfway through baking. Transfer loaves to wire rack and let cool completely, about 1 hour. (Loaves can be wrapped in plastic and stored at room temperature for up to 24 hours.)

4. Slice loaves in half horizontally. Spread one-fourth of olive salad on cut side of each loaf top and bottom, pressing firmly with rubber spatula to compact. Layer 2 ounces salami, 1½ ounces provolone, 3 ounces mortadella, 1½ ounces provolone, and 2 ounces capicola in order on each loaf bottom. Cap with loaf tops and individually wrap sandwiches tightly in plastic.

5. Place baking sheet on top of sandwiches and weigh down with heavy Dutch oven or two 5-pound bags of flour or sugar for 1 hour, flipping sandwiches halfway through pressing. Unwrap and slice each sandwich into quarters and serve. (Pressed, wrapped sandwiches can be refrigerated for up to 24 hours. Bring to room temperature before serving.)

NOTES FROM THE TEST KITCHEN

PRESS FOR SUCCESS
Pressing the assembled sandwiches for an hour helps the olive salad properly soak into the bread.

TEMPEH REUBENS

☑ **WHY THIS RECIPE WORKS:** When you think of a Reuben sandwich, your first thought is probably all about the corned beef and the particular character of that cured and salted meat. But is a Reuben really all about the meat? Given its unique combination of tangy Russian dressing, melty Swiss cheese, and hearty rye bread, we knew it was worth trying to make this deli classic vegetarian-friendly. We chose hearty tempeh as our corned beef replacement for its firm texture and its ability to stand up to strong flavors. To impart the tempeh with the true flavor of corned beef, we decided to "corn" it. Then we browned the tempeh in a skillet to give it a nice crust. To make a quick Russian dressing, we started with prepared cocktail sauce and mixed it with creamy mayonnaise, crunchy pickles, and some tart pickle juice. We topped the sandwiches with sauerkraut and Swiss cheese and toasted them in a skillet until the cheese was melted and the bread was crisp and golden brown.

Pity the vegetarian at the neighborhood deli—just about every delicious option is packed with meat. One of my favorites, the Reuben, is most famous for the distinctive taste of its corned beef, but was it possible to translate that essence into a meatless sandwich that packed just as much flavor? I knew that although really good traditional Reubens are practically ubiquitous these days, creating a vegetarian take on this classic would be a tricky undertaking. The main challenge, of course, would be replacing the unique flavor and texture of the central corned beef with a vegetarian alternative. In addition, I wanted to make sure the other elements of the sandwich were perfectly balanced, with none of the weaknesses that Reubens frequently fall victim to, such as chilly centers, unmelted cheese, soggy rye, watery sauerkraut, and sugary supermarket dressing.

To replace the beef, I looked to tempeh. Tempeh, a mainstay of many vegetarian diets, is made by fermenting cooked soybeans and then forming the mixture into a firm, dense cake. This helps the tempeh hold its shape when cooked, which makes it a good meat substitute and a great choice for sandwiches. It has a strong, nutty taste and it also absorbs flavors easily, which gave me the idea of corning it just like corned beef. I cut the tempeh into thick steaks and marinated it in a traditional corning brine with allspice, salt, peppercorns,

thyme, and paprika. Compared with traditional corned beef, which takes upward of 4 hours of brining, corning tempeh was remarkably easy—just a 10-minute simmer was enough to impart the distinctive flavor without making it too salty. To keep the sandwiches from getting too soft or soggy I then seared the tempeh to give it a perfect brown crust and crisp texture.

Once I had the base of my sandwich figured out, I turned to the condiments that make a Reuben unique. Bottled Russian and Thousand Island dressings are nearly identical: Both are made from mayonnaise, ketchup, pickle relish, vinegar, and sugar, and both were unacceptably sweet in my sandwich. A homemade dressing using the same ingredients—minus the sugar—was much better, but my tasters wanted more punch. Hot peppers tasted out of place, but horseradish (an ingredient sometimes found in Russian dressings) provided welcome heat. To streamline ingredients, I tried replacing the ketchup and horseradish with prepared cocktail sauce, and my tasters couldn't tell the difference. While most recipes use pickle relish, tasters preferred the fresher flavor and crunch of hand-chopped pickles. Finally, replacing the vinegar with pickle juice balanced tang with sweetness. The result was a flavorful homemade sauce with a satisfying crunch that was worlds better than anything you can buy in a supermarket.

Now it was time to put everything together. I spread the dressing on rye bread, and to combat soggy sandwich syndrome, I drained the sauerkraut before layering it with the corned tempeh and cheese. (We prefer the sauerkraut sold in pouches in the refrigerated sections in most supermarkets to most jarred or canned varieties.) But the sauerkraut still exuded enough moisture to saturate the bread, so next I tried cooking the sauerkraut in a skillet before assembling the sandwiches. This allowed the excess moisture to evaporate; plus, the hot sauerkraut helped warm the rest of the ingredients, which made it easier for all the layers to come together by the time the bread was sufficiently browned in the skillet. Cooking the sauerkraut also presented an opportunity to add flavor, and I found that 2 tablespoons of cider vinegar and a little brown sugar improved the store-bought sauerkraut considerably.

I was almost there, but the cheese—I was using regular deli slices of Swiss—still wasn't melting fully. The test kitchen uses shredded cheese to make grilled cheese sandwiches, and switching to shredded Swiss helped a little. I then tried covering the skillet; the higher temperature under the lid was just what I needed. Transferring my Reubens to plates, I could see that the cheese was melted and the bread was crisp and golden brown. I had kept all the hallmarks of this deli classic while making it new and fresh with my vegetarian twists.

—SARA MAYER, *America's Test Kitchen Books*

Tempeh Reubens

SERVES 4

- 10 tablespoons cider vinegar
- ½ cup water
- 2 teaspoons ground allspice
- 1½ teaspoons salt
- 1 teaspoon black peppercorns, cracked
- 1 teaspoon dried thyme
- 1 teaspoon paprika
- 1 pound tempeh, cut into 3½-inch-long by ⅜-inch-thick slabs
- 1 cup sauerkraut, drained and rinsed
- 1 teaspoon packed brown sugar
- ¼ cup vegetable oil
- ¼ cup mayonnaise
- ¼ cup finely chopped sweet pickles plus 1 teaspoon pickle brine
- 2 tablespoons cocktail sauce
- 4 tablespoons unsalted butter, melted
- 8 slices hearty rye bread
- 4 ounces Swiss cheese, shredded (1 cup)

1. Combine ½ cup vinegar, water, allspice, salt, peppercorns, thyme, and paprika in large saucepan and bring to simmer over medium heat. Add tempeh, cover, reduce heat to medium-low, and simmer until liquid is mostly absorbed, 10 to 15 minutes, turning tempeh halfway through cooking. Transfer tempeh to plate and let cool for 10 minutes.

2. Meanwhile, cook sauerkraut, remaining 2 tablespoons vinegar, and sugar in 12-inch nonstick skillet over medium-high heat, stirring occasionally, until liquid evaporates, about 3 minutes; transfer to bowl. Wipe out skillet with paper towels.

3. Heat 2 tablespoons oil in now-empty skillet over medium heat until shimmering. Add 4 pieces tempeh and cook until golden brown on first side, 2 to 4 minutes. Flip tempeh, reduce heat to medium-low, and continue to cook until golden brown on second side, 2 to 4 minutes; transfer to clean plate. Wipe out skillet with paper towels and repeat with remaining 2 tablespoons oil and remaining tempeh. Wipe out skillet with paper towels.

4. Whisk mayonnaise, pickles and brine, and cocktail sauce together in bowl. Brush melted butter evenly over 1 side of each slice of bread. Flip bread over and spread mayonnaise mixture evenly over second side. Assemble 4 sandwiches by layering ingredients as follows on top of mayonnaise mixture: half of Swiss, tempeh, sauerkraut, remaining Swiss. Press gently on sandwiches to set.

5. Heat now-empty skillet over medium-low heat for 2 minutes. Place 2 sandwiches in pan and cook until golden brown on first side, about 2 minutes. Flip sandwiches, cover skillet, and cook until second side is golden brown and cheese is melted, about 2 minutes. Transfer sandwiches to serving platter. Wipe out skillet with paper towels and cook remaining 2 sandwiches. Serve.

NOTES FROM THE TEST KITCHEN

CUTTING TEMPEH INTO SLABS

1. Cut each piece crosswise into two 3½-inch-long pieces.

2. Next cut each piece horizontally into ⅜-inch-thick slabs.

PHILLY-STYLE PORTOBELLO AND CHEESE SANDWICHES

✓ **WHY THIS RECIPE WORKS:** Philly cheesesteaks are famous well beyond the boundaries of Pennsylvania, and for good reason: These rich, decadent sandwiches are the perfect combination of paper-thin sliced steak and gooey, melty cheese. We wanted to make a healthier, vegetarian take on the cheesesteak. First we swapped out the steak for meaty, umami-rich portobello mushrooms. To give the sandwich a more complex and satisfying texture, we added hearty, subtly bitter broccoli rabe. We sautéed the broccoli rabe with some garlic and pepper flakes for heat and then tossed it with vinegar before letting it sit while we cooked the mushrooms. To mimic the traditional thinly shaved steak, we cut the mushrooms into thin slices and sautéed them until they were nicely browned and flavorful. Once the mushrooms were cooked, we stirred in the broccoli rabe. To bind it all together, we let slices of American cheese melt into the vegetables to make a rich, cohesive filling that we piled high on toasted sub rolls.

A true cheesesteak contains beef that's sliced paper-thin and generously heaped into a soft-crumbed roll along with your melty cheese of choice, often provolone or American. But all that richness can be a little overwhelming, and if not done well, a cheesesteak can become just a dense, greasy pile of meat and cheese. I wanted to stay true to the Philly spirit while lightening up the profile of this hefty sandwich. As a bonus, I also wanted to make it vegetarian-friendly and amp up the health and flavor quotients. In order to adapt this meat-centric dish to be healthier and vegetarian, I first had to find a replacement for the steak that had the heft and the richness of the beef and enough flavor to hold its own against a blanket of creamy melted cheese.

Portobello mushrooms were a natural fill-in for chewy, rich steak. Their large size allows for long slices and their rich, earthy flavor is a great replacement for the heartiness of meat. I made sure to carefully remove the gills before using them to avoid any muddy flavor. Super-thin slicing is key to the success of steak in a traditional Philly cheesesteak—this allows the meat and the cheese to combine smoothly. I cut the portobellos into similarly thin slices to mimic this consistency. This also had the added bonus of allowing as much water as possible to cook off of the mushrooms as they sautéed, which helped with browning and texture.

I knew I wanted to add something a little different to my take on the cheesesteak, so I went looking for another layer that might work with the rich flavor profile and found inspiration in Philly's other famous sandwich—Italian roast pork with broccoli rabe and provolone. Peppery broccoli rabe brings great flavor and complexity to any dish, but it requires some extra attention to soften its bitter edge. I tamed it by first trimming off the tough bottom stalks, then chopping the rest into small pieces, and steaming those pieces with garlic and hot pepper flakes. Next, I stirred in some vinegar for balance. Then, I sautéed the broccoli rabe with the cooked mushrooms to bring all the flavors together. I now had a delicious vegetarian sandwich filling full of interesting flavors; the next question was how to smother it all in cheese without losing those flavors that I'd so carefully developed.

My first choice for cheese was provolone, but its distinctive taste clashed with the bite of the broccoli rabe; plus, my tasters insisted that the gooey, melty quality of American cheese was essential to a Philly-style sandwich. In order to get the ideal cheese-to-vegetable ratio, I melted the American cheese over the mushrooms and broccoli rabe right in the skillet and folded it in to bind everything together before scooping it into the toasted sub rolls. I'd created a new hybrid vegetarian take on two great Philadelphia sandwiches with all the heartiness, creaminess, flavor, and indulgence that those dishes are famous for, minus the meat.

—SARA MAYER, *America's Test Kitchen Books*

Philly-Style Broccoli Rabe, Portobello, and Cheese Sandwiches
SERVES 4

- 3 tablespoons vegetable oil
- 2 garlic cloves, sliced thin
- ⅛ teaspoon red pepper flakes
- ¾ pound broccoli rabe, trimmed and cut into ½-inch pieces
- 2 tablespoons water
- Salt and pepper
- 2 tablespoons balsamic vinegar
- 6 portobello mushroom caps, gills removed, halved, and sliced thin
- 10 slices (10 ounces) deli American cheese
- 4 (8-inch) Italian sub rolls, split lengthwise and toasted

1. Heat 1 tablespoon oil in 12-inch nonstick skillet over medium heat until shimmering. Add garlic and pepper flakes and cook for 1 minute. Stir in broccoli rabe, water, and ½ teaspoon salt. Cover and cook until broccoli rabe is bright green and crisp-tender, 3 to 4 minutes. Off heat, stir in vinegar, then transfer to bowl.

2. Heat remaining 2 tablespoons oil in now-empty skillet over medium-high heat until shimmering. Add mushrooms (skillet will be very full), cover, and cook, stirring occasionally, until mushrooms release their liquid, 6 to 8 minutes. Uncover and continue to cook until moisture has evaporated and mushrooms begin to brown, 6 to 8 minutes.

3. Stir broccoli rabe back into skillet and season with salt and pepper to taste. Reduce heat to low and shingle cheese over vegetables. Cook until cheese is melted, about 2 minutes. Fold melted cheese thoroughly into mushroom mixture. Divide mixture evenly among toasted rolls. Serve.

ANCHO-ORANGE PORK BURRITOS

✔ **WHY THIS RECIPE WORKS:** Traditional Mexican *chilorio* is made by slow-cooking pork until it's fall-apart tender, then shredding it and cooking it again in a chile sauce. We decided to use this ultraflavorful pork preparation as inspiration for a unique burrito filling. To achieve moist, tender, and richly flavored pork, we cooked boneless pork butt slowly and gently in the oven in an aromatic sauce base of orange juice, vinegar, and chipotle and ancho chiles. To keep the recipe streamlined, we pureed our braising liquid into a sauce. To ensure that the pork was the star, we used just herb-studded rice, no cheese or beans, when assembling our burritos.

Here in the northeast, a good burrito is hard to find. I've been to my fair share of Mexican restaurants, from casual sit-down chains to fast-food joints to tiny mom-and-pop operations. Almost all of them offer burritos. Almost none of those burritos are any good. More often than not, the fillings are underwhelming, overcheesed, and covered in gloppy guacamole in an attempt to give them some flavor. So I knew I had my work cut out for me: I wanted to create a burrito filling that was so flavorful, it wouldn't require any excess gussying up to make it taste good.

Since pork burritos are my favorite, I decided to make a pork filling. I wanted to give my burrito a somewhat authentic flavor profile, so I went on the hunt for Mexican pork preparations that I could modify for the American home kitchen.

During my research, I came across several recipes for *chilorio*, a dish of shredded pork in a chile sauce. Generally, the recipes were fairly similar: a well-marbled cut would be slow-simmered with aromatics and sometimes orange juice until fall-apart tender. Then the meat would be pulled into bite-size pieces and cooked again in a separate chile sauce. Hailing from the northern Mexican state of Sinaloa, this preparation is so popular, it's sold premade (and even canned) at some markets in Mexico. I chose a few recipes that included orange juice as my starting point—I thought the combination of tangy, bright citrus and earthy, smoky chiles would be just the thing for my burrito filling.

The test kitchen's favorite cut for pulled pork is a butt roast—its plentiful connective tissue makes it well suited to long, slow cooking. I put the pork in a Dutch oven with some orange juice and let it braise in a low oven. While the pork cooked, I made my chile sauce with a combination of ancho and chipotle chiles, a host of aromatics and spices, vinegar (a traditional addition), and a bit of tomato paste for depth. I let the sauce simmer on the stove to thicken it and meld the flavors. Once the pork was done, I shredded it and tossed the meat with the sauce.

The result was lacking. The porky depth I was hoping for simply wasn't there, and making the sauce on the stovetop seemed fussy. I wondered if I could put my braising liquid to work to solve both problems.

For my next test, I put all the ingredients in the pot with the pork, hoping that the sauce would saturate the pork with flavor while the rich pork fat infused the sauce with savory depth. When the pork came out of the oven a couple hours later, I knew I was on to something. I spooned the pork into a bowl to shred. I strained the remainder of the pot's contents into a fat separator, removed the bay leaves, and transferred the solids and the defatted liquid to the blender. A minute later, I had a beautifully rich, deep red-orange sauce that was ready to mix with the shredded pork.

ANCHO-ORANGE PORK BURRITOS

I was ready to assemble my burritos. I cooked up some plain white rice, grated some mild Monterey Jack, and filled and rolled fresh flour tortillas. Tasters' comments were unanimous: The pork tasted great, but the cheese was out of place and the bland rice took away from the flavor. I decided to eliminate the cheese altogether, and went to work jazzing up the rice just enough so that it could stand up to, but not overpower, the flavorful pork.

In the end, cilantro and a few scallions stirred into the rice complemented the pork nicely.

Finally, I had the perfect burrito: deeply flavorful, chile-infused pork, herb-studded rice, and a warm flour tortilla—no condiments necessary.

—LAWMAN JOHNSON, *America's Test Kitchen Books*

Ancho-Orange Pork Burritos

SERVES 8

- ¾ cup orange juice (2 oranges)
- ½ cup distilled white vinegar
- 4 dried ancho chiles, stemmed, seeded, and torn into ½-inch pieces (1 cup)
- 2 tablespoons tomato paste
- 2 tablespoons minced canned chipotle chile in adobo sauce
- 5 garlic cloves, lightly crushed and peeled
- 2 bay leaves
- 2 teaspoons ground cumin
- 2 teaspoons dried oregano
  Salt and pepper
- 4 pounds boneless pork butt roast, trimmed and cut into 2-inch pieces
- 2 cups water
- 1½ cups long-grain white rice, rinsed
- ¼ cup minced fresh cilantro
- 2 scallions, sliced thin
- 8 (10-inch) flour tortillas

1. Adjust oven rack to lower-middle position and heat oven to 300 degrees. Whisk orange juice, vinegar, anchos, tomato paste, chipotle, garlic, bay leaves, cumin, oregano and 1 teaspoon salt together in Dutch oven.

Season pork with salt and pepper, stir into pot, and arrange in single layer. Cover and cook in oven until pork is very tender, about 2 hours.

2. Transfer pork to large bowl using slotted spoon and let cool slightly. Using 2 forks, shred pork into bite-size pieces. Strain braising liquid into fat separator, reserving solids, and let settle for 5 minutes. Discard bay leaves and transfer solids to blender. Add 1½ cups defatted liquid to blender and process until smooth, about 1 minute. Combine sauce and pork in now-empty Dutch oven. (Pork can refrigerated for up to 3 days or frozen for up to 1 month. Before assembling burritos, reheat mixture over medium heat until hot.)

3. Meanwhile, bring water, rice, and 1 teaspoon salt to boil in medium saucepan over medium-high heat. Cover, reduce heat to low, and cook until rice is tender and water is absorbed, about 20 minutes. Remove rice from heat and let sit, covered, for 10 minutes. Add cilantro and scallions and fluff with fork to incorporate; cover to keep warm.

4. Wrap tortillas in damp dish towel and microwave until warm and pliable, about 1 minute. Lay warm tortillas on counter. Mound warm rice and pork across center of tortillas, close to bottom edge. Working with 1 tortilla at a time, fold sides then bottom of tortilla over filling, pulling back on it firmly to tighten it around filling, then continue to roll tightly into burrito. Serve.

NOTES FROM THE TEST KITCHEN

COOKING WITH TORTILLAS

When tortillas are incorporated into a dish, such as our Ancho-Orange Pork Burritos, they are often softened by briefly frying them, one at a time, in hot oil. This helps to make the tortillas pliable and decreases the risk that they'll crack or fall apart in the sauce. Since frying tortillas one at a time is time-consuming and messy, we often warm the tortillas all at once in the microwave instead.

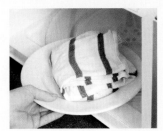

Wrap tortillas in damp dish towel and microwave until warm and pliable, about 1 minute.

TENDER, JUICY GRILLED BURGERS

☑ **WHY THIS RECIPE WORKS:** Creating a juicy and loosely textured burger that could withstand the rigors of grilling called for a number of tactics. First, we ground our own meat in the food processor, which let us choose the cut (steak tips), grind (coarse), and consistency (loose) of the burger. Incorporating a little salt and butter before shaping added richness, boosted juiciness, and flavored the burgers. Finally we shaped the burgers (with a dimple in their centers to prevent bulging) and froze them for 30 minutes, which held them together as they cooked and let them stay on the grill a few minutes longer for excellent char and perfect centers.

One of the best things about summer is the chance to eat a really great burger off the grill. By that I mean a burger with an ultracraggy crust, a rich beefy taste, and an interior so juicy and tender that it practically falls apart at the slightest pressure.

The problem is, such a burger is actually pretty hard to come by. While the typical specimen may have a nicely browned crust, it's also heavy and dense with a pebbly texture. The reason is no mystery: Most cooks use preground meat, which is usually ground so fine that a certain amount of graininess is inevitable. Furthermore, they tend to shape the meat into tightly packed disks that guarantee dense texture.

I decided to tackle these issues head on and find an approach to a truly excellent backyard burger.

It was a given that I'd need to grind my own meat. Besides being ground too fine, commercial burger meat is also manhandled during processing. This overmanipulation draws out a lot of the sticky protein myosin, so even if you form your patties with a gentle hand, your results have already been compromised.

In the test kitchen, we've found it easy to grind meat ourselves with a food processor. The method we've developed (no matter the cut) calls for trimming gristle and excess fat from the meat, cutting the meat into ½-inch pieces, freezing it for about 30 minutes to firm it up so that the blades cut it cleanly instead of smashing and smearing it, and finally processing it in small batches to ensure an even, precise grind.

I narrowed the cut of meat to three options: chuck, boneless short ribs, and sirloin steak tips. Chuck had great flavor, but it contained a lot of sinewy connective tissue that had to be painstakingly removed before grinding. Deeply marbled short ribs were gloriously fatty and rich—but a bit too rich for several tasters, so they were also out. Somewhat leaner steak tips had great meaty flavor and required virtually no trimming. They came up a bit short in terms of richness, but I had a trick up my sleeve for fixing that.

In our standard burger recipe, we call for tossing the ground meat with melted butter to impart deeper flavor and richness. However, pouring melted butter over my near-frozen meat was somewhat problematic; the butter started to solidify on contact, making it tricky to evenly distribute. I realized that there was a way to incorporate the butter that would not only enable even distribution but also be easier: adding it to the food processor when grinding the meat.

Now I was ready to sort out the mechanics of shaping and grilling. I determined that 6 ounces was the ideal portion size with patties that were ¾ inch thick, which I figured were just thick enough to allow decent char on the exterior without overcooking at the center. I knew from experience that I needed to make a small depression in the center of each patty before grilling to ensure that they finished flat instead of ballooning outward.

But before I could even add those divots, I had to sort out my biggest obstacle: How could I form my burgers so that they wouldn't fall apart on the grate but at the same time achieve that essential open texture? Too much manipulation of ground meat translates to tough burgers, but if I could draw out just a little sticky myosin, maybe it would help hold the burgers together without making them tough.

Kneading the ground meat was impractical, but salt, like kneading, also draws out myosin. Adding the salt and using a fork to toss the meat allowed me to evenly distribute the salt without overworking the meat. Sadly, by the time I'd added enough salt for the necessary structure, the resulting burgers were tough and springy.

However, working salt into the interior of the meat did have an upside: It thoroughly seasoned the meat and made it juicier. This made good sense: Just as the salt in a brine helps meat retain moisture as it cooks, the salt mixed into the ground meat ensured that it stayed juicy and moist on the grill. I just had to be precise, adding only as much salt as I could get away with before adversely affecting the burgers' texture.

I had made great progress, but if I couldn't find a way to keep my burgers intact, it didn't matter how good they tasted. My loosely formed patties held together pretty well for the first few seconds on the grill, but as soon as the meat lost its chill from the refrigerator, the patties fell apart. I needed an approach that would hold the patties together long enough for them to develop a crust. When I thought about it that way, the answer became obvious: Freeze them. For my next test, I placed the burgers in the freezer until they were just firm but not frozen solid and then headed out to the grill. As I'd hoped, by the time they'd thawed at their centers, they had developed enough crust to ensure that they held together. In fact, because they were cold, I found that they could stay on the grill a few minutes longer per side—gaining even more tasty char and making flipping all the more fail-safe—without going beyond medium-rare.

All that remained were the details of the fire itself. To ensure that the burgers charred on the exterior dramatically and quickly, a hot fire proved best. Since they took up very little real estate on the grate, I corralled a few quarts of charcoal inside a disposable aluminum roasting pan (perforated to let in oxygen so that they would burn) underneath the burgers to guarantee a cooking space that was plenty hot. (On a gas grill, this translated to setting all the burners to high and preheating the grill for 15 minutes.)

Whether served with the classic fixings like lettuce and tomato or something fancier, this was a grilled burger that actually lived up to my ideal.

—DAN SOUZA, *Cook's Illustrated*

Tender, Juicy Grilled Burgers

SERVES 4

This recipe requires freezing the meat twice, for a total of 65 to 80 minutes, before grilling. When stirring the salt and pepper into the ground meat and shaping the patties, take care not to overwork the meat or the burgers will become dense. Sirloin steak tips are also sold as flap meat. Serve the burgers with your favorite toppings.

- 1½ **pounds sirloin steak tips, trimmed and cut into ½-inch chunks**
- 4 **tablespoons unsalted butter, cut into ¼-inch pieces**
  Kosher salt and pepper
- 1 **(13 by 9-inch) disposable aluminum pan (if using charcoal)**
- 4 **hamburger buns**

NOTES FROM THE TEST KITCHEN

MAKE A BURGER THAT GOES SPLAT

Store-bought burger meat cooks up dense and tough. It's ground very fine and then wrapped up tightly for retail—factors that cause too much of the sticky protein myosin to be released. By grinding meat ourselves, we can keep it coarse and pack it gently into patties that stay fall-apart tender.

A TOUGH SELL
This burger made with preground meat held together even when we dropped a 10-pound Dutch oven on it.

SMASHINGLY TENDER
Meat ground at home delivers a much more tender burger, one that splattered easily under the Dutch oven's weight.

ADD SALT FOR JUICIER BURGERS

Mixing ground meat with too much salt will make burgers tough, but ¾ teaspoon helps the meat retain its juices.

1. Place beef chunks and butter on large plate in single layer. Freeze until meat is very firm and starting to harden around edges but still pliable, about 35 minutes.

2. Place one-quarter of meat and one-quarter of butter cubes in food processor and pulse until finely ground (about size of rice grains), 15 to 20 pulses, stopping and redistributing meat around bowl as necessary to ensure beef is evenly ground. Transfer meat to baking sheet. Repeat grinding with remaining 3 batches of meat and butter. Spread mixture over sheet and inspect carefully, discarding any long strands of gristle or large chunks of hard meat, fat, or butter.

3. Sprinkle 1 teaspoon pepper and ¾ teaspoon salt over meat and gently toss with fork to combine. Divide meat into 4 balls. Toss each between hands until uniformly but lightly packed. Gently flatten into patties

¾ inch thick and about 4½ inches in diameter. Using your thumb, make 1-inch-wide by ¼-inch-deep depression in center of each patty. Transfer patties to platter and freeze for 30 to 45 minutes.

4A. FOR A CHARCOAL GRILL: Using skewer, poke 12 holes in bottom of disposable pan. Open bottom vent completely and place disposable pan in center of grill. Light large chimney starter filled two-thirds with charcoal briquettes (4 quarts). When top coals are partially covered with ash, pour into disposable pan. Set cooking grate in place, cover, and open lid vent completely. Heat grill until hot, about 5 minutes.

4B. FOR A GAS GRILL: Turn all burners to high, cover, and heat grill until hot, about 15 minutes. Leave all burners on high.

5. Clean and oil cooking grate. Season 1 side of patties liberally with salt and pepper. Using spatula, flip patties and season other side. Grill patties (directly over coals if using charcoal), without moving them, until browned and meat easily releases from grill, 4 to 7 minutes. Flip burgers and continue to grill until browned on second side and meat registers 125 degrees for medium-rare or 130 degrees for medium, 4 to 7 minutes longer.

6. Transfer burgers to plate and let rest for 5 minutes. While burgers rest, lightly toast buns on grill, 1 to 2 minutes. Transfer burgers to buns and serve.

THICK-CUT PORTERHOUSE STEAKS

✔ **WHY THIS RECIPE WORKS:** With such a mammoth cut of meat, it is hard to achieve even cooking. To help our thick-cut steaks stay pink, juicy, and tender, we started them in a low-temperature oven (275 degrees). Then we seared the steaks in a hefty 3 tablespoons of oil over high heat to get an even exterior crust. By searing them quickly, we were able to keep the meat under the crust from turning gray for perfectly rosy meat throughout.

The porterhouse is a meaty beast. The combination of a flavorful, fat-marbled strip steak and a buttery tenderloin attached to (and separated by) a great big bone is grand, expansive, and expensive—a fresh alternative to the traditional holiday roast. But with stakes this high, I knew that I needed a foolproof method to make sure I got my money's worth and to give Christmas dinner its due.

To serve eight hungry people, I'd need two 3-pound steaks, each about 2 inches thick. Cooking steaks this thick presents a serious challenge for the home cook: By the time you've given it enough heat to create a good crust and the center of the steak is a nice medium-rare, the outer edges of the meat are overcooked, with an unappetizing band of pallid gray meat.

For most boneless steaks, the test kitchen has found a way to prevent the gray band: We lay them on a wire rack set in a rimmed baking sheet and then roast them in a low, 275-degree oven before searing them in a ripping-hot pan to create a crust. The slow roasting gradually brings the steaks up to temperature, allowing for even cooking with no gray band; because the steaks are elevated on the rack, hot air can circulate all around them. This method also dries the steaks' exterior so that the final searing happens fast and furiously, further reducing the chance of overcooking.

I quickly realized that the first part of this method worked great with my big bone-in steaks (especially when I positioned them with the more delicate tenderloin portions facing each other in the center of the rack, where they were slightly insulated and thus cooked more gently than the more resilient strip portions that were positioned on the hotter outer part of the rack), but the wheels came off during the searing step.

The problem was that the meat shrank away from the bone while it was in the oven, which meant the bone now protruded beyond the surface of the meat. This prevented the full surface of each side of the steaks from coming into direct contact with the hot pan when I tried to sear them. Not good: If the steaks weren't able to lie flat against the skillet, there's no way they'd get a good, hard sear. I tried broiling the steaks in the oven as an alternative to pan searing, but it took much too long to develop a decent crust, meaning that I risked overcooking the interior, or worse, inviting the ugly gray band back into the meat. I'd have to find a different way to create a dark, delicious crust in the skillet.

I took a deep breath and a step back to reconsider the process. If all the meat wasn't coming into direct contact with the heat of the pan (because the bone was in the way), then maybe I could bring the heat to the steak. But how?

By adding more oil, that's how. Oil is a perfect heat conductor; if I could use it to create a bridge between the hot pan and the roasted steaks, I'd have a win. Jumping from 1 to 3 tablespoons of vegetable oil in

THICK-CUT PORTERHOUSE STEAKS

the skillet—turning the process into a kind of hybrid sear and pan-fry—was the fix that produced a nice, even crust on these big steaks. For good measure, I also seared the steaks on their curved edges for a few minutes to crisp some of the exterior fat.

I was feeling pretty confident about my porterhouse steaks, and they certainly looked spectacular, but my scrupulous tasters would have the final say. It wasn't easy to let the steaks rest for about 10 minutes (an essential step to prevent the meat from being dry on the plate), so I occupied myself by whipping up a quick batch of the test kitchen's easy, elegant Blender Béarnaise Sauce (recipe follows). Hey, this was a holiday dinner, after all.

I carved the steaks, first separating the two sides of meat from the bone and then cutting the pieces cross-wise into strips, and called over my hungry colleagues. The steaks were a picture-perfect medium-rare, pink on the inside with a gorgeous, even mahogany crust, and the sauce was creamy, herby, and flavorful. The combination was a huge hit. With a steak this special, it's quite possible that my family will never go back to roast beef for our Christmas dinner.

—MORGAN BOLLING, *Cook's Country*

Thick-Cut Porterhouse Steaks

SERVES 8

Porterhouse steaks have a bone dividing the smaller tenderloin and the larger strip. We use kosher salt because it's easy to sprinkle evenly over the meat. Let the oil heat in the pan until it is just smoking before adding the steaks. If serving with béarnaise sauce, make the sauce while the steaks rest.

- 2 (2½- to 3-pound) porterhouse steaks, 2 inches thick, trimmed
  Kosher salt and pepper
- 3 tablespoons vegetable oil

1. Adjust oven rack to middle position and heat oven to 275 degrees. Set wire rack in aluminum foil–lined rimmed baking sheet. Pat steaks dry with paper towels and season liberally with salt and pepper. Place steaks side by side on prepared rack with tenderloins facing center, about 1 inch apart. Transfer steaks to oven. Cook until thermometer inserted sideways 3 inches from tip of strip side of steak registers 115 to 120 degrees (for

medium-rare), 70 to 90 minutes, rotating sheet halfway through cooking.

2. Pat steaks dry with paper towels. Heat oil in 12-inch skillet over high heat until just smoking. Place 1 steak in skillet and sear until well browned, about 2 minutes per side, lifting occasionally to redistribute oil. Using tongs, stand steak upright to sear edges, 1 to 2 minutes. Return steak to wire rack, tent loosely with foil, and repeat with remaining steak. Let steaks rest for 10 minutes.

3. Transfer steaks to carving board. Carve strip steaks and tenderloins from bones. Place T-bones on platter. Slice steaks thin against grain, then reassemble sliced steaks on both sides of bones. Season with salt and pepper to taste. Serve.

Blender Béarnaise Sauce

MAKES 1¼ CUPS

When making the béarnaise with an immersion blender, we prefer to make it in a 2-cup liquid measuring cup, but another container of equal volume and diameter will also work. It's important to make sure the butter is still hot (about 180 degrees) so that the egg yolks cook sufficiently.

- ½ cup white wine vinegar
- 2 sprigs fresh tarragon, plus 1½ tablespoons minced
- 1 shallot, sliced thin
- 3 large egg yolks
- 1½ teaspoons lemon juice
  Salt
  Pinch cayenne pepper, plus extra for seasoning
- 16 tablespoons unsalted butter, melted and still hot
  Hot water

1. Bring vinegar, tarragon sprigs, and shallot to simmer in small skillet over medium heat. Cook until vinegar is reduced to about 2 tablespoons, 5 to 7 minutes; remove from heat. Using fork, discard shallot slices and tarragon sprigs.

2A. FOR A BLENDER: Process egg yolks, lemon juice, ¼ teaspoon salt, cayenne, and vinegar mixture in blender until frothy, about 10 seconds. With blender running, slowly drizzle in hot butter until fully emulsified, about 2 minutes.

2B. FOR AN IMMERSION BLENDER: Combine egg yolks, lemon juice, ¼ teaspoon salt, cayenne, and vinegar mixture in 2-cup liquid measuring cup. Add hot butter. Quickly place blender in bottom of cup and blend until sauce begins to emulsify. Slowly pull blender toward surface until sauce is fully emulsified, about 30 seconds.

3. Stir in minced tarragon. Adjust consistency with hot water as needed, 1 teaspoon at a time, until sauce slowly drips from spoon. Season with salt and extra cayenne to taste.

MEXICAN-STYLE GRILLED STEAK (CARNE ASADA)

✔ **WHY THIS RECIPE WORKS:** To create a recipe for a carne asada platter that satisfies like those found in Mexico, we started with skirt steak. Since it's most tender and juicy when cooked to medium, it allowed us to create plenty of char on its exterior without overcooking it. We eschewed the standard lime juice marinade in favor of a dry salting to promote faster browning on the grill and then gave the steak a squeeze of fresh lime before serving. To speed up charring even more and create a large enough area of concentrated heat to cook all four steaks at once, we cut the bottom from a disposable aluminum roasting pan and used it to corral the coals. For heady garlic flavor, we treated the cooked steaks like bruschetta, rubbing their rough crusts with a smashed garlic clove. Red chile salsa and refried beans completed our platter.

Carne asada began as a plate of seared strips of lime-and-salt-seasoned beef jerky, folded enchiladas, beans, and queso fresco. At some point a fresh grilled or seared steak was swapped in and the number of sides was upped. Thus *carne asada de Tampico* was born.

For my version, I wanted to stick close to the original while keeping it approachable to the home cook. A juicy, thin, well-charred steak was a must, and I settled on two extras: salsa and some quick refried beans.

Mexican cookbooks were divided on the best cut for the job. Some went the thriftier route, calling for chuck roast, but pricier tenderloin and strip steak appeared, too. I tested them all, marinated in salt and lime juice and grilled until charred. Inexpensive chuck may have been ideal for the jerky version, but its tough connective tissue and pockets of sinew and fat made it a flop for the update. Supertender steaks didn't fare much better. While I wasn't cooking any of the steaks

to well-done as a number of traditional recipes suggested, to get good charring on a thin steak, medium was the most realistic goal. Cooked to this degree, both tenderloin and strip were inevitably dry and mealy. Flank steak was better, but it was hard to pound thin enough, so it also fell out of the running.

Left at the top of the heap were skirt steak and sirloin steak tips. Not only do these cuts have a beefier flavor, but because of their muscle structure, they were tender when grilled to medium. In the end, skirt steak won out for both flavor and texture, and since it's inherently thin, all I needed to do was give it a few good whacks with a meat pounder.

Next I focused on the marinade. Purist recipes call for lime juice and maybe salt. Outside this circle, recipes went to the other extreme, calling for everything from wine, herbs, and garlic to cumin, chiles, and even soy sauce. I tried every combination that I found. The verdict? Steaks bathed in unexpected ingredients like red wine and soy sauce garnered few fans. My tasters liked simple—though not dead simple. While salt and lime alone were OK, a little warmth from cumin and sharpness from garlic were welcome. A 45-minute soak allowed the salt to penetrate the meat, helping make it more tender and juicy, but any longer and the acidic mixture broke down the structure and made the meat mushy. When the time was up, I removed the steaks from the marinade, patted them dry, and fired up the grill.

For the grill setup, I needed a ripping-hot fire to ensure that the meat charred well before the interior overcooked. Loading a chimney starter full of coals (about 6 quarts of charcoal briquettes) was essential. First I tried steeply banking the coals on one side to put concentrated heat close to the cooking grate, but with the coals packed into such a small footprint, I couldn't cook more than one steak at a time. I needed coals mounded into a relatively thick layer for intense heat but spread out just enough to cook all the steaks at once. Arranging them just so was too fussy; I needed something to corral the coals.

A disposable aluminum roasting pan seemed like just the answer, but even when I punched numerous holes in the bottom to allow for airflow, the heat was tempered too much. I eventually grabbed kitchen shears and cut the bottom out, leaving just the pan collar to contain the coals. This setup delivered the fastest browning yet—about 4 minutes per side—but I still ended up with overcooked meat. I had a hunch that my marinade might be part of the problem.

In order for browning to kick into high gear, the surface of a steak must dry out. The soaking step was introducing unwanted moisture, so I ditched the marinade and instead treated the steaks to a dry rub of salt, cumin, and minced garlic. I also refrigerated them uncovered on a wire rack for 45 minutes to further encourage a dry exterior before grilling. These steaks browned and crisped in record time—just longer than 2 minutes per side—leaving the interior moist and tender. To work in the lime flavor, I simply gave the grilled steaks a squeeze of citrus before serving. This all worked great, except that without added moisture the garlic in the rub burned. So I stole a technique often used for bruschetta: I took a smashed garlic clove and rubbed it over the steaks' charred crusts after they came off the grill. This simple step brought a burst of fresh garlic flavor and aroma to the meat.

Many carne asada recipes call for a tomatillo salsa, but it was the versions that had a red chile salsa that really stuck with me. The chiles' fruity, slightly smoky flavor added incredible depth to the steak. I started by toasting dried guajillo chiles—which have the right bright, slightly tangy flavor with a hint of heat—in a hot skillet before grinding them in a blender. From there I added a can of fire-roasted diced tomatoes, water, garlic, vinegar, oregano, pepper, clove, cumin, and salt.

Finally, no carne asada platter would be complete without beans. I opted for creamy refried beans over the brothy boiled kind. A quick homemade version with canned pinto beans, onion, garlic, and rich meaty depth from bacon was easy to prepare and tasted far superior to the canned stuff. My recipe was streamlined and simple since I could prepare the salsa and beans in the time the meat sat in the refrigerator. Combined with the juicy, perfectly charred steak, this was carne asada that lived up to the Mexico City favorite.

—DAN SOUZA, *Cook's Illustrated*

Mexican-Style Grilled Steak (Carne Asada)

SERVES 4 TO 6

Two pounds of sirloin steak tips, also sold as flap meat, may be substituted for the skirt steak. Serve with Red Chile Salsa and Simple Refried Beans (recipes follow).

- 2 teaspoons kosher salt
- ¾ teaspoon ground cumin
- 1 (2-pound) skirt steak, trimmed, pounded ¼ inch thick and cut with grain into 4 equal steaks
- 1 (13 by 9-inch) disposable aluminum roasting pan (if using charcoal)
- 1 garlic clove, peeled and smashed
  Lime wedges

1. Combine salt and cumin in small bowl. Sprinkle salt mixture evenly over both sides of steaks. Transfer steaks to wire rack set in rimmed baking sheet and refrigerate, uncovered, for at least 45 minutes or up to 24 hours.

2A. FOR A CHARCOAL GRILL: Use kitchen shears to remove bottom of disposable pan and discard, reserving pan collar. Open bottom vent completely. Light large chimney starter filled with charcoal briquettes (6 quarts). When top coals are partially covered with ash, place disposable pan collar in center of grill over bottom vent and pour coals into even layer in collar. Set cooking grate in place, cover, and open lid vent completely. Heat grill until hot, about 5 minutes.

2B. FOR A GAS GRILL: Turn all burners to high, cover, and heat grill until hot, about 15 minutes. Leave all burners on high.

3. Clean and oil cooking grate. Place steaks on grill (if using charcoal, arrange steaks over coals in collar) and cook, uncovered, until well browned on first side, 2 to 4 minutes. Flip steaks and continue to cook until well browned on second side and meat registers

---

NOTES FROM THE TEST KITCHEN

MEDIUM-RARE? NOT WITH THIS STEAK

Cooking most steaks to 125 degrees, or medium-rare, delivers the juiciest, most tender results. But skirt steak is one exception. When a piece of beef is heated, its muscle fibers shrink in width, separating them from one another and making them easier to chew. For cuts like strip steak, which have comparatively thin fibers, the amount of shrinking, and thus tenderizing, that occurs when the meat is cooked to 125 degrees is sufficient. But skirt steak has wider muscle fibers that need to shrink further, and thus require cooking to 130 degrees, before they are acceptably tender.

However, this tenderizing effect doesn't continue the more you cook the steak. Once any cut of meat hits 140 degrees, muscle fibers begin to shrink not just in width but also in length, and that causes the meat to toughen again. This lengthwise shrinking also squeezes out juices, which means your steak will end up not just tough but also dry.

130 degrees, 2 to 4 minutes longer. Transfer steaks to carving board, tent loosely with aluminum foil, and let rest for 5 minutes.

4. Rub garlic thoroughly over 1 side of steaks. Slice steaks against grain into ¼-inch-thick slices and serve with lime wedges.

Red Chile Salsa
MAKES 2 CUPS

Our favorite brand of fire-roasted tomatoes is DeLallo. Serve the salsa alongside the steak.

- 1¼ ounces dried guajillo chiles, wiped clean
- 1 (14.5-ounce) can fire-roasted diced tomatoes
- ¾ cup water
- ¾ teaspoon salt
- 1 garlic clove, peeled and smashed
- ½ teaspoon white vinegar
- ¼ teaspoon dried oregano
- ⅛ teaspoon pepper
  - Pinch ground clove
  - Pinch ground cumin

Toast guajillos in 10-inch nonstick skillet over medium-high heat until softened and fragrant, 1 to 2 minutes per side. Transfer to large plate and, when cool enough to handle, remove stems and seeds. Place guajillos in blender and process until finely ground, 60 to 90 seconds, scraping down sides of blender jar as needed. Add tomatoes and their juice, water, salt, garlic, vinegar, oregano, pepper, clove, and cumin to blender and process until very smooth, 60 to 90 seconds, scraping down sides of blender jar as needed. (Salsa can be stored in the refrigerator for up to 5 days or frozen for up to 1 month.)

Simple Refried Beans
MAKES ABOUT 1½ CUPS

- 2 slices bacon
- 1 small onion, chopped fine
- 2 garlic cloves, minced
- 1 (15-ounce) can pinto beans (do not rinse)
- ¼ cup water
  - Kosher salt

Heat bacon in 10-inch nonstick skillet over medium-low heat until fat renders and bacon crisps, 7 to 10 minutes, flipping bacon halfway through. Remove bacon and reserve for another use. Increase heat to medium, add onion to fat in skillet, and cook until lightly browned, 5 to 7 minutes. Add garlic and cook until fragrant, about 30 seconds. Add beans and their liquid and water and bring to simmer. Cook, mashing beans with potato masher, until mixture is mostly smooth, 5 to 7 minutes. Season with salt to taste, and serve.

ROSEMARY-GARLIC TOP SIRLOIN ROAST

WHY THIS RECIPE WORKS: We took a relatively humble sirloin roast and transformed it into an elegant holiday meal with a few simple refinements. Cutting the large, oddly shaped roast in half and then tying it along its length gave us two round, attractive cylinders that cooked through in just 2 hours (half of the time a prime rib would require). Salting the roasts overnight seasoned them well and helped keep them moist during cooking, while roasting them in a low 225-degree oven avoided overcooking the exterior before the interior cooked through. We took a three-step approach to creating a flavorful, attractive exterior. We first seared the roasts on all sides after their long salting and then coated them with an aromatic garlic, anchovy, herb, and olive oil paste. Finishing the roasts with a brief stint in a 500-degree oven deepened the paste's color and flavor and helped crisp it for contrasting texture.

In many families, "holiday roast" means one thing: prime rib. It's a great cut of meat and it's a knockout for presentation, but it's also a budget-buster and takes literally half a day if you want to cook it right. This year, I wanted to serve a roast that would be gentle on the wallet and not too time-consuming, but I didn't want to make sacrifices. My roast had to have a rich, beefy flavor and a tender, juicy interior. And, of course, it would have to present well at the table.

To meet my goal, I knew exactly where I should start: the sirloin. The particular cut that I had in mind was the boneless top sirloin center-cut roast. It has plenty of beefy flavor, a reasonable amount of marbling, and an impressively tender texture. And at about $8 per pound, it filled most of my requirements.

ROSEMARY-GARLIC TOP SIRLOIN ROAST

That said, the top sirloin roast also has its share of flaws—which explains why it can be had on the cheap. First, it has an irregular profile, with two sides that slope and one that tapers into a narrower end, and it can be quite large, as much as 8 inches in diameter. That's fine if you are serving it for more run-of-the-mill entertaining, but these two traits make for less-than-beautiful, overly large slices. Second, this sirloin roast lacks a fat cap, which means it's frequently dry and doesn't brown as readily. Still, the pros were so promising that I knew this would be a holiday roast that could hold its own if I could just deal with the cons.

The shape problem, I realized, had a reasonably easy solution: Divide and conquer. Slicing a top sirloin center-cut roast in half down the center, following the grain, yielded two roasts with more compact profiles. Tying them with kitchen twine every few inches turned them into almost perfectly round, attractive cylinders that were a much more reasonable 4 inches across.

From here, I followed a basic cooking method. I salted the two roasts and let them sit for a day in the refrigerator, uncovered, to season the meat and ensure maximum juiciness. This also caused the exteriors to dry out, which would encourage browning. The next day I placed the roasts on a wire rack set in a baking sheet, and roasted them in a 225-degree oven. I pulled the roasts from the oven when they were just shy of medium-rare at the center. The roasts rested while I waited for the oven to preheat to 500 degrees and then went back in the oven for 10 minutes to brown and develop both flavor and visual appeal.

This first attempt wasn't bad at all. The roasts were juicy and tender and had great beefy flavor, and I was pleased to find that the narrow shape allowed them to reach medium-rare in less than 2 hours (a far cry from prime rib's 4-plus hours). That said, while a high-heat finish might be a great way to brown a prime rib or pork rib roast, it wasn't doing much for my top sirloin.

The fat cap on roasts like prime rib will readily brown in a hot oven, but these roasts—without any sort of fat cap—had barely a hint of browning in the 10 minutes I'd given them at 500 degrees. Roasting them longer eventually produced some appreciable browning but also created a substantial band of gray overcooked meat just beneath the surface.

A more effective approach was to quickly sear the roasts on all sides in a hot skillet before tying them and cooking them through, since searing them cold, rather than after they were cooked, helped minimize overcooking. This somewhat deepened the meaty flavor and improved the appearance, but still, top sirloin roast couldn't match a prime rib, whose fat cap isn't just visually pleasing but also adds richness and crisps up beautifully.

Adding a substantial amount of fat to the roasts myself—rubbing them liberally with either oil or butter before cooking—helped a little but not enough. These roasts needed something that would contribute to an elegant appearance and add flavor along with some textural contrast. What could achieve all three? I hoped the answer was a paste.

I started by reaching for a few intensely flavored kitchen staples: a handful of garlic cloves, since they would provide flavor and also give some substance to the paste; a half-dozen anchovy fillets, just enough to lend an umami meatiness without contributing noticeable fishiness; rosemary; and red pepper flakes. I processed the ingredients plus ¼ cup of olive oil to a smooth paste in the food processor. I followed the same salting and cooking procedure as before, but this time when the roasts were resting, I spread the paste evenly over their exteriors. I came back around to the idea of a 10-minute high-heat finish, this time not with the goal of browning the meat but instead browning the paste. In terms of flavor, the results weren't bad, but it fell a bit flat. The paste also didn't brown particularly well, which meant it looked somewhat drab and wasn't adding any contrasting texture. Six anchovies and four garlic cloves may not seem like much, but I realized that their added moisture was the likely culprit.

I considered sautéing the paste to remove that moisture, but with my goal of keeping things easy in mind, I tried a simpler approach first. I applied the paste to the roasts before they went into the 225-degree oven. This was just the answer. The paste slowly dried out during the 2-hour cooking time, and once it hit the 500-degree oven, it quickly browned. A bite confirmed I'd hit the bull's-eye. The paste not only added texture and visual appeal but also had a more concentrated, complex flavor.

With their flavorful, attractive coating and tender, juicy interiors, these elegant roasts had it all—except of course for time-consuming steps and a hefty price tag.

—ANDREW JANJIGIAN, *Cook's Illustrated*

Rosemary-Garlic Top Sirloin Roast

SERVES 8 TO 10

This recipe requires refrigerating the salted meat for at least 24 hours before cooking. The roast, also called a top sirloin roast, top butt roast, center-cut roast, spoon roast, shell roast, or shell sirloin roast, should not be confused with a whole top sirloin butt roast or top loin roast. Do not omit the anchovies; they provide great depth of flavor with no overt fishiness. Monitoring the roast with a meat-probe thermometer is best. If you use an instant-read thermometer, open the oven door as little as possible and remove the roast from the oven to take its temperature.

- 1 (5- to 6-pound) boneless top sirloin center-cut roast
- 2 tablespoons kosher salt
- 4 teaspoons plus ¼ cup extra-virgin olive oil
- 3 tablespoons chopped fresh rosemary
- 4 garlic cloves, minced
- 6 anchovy fillets, rinsed and patted dry
- 1 teaspoon pepper
- ¼ teaspoon red pepper flakes
  Coarse sea salt

1. Cut roast lengthwise along grain into 2 equal pieces. Rub 1 tablespoon kosher salt over each piece. Transfer to large plate and refrigerate, uncovered, for at least 24 hours or up to 4 days.

2. Adjust oven rack to middle position and heat oven to 225 degrees. Heat 2 teaspoons oil in 12-inch skillet over high heat until just smoking. Brown 1 roast on all sides, 6 to 8 minutes. Return browned roast to plate. Repeat with 2 teaspoons oil and remaining roast. Let cool for 10 minutes.

3. While roasts cool, process rosemary, garlic, anchovies, and remaining ¼ cup oil in food processor until smooth paste forms, about 30 seconds, scraping down sides of bowl as needed. Add pepper and pepper flakes and pulse to combine, 2 to 3 pulses.

4. Using 5 pieces of kitchen twine per roast, tie each roast crosswise at equal intervals into loaf shape. Transfer roasts to wire rack set in rimmed baking sheet and rub roasts evenly with paste.

5. Roast until meat registers 125 degrees for medium-rare or 130 degrees for medium, 2 to 2¼ hours. Remove roasts from oven, leaving on wire rack, and tent loosely with aluminum foil; let rest for at least 30 minutes or up to 40 minutes.

6. Heat oven to 500 degrees. Remove foil from roasts and cut and discard twine. Return roasts to oven and cook until exteriors of roasts are well browned, 6 to 8 minutes.

7. Transfer roasts to carving board. Slice meat ¼ inch thick. Season with sea salt to taste, and serve.

VARIATIONS

Coffee-Chipotle Top Sirloin Roast

Omit rosemary and red pepper flakes. Add 1 tablespoon ground coffee, 1 tablespoon minced canned chipotle chile in adobo sauce, 2 teaspoons ground coriander, 2 teaspoons paprika, 1 teaspoon unsweetened cocoa powder, and 1 teaspoon ground mustard to food processor with oil in step 3.

Fennel-Coriander Top Sirloin Roast

Omit rosemary and red pepper flakes. Add 2 teaspoons ground fennel, 2 teaspoons ground coriander, 2 teaspoons paprika, and 1 teaspoon dried oregano to food processor with oil in step 3.

SMOKED BEEF TENDERLOIN

✓ **WHY THIS RECIPE WORKS:** To get a well-seasoned, evenly smoked, medium-rare beef tenderloin, we started by trimming a whole tenderloin ourselves, tied it for even cooking, and then hit the roast with a fresh herb salt to absorb flavor from the seasoning overnight. Then we oiled the roast, seared it over high heat, and slow-cooked it for 30 minutes to allow the wood smoke flavor to permeate the meat. We finished the thicker end of the roast over the hotter side of the grill for even cooking. To enhance the herb flavor and to complement the smoky meat, we made a quick dressing with freshly grill-smoked scallions.

Here's a little secret about a whole beef tenderloin: Because it has a relatively uniform shape once trimmed and tied—unlike, say, a turkey or a bone-in rib roast—this large cut is a cinch to cook evenly. All you have to do is season and sear it well, cook it gently, and make sure you don't overcook it (it's a very expensive piece of meat, after all). It's also easy to carve, since there is little fat and no bones to navigate. These are significant advantages for a cut of meat that, as fans of filet mignon know, has a buttery texture that is as tender as it gets.

So, what's its downside? Flavor. Beef tenderloin is a mild-tasting cut (and that's putting it mildly). My move this round: to ramp up the flavor by smoking the roast on the grill. The test kitchen has grilled whole tenderloins before, but adding smoke was uncharted territory. Drawing on past test kitchen experience, I knew I'd start with a trimmed tenderloin, which has the small, fatty side muscle—the "chain," in butcherspeak—and the chewy silverskin removed. I tucked the narrow end under to create a uniform shape and tied the roast with kitchen twine at 1-inch intervals. Then I hit it aggressively with salt and pepper and let the roast sit with the seasoning for 2 hours (it would be fine for up to 24 hours) so that the salt could work its way deep inside the roast.

I prepared a two-level fire on the grill and then wrapped some soaked wood chips in a foil packet and laid it on the hot coals. Once the chips were smoking, I followed our past grilling method and seared the roast directly over the smoldering chips until it was nice and brown on all sides. Then I moved the beef to the cooler side of the grill so that it could finish cooking evenly in the smoky, gentle heat. I took the roast off the grill when the center reached 125 degrees

(for medium-rare) and let it rest for 30 minutes before slicing. I collected my colleagues to taste: Really good, they said, but not great. The smoke added depth and nuance, but it was a little harsh, and while the meat was well seasoned, it could use another jolt of flavor.

After some consultation with my colleagues, I realized that placing the foil packet of chips on top of the charcoal was hurting me: Because the tenderloin has such a mild flavor, this wood-chip arrangement was infusing the meat with too much smoke, giving the meat a harsh edge. I achieved a much more measured, subtle smoke flavor when I placed the packet on the bottom of the grill and then poured the hot charcoal on top. This way the smoke flavor was much less aggressive. As for other flavorings, I tested adding different herbs, spices, and other ingredients to the mix to augment, but not overwhelm, the smoke flavor. On the tested-and-rejected list were cayenne, canned chipotles in adobo, sage, steak sauce, dried porcini mushrooms, and oregano. A combination of fragrant fresh rosemary and thyme, rubbed into the salt to extract the herbs' full flavor, worked best for the initial seasoning of the beef. But I didn't want to stop there. I decided to make a sauce to serve alongside.

I simmered a healthy handful of chopped garlic in olive oil with pepper flakes and more rosemary and thyme. Then I discarded the herbs and added minced parsley, a little balsamic vinegar, pepper, and some reserved herb salt. To build layers of flavor, I used some of this potent mixture to baste the meat while it smoked, and I threw two bunches of scallions on the grill with the beef. I finely chopped the smoky scallions and stirred them into the sauce. I called my tasters again, and they couldn't believe how deeply flavored the beef now was. This recipe is poised to steal the show at your next big summer gathering.

—DIANE UNGER, *Cook's Country*

Smoked Beef Tenderloin
SERVES 12 TO 16

For the most economical choice, buy a whole, untrimmed tenderloin and trim it yourself. Note that the roast needs to sit for at least 2 hours or up to 24 hours after seasoning but before cooking. If you'd like to use wood chunks instead of wood chips when using a charcoal grill, substitute two medium wood chunks, soaked in water for 1 hour, for the wood chip packet.

SMOKED BEEF TENDERLOIN

HERB SALT

- 2 tablespoons kosher salt
- 1 tablespoon minced fresh rosemary
- 2 teaspoons minced fresh thyme

BEEF AND SCALLIONS

- 1 (6- to 7-pound) whole beef tenderloin, trimmed
- 2 bunches scallions, trimmed

  Pepper
- 1½ cups wood chips

SAUCE

- ¾ cup extra-virgin olive oil
- 6 garlic cloves, chopped
- 1 sprig fresh rosemary
- 1 sprig fresh thyme
- ¼ teaspoon red pepper flakes
- ¼ cup minced fresh parsley
- 1 tablespoon balsamic vinegar

  Kosher salt and pepper

1. FOR THE HERB SALT: Rub salt, rosemary, and thyme together in bowl using your fingers.

2. FOR THE BEEF AND SCALLIONS: Tuck tail end of tenderloin under by 2 to 4 inches to create more even shape, then tie with kitchen twine to secure. Tie remainder of tenderloin at 1-inch intervals. Sprinkle tenderloin all over with 2 tablespoons herb salt (reserve remaining herb salt in covered container for later use). Wrap tenderloin in plastic wrap and refrigerate for at least 2 hours or up to 24 hours. Tie scallions into 2 separate bunches with kitchen twine.

3. FOR THE SAUCE: Combine oil, garlic, rosemary sprig, thyme sprig, and pepper flakes in small saucepan. Bring to gentle simmer over low heat, stirring occasionally, and cook until garlic just begins to brown and herbs are fragrant, 8 to 10 minutes. Remove from heat, transfer to bowl, and let cool completely. Discard rosemary and thyme sprigs. Stir in parsley, vinegar, 1 teaspoon pepper, and 1 teaspoon reserved herb salt.

4. Brush tenderloin all over with 3 tablespoons sauce, then sprinkle with 1 tablespoon pepper. Brush scallion bunches with 1 tablespoon sauce. Reserve remaining ¾ cup sauce for serving.

5. Soak wood chips in water for 15 minutes, then drain. Using large piece of heavy-duty aluminum foil, wrap soaked wood chips in foil packet and cut several vent holes in top.

PREPARING AN UNTRIMMED TENDERLOIN

1. REMOVE CHAIN: The chain is the fatty strip that runs along the side of a tenderloin. Use a boning or chef's knife to remove it.

2. REMOVE SILVERSKIN: Insert the tip of your knife under the sinewy silverskin and then grab it and cut upward against silverskin to remove it. Use a paper towel for a better grip.

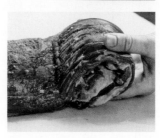

3. TIE WITH TWINE: Fold the narrow end under to make an even shape that will cook more consistently. Tie the roast at 1-inch intervals with kitchen twine.

6A. FOR A CHARCOAL GRILL: Open bottom vent halfway. Light large chimney starter three-quarters filled with charcoal briquettes (4½ quarts). Place wood chip packet on 1 side of grill. When top coals are partially covered with ash, pour evenly over half of grill on top of wood chip packet. Set cooking grate in place, cover, and open lid vent halfway. Heat grill until hot and wood chips are smoking, about 5 minutes.

6B. FOR A GAS GRILL: Remove cooking grate and place wood chip packet directly on primary burner. Set grate in place, turn all burners to high, cover, and heat grill until hot and wood chips are smoking, about 15 minutes. Leave primary burner on high and turn off other burners. (Adjust primary burner as needed to maintain grill temperature of 350 to 375 degrees).

7. Clean and oil cooking grate. Place tenderloin and scallions on hotter side of grill. Cook (covered if using gas) until scallions are lightly charred, about 3 minutes, and tenderloin is browned on first side, about 5 minutes. Flip scallions and tenderloin and continue to cook on second sides until scallions are lightly charred, about 3 minutes, and meat is browned, about 5 minutes. Transfer scallions to plate. Move tenderloin to cooler side of grill. Cover, positioning lid vent over meat, and cook for 30 minutes.

8. Move thicker part of tenderloin over hotter side of grill and continue to cook, covered, until tenderloin registers 125 degrees for medium-rare, 10 to 20 minutes longer. Transfer tenderloin to carving board, tent loosely with foil, and let rest for 30 minutes.

9. Chop scallions and stir into reserved sauce. Season with salt and pepper to taste. Remove twine and carve meat into ¼-inch-thick slices. Season meat lightly with herb salt and pepper and drizzle with sauce. Serve.

INDOOR BARBECUE BEEF SHORT RIBS

✔ **WHY THIS RECIPE WORKS:** To get the big flavors and fall-off-the-bone texture of Texas-style barbecue without spending hours tending to a smoker, we brought the operation inside. Braising the ribs in a mixture of liquid smoke, barbecue sauce, Worcestershire sauce, and coffee resulted in smoky, tender meat in 3 hours of unattended cooking. To achieve the trademark "bark" of Texas barbecue, we brushed the ribs with a barbecue sauce "glue" and applied a rub of black pepper, salt, chili powder, and brown sugar. Then we cranked the oven to 425 degrees and roasted the ribs for 30 minutes more for a flavorful, crusty exterior.

In central Texas barbecue, beef reigns supreme. Think gargantuan beef ribs, tender brisket, and, in certain circles, English-style short ribs. The block-like hunks of meat take to the pit like a duck to water, turning succulent and flavorful in the low, smoky heat. You will pay top dollar for smoked short ribs at such vaunted Texas barbecue haunts as Louie Mueller Barbecue and Franklin Barbecue—and they are worth every penny (and the interminable wait you will likely endure).

Could I get similar results on a faster timetable from the oven? I wanted authentic Texas-style results: tender meat coated with a thick, peppery "bark"—the true signifier of good 'cue.

Most recipes call for roasting the ribs and then slathering them with smoky-tasting sauce or liquid smoke. This approach works fairly well, but I wanted resonant flavor.

In a recipe search I uncovered a few unexpected ideas, including simmering the ribs with wood chips or thick slabs of bacon (neither proved effective). Most promising was a method in which the ribs were slowly braised in a seasoned liquid to tenderize and render their fat, and then drained, coated in spices, and finished in the oven. When I tried it, the ribs readily absorbed flavors from the braising liquid and the final roasting step worked well, especially when I sprinkled on a Texas-style spice crust that was heavy on the black pepper.

With a general method in hand, I pressed on. Six pounds of English-style ribs, sawed into 4- to 5-inch lengths, would serve four. Once trimmed, they fit easily into a large roasting pan. I cooked the ribs sealed tightly under foil at temperatures ranging from 250 to 400 degrees and found the best compromise between time and tenderness at 300 degrees. In 3 hours, the ribs were tender and nearly falling off the bone.

My braising liquid started out simple: water, a tablespoon of liquid smoke, and salt. It did the job, but I knew I could do better. I stuck with a base of water—beef broth surprisingly provided very little flavor enhancement—but increased the liquid smoke to a whopping ¼ cup. I added Worcestershire sauce and some bottled barbecue sauce. Brown sugar, combined with a pinch of ground clove, emphasized the smokiness. Coffee is common in barbecue sauces, and adding a few tablespoons of instant espresso powder to the braising liquid had a galvanizing effect. The ribs didn't taste of coffee, just smokier and more satisfying.

These fully seasoned, ultratender ribs were now ready for a topcoat of baked-on spice rub. Spice rubs in central Texas are traditionally kept to a minimum, usually just coarse-ground black pepper, chili powder, paprika, garlic powder, and brown sugar. I tested a handful of rubs before settling on one made from black pepper, salt, chili powder, and brown sugar (cayenne appealed to some of my tasters but left others gasping, so I'll leave that option up to you).

To get the spice rub to cling more readily, I coated the ribs with a liquid smoke–enhanced swipe of barbecue sauce before applying the rub. I found that roasting the ribs for 30 minutes at 425 degrees crisped the exterior without drying out the meat or causing the sugar in the spice rub to burn. These indoor-cooked ribs now looked like they had spent the day in a Texas smoker despite taking less than 4 hours in my oven.

—MATTHEW CARD, *Cook's Country*

ANTICIPATING SHRINKAGE

The meat on a short rib shrinks a lot during cooking, so make sure to buy ribs that are 4 to 5 inches long when raw. That way, you'll have plenty of meat on the bone when it's time to eat.

ENGLISH-STYLE SHORT RIBS
When raw, the bone is barely visible.

Indoor Barbecue Beef Short Ribs

SERVES 4 TO 6

Our favorite store-bought barbecue sauce is Bull's-Eye Original Barbecue Sauce.

    4   cups water
    ¾   cup barbecue sauce, plus extra for serving
    ¼   cup plus ½ teaspoon liquid smoke
    ¼   cup Worcestershire sauce
    5   tablespoons packed brown sugar
    2   tablespoons instant espresso powder
        Salt and pepper
    ¼   teaspoon ground cloves
    6   pounds bone-in English-style short ribs, bones
        4 to 5 inches long, 1 to 1½ inches of meat on
        top of bone, trimmed
    2   teaspoons chili powder
    ¼   teaspoon cayenne pepper (optional)

1. Adjust oven rack to middle position and heat oven to 300 degrees. Bring water, ¼ cup barbecue sauce, ¼ cup liquid smoke, Worcestershire sauce, 3 tablespoons sugar, espresso powder, 1 teaspoon salt, and cloves to boil in medium saucepan over medium-high heat. Remove from heat once boiling.

2. Arrange ribs meat side down in large roasting pan. Pour hot water mixture over ribs. Wrap pan tightly with aluminum foil and transfer to oven. Roast until ribs are easily pierced with paring knife, about 3 hours.

3. Remove pan from oven and increase oven temperature to 425 degrees. Line rimmed baking sheet with foil. Combine remaining ½ cup barbecue sauce and remaining ½ teaspoon liquid smoke in small bowl. In separate bowl, combine chili powder, cayenne, if using, 2 teaspoons pepper, 1½ teaspoons salt, and remaining 2 tablespoons sugar.

4. Place ribs meat side up on prepared sheet. Brush ribs liberally with barbecue sauce mixture, then sprinkle tops and sides with spice mixture. Roast until ribs are crispy and dark brown, about 30 minutes. Let ribs rest for 15 minutes. Serve, passing extra barbecue sauce separately.

BROILED PORK TENDERLOIN

✓ WHY THIS RECIPE WORKS: Recipes for broiled pork tenderloin promise roasts with well-browned exteriors and juicy centers but are more likely spottily browned with undercooked interiors. Using a disposable aluminum pan to cook the pork reflected the radiant heat of the broiler toward the pork, enhancing browning and ensuring that the interior didn't overcook by the time deep browning had been achieved. Since some ovens preheat faster than others and are likely to cycle off if preheated at such an intense heat for too long, we evened the playing field by preheating the oven to 325 degrees before putting in the roasts and turning on the broiler. Because of the broiler's intense heat, we found that there was a lot of carryover cooking, so we pulled the roasts from the oven when they hit 125 to 130 degrees to ensure that they were a perfect medium-rare (145 degrees) after their 10-minute rest.

The problem with most broiled pork tenderloin recipes is that they treat the broiler as a one-size-fits-all approach, when in reality no two behave exactly the same way. This became clear when I took a typical recipe for broiled pork tenderloin and made it in different ovens in the test kitchen. The results were all over the map—and none were perfect. One was beautifully browned but overcooked inside; another was burned in patches; a third came out tender and juicy inside but with an unappetizing drab gray exterior.

My goal was twofold: to create a recipe for richly browned, juicy pork tenderloin and to figure out a way to minimize differences among broilers so every oven would produce consistent results.

I began with a pair of 1-pound tenderloins. I folded the tenderloins' tail ends underneath their middles and tied the meat at 2-inch intervals to give them uniform shape. After brushing the roasts with oil and seasoning them with salt and pepper, I placed them on a baking sheet.

I knew from experience that closer to the broiler was not necessarily better. The key would be to find the position where the exterior browned evenly and the interior cooked through at roughly the same pace.

The best results came from cooking the roasts 4 to 5 inches from the broiler element. And because the broiler's intense heat was causing the roasts' internal temperature to rise 15 to 25 degrees after cooking, I pulled them from the oven when they registered 125 to 130 degrees to ensure that they reached the ideal serving temperature (145 degrees) after a 10-minute rest.

On to the next challenge: producing even and deep browning. We often use baking soda to creating an alkaline environment, therefore accelerating the Maillard reaction, which browns food and creates numerous flavor and aroma compounds in the process. For even distribution, I made a paste with just ¼ teaspoon of baking soda, salt, and a little oil. This treatment boosted browning but still wasn't enough. I couldn't get the broiler any hotter, so what else could I do?

I took a break to think more about how broilers actually work. Unlike roasting or baking, in which a heating element heats the walls of the oven, which heats the air within (a phenomenon called convection), broiling cooks food directly with invisible infrared light waves, or radiant heat. I realized that the broiler's heat waves weren't hitting just the pork but also the baking sheet, the oven racks, and the oven walls. What if I was able to direct more of those waves toward the meat?

With that in mind, I ditched the baking sheet for a disposable aluminum roasting pan. And sure enough, tenderloins broiled in it came out with beautiful browning on the top and the sides facing the reflective surface. For browning all the way around, I tried flipping the roasts halfway through broiling, but they overcooked. In the end, I found that deeply browning just the top of each roast achieved decent flavor. It seemed like a good point at which to try my recipe out under some other broilers.

Not at all surprisingly, many had subpar browning by the time they were cooked through. After poring over a stack of oven manuals, I pinpointed the source of the problem. Every manual had a different recommendation for preheating the broiler, from as long as 8 minutes to as few as 2 minutes.

Broilers that were preheated for too long were likely shutting off midway through cooking. This is because most ovens these days are designed with a built-in maximum temperature (typically around 550 degrees). Once the air temperature rises beyond that point, the oven (and broiler) will automatically turn off, wait for the temperature to drop, and then turn back on again. Because the broiler was also heating up the air in the oven, this would mean that the meat could continue to cook in the residual heat (by convection)—but it wouldn't continue to brown under radiant heat from the broiler.

I could err on the side of caution and preheat the broiler for only a minute or two—but slower-to-heat broilers would still give me roasts that weren't browned enough. I suddenly had a radical thought: What if I preheated the oven first and then switched on the broiler and slid in the meat? This would preheat the oven and also heat the broiler, which would narrow the jump the broiler had to make to fully come up to temperature. I settled on 325 degrees: Any higher and the ovens might still cycle on and off during broiling.

I preheated several ovens as I prepped more pork and then put the meat into the oven and switched on the broilers. I suspected that my new method was so effective that I would be able to brown the meat on both sides. After 5 minutes, I flipped the roasts and then removed them once they reached 125 to 130 degrees. Happily, every roast boasted rich browning—plus they were all equally tender and juicy.

—LAN LAM, *Cook's Illustrated*

Broiled Pork Tenderloin

SERVES 4 TO 6

We prefer natural pork, but if you use enhanced pork (injected with a salt solution), reduce the salt in step 2 to 1½ teaspoons. A 3-inch-deep aluminum roasting pan is essential. Do not attempt this recipe with a drawer broiler. If you like, serve the pork with our Sun-Dried Tomato and Basil Salsa (recipe follows).

- 2 (1-pound) pork tenderloins, trimmed
- 2 teaspoons kosher salt
- 1¼ teaspoons vegetable oil
- ½ teaspoon pepper
- ¼ teaspoon baking soda
- 1 (13 by 9-inch) disposable aluminum roasting pan

1. Adjust oven rack 4 to 5 inches from broiler element and heat oven to 325 degrees. Fold thin tip of each tenderloin under about 2 inches to create uniformly shaped roasts. Tie tenderloins crosswise with kitchen twine at 2-inch intervals, making sure folded tip is secured underneath. Trim excess twine close to meat to prevent it from scorching under broiler.

2. Mix salt, oil, and pepper in small bowl until salt is evenly coated with oil. Add baking soda and stir until well combined. Rub mixture evenly over pork. Place tenderloins in disposable pan, evenly spaced between sides of pan and each other.

3. Turn oven to broil. Immediately place meat in oven and broil tenderloins for 5 minutes. Flip tenderloins and continue to broil until golden brown and meat registers 125 to 130 degrees, 8 to 14 minutes. Remove disposable pan from oven, tent loosely with aluminum foil, and let rest for 10 minutes. Remove twine, slice tenderloins into ½-inch-thick slices, and serve.

Sun-Dried Tomato and Basil Salsa
MAKES ABOUT 1 CUP

We like the sweet flavor and pliable texture of oil-cured sun-dried tomatoes.

- ¼ **cup oil-packed sun-dried tomatoes, rinsed and chopped fine**
- ¼ **cup chopped fresh basil**
- ¼ **cup chopped fresh parsley**
- ¼ **cup extra-virgin olive oil**
- 2 **tablespoons balsamic vinegar**
- 1 **small shallot, minced**
- **Salt and pepper**

Combine all ingredients in bowl and season with salt and pepper to taste.

NOTES FROM THE TEST KITCHEN

AVOID OVERCOOKING
As the roasts rest, their internal temperature rises 10 to 15 degrees more than it would in a typical roasting recipe. For the ideal 145-degree serving temperature, take them out of the oven when they hit about 125 degrees.

SMOKY PULLED PORK ON A GAS GRILL

✓ **WHY THIS RECIPE WORKS:** It's often difficult to imbue pulled pork with rich, smoky flavor when cooking on a gas grill. We started by cutting our pork butt into three pieces to increase the surface area that the smoke could cling to. After salting the pork overnight, we took it directly from the fridge to the grill: The meat's cool temperature allowed more smoke to condense onto its surface. Instead of inundating the meat with smoke at the beginning, we got the most out of the wood chips by soaking half of them in water to delay when they began to smoke. We fashioned foil packets that were the right size and shape to sit on the grill, with just the right size and number of openings to allow in enough oxygen so that the chips smoldered, but not so much that they caught fire. Finally, we stirred together a bright and spicy vinegar sauce that highlighted the pungent smoke flavors of our pulled pork.

As barbecue purists will tell you, it's hard—if not impossible—to produce the same quality of smoke on a gas grill as you can over charcoal. But this year, on behalf of those who embrace convenience (or simply don't have a charcoal grill), I decided to challenge the assumption that a gas grill is an inferior choice for smoking meat. The only ground rule I set for myself: I would not resort to cheating by using liquid smoke or any presmoked material (such as smoked tea leaves).

I started by trimming a 5-pound pork butt roast of excess fat, and then I cut it into thirds. This would not only lessen the cooking time (which is usually about 7 hours) but also increase the number of surfaces that smoke could cling to. I decided to sprinkle on just salt to make it easier to assess smoke flavor. I rubbed on plenty, wrapped the pieces tightly in plastic wrap, and left them to sit overnight in the refrigerator. This would give the meat time to absorb the salt, seasoning it and changing its protein structure so that it could retain more of its juices during cooking.

The next day, I moved out to the grill. For the bulk of the cooking time, I wanted to keep the meat between 160 and 180 degrees, the range in which the connective tissue will slowly break down. A couple of water-filled pie plates under the cooking grate would catch any juices that dripped and prevent them from burning.

The plates would also create a moist environment that would keep the exterior of the pork from drying out and help smoke stick to the meat. A few quick tests established a cooking time of 4 to 5 hours. With the framework settled, I was ready to face the main challenge: perfecting the smoke.

I started by taking a close look at our procedures for using wood chips on a gas grill. The goal is to get chips to smolder slowly and consistently; if they ignite and burn up quickly, some of the compounds in the wood that would normally add desired flavor to the meat instead go up in flames, and what doesn't burn off adds a sooty, acrid flavor to the food. We usually address this concern by soaking the chips in water for 15 minutes and then wrapping the soaked chips in a foil packet and poking a few holes in it to let out the smoke.

While these directions have always delivered acceptable results, they also seemed open to interpretation. One critical piece of business was to come up with a very specific set of instructions for making the packets that would ensure uniformity from cook to cook and, in turn, produce a consistent amount of smoke. When barbecuing meat over a long period of time, we have typically called for 4 cups of chips, so I settled on 4 cups of chips weighing 9½ ounces.

I divided the chips between two foil packets that I folded into 8 by 4½-inch rectangles, each of which sat nicely over the burner. I then cut two evenly spaced 2-inch slits into the foil, which produced a consistent stream of smoke. Because I was so carefully controlling the oxygen availability, soaked or not, the chips in my packets weren't going up in flames.

Knowing that I had a set amount of smoke to work with, my next question was, would it be better to use two packets of unsoaked chips, which would allow me to inundate the meat with smoke at the beginning of cooking, or would producing a smaller stream of smoke over a longer period by using one packet of soaked chips and one packet of unsoaked chips be better?

The only way to know which approach was best was to smoke some pork. I cooked one batch over two packets of dry chips, and another batch over one packet of soaked chips and one dry. The batch with one dry and one soaked packet stretched out the smoke over a longer period of time, ensuring that the pork could absorb maximum smoke gradually without off-flavors.

The results were impressively smoky, but tasters still wondered if I could boost the smokiness just a little more. Since I was at the upper limit for how much wood I could fit on the grill, I focused on finding a way to get more of the existing smoke into the meat. As it cooked, the pork was releasing juices into the water-filled pan below—juices that were infused with smoky flavor. Why should it all go to waste? When the smoke petered out after the first 1½ hours of cooking, I transferred the meat to a disposable aluminum roasting pan. This way, any juices that released during the remaining cooking time would be collected. I stirred a portion of the juices back into the meat after shredding it.

I also wondered if there was a way to get more smoke to cling to the meat, instead of letting it escape through the vents and into the air. A coworker noted that my clothes actually smelled smokier on cold days. She was onto something: On cooler days, the surface of my coat was cold, and when the smoke particles came in contact with it, they quickly changed from gas to solid, thus clinging to my coat rather than drifting off into the air above. Could the same logic be applied to the pork? For my next test, instead of pulling the pork from the fridge when I headed outside to set up the grill, which caused its surface temperature to rise about 10 degrees before I set it on the grates, I waited to pull it from the fridge until I was ready to start cooking. Once this final batch was cool enough to handle, I shredded the meat and waited for my tasters to comment. By their expressions, I could tell that with these last tweaks I'd really nailed a deep smoke flavor.

It was time to focus on the dry rub and the sauce. A mixture of paprika, brown sugar, and pepper rubbed onto the pork along with the salt added depth without taking over and also provided some color and helped create an appealing bark-like crust. As for the sauce, a combination of cider vinegar, ketchup, brown sugar, and red pepper flakes cut cleanly through the pork's richness and helped amplify the smoky flavor.

I had one final test to go: I asked my tasters to compare my gas-grilled pulled pork with pulled pork made on a charcoal grill in a blind tasting. The moment of truth: Tasters unanimously agreed that my gas-grilled version boasted not just as much smoke flavor but, in fact, more. That's right, barbecue purists: more smoke flavor.

With this method, gas grill owners—or at least those who are willing to be very precise—never have to feel sheepish about making pulled pork. My pulled pork is as good and smoky as backyard barbecue gets.

—LAN LAM, *Cook's Illustrated*

SMOKY PULLED PORK ON A GAS GRILL

Smoky Pulled Pork on a Gas Grill

SERVES 8 TO 10

Pork butt roast is often labeled Boston butt in the supermarket. We developed this recipe with hickory chips, though other varieties of hardwood can be used. (We do not recommend mesquite chips.) Before beginning, check your propane tank to make sure that you have at least a half-tank of fuel. If you happen to run out of fuel, you can move the pork to a preheated 300-degree oven to finish cooking. Serve the pulled pork on white bread or hamburger buns with pickles and coleslaw.

PORK

    Kosher salt and pepper

2 teaspoons paprika

2 teaspoons packed light brown sugar

1 (5-pound) boneless pork butt roast, trimmed

9½ ounces wood chips (4 cups)

2 (9-inch) disposable aluminum pie plates

1 (13 by 9-inch) disposable aluminum roasting pan

VINEGAR SAUCE

2 cups cider vinegar

2 tablespoons ketchup

2 teaspoons packed light brown sugar

1 teaspoon red pepper flakes

1 teaspoon kosher salt

1. FOR THE PORK: Combine 5 teaspoons salt, 2½ teaspoons pepper, paprika, and sugar in small bowl. Cut pork against grain into 3 equal slabs. Rub salt mixture into pork, making sure meat is evenly coated. Wrap pork tightly in plastic wrap and refrigerate for at least 6 hours or up to 24 hours.

2. Just before grilling, soak 2 cups wood chips in water for 15 minutes, then drain. Using large piece of heavy-duty aluminum foil, wrap soaked chips in 8 by 4½-inch foil packet. (Make sure chips do not poke holes in sides or bottom of packet.) Repeat with remaining 2 cups unsoaked chips. Cut 2 evenly spaced, 2-inch slits in top of each packet.

3. Remove cooking grate and place wood chip packets directly on primary burner. Place disposable pie plates, each filled with 3 cups water, directly on other burner(s). Set grate in place, turn all burners to high, cover, and heat grill until hot and wood chips are smoking, about 15 minutes. Turn primary burner to medium and turn off other burner(s). (Adjust primary burner as needed to maintain grill temperature of 300 degrees.)

4. Clean and oil cooking grate. Place pork on cooler side of grill, directly over water pans; cover; and smoke for 1½ hours.

5. Transfer pork to disposable pan. Return disposable pan to cooler side of grill and continue to cook until meat registers 200 degrees, 2½ to 3 hours.

6. Transfer pork to carving board and let rest for 20 minutes. Pour juices from disposable pan into fat separator and let stand for 5 minutes.

7. FOR THE VINEGAR SAUCE: While pork rests, whisk all ingredients together in bowl. Using 2 forks, shred pork into bite-size pieces. Stir ⅓ cup defatted juices and ½ cup sauce into pork. Serve, passing remaining sauce separately.

NOTES FROM THE TEST KITCHEN

THE IMPORTANCE OF A JUST-SO PACKET

In the past, we've found that sealing wood chips in a foil packet with a few slits cut into it is the best method for producing smoke on a gas grill. We confirmed that that's still the case, but we also found that our directions for making a packet have been too vague. By ironing out the details, we ensure consistent, steady smoke from one packet to the next.

- Eight by 4½-inch packets hold 4.75 oz of chips, the maximum amount that will fit on the burner.
- Two 2-inch-long slits let in just enough oxygen for a steady smolder. (Be careful that the slits don't get blocked by the grate's bars.)
- Weigh the chips—don't measure by volume—since chips vary greatly in size.
- Since the pork can absorb only so much smoke at any moment, soak half of the chips to draw out the smoke over a longer period.

MU SHU PORK

✔ **WHY THIS RECIPE WORKS:** Making Mandarin pancakes—the traditional wrapper for mu shu pork filling—may sound daunting and time-consuming, but we discovered that they were remarkably easy, thanks to the hot water that we used to make the dough. Using hot water was important for two reasons: It made the dough less sticky because starches absorb hot water more quickly than cold water, and it made the dough easier to roll out because the gluten proteins relaxed and didn't snap back. While the dough rested, we prepped the pork and vegetable filling. We brined sliced pork tenderloin in soy sauce, which kept it tender and moist, while sherry, sugar, ginger, and white pepper punched up the flavor. Rehydrated shiitake mushrooms provided a pleasantly chewy texture, and their soaking liquid added depth to our stir-fry sauce. We also added cabbage and sliced bamboo shoots to bulk up the vegetable portion of the meal.

I'm happy to eat just about any pork stir-fry at a Chinese restaurant, but mu shu pork has always been my favorite, thanks to the dish's most unique element: the Mandarin pancakes. Elastic but tender and paper-thin, these wheat rounds are the ideal utensil for wrapping up the stir-fried mix of soy- and ginger-flavored pork, delicately crisp-tender shredded vegetables, and scrambled eggs. A smear of salty-sweet hoisin sauce on the pancakes bolsters its flavor.

As often as I order mu shu pork in restaurants, though, I've always hesitated to make it at home because I figured that the pancakes might be troublesome. But my skepticism turned to curiosity when I consulted a few recipes: The pancakes contained just three ingredients—water, flour, and sesame oil—and came together in less than an hour (including a half-hour of hands-off time for the dough to rest). I could definitely manage that.

The stir-fry would be a simple affair, and I stuck pretty closely to the lead of most recipes I found. I cut a pork tenderloin (its supple texture is ideal in stir-fries) into thin strips and tossed them with soy sauce, dry sherry (a widely available substitute for more traditional Chinese rice wine), and fresh ginger. I also used the same liquids (thickened with a touch of cornstarch) to whisk up a sauce. While the meat marinated, I scrambled a couple of eggs in a large, oiled nonstick skillet until they were just shy of cooked through (they'd finish

cooking when I added them back to the skillet with the sauce) and then set them aside while I stir-fried the pork, spreading the strips in a flat layer so that they would brown nicely. Beyond that, it was simply a matter of stir-frying the vegetables, adding the sauce, and then returning the proteins to the pan to warm through.

For the vegetables, authentic recipes called for just wood ear mushrooms and dried lily buds—and while my tasters and I enjoyed their pleasantly resilient chew, we found the mixture rather Spartan. (I later learned that mu shu pork is traditionally just one part of a banquet meal in which other dishes contribute the vegetable quota.) Both ingredients were also hard to come by, so I replaced them with dried shiitakes (rehydrated in hot water) and canned bamboo shoots. I also worked in shredded green cabbage and thin-sliced scallion whites.

The meat was moist and the vegetables crisp-tender, but the soy-sherry mixture lacked depth—and I wasn't convinced that a smear of hoisin would do enough to perk it up. So I made a few adjustments: In addition to seasoning the sauce with sugar and white pepper (which has clean, delicate heat), I reserved and stirred in the umami-rich shiitake soaking liquid. Finally, I got the scallion whites good and brown in the pan to tease out more flavor. Those fixes produced a stir-fry that was good enough to eat on its own—but I still had the most important element to tend to.

The traditional method for making Mandarin pancakes is to combine flour with boiling water, knead the dough, and let it rest for about 30 minutes, which gave me time to prep the stir-fry ingredients. The next step is to shape small disks, sandwich pairs of those disks together with sesame oil, and roll out the sandwiched disks really thin. Finally, when the double pancakes are cooked on each side in a hot, dry skillet, something sort of magical happens: Water in the dough turns into steam, which makes the two layers of dough easy to pull apart into paper-thin pancakes.

Even though I had doubts about the dough at first—it felt dry initially, then tackier, and finally smooth after it rested—my results were flawless. But I had questions: For one, must the water be boiling hot or could it be cool? And was there more to sandwiching the dough than just the efficiency of rolling and cooking two pancakes at once?

I had a preliminary answer to my first query when I made a new batch of dough with cool water—and found it unmanageably sticky. Kneading and then resting the dough helps give the starches time to absorb the water. And from the Play-Doh-like smoothness of the hot-water dough, I could tell that the water had been soaked up. But the tackiness of this batch suggested that the cool water wasn't being readily absorbed. I did some digging and discovered that starch soaks up hot water faster than it does cool water. Hot water also produces dough that's easier to roll out because it makes the network of proteins that give the dough structure, known as gluten, looser and thus less prone to snapping back.

As for sandwiching the pancakes, I tried rolling out individual rounds instead of double ones. The first problem: By the time they were appropriately thin, the wrappers were too delicate to pull off the counter. What's more, when I cooked each pancake on both sides, the dough dried out and lost a bit of the supple stretch it has when one side doesn't directly touch the heat.

Satisfied that I understood the mechanics of Mandarin pancakes, I prepared one last batch for a make-ahead test. Both the refrigerated and frozen pancakes revived nicely in the microwave, which meant that I could count on mu shu pork when I needed to throw together a quick weeknight stir-fry.

—ANDREA GEARY, *Cook's Illustrated*

NOTES FROM THE TEST KITCHEN

NO SUBSTITUTIONS

Don't be tempted to substitute tortillas or other wrappers for homemade Mandarin pancakes; there is no replacement for their thin, delicate, stretchy texture. Plus, the pancakes can be made well in advance and refrigerated or frozen.

PANCAKES MADE TWO BY TWO

Cooking two rounds together produces pancakes twice as fast.

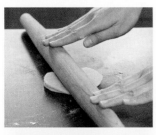

SANDWICH: Brush 6 disks with sesame oil. Top with unoiled disks. Press pairs together, then roll into thin rounds.

COOK: Heat each round until air pockets form between layers and underside is dry. Flip and cook second side.

PULL APART: When pancakes are cool enough to handle, peel apart into 2 pieces.

Mu Shu Pork

SERVES 4

We strongly recommend weighing the flour for the pancakes. For an accurate measurement of boiling water, bring a full kettle to a boil and then measure ¾ cup.

PANCAKES

- 1½ cups (7½ ounces) all-purpose flour
- ¾ cup boiling water
- 2 teaspoons toasted sesame oil
- ½ teaspoon vegetable oil

STIR-FRY

- 1 ounce dried shiitake mushrooms, rinsed
- ¼ cup soy sauce
- 2 tablespoons dry sherry
- 1 teaspoon sugar
- 1 teaspoon grated fresh ginger
- ¼ teaspoon white pepper
- 1 (12-ounce) pork tenderloin, trimmed, halved horizontally, and sliced thin against grain
- 2 teaspoons cornstarch
- 2 tablespoons plus 2 teaspoons vegetable oil
- 2 eggs, beaten
- 6 scallions, white and green parts separated and sliced thin on bias
- 1 (8-ounce) can bamboo shoots, rinsed and sliced into matchsticks
- 3 cups thinly sliced green cabbage
- ¼ cup hoisin sauce

1. FOR THE PANCAKES: Using wooden spoon, mix flour and boiling water in bowl to form rough dough. When cool, transfer dough to lightly floured surface and knead until it forms ball that is tacky but no longer sticky, about 4 minutes (dough will not be perfectly smooth). Cover loosely with plastic wrap and let rest for 30 minutes.

2. Roll dough into 12-inch-long log on lightly floured surface and cut into 12 equal pieces. Turn each piece cut side up and pat into rough 3-inch disk. Brush 1 side of 6 disks with sesame oil; top each oiled side with unoiled disk and press lightly to form 6 pairs. Roll disks into 7-inch rounds, lightly flouring work surface as needed.

3. Heat vegetable oil in 12-inch nonstick skillet over medium heat until shimmering. Using paper towels, carefully wipe out oil. Place pancake in skillet and cook without moving it until air pockets begin to form between layers and underside is dry, 40 to 60 seconds. Flip pancake and cook until few light brown spots appear on second side, 40 to 60 seconds. Transfer to plate and, when cool enough to handle, peel apart into 2 pancakes. Stack pancakes moist side up and cover loosely with plastic. Repeat with remaining pancakes. Cover pancakes tightly and keep warm. Wipe out skillet with paper towel. (Pancakes can be wrapped tightly in plastic wrap, then aluminum foil, and refrigerated for up to 3 days or frozen for up to 2 months. Thaw wrapped pancakes at room temperature. Unwrap and place on plate. Invert second plate over pancakes and microwave until warm and soft, 60 to 90 seconds.)

4. FOR THE STIR-FRY: Microwave 1 cup water and mushrooms in covered bowl until steaming, about 1 minute. Let sit until softened, about 5 minutes. Drain mushrooms through fine-mesh strainer and reserve ⅓ cup liquid. Discard mushroom stems and slice caps thin.

5. Combine 2 tablespoons soy sauce, 1 tablespoon sherry, sugar, ginger, and pepper in large bowl. Add pork and toss to combine. Whisk together reserved mushroom liquid, remaining 2 tablespoons soy sauce, remaining 1 tablespoon sherry, and cornstarch; set aside.

6. Heat 2 teaspoons oil in now-empty skillet over medium-high heat until shimmering. Add eggs and scramble quickly until set but not dry, about 15 seconds. Transfer to bowl and break eggs into ¼- to ½-inch pieces with fork. Return now-empty skillet to medium-high heat and heat 1 tablespoon oil until shimmering. Add scallion whites and cook, stirring frequently, until well browned, 1 to 1½ minutes. Add pork mixture. Spread into even layer and cook without moving until well browned on 1 side, 1 to 2 minutes.

Stir and continue to cook, stirring frequently, until all pork is opaque, 1 to 2 minutes longer. Transfer to bowl with eggs.

7. Return now-empty skillet to medium-high heat and heat remaining 1 tablespoon oil until shimmering. Whisk mushroom liquid mixture to recombine. Add mushrooms and bamboo shoots to skillet and cook, stirring frequently, until heated through, about 1 minute. Add cabbage, all but 2 tablespoons scallion greens, and mushroom liquid mixture and cook, stirring constantly, until liquid has evaporated and cabbage is wilted but retains some crunch, 2 to 3 minutes. Add pork and eggs and stir to combine. Transfer to platter and top with scallion greens.

8. Spread about ½ teaspoon hoisin in center of each warm pancake. Spoon stir-fry over hoisin and serve.

STUFFED PORK LOIN

✓ **WHY THIS RECIPE WORKS:** Stuffing pork loin with verdant herbs creates a great-looking springtime centerpiece. To give every bite of this inherently bland cut plenty of flavor, we butterflied it and coated its interior with a potent herb, caper, and Parmesan paste and then rolled and tied it up. Searing the pork loin on the stovetop before finishing it in a low 275-degree oven yielded a tender interior with a mahogany exterior crust. We used an instant-read thermometer to ensure that the meat didn't overcook. To take advantage of flavorful pan drippings, we made a quick pan sauce with chicken broth, heavy cream, and a squirt of lemon.

Pork loin can be disappointing. Lean and mild, it's too often overcooked, leading to sad suppers of dry, flavorless meat that no amount of marinade, sauce, crust, or stuffing can save. I set out to make a moist, flavorful pork loin roast that would restore my faith in this readily available cut and serve as a resplendent centerpiece for a happy gathering.

The test kitchen has been down the pork loin route before, so I had a few guidelines to help me get started. We like to pull the meat from the oven when it reaches 135 degrees, as carryover cooking will take the internal temperature to 140 degrees, at which point the pork is perfectly cooked. I made the decision to go with

HERB-STUFFED PORK LOIN

a boneless roast here, as they are easier to find and to work with than the bone-in variety. But to make it remarkable, I knew I'd have to add flavor.

I started with two beautiful boneless loin roasts. I'd need a way to deeply season them: I tested brining the pork versus rubbing it with a salt mixture and letting it sit, refrigerated, for several hours. After a few tests it became clear that salting the meat was much easier, as I didn't have to wrestle a big brine bucket in and out of the refrigerator.

Cooking the pork to the proper temperature was relatively easy; a handful of tests showed that searing the roast in a skillet on the stovetop before roasting it in a low, 275-degree oven was the surest path to perfectly cooked pork. The sear added a little of the depth of flavor that this cut so sorely needed. And the low oven temperature cooked the lean meat gently while minimizing the chance of overcooking. For an even better sear, I added a little sugar to the salt rub.

As for pairing the pork with flavorful ingredients, I started by testing different sauces to serve with the roast. After a few days of sampling sauces, my tasters whittled down the options for this springtime roast to two Italian favorites: pesto (made with olive oil, garlic, Parmesan, and basil) and *salsa verde* (consisting of parsley, anchovies, capers, and lemon). I took a little culinary liberty and combined the two into a serious but lively sauce: briny, herby, bright, and complex.

My tasters liked the sauce so much, in fact, that they wanted more of it. Could I stuff the roast with more of this bright green elixir? I tried cutting a pocket into the roast, stuffing it, and tying it up with twine; this worked OK, but the pocket didn't hold much stuffing. A better option was opening the roast like a book, pounding it to an even thickness, and smearing on a good coating of the sauce. Then I rolled up the roast, tied it to hold its shape, seared it, and put it in the oven.

Wow. Now the bright sauce seasoned the roast inside and out, imparting a wide range of flavors to every bite. Backtracking slightly, I found that butterflying the roast before rubbing on the salt/sugar mixture allowed even more of the seasoning to infuse the meat. What's more, I could do this ahead of time; the rub needs at least an hour to work its magic, but you can rub and refrigerate the roast up to a day before you cook it. I was almost done.

While waiting for my next pork loin to rest, I threw together a quick pan sauce, taking advantage of the flavorful pork drippings by cooking them down with garlic, shallot, chicken broth, and wine. I sliced into the roast and knew I was finally in business: a mahogany crust, juicy meat, a bright herby stuffing, and an easy, tasty sauce for serving.

—MORGAN BOLLING, *Cook's Country*

Herb-Stuffed Pork Loin

SERVES 8

Plan ahead: The roast must be seasoned at least 1 hour or up to 24 hours in advance. You will need an ovensafe nonstick skillet for this recipe.

- 1 (3- to 3½-pound) boneless center-cut pork loin roast
- 1 tablespoon packed brown sugar
  Kosher salt and pepper
- 6 tablespoons extra-virgin olive oil
- 8 garlic cloves (3 sliced thin, 5 unpeeled)
- 2 ounces Parmesan cheese, grated (1 cup)
- ¾ cup minced fresh parsley
- ½ cup chopped fresh basil
- ¼ cup capers, minced
- 3 anchovy fillets, rinsed and minced
- 1 teaspoon grated lemon zest plus 2 teaspoons juice
- 1 shallot, peeled and halved
- 2 sprigs fresh rosemary
- 1½ tablespoons all-purpose flour
- ¼ cup dry white wine
- 2 cups chicken broth
- ¼ cup heavy cream

1. Position roast fat side up on cutting board. Insert knife two-thirds of the way up from bottom of roast along 1 long side and cut horizontally, stopping ½ inch before edge to create flap. Open up flap. At hinge, cut down into thicker portion of roast, stopping ½ inch from bottom. Pivot knife parallel to cutting board and cut horizontally in opposite direction, stopping ½ inch before edge, to create second flap. Open up this flap and lay meat flat. If meat is of uneven thickness, cover roast

BUTTERFLYING AND STUFFING A PORK LOIN

1. OPEN: With fat side up, cut into the loin two-thirds up from the bottom, stopping ½ inch from the edge. Peel back the top flap and cut down, stopping ½ inch from the bottom.

2. FLATTEN: Now cut back into the thicker mass, again stopping ½ inch from the edge. Open up loin, flatten, season, and refrigerate for 1 to 24 hours.

3. FILL: Spread the filling evenly over the interior side, leaving a ½-inch border on all sides.

4. ROLL: Carefully roll the roast leaving the fat side up. Tie at 1-inch intervals.

CENTER-CUT LOIN ROAST

The center cut-loin roast is juicy, tender, and evenly shaped with somewhat less fat then the center-cut rib roast. Make sure to buy a center-cut roast with a decent fat cap on top.

with plastic wrap and pound to even thickness with meat pounder.

2. Combine sugar and 1 tablespoon salt in bowl. Sprinkle roast all over with sugar-salt mixture. Transfer roast to gallon-size zipper-lock bag, seal, and refrigerate for at least 1 hour or up to 24 hours.

3. Adjust oven rack to middle position and heat oven to 275 degrees. Heat ¼ cup oil and sliced garlic cloves in ovensafe 12-inch nonstick skillet over medium-high heat until garlic begins to brown slightly, about 3 minutes. Transfer garlic and oil to bowl and let cool for 5 minutes. Stir Parmesan, parsley, basil, capers, anchovies, lemon zest, and ½ teaspoon pepper into garlic oil.

4. Place roast on cutting board, cut side up. Spread herb mixture evenly over surface of roast, leaving ½-inch border on all sides. Starting from short side farthest from exterior fat cap, roll tightly, then tie with kitchen twine at 1-inch intervals. Season roast with pepper.

5. Heat remaining 2 tablespoons oil in now-empty skillet over medium-high heat until just smoking. Brown roast on all sides, about 10 minutes. Flip roast seam side down in skillet. Add shallot, rosemary sprigs, and unpeeled garlic cloves to skillet and transfer to oven. Cook until thickest part of roast registers 135 degrees, 65 to 70 minutes. Transfer roast to carving board, tent loosely with aluminum foil, and let rest for 30 minutes. Do not clean skillet.

6. Meanwhile, use spoon to smash garlic in skillet (skillet handle will be hot). Place skillet over medium-high heat and cook until shallot and garlic are sizzling. Stir in flour and cook, stirring, for 1 minute. Add wine and cook until nearly evaporated, about 2 minutes. Add broth and cream and bring to boil. Reduce heat to medium-low and simmer until sauce is reduced to about 1 cup and thickened, 10 to 12 minutes. Strain through fine-mesh strainer set over small saucepan; discard solids. Stir in lemon juice. Season with salt and pepper to taste. Cover and keep warm.

7. Discard twine and slice roast ½ inch thick. Serve, passing sauce separately.

FRENCH-STYLE PORK CHOPS WITH APPLES AND CALVADOS

✓ **WHY THIS RECIPE WORKS:** Pork and apples is a classic and familiar pairing. We turned to the French recipe for *porc à la Normande* to inspire a more elegant rendition. Using thick bone-in chops allowed us more leeway to avoid overcooking, while salting them an hour before cooking helped keep them moist. An evenly heated pan is key to a good sear on these big chops, so we heated our skillet over medium heat for a full 5 minutes before turning up the heat. Cutting the apples into attractive rings provided a bed to raise the chops off the skillet's bottom to allow for even cooking once transferred to the oven. For a sauce with layered apple flavor, we relied on a combination of sweet cider vinegar, Calvados, and a few chopped apples, which broke down and helped produce the right texture. Butter gave the sauce richness, while chicken broth and bacon lent a balancing savoriness. We found that flambéing the sauce was critical to creating an elegantly complex sauce, and doing it in two batches kept the job easy.

Dishes featuring the classic duo of pork and apples usually aren't anything special—think weeknight chops and applesauce. But porc à la Normande is a different story. A dish that has graced French tables for hundreds of years, it features an elegant presentation of pork, accompanied by sautéed apples cut into chunks, rings, or even *tournées* (oblong football shapes), while a sauce, complex with layers of apple flavor and a touch of richness, brings it all together.

When I tried a few versions, the potential and the pitfalls were clear. The pork was usually dry and the apples undercooked. Many of the sauces—the component that should really take this dish from everyday to exceptional—were too sweet and tasted flat. And every recipe required hours and an arsenal of pots. My challenge: deliver an elegant version with perfectly cooked pork and apples and a savory-rich sauce with complex apple flavor without requiring a lot of time or cookware.

The issue of dry pork starts with the selection of chops. I opted for center-cut bone-in rib chops since, unlike sirloin or blade chops, they contain just one muscle group (the loin), which makes them easier to cook evenly. Using 1-inch-thick chops would give me some leeway to help avoid overcooking, and salting the chops for an hour would help them retain their juices.

When the hour was up, I followed our protocol for cooking thick cuts: Sear on the stovetop, transfer to a wire rack set in a baking sheet, and finish in a 300-degree oven. These chops browned nicely and cooked up juicy and tender, so I moved on to the apples.

Cutting the apples into ½-inch-thick rings was clearly the way to go. Rings looked more elegant than chunks and would be easier to brown and cook through evenly (and less fussy to prepare) than tournées. I could have simply cooked the apples on the stovetop while the chops were in the oven, but I saw an opportunity for efficiency, as well as a flavor boost. Why not ditch the wire-rack-and-sheet-pan setup for the chops and instead use the apples to elevate the chops so they would cook evenly?

I browned some apple rings on one side, flipped them over, and added some chicken broth for even cooking and more flavor. Next, I placed my browned chops on top of the apples and moved the whole setup to the oven. The apples picked up fantastic meaty flavor while the chops, elevated off the skillet's bottom, cooked perfectly.

The bulk of the sauce would be made from some form of apple-y liquid. I settled on apple cider. Apple juice lacks complexity because it's filtered, while hard ciders vary greatly and pack much less apple punch. All the recipes I'd tried also included Calvados, for good reason. This apple brandy from Normandy would provide an essential woodsy apple essence. For yet another hit of fruitiness, I chopped a couple of apples and added them to the pot with the liquids. They broke down as the sauce reduced and helped give it body as well as apple flavor.

Another thing about the traditional recipes: Many of them call for flambéing the sauce, igniting it after adding the Calvados. In the past we've touted the flavor flambéing adds to a dish, but I wondered if it was really necessary here since I'd be adding a number of flavorful ingredients. I decided to skip it. I sautéed some shallots; added a glug of Calvados, followed by cider, chicken broth, and the chopped apples; and brought the sauce to a simmer. Once it had reduced to a spoon-coating consistency, I stirred in some crème fraîche for richness.

This sauce was good, but I wanted great. Cooking two slices of chopped bacon and sautéing the shallots in the rendered fat boosted the savoriness. Nutmeg and thyme lent warmth and herbal depth. And instead of the crème fraîche, which gave the sauce a muddy appearance, I whisked in butter plus cider vinegar. This sauce had a great consistency when I quickly sampled it, but come serving time, after I'd prepared the chops and apples, I hit a snag: The butter had floated to the surface instead of staying emulsified.

I could have whisked for much longer to break the butter into droplets tiny enough to stay emulsified, or I could have whisked in the butter just before serving, but I came up with an easier solution. My inspiration came from my restaurant days of making chicken and beef stock. The chef had told us to gently simmer and avoid a hard boil. If a stock bubbles too vigorously, the fat will emulsify and make the stock cloudy. What he'd advised against then was exactly what I needed now: emulsification. I made another batch, this time adding the butter along with the cider and letting the sauce reduce at a vigorous simmer. Voilà, by serving time the sauce was still picture-perfect. However, it was a little boozy and lacked complexity.

Maybe the flambé step was more important than I'd thought. Or could I get away with simply boiling the Calvados for several minutes to simulate the rapid evaporation caused by flambéing, instead of actually lighting it on fire? I ran a side-by-side test: my working recipe with a flambéing step added, and a version for which I boiled the mixture after adding the Calvados. Tasters' votes were unanimous: Both were more complex than my previous versions, but the flambéed sauce was noticeably the most complex. Adding the Calvados in two stages, flambéing after each addition, kept the height of the flames and their burning time to a minimum.

Requiring just a couple of pots and an hour and a half start to finish, the whole recipe came together pretty easily. And thanks to its little bit of French-style flair, it had moved from ordinary to impressive.

—LAN LAM, *Cook's Illustrated*

NOTES FROM THE TEST KITCHEN

FOR AN EMULSIFIED SAUCE, BREAK THE RULES
As the sauce in this recipe sits for 30 minutes while the chops and apples are prepared, butter that's simply whisked in after the sauce has been reduced (the standard procedure for most butter-enriched sauces) will separate out. To keep the butter emulsified longer, one option would have been to whisk more thoroughly to break the butter into even tinier droplets that would stay suspended for more than a few minutes. Or, we could have whisked in the butter just before serving. Instead, we came up with an even easier approach, drawing inspiration from—and then breaking—a classic French rule for making stock.

French tomes dictate that you should never allow a stock to vigorously simmer: The bubbling action can break up the fat so that it disperses throughout the liquid, turning the stock cloudy. But since breaking up the fat was what we wanted to do for our sauce, we added the butter at the start of the long reduction time and then turned up the heat to keep the sauce at a vigorous simmer. The constant agitation during the 30 minutes broke the butter into tiny droplets that stayed so well emulsified that the sauce won't break for a full hour.

WHY WE FLAMBÉ
We found that flambéing this sauce not only removes some alcohol but also makes a real difference in flavor, producing a more complex-tasting sauce through caramelization, the Maillard reaction, and changing the shape of the flavor molecules, which leads to a changed flavor perception. Adding the alcohol in two stages keeps the size of the flames manageable and shortens the amount of time it burns.

French-Style Pork Chops with Apples and Calvados
SERVES 4

We prefer natural pork, but if the pork is enhanced (injected with a salt solution), decrease the salt in step 1 to ½ teaspoon per chop. To ensure that they fit in the skillet, choose apples that are approximately 3 inches in diameter. Applejack or regular brandy can be used in place of the Calvados. Before flambéing, be sure to roll up long shirtsleeves, tie back long hair, and turn off the exhaust fan and any lit burners. Use a long match or wooden skewer to flambé the Calvados. The amount of vinegar to add in step 4 will vary depending on the sweetness of your cider.

- 4 (12- to 14-ounce) bone-in pork rib chops, 1 inch thick
  Kosher salt and pepper
- 4 Gala or Golden Delicious apples, peeled and cored
- 2 slices bacon, cut into ½-inch pieces
- 3 shallots, sliced
  Pinch ground nutmeg
- ½ cup Calvados
- 1¾ cups apple cider
- 1¼ cups chicken broth
- 4 sprigs fresh thyme, plus ¼ teaspoon minced
- 2 tablespoons unsalted butter
- 2 teaspoons vegetable oil
- ½–1 teaspoon apple cider vinegar

1. Evenly sprinkle each chop with ¾ teaspoon salt. Place chops on large plate, cover loosely with plastic wrap, and refrigerate for 1 hour.

2. While chops rest, cut 2 apples into ½-inch pieces. Cook bacon in medium saucepan over medium heat until crisp, 5 to 7 minutes. Add shallots, nutmeg, and ¼ teaspoon salt; cook, stirring frequently, until shallots are softened and beginning to brown, 3 to 4 minutes. Off heat, add ¼ cup Calvados and let warm through, about 5 seconds. Wave lit match over pan until Calvados ignites, then shake pan gently to distribute flames. When flames subside, 30 to 60 seconds, cover pan to ensure flame is extinguished, 15 seconds. Add remaining ¼ cup Calvados and repeat flambéing (flames will subside after 1½ to 2 minutes). (If you have trouble igniting second addition, return pan to medium heat, bring to bare simmer, and remove from heat and try again.) Once flames have extinguished, increase heat to medium-high; add cider, 1 cup broth, thyme sprigs, butter, and chopped apples; and bring to rapid simmer. Cook, stirring occasionally, until apples are very tender and mixture has reduced to 2⅓ cups, 25 to 35 minutes. Cover and set aside.

3. Adjust oven rack to middle position and heat oven to 300 degrees. Slice remaining 2 apples into ½-inch-thick rings. Pat chops dry with paper towels and evenly sprinkle each chop with pepper to taste. Heat oil in 12-inch skillet over medium heat until beginning to smoke. Increase heat to high and brown chops on both sides, 6 to 8 minutes total. Transfer chops to large plate and reduce heat to medium. Add apple rings and cook until lightly browned, 1 to 2 minutes. Add remaining ¼ cup broth and cook, scraping up any browned bits with rubber spatula, until liquid has evaporated, about 30 seconds. Remove pan from heat, flip apple rings, and place chops on top of apple rings. Place skillet in oven and cook until chops register 135 to 140 degrees, 11 to 15 minutes.

4. Transfer chops and apple rings to serving platter, tent loosely with foil, and let rest for 10 minutes. While chops rest, strain apple/brandy mixture through fine-mesh strainer set in large bowl, pressing on solids with ladle or rubber spatula to extract liquid; discard solids. (Make sure to use rubber spatula to scrape any apple solids on bottom of strainer into sauce.) Stir in minced thyme and season sauce with vinegar, salt, and pepper to taste. Transfer sauce to serving bowl. Serve chops and apple rings, passing sauce separately.

ONE-PAN PORK CHOPS AND ROASTED VEGETABLES

WHY THIS RECIPE WORKS: A one-pan meal means fewer dishes to wash, but trying to reconcile different cooking times for meat and vegetables is a challenge. We usually like to sear pork chops to develop flavorful browning, but for a baking-sheet supper, this was a nonstarter. Instead, we added flavor with a pungent spice rub of salt, pepper, paprika, and coriander. While the chops sat in their rub, we roasted the vegetables—sweet carrots, earthy potatoes, anise-like fennel, and a handful of garlic cloves. Then we topped the vegetables with the spice-rubbed pork chops for a final 10 minutes of cooking. The chops stayed moist, and their elevated perch allowed air to circulate for even cooking. One-inch-thick chops work best with this method.

We are always looking for ways to streamline recipes to make life easier for the home cook. So a one-pan meal of pork chops with roasted potatoes and carrots sounded great: simple, tasty, and easy to clean up. But once I lined up all the ingredients in the test kitchen, it quickly became clear that I'd have a few problems to solve.

The most obvious issue was cooking time: Thin pork chops cook in as little as 5 minutes, but even large, 1-inch-thick, center-cut, bone-in chops cook in only 10 to 15 minutes. Roasting vegetables to a soft, tender stage would require at least twice that time.

My other problem was flavor: I knew before starting that browning the chops on the stovetop—which we often do to build flavor—didn't make sense here. I'd have to sear them first in an ovensafe skillet and then transfer them along with the vegetables to the oven. But four big pork chops and 2 pounds of vegetables (enough to feed four) wouldn't fit comfortably even in a large skillet. I'd have to come up with another way to add flavor.

But for now, I'd focus on the cooking time. My plan was to partially roast the vegetables in the oven on a rimmed baking sheet (which promotes fast cooking and browning) and then add the large chops on top of the vegetables after about 30 minutes—and not use a skillet at all.

I tossed sliced Yukon Gold potatoes, coarsely cut carrots and fennel bulb, and a big handful of peeled garlic cloves with a tablespoon of extra-virgin olive oil

ONE-PAN PORK CHOPS AND ROASTED VEGETABLES

and some minced fresh rosemary. Then I dumped the mixture onto the baking sheet and slid it into the oven. After a few tests, I found that roasting at 450 degrees on the upper-middle rack allowed the vegetables to brown at such a pace that I didn't need to open the oven to stir them during cooking—a definite plus.

While the vegetables were roasting, I focused my attention on adding flavor to the main ingredient, the chops. Since stovetop searing was off the table, I tried rubbing the chops with sugar to see if that would help them brown in the oven, but it still took too long: The chops were basically jerky by the time they picked up significant color. I decided instead to use a potent spice rub. I tried several combinations, and my tasters voted in favor of a fragrant blend of sweet paprika, coriander, salt, and pepper. This mix added a subtle but energetic pop of flavor to the pork and gave it an attractive color (thanks to the paprika). Now that the meat had some real flavor, I could work out the timing.

After about 25 minutes in the oven, the vegetables were almost—but not quite—tender. Working quickly, I balanced the raw, spice-rubbed chops on top of the vegetables and returned the pan to the oven. Elevating the chops on top of the vegetables allowed air to circulate under the meat, which sped up the cooking. What's more, as the pork juices and seasonings dripped down onto the vegetables, they took on beautiful meaty flavors. The hot vegetables, in turn, helped speed up the cooking time of the chops; after just 10 to 15 minutes, the chops hit a perfect 140 degrees and the vegetables were nicely tender.

The chops and vegetables were well seasoned, but I wanted a jolt of freshness to tie the meat and vegetables together. I turned to common pantry ingredients—red wine vinegar, a bit of minced shallot, some extra-virgin olive oil, and a little sugar for balance—and then whisked in a couple of tablespoons of fresh parsley and drizzled the bright green sauce over the finished dish.

This dish was delicious and easy, and done in 40 minutes of roasting—just right for an easy weeknight supper.

—CHRISTIE MORRISON, *Cook's Country*

One-Pan Pork Chops and Roasted Vegetables
SERVES 4

This recipe was developed using kosher salt. If you substitute table salt, reduce the amount of salt in each part of the recipe by half.

- 4 (10-ounce) bone-in center-cut pork chops, 1 to 1¼ inches thick, trimmed
- ⅓ cup extra-virgin olive oil
  Kosher salt and pepper
- 1 teaspoon paprika
- 1 teaspoon ground coriander
- 1 pound Yukon Gold potatoes, unpeeled, halved lengthwise and cut crosswise into ½-inch-thick slices
- 1 pound carrots, peeled and cut into 3-inch lengths, thick ends quartered lengthwise
- 1 fennel bulb, stalks discarded, bulb halved, cored, and cut into ½-inch-thick wedges
- 10 garlic cloves, peeled
- 2 teaspoons minced fresh rosemary
- 2 tablespoons minced fresh parsley
- 1 small shallot, minced
- 4 teaspoons red wine vinegar
- ⅛ teaspoon sugar

1. Adjust oven rack to upper-middle position and heat oven to 450 degrees. Pat pork dry with paper towels and rub with 1 teaspoon oil. Combine 2 teaspoons salt, 1 teaspoon pepper, paprika, and coriander in small bowl. Season pork chops all over with spice mixture; set aside.

2. Toss potatoes, carrots, fennel, garlic, rosemary, 1 tablespoon oil, 1½ teaspoons salt, and ¼ teaspoon pepper together in large bowl. Spread vegetables in single layer on rimmed baking sheet. Roast vegetables until just tender, about 25 minutes.

3. Carefully place pork chops on top of vegetables and return to oven. Roast until chops register 140 degrees and vegetables are fully tender, 10 to 15 minutes longer, rotating sheet halfway through roasting.

4. Meanwhile, combine parsley, shallot, vinegar, sugar, ½ teaspoon salt, ¼ teaspoon pepper, and remaining ¼ cup oil in bowl. Transfer vegetables and pork to platter and drizzle with vinaigrette. Serve.

POULTRY AND SEAFOOD

GRILLED CHICKEN SOUVLAKI

✔ **WHY THIS RECIPE WORKS:** Nicely charred, lemony chicken drizzled with creamy *tzatziki* wrapped in a soft pita makes a perfect summer weeknight meal, but achieving evenly cooked, moist chicken on skewers can be a challenge. We started by brining the chicken to help it retain moisture and to season it throughout. To keep the pieces on the ends of the skewers from cooking faster than the pieces in the middle, we used chunks of red onion and bell pepper as "shields." We reserved a bit of our lemony marinade mixture to toss with the chicken after grilling for a bright, fresh hit of flavor. We warmed and softened the pitas by moistening them and steaming them in a foil packet on the grill. Our cool tzatziki made a perfect counterpoint to our charred chicken.

Souvlaki is basically a Greek term for meat grilled on a stick. Just about every meat-eating culture has a version, but when it comes to being documented masters (if not the originators) of the technique, Greek credentials are hard to beat. Homer's *Iliad* and *Odyssey* are rich with detailed accounts of the heroes skewering meat and cooking it over fire, souvlaki-style.

In modern Greece, souvlaki is usually made with pork, but at Greek restaurants here in the United States, boneless, skinless chicken breast is common. The chunks of white meat are marinated (often overnight) in a tangy mixture of lemon juice, olive oil, oregano, parsley, and sometimes garlic before being skewered and grilled until nicely charred. Souvlaki is best served on a lightly grilled pita, slathered with tzatziki, a yogurt-based sauce, wrapped snugly, and eaten out of hand. The creamy sauce, freshened with herbs and cucumber, complements the char of the chicken, and the soft pita pulls it all together.

At least as appealing as the dish itself is how easily it translates to a home grill. The ingredients are readily available, and small chunks of boneless chicken cook quickly, making souvlaki a prime candidate for weeknight backyard fare. I just needed to come up with a good recipe.

The first round of grilling left the boneless, skinless chicken breasts bland and dry with a mushy outside. The long soak in the acidic marinade was to blame. Tests have shown us that, over time, acid weakens the protein bonds on the surface of meat, which causes that mushy texture. What's more, the marinade never penetrates much below the meat's surface, so its flavor is superficial at best. Bottom line: The long marinating step had to go.

In the next test, I went to the other extreme: I tossed the 1-inch cubes of chicken with lemon juice and olive oil and then immediately skewered and grilled them over very hot coals. It was only a modest success. The pasty exterior was gone, but the meat was still bland and dry, especially those more exposed chunks that had been on either end of each skewer.

So I mixed up a brine. Soaking meat in a saltwater solution before cooking encourages it to take up extra moisture, and the salt, some of which is also absorbed, seasons the meat. Brining the chicken after cutting it into chunks would be particularly effective, as there would be more exposed surface area in contact with the solution.

I soaked the chicken for 30 minutes while the grill heated and then drained it, patted it dry, and tossed it with olive oil, lemon juice, dried oregano, parsley, and black pepper. I also added a bit of honey, which I suspected would add complexity and help with browning. The one thing I left out was garlic. In previous tests most of it had fallen off, and what had remained on the meat burned. I'd try to make up for it in the tzatziki. In the meantime, I threaded the dressed chunks onto skewers and grilled them over very hot coals for about 15 minutes, at which point they were cooked through and well charred.

The brine had helped, as most of the chicken was now moist, but those end pieces were still parched. That brought up a fundamental problem with the meat-on-a-stick method: Meat that's packed tightly on a skewer doesn't cook evenly. The middle pieces are insulated from the fierce heat, while the exposed end pieces cook faster. Poking around with a thermometer, I found that the end pieces reached the target 160 degrees at least 4 minutes before the middle ones did.

I came up with another idea. Instead of packing only meat onto the skewers, I started each one with a stack of bell pepper chunks, then threaded on the chicken pieces, and finished each skewer with two chunks of red onion. The vegetables functioned as shields, protecting the end pieces of chicken from the heat so they cooked at the same rate as the middle pieces. A bonus: They added more char flavor to the wrap and broke up the all-meat filling with some crunch.

What was missing from the chicken was the lemon punch that I associate with souvlaki, so I made a quick adjustment. Instead of using all the lemon–olive oil mixture to coat the raw chicken, I reserved ¼ cup of it to use after cooking. When the skewers came off the grill, I unloaded the chicken and vegetables into a bowl with the reserved sauce. Covering the bowl and letting the contents steam for a bit to absorb the sauce resulted in bright-tasting chicken and vegetables.

Next up: the sauce. Tzatziki is plain yogurt flavored with garlic, cucumber, herbs, salt, and maybe a bit of acid like lemon juice or vinegar. Since raw garlic can be too assertive, I used a trick from Caesar salad dressing: grating the garlic to a paste and briefly steeping it in lemon juice before adding both to the sauce. The acid converts the harsh-tasting garlic compound, allicin, into mellower compounds in the same way that cooking does.

Thick Greek yogurt is typically used and the cucumbers, either grated or minced, are usually pretreated with salt to remove excess moisture. But the mixture of yogurt and salted cucumbers was so heavy and thick that it dominated the wrap. To thin out the sauce, I skipped salting the cucumbers and relied on the salt in the tzatziki to pull water from the cucumbers into the yogurt as it sat (from that point on, I prepared the sauce before the chicken). When it came time to assemble the wraps, the tzatziki had a thinner consistency.

Finally, I wrapped a stack of four pitas tightly in foil after moistening the top and bottom surfaces of the stack with water. I placed the packet on a cooler side of the grill, so the bread could steam while the chicken cooked. By the time the chicken had rested, the pitas were soft, warm, and floppy—perfect for wrapping.

—ANDREA GEARY, *Cook's Illustrated*

Grilled Chicken Souvlaki

SERVES 4

This tzatziki is fairly mild; if you like a more assertive flavor, double the garlic. A rasp-style grater makes quick work of turning the garlic into a paste. We like the chicken in a wrap, but you may skip the pita and serve the chicken, vegetables, and tzatziki with rice. You will need four 12-inch metal skewers.

NOTES FROM THE TEST KITCHEN

A VEGETABLE SHIELD
The age-old problem with grilling meat on a stick: The end pieces overcook. We protect the chicken by threading pepper and onion pieces on the ends. The charred vegetables taste great in the sandwich, too.

SOFTENING SUPERMARKET PITA
To soften up dry, tough supermarket pita, we moisten two of the pitas with a little water and then stack them on either side of two unmoistened pieces. Then we steam them in a foil-wrapped stack on the cooler side of the grill while the cooked chicken rests.

TZATZIKI SAUCE

- 1 tablespoon lemon juice
- 1 small garlic clove, minced to paste
- ¾ cup plain Greek yogurt
- ½ cucumber, peeled, halved lengthwise, seeded, and diced fine (½ cup)
- 3 tablespoons minced fresh mint
- 1 tablespoon minced fresh parsley
- ⅜ teaspoon salt

CHICKEN

- Salt and pepper
- 1½ pounds boneless, skinless chicken breasts, trimmed and cut into 1-inch pieces
- ⅓ cup extra-virgin olive oil
- 2 tablespoons minced fresh parsley
- 1 teaspoon finely grated lemon zest plus ¼ cup juice (2 lemons)
- 1 teaspoon honey
- 1 teaspoon dried oregano
- 1 green bell pepper, stemmed, seeded, quartered, and each quarter cut into 4 chunks
- 1 small red onion, ends trimmed, peeled, halved lengthwise, and each half cut into 4 chunks
- 4 (8-inch) pita breads

1. FOR THE TZATZIKI SAUCE: Whisk lemon juice and garlic together in small bowl. Let stand for 10 minutes. Stir in yogurt, cucumber, mint, parsley, and salt. Cover and set aside.

2. FOR THE CHICKEN: Dissolve 2 tablespoons salt in 1 quart cold water. Submerge chicken in brine, cover, and refrigerate for 30 minutes. While chicken is brining, combine oil, parsley, lemon zest and juice, honey, oregano, and ½ teaspoon pepper in medium bowl. Transfer ¼ cup oil mixture to large bowl and set aside to toss with cooked chicken.

3. Remove chicken from brine and pat dry with paper towels. Toss chicken with remaining oil mixture. Thread 4 pieces of bell pepper, concave side up, onto one 12-inch metal skewer. Thread one-quarter of chicken onto skewer. Thread 2 chunks of onion onto skewer, and place skewer on plate. Repeat skewering remaining chicken and vegetables on 3 more skewers. Lightly moisten 2 pita breads with water. Sandwich 2 unmoistened pita breads between moistened pitas and wrap stack tightly in lightly greased heavy-duty aluminum foil.

4A. FOR A CHARCOAL GRILL: Open bottom vent completely. Light large chimney starter mounded with charcoal briquettes (7 quarts). When top coals are partially covered with ash, pour evenly over half of grill. Set cooking grate in place, cover, and open lid vent completely. Heat grill until hot, about 5 minutes.

4B. FOR A GAS GRILL: Turn all burners to high, cover, and heat grill until hot, about 15 minutes. Leave primary burner on high and turn off other burner(s).

5. Clean and oil cooking grate. Place skewers on hotter side of grill and cook, turning occasionally, until chicken and vegetables are well browned on all sides and chicken registers 160 degrees, 15 to 20 minutes. Using fork, push chicken and vegetables off skewers into bowl of reserved oil mixture. Stir gently, breaking up onion chunks; cover with foil and let sit for 5 minutes.

6. Meanwhile, place packet of pitas on cooler side of grill. Flip occasionally to heat, about 5 minutes.

7. Lay each warm pita on 12-inch square of foil. Spread each pita with 2 tablespoons tzatziki. Place one-quarter of chicken and vegetables in middle of each pita. Roll into cylindrical shape and serve.

MAHOGANY CHICKEN THIGHS

✔ **WHY THIS RECIPE WORKS:** The dark meat of chicken thighs may be flavorful, but too often it's riddled with pockets of fat. Braising can help, but we wanted crispy skin, too. We developed a hybrid cooking method that helped us to achieve all of our goals. Gently simmering the thighs in a potent mixture of soy sauce, sherry, ginger, and garlic rendered the fat, melted the tough connective tissues into rich gelatin, and boosted the flavor. Although the meat ended up "overcooked" by usual standards, the plentiful gelatin ensured that it was moist and tender. A brief flash under the broiler crisped the skin and enhanced the rich mahogany color.

In the test kitchen, we love to work with chicken thighs, but we're aware that not everyone shares our enthusiasm. Even those who admit that a roasted thigh delivers more flavorful meat than a roasted breast might steer clear of the dark meat, lest they encounter the pockets of fat and chewy connective tissue that tend to hide beneath the crispy skin.

There is a cooking method that directly addresses those flaws: braising, which melts the fat and breaks down the connective tissue into soft, rich gelatin. Both roasting and braising coat the muscle fibers and leave the meat moist and silky. But braised chicken thighs have one big drawback: flabby, pale, waterlogged skin. To tempt white meat devotees to the dark side, we'd have to develop a method that delivered the best of both worlds: the moist meat of braising—with no pockets of fat or connective tissue—and the crispy skin of roasting.

A hybrid approach seemed like the best bet. First we'd braise the chicken to render the skin's fat and melt down the sinew—and we'd do so in a flavorful liquid that would season the meat. Then we'd blast the chicken with dry heat to crisp that rendered skin.

In a Dutch oven we stirred together 1 cup of soy sauce and six smashed cloves of garlic, as both contain water-soluble flavor compounds that would penetrate the surface of the meat. We nestled eight chicken thighs into the pot, skin side down to encourage the fatty layer under the skin to render, and added 1½ cups of water—enough to just cover them. We brought it all

MAHOGANY CHICKEN THIGHS

to a simmer on the stove and then transferred the pot to a 350-degree oven for its gentler, more even heat.

After 40 minutes, the chicken had reached 175 degrees, the temperature at which we usually pull roasted chicken thighs from the oven. We transferred the pieces skin side up to a wire rack set in a rimmed baking sheet before returning them to the oven, this time setting them just below the fierce heat of the broiler.

The moist heat had melted most, though not all, of the fat and connective tissue, so the meat wasn't as tender as we'd like. Its flavor was also one-dimensional. As for the skin, it wasn't quite crispy, but it was attractive; the soy sauce had dyed it (and the meat) a deep mahogany color that intensified under the broiler.

To add complexity to the soy flavor, we whisked in sherry, white vinegar, a big piece of smashed ginger, and sugar and molasses for sweetness (both would also caramelize and boost that mahogany hue). Turning the chicken skin side up halfway through braising allowed the rendered skin to dry before broiling, which helped it crisp a little more. We also swapped the Dutch oven for a 12-inch skillet, which we could use for both braising and broiling.

On to the bigger question: how to rid the meat of the fatty, chewy bits once and for all and make it more tender. Clearly, 40 minutes was ample time for the thighs to cook through, but their connective tissue was another matter. This portion starts breaking down at 140 degrees, does so slowly, and—if these tests had taught us anything—can't be rushed.

Realizing that we needed to hold the meat in the collagen breakdown sweet spot—above 140 degrees but below the temperature at which the meat would be overcooked—for longer, we lowered the oven temperature by 50 degrees and increased the braising time to an hour. We thought that the lower heat would prevent the meat's temperature from climbing too rapidly, but alarmingly, the braised pieces registered 195 degrees—and we still had the broiling step to go. We were sure we'd way overshot the mark, but finished the batch anyway.

But this mistake turned out to be a happy accident. These thighs were by far the best yet: beautifully moist and tender. Yes, the meat was overcooked according to our usual standards, but the extended braising time had broken down the connective tissue so thoroughly that there was loads of gelatin to bathe the muscle fibers, resulting in meat that was supple and juicy.

Now it was time to go back to the skin, which was still less than perfectly crispy. It was an easy fix, though: We simply lowered the oven rack to the middle position, which put more distance between the broiler element and the meat and gave the skin more time to brown and crisp.

We celebrated the victory by using a portion of the leftover braising liquid to make a quick sauce (thickened with a little cornstarch for body).

Now that we know how to get the best out of chicken thighs, we're planning on spending a lot more time on the dark side.

—ANDREA GEARY, *Cook's Illustrated*

Mahogany Chicken Thighs

SERVES 4 TO 6

For best results, trim all visible fat and skin from the underside of the thighs. Serve with steamed rice and vegetables.

- 1½ cups water
- 1 cup soy sauce
- ¼ cup dry sherry
- 2 tablespoons sugar
- 2 tablespoons molasses
- 1 tablespoon distilled white vinegar
- 8 (5- to 7-ounce) bone-in chicken thighs, trimmed
- 1 (2-inch) piece ginger, peeled, halved, and smashed
- 6 garlic cloves, peeled and smashed
- 1 tablespoon cornstarch

1. Adjust oven rack to lower-middle position and heat oven to 300 degrees. Whisk 1 cup water, soy sauce, sherry, sugar, molasses, and vinegar together in ovensafe 12-inch skillet until sugar is dissolved. Arrange chicken, skin side down, in soy mixture and nestle ginger and garlic between pieces of chicken.

2. Bring soy mixture to simmer over medium heat and simmer for 5 minutes. Transfer skillet to oven and cook, uncovered, for 30 minutes.

3. Flip chicken skin side up and continue to cook, uncovered, until chicken registers 195 degrees, 20 to 30 minutes longer. Transfer chicken to platter, taking care not to tear skin. Pour cooking liquid through fine-mesh strainer into fat separator and let settle for 5 minutes. Heat broiler.

4. Whisk cornstarch and remaining ½ cup water together in bowl. Pour 1 cup defatted cooking liquid into now-empty skillet and bring to simmer over medium heat. Whisk cornstarch mixture into cooking liquid and simmer until thickened, about 1 minute. Pour sauce into bowl and set aside for serving.

5. Return chicken skin side up to now-empty skillet and broil until well browned, about 4 minutes. Return chicken to platter, and let rest for 5 minutes. Serve, passing reserved sauce separately.

SMOKED BOURBON CHICKEN

WHY THIS RECIPE WORKS: For smoked chicken imbued with the unmistakable flavor of bourbon, we cooked the marinade, which got the most flavor compounds into our chicken. Slashing the chickens also allowed for better penetration of the marinade flavors before grilling. Splitting our chickens into halves allowed the skin and meat to have maximum exposure to smoke from the grill, and basting them with our marinade throughout cooking let the marinade flavor and smoke flavor develop in our chicken even more.

It used to be that bourbon was thought of only as a drink. While that may be its highest and best use, this classic American spirit has long been used in cooking, too. It seems to have started with adding a shot or two to barbecue sauces and has progressed to recipes like Smoked Bourbon Chicken. This sounded to me like a perfect combination of Southern flavors, so I decided to develop my own version.

I found plenty of recipes for this dish, but their approaches were all over the map. I tried them all and got varied results. In the end, none were very successful; all featured either dried-out chicken or meek bourbon flavor or both.

My first decision, based on that first round of testing, was to use two whole chickens but split them rather than leave them whole, so I could cook each half skin side up for crispier skin.

The next issue I tackled was the bourbon flavor. Recipes that relied on either a pregrill bourbon brine or a postgrill coating with a bourbon-spiked barbecue sauce had failed to imbue much of that flavor. But using a marinade, with its concentrated flavor components,

had yielded promising results. I cobbled together a marinade that, along with bourbon, used brown sugar, shallots, garlic, and soy sauce. After an hour of marinating, I set up a grill fire with areas of high direct heat and lower indirect heat, put a foil packet containing a cup of soaked wood chips on top of the hot coals, and then put the chicken on the cooler side of the grill and covered it. An hour later the chicken halves were ready, with mixed results. I did get good bourbon flavor, but the marinade was lacking balance and impact.

I decided to try a method we'd used before, cutting slashes into the meat to create more surface area to absorb flavors. When I tried this, I definitely got more flavor into the chicken. But I still didn't feel that the marinade was living up to its potential, so I called our science editor for some advice. He explained that soy sauce has aroma compounds that can be intensified when heated, and heating the marinade for a mere minute right after I mixed it together could potentially improve the overall flavor in the chicken. Accordingly, for my next version I brought the marinade to a boil in a saucepan, let it cool to room temperature, and then added the chicken. Bingo. This batch of chicken had smokiness, a pleasantly bold bourbon flavor, and deep, well-rounded seasoning.

Now I was ready to deal with the dryness. Since I was already marinating with a potent combination including soy sauce, brining didn't seem like the right approach. I turned instead to a staple of barbecue recipes: a mopping sauce. Mopping sauces are applied during grilling to long-cooking recipes, such as ribs. They help keep the meat moist by preventing the surface temperature from going above 212 degrees. In addition, since smoke is attracted to moisture, keeping the chicken skin damp should enhance the smoky flavor. I put another batch of chicken on the grill and diligently basted every 15 minutes until the skin was a deep mahogany (an added effect of the constant basting) and the chicken had come to the right temperature. After I brought the chicken inside, tasters gathered around the carving board, eagerly looking at the impressively dark, browned chicken halves. This time, heads nodded in agreement: The bourbon flavor was definitely there, as was smoke, and the chicken was moist. Finally chicken, bourbon, and smoke had met in a recipe that was not just good, but smokin' good.

—CRISTIN WALSH, *Cook's Country*

Smoked Bourbon Chicken

SERVES 4

Use a bourbon you'd be happy drinking. Use all the basting liquid in step 5.

1¼ cups bourbon
1¼ cups soy sauce
½ cup packed brown sugar
1 shallot, minced
4 garlic cloves, minced
2 teaspoons pepper
2 (3½- to 4-pound) whole chickens,
   giblets discarded
1 cup wood chips
4 (12-inch) wooden skewers

1. Bring bourbon, soy sauce, sugar, shallot, garlic, and pepper to boil in medium saucepan over medium-high heat and cook for 1 minute. Remove from heat and let cool completely. Set aside ¾ cup bourbon mixture for basting chicken. (Bourbon mixture can be refrigerated up to 3 days in advance.)

2. With chickens breast side down, using kitchen shears, cut through bones on both sides of backbones; discard backbones. Flip chickens over and, using chef's knife, split chickens in half lengthwise through centers of breastbones. Cut ½-inch-deep slits across breasts, thighs, and legs, about ½ inch apart. Tuck wing-tips behind backs. Divide chicken halves between two 1-gallon zipper-lock bags and divide remaining bourbon mixture between bags. Seal bags, turn to distribute marinade, and refrigerate for at least 1 hour or up to 24 hours, flipping occasionally.

3. Just before grilling, soak wood chips in water for 15 minutes, then drain. Using large piece of heavy-duty aluminum foil, wrap soaked chips in foil packet and cut several vent holes in top. Remove chicken halves from marinade and pat dry with paper towels; discard marinade. Insert 1 skewer lengthwise through thickest part of breast down through thigh of each chicken half.

4A. FOR A CHARCOAL GRILL: Open bottom vent halfway. Light large chimney starter filled with charcoal

NOTES FROM THE TEST KITCHEN

HOW TO CUT A CHICKEN IN HALF

1. REMOVE BACKBONE: Using poultry shears, cut through bones on both sides of backbone; discard backbone.

2. CUT THROUGH BREAST: Flip chicken over and use chef's knife to halve chicken through center of breastbone.

briquettes (6 quarts). When top coals are partially covered with ash, pour into steeply banked pile against side of grill. Place wood chip packet on coals. Set cooking grate in place, cover, and open lid vent halfway. Heat grill until hot and wood chips are smoking, about 5 minutes.

4B. FOR A GAS GRILL: Remove cooking grate and place wood chip packet directly on primary burner. Set grate in place, turn all burners to high, cover, and heat grill until hot and wood chips are smoking, about 15 minutes. Leave primary burner on high and turn off other burners. (Adjust primary burner as needed to maintain grill temperature between 350 to 375 degrees.)

5. Clean and oil cooking grate. Place chicken halves skin side up on cooler side of grill with legs pointing toward fire. Cover and cook, basting every 15 minutes with reserved bourbon mixture, until breasts register 160 degrees and thighs register 175 degrees, 75 to 90 minutes, switching placement of chicken halves after 45 minutes. (All of bourbon mixture should be used.) Transfer chicken to carving board, tent loosely with foil, and let rest for 20 minutes. Carve and serve.

COQ AU RIESLING

WHY THIS RECIPE WORKS: For our take on the elegant white wine version of *coq au vin*, starting with a whole chicken and then breaking it down ourselves was a must, not only to obtain evenly sized parts that would cook at the same rate but also so that we could use the back and wings to enrich the sauce. The fond created from browning the chicken skin was also essential for flavor but required browning the chicken parts in batches. Plus, the skin turned flabby during braising. The solution? Removing the skin from the meat, browning it in one batch, and then discarding it before serving. Adding about three-quarters of a bottle of dry Riesling along with a cup of water produced a sauce that was nuanced and balanced. Finally, we finished the sauce with crème fraîche for just the right silkiness and body.

For most American cooks, coq au vin means chicken stewed in red wine with bacon, mushrooms, and onions—the version first popularized on Julia Child's television show *The French Chef*. But in France, coq au vin is often made with white wine. In traditional approaches, you cut a whole chicken into pieces and marinate it overnight. The next day you cook lardons, or pieces of fatty pork, in a Dutch oven, set them aside to sear the chicken, and then set aside the chicken and sauté a *mirepoix* of carrots, celery, and onions with flour and herbs. Then wine and broth go into the pot and the chicken is added back in and simmered until tender. The cooking liquid, now thickened to a rich nap, is strained so that it's velvety smooth. The main difference: The red version is usually garnished with sautéed mushrooms and pearl onions, while the white typically skips the onions and is finished with cream or crème fraîche.

I was sold on the promise of a richer, more subtle and elegant dish. I was also determined that my version would be far less of a project than the original.

I quickly discovered that many of the old practices were not necessary. Marinating the chicken in wine was not only unnecessary but ill-advised. The acidity of the wine tended to literally cook the exterior of the meat, denaturing the proteins in the same way that heat would and thereby making them less able to hold on to moisture. I came to a similar conclusion about the long cooking times in traditional recipes. While probably essential for tough meat, with today's birds it robbed the chicken of both flavor and moisture.

Next I moved on to testing more modern, streamlined recipes. Many eschewed the whole-bird approach in favor of using prepackaged parts. While this was simpler, it also made ensuring even cooking difficult, since the parts in a package may come from different chickens of varying sizes. I wanted a manageable, pared-down approach, but not at such expense. Cutting up a whole chicken was mandatory. I would just have to figure out how to speed up things elsewhere.

I began prepping a new batch, and as soon as I'd finished breaking down the chicken, I realized another advantage to a whole bird beyond ensuring even-size pieces: I had the back and wings to put to use. By browning them in the pot along with the other parts and leaving them there during the simmering time, I found that I could give the sauce a good boost of meaty flavor. It was enough of an improvement that I realized the store-bought chicken broth I'd been adding along with the wine wasn't even necessary, so I swapped in a few cups of water instead.

Since I wasn't marinating the chicken and was cooking the meat for only about 30 minutes, most of my effort and time went into browning the bacon and chicken parts and sautéing the mirepoix. Searing the chicken pieces had to be done in at least two batches to avoid crowding, and each batch took about 10 minutes. Plus, all the moving in and out of the pot made for a lot of dirty dishes.

Throughout these early tests, I noticed that most tasters, myself included, were removing the skin before eating the chicken, since it had turned unappealingly wet and flabby from the 30-minute simmer. If the skin was going to be discarded anyway, why not separate it from the meat and sear it by itself? This would not only save diners the trouble of removing it themselves but, more important, allow me to sear all the skin in a single batch. When the simmering time was up, the skin could be easily strained off with the other flavor additions.

Next time around I added the skin to the pot along with the back and wings. When the skin was well browned and the pot had developed a decent fond, I returned the bacon to the pot, added the mirepoix, and carried on as usual. The results were as good as when I'd seared the skin-on pieces, but the whole process took a fraction of the time. I was able to shave off more time by cooking the bacon alone in the pot until its fat began to render and then leaving it there to brown along with the skin, back, and wings.

COQ AU RIESLING

Now I just needed to refine the sauce. Most recipes call for almost a full bottle of wine, but when I added that much, most tasters found the sauce too sour and the acidity overpowered the chicken. When I cut back the wine to 2½ cups, the sauce was much more balanced. As for the quality and the variety of the wine, we found that—as is usually the case when cooking with wine—there's no sense spending a lot, but that if you wouldn't want to drink the wine, you wouldn't want to use it for cooking either. Bottles in the $7-to-$10 range did the trick.

As for finishing with either cream or crème fraîche, tasters preferred the tartness of the latter. Plus, unlike cream, the thicker dairy didn't loosen up the sauce too much. For the garnish, mushrooms are typically sautéed in butter in a separate skillet until brown, but I saw one last chance to simplify. It was just as effective to cook them in a few tablespoons of reserved chicken fat in the Dutch oven before returning the strained sauce to the pot. With that, I had my own take on coq au Riesling that was as streamlined to prepare as it was elegant.

—ANDREW JANJIGIAN, *Cook's Illustrated*

Coq au Riesling

SERVES 4 TO 6

A dry Riesling is the best wine for this recipe, but a Sauvignon Blanc or Chablis will also work. Avoid a heavily oaked wine such as Chardonnay. Serve the stew with egg noodles or mashed potatoes.

1	(4- to 5-pound) whole chicken, cut into 8 pieces (4 breast pieces, 2 drumsticks, 2 thighs), wings and back reserved
	Salt and pepper
2	slices bacon, chopped
3	shallots, chopped
2	carrots, peeled and chopped coarse
2	celery ribs, chopped coarse
4	garlic cloves, peeled and lightly crushed
3	tablespoons all-purpose flour
2½	cups dry Riesling
1	cup water
2	bay leaves
6	sprigs fresh parsley, plus 2 teaspoons minced
6	sprigs fresh thyme
1	pound white mushrooms, trimmed and halved if small or quartered if large
¼	cup crème fraîche

1. Remove skin from chicken breast pieces, drumsticks, and thighs and set aside. Sprinkle both sides of chicken pieces with 1¼ teaspoons salt and ½ teaspoon pepper; set aside. Cook bacon in large Dutch oven over medium-low heat, stirring occasionally, until beginning to render, 2 to 4 minutes. Add chicken skin, back, and wings to pot; increase heat to medium; and cook, stirring frequently, until bacon is browned, skin is rendered, and chicken back and wings are browned on all sides, 10 to 12 minutes. Remove pot from heat and carefully transfer 2 tablespoons fat to small bowl and set aside.

2. Return pot to medium heat. Add shallots, carrots, celery, and garlic and cook, stirring occasionally, until vegetables are softened, 4 to 6 minutes. Add flour and cook, stirring constantly, until no dry flour remains, about 30 seconds. Slowly add wine, scraping up any browned bits. Increase heat to high and simmer until mixture is slightly thickened, about 2 minutes. Stir in water, bay leaves, and parsley and thyme springs and bring to simmer. Place chicken pieces in even layer in pot, reduce heat to low, cover, and cook until breasts register 160 degrees and thighs and legs register 175 degrees, 25 to 30 minutes, stirring halfway through cooking. Transfer chicken pieces to plate as they come up to temperature.

3. Discard back and wings. Strain cooking liquid through fine-mesh strainer set over large bowl, pressing on solids to extract as much liquid as possible; discard solids. Let cooking liquid settle for 10 minutes.

Using wide shallow spoon, skim fat from surface and discard.

4. While liquid settles, return pot to medium heat and add reserved fat, mushrooms, and ¼ teaspoon salt; cook, stirring occasionally, until lightly browned, 8 to 10 minutes.

5. Return liquid to pot and bring to boil. Simmer briskly, stirring occasionally, until sauce is thickened to consistency of heavy cream, 4 to 6 minutes. Reduce heat to medium-low and stir in crème fraîche and minced parsley. Return chicken to pot along with any accumulated juices, cover, and cook until just heated through, 5 to 8 minutes. Season with salt and pepper to taste, and serve.

VIETNAMESE-STYLE CARAMEL CHICKEN

✓ **WHY THIS RECIPE WORKS:** Traditional Vietnamese-style caramel chicken promises a dish that balances a bittersweet caramel with salty and spicy flavors, but most recipes miss the mark. Cooking the caramel until it was a deep, dark color was the key to achieving the right complex bittersweetness, while fish sauce (in a 1:4 ratio of fish sauce to caramel) lent the traditional balancing salty component. A combination of ginger and black pepper provided the right amount of heat. Cutting the boneless, skinless chicken thighs in half, rather than into smaller bits as called for in many of the recipes we found, gave the chicken more time to absorb the sauce, while a quick soak in a baking soda–water bath helped the chicken stay juicy over a longer cooking time, turning the meat ultratender.

In an American kitchen, caramel sauce is the sweet treat that we like to pour over ice cream and other desserts. In Vietnam, it's a different thing entirely. There, *nuoc mau*, or "colored water," as it's known, is commonly prepared in large batches and added to a variety of savory dishes. To make the caramel, the sugar is cooked long enough that the results are a little sweet and also bitter. Stirring in a good amount of fish sauce adds an essential savory, salty flavor, while ginger, pepper, or chile lend heat. In the best versions, the result is a potent yet perfectly balanced sauce that lends a rich brown color to everything from meat to catfish to tofu.

I've always been drawn to the chicken-based version, but when I tried a few recipes, none of the results lived up to the promise. The chicken, which is braised in the sauce, was usually leathery, and the sauce was either gloppy or so thin that it slid off the meat. When it came to flavor, most of the recipes fell into one of two camps: either too sweet or too salty and pungent. I wanted an authentic but approachable recipe that produced tender, juicy chicken bathed in just the right amount of a sauce that balanced bitter, sweet, salty, and spicy.

I started with the sauce. Modern recipes were convenient but trying to evenly caramelize sugar over the large surface of a skillet proved difficult. So instead I followed the lead of traditional Vietnamese recipes and pulled out a deep, small saucepan for the caramel. Once it was prepared, I'd move the sauce to a skillet to braise the chicken.

Traditional recipes call for cooking the caramel until it's almost black, but I decided to start more cautiously. I brought 7 tablespoons of sugar and 3 tablespoons of water to a boil in my saucepan over moderately high heat until it started to turn golden. As the sugar began to take on color more rapidly, I turned down the heat and swirled the pan occasionally to ensure that the caramel cooked evenly. When a reddish-brown hue was just starting to develop, I turned off the heat and carefully added another ¾ cup of hot water to stop the cooking (adding hot water rather than cold ensured that the mixture didn't harden). After the caramel sputtered and bubbled for a few seconds, I moved on to adding the fish sauce.

The hallmark of nuoc mau is its careful balance of bittersweet and salty, so determining the correct ratio of fish sauce to caramel was key. After a lot of tinkering, I found that just ¼ cup of fish sauce produced the right savory, salty punch without tasting fishy. But something was off. The caramel's flavor was more purely sweet—closer to a dessert sauce—than the bittersweet flavor I was after.

I started up another batch and went against all my instincts, leaving it on the heat even after I saw the wisps of smoke. Soon, the bubbles took on an orange hue. I swirled the pan and saw that the color beneath was like molasses or black coffee. I immediately turned off the heat and added in the water and fish sauce. The key was to use an instant-read thermometer—I learned that the desired dark-molasses color corresponded to temperatures between 390 and 400 degrees. Hands down, the darker batch was superior to anything I'd tried yet. It was still slightly sweet, but it also had a notable bitterness that added complexity and brought the whole sauce into remarkable balance. For a final touch, I stirred in a couple of tablespoons of freshly grated ginger for warmth and brightness.

It was time for the chicken. I followed the lead of many modern recipes, which call for boneless, skinless chicken thighs cut into small pieces. While small bits of meat provided a lot of great surface area for the sauce to cling to, the flavor was only skin deep—the chicken had cooked through too quickly to absorb much flavor. I found that I achieved a happy medium by cutting boneless, skinless thighs in half.

In some recipes the meat was just cooked through, while others called for cooking it so long that it was nearly falling apart. I liked the latter approach since it meant more time for sauce absorption, but tasters found the resulting chicken dry. Luckily, I had a solution. In the past, we've found that treating meat with baking soda can help. The soda raises the meat's pH, which causes enzymes called calpains to become more active and cut the meat's muscle fibers. As the fibers break down, the meat's texture softens and its looser consistency retains water better. The net result: juicier, more tender meat.

I dissolved 1 tablespoon of baking soda in 1¼ cups of cold water and let the chicken soak for 15 minutes before rinsing it and adding it to the sauce in a 12-inch skillet. Even when simmered for more than 30 minutes, the chicken was still juicy—plus, it was pull-apart tender and fully infused with the flavor of the sauce.

I was really close, but the sauce wasn't clinging to the chicken like I'd hoped. As the chicken cooked, it released its juices, thinning out the sauce. Whisking in 2 teaspoons of cornstarch gave my sauce just enough body. In addition to the ginger, a few tasters asked for a little more spice. A small amount of ground black pepper added depth and the right amount of gentle heat.

For the last detail, I steamed some broccoli to provide a pleasant textural and visual contrast to the chicken. Finally, this was the complex, addictive dish that I'd been imagining.

—ANNIE PETITO, *Cook's Illustrated*

Vietnamese-Style Caramel Chicken with Broccoli

SERVES 4 TO 6

The saltiness of fish sauce can vary; we recommend Tiparos. When taking the temperature of the caramel in step 2, tilt the pan and move the thermometer back and forth to equalize hot and cool spots; also make sure to have hot water at the ready. This dish is intensely seasoned, so serve it with plenty of steamed white rice.

1 tablespoon baking soda

2 pounds boneless, skinless chicken thighs, trimmed and halved crosswise

7 tablespoons sugar

¼ cup fish sauce

2 tablespoons grated fresh ginger

1 pound broccoli, florets cut into 1-inch pieces, stalks peeled and sliced ¼ inch thick

2 teaspoons cornstarch

½ teaspoon pepper

½ cup chopped fresh cilantro leaves and stems

1. Combine baking soda and 1¼ cups cold water in large bowl. Add chicken and toss to coat. Let stand at room temperature for 15 minutes. Rinse chicken in cold water and drain well.

2. Meanwhile, combine sugar and 3 tablespoons water in small saucepan. Bring to boil over medium-high heat and cook, without stirring, until mixture begins to turn golden, 4 to 6 minutes. Reduce heat to medium-low and continue to cook, gently swirling saucepan, until sugar turns color of molasses and registers between 390 and 400 degrees, 4 to 6 minutes longer. (Caramel will produce some smoke during last 1 to 2 minutes of cooking.) Immediately remove saucepan from heat and carefully pour in ¾ cup hot water (mixture will bubble and steam vigorously). When bubbling has subsided, return saucepan to medium heat and stir to dissolve caramel.

3. Transfer caramel to 12-inch skillet and stir in fish sauce and ginger. Add chicken and bring to simmer over medium-high heat. Reduce heat to medium-low, cover, and simmer until chicken is fork-tender and registers 205 degrees, 30 to 40 minutes, flipping chicken halfway through simmering. Transfer chicken to serving dish and cover to keep warm.

4. Bring 1 inch water to boil in Dutch oven. Lower insert or steamer basket with broccoli into pot so it rests above water; cover and simmer until broccoli is just tender, 4½ to 5 minutes. Transfer broccoli to serving dish with chicken.

5. While broccoli cooks, bring sauce to boil over medium-high heat and cook until reduced to 1¼ cups, 3 to 5 minutes. Whisk cornstarch and 1 tablespoon water together in small bowl, then whisk into sauce; simmer until slightly thickened, about 1 minute. Stir in pepper. Pour ¼ cup sauce over chicken and broccoli. Sprinkle with cilantro and serve, passing remaining sauce separately.

NOTES FROM THE TEST KITCHEN

TAKING SOME SWEET OUT OF CARAMEL

Most of us think of caramel as a sweet sauce. But if cooked long enough, caramel will become less sweet and more complex. Here's what happens: When sugar is heated, a cascade of chemical reactions occurs that transforms some—and eventually all—of its single type of molecule into literally hundreds of different compounds that bring new flavors, aromas, and colors. At first these compounds are mild and buttery in flavor, and the caramel still tastes very sweet. With continued cooking, even more sugar molecules break down, and the caramel begins to taste markedly less sweet; meanwhile bitter, potent-tasting molecules also begin to form (along with those that bring a darker color). We found that cooking sugar to between 390 and 400 degrees produced a caramel with subtle sweetness and an appealingly bitter edge. Any additional cooking, though, made the caramel taste acrid and burnt.

SIMPLY SWEET
Only some sucrose molecules have broken down. Color is amber, and flavor is mild and still very sweet.

BITTERSWEET
More sucrose has broken down. Color is molasses-like, and flavor is less sweet and more complex.

MAKE-AHEAD CURRIED CHICKEN AND BROWN RICE

✓ **WHY THIS RECIPE WORKS:** Looking to develop a chicken and rice dish that was out of the ordinary, we paired meaty chicken thighs and hearty brown rice with a fragrant curry sauce. For a complexly flavored sauce that was easy to throw together, we used store-bought red curry paste enhanced with sautéed onion and scallions. Blooming the scallions and curry paste in oil brought out their flavors further and chicken broth added richness. Left to soak overnight, the rice tenderized and absorbed some of the flavor of the sauce. We seasoned the chicken thighs and marinated them overnight with oil and fresh lemon grass, which infused the chicken with flavor. On the second day, when we were finishing the dish in the oven, we stirred in coconut milk toward the end of cooking, which gave the sauce richness and a silky texture.

A good dish of curried chicken should have complex layers of flavor but at the same time be light and clean-tasting. Too many chicken curry recipes rely on overpowering amounts of spice and cloyingly thick sauces. These challenges become even more pronounced when you try to make a curry recipe ahead of time; the extra time can play havoc with the flavors and balance of ingredients if you're not careful. I wanted to create a mild but flavor-packed curried chicken dish, with a light but substantial sauce that would hold its own—and I wanted to be able to cook the rice to accompany the chicken right in the same dish for an even simpler and more approachable dinner. I also had a hunch that, if done right, making this recipe ahead of time would not only make it more convenient, it would also greatly improve the complex, multi-layered flavors of the curry and the integration of the various different ingredients.

Most of the one-dish chicken and rice dishes I looked at relied on boneless, skinless chicken breasts for convenience, so those were the first option I considered, but because chicken breasts are so lean, without special treatment it's hard to prevent the meat from drying out. They also have a very mild flavor, so they usually have to be browned to ensure deep chicken flavor, which adds a step (and a dirty pan) to the cooking process, and I wanted to avoid that. This led me to reconsider my choice of chicken cut—what if I went with boneless, skinless chicken thighs instead? The darker, more flavorful meat would help me avoid the need to sear the chicken and would also add depth to the dish. Sticking with boneless and skinless chicken thighs avoided problems with soggy skin and kept everything as simple as possible.

Once I'd decided on the chicken cut, I started thinking about the flavors of my dish. The complex flavors of a curry come from a variety of spices, chiles, and aromatics working in combination. Building this mix from the ground up can lead to quite an intimidating ingredient list. To keep mine manageable, I turned to premixed store-bought red curry paste, which I augmented with onion and scallions. I sautéed those ingredients together to bloom the spices and then stirred in chicken broth to make a fragrant, rich cooking liquid that I could use to make the base of my dish, the rice. To avoid the texture and flavor issues that tend to accompany short-grain rice, I opted instead for long-grain rice. Long-grain rice is far better at withstanding long soaking times without the danger of turning to mush, which was important if I was going to assemble my dish hours ahead of time. For even more flavor, I chose to use brown rice. Soaking the rice overnight in the flavorful broth not only infused it with plenty of curry spice but also tenderized the hearty brown rice, making it much easier to cook alongside the chicken in the finished casserole. For the final flavor addition to the rice, I wanted to add chopped red bell pepper, but bell peppers can be tricky to deal with. They need time to soften and cook through, but if they get overcooked they become mushy and blown out. I found that the best method was to add them to the cooled rice and broth so they could soak and soften along with the rice. They cooked to just the right texture in the oven the next day, melting into the rice and adding a great sweetness to the heat of the curry paste.

With the rice taken care of, I turned back to the chicken. I wanted to pack in even more flavor, so I tried cooking the chicken in coconut milk, a star ingredient in curries of many origins that adds incredible richness to a dish. Unfortunately, this made the dish greasy and heavy, and by the time it was finished cooking, it had actually lost much of the coconut flavor I was looking for, so I had to reevaluate. I knew I still wanted to incorporate the coconut milk, but I decided to wait until the second day when I put the whole dish together. In the meantime, I marinated the chicken with a little olive oil and some prepared lemon grass, a classic ingredient in curry recipes. The lemon grass flavor in the chicken would complement, but still taste distinctive from, the hotter spices of the red curry paste in the rice. Then, the next day, I nestled the marinated chicken in the soaked, curried rice and put my one-dish meal in the oven. After the chicken and rice were nearly done cooking together, I stirred in a small amount of light coconut milk during the last 15 minutes of baking. This was the perfect way to bring in all the flavor and richness I wanted from the coconut milk without any greasiness.

The steps I had taken on the first day made it easy to bring everything together in one dish on the second day. Soaking the rice overnight meant that it needed less time to cook through, so I was able to put the chicken right in with the rice to bake. Stirring a few times as the dish baked ensured that all the grains of rice came out tender, and by the time it was done, the chicken was perfectly cooked. My last-minute addition of light coconut milk absorbed right into the flavorful rice for a final dish that supported all my hunches about how to produce a great make-ahead version of curried chicken and rice with rich flavor and an easy, no-fuss approach.

—SARA MAYER, *America's Test Kitchen Books*

Make-Ahead Curried Chicken and Brown Rice with Red Peppers

SERVES 6

Using light coconut milk is important because it keeps the rice from becoming too greasy.

2	tablespoons extra-virgin olive oil
1	onion, chopped
	Salt and pepper
2	scallions, minced
2	tablespoons red curry paste
2½	cups chicken broth
1½	cups long-grain brown rice, rinsed
2	red bell peppers, stemmed, seeded, and cut into ½-inch pieces
2	pounds boneless, skinless chicken thighs, trimmed
1	lemon grass stalk, trimmed to bottom 6 inches and minced (2 tablespoons)
½	cup canned light coconut milk
1	tablespoon minced fresh cilantro
	Lime wedges

1. Heat 1 tablespoon oil in 12-inch skillet over medium heat until shimmering. Add onion and ½ teaspoon salt and cook until softened and lightly browned, 5 to 7 minutes. Stir in scallions and curry paste and cook until fragrant, about 30 seconds. Stir in 1 cup broth, scraping up any browned bits.

2. Transfer broth mixture to 13 by 9-inch baking dish, stir in rice and remaining 1½ cups broth, and let cool to room temperature, about 20 minutes. Stir in bell peppers.

3. Pat chicken dry with paper towels, season with salt and pepper, and place in zipper-lock bag. Add lemon grass and remaining 1 tablespoon oil to bag, press out air, and seal; toss to coat chicken.

4. Wrap dish tightly with plastic wrap and refrigerate rice mixture and chicken separately for at least 8 hours or up to 24 hours.

5. Adjust oven rack to middle position and heat oven to 375 degrees. Unwrap dish and nestle chicken into rice. Cover dish tightly with greased aluminum foil and bake casserole until liquid is almost fully absorbed and rice and chicken are tender, about 1 hour, stirring thoroughly 3 times during baking. Stir in coconut milk and bake, covered, until liquid is fully absorbed, about 15 minutes. Let sit, covered, for 10 minutes. Sprinkle with cilantro and serve with lime wedges.

NOTES FROM THE TEST KITCHEN

MARRYING CHICKEN AND RICE

It took a few tricks to get perfectly cooked boneless, skinless chicken thighs and hearty brown rice in a single dish.

We soaked the rice overnight, which meant that it needed less time to cook through. We also stirred it a few times as it baked to ensure that all the grains came out tender.

MAKE-AHEAD CHICKEN POT PIE

✓ **WHY THIS RECIPE WORKS:** The convenience of frozen pot pies hold a lot of appeal, but store-bought versions are always disappointing. We set out to create a great-tasting make-ahead version that would hold up to freezing and reheating. For the sauce, we lightly browned onions, carrots, and celery in butter before mixing in tomato paste for color and flavor. We added some flour to thicken things up before stirring in the chicken broth. For the chicken, we poached boneless, skinless thighs in the sauce. Once the chicken was tender, we removed it from the pot, shredded it, and returned it to the sauce along with heavy cream for richness and sherry for a deeper flavor. For the topping, we turned to convenient store-bought pie dough, which comes in packages of two and was easy to trim to fit over the filling. To ensure a crisp crust, we created an aluminum foil barrier so the filling could heat through while the crust thawed and baked.

Chicken pot pie is comfort food at its best, but it can also be a lot of work to make. I wanted to streamline chicken pot pie and turn it into something that would retain all the golden, flaky pastry and velvety rich filling of classic chicken pot pie, but in a make-ahead form that I could pull out of the freezer any weeknight.

I followed the classic method for sautéing vegetables and making a creamy sauce in the same pan, browning my vegetables and aromatics together before adding tomato paste and flour. Next I added some chicken broth and tackled the meat of the dish—the actual chicken. Many classic recipes call for poaching or roasting a whole chicken as a separate step in the cooking process, but that seemed like way too much work, so I turned to boneless, skinless chicken parts poached right in the sauce I was already making. By incorporating the chicken into the making of the sauce I combined two steps into one and this change also added extra flavor to both the sauce and the chicken. I started with a mix of boneless, skinless breasts and thighs, but while the darker meat of the thighs remained moist and flavorful as it cooked, the breasts ended up dry and stringy, so I decided to use all thighs. Once they were cooked, I removed the thighs from the sauce to shred them into bite-size pieces and then added them back to the sauce along with heavy cream and sherry to make a rich filling. I also added the more delicate elements of

MAKE-AHEAD CHICKEN POT PIE

the filling—peas and fresh parsley—at the very end of this step, to keep from overcooking them.

Things were looking pretty good so far, but my problems weren't over. Despite the great filling I'd cooked up, my first few attempts at baking my make-ahead chicken pot pie came out unpleasantly dry and mealy. It turns out that freezing and storing the dish has a big impact on the moisture level. Because of this, the filling in my final recipe had to be much looser and saucier than normal; the extra liquid ensured that it wouldn't become too thick and gummy during baking after being frozen.

Now that I'd developed the perfect freeze-ahead pot pie filling, I had to tackle the crust. Homemade pie crust seemed like too much labor for a simplified dinner option, so I turned to store-bought refrigerator pie crusts. I cut vents in the pastry and trimmed them to fit on top of my pot pies, then wrapped everything up and put the pies away in the freezer. A few weeks later I came back to see how they would bake up. I placed a frozen, unwrapped pot pie on a foil-rimmed baking sheet and baked it, but it immediately became clear that there were some new issues to deal with at this stage in the recipe. The biggest one was that during baking, the filling bubbled up through the vents in the crust, making the pie gummy, wet, and messy. The solution came from a box—of tin foil: I added a barrier of aluminum foil between the crust and the pot pie filling, which would let the filling warm up while protecting the crust from too much moisture. I also kept the whole pot pie covered with foil for the first half of the baking time, which let the crust defrost without allowing it to burn. Then I uncovered the dish for the second half of baking to ensure that the crust would be fully browned by the time dinner was ready to serve. The pie needed both the covered and uncovered baking time to ensure that all the elements were done at the same time.

When the pie was fully cooked, it was easy to simply slide the aluminum foil out from between the perfectly browned crust and fully heated filling. I now had freezer-friendly chicken pot pies to enjoy whenever the mood struck; these pot pies can be baked right away, if you want, but they can also be frozen and stored for up to a month before baking. Since the recipe makes two, you can even have one for dinner tonight and one that's just as delicious for dinner a month from now—all with less than 2 hours of prep time.

—MEAGHEN WALSH, *America's Test Kitchen Books*

Make-Ahead Chicken Pot Pie

MAKES 2 PIES, EACH SERVING 4

You will need two 9½-inch disposable aluminum deep-dish pie pans for this recipe.

- 1 tablespoon unsalted butter
- 2 onions, chopped fine
- 1 pound carrots, peeled and sliced ¼ inch thick
- 2 celery ribs, sliced ¼ inch thick
  Salt and pepper
- 2 teaspoons tomato paste
- 2 teaspoons minced fresh thyme or ½ teaspoon dried
- ½ cup all-purpose flour
- 2½ cups chicken broth
- 3 pounds boneless, skinless chicken thighs, trimmed
- ½ cup heavy cream
- 2 tablespoons dry sherry
- 1 cup frozen peas
- ¼ cup minced fresh parsley
- 1 package store-bought pie dough
- 1 large egg, lightly beaten

1. Melt butter in Dutch oven over medium heat. Add onions, carrots, celery, 1 teaspoon salt, and ½ teaspoon pepper and cook until softened and lightly browned, 8 to 10 minutes. Stir in tomato paste and thyme and cook until browned, about 2 minutes. Stir in flour and cook for 1 minute.

2. Slowly whisk in chicken broth, scraping up any browned bits and smoothing out any lumps. Add chicken and bring to simmer. Reduce heat to medium-low, cover, and simmer, stirring occasionally, until chicken registers 175 degrees and sauce is thickened, 25 to 30 minutes. Off heat, transfer chicken to cutting board, let cool slightly, then shred into bite-size pieces using 2 forks.

3. Stir heavy cream and sherry into sauce, then stir in shredded chicken with any accumulated juices. Season with salt and pepper to taste. Spray pie pans with vegetable oil. Divide filling evenly between 2 pans and let cool to room temperature, about 30 minutes. Divide peas and parsley evenly between pans and stir into fillings.

4. Cut out two 12-inch square sheets of aluminum foil and grease both sides lightly. Press sheet of foil flush to surface of each filling, letting excess hang over edges of pans. Unroll each pie dough round, trim to 9-inch round (if necessary), and cut four 2-inch vents in center. Gently place 1 pie dough round on each pan. (To bake casserole right away, skip cooling in step 3.

Brush pastry top with beaten egg, place pot pie on foil-lined rimmed baking sheet, and bake, uncovered, in preheated 400-degree oven until crust is golden, 35 to 40 minutes. Let cool for 15 minutes. Loosen foil from edges of pan. Holding pie crust in place, gently pull foil out from underneath. Serve.)

5. Wrap pans tightly with plastic wrap and cover with foil. Freeze casseroles for up to 1 month. (Do not thaw before reheating.)

6. Unwrap pot pie, brush top with beaten egg, cover with greased foil, and place on foil-lined rimmed baking sheet. Place pot pie on middle rack of cold oven, turn oven to 400 degrees, and bake for 40 minutes. Uncover and continue to bake until crust is golden, 35 to 40 minutes. Let cool for 15 minutes. Loosen foil from edges of pan. Holding pie crust in place, gently pull foil out from underneath. Serve.

ROAST HERITAGE TURKEY

✓ **WHY THIS RECIPE WORKS:** Heritage turkeys lead a much longer and more active life than their supermarket brethren, leading to dark meat that is well exercised and collagen-rich. Plus, they have a shallower breast and longer legs, making traditional cooking methods unsuccessful. We needed a heritage turkey–friendly approach. Before roasting, we seasoned under the skin and let the turkey parts sit uncovered in the refrigerator overnight to improve flavor and tenderness and boost crisping of the skin. We broke the bird down in order to separate the dark and white meat so that we could give the dark meat a head start in a low oven to begin tenderizing. We added the breast partway through and flipped the pieces to ensure even cooking. After letting them rest for 30 to 60 minutes, we returned them to a 500-degree oven to quickly crisp the skin.

During the past few holiday seasons, we've become increasingly curious about heritage turkey. In 1997, these turkeys were nearly extinct in the United States, but a concerted effort by breeders and farmers brought them back. The revival is understandable: Heritage turkeys come from special stock that promises to be superior to its supermarket counterpart. These old-breed turkeys spend lots of time outdoors, eat a varied diet, and grow slowly. This purportedly translates to richly flavored meat.

I ordered a half-dozen heritage turkeys from farms across the country, each one boasting a slightly different pedigree. They did all have one thing in common: None looked like the familiar supermarket bird. They had notably longer legs and smaller breasts—so success using a standard cooking method seemed unlikely. Still, it was the logical place to start, so I forged ahead with a typical approach that started the bird at high heat and ended with low heat.

I cooked the birds breast side down at 400 degrees for 45 minutes and then breast side up at 325 degrees until the breast hit 165 degrees. Two things became clear. First, the flavor of the breast meat on these turkeys was richer than any white meat I'd ever tasted. And second, I had no idea how to cook these birds: The dark meat on some of them was so underdone that I had to separate the leg quarters and return them to the oven. Once fully cooked, however, the dark meat also proved exceptional—tender as well as deeply flavored.

I needed a technique that could deal with the unique build of these birds to deliver just-cooked white meat and well-done dark meat. I had an idea about how to do it.

One of the best ways to tenderize tough cuts of poultry is a braise. A braising liquid quickly transfers heat to the meat because it is densely packed with molecules (which is where the heat is stored). The air in a hot oven, on the other hand, has comparatively few molecules and thus transfers heat more slowly. I wondered if I could take advantage of the disparity in speed between braising and roasting by submerging the back, legs, and wings of the turkey in broth while keeping the breast elevated. This seemed like a smart idea, until all of a sudden it didn't. There I was, standing in the kitchen in front of a roasting pan filled almost to the brim with a sea of chicken broth. Emerging like islands from the deep were the knee of each leg and only the top half of the breast. My plan had been foiled by heritage turkey anatomy—because the breast was so shallow and the legs so long, there was no way to submerge the dark meat without covering much of the white in the process.

Or was there? I grabbed my knife and made slits between the breast and thigh on both sides of the turkey, allowing the legs to lie flatter so that I could add less liquid. My hope was that after braising I could truss the legs back into place and then roast the bird to finish cooking the breast and brown the skin. No dice. As the dark meat braised, the leg muscles contracted and hoisted the legs out of the liquid like surfacing submarines.

I reworked my plan of attack. Breaking down the turkey would allow me to customize cooking the dark and white meat for the best possible results, but I wanted to keep it simple. I grabbed my knife and cut off both leg quarters.

One immediate benefit of this quick butchering was ease of seasoning. Rubbing salt on the skin of a bird makes the skin salty, but if you want seasoned meat, you have to get under the skin and rub salt directly onto the breast and legs. My broken-down bird provided ample routes of entry for this endeavor. After seasoning the turkey parts, I let them rest overnight in the refrigerator, a step that leads to better-seasoned, more-tender meat, as well as drier skin that readily crisps and browns.

It was time to roast, and here I had a big decision to make. Should I start with high heat to brown the skin and then lower the oven to finish cooking gently, or do the reverse and go low to high? High to low turned out to be too fussy: After the browning stage, the breast, which had started cooking, had to be set aside while the dark meat got its jump start and then go back in. Low to high—starting the dark meat, adding the breast partway through, and then browning—was much more streamlined. I also noticed that the skin browned better and stayed more crisp when I saved the high-heat stage for the end.

I set the breast aside and placed the leg quarters, skin side down, in a 250-degree oven for their head start. I tested a flock of turkeys to determine the ideal temperature for the legs to reach before I flipped them over and added the breast: 140 degrees. This may seem like a big head start, given that the legs needed to reach only 175 degrees, but it actually made good sense. At 140 degrees collagen is just beginning to break down, and from there it happens very, very slowly so the temperature rises only gradually. By the time the breast was cooked through, the legs had finally fully tenderized. To ensure that the breast cooked evenly, I started it skin side down and then flipped it for the final couple of hours of cooking. After pulling the parts from the oven, I let them rest to allow the juices to redistribute and the meat to cool a bit so it wouldn't overcook during a final blast at 500 degrees. This setup did the trick. Just 10 minutes in the hot oven turned the skin brown, burnished, and crispy. The white meat was moist, the dark meat was tender and juicy, and the salting step had highlighted the bird's meaty, savory qualities.

While my turkey was slowly roasting, I put the reserved back and neck to work in a simple gravy. Since I didn't have any drippings, I browned the back and neck, built the gravy, and then reduced the mixture with the back and neck in the pot to eke out all their flavor before straining. Though, now that I'd tasted my heritage turkey, I wasn't so certain it needed gravy at all.

—DAN SOUZA, *Cook's Illustrated*

Roast Heritage Turkey

SERVES 8 TO 10

This recipe requires refrigerating the salted turkey for 24 to 48 hours before cooking. If you're making our Gravy for Roast Heritage Turkey (recipe follows), reserve the turkey backbone and neck.

1 **(10- to 12-pound) heritage breed turkey,**
   neck removed
   Kosher salt

1. Place wire rack in rimmed baking sheet and lightly grease rack. With turkey breast side up, using sharp knife, slice through skin between breast and thigh down to joint on both sides. Using your hands, pull each leg quarter back to expose joint between leg and breast. Remove legs by cutting through hip joint and then skin. Slice through membrane connecting breast to backbone. Bend backbone away from breast to break where it meets rib cage; use knife to remove completely.

2. Using your fingers, gently loosen skin covering legs and breasts. Rub 1½ teaspoons salt evenly inside cavity of turkey breast, 1½ teaspoons salt under skin of each breast, and 1½ teaspoons salt under skin of each leg.

NOTES FROM THE TEST KITCHEN

TRIM THE RIB BONES

While some turkey breasts are sold pretrimmed, you may need to use kitchen shears to neatly trim the wings, rib bones, and backbone pieces on both sides of the breast to ensure that the turkey will fit into the pot.

Tuck wings underneath breast. Place turkey legs and breast, skin side up, on prepared wire rack. Refrigerate turkey parts, uncovered, for at least 24 hours or up to 48 hours.

3. Adjust oven rack to lower-middle position and heat oven to 250 degrees. Transfer breast to large plate and set aside while leg quarters start roasting. Flip leg quarters skin side down and transfer to oven; roast until thighs register 140 degrees, 45 to 75 minutes.

4. Flip leg quarters skin side up and place breast, skin side down, on wire rack next to leg quarters. Return to oven and roast for 1 hour.

5. Flip breast skin side up and continue to roast until breast registers 155 degrees and thighs register 175 degrees, 1¼ to 2¼ hours longer. Remove turkey from oven and let rest for at least 30 minutes or up to 60 minutes.

6. While turkey is resting, increase oven temperature to 500 degrees. Stack turkey assembly on second baking sheet to prevent excess smoking. Return turkey to oven and roast until skin is golden brown and crispy, 10 to 15 minutes.

7. Transfer turkey to carving board and let rest for 20 minutes. Carve turkey and serve.

Gravy for Roast Heritage Turkey

MAKES ABOUT 1 QUART

If the gravy reduces too quickly, add water and continue to cook for the full hour.

> 2 teaspoons vegetable oil
> Reserved turkey backbone and neck from Roast Heritage Turkey
> 4 tablespoons unsalted butter
> 1 small onion, sliced thin
> 1 celery rib, sliced thin
> ¼ cup all-purpose flour
> ½ cup dry white wine
> 4 cups chicken broth
> 3 cups water
> 3 bay leaves
> Salt and pepper

1. Heat oil in Dutch oven over medium heat until shimmering. Add reserved turkey backbone and neck and cook until well browned on all sides, 8 to 10 minutes. Transfer to large plate and set aside. Reduce heat to medium-low and add butter, onion, and celery. Cook, stirring frequently, until vegetables are softened and browned, 5 to 7 minutes. Stir in flour and cook, stirring constantly, until fragrant and lightly browned, about 1 minute. Whisk in wine and cook until thickened, about 1 minute. Whisking constantly, gradually add broth, water, and bay leaves. Return backbone and neck to pot and bring to simmer over high heat. Reduce heat to medium-low and simmer, uncovered, flipping backbone and neck occasionally, until liquid is thickened and measures about 1 quart, about 1 hour.

2. Discard backbone and neck. Strain gravy through fine-mesh strainer, pushing on solids to extract as much liquid as possible. Season with salt and pepper to taste.

TURKEY IN A POT WITH GRAVY

✓ **WHY THIS RECIPE WORKS:** For a turkey breast with supermoist meat, we borrowed the French technique of cooking *en cocotte*. We browned the breast first to add color to the skin and flavor to the pot. We roasted the turkey with the vegetables, tightly covered in a low (250-degree) oven, to 155 degrees. Then we uncovered the bird, brushed it with butter, and broiled it to help crisp the skin. The drippings and vegetables formed a flavorful base to build a delicious gravy while the turkey rested.

First, dispense with the obvious: Serving a turkey breast instead of a whole turkey changes the look of the Thanksgiving table. But consider how quickly that photo op fades once carving commences. The breast, alone, is much easier to cook and to carve. This year, I was willing to forgo the full bird for a moist, perfect breast—if only I could figure out how.

Cooking a whole bird in a pot is a French technique called en cocotte in which poultry is cooked over low heat in a covered pot for an extended period of time; it produces very moist, tender meat. A whole chicken is the most common choice, but I wondered if that same technique would work with a bone-in turkey breast. My goal was a tender, moist turkey breast with crispy skin plus a delicious gravy to seal the deal.

Bone-in turkey breasts tend to vary in size, weighing anywhere from 5 to 10 pounds. After several initial tests, I figured out that 6 to 7 pounds was the ideal size;

it's large enough to feed a small crowd (up to eight people), but small enough to fit into a 7-quart Dutch oven, particularly if the rib bones are trimmed.

Browning the turkey breast was an essential step in developing deep flavor. Due to the shape of the breast, it took a little finagling, but I was able to brown the breast in around 15 minutes, tilting it on its sides to brown all over. My next step, after removing the browned breast from the pot, was to add some diced onion, carrot, and celery to the same pot, along with garlic, thyme, and a bay leaf. This would not only begin building a gravy but also add moisture to the pot for deglazing the flavorful fond left from the browning. When the vegetables were well browned, I set the turkey breast over the vegetables, meaty side up, and then covered the pot with foil and a tight lid and transferred it to a low oven. The turkey breast took between 1½ and 1¾ hours to come up to the target temperature of 155 degrees.

The meat was moist and juicy, but unfortunately, the skin was nowhere near as crispy as I wanted it after the turkey had been steaming in the pot. To fix the flabby skin issue, I turned to the broiler. I pulled the turkey out of the oven at 155 degrees, waited for the broiler to come up to temperature, brushed the skin with melted butter to help browning, and returned my potted turkey, still on the middle rack, to the broiler. With a close eye through the glass oven door, I let the turkey brown for about 10 minutes. The skin that had been flabby before now had a lovely crispy texture. With the meat tender and juicy and the skin crispy, all that was left was to focus on the gravy.

Initially, I tried straining and defatting the juices left in the pot and then thickening them with either a roux or a slurry. But the resulting gravy lacked complexity. For my next try, I took a new approach. After removing the turkey from the pot, I reduced the pan juices until they had all but evaporated, concentrating the turkey flavor and producing a mahogany fond on the bottom of the pot. I stirred some flour into this rich mixture to make a roux and then added a full quart of chicken broth to the pot. I brought the mixture to a simmer and cooked it until the mixture had reduced and concentrated, which took about 15 minutes. After straining and seasoning, I finally had it all: perfectly cooked, incredibly moist and tender meat; crispy skin; and intensely flavored gravy, all from one pot. Satisfied, I gathered my tasters. Their opinion? "Tastes like Thanksgiving should taste."

—DIANE UNGER, *Cook's Country*

Turkey in a Pot with Gravy
SERVES 6 TO 8

Try to purchase a turkey breast with the wings already removed so it's sure to fit into your pot. Otherwise, remove the wings before proceeding with the recipe. A carving fork works well for turning the turkey and removing it from the pot.

- 1 (7-pound) bone-in whole turkey breast, wings discarded, trimmed
  Salt and pepper
- 2 tablespoons olive oil
- 1 onion, chopped
- 1 carrot, chopped
- 1 celery rib, chopped
- 6 garlic cloves, peeled and crushed
- 1 teaspoon minced fresh thyme
- 1 bay leaf
- 1 tablespoon unsalted butter, melted
- ¼ cup all-purpose flour
- 4 cups chicken broth

1. Adjust oven rack to middle position and heat oven to 250 degrees. Using kitchen shears, trim any rib bones that extend beyond underside of turkey breast. (If any backbone pieces are still attached to underside of turkey, remove them.) Pat turkey dry with paper towels and season with salt and pepper.

2. Heat oil in large Dutch oven over medium-high heat until just smoking. Add turkey, skin side down, and cook until well browned, 12 to 16 minutes, rolling it from side to side as needed for even browning. Transfer turkey to plate and set aside. Pour off all but 2 tablespoons fat from pot. Add onion, carrot, celery, garlic, thyme, and bay leaf to pot and cook until vegetables are well browned, 7 to 10 minutes.

3. Return turkey and accumulated juices to pot, skin side up. Off heat, place large sheet of aluminum foil over pot and press edges to seal, then cover tightly with lid. Transfer pot to oven and cook until thickest part of breast registers 155 degrees, 1½ to 1¾ hours.

4. Remove pot from oven and heat broiler. Uncover pot (handles will be very hot) and brush turkey with melted butter. When broiler is heated, return pot to oven and broil until skin is golden brown, 8 to 15 minutes, rotating pot as needed for even browning. Remove pot

TURKEY IN A POT WITH GRAVY

from oven. Transfer turkey to carving board, tent loosely with foil, and let rest while making gravy.

5. Place pot over medium-high heat, bring to boil, and cook until almost all liquid has evaporated, 8 to 15 minutes. Stir in flour and cook until lightly browned, about 2 minutes. Slowly whisk in broth and bring to boil. Reduce heat to medium and cook at strong simmer, stirring often, until gravy is thickened and measures about 2 cups, 15 to 18 minutes. Strain gravy through fine-mesh strainer set over medium saucepan; discard solids. Season gravy with salt and pepper to taste. Carve turkey. Rewarm gravy and serve with turkey.

GRILLED FISH TACOS

✓ **WHY THIS RECIPE WORKS:** For a fish taco with fresh, bold flavors, we fired up the grill. For simplicity we opted for skinless fillets instead of the traditional whole butterflied fish. Meaty swordfish held up on the grill better than flaky options like snapper and cod. A thick paste featuring ancho and chipotle chile powders, oregano, and just a touch of citrus developed deep, flavorful charring on the grill without promoting sticking. Refreshing grilled pineapple salsa, avocado, and crunchy iceberg lettuce completed our tacos with flavor and texture contrasts.

Batter-fried fish tacos have their place, but when we don't want to deal with a pot of hot oil, we go for the grilled kind. Nicely charred, moist fillets with a few cool, crunchy garnishes and a squeeze of lime have the potential to be lighter on both the fuss and the stomach.

For grilled fish tacos with more punch, we looked for inspiration in preparations popular in the Yucatán Peninsula and along the Pacific coast of Mexico. Here they split a whole fish in half lengthwise, bathe it in a deep red chile–citrus mixture, then grill it wrapped in banana leaves or in a grill basket. This flavor-packed fish is served on a platter whole, to be flaked off and eaten with tortillas and some simple sides. We wanted grilled fish tacos featuring a similarly bold flavor profile, but a simpler approach.

Our first task was finding the best substitute for the whole fish. Traditional recipes usually start with a whole butterflied snapper or grouper. We knew we wanted to grill smaller portions, but a quick test in which we grilled both snapper and grouper fillets confirmed they

weren't going to work out. Keeping the skin on was key with these flakier fish to prevent sticking, and that meant at serving time almost all of their charred flavor went into the trash with the skin. Relying on banana leaves or a grilling basket, like the traditional recipes, would circumvent sticking, but tracking down such an obscure item or requiring special equipment were both out of the question. We needed a different variety of fish.

Fish with a denser, meatier texture were more promising, so we gave mahi-mahi, tuna, swordfish, and halibut a chance. In the end, swordfish was the favorite. It's easy to find, it stands up well to flipping on the grill, and steaks had enough time to pick up plenty of flavorful char before the interior cooked through. Cutting the fish into 1-inch-wide strips made it even easier to handle and also meant that the fish could go from grill to taco without any further prep.

Some of the more modern recipes we found called for marinating the fish in lots of citrus juice with a hit of warm chile spice and other seasonings. But we quickly discovered this sort of pretreatment created more problems than benefits. First, the flavor was lackluster since the fish spent only about 30 minutes in the marinade, and letting it sit longer led to fish that cooked in its high-acid bath. Worse, the significant amount of sugar in the fruit juice meant that, even with oil in the marinade, the fish had to be chiseled off the cooking grate. We briefly considered putting a piece of foil between the fish and the grate, but it prevented the fish from picking up flavorful char. We moved on to option two.

Many of the traditional recipes we'd found called for coating the fish in a thick paste featuring ground annatto seeds (the same spice used to color yellow cheese) or ground dried chiles, various warm spices, and just enough citrus juice to make it spreadable. But we knew we'd have to vary from tradition at least a little. Annatto seeds, which come from the tropical achiote tree, might be easy to find in Mexico, but they can be tough to ferret out stateside. We hoped that landing on the right mix of chiles and spices could make up for the loss of the annatto's earthy, peppery flavor.

Starting with whole dried chiles is the authentic approach, but the fuss of toasting them in a dry skillet or softening them in oil, then grinding them to a powder was more work (not to mention shopping effort) than we cared to deal with. At the other end of the spectrum—and also not an option in our minds—was chili powder. With its blend of ground chiles and other spices and herbs, it made a paste that was passable but not distinctive.

Instead, we created a blend of chile powders and ground herbs, singling out ancho chile powder for its fruitiness and chipotle chile powder for smoky heat and earthiness, while some oregano and ground coriander boosted complexity. Blooming this mixture in oil, along with some minced garlic and salt, rounded out the flavors. But it still needed a bigger punch of savory sweetness. Adding a few tablespoons of tomato paste took care of that.

The last component: the citrus juice. Looking back at the recipes we'd compiled, sour or Seville oranges appeared most frequently. Instead, we employed a commonly suggested substitute: orange juice with a little lime juice added to give it the right tart, bright acidity.

After coating the fish in the paste, we let it sit in the refrigerator while the grill heated up to give the salt time to penetrate and season the fish. Despite fish's reputation for delicacy, we found there was no need to hold back on heat. A heaping chimney of charcoal (about 7 quarts) gave the coating great char that further deepened the swordfish's flavor and just cooked it through. We were also happy to find that as long as we thoroughly oiled the grate, the paste didn't exacerbate any sticking issues. In fact, the grittiness of the chile powder and herbs kept the fish from sticking.

All that was left was coming up with the right combination of garnishes. Fresh, crunchy iceberg lettuce and rich, silky avocado were both in. A fresh fruit salsa also sounded promising. Mango and papaya both had potential, but pineapple won out for its acidity and sweetness, which balanced the spicy earthiness of the fish. A little jalapeño for some fresh heat and bell pepper and cilantro for color and freshness rounded out the salsa.

Since there was plenty of room on the grill, we threw the pineapple and jalapeño on the cooking grate opposite the fish, an easy step that caramelized the fruit and deepened the chile's flavors and brought more of the flavor of the grill to our tacos. Once the fish and salsa ingredients came off the grate, we quickly warmed the tortillas over the fire.

Loaded up with the smoky, boldly flavored fish, salsa, and garnishes, these tacos were satisfying yet still refreshingly light. They didn't need anything else but a cold beer to drink alongside.

—DAVID PAZMIÑO, *Cook's Illustrated*

NOTES FROM THE TEST KITCHEN

DON'T FLAKE OUT

When grilling fish, avoid flaky varieties like grouper, hake, cod, or snapper, which will stick to the grill and fall apart when you try to flip them.

SHREDDED SNAPPER

For fillets that stay intact, choose a denser variety like swordfish, mahi-mahi, tuna, or halibut.

Grilled Fish Tacos

SERVES 6

Mahi-mahi, tuna, and halibut fillets are all suitable substitutes for the swordfish, but to ensure the best results buy 1-inch-thick fillets and cut them in a similar fashion as the swordfish.

 3 **tablespoons vegetable oil**
 1 **tablespoon ancho chile powder**
 2 **teaspoons chipotle chile powder**
 1 **teaspoon dried oregano**
 1 **teaspoon ground coriander**
 2 **garlic cloves, minced**
    Salt
 2 **tablespoons tomato paste**
 ½ **cup orange juice**
 6 **tablespoons lime juice (3 limes)**
 2 **pounds skinless swordfish steaks, 1 inch thick, cut lengthwise into 1-inch-wide strips**
 1 **pineapple, peeled, cored, quartered lengthwise, and each quarter sliced in half lengthwise**
 1 **jalapeño chile**
18 **(6-inch) corn tortillas**
 1 **red bell pepper, stemmed, seeded, and cut into ¼-inch pieces**
 2 **tablespoons minced fresh cilantro, plus extra for serving**
 ½ **head iceberg lettuce, cored and sliced thin**
 1 **avocado, halved, pitted, and sliced thin**
    Lime wedges

1. Heat 2 tablespoons oil, ancho chile powder, and chipotle chile powder in 8-inch skillet over medium heat, stirring constantly, until fragrant and some bubbles form, 2 to 3 minutes. Add oregano, coriander, garlic, and 1 teaspoon salt and continue to cook until fragrant, about 30 seconds longer. Add tomato paste and, using spatula, mash tomato paste with spice mixture until combined, about 20 seconds. Stir in orange juice and 2 tablespoons lime juice. Cook, stirring constantly, until thoroughly mixed and reduced slightly, about 2 minutes. Transfer chile mixture to large bowl and let cool for 15 minutes.

2. Add swordfish to bowl with chile mixture and stir gently with rubber spatula to coat fish. Cover and refrigerate for at least 30 minutes or up to 2 hours.

3A. FOR A CHARCOAL GRILL: Open bottom vent completely. Light large chimney starter mounded with charcoal (7 quarts). When top coals are partially covered with ash, pour coals evenly across bottom of grill. Set cooking grate in place. Cover and open lid vent completely. Heat grill until hot, about 5 minutes.

3B. FOR A GAS GRILL: Turn all burners to high, cover, and heat grill until hot, about 15 minutes. Turn all burners to medium-high.

4. Clean and thoroughly oil cooking grate. Brush both sides of pineapple with remaining 1 tablespoon oil. Place fish on half of grill. Place pineapple and whole jalapeño on other half. Cover and cook until fish, pineapple, and jalapeño have begun to brown, 3 to 5 minutes. Using thin spatula, turn fish, pineapple, and jalapeño. Cover and continue to cook until the second half of pineapple and jalapeño have browned and swordfish registers 140 degrees, 3 to 5 minutes. Transfer fish to large platter, flake into pieces, and tent with foil. Transfer pineapple and jalapeño to cutting board.

5. Clean cooking grate. Place half of tortillas on grill. Cook on each side until softened and speckled with brown spots, 30 to 45 seconds per side. Wrap tortillas in dish towel or foil to keep warm. Repeat with remaining tortillas.

6. When cool enough to handle, finely chop pineapple and jalapeño. Transfer to medium bowl and stir in bell pepper, cilantro, and remaining ¼ cup lime juice. Season with salt to taste. Top tortillas with flaked fish, salsa, lettuce, and avocado. Serve with lime wedges and extra cilantro.

MAKE-AHEAD CRISPY BREADED COD FILLETS

✓ **WHY THIS RECIPE WORKS:** If you're looking for tender, moist fish with a tasty crumb crust that doesn't fall off, you've got to have a few tricks up your sleeves. If you also want to make the dish ahead of time, it's even more challenging. We began from the top: the breading. Traditional bread crumbs are prone to sogginess, but in the test kitchen we've had great success with extra-crispy panko bread crumbs. However, even panko lost its crispness after a night in the refrigerator. Toasting the panko on the stovetop with melted butter (plus some aromatics for flavor) solved the problem. To get it to stick to the fillets, we spread a mixture of egg yolk and mayonnaise on top of the fish before pressing on the crumbs. Now we had a nice, crispy crust that wouldn't fall off and we turned to baking the fillets. The best treatment for the delicate fish turned out to be a lower temperature and slightly longer cooking process than many traditional recipes recommended. We also raised the fish above the baking sheet with a rack to help it cook evenly for a perfect weeknight dinner.

Baked fish has many virtues: It's mild, healthy, and quick cooking. Add a crunchy, flavorful crumb topping and there's a lot to like—in theory. In the real world, though, baked fish is often dry and overcooked yet somehow still frequently found sitting in a pool of liquid. I've also eaten more than my share of wet, boring crumb toppings—assuming they haven't entirely fallen off the fillet. Surely moist, flavorful fish with a crisp crown of crumbs is not an unreasonable goal. To raise the stakes, I also wanted to make this dinner more convenient by figuring out a way to prepare it up to a day in advance so I could walk in the door, turn on the oven, and pop the fish right in. I set out to make these dreams a reality.

My main priority was the breading. Fresh bread crumbs are prone to sogginess, so for more crunch in the topping, I went with a proven test kitchen favorite: super-crunchy Japanese panko crumbs. To get them to stick firmly to the fish, I smeared the tops of the fillets with mayonnaise before pressing on the crumbs. Now the crumbs were firmly anchored, but let's face it, white fish is lean and the flavor is subtle. I had the texture down, but tasters thought that the dish tasted bland. After several tests, I found that adding an egg yolk to the mayonnaise enriched the fish nicely, while pepper and lemon zest rounded out the flavors. Unfortunately, when I turned to my goal of preparing the fish ahead of time, it turned out that the great crunch of the panko bread crumbs couldn't survive a whole night sitting in the refrigerator—they were ending up pale and soft. Obviously, I'd have to brown the panko before baking the fish. For my next test, I sautéed the panko in melted butter (fortified with garlic, thyme, salt, and shallot) until it was deep golden. I let it cool and then "glued" it onto the fillets with the enriched mayonnaise. Now the crumbs not only stayed put but also tasted delicious; even a day later, the toasted topping was crispy and crunchy.

Next, I turned to the fish fillets—it didn't matter how great my bread crumbs were if the fish itself wasn't perfect. I knew that as fish cooks, its proteins denature and its natural juices get squeezed out, which explains why overcooked fish is dry yet sits in a puddle of its own juice. Most recipes use relatively hot ovens (375 to 450 degrees), but when the window for perfect doneness is small, as it is for fish fillets, isn't this approach just asking for trouble? My strategy was to slow down the cooking so I could get the fish out of the oven before it overcooked. As extra insurance, I used fillets that were at least 1 inch thick, and therefore less likely to overcook than thin fillets.

I put my fish fillets in a baking dish, set them in a 300-degree oven, and waited, thermometer at the ready. I checked the temperature of the fillets at 5-minute intervals until they reached the optimum temperature (140 degrees). The fish wasn't bad, but it was slightly tough and soggy on the underside. A fellow test cook suggested elevating the fish on a wire rack, which would allow gentle heat to circulate all around it and also lift it out of its juices. So I switched from a baking dish to a rimmed baking sheet outfitted with a rack (greased so the fish wouldn't stick). After about 50 minutes, the fish was perfectly cooked with a well-seasoned, crispy crumb coating that stayed put even through chilling and cooking. The fish could be prepared up to 24 hours ahead of time and refrigerated, with less than an hour to take it from the fridge to the table. Flavorful, satisfying, and simple? This baked fish just earned a place in my weekly repertoire.

—STEPHANIE PIXLEY, *America's Test Kitchen Books*

NOTES FROM THE TEST KITCHEN

KEEPING BREADING CRISP

For a buttery bread-crumb topping that stayed crisp even overnight, we started with extra-crispy panko bread crumbs. Toasting them in butter kept them from turning soggy and gave them great flavor.

To glue the topping securely to the cod fillets, we used mayonnaise whisked with an egg yolk and seasoned with lemon juice and pepper.

Make-Ahead Crispy Breaded Cod Fillets
SERVES 4

You can substitute haddock or halibut for the cod.

- **3 tablespoons unsalted butter**
- **1 large shallot, minced**
- **Salt and pepper**
- **1 garlic clove, minced**
- **1 teaspoon minced fresh thyme or ¼ teaspoon dried**
- **¾ cup panko bread crumbs**
- **2 tablespoons minced fresh parsley**
- **2 tablespoons mayonnaise**
- **1 large egg yolk**
- **½ teaspoon grated lemon zest**
- **4 (6- to 8-ounce) skinless cod fillets, 1 to 1½ inches thick**

1. Melt butter in 12-inch skillet over medium heat. Add shallot and ½ teaspoon salt and cook until softened, about 3 minutes. Stir in garlic and thyme and cook until fragrant, about 30 seconds. Add panko and ¼ teaspoon pepper and cook, stirring constantly, until evenly browned, about 4 minutes. Transfer panko mixture to shallow dish and let cool for 10 minutes. Stir in parsley.

2. Whisk mayonnaise, egg yolk, lemon zest, and ¼ teaspoon pepper together in bowl. Pat cod dry with paper towels and season with salt and pepper. Brush tops of fillets evenly with mayonnaise mixture. Working with 1 fillet at a time, dredge coated side in panko mixture, pressing gently to adhere. Place fillets, crumb side up, on large plate.

3. Cover and refrigerate cod for at least 1 hour or up to 24 hours.

4. Adjust oven rack to middle position and heat oven to 300 degrees. Set wire rack in rimmed baking sheet and spray with vegetable oil spray. Transfer cod to prepared rack and bake until fish flakes apart when gently prodded with paring knife and registers 140 degrees, 45 to 55 minutes, rotating sheet halfway through baking. Serve.

BRAISED HALIBUT WITH LEEKS AND MUSTARD

✔ WHY THIS RECIPE WORKS: Braising, which requires cooking the fish in a small amount of liquid so that it gently simmers and steams, has a lot going for it: As a moist-heat cooking method, it is gentle and forgiving, all but guaranteeing moist, succulent fish. Plus, it makes a one-pot meal as the cooking liquid becomes a sauce, and it's easy to add vegetables to the pan to cook at the same time. We chose halibut for its sweet delicate flavor and firm texture that made for easier handling. Because the portion of the fillets submerged in liquid cooks more quickly than the upper half that cooks through in the steam, we cooked the fillets for a few minutes in the pan on just one side and then braised the fillets parcooked side up to even out the cooking. Vegetables that held their shape but cooked through quickly worked best. For the cooking liquid, wine supplemented by the juices released by the fish and vegetables during cooking delivered a sauce with balanced flavor and just the right amount of brightness. Butter gave it some much-needed richness and the right velvety texture.

Braising is a great way to cook large pork and beef roasts, but you rarely see recipes for braised fish. Why is that? Sure, braising is ideal for making tough cuts of meat succulent—cooking them slowly over long periods with a little bit of liquid will turn them meltingly tender. But at its core, braising is simply a gentle, moist-heat cooking method, which actually makes it ideally suited to producing moist, supple fish. And unlike poaching—a more familiar moist-heat approach to cooking fish—the cooking liquid isn't thrown out but instead is used as the basis for a sauce. Add a vegetable

to the pot and you've got an entrée, sauce, and side that just needs rice or some good bread.

Of the braised fish recipes I did find, some called for doing all the cooking in the oven, others on the stove. The vegetables, fish, and liquid all varied quite a bit, and Dutch ovens, skillets, and sauté pans, with and without lids, were all used (a lid is a must on the stovetop to trap the steam, but not required in the oven). Yet no matter the approach, they all had problems. Timing was the biggest issue: Either the vegetables were perfectly done while the fish was overcooked and dry, or the vegetables were underdone and the fish was just right. The sauces were generally thin and bland. Despite braised fish's potential, no recipe could deliver. As someone who is always up for a good challenge, I set out to get it right.

I started with the fish. After a few initial rounds, I eliminated thin, flaky fillets like flounder and sole; they fell apart far too easily when I transferred them from cooking vessel to plate. Lean tuna steaks were also a no-go because they dried out, and the strong flavors of oily fish like salmon and mackerel overwhelmed the sauce. Halibut was my favorite. Its dense flesh is easy to manipulate in the pan and it has a clean, sweet flavor that would pair well with a simple sauce and most any vegetable. (The recipe also worked with similar firm-fleshed white fish such as sea bass or striped bass.)

For the cookware, I skipped the Dutch oven and sauté pan in favor of a 12-inch skillet. My halibut fillets needed gentle handling to stay in one piece, and the low sides of a skillet would allow me to easily slide spatulas under the fish. And while long-cooking meat braises benefit from the steady, even heat of the oven, my fish would cook through so quickly that keeping it on the stovetop was the much more logical choice.

I decided to follow the lead of most meat braises and quickly sear my fish to give it some color and a deeper flavor. I heated some oil in the skillet, seasoned the fillets with salt and pepper, and seared each side for a couple of minutes until browned. I then removed the fish from the pan and added leeks, a vegetable that would hold its shape but be quick-cooking enough to be done at the same time as the fish. The leeks' mild allium flavor would also complement the halibut nicely.

I sliced the leeks and then wilted them in a little oil before resting the fillets neatly on top. The bed of leeks lifted the fish off the pan's bottom, allowing for more even cooking while also infusing the fillets with flavor.

BRAISED HALIBUT WITH LEEKS AND MUSTARD

I added just enough white wine and water to bring the liquid halfway up the sides of the fish. (White wine was a natural choice, and cutting it with water would mellow its sharpness.) I covered the fillets and waited until they were cooked through, which took about 20 minutes.

While the result wasn't bad, the sauce was too thin, bland, and lean-tasting, and the fish, though perfectly moist at the center, was a bit dry and overcooked on the exterior. The reason for the diluted sauce was pretty clear: I'd underestimated how much liquid the fish and leeks would release as they cooked. As for the fish's slightly dry exterior, I had the searing step to blame. While a pork or beef roast might be more forgiving, lean fish didn't have that wiggle room for doneness.

For the next test, I placed the leeks in the skillet along with a dollop of Dijon mustard and let them wilt before adding just enough wine to cover the vegetables. I then placed the fillets (not seared this time) on top and proceeded. I had hoped that the liquid released by the fish and vegetables would temper the wine's flavor and produce just the right amount of sauce. I was headed in the right direction, but the wine came across as a bit harsh and, not too surprisingly, the sauce's consistency was still too thin. And while the fish had improved from the previous batch—it wasn't dried out on both sides—it was slightly overcooked on just the underside this time.

I saw a way to fix the lean flavor and thin texture of the sauce in one fell swoop. In a traditional meat braise, the sauce thickens and becomes silky because tough cuts of meat possess a lot of collagen, which transforms into gelatin over the duration of the braise. This gelatin gives the cooking liquid body. Halibut, of course, doesn't have much collagen, so I needed another source of thickening power. Taking a cue from traditional pan sauces, I turned to butter. While a couple of tablespoons will thicken and enrich a pan sauce, I was working with a lot more liquid here. Six tablespoons delivered the flavor and texture I was after.

As for the unevenly cooked fish, I'd been expecting the foolproof, moist-throughout results that poaching delivers, but I realized I'd run into a problem unique to braising. With poaching, the fish is fully submerged in liquid, but in the case of braising, I was dealing with multiple cooking mediums. Here the simmering liquid was cooking the submerged portion more quickly than the upper portion, which was cooking through in the steam. I needed to give the upper portion a jump start, so I cooked the fillets, skinned side up, in the skillet for 3 or 4 minutes on one side, just until opaque but not browned (rather than add more fat to the pan, I simply used the butter I needed for thickening the sauce for this step). I set them aside while I wilted the leeks and added the wine. Then I returned the fish to the pan, this time cooked side up, before proceeding as before. After transferring the cooked fish and vegetables to a platter, I simmered the sauce for a couple of minutes to reduce it to just the right consistency. This time I nailed it. The fish was perfectly cooked throughout and the sauce was silky, with just the right subtle flavor to complement the leeks and halibut. All my braised fish dinner needed was a little fresh parsley and a squeeze of lemon juice for freshness before it was ready for the table.

—LAN LAM, *Cook's Illustrated*

NOTES FROM THE TEST KITCHEN

SECRETS TO PERFECT BRAISED FISH

In tests comparing steamed halibut to completely submerged in water and simmering it, we found that steaming took 57 percent longer. Why? For the fish to cook, molecules have to transfer their energy to the food through direct contact. Far more molecules come in contact with the food in the simmering water than they do in the steam.

So it's no surprise that in our early tests for braised fish fillets, by the time the steamed portion had cooked through, the simmered portion had overcooked.

To address this discrepancy, we parcook one side of the fillets by sautéing them briefly, and then we arrange them atop a bed of wine and vegetables, raw side down, for the braise. This gives the upper portion that cooks through more slowly by steam a jump start. The result: perfectly moist, evenly cooked fillets.

READY: Give one side of the fish a head start by cooking it gently in butter.

SET: Transfer the fillets to a plate, raw side down, while you prepare the braising liquid.

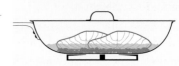

BRAISE: Cook the fish, raw side down, on a bed of vegetables and wine. The parcooked side steams more slowly, and the raw side simmers more quickly.

Braised Halibut with Leeks and Mustard

SERVES 4

We prefer to prepare this recipe with halibut, but a similar firm-fleshed white fish such as striped bass or sea bass that is between ¾ and 1 inch thick can be substituted. To ensure that your fish cooks evenly, purchase fillets that are similarly shaped and uniformly thick.

    4   (6- to 8-ounce) skinless halibut fillets, ¾ to 1 inch thick
         Salt and pepper
    6   tablespoons unsalted butter
    1   pound leeks, white and light green parts only, halved lengthwise, sliced thin, and washed thoroughly
    1   teaspoon Dijon mustard
    ¾   cup dry white wine
    1   teaspoon lemon juice, plus lemon wedges for serving
    1   tablespoon minced fresh parsley

1. Sprinkle fish with ½ teaspoon salt. Melt butter in 12-inch skillet over low heat. Place fish in skillet, skinned side up, increase heat to medium, and cook, shaking pan occasionally, until butter begins to brown (fish should not brown), 3 to 4 minutes. Using spatula, carefully transfer fish to large plate, raw side down.

2. Add leeks, mustard, and ½ teaspoon salt to skillet and cook, stirring frequently, until leeks begin to soften, 2 to 4 minutes. Add wine and bring to gentle simmer. Place fish, raw side down, on top of leeks. Cover skillet and cook, adjusting heat to maintain gentle simmer, until fish registers 135 to 140 degrees, 10 to 14 minutes. Remove skillet from heat and, using 2 spatulas, transfer fish and leeks to serving platter or individual plates. Tent loosely with aluminum foil.

3. Return skillet to high heat and simmer briskly until sauce is thickened, 2 to 3 minutes. Remove pan from heat, stir in lemon juice, and season with salt and pepper to taste. Spoon sauce over fish and sprinkle with parsley. Serve immediately with lemon wedges.

VARIATION

Braised Halibut with Carrots and Coriander

Substitute 1 pound carrots, peeled and shaved with vegetable peeler lengthwise into ribbons, and 4 shallots, halved and sliced thin, for leeks. Substitute ½ teaspoon ground coriander seed for Dijon mustard. Increase lemon juice to 1½ teaspoons and substitute cilantro for parsley.

CRISPY SALT AND PEPPER SHRIMP

✓ **WHY THIS RECIPE WORKS:** To keep our shell-on, deep-fried salt and pepper shrimp shells crispy and crunchy rather than tough, we employed several tricks. First, we chose shrimp that were not overly large, which ensured that the shells were thinner relative to those on more jumbo specimens. Next, we coated them in a thin layer of cornstarch to dry out their shells, which helped make them brittle upon frying. Then we cooked them in small batches in very hot oil, which ensured that any remaining water in the shells was driven off. To season the shrimp and keep them moist, we tossed them with salt and a little rice wine and let them sit briefly before dredging and frying. For an extra jolt of spiciness, after frying the shrimp, we also dredged and fried a couple of thinly sliced jalapeños. And to give the dish lots of depth, we added black peppercorns, Sichuan peppercorns, cayenne, and sugar to the coating and fried more of the same with ginger and garlic to make a flavorful paste. Finally, we tossed the shrimp in this aromatic paste to unify the dish and distribute the flavorings evenly.

Shrimp that are dipped in a batter and fried until golden and crisp are undeniably good, but I'd argue that the Chinese take—salt and pepper shrimp—boasts an exterior that's even more tempting. The key ingredient to that texture might surprise you: It's not a batter but simply the shrimp shells themselves. Instead of being removed before cooking, they're left intact on the meat. When the shrimp cook in the hot oil, the meat cooks up plump and moist, and the shells become as shatteringly crisp—and appealing to eat—as fried chicken skin.

That texture, along with the combination of pepper, garlic, and ginger (and, of course, salt) that gives this dish its killer savory-spicy profile, compels me to order salt and pepper shrimp anytime I'm in a Chinese restaurant. They're also what prompted me to look for recipes to make at home, so I gathered a half-dozen salt and pepper shrimp recipes and found that all followed the same basic approach: Salt the shrimp, dredge them in cornstarch or a simple batter, and then fry them in hot oil, adding the flavorings along the way.

Easy enough, I thought, until I tried a few of the recipes. It turns out that achieving shrimp shells with a delicately brittle texture and juicy meat was no easy task. Most times, no matter how long I fried the shrimp, and whether or not I coated them, the shells were leathery. So my goal was clear: find a frying technique that produced tender meat encased in a shell so delicately crisp, even the shell-on naysayers wouldn't be able to pass it up.

Though restaurant versions seem to be made with relatively small shrimp, I'd been following the lead of published recipes, using larger shellfish that came 21 to 25 per pound. I compared batches of smaller 26- to 30-count and 31- to 40-count shrimp with the bigger crustaceans. For simplicity's sake, I cooked them plain in a pot of 350-degree vegetable oil for 5 minutes or so until they turned opaque. Sure enough, the shells on both batches of the smaller shrimp, while not perfectly crisp, developed spots where they were nicely browned and brittle. The shells on the 31- to 40-count batch seemed the most crispy, so I settled on this size.

Now that I was starting off with thinner shells, I wondered if a coating would help them crisp more uniformly. First I tried dipping them in a batter made of flour, egg white, and water. While the coating itself came out pleasantly brittle, it did little to help crisp up the shell it surrounded. In fact, the opposite was true: The batter-coated shrimp had the toughest shells of any I'd cooked yet. Simply dredging the shrimp in cornstarch worked much better, leading to shells that were much crunchier than those in any of my previous batches.

The main structural element in the shells of shrimp is a polysaccharide called chitin. Chitin does not break down when heated, which means that it doesn't soften or fall apart when cooked. However, chitin is flexible, thanks to its water content; thus, in order to make it crisp, it's necessary to drive off as much of that water as possible. While the batter formed a thick barrier that hindered moisture from escaping, and shells with no coating relied solely on the heat of the oil to drive off water, the cornstarch actively pulled moisture from the shells even before they hit the fryer.

I knew that getting—and keeping—the oil as hot as possible would aid in thoroughly drying out the shells. It also would dry them quickly so the shrimp wouldn't have a chance to overcook. I found that I could raise its temperature to 385 degrees without causing the oil to smoke. Adding too much food to the oil at one time is a sure way to drop the temperature, so I fried the shrimp in batches, holding the finished shrimp in a warm oven on a wire rack while the remainder fried. With all these adjustments, the shells were now as brittle and crisp as the best of any restaurant version I'd sampled.

Of course salt and pepper shrimp wasn't about only the shells: It was time to focus on the meat beneath, which was a bit more tough and chewy than I wanted. To give the dish its signature salty punch, most recipes call for rubbing the raw shrimp with salt and letting them sit for about 10 minutes, a step that I knew would not only give the salt time to penetrate the flesh and thoroughly season it but also allow it to hold on to more of its juices. A few sources also called for tossing the shrimp with a couple of tablespoons of rice wine. This seemed like a great idea, since a little bit of this savory liquid would help the salt get under the shell to make contact with the meat and might contribute some flavor of its own. When I tried both approaches, tasters confirmed that the shrimp tossed with salt and rice wine was juicier as well as more flavorful. To ensure that the added moisture didn't affect frying, I patted the shrimp dry before coating them in starch.

It was time to incorporate the garlic and ginger that flavor the dish. I made an aromatic "paste" by reserving 2 tablespoons of the frying oil, cooking the minced garlic and ginger in it for around 45 seconds, and then dropping in the fried shrimp and briefly tossing them with the mixture before serving.

All that remained was to work in some trademark heat and pungency. Some recipes call for merely grinding black peppercorns over the fried shrimp before serving, but I preferred to add the pepper to the cornstarch before tossing the shrimp in it for better distribution. I was intrigued by recipes that also included Sichuan peppercorns, which have a distinctive piney, citrusy taste, so I introduced a generous grind of these to the cornstarch as well, along with a little cayenne and sugar. These heady flavors were even more evident when I set aside some of the seasoning mix and added it to the reserved frying oil with the garlic and ginger before tossing in the fried shrimp.

But I still wasn't quite satisfied. I wanted a bit more heat, as well as some herbal flavors. The solution: I thinly sliced a couple of fresh jalapeños, coated them in cornstarch, and quickly fried them after I'd removed the shrimp. I then sprinkled them over the finished dish. My tasters also approved of two final tweaks: Sliced scallions added to the aromatic paste with the fried shrimp, and an extra ½ teaspoon of salt sprinkled into the oil at the same time.

—ANDREW JANJIGIAN, *Cook's Illustrated*

Crispy Salt and Pepper Shrimp

SERVES 4 TO 6

In this recipe the shrimp are meant to be eaten shell and all. To ensure that the shells fry up crisp, avoid using shrimp that are overly large or jumbo. We prefer 31- to 40-count shrimp, but 26- to 30-count may be substituted. Serve with steamed rice.

1½	pounds shell-on shrimp (31 to 40 per pound)
2	tablespoons Chinese rice wine or dry sherry
	Kosher salt
2½	teaspoons black peppercorns
2	teaspoons Sichuan peppercorns
2	teaspoons sugar
¼	teaspoon cayenne pepper
4	cups vegetable oil
5	tablespoons cornstarch
2	jalapeño chiles, stemmed, seeded, and sliced into ⅛-inch-thick rings
3	garlic cloves, minced
1	tablespoon grated fresh ginger
2	scallions, sliced thin on bias
¼	head iceberg lettuce, shredded (1½ cups)

1. Adjust oven rack to upper-middle position and heat oven to 225 degrees. Toss shrimp, rice wine, and 1 teaspoon salt together in large bowl and set aside for 10 to 15 minutes.

2. Grind black peppercorns and Sichuan peppercorns in spice grinder or mortar and pestle until coarsely ground. Transfer peppercorns to small bowl and stir in sugar and cayenne.

3. Heat oil in large Dutch oven over medium heat until oil registers 385 degrees. While oil is heating, drain shrimp and pat dry with paper towels. Transfer shrimp to bowl, add 3 tablespoons cornstarch and 1 tablespoon peppercorn mixture, and toss until well combined.

4. Carefully add one-third of shrimp to oil and fry, stirring occasionally to keep shrimp from sticking together, until light brown, 2 to 3 minutes. Using wire skimmer or slotted spoon, transfer shrimp to paper towel–lined plate. Once paper towels absorb any excess oil, transfer shrimp to wire rack set in rimmed baking sheet and place in oven. Return oil to 385 degrees and repeat in 2 more batches, tossing each batch thoroughly with coating mixture before frying.

5. Toss jalapeño rings and remaining 2 tablespoons cornstarch in medium bowl. Shaking off excess

NOTES FROM THE TEST KITCHEN

HOW FRYING MAKES SHRIMP SHELLS GOOD ENOUGH TO EAT

Most of us peel shrimp before eating it—and for good reason. Made of an elastic substance known as chitin, the shell can be tough. But great salt and pepper shrimp feature a fried shell as crispy—and appealing to eat—as the skin on fried chicken.

Chitin does not break down when exposed to heat. Its rubbery texture is entirely caused by moisture. To crisp the shells, it is necessary to dehydrate them as much as possible—something that can be accomplished only by a dry heat method like frying. (Moist methods will leave the shells chewy and flexible; think shrimp boil.) For this reason, we eschew a wet batter and instead toss the shrimp in seasoned cornstarch. This light, dry coating helps pull moisture from the shells, which evaporates in the hot oil, leaving them brittle and crisp. Note: Since older, larger shrimp have thicker, tougher shells, it's also important to start with relatively small shrimp; we prefer 31- to 40-count specimens.

BOILED = TOUGH
Moist heat makes shrimp shells rubbery.

FRIED = CRISP
Dry heat dehydrates—and, thus, crisps—the shells.

cornstarch, carefully add jalapeño rings to oil and fry until crispy, 1 to 2 minutes. Using wire skimmer or slotted spoon, transfer jalapeño rings to paper towel–lined plate. After frying, reserve 2 tablespoons frying oil.

6. Heat reserved oil in 12-inch skillet over medium-high heat until shimmering. Add garlic, ginger, and remaining peppercorn mixture and cook, stirring occasionally, until mixture is fragrant and just beginning to brown, about 45 seconds. Add shrimp, scallions, and ½ teaspoon salt and toss to coat. Line platter with lettuce. Transfer shrimp to platter, sprinkle with jalapeño rings, and serve immediately.

SHRIMP AND GRITS

SHRIMP AND GRITS

✓ WHY THIS RECIPE WORKS: This Carolina classic is famous for its tender shrimp, silky gravy, and creamy grits. To control the cooking of the shrimp, we parcooked them in rendered bacon fat. We set them aside while creating a light gravy of flavorful (and quick) shrimp stock, bacon, garlic, lemon, and Tabasco; we then finished cooking the shrimp directly in the gravy. We found that toasting the grits before adding liquid helped bring out the most corn flavor. Chopped scallions finished the dish with a jolt of freshness.

Today the savory Southern dish known as shrimp and grits is ubiquitous on restaurant menus and, increasingly, in home kitchens around the United States. But until recently, it was unknown outside a small swath of the southeastern U.S. coast. There, the entrenched combination was an inevitable outcome of abundance—the Carolina shores teemed with shrimp, and grits were plentiful and cheap. Together, they've been known locally for generations as "breakfast shrimp."

Early versions of this dish, including the first known published recipe in *200 Years of Charleston Cooking* (1930), called for little more than butter, shrimp, and grits. Though countless adaptations have been explored over the years, I planned to keep it simple. I prepared five existing recipes, including the Charleston Cooking version. Some were better than others, but none was exactly what I sought. I wanted to taste shrimp above anything else, I wanted creamy grits, and I wanted a lively, relatively light sauce.

The recipes were split on what liquid to use for the sauce. Some called for chicken stock, others clam juice. The shrimpiest used a simple, flavorful shrimp stock made by simmering shrimp shells in water for just a few minutes. I was happy to follow suit, for flavor and thrift; my shrimp shells were otherwise destined for the trash bin.

I used a butter-and-flour roux to thicken the stock and reduced it to the silky consistency I wanted. I added the shrimp partway through so they could poach in the sauce and then finished with two standard add-ins: a squirt of lemon juice for brightness and some crumbled bacon.

Easy, yes, but rife with potholes, too. Finicky shrimp can overcook in a matter of seconds and turn from supple to rubbery. What's more, while the shrimp poached in the sauce, they released liquid, thinning it out and compromising its structure.

I decided to try a two-step process, rendering chopped bacon in the pan and lightly sautéing the shrimp in this fat until just pink for a base of flavor. I removed the shrimp well before they were cooked through and in the same skillet stirred together a tablespoon of butter and 2 tablespoons of flour to cook for 1 minute. Then I whisked in shrimp stock to simmer and reduce. When the stock reached the correct consistency (just thick enough to coat the back of a spoon), I returned my shrimp to the skillet to cook through.

Success. Parcooking the shrimp this way prevented them from releasing too much liquid in my sauce, and I could finish them off right before I was ready to serve the dish.

The well-known Southern formula to cook grits is to start with a 4:1 ratio of liquid to grits. You boil the liquid and slowly whisk in the grits, stirring often and cooking them until they're soft and creamy before finishing with butter, salt, and pepper. But I wanted to explore other options for creaminess, corniness, and texture. In the end, I made only one tweak to the tried-and-true: Toasting the grits in butter before adding the liquid (a mix of water and milk was best) helped coax out the corn flavor I was after. I also went with a little more liquid, a covered pot, and a slightly longer cooking time to arrive at just the right creamy texture.

My final recipe had few bells and whistles, but the result thrilled my tasters. This dish was simple to prepare and entirely satisfying. Exactly what I was after.

—MORGAN BOLLING, *Cook's Country*

NOTES FROM THE TEST KITCHEN

FRESH VERSUS FROZEN
Just because shrimp are raw at the store doesn't mean they're fresh; roughly 90 percent of the shrimp sold in the United States comes from outside the country. So unless you live near a coastal area, you can bet the shrimp you're seeing were frozen and then defrosted. The problem is, once shrimp have been defrosted, their quality deteriorates quickly—and there is no way of telling how long they've been sitting in the case. We prefer to buy frozen shrimp and defrost them ourselves.

SERVES 4

We prefer untreated shrimp—those without added sodium or preservatives like sodium tripolyphosphate (STPP). Most frozen E-Z peel shrimp have been treated (the ingredient list should tell you). If you're using treated shrimp, do not add the salt in step 4. If you use our winning grits (Anson Mills Pencil Cob) or other fresh-milled grits, you will need to increase the simmering time by 25 minutes.

GRITS

    3 tablespoons unsalted butter
    1 cup old-fashioned grits
  2¼ cups whole milk
    2 cups water
       Salt and pepper

SHRIMP

    3 tablespoons unsalted butter
  1½ pounds extra-large shrimp (21 to 25 per pound),
       peeled and deveined, shells reserved
    1 tablespoon tomato paste
  2¼ cups water
    3 slices bacon, cut into ½-inch pieces
    1 garlic clove, minced
       Salt and pepper
    2 tablespoons all-purpose flour
    1 tablespoon lemon juice
    ½ teaspoon Tabasco sauce, plus extra for serving
    4 scallions, sliced thin

1. FOR THE GRITS: Melt 1 tablespoon butter in medium saucepan over medium heat. Add grits and cook, stirring often, until fragrant, about 3 minutes. Add milk, water, and ¾ teaspoon salt. Increase heat to medium-high and bring to boil. Reduce heat to low, cover, and simmer, whisking often, until thick and creamy, about 25 minutes. Remove from heat, stir in remaining 2 tablespoons butter, and season with salt and pepper to taste. Cover and keep warm.

2. FOR THE SHRIMP: Meanwhile, melt 1 tablespoon butter in 12-inch nonstick skillet over medium heat. Add shrimp shells and cook, stirring occasionally, until shells are spotty brown, about 7 minutes. Stir in tomato paste and cook for 30 seconds. Add water and bring to boil. Reduce heat to low, cover, and simmer for 5 minutes.

3. Strain shrimp stock through fine-mesh strainer set over bowl, pressing on solids to extract as much liquid as possible; discard solids. You should have about 1½ cups stock (add more water if necessary to equal 1½ cups). Wipe out skillet with paper towels.

4. Cook bacon in now-empty skillet over medium-low heat until crisp, 7 to 9 minutes. Increase heat to medium-high and stir in shrimp, garlic, ½ teaspoon salt, and ½ teaspoon pepper. Cook until edges of shrimp are just beginning to turn pink, but shrimp are not cooked through, about 2 minutes. Transfer shrimp mixture to bowl.

5. Melt 1 tablespoon butter in now-empty skillet over medium-high heat. Whisk in flour and cook for 1 minute. Slowly whisk in shrimp stock until incorporated. Bring to boil, reduce heat to medium-low, and simmer until thickened slightly, about 5 minutes.

6. Stir in shrimp mixture, cover, and cook until shrimp are cooked through, about 3 minutes. Off heat, stir in lemon juice, Tabasco, and remaining 1 tablespoon butter. Season with salt and pepper to taste. Serve over grits, sprinkled with scallions, and passing extra Tabasco.

SHRIMP A LA DIABLA

✔ **WHY THIS RECIPE WORKS:** For a take on *shrimp a la diabla* that lived up to its devilish name, we made a spicy sauce using a combination of guajillo chiles and chipotle chile in adobo. Toasting the guajillos brought out their flavor nicely. For the tomato component of the sauce, we found that canned tomato sauce gave us better texture and more consistent results than cooking down fresh tomatoes. Cooking the shrimp directly in the sauce not only kept this a one-pot dish, but also allowed the shrimp to pick up all the rich, spicy flavors of the sauce.

Found throughout Mexico, shrimp a la diabla, or "devilish shrimp," features the popular shellfish served in a chile sauce that's nothing short of fiery. Since I love spicy food, I knew I had to try this dish.

I started with the sauce. The recipes I found were all over the map in terms of chiles, calling for everything from dried guajillos and arbols to fresh jalapeños and serranos. Some recipes called only for chipotle chiles in adobo or some type of preground chile powder and hot sauce. I selected a broad range of recipes and got to work.

Since the chiles were so central to the flavor of the sauce, chile powders were out—their flavors weren't potent enough to carry the dish. Tasters liked the sauces made with dried guajillo chiles, deeming the flavor of the chiles deep and almost smoky, with a pleasantly fruity undertone. They also gave the sauce a beautiful dark red hue. But these sauces still needed some spicing up—literally. Not one of them had enough heat to be properly deemed "a la diabla."

But before I added heat, I needed to decide on the tomato element of the sauce. Many recipes called for fresh tomatoes, but I found that these produced inconsistent results. I knew that seasonal differences would only exacerbate this problem. Canned tomato sauce was easy and convenient, and it gave the sauce a thick, hearty texture that tasters liked.

With the tomatoes, settled, I moved on to amping up the heat levels of the sauce. My first move was to add more guajillos—way more. I made six batches of sauce, increasing the guajillo count by one for each batch—from a mere three chiles to a generous eight. The sauce with eight chiles was tasters' favorite. Although the heat level was now much closer to where I wanted it (just short of tongue-sizzling), I wanted to round out the subtly smoky flavor profile of the guajillos. Just a tablespoon of minced chipotle chile in adobo sauce did the trick. I toasted the guajillos to bring out their latent flavors, then cooked the guajillos with the chipotle, tomato sauce, oregano, and water in a Dutch oven. Finally, I pureed the sauce in the blender and moved on to the next part of the dish: the shrimp.

Almost all of the recipes I found called for softening onion or garlic in butter, then sautéing the shrimp slightly before adding the sauce to the pan. I sautéed an onion and a few cloves of garlic, added the shrimp to the pan, and then added my sauce a minute later. The flavor of the sauce and the shrimp were great, but tasters weren't fond of the pieces of onion in the otherwise smooth sauce. Plus, I wondered whether dirtying a second pan was really necessary—the shrimp didn't develop much flavor in the minute or two they spent in sauté pan, and the sauce was coming together so easily that it seemed a shame to overcomplicate the recipe if I didn't have to.

For my next test, I simply incorporated the onion and garlic into the sauce, blooming them along with chipotle and oregano. I pureed the sauce, put it back in the pot, and stirred in the shrimp. After about 5 minutes, the shrimp were perfectly cooked and had absorbed some of the sauce's rich, multidimensional flavor. With just a spritz of lime, my shrimp a la diabla was balanced, bright, and above all, fiery hot.

—DANIELLE DESIATO, *America's Test Kitchen Book*

Shrimp a la Diabla

SERVES 4 TO 6

Serve with rice.

- 8 **dried guajillo chiles, stemmed, seeded and torn into ½-inch pieces (1 cup)**
- 2 **tablespoons extra-virgin olive oil, plus extra for serving**
- 1 **onion, chopped fine**
  Salt and pepper
- 3 **garlic cloves, minced**
- 1 **tablespoon minced canned chipotle chile in adobo sauce**
- 2 **teaspoons dried oregano**
- 1 **(8-ounce) can tomato sauce**
- 1 **cup water**
- 2 **pounds extra-large shrimp (21 to 25 per pound), peeled and deveined**
- ¼ **cup chopped fresh cilantro or parsley**
- 1 **tablespoon lime juice, plus lime wedges for serving**

1. Toast guajillo chiles in Dutch oven over medium heat, stirring frequently, until fragrant, 2 to 6 minutes; transfer to bowl.

2. Heat oil in now-empty pot over medium-high heat until shimmering. Add onion and ½ teaspoon salt and cook until softened, about 5 minutes. Stir in garlic, chipotle, and oregano and cook until fragrant, about 30 seconds. Stir in tomato sauce, water, and toasted chiles, bring to simmer, and cook until chiles are softened, about 10 minutes.

3. Transfer mixture to blender and process until smooth, about 30 seconds. Return sauce to now-empty pot and stir in shrimp. Cover and cook over medium-low heat until shrimp are cooked through and completely opaque, 5 to 7 minutes.

4. Transfer shrimp to individual plates. Stir cilantro and lime juice into sauce and season with salt and pepper to taste. Spoon sauce over shrimp, drizzle with extra oil, and serve with lime wedges.

BREAKFAST, BRUNCH, AND BREADS

HUEVOS RANCHEROS

HUEVOS RANCHEROS

✓ **WHY THIS RECIPE WORKS:** This spicy dish of eggs, charred chiles, and tortillas makes for an eye-opening breakfast but is often hard to put together for four people. For maximum flavor with little effort, we roasted diced tomatoes with brown sugar, lime juice, green chiles, chili powder, and garlic that we bloomed in oil in the microwave. We spread that flavorful mixture in a 13 by 9-inch baking dish, made divots in the mixture to hold our eggs (eight divots in all), sprinkled cheese over the divots, added our eggs, and baked the eggs for about 15 minutes, until just set. Topped with avocado, scallion, and cilantro and served with warm corn tortillas, huevos rancheros will get your day started with a bang.

There are those who throw off the sheets for a sweet stack of fluffy pancakes or a syrup-soaked waffle, but I am not one of them. Instead, I stir for savory—think corned beef hash, bacon and eggs, or my favorite breakfast: huevos rancheros. I find the dish's fine-tuned combination of sunny-side up eggs, spicy sauce, tender tortillas, and rich cheese unbeatable (especially once it's all doused in hot sauce).

However, preparing the dish's numerous components requires more effort and attention to detail than I am usually willing to commit to first thing in the morning. Is there an easy (or at least easier) way to make huevos rancheros?

Huevos rancheros wended its way northward from Mexico through the border states before becoming near-ubiquitous on breakfast menus around the United States. Perhaps because of its wayward migration, there's no singularly defined version. The tortillas remain constant, of course, but the eggs can be fried or poached, and sauces range from simple salsas and pico de gallo to both red and green moles and, finally, enchilada-style or ranchero sauces. After preparing a few promising recipes, I preferred this latter sauce, which is traditionally made from roasted tomatoes, onion, garlic, chiles, and seasonings.

Instead of just browning the vegetables in a skillet, though, I wanted to replicate the deep char that Mexican cooks get using a cast-iron (or earthenware) griddle called a *comal*. In the past, the test kitchen has turned to the broiler for this type of aggressive searing, so that's where I started, too. But broiling requires frequent stirring and close attention to avoid incineration

(speckled charring is perfect, burning not so much). The last thing I wanted to do first thing in the morning was prepare anything requiring such high-wire focus.

Instead of broiling, I wondered if a hot oven might give me similar results. I tossed the sauce components—by this point, I had narrowed it down to diced canned tomatoes (drained), onion, jalapeño chiles, and garlic—with salt, pepper, and olive oil and roasted the mix on a rimmed baking sheet at temperatures ranging from 400 to 500 degrees. The high end of the spectrum did the trick, browning the vegetables and concentrating their flavor in the same fashion as broiling—just a lot more conveniently (it requires only one quick stir midway through to ensure even browning). Sure, it took a little longer to roast than to broil—about 40 minutes all said—but I put that time to good use making coffee and reading the newspaper.

While some recipes call for dried chiles (usually pasilla or ancho), I knew that the stemming, toasting, soaking, and pureeing would be too much work here. I tested standard chili powder and was pleased to find that 3 tablespoons contributed the kick I wanted, especially when I added it to the vegetables before roasting so it could toast and intensify in the oven's high, dry heat. In an attempt to simplify my recipe, I made a batch in which I omitted the fresh jalapeños from the mix and added a can of green chiles instead. The sauce tasted great with the canned chiles, which required no effort besides popping the lid off the can. To fine-tune the sauce, I added a tablespoon each of brown sugar and fresh lime juice.

In my early batches, I pureed the sauce to a smooth, silky consistency. It tasted right, but there was little textural contrast to the eggs. Why not leave the sauce chunky? Straight from the oven, it was too thick—more side dish than sauce—so I mixed it with a portion of the tangy liquid I'd drained from the tomatoes. This batch proved the best to date and was easier, too. With about 5 minutes of hands-on prep and 40 minutes of oven time, I had a terrific-tasting sauce for my eggs.

The eggs for huevos rancheros are usually fried sunny-side up. Ever tried frying eight eggs at once? It's nearly impossible unless you're a line cook. The first egg in the pan is largely set by the time the last egg is cracked and chances are high that at least one of the yolks cracks in the haste of getting the eggs into the pan. The same problems hold true for poached eggs.

Looking afield for inspiration, I remembered a colorfully named Italian dish called "eggs in purgatory" in which eggs are poached directly in a pan of simmering sauce. Rather than hauling out a skillet, I looked to the pan of roasted sauce. I could skip dirtying an extra pan and simply cook the eggs there too. A roomy 13 by 9-inch baking dish worked perfectly—I easily nestled eight eggs in the sauce in two tidy rows. I first left the oven at the temperature at which I had roasted the vegetables—500 degrees—but the eggs cooked unevenly. A much better temperature was 400 degrees; within 13 to 16 minutes, the eggs were just set (and they continued to cook a little further via carryover cooking).

Garnishes for huevos rancheros range broadly and after trying a host of options, I settled on a blend of scallions and cilantro to brighten the sauce and some spicy pepper Jack cheese and avocado to complement it. Finally, I had a recipe for huevos rancheros that didn't require waking before dawn or an armload of ingredients to prepare.

—MATTHEW CARD, *Cook's Country*

Huevos Rancheros

SERVES 4

Use a heavyweight rimmed baking sheet; flimsy sheets will warp. Serve with refried beans and hot sauce.

    2 (28-ounce) cans diced tomatoes
    1 tablespoon packed brown sugar
    1 tablespoon lime juice
    1 onion, chopped
    ½ cup chopped canned green chiles
    ¼ cup extra-virgin olive oil
    3 tablespoons chili powder
    4 garlic cloves, sliced thin
       Salt and pepper
    4 ounces pepper Jack cheese, shredded (1 cup)
    8 large eggs
    1 avocado, halved, pitted, and diced
    3 scallions, sliced thin
    ⅓ cup minced fresh cilantro
    8 (6-inch) corn tortillas, warmed

1. Adjust oven rack to middle position and heat oven to 500 degrees. Line rimmed baking sheet with parchment paper. Drain tomatoes in fine-mesh strainer set over bowl, pressing with rubber spatula to extract as much juice as possible. Reserve 1¾ cups tomato juice and discard remainder. Whisk sugar and lime juice into reserved tomato juice and set aside.

2. In separate bowl, combine onion, chiles, oil, chili powder, garlic, ½ teaspoon salt, and drained tomatoes. Transfer tomato mixture to prepared baking sheet and spread in even layer to edges of sheet. Roast until charred in spots, 35 to 40 minutes, stirring and redistributing into even layer halfway through baking. Reduce oven temperature to 400 degrees.

3. Transfer roasted tomato mixture to 13 by 9-inch baking dish and stir in tomato juice mixture. Season with salt and pepper to taste, then spread into even layer. Sprinkle pepper Jack over tomato mixture. Using spoon, hollow out 8 holes in tomato mixture in 2 rows. Crack 1 egg into each hole. Season eggs with salt and pepper.

4. Bake until whites are just beginning to set but still have some movement when dish is shaken, 13 to 16 minutes. Transfer dish to wire rack, tent loosely with aluminum foil, and let sit for 5 minutes. Spoon avocado over top, then sprinkle with scallions and cilantro. Serve with warm tortillas.

TO MAKE AHEAD: The sauce can be made 24 hours in advance. Microwave until hot, about 2 minutes (stirring halfway), before transferring to baking dish and proceeding with recipe.

NOTES FROM THE TEST KITCHEN

ROAST THE VEGETABLES: BAKE THE EGGS
To evoke the charred flavors in traditional huevos rancheros, we roast vegetables in a hot oven before layering them into a baking dish with cheese sprinkled over. Cracking eggs into wells in the mixture allows us to bake eight servings at once—no more standing at the stove frying egg after egg for an impatient crowd.

SWEET POTATO AND CHORIZO HASH

✔ **WHY THIS RECIPE WORKS:** We set out to create a twist on breakfast hash using the classic Mexican combination of chorizo and potatoes. Mexican-style chorizo was easy to incorporate into the hash and had a bold, intense flavor that we liked. Using both russet potatoes and sweet potatoes created a well-rounded flavor and ensured that the hash crisped nicely. Parcooking the potatoes shortened their cooking time considerably. As for the eggs, we kept the recipe streamlined by poaching them right in the hash: We made indentations in the potato mixture, cracked the eggs into the divots, and then covered the pan so the eggs would cook through.

In Mexico, it's not uncommon to see tacos filled with chorizo and potatoes. The combination is incredibly flavorful: deeply browned, spicy chorizo, crisp potatoes unabashedly coated in the chorizo fat, all wrapped up in lightly charred, soft corn tortillas. It's straightforward, hearty, and savory. But who says chorizo and potatoes have to be relegated to the realm of lunch or dinner? I wanted to use this classic combination as inspiration for a new twist on breakfast hash.

First, I needed to nail down the chorizo. There are several kinds of chorizo available, and although they're all derived from the same sausage, each type has its own characteristics. Spanish chorizo is a dry-cured, coarsely ground pork sausage; it's usually bright red and has a smoky flavor from smoked paprika. Colombian or Argentinean chorizo is not cured, but instead is made from coarsely ground fresh pork seasoned with garlic and herbs. Mexican chorizo differs from the other two in several ways. It's more finely ground and has a pronounced spicy tanginess from chili powder and vinegar. Although it's usually pork, it can also be made from beef, and it's almost always removed from the casings before cooking. For my recipe, I would use Mexican-style chorizo, since I wanted to crumble it and incorporate it into my hash.

Next up: the potatoes. Although russet potatoes crisp up beautifully, I wanted to build some more nuanced flavor by using sweet potatoes. I threw together a working recipe, diced up a couple of pounds of sweet potatoes, browned my chorizo, and let everything cook. It was a failure: The low-starch sweet potatoes turned out soft and mushy, not at all what I wanted in a hash. Plus, I had lost some of the savory appeal that had drawn me to the combination of chorizo and potatoes in the first place. Back to the drawing board.

Since I didn't want to omit the sweet potatoes altogether, I thought maybe I could split the difference and use half sweet potatoes and half russet potatoes. This worked perfectly: The russets became browned and crisp, while the sweet potatoes gave the dish some earthy depth. I borrowed a trick from previous hash recipes and parcooked the potatoes in the microwave with a little bit of oil before adding them to the pan. This decreased the cooking time significantly—a big plus for a breakfast dish—and ensured that the potatoes were fully cooked by the time they reached the perfect level of browning.

To boost the flavor of the hash, I started with basic aromatics like onion, garlic, and thyme. But tasters wanted a bit more spicy depth. Digging around the pantry, I came across two staple Mexican ingredients, cumin and canned chipotle chile in adobo sauce. A little bit of both ingredients went a long way in getting the flavor where I wanted it. I also added a splash of heavy cream to give the hash some richness.

Next, I turned my attention to an essential element of any good hash: perfectly cooked eggs. And since I'd made enough hash to serve four people, I would need to make eight eggs. Frying them one or two or even four at a time was not an option; I wanted everything to be ready at once. Why not cook them in the same skillet as the hash? I made four indentations in the potato-chorizo mixture, cracked two eggs into each, and waited. Unfortunately, by the time the whites had cooked through, the yolks were overdone. Luckily, this was a simple problem to solve: Covering the pan after I'd added the eggs encouraged the eggs to cook more evenly, producing the perfectly soft, slightly runny yolks I was after.

As a final touch, I sprinkled some fresh chives over the top of the hash. Deeply flavorful, just spicy enough, with lots of crispy bites of chorizo and potato offset by the rich egg yolks—this breakfast hash was everything I wanted it to be.

—LAWMAN JOHNSON, *America's Test Kitchen Books*

SERVES 4

If you notice that the potatoes aren't getting brown in step 3, turn up the heat.

  1   pound russet potatoes, peeled and cut into
       ½-inch pieces
  1   pound sweet potatoes, peeled and cut into
       ½-inch pieces
  1   tablespoon vegetable oil
       Salt and pepper
  8   ounces Mexican-style chorizo sausage,
       casings removed
  1   onion, chopped fine
  3   garlic cloves, minced
  1½   teaspoons minced canned chipotle chile in
       adobo sauce
  ¾   teaspoon minced fresh thyme or ¼ teaspoon dried
  ½   teaspoon ground cumin
  ½   cup heavy cream
  8   large eggs
  1   tablespoon minced fresh chives

1. Toss russet potatoes, sweet potatoes, oil, ½ teaspoon salt, and ¼ teaspoon pepper together in bowl. Cover and microwave until potatoes are translucent around edges, 7 to 9 minutes, stirring halfway through microwaving.

2. Meanwhile, cook chorizo in 12-inch nonstick skillet over medium-high heat, breaking up meat with wooden spoon, until beginning to brown, about 5 minutes. Stir in onion and cook until onion is softened and lightly browned, 5 to 7 minutes. Stir in garlic, chipotle, thyme, and cumin and cook until fragrant, about 30 seconds.

3. Stir in cream and hot potatoes. Using back of spatula, gently pack potatoes into skillet and cook undisturbed for 2 minutes. Flip hash, 1 portion at a time, and lightly repack into skillet. Repeat flipping process every few minutes until potatoes are nicely browned, 6 to 8 minutes.

4. Off heat, use spoon to make 4 indentations (2 to 3 inches wide) in hash, pushing hash up into center and around edges of skillet (bottom of skillet should be exposed in each divot). Crack 2 eggs into each indentation and season with salt and pepper. Cover and cook over medium-low heat until whites are just set and yolks are still runny, 4 to 8 minutes. Sprinkle with chives and serve immediately.

BREAKFAST PIZZA

✔ **WHY THIS RECIPE WORKS:** Breakfast pizza is an easy, unexpected crowd favorite for a Sunday brunch, but it comes with a challenge: achieving a crisp, golden-brown crust without overcooking the eggs. To get there, we pressed room-temperature dough into a lightly oiled sheet pan and parbaked it for 5 minutes to give the crust a head start before we added the toppings. The remaining minutes in the oven cooked the eggs just right, with golden, just-set yolks. The surprising addition of cottage cheese tethered all the ingredients together with a silky creaminess.

Pizza, simply put, is bread with stuff on it. Who's to say that stuff can't be breakfast—bacon and eggs? I wanted to create a simple but satisfying breakfast pizza with a crisp crust, crunchy bacon, golden-yolked eggs, and, instead of a red sauce, a creamy, breakfast-friendly layer of cheese to kick off a weekend morning.

My challenge was to achieve a crisp, golden-brown crust without overcooking the eggs—two contrasting goals.

Pizza parlors use specialized ovens that reach temperatures of 700 degrees or more to get perfect crisp-chewy crust in a short burst of time, but I knew that I was limited to a home oven, where 500 degrees is the max. My coworkers suggested a pizza stone, which can help an oven maintain consistently high temperatures and help a home cook produce a crisp crust, but I didn't want to spend the extra time heating one up. I was determined to do this on a baking sheet, but I was concerned that the store-bought pizza dough I chose for convenience would take 15 minutes to cook—much too long for the soft egg yolks I wanted.

But I had to start somewhere. So I pressed and rolled my pizza dough and patted it into a lightly oiled baking sheet. I sprinkled on some seasoned ricotta for creaminess, a few crumbles of cooked bacon, and some grated mozzarella. I carefully broke eggs on top and slid the whole thing into the oven to bake for 15 minutes. This routine was a bust: I had blond, flabby crust topped with chalky eggs.

I picked bits of crisp bacon off the pizza and considered my next move. What if I prebaked a pizza with everything except the eggs, giving the cheese a chance to melt and the crust more time to crisp up, and then added the eggs for the last few minutes? Another fail. Cracking the eggs over partially melted cheese was nearly impossible. They just slid right off.

BREAKFAST PIZZA

I took a step back and considered. Maybe it wasn't just a problem of timing, but of architecture, too. What if I built a solid foundation by parbaking the dough first? I'd do this on the lowest rack, closest to the heating element, to help ensure crispness. Then, after a few minutes, when the dough was puffed and firm, I would add my toppings. Introducing the shredded cheese at this stage allowed me to shape it into wells where I could safely nestle the eggs. With some finessing (and several pizzas), I determined that 5 minutes was all I needed to parbake the naked crust, plus another 9 to 12 minutes for the toppings.

I still faced a lingering texture problem. The ricotta that I'd hoped would create a creamy layer between the pizza crust and the other toppings was separating in the heat of the oven, becoming grainy and dry. A colleague offered a bold suggestion for a solution: cottage cheese.

Wait, what? I was not eager to vandalize this pizza with lumpy white glop. But we've tried stranger things in the test kitchen, and I couldn't think of a compelling reason not to try it. Cottage cheese is cheese after all—and a creamy one at that.

I popped open a tub and spread ½ cup over the parbaked dough before piling on the other toppings. To my surprise and delight, the curds melted and the cottage cheese transformed into a creamy, silky layer, deftly tethering everything together. Even professed cottage cheese haters found this pizza, and the variations I created, irresistible.

—CECELIA JENKINS, *Cook's Country*

Breakfast Pizza

SERVES 6

Small-curd cottage cheese is sometimes labeled "country-style." Room-temperature dough is much easier to shape than cold, so pull the dough from the fridge about 1 hour before you start cooking.

NOTES FROM THE TEST KITCHEN

BUILDING A BREAKFAST PIZZA
For a crisp crust, we parbake the dough for 5 minutes, until the bottom is just beginning to brown. We then add the toppings, creating wells to keep the eggs in place.

---

3 tablespoons extra-virgin olive oil, plus extra for drizzling

6 slices bacon

8 ounces mozzarella cheese, shredded (2 cups)

1 ounce Parmesan cheese, grated (½ cup)

4 ounces (½ cup) small-curd cottage cheese

¼ teaspoon dried oregano

Salt and pepper

Pinch cayenne pepper

1 pound store-bought pizza dough, room temperature

6 large eggs

2 scallions, sliced thin

2 tablespoons minced fresh chives

1. Adjust oven rack to lowest position and heat oven to 500 degrees. Grease rimmed baking sheet with 1 tablespoon oil.

2. Cook bacon in 12-inch skillet over medium heat until crisp, 7 to 9 minutes. Transfer to paper towel–lined plate; when cool enough to handle, crumble bacon. Combine mozzarella and Parmesan in bowl; set aside. Combine cottage cheese, oregano, ¼ teaspoon pepper, cayenne, and 1 tablespoon oil in separate bowl; set aside.

3. Press and roll dough into 15 by 11-inch rectangle on lightly floured counter, pulling on corners to help make distinct rectangle. Transfer dough to prepared sheet and press to edges of sheet. Brush edges of dough with remaining 1 tablespoon oil. Bake dough until top appears dry and bottom is just beginning to brown, about 5 minutes.

4. Remove crust from oven and, using spatula, press down on any air bubbles. Spread cottage cheese mixture evenly over top, leaving 1-inch border around edges. Sprinkle bacon evenly over cottage cheese mixture.

5. Sprinkle mozzarella mixture evenly over pizza, leaving ½-inch border. Create 2 rows of 3 evenly spaced small wells in cheese, each about 3 inches in diameter (6 wells total). Crack 1 egg into each well, then season each with salt and pepper.

6. Return pizza to oven and bake until crust is light golden around edges and eggs are just set, 9 to 10 minutes for slightly runny yolks or 11 to 12 minutes for soft-cooked yolks, rotating sheet halfway through baking.

7. Transfer pizza to wire rack and let cool for 5 minutes. Transfer pizza to cutting board. Sprinkle with scallions and chives and drizzle with extra oil. Slice and serve.

Chorizo and Manchego Breakfast Pizza

Substitute 6 ounces chorizo sausage, halved lengthwise and cut into ½-inch slices, for bacon and 1 cup shredded Manchego cheese for Parmesan. Cook chorizo in 12-inch skillet over medium heat until lightly browned, 7 to 9 minutes. Let cool completely before proceeding.

Sausage and Red Bell Pepper Breakfast Pizza

Substitute 6 ounces bulk breakfast sausage for bacon and extra-sharp cheddar for mozzarella. Combine sausage; 1 stemmed, seeded, and chopped red bell pepper; 1 chopped onion; and ¼ teaspoon salt in 12-inch skillet. Cook over medium heat, breaking up sausage with spoon, until sausage begins to brown and bell pepper and onion are translucent, about 6 minutes. Transfer to paper towel–lined plate. Let mixture cool completely before proceeding.

WHOLE-WHEAT BLUEBERRY MUFFINS

✔ WHY THIS RECIPE WORKS: One hundred percent whole-wheat muffins can often be dense, squat sinkers that nobody wants to eat. Our goal was to fix that problem, producing a whole-wheat muffin with hearty flavor but a light crumb. After combining two leaveners and incorporating ingredients with high amounts of moisture (buttermilk, eggs, and blueberries) and a mix of melted butter and oil with 100 percent whole-wheat flour, we were ecstatic to find our blueberry muffins as tender as they were flavorful. After a sprinkle of streusel on the top of the muffin, we now had a tender, slightly sweet whole-wheat muffin with that signature nutty, whole-wheat flavor.

In the past few years, baking with whole-wheat flour has become increasingly popular. Not only is it better for you nutritionally, providing more fiber and bran, but it also provides a unique sweet, nutty flavor that white flour simply can't match. Unfortunately, baked goods that use solely whole-wheat flour (as opposed to a mixture of whole-wheat and white) too often emerge from the oven with a dense, almost brick-like texture. As a fan of the flavor of whole wheat, though, I was on a mission to make a 100 percent whole-wheat blueberry muffin that was just as tender and light as its white all-purpose alternative.

I pored over "healthy" cookbooks for five recipes that would knock the socks off my tasters. I was going to show them that these muffins weren't as dry, dense, and squat as people had said they were. Well, not so fast. The five-recipe test I did was pretty underwhelming. Some of the muffins were overly greasy, one tasted "soapy," another tasted bitter, one was disguised as a scone, and another was so sweet that we thought we were eating a cupcake from our neighborhood bakery.

But there was one recipe that gave me some inspiration. It used whole-wheat flour, brown sugar, baking powder, baking soda, buttermilk, and vegetable oil. Tasters preferred this recipe out of all five because it was surprisingly moist. Unfortunately, it was also pretty dense and quite squat, common side effects of baking with whole-wheat flour.

At this point, I decided to abandon other people's recipes and instead look back at the test kitchen's own standard blueberry muffin, which is made with all-purpose flour. Maybe there was something there that would help me.

Interestingly, this recipe had similar ingredients to the one that gave the best results in the five-recipe test, but there were also differences. It used white sugar instead of brown, used one leavener (baking powder) where the other used two (baking soda in addition to powder), included an egg in the recipe, and used melted butter in addition to vegetable oil. I baked up a batch of muffins from our classic recipe, simply substituting 100 percent whole-wheat flour for the all-purpose flour in the original. Quite surprisingly, these muffins were better—lighter in texture and much more tender—than any of those made with the best of the recipes supposedly designed for whole wheat.

I was at a loss to figure out why, so I turned to our science editor for some insight. He immediately saw a number of reasons for the success of this muffin.

First, there is an unusually high amount of liquid in this recipe—not just the cup of buttermilk, but also 1½ cups of blueberries, two eggs, and 4 tablespoons each of melted butter and vegetable oil. This high water content, he explained, produces more steam during baking, which serves as another kind of leavening. The liquid also softens the bran in the whole wheat, which helps create a lighter, more tender, less dense muffin.

The combination of melted butter and oil also reduces gluten development and helps tenderize the muffin. Likewise, the acid from the buttermilk lowers the pH, again inhibiting gluten development and therefore producing a more tender muffin.

Looking at the two recipes, our science editor also suggested that I might get even better results if I took a hint from the five-recipe test winner and tried using baking soda in addition to baking powder. The whole-wheat flour, he figured, could use that additional leavening power. Sure enough, when I did a side-by-side test of my working recipe using just baking powder versus powder plus soda, there was a clear difference. The muffins that used both leaveners were lighter in texture, the top was domed, and they were more golden brown in color. Our science editor explained that the baking soda was helping neutralize the acid in the buttermilk, which in turn allowed the baking powder to function more effectively. Without the added baking soda, much of the baking soda already in the baking powder was being neutralized and losing its leavening power.

Inspired by this, I decided to do a couple more side-by-side tests comparing elements from the two recipes.

First I tried muffins made with brown versus white sugar. As it turned out, the combination of brown sugar and whole-wheat flour made a sour muffin with traces of bitterness that tasters didn't enjoy. White sugar it would be. Next I compared muffins made with buttermilk, yogurt, and sour cream, respectively. The sour cream produced an unappealingly pasty and tangy muffin, but yogurt and buttermilk were both good. Given that result, I chose to stick with the original buttermilk.

I was satisfied with the texture and flavor of this muffin, but there was still one thing missing: a satisfying topping. Because these muffins were relatively low in sugar, tasters felt that they could benefit from a bit of extra sweetness before baking. I turned to our trusty streusel topping and it satisfied us all. After a few tweaks to the butter, sugar, and flour ratios, I eventually had a crumbly, slightly sweet topping for my now light and delicate 100 percent whole-wheat blueberry muffins. (And, yes, you read that correctly.)

—ASHLEY MOORE, *Cook's Country*

Whole-Wheat Blueberry Muffins

MAKES 12 MUFFINS

Do not overmix the batter. You can substitute frozen (unthawed) blueberries for fresh in this recipe.

STREUSEL

- 3 tablespoons granulated sugar
- 3 tablespoons packed brown sugar
- 3 tablespoons whole-wheat flour
  Pinch salt
- 2 tablespoons unsalted butter, melted

MUFFINS

- 3 cups (16½ ounces) whole-wheat flour
- 2½ teaspoons baking powder
- ½ teaspoon baking soda
- 1 teaspoon salt
- 1 cup (7 ounces) granulated sugar
- 2 large eggs
- 4 tablespoons unsalted butter, melted
- ¼ cup vegetable oil
- 1¼ cups buttermilk
- 1½ teaspoons vanilla extract
- 7½ ounces (1½ cups) blueberries

NOTES FROM THE TEST KITCHEN

SWAP STRATEGICALLY

You can't simply swap whole-wheat flour into a regular muffin recipe and expect it to work. But if you know the science behind baking and account for the variables, you can make great blueberry muffins using 100 percent whole-wheat flour.

THE WRONG WHOLE-WHEAT MUFFIN
Makes for a fine doorstop . . . but bad eating.

WHOLE-WHEAT FLOUR: COMPLETE KERNEL

Whole-wheat flour contains the entire wheat kernel, including the germ, which means that it's higher in fiber, fat, and protein than all-purpose flour. Because the protein in the germ doesn't form gluten, whole-wheat flour is often bolstered with all-purpose flour or bread flour in baking recipes. Whole-wheat flour is prone to rancidity; store it in a zipper-lock bag in the freezer.

1. FOR THE STREUSEL: Combine granulated sugar, brown sugar, flour, and salt in bowl. Add melted butter and toss with fork until evenly moistened and mixture forms large chunks with some pea-size pieces throughout; set aside.

2. FOR THE MUFFINS: Adjust oven rack to middle position and heat oven to 400 degrees. Spray 12-cup muffin tin, including top, generously with vegetable oil spray. Whisk flour, baking powder, baking soda, and salt together in large bowl. Whisk sugar, eggs, melted butter, and oil together in separate bowl until combined, about 30 seconds. Whisk buttermilk and vanilla into sugar mixture until combined.

3. Stir sugar mixture into flour mixture until just combined. Gently stir in blueberries until incorporated. Using ¼-cup dry measuring cup, divide batter evenly among prepared muffin cups (cups will be filled to rim); sprinkle muffin tops evenly with streusel.

4. Bake until golden brown and toothpick inserted in center comes out with few crumbs attached, 18 to 20 minutes, rotating muffin tin halfway through baking. Let muffins cool in muffin tin on wire rack for 5 minutes. Remove muffins from muffin tin and let cool 5 minutes longer. Serve.

NOTES FROM THE TEST KITCHEN

SQUEEZING ZUCCHINI

Zucchini is more than 95 percent water, so it's no wonder that zucchini bread is notoriously soggy. This technique rids the zucchini of much of its moisture and concentrates the flavor at the same time.

1. Using the coarse holes on a box grater, grate the zucchini, peel and all.

2. Place the grated zucchini in a clean dish towel and wring out as much liquid as possible.

ZUCCHINI BREAD

✔ WHY THIS RECIPE WORKS: Baked goods are a great way to use up zucchini. Because of its high moisture content, zucchini produces a moist cake. However, if not used correctly, zucchini can leave baked goods extremely wet and gummy. By removing a majority of the juice from the zucchini, along with most other sources of moisture, and lowering the fat, we were able to up our zucchini content from 12 ounces to 1½ pounds without sacrificing a properly moist and tender crumb.

In the health food–crazed 1960s and '70s, recipes for zucchini bread popped up everywhere. With bits of healthy green vegetable speckling the crumb, the bread was a sweet treat you could not only enjoy but also feel virtuous about eating. But while other food fads have come and gone, zucchini bread has remained hugely popular—and for an entirely different reason: The high water content of the vegetable makes it ideal for producing the soft, moist crumb that is the hallmark of a great quick bread.

But zucchini can also be a liability, as too much leads to a soggy loaf. That's why, in spite of the oft-stated goal of using up surplus squash, most recipes top out at a mere 10 to 12 ounces. And funnily enough, despite being associated with a health-food movement, the recipes tend to call for copious amounts of oil that turn the loaf greasy and overly rich.

Packing more zucchini into the bread would hopefully pave the way for scaling back the ½ to ¾ cup of oil that most recipes call for, so I set a goal of doubling the usual amount of squash. Simply folding coarsely grated zucchini shreds into the batter is common, but wringing them out in a towel first seemed like a better approach: The drier the zucchini was, the more I could squeeze into a loaf without sogging it out. Sure enough, a full ½ cup of pale green liquid dripped out of 1½ pounds of squash. Encouraged, I ran a few more zucchini along the fine holes of the grater before wringing them out, reasoning that the increased surface area of the smaller pieces would help expel more liquid. Indeed, I got ¾ cup of juice from this batch.

I used coarse and finely ground zucchini (both wrung out), as well as 1½ pounds of unsqueezed coarse shreds as a control, in a typical zucchini bread recipe minus

ZUCCHINI BREAD

most of the fat: all-purpose flour, generous amounts of baking soda and powder for lift, sugar, touches of salt and cinnamon, eggs, a handful of toasted walnuts, and just ¼ cup of oil. I scraped the batters into greased loaf pans before putting them into 325-degree ovens. The bread made with unsqueezed shreds emerged predictably wet and gummy, and the finely shredded loaf was just as dense—the thin shreds had clumped together, compressing the crumb. Fortunately, the coarsely grated squeezed squash produced a crumb that was supermoist, more open, and significantly less gummy. Plus, it wasn't greasy at all. I'd stick with the squeezed coarse shreds.

Now what about this loaf's flavor? Here I was pleasantly surprised. As low-key as zucchini may be, I had feared that an overload would give the bread a vegetal taste. But despite the significant amount, the bread had a sweet, mildly earthy taste; mineral or strong vegetal flavors were absent. It turns out that by removing much of the moisture, I had also removed some of the key compounds, called Amadori compounds, responsible for zucchini's vegetal flavor, which are concentrated in the juice, not the flesh.

I just needed to get rid of a remaining trace of gumminess. I swapped a portion of the all-purpose flour for whole-wheat flour, since the bran and germ in whole-wheat flour allow it to absorb more moisture than the all-purpose kind. I was gratified to find that not only was this latest loaf no longer sticky but it also boasted a nice coarseness from the whole wheat. It just needed some complexity. No problem: I simply switched from granulated sugar to molasses-y brown sugar, increased the cinnamon to 1 tablespoon, and added nutmeg and vanilla.

With its light, moist crumb that's low on oil and chock-full of zucchini (and even boasts a whole-grain element), this bread might even pass as a "health" food. I just consider it the best zucchini bread I've ever tasted.

—SARAH MULLINS, *Cook's Illustrated*

Zucchini Bread
MAKES 1 LOAF

Use the large holes of a box grater to shred the zucchini. The test kitchen's preferred loaf pan measures 8½ by 4½ inches; if you use a 9 by 5-inch loaf pan, start checking for doneness 5 minutes early.

- 1½ pounds zucchini, shredded
- 1¼ cups packed (8¾ ounces) brown sugar
- ¼ cup vegetable oil
- 2 large eggs
- 1 teaspoon vanilla extract
- 1½ cups (7½ ounces) all-purpose flour
- ½ cup (2¾ ounces) whole-wheat flour
- 1 tablespoon ground cinnamon
- 1½ teaspoons salt
- 1 teaspoon baking powder
- 1 teaspoon baking soda
- ½ teaspoon ground nutmeg
- ¾ cup walnuts, toasted and chopped (optional)
- 1 tablespoon granulated sugar

1. Adjust oven rack to middle position and heat oven to 325 degrees. Grease 8½ by 4½-inch loaf pan.

2. Place zucchini in center of dish towel. Gather ends together and twist tightly to drain as much liquid as possible, discarding liquid (you should have ½ to ⅔ cup liquid). Whisk brown sugar, oil, eggs, and vanilla together in medium bowl. Fold in zucchini.

3. Whisk all-purpose flour, whole-wheat flour, cinnamon, salt, baking powder, baking soda, and nutmeg together in large bowl. Fold in zucchini mixture until just incorporated. Fold in walnuts, if using. Pour batter into prepared pan and sprinkle with granulated sugar.

4. Bake until top bounces back when gently pressed and toothpick inserted in center comes out with few moist crumbs attached, 65 to 75 minutes. Let bread cool in pan on wire rack for 30 minutes. Remove bread from pan and let cool completely on wire rack. Serve.

VARIATION

Cocoa Zucchini Bread with Dried Cherries
Substitute cocoa powder for cinnamon and ground cloves for nutmeg. Prepare bread with walnuts and add ¾ cup dried cherries, chopped, to batter with walnuts.

SAVORY CORN MUFFINS

✓ **WHY THIS RECIPE WORKS:** For a corn muffin with great cornmeal flavor and proper muffin structure, we used a ratio of 2 parts cornmeal to 1 part flour. We ditched the copious amount of sugar found in most recipes for a truly savory muffin. To help make up for the moisture that sugar normally provides, we used a mix of milk, butter, and sour cream for the right amount of water and fat. Finally, in order to get extra liquid into the batter, we precooked a portion of the cornmeal with additional milk to make a polenta-like porridge, which produced a super-moist muffin.

A great sweet cornmeal muffin might be easy to come by, but a passable version of the savory type is the Bigfoot of the muffin world: We've all heard of its existence, but good luck finding physical evidence to support the claim. Most often, these muffins are unappealing, with insufficient cornmeal flavor and/or a dense, heavy crumb. Could I tip the scales in favor of the cornmeal?

I knew the reason for the flavor deficit: Recipes generally call for only 1 part cornmeal to 1 part wheat flour. Using more cornmeal would surely produce the distinctive flavor I wanted. But it would also affect texture: Wheat flour helps form an elastic network of gluten that provides structure and traps gas during baking. Cornmeal, on the other hand, can't form gluten. For an attractive rise, some wheat flour would be essential, but I wanted to use as little as possible to keep the cornmeal flavor at the fore.

I tested several proportions before settling on 2 cups cornmeal to 1 cup flour, along with milk, melted butter, baking powder and soda, salt, and eggs. These muffins boasted excellent flavor with enough gluten to push the batter above the rim of the muffin tin, but they were way too dry.

Muffins stay moist with the help of a few key ingredients; namely, water, fat, and sugar. Because a batter that's too runny won't form the proper shape during baking, I wanted to avoid, at least for the moment, increasing the milk I was already using or even adding water. Instead I tried sour cream, which has some water

and a lot of fat. But the thick dairy wasn't enough to turn the tide: These muffins were still on the dry side. Next on the docket? Sugar.

Yes, sugar makes things sweet, but it also has a huge impact on the moisture level of baked goods. That's because sugar is hygroscopic, meaning that it attracts and traps moisture. It's not uncommon for a sweet muffin to call for more than 1 cup of sugar, an absolute nonstarter for my savory muffins. But a little sugar could provide some moisture retention without making the muffins sweet. I started small, maxing out at 3 tablespoons of sugar before the muffins began to taste too sweet.

But frustratingly, even with the help of sour cream and sugar, the crumb was still dry. In the past, we've improved moistness by adding a surplus of liquid to other types of batter and then letting it rest to thicken up prior to baking. The upshot is extra liquid in the mix without having to sacrifice the attractive dome achieved by a drier, stiffer batter. I tried it, increasing the milk and letting the batter rest for 20 minutes. No dice: The cornmeal-rich batter never fully absorbed the extra liquid and the muffins baked up flat.

Then I had a thought: Could I add more moisture without thinning the batter by precooking the cornmeal with extra milk? I'd give it a try. I microwaved ½ cup of the cornmeal with 1¼ cups of milk (almost double the amount I'd used previously) until a thick, polenta-like porridge formed. I then whisked in the rest of the ingredients, divided the batter among the muffin tin cups, and placed the tin in the oven. Fifteen minutes later, I pulled out 12 exceptional muffins: golden brown, rich with buttery cornmeal flavor, and, most important, perfectly moist.

Why did this work? The starch granules in cornmeal absorb only a limited amount of moisture (less than 30 percent of their own weight) when mixed into a cold liquid. But when the liquid is heated, it weakens the starch granules so that they are able to soak up more fluid. Using this technique, I could add nearly twice the amount of liquid to my batter without turning it too thin to form a dome.

And just like that, I had my proof: Great savory cornmeal muffins really do exist.

—DAN SOUZA, *Cook's Illustrated*

MAKES 12 MUFFINS

Don't use coarse-ground or white cornmeal.

- 2 **cups (10 ounces) cornmeal**
- 1 **cup (5 ounces) all-purpose flour**
- 1½ **teaspoons baking powder**
- 1 **teaspoon baking soda**
- 1¼ **teaspoons salt**
- 1¼ **cups whole milk**
- 1 **cup sour cream**
- 8 **tablespoons unsalted butter, melted and cooled slightly**
- 3 **tablespoons sugar**
- 2 **large eggs, beaten**

1. Adjust oven rack to upper-middle position and heat oven to 425 degrees. Grease 12-cup muffin tin. Whisk 1½ cups cornmeal, flour, baking powder, baking soda, and salt together in medium bowl.

2. Combine milk and remaining ½ cup cornmeal in large bowl. Microwave milk-cornmeal mixture for 1½ minutes. Whisk thoroughly and continue to microwave, whisking every 30 seconds, until thickened to batter-like consistency (whisk will leave channel in bottom of bowl that slowly fills in), 1 to 3 minutes longer. Whisk in sour cream, melted butter, and sugar until combined. Whisk in eggs until combined. Fold in flour mixture until thoroughly combined. Using portion scoop or large spoon, divide batter evenly among prepared muffin cups (about ½ cup batter per cup; batter will mound slightly above rim).

3. Bake until tops are golden brown and toothpick inserted in center comes out clean, 13 to 17 minutes, rotating muffin tin halfway through baking. Let muffins cool in muffin tin on wire rack for 5 minutes. Remove muffins from muffin tin and let cool 5 minutes longer. Serve warm.

VARIATION

Savory Corn Muffins with Cheddar and Scallions
Add ½ teaspoon pepper, ¼ teaspoon dry mustard, and pinch cayenne to dry ingredients in step 1. Whisk in 1½ cups shredded cheddar cheese and 5 thinly sliced scallions with eggs.

POTATO BISCUITS WITH CHIVES

✔ WHY THIS RECIPE WORKS: To achieve a supremely flaky biscuit, we turned to an unexpected ingredient: potato. Since potatoes don't have gluten (the chewy protein that gives structure to bread), adding them to baked goods results in a tender crumb. Potato starch also holds on to more water than wheat starch, which keeps these biscuits moist. And luckily, we found that instant potato flakes work even better than real mashed potatoes. To flavor these biscuits, we chose some traditional potato partners: buttermilk and chives.

Anyone who loves a good biscuit, as I do, can quickly list its requisite qualities: It is light, flaky, tender, and rich. Here at the test kitchen we've made every manner of biscuit—or so I thought, until I came across a recipe for a particular breed of stamped biscuits using mashed potatoes. A resourceful idea, to be sure, but wouldn't adding heavy, wet mashed potatoes to biscuit dough work against producing a light biscuit? I needed to find out.

I fished around for more recipes, ultimately coming up with a handful that called for leftover mashed potatoes and several that built the cooking and mashing of the spuds right into the recipe. After baking up a few of each, I had my answer: Most of these potato biscuits were squat and heavy, resembling crackers more than the high, light biscuits I love. Those that used leftover mashed potatoes had inherent problems—how much butter or cream was in the mash? What kind of potatoes were used?

There were too many variables. The results were more consistent in recipes that used fresh mashed potatoes, but something about this approach bothered me. Biscuits are by nature one of the quickest, easiest baked goods out there—cooking, draining, mashing, and then cooling potatoes didn't fit into that time line. Were potato biscuits even worth salvaging? I took a break from the kitchen and hit the books.

A little research unearthed the potential benefits: Adding potato to baked goods, whether bread, rolls, or, yes, biscuits, is said to produce a superlatively tender texture. How? Gluten, the protein that makes bread products chewy, is formed when the proteins in wheat flour mix with liquid and link together. Granules of potato starch interrupt the protein structure, meaning less gluten is formed, resulting in extra tenderness in the finished product. Interesting.

But how could I reap the benefits of potato starch without the moisture of the potatoes wreaking havoc on the biscuits? In the end, I found my answer in a box: instant mashed potatoes. Dehydrated potato flakes have all the starch of whole potatoes but are devoid of water and much more consistent than real spuds. Best of all, they're instant—absolutely perfect for my speedy biscuit time line.

I started off working with my favorite test kitchen stamped biscuit recipe, which calls for combining all-purpose flour, sugar, salt, baking powder, and baking soda in the food processor, cutting in butter and shortening, and then stirring in buttermilk before rolling and stamping out the biscuits. After starting the biscuits in a hot oven for maximum rise, you reduce the temperature slightly and let them gently finish baking. Finally, when they're hot from the oven, you brush the tops of the biscuits with melted butter for extra richness and gloss. A few experiments revealed that for every 2 tablespoons of potato flakes I added, I needed to subtract 1 tablespoon of flour from the recipe to give the biscuit dough the proper texture. Working in increments, I got all the way up to ¾ cup of potato flakes, which produced an incredibly flaky biscuit—any more than that and flaky began to border on crumbly.

These biscuits were delicious, no doubt, but there were a few skeptics in the test kitchen who questioned whether mine were any better than regular biscuits. To prove my case, I whipped up another batch of potato biscuits and laid them out next to a freshly baked tray of traditional buttermilk biscuits. The results? Both were good, but tasters appreciated the lighter, flakier texture of the ones made with potato flakes. The one complaint: My biscuits weren't quite as tall as the traditional ones. Since potato starch has no gluten, my dough had less structure, so the biscuits couldn't rise quite as high. Luckily, an extra teaspoon of baking powder did the trick, making tender and tall biscuits, and there were no more doubters to be found.

To pair with the subtly earthy flavor of the potato, I added fresh chives to the biscuits. This batch went over so well that I developed a couple of variations, turning to other classic potato pairings. I added sharp cheddar cheese and sliced scallions to one, and to the other, crispy, salty, crumbled bacon. Just when I thought a biscuit was a biscuit, I found a reason to rekindle my love.

—REBECCAH MARSTERS, *Cook's Country*

Potato Biscuits with Chives
MAKES 12 BISCUITS

We like the texture of biscuits made with both butter and shortening, but if you prefer to use all butter, omit the shortening and use 12 tablespoons of chilled butter in step 1.

- 2½ cups (12½ ounces) all-purpose flour
- ¾ cup instant potato flakes
- ⅓ cup chopped fresh chives
- 4 teaspoons baking powder
- ½ teaspoon baking soda
- 1 tablespoon sugar
- 1 teaspoon salt
- 8 tablespoons unsalted butter, cut into ½-inch pieces and chilled, plus 2 tablespoons unsalted butter, melted
- 4 tablespoons vegetable shortening, cut into ½-inch pieces and chilled
- 1¼ cups buttermilk, chilled

1. Adjust oven rack to middle position and heat oven to 450 degrees. Line rimmed baking sheet with parchment paper. Process flour, potato flakes, chives, baking powder, baking soda, sugar, and salt in food processor until combined, about 15 seconds. Add chilled butter and shortening and pulse until mixture resembles coarse crumbs, 7 to 9 pulses.

2. Transfer flour mixture to large bowl. Stir in buttermilk with rubber spatula until combined, turning and pressing until no dry flour remains. Turn out dough onto lightly floured surface and knead briefly, 8 to 10 times, to form smooth, cohesive ball. Roll out dough into 9-inch circle, about ¾ inch thick.

3. Using floured 2½-inch round cutter, stamp out 8 to 9 biscuits and arrange upside down on prepared sheet. Gather dough scraps and gently pat into ¾-inch-thick circle. Stamp out remaining 3 to 4 biscuits and transfer to sheet.

4. Bake until biscuits begin to rise, about 5 minutes, then rotate sheet and reduce oven temperature to 400 degrees. Continue to bake until golden brown, 10 to 12 minutes longer. Brush biscuit tops with melted butter. Transfer to wire rack and let cool for 5 minutes before serving.

POTATO BISCUITS WITH CHIVES

BUTTER FAN ROLLS

BUTTER FAN ROLLS

✓ **WHY THIS RECIPE WORKS:** The success of these rolls lies in the layers. Some easy countertop construction produces delicious rolls with buttery layers that are fun to pull apart and eat. In order to keep the fans from becoming crunchy the rolls baked, we moved the muffin tin to the upper-middle position in the oven, placing them further from the heat source. We used whole milk along with sugar and butter to give these rolls plenty of richness.

If ever a roll was aptly named, it's the butter fan roll: buttery layers of yeasty bread fanned out like, well, a fan—designed to be fancy enough for a dinner party but begging to be pulled apart and slathered with butter and jam for breakfast, too. After seeing these cute, tender, buttery little buns in bread baskets and bakery store windows throughout the Northeast, I set out to make my own homemade version.

Just looking at them, I had a feeling these rolls would take some doing—after all, you don't get such striking, layered, fanned-out mini loaves like these without a little countertop construction work. But how, exactly, is this unique shape achieved? I turned to a handful of existing recipes to find out.

After spending an afternoon in the kitchen, I had a wide range of rolls to sample. Some were tiny and tightly stacked. Others were big and floppy, with wings rather than fans. Some had robust buttery flavor, while others were bland. Some were soft and cakey, others dry and almost crunchy. But all followed a similar procedure: Mix and briefly knead the dough and let it rise once. Then punch down the dough, roll it out, cut it into strips, stack the strips, nestle them into muffin tins, let the dough rise again, and bake them off.

This all sounds like a lot of work, and they do take some attention, but butter fan rolls aren't nearly as taxing or complicated as their appearance led me to expect.

Where I tripped up, however, was in the baking. My early experiments became games of chance: I produced rolls that were sometimes undercooked in the middle, sometimes overcooked at the ends, often too brown on the bottom, at times soggy in the center—never perfect. Having nailed many dinner rolls in my day, I was vexed.

The beautiful fanned-out shape that defines these rolls was creating a problem of texture and consistency. I wanted soft, tender rolls that were completely cooked throughout, with faintly crisp—not crunchy—tips.

After a few experiments baking the rolls on the center rack of the oven at a range of temperatures (I tried 325, 350, and 375 degrees), and for a range of times (I tried 12, 15, and 18 minutes), I just couldn't crack the consistency code. When the oven was too hot, I'd have crisp tips but overcooked rolls. When it was too cool, I'd have nicely baked rolls but with soft tips.

Setting aside questions of temperature, I focused on location, moving the oven rack from the middle position to the upper-middle position. Placing the muffin tins just a bit farther from the heating element allowed the rolls to cook through a bit more gently, while the radiant heat reflected from the roof of the oven created the lightly crisp edges I was looking for. I'd found the sweet spot.

Satisfied, but still curious, I wanted to try one more adjustment for convenience's sake. Even though these buns are sometimes called Yankee buttermilk rolls, I couldn't help wondering whether the buttermilk was really necessary. Could these rolls be made with regular whole milk, or even skim?

Answer: Yes in both cases. In fact, my tasters had to work hard to discern any more than a very slight difference. When pressed, they preferred the slightly less-tangy flavor of the rolls made with whole milk.

—CRISTIN WALSH, *Cook's Country*

Butter Fan Rolls

MAKES 12 ROLLS

Do not overflour the counter when rolling out the dough in step 3, and use a bench scraper to square off the edges of the rectangle. Make sure to plan ahead: This dough takes about 3 hours to rise before baking.

- ¾ cup warm milk (110 degrees)
- ¼ cup (1¾ ounces) sugar
- 1 large egg plus 1 large yolk, room temperature
- 1 tablespoon instant or rapid-rise yeast
- 3½ cups (17½ ounces) all-purpose flour
- 2 teaspoons salt
- 8 tablespoons unsalted butter, cut into 8 pieces and softened, plus 4 tablespoons unsalted butter, melted

1. In bowl of stand mixer, combine milk, sugar, egg and yolk, and yeast and let sit until foamy, about 3 minutes. Add flour and salt. Fit stand mixer with dough hook and knead on medium-low speed until dough is shaggy, about 2 minutes.

2. With mixer running, add softened butter 1 piece at a time until incorporated. Continue to knead until dough is smooth, about 5 minutes. Transfer dough to greased large bowl, cover tightly with plastic wrap, and let rise at room temperature until doubled in size, about 1½ hours.

3. Grease 12-cup muffin tin. Press down on dough to deflate and transfer to lightly floured counter (do not overflour counter). Divide dough into 2 equal balls (about 1 pound each). Roll one dough ball into 15 by 12-inch rectangle with long side parallel to counter's edge.

4. Using pizza wheel, cut dough vertically into 6 (2½- by 12-inch) strips. Brush tops of 5 strips evenly with 1 tablespoon melted butter, leaving 1 strip unbuttered. Stack strips squarely on top of each other, buttered to unbuttered side, finishing with unbuttered strip on top.

5. Using sharp knife, cut stacked dough strips crosswise into 6 equal stacks. Place stacks, cut side up, in each of 6 muffin cups. Repeat with remaining dough ball and 1 tablespoon melted butter. Cover tin loosely with plastic and let dough rise at room temperature until doubled in size, 1¼ to 1½ hours. Adjust oven rack to upper-middle position and heat oven to 350 degrees.

6. Bake until golden brown, 20 to 25 minutes, rotating muffin tin halfway through baking. Brush rolls with remaining 2 tablespoons melted butter. Let cool in muffin tin for 5 minutes. Remove rolls from muffin tin and transfer to wire rack. Serve warm or at room temperature.

NOTES FROM THE TEST KITCHEN

SLASHING RUSTIC LOAVES

The slashes on rustic loaves aren't just about aesthetics. Slashes create weak spots in a loaf's surface, which allow the interior crumb to expand fully in the right direction. Without the slashes, the loaf will expand outward wherever it finds a weak spot, resulting in an odd shape and an uneven crumb.

Torpedo- or oval-shaped loaves should be scored along their length with long ½-inch-deep slashes made at a shallow, 30-degree angle. For even, smooth cuts, it's important to use a swift, fluid motion. If the blade is held upright or the cut is too deep, it will close up during baking. Scoring of this type is most easily done with a curved-blade *lame*. Since the openings taper, the ends of each cut should overlap just slightly to ensure that the loaf expands evenly.

AUTHENTIC BAGUETTES AT HOME

✔ WHY THIS RECIPE WORKS: The problem with most baguette recipes, we discovered, is that all the small details that matter are glossed over. For an authentic wheaty flavor, we added a bit of whole-wheat flour (sifted to remove some of the larger pieces of bran that would otherwise add bitterness and make the loaf dense) to the white flour. Mixing the dough in a machine and then using a series of gentle folds to develop the dough created the perfect tender, irregular internal crumb. Next we employed a long, slow rise in the refrigerator, which delivered the complex flavor of fermentation while making the recipe flexible, since we could bake the loaves anytime within a three-day window. To shape the loaves perfectly without overworking the dough, we employed a multistep approach that gradually transformed them into baguettes. Finally, we ensured a crispy, crackly crust by moistening the *couche*, the pleated linen cloth that holds the loaves as they proof, and by starting the loaves beneath a pair of upturned disposable roasting pans to trap steam as it evaporated from the exterior of the dough.

I think home cooks rarely make baguettes for two reasons: One, they are intimidated, and two, they don't know what they are missing. A great baguette is hard to come by, at least outside France. Even if a nearby bakery makes a great baguette, you have to buy one within hours of baking or else it's rock hard. If you want a great baguette, you should make it yourself.

But when I tested some promising recipes, not one produced loaves that attained that ideal. Many had a pale, soft crust and weak flavor; others were dense and uniform on the inside. I'd need to develop my own recipe—and what better place to begin than the baguette's home turf?

In Paris, I learned that the darker the crust, the deeper the flavor. Excess exterior flour will dull flavor and compromise crispiness. Irregular interior holes indicate that the dough has been handled gently and thus will have a tender crumb. Almond-shaped slashes that open wide also signify tenderness and a fully expanded interior, while color that changes from pale to dark within those cuts is a sign of complex flavor. A great baguette should have the flavor of sweet wheat, with just a subtle hint of tangy, complex fermented flavor.

The problem with recipes wasn't so much what they instructed me to do but how little instruction and explanation they provided. So much of what goes into making a good baguette is in the mechanics of the thing—shaping, proofing, scoring, steaming in the oven—and this wasn't conveyed in recipes. My role was clear: Cull what I could from recipes and then apply what I learned to create a step-by-step, authentic baguette recipe for the home oven.

The standard baguette ingredient list is simple: flour, water, salt, and yeast. I settled on 1 pound of flour, 1 teaspoon of yeast, 1½ teaspoons of salt, and 12 ounces of water, enough for a moderately wet dough. (I also added a teaspoon of diastatic malt powder to help the loaf brown deeply.) As for mixing and kneading, I found that less is more. Using a stand mixer to do both jobs left the crumb too uniform and tight. Mixing by hand and then giving the dough several folds during the initial proofing to develop the structure gave me better results, but it was difficult to evenly combine the ingredients. I settled on mixing the dough in the machine and then folding the dough several times during the initial proofing.

Next up was fermentation, which is when the yeast consumes sugar and starches in the flour to produce gas and alcohol, giving the loaf both lift and flavor. The simplest approach calls for doing everything from mixing through baking in a single day, allowing 2 to 3 hours for fermentation. Another option is the slow rise, or cold-fermentation method, in which the dough is placed in the fridge for a day or more before shaping and baking. The straight dough method gave me baguettes with little character, but the slow-rise baguettes were far more flavorful and offered another benefit: convenience. The dough needed at least 24 hours in the fridge, but it could sit for as long as 72 hours. Plus, this dough could be portioned out to make baguettes "on demand" as desired within that window.

When I used this method, the flavor was good, but my loaves were missing that wheaty taste that I'd experienced with the Parisian baguettes. This is because much of the wheat grown in North America is destined for the Far East, where people want pure white dumplings and noodles, the growth of wheat varieties high in naturally occurring yellow carotenoids pigment are discouraged. To mimic the more intense wheatiness of French flours, I added a bit of whole-wheat flour to my recipe.

NOTES FROM THE TEST KITCHEN

BAGUETTE BAKER'S KIT
Baguettes require a few specialty items, though we did find some alternatives.

DIASTATIC MALT POWDER
Because of the long proofing time, nearly all the sugars in baguette dough will be consumed by yeast. Since sugars are responsible for browning, this will leave the crust pale and dull-tasting. Adding diastatic malt powder, a naturally occurring enzyme that converts the starches in flour to sugar, guarantees a supply of sugar at baking time and thus a crust that browns quickly and deeply (it also improves the texture of the loaf). It's not essential, but it makes a difference. Purchase diastatic malt powder (available from Amazon, $7.63 for 1 pound), not plain malt powder or malt syrup.

COUCHE
To proof shaped baguettes, bakers cradle them in the folds of a piece of heavy raw linen called a couche. A couche wicks away moisture, helping create a crisp crust, and releases the dough without tugging it out of shape as cotton or synthetic will. Our favorite, the San Francisco Baking Institute 18" Linen Canvas (Couche) ($8 for 36 by 18-inch couche), has good body without being too stiff. Alternatively, you can use a double layer of 100 percent linen tea towels that are at least 16 inches long and 12 inches wide.

FLIPPING BOARD
To move baguettes from the couche to the oven, professional bakers use a long narrow piece of wood called a flipping board or transfer peel. While the boards aren't expensive ($12 from breadtopia.com), we found that a homemade substitute, made by taping together two pieces of clean, stiff cardboard (16 inches long by 4 inches wide) with packaging tape, works equally well.

LAME
Baguettes require scores that taper at the ends and open wide at the center, with an edge that peels back into a crisp ridge or "ear" that lends both flavor and texture. To achieve this, you must cut the loaf at a low angle, something much more easily done with the curved blade of a lame. Our favorite, the Breadtopia Bread Lame ($9.50), scored baguettes perfectly, and its blades are easy to change. Plus, it came with 10 extra blades. Alternatively, an unused box cutter blade will work.

So I tried substituting ¼ cup of whole-wheat flour for some of the white flour. Tasters welcomed the wheatiness, but they also noted a hint of bitterness and found these baguettes more dense and less crispy. The bran in the wheat flour was adding a bitter flavor and its sharp edges were cutting gluten strands, weakening the structure. Happily, there was a solution: Sifting the wheat flour removed some of the larger pieces of bran (but not the germ). Subbing in this sifted flour gave me baguettes with the same texture as that of all-white-flour loaves, but with far better flavor.

Now that I had a dough I was happy with, I could focus on shaping, which I had learned has a major impact here. Turning that mass of dough into a baguette shape gradually was critical. If done too quickly, you'll overwork the dough, or you won't get the right shape—or both. As I worked out my own step-by-step method, I found that the key was using a gentle touch and avoiding trapping large pockets of air. I settled on a three-stage process—preshape, fold, stretch—and a few key tricks that ensured ideal results. For instance, pressing the dough into a square and then rolling it like a log was the gentlest way to start the shaping process, while moving the semiformed loaf back and forth at the center until its ends widened, giving it a dog-bone shape, tightened the loaf and also pushed large air bubbles out either end.

I also learned that to score the loaves properly, I needed to keep the blade at a shallow angle. A *lame*, a traditional baguette scoring tool with a slightly curved blade, made producing slashes that baked up into the right almond-shaped openings easy, and it also created the proper ridge, or "ear," along one side of the slash that baked up deliciously crispy.

It was time to move on to the crust. At bakeries, shaped loaves are proofed in the folds of a piece of heavy linen known as a couche. The couche helps the baguette retain its shape and wicks away moisture from the exterior to encourage a crispy crust. But the thick crusts on my loaves suggested that they might be losing a little too much moisture.

Steam within the oven serves three important functions in bread baking. First, it keeps the exterior of the bread moist when it begins to bake, preventing the crust from hardening before the interior has fully expanded. Second, it ensures good color since the enzymes that convert some of the starches into sugars, which in turn lead to browning, need water to function. And finally, steam promotes crispiness. The remaining starches on the loaf's surface absorb the steam and cook into a crispy crust; without it, they simply dry out, leaving the crust dull and raw-tasting.

Misting the back of my couche lightly with water was a step in the right direction, but still the crust wasn't quite right. For my next test, I covered my baguettes with a pair of large, overturned disposable roasting pans (doubled up for a better seal). After 10 minutes, I pulled off the pans and continued to bake the baguettes. Tearing into a baguette confirmed it: It was shatteringly crispy. This was a baguette that could sit proudly on anyone's table.

—ANDREW JANJIGIAN, *Cook's Illustrated*

Authentic Baguettes at Home

MAKES FOUR 15-INCH-LONG BAGUETTES

If you can't find King Arthur all-purpose flour, substitute bread flour. For best results, weigh your ingredients. This recipe makes enough dough for four loaves, which can be baked anytime during the 24- to 72-hour window after placing the dough in the fridge.

- ¼ cup (1⅓ ounces) whole-wheat flour
- 3 cups (15 ounces) King Arthur all-purpose flour
- 1½ teaspoons salt
- 1 teaspoon instant or rapid-rise yeast
- 1 teaspoon diastatic malt powder (optional)
- 1½ cups (12 ounces) water
- 2 (16 by 12-inch) disposable aluminum roasting pans

1. Sift whole-wheat flour through fine-mesh strainer into bowl of stand mixer; discard bran remaining in strainer. Add all-purpose flour, salt, yeast, and malt powder, if using, to bowl of stand mixer. Fit stand mixer with dough hook, add water, and knead on low speed until cohesive dough forms and no dry flour remains, 5 to 7 minutes. Transfer dough to lightly oiled large bowl, cover with plastic wrap, and let rest at room temperature for 30 minutes.

2. Holding edge of dough with your fingertips, fold dough over itself by gently lifting and folding edge of dough toward center. Turn bowl 45 degrees; fold again. Turn bowl and fold dough 6 more times (total of 8 folds). Cover with plastic and let rise for 30 minutes. Repeat folding and rising every 30 minutes, 3 more times. After fourth set of folds, cover bowl tightly with plastic and refrigerate for at least 24 hours or up to 72 hours.

AUTHENTIC BAGUETTES AT HOME

SHAPING AND BAKING BAGUETTES

Once your dough has gone through the initial rising, folding, and resting stages, it's ready to be shaped.

1. On lightly floured counter, roll each piece of refrigerated and rested dough into loose 3- to 4-inch-long cylinder. Move dough to floured baking sheet and cover with plastic. Let rest at room temperature for 30 minutes.

2. Gently press 1 piece of dough into 6 by 4-inch rectangle with long edge facing you. Fold upper quarter of dough toward center and press to seal. Rotate dough 180 degrees and repeat folding step to form 8 by 2-inch rectangle.

3. Fold dough in half toward you, using thumb of your other hand to create crease along center of dough, sealing with heel of your hand as you work your way along the loaf. Do not seal ends of loaf.

4. Cup your hand over center of dough and roll dough back and forth gently to form dog-bone shape. Working toward ends, gently roll and stretch dough until it measures 15 inches long by 1¼ inches wide.

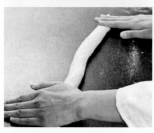

5. Moving your hands in opposite directions, use back-and-forth motion to roll ends of loaf under your palms to form sharp points.

6. Transfer dough to floured couche, seam side up. On either side of loaf, pinch edges of couche into pleat.

7. Place second loaf on opposite side of pleat. Fold couche edges over loaves to cover, then place sheet inside large plastic bag, and tie or fold under to enclose. Let rise for 45 minutes to 1 hour. While bread rises, preheat baking stone.

8. Unfold couche. Use flipping board to roll each loaf so seam side is down. Hold long edge of board between loaf and couche at 45-degree angle. Lift couche and flip loaf seam side up onto board. Invert loaf onto parchment-lined peel.

9. Holding lame concave side up at 30-degree angle to loaf, make series of three 4-inch-long, ½-inch-deep slashes along length of each loaf, using swift, fluid motion, overlapping each slash slightly.

10. Transfer loaves, on parchment, to baking stone, cover with stacked inverted disposable pans; bake for 5 minutes. Remove pans and bake until loaves are evenly browned, 12 to 15 minutes longer, rotating parchment halfway through baking.

3. Transfer dough to lightly floured counter, pat into 8-inch square (do not deflate), and divide in half. Return 1 piece of dough to container, wrap tightly with plastic, and refrigerate (dough can be shaped and baked anytime within 72-hour window). Divide remaining dough in half crosswise, transfer to lightly floured rimmed baking sheet, and cover loosely with plastic. Let rest for 45 minutes.

4. On lightly floured counter, roll each piece of dough into loose 3- to 4-inch-long cylinder; return to floured baking sheet and cover with plastic. Let rest at room temperature for 30 minutes.

5. Lightly mist underside of couche with water, drape over inverted baking sheet, and dust with flour. Gently press 1 piece of dough into 6 by 4-inch rectangle on lightly floured counter, with long edge facing you. Fold upper quarter of dough toward center and press gently to seal. Rotate dough 180 degrees and repeat folding step to form 8 by 2-inch rectangle.

6. Fold dough in half toward you, using thumb of your other hand to create crease along center of dough, sealing with heel of your hand as you work your way along the loaf. Without pressing down on loaf, use heel of your hand to reinforce seal (do not seal ends of loaf).

7. Cup your hand over center of dough and roll dough back and forth gently to tighten (it should form dog-bone shape).

8. Starting at center of dough and working toward ends, gently and evenly roll and stretch dough until it measures 15 inches long by 1¼ inches wide. Moving your hands in opposite directions, use back and forth motion to roll ends of loaf under your palms to form sharp points.

9. Transfer dough to floured couche, seam side up. On either side of loaf, pinch edges of couche into pleat, then cover loosely with large plastic garbage bag.

10. Repeat steps 4 through 9 with second piece of dough and place on opposite side of pleat. Fold edges of couche over loaves to cover completely, then carefully place sheet inside bag, and tie or fold under to enclose.

11. Let stand until loaves have nearly doubled in size and dough springs back minimally when poked gently with your fingertip, 45 to 60 minutes. While bread rises, adjust oven rack to middle position, place baking stone on rack, and heat oven to 500 degrees.

12. Line pizza peel with 16 by 12-inch piece of parchment paper with long edge perpendicular to handle. Unfold couche, pulling from ends to remove pleats. Gently pushing with side of flipping board, roll 1 loaf over, away from other loaf, so it is seam side down. Using your hand, hold long edge of flipping board between loaf and couche at 45-degree angle, then lift couche with your other hand and flip loaf seam side up onto board.

13. Invert loaf onto parchment-lined peel, seam side down, about 2 inches from long edge of parchment, then use flipping board to straighten loaf. Repeat with remaining loaves, leaving at least 3 inches between loaves.

14. Holding lame concave side up at 30-degree angle to loaf, make series of three 4-inch-long, ½-inch-deep slashes along length of loaf, using swift, fluid motion, overlapping each slash slightly. Repeat with second loaf.

15. Transfer loaves, on parchment, to baking stone, cover with stacked inverted disposable pans, and bake for 5 minutes. Carefully remove pans and bake until loaves are evenly browned, 12 to 15 minutes longer, rotating parchment halfway through baking. Transfer to cooling rack and let cool for at least 20 minutes before serving. Consume within 4 hours.

NEW YORK BAGELS

✓ WHY THIS RECIPE WORKS: Chewy yet tender, with a fine crumb, our bagels have a crisp, evenly browned exterior and a slightly malty flavor. To get the right amount of chew, we used high-protein bread flour, supplemented with vital wheat gluten, along with a minimum amount of water. To further increase the chew, we incorporated a number of gluten-strengthening shaping techniques: rolling with a rolling pin, forming the dough into a rope, and twisting the dough around itself before shaping it into a ring. And to ensure even, rapid browning, we added baking soda to the boiling water. To create a crisp crust, we baked the bagels on a rack set in a rimmed baking sheet, with boiling water poured onto the pan to create steam.

The average bagel is nothing special and not hard to come by: a uniformly soft, swollen, tasteless ring that's mass-produced and sold at supermarkets, convenience stores, coffee shops, and bagel chains nationwide.

But a proper New York bagel—that's in a class by itself. In New York City these rings have a fine, uniform crumb and a substantial chew. Their exterior is glossy and lightly browned with a thin, crackly-crisp shell, and their flavor is complex: wheaty, with both a faint sourness and a malty sweetness.

Unfortunately, bagels like these are all but impossible to find outside the New York City area. That's not because the city's water makes bagels better, as many devotees claim; it's because good bagel shops use specialized ingredients, equipment, and techniques that help the dough develop a crisp exterior, satisfying chew, and complex flavor. Replacing those ingredients, tools, and techniques with home baker–friendly alternatives was precisely the challenge I faced.

Bagel dough differs from most other bread doughs in three significant ways, each of which helps produce a bagel's fine, even crumb and chew. First, the dough contains less water—usually between 50 and 55 percent, versus about 60 to 70 percent in loaf breads. Minimizing the water reduces the network of proteins that give baked goods their elasticity and thus yields very stiff dough that bakes up chewy. Second, while most bread doughs proof twice, bagel dough is shaped into rings immediately after mixing and is proofed only once to prevent its yeast from developing too much gas, which would make the bagel's crumb airy. Third, bagels are often proofed in the refrigerator for the better part of 24 hours, a process known as cold fermentation. Not only does the colder temperature further minimize the yeast's gas production, but it also encourages the yeast to produce a more intricate mix of flavor compounds.

The only downside to working with the drier, stiffer dough was that it strained the mixer. So I moved the operation to the food processor, the sharp blades of which easily handled the dense, stiff mass. I also made two other tweaks: I used ice water to keep the dough as cool as possible during mixing, and I let the shaped bagels ferment at room temperature for an hour before chilling to give the yeast a chance to jump-start the fermentation process a bit.

The other ingredient that influenced the bagels' texture was the flour, as the chewiest results came from doughs made with high-gluten flour. This product, a staple in bread bakeries and available only via mail order, contains a high proportion (14 to 15 percent) of the gluten-forming proteins, glutenin and gliadin, that make up the strong elastic networks in chewy New York bagels and pizza. Bread flour was surely the best supermarket alternative, since it's the highest-protein flour that's widely available. Adding vital wheat gluten, a powdered form of wheat gluten often used to create a stronger elastic network, brought the texture of these bagels closer to that of the high-gluten-flour bagels—but still not close enough.

Traditionally, bagels are shaped by stretching each round into a log, which purposely puts a lot of stress on the dough to tighten the gluten network, and then wrapping it around your palm and pressing both ends together to seal. To stress the dough even further, I flattened out the ball with a rolling pin and then rolled it up like a carpet before stretching it out, which strengthened the dough and pressed out any large air bubbles. I'd also seen some bagels with a subtle spiral pattern in the dough, and testing proved that it wasn't merely cosmetic: When I twirled the ends of the dough in opposite directions before sealing them, that twist further tightened up the gluten network and gave the bagels true New York–caliber chew.

In bakeries, bagels undergo a two-step boil-and-bake process: They are dropped into malt syrup–infused boiling water for about 20 seconds and then placed on water-soaked wood boards lined with burlap and sprinkled with cornmeal (to prevent sticking) that sit directly on the hot oven floor. Once the bagels have started to brown, they're flipped directly onto the oven floor to finish browning.

Boiling bagels "wakes up" their yeast (sluggish from being kept cold) so that they spring up during baking. It also hydrates and cooks the starches on the bagel's exterior to create the glossy, crisp crust. And finally, it lends the dough that subtle malt sweetness. Bagel boards are mostly about crust development. They protect the exterior from burning during the first half of baking and give off steam that performs three functions: It keeps the dough's exterior moist and pliable so that it can expand, it further cooks the surface starches, and it efficiently transfers heat so that the bagels crisp.

To mimic the professional setup, I placed a wire rack (coated with vegetable oil spray) in a rimmed baking sheet and slid a baking stone into the oven to act as the "hearth." As for a source of steam, I figured the rimmed baking sheet could hold enough water.

My ersatz setup got me almost all the way there: The ½ cup of boiling water I poured into the baking sheet provided plenty of steam. But once I transferred the bagels to the hot stone and removed the pan of water from the oven, they started to burn and turn leathery.

I thought back to the malt-infused boiling water. Browning is influenced by pH—acidic foods don't darken as readily as alkaline ones do—so I removed the slightly acidic malt syrup from the water and instead added a tablespoon of alkaline baking soda (an addition

NEW YORK BAGELS

SHAPING BAGELS LIKE A PRO

Thoroughly working the dough during shaping helps a New York bagel develop its characteristic chew.

1. Pat and roll dough ball (lightly coated with flour) with rolling pin into 5-inch round. Roll into tight cylinder, starting with far side of dough.

2. Roll and stretch dough into 8- to 9-inch-long rope, starting at center of cylinder (don't taper ends).

3. Twist rope to form tight spiral by rolling ends of dough under hands in opposite directions.

4. Wrap rope around fingers, overlapping ends by 2 inches, to create ring. Pinch ends together.

5. Press and roll seam (positioned under your palm) using circular motion on counter to fully seal.

I'd seen in some recipes), plus a little sugar. That just about did it, as these bagels baked up with a nice, glossy tan and a lightly crisp exterior. Not surprisingly, they lacked that distinct malt flavor, but the fix was easy: I added the syrup to the dough instead.

Complexly flavored with a delicate crisp crust and substantial chew, these plain bagels rivaled some of the best I've had in New York.

—ANDREW JANJIGIAN, *Cook's Illustrated*

New York Bagels

MAKES 8 BAGELS

This recipe requires refrigerating the shaped bagels for 16 to 24 hours before baking them. This recipe works best with King Arthur bread flour, although other bread flours will work. Vital wheat gluten and malt syrup are available in most supermarkets in the baking and syrup aisles, respectively. If you cannot find malt syrup, substitute 4 teaspoons of molasses. The bagels are best eaten within a day of baking; fully cooled bagels can be transferred to heavy-duty zipper-lock bags and frozen for up to one month.

- 1 cup plus 2 tablespoons (9 ounces) ice water
- 2 tablespoons malt syrup
- 2⅔ cups (14⅔ ounces) bread flour
- 4 teaspoons vital wheat gluten
- 2 teaspoons instant or rapid-rise yeast
- 2 teaspoons salt
- ¼ cup (1¼ ounces) cornmeal
- ¼ cup (1¾ ounces) sugar
- 1 tablespoon baking soda

1. Stir ice water and malt syrup together in 2-cup liquid measuring cup until malt syrup has fully dissolved. Process flour, wheat gluten, and yeast in food processor until combined, about 2 seconds. With processor running, slowly add ice water mixture; process until dough is just combined and no dry flour remains, about 20 seconds. Let dough stand for 10 minutes.

2. Add salt to dough and process, stopping processor and redistributing dough as needed, until dough forms shaggy mass that clears sides of workbowl (dough may not form one single mass), 45 to 90 seconds. Transfer dough to unfloured counter and knead until smooth, about 1 minute. Divide dough into 8 equal pieces (3½ ounces each) and cover loosely with plastic wrap.

3. Working with 1 piece of dough at a time and keeping remaining pieces covered, form dough pieces into smooth, taut rounds. (To round, set piece of dough on unfloured counter. Loosely cup your hand around dough and, without applying pressure to dough, move your hand in small circular motions. Tackiness of dough against counter and circular motion should work dough into smooth, even ball, but if dough sticks to your hands, lightly dust your fingers with flour.) Let dough balls rest on counter, covered, for 15 minutes.

4. Sprinkle rimmed baking sheet with cornmeal. Working with 1 dough ball at a time and keeping remaining pieces covered, coat dough balls lightly with flour and then, using your hands and rolling pin, pat and roll dough balls into 5-inch rounds. Starting with edge of dough farthest from you, roll into tight cylinder. Starting at center of cylinder and working toward ends, gently and evenly roll and stretch dough into 8- to 9-inch-long rope. Do not taper ends. Rolling ends of dough under your hands in opposite directions, twist rope to form tight spiral. Without unrolling spiral, wrap rope around your fingers, overlapping ends of dough by about 2 inches under your palm, to create ring shape. Pinch ends of dough gently together. With overlap under your palm, press and roll seam using circular motion on counter to fully seal. Transfer rings to prepared sheet and cover loosely with plastic, leaving at least 1 inch between bagels. Let bagels stand at room temperature for 1 hour. Cover sheet tightly with plastic and refrigerate for 16 to 24 hours.

5. One hour before baking, adjust oven rack to upper-middle position, place baking stone on rack, and heat oven to 450 degrees.

6. Bring 4 quarts water, sugar, and baking soda to boil in large Dutch oven. Set wire rack in rimmed baking sheet and spray rack with vegetable oil spray.

7. Transfer 4 bagels to boiling water and cook for 20 seconds. Using wire skimmer or slotted spoon, flip bagels over and cook 20 seconds longer. Transfer bagels to prepared wire rack, with cornmeal side facing down. Repeat with remaining 4 bagels.

8. Place sheet with bagels on preheated baking stone and pour ½ cup boiling water into bottom of sheet. Bake until tops of bagels are beginning to brown, 10 to 12 minutes. Using metal spatula, flip bagels and continue to bake until golden brown, 10 to 12 minutes longer. Remove sheet from oven and let bagels cool on wire rack for at least 15 minutes. Serve warm or at room temperature.

BALLPARK PRETZELS

WHY THIS RECIPE WORKS: Making this ballpark favorite at home is easier than you'd think, as long as you follow some tricks that we discovered. First, using bread flour helped achieve a proper soft yet chewy pretzel. To get the deep mahogany color we were looking for, we added brown sugar to the dough and then gave the pretzels a quick dip in an alkaline boiling water and baking soda mixture. After letting the pretzels dry, we baked them to a tender, chewy crumb.

With their mahogany-brown crusts, tender insides, and salty bite, soft pretzels are pretty much irresistible. Something this good shouldn't be available only on those rare occasions when I make it to a ball game. I found plenty of recipes and whittled down the list to several promising candidates. All followed the same process of making a dough with flour, water, a sweetener, salt, and yeast. The dough was left to rise and then twisted into the classic pretzel shape. From there, recipes varied: Some called for baking the pretzels straight away; others required a boil in water first.

I called my tasters to weigh in. While the test revealed one step as essential—the prebake boil for a chewy interior—the rest was up in the air. Most of these "made at home" pretzels were dull. And even the best-tasting lacked that essential deep mahogany crust.

I wasn't surprised. I knew that professional bakers get that dark mahogany exterior with its distinctive flavor by treating the dough with lye, which helps a small piece of dough, like a pretzel, achieve a rich brown exterior during a relatively short baking time. Of course, most home cooks don't have lye on hand, nor would they want to. It's tricky to work with—abrasive and caustic. But every home cook has, knowingly or not, worked with a more subdued and friendlier alkali: baking soda. Could I achieve a beautiful brown pretzel crust at home with this common ingredient?

Choosing the best of the tested recipes as my launching point, I stirred 1½ cups of warm water, 2 tablespoons of oil, 2 tablespoons of sugar, and 2 teaspoons of yeast in a mixing bowl until the yeast was activated and the mixture was foamy. To that I added 3¾ cups of all-purpose flour and some salt and then used a dough hook to knead until I had a silky-smooth dough. I set the dough aside to rest, and after it had doubled in size, about an hour later, I started shaping pretzels.

When 12 pretzels were twisted and pressed, I heated a solution of 1 cup of baking soda and 4 cups of water in a pot, dipped the pretzels into the simmering solution a few at a time (a surprisingly easy process), and then divided them among two greased baking sheets and sprinkled them with kosher salt. After baking at 425 degrees for 15 minutes, the pretzels were darkened and shiny on the outside, exactly what I had hoped for.

Unfortunately, their beauty was only crust-deep. The exterior had an unpleasant soapy flavor and the inside was bland and too tender. As one taster put it, "There's no chew!" and another added, "It's like a dinner roll pretzel." What's more, the pretzels were sticking to the baking sheets. To get the pretzels off the sheets, I had to tear them to shreds.

I decided to change direction and work from the inside out, addressing the poor interior texture and flavor first. I wondered if bread flour, with its higher gluten content, could provide more of that distinctive chew that tasters were looking for. Answer: Yes. It had a nice chew yet was still soft. And to combat the dinner roll flavor, I tested various sweeteners, thinking that something else might provide more complexity. Dark brown sugar beat out light brown sugar, white sugar, and honey; tasters felt that it most closely mimicked the sweet, subtly malty flavor that ballpark pretzels have.

On to the exterior issues, specifically the challenges created by the baking soda solution. It was clear that the previously tested ratio of 1 cup baking soda to 4 cups water was too strong and was leaving that unpleasant soapy residual taste on the crust. I dipped four different batches in four different baking-soda-and-water solutions of varying strengths. I found that the solution that created the best dark crust with no off-putting flavor was relatively weak, with only ¼ cup baking soda to 4 cups water.

But one problem remained: The baking soda-and-water solution made the surface of the pretzels especially sticky, causing them to cement themselves to the baking sheet. I tried creating a barrier between the baking sheet and pretzels by sprinkling salt on the greased sheets before placing the boiled pretzels on them. Though tasters raved about the added seasoning, which covered all sides of the pretzel, it didn't prevent the pretzels from staying glued to the metal surface. In the end, the answer was simple: A 5-minute rest on a wire rack to allow the bottoms of the pretzels to dry off postsimmer prevented sticking.

Making pretzels requires more effort than opening a Cracker Jack box, but the delicious reward of a ballpark pretzel at home makes the extra effort worth it. Serve them warm with a side of mustard, and you're ready to play ball.

—CRISTIN WALSH, *Cook's Country*

Ballpark Pretzels

MAKES 12 PRETZELS

We use kosher salt on the exterior of our pretzels, but coarse pretzel salt may be substituted. However, be sure to still use kosher salt in the dough. Keep in mind that the dough needs to rise for 60 minutes, and then the shaped pretzels require a 20-minute rise before boiling and baking. These pretzels are best served warm, with mustard.

1½   **cups warm water (110 degrees)**
3   **tablespoons vegetable oil**
2   **tablespoons packed dark brown sugar**
2   **teaspoons instant or rapid-rise yeast**
3¾   **cups (20⅔ ounces) bread flour**
   Kosher salt
¼   **cup baking soda**

1. Lightly grease large bowl. In bowl of stand mixer, combine warm water, 2 tablespoons oil, sugar, and yeast and let sit until foamy, about 3 minutes. Combine

---

NOTES FROM THE TEST KITCHEN

SHAPE SHIFTER

1. After rolling each ball into 22-inch rope, bend into U shape with ends facing away.

2. Cross rope ends in middle of U, then cross again. fold ends over top toward bottom of U and press ends firmly into bottom of curve, about 1 inch apart

flour and 4 teaspoons salt in separate bowl. Add flour mixture to yeast mixture. Fit stand mixer with dough hook and knead on low speed until dough comes together and clears sides of bowl, 4 to 6 minutes.

2. Turn out dough onto lightly floured counter and knead by hand until smooth, about 1 minute. Transfer dough to greased bowl and cover with plastic wrap. Let dough rise at room temperature until almost doubled in size, about 60 minutes.

3. Gently press center of dough to deflate. Transfer dough to lightly greased counter, divide into 12 equal pieces, and cover with plastic.

4. Lightly flour 2 rimmed baking sheets. Working with 1 piece of dough at a time, roll into 22-inch-long rope. Shape rope into U with 2-inch-wide bottom curve and ends facing away from you. Crisscross ropes in middle of U, then fold ends toward bottom of U. Firmly press ends into bottom curve of U 1 inch apart to form pretzel shape. Transfer pretzels to prepared sheets, knot side up, 6 pretzels per sheet. Cover pretzels loosely with plastic and let rise at room temperature until slightly puffy, about 20 minutes.

5. Adjust oven racks to upper-middle and lower-middle positions and heat oven to 425 degrees. Dissolve baking soda in 4 cups water in Dutch oven and bring to boil over medium-high heat. Using slotted spatula, transfer 4 pretzels, knot side down, to boiling water and cook for 30 seconds, flipping halfway through cooking. Transfer pretzels to wire rack, knot side up, and repeat with remaining 8 pretzels in 2 additional batches. Let pretzels rest for 5 minutes.

6. Wipe flour from sheets and grease with remaining 1 tablespoon oil. Sprinkle each sheet with ½ teaspoon salt. Transfer pretzels to prepared sheets, knot side up, 6 pretzels per sheet. Sprinkle 1 teaspoon salt evenly over pretzels.

7. Bake pretzels until mahogany brown and any yellowish color around seams has faded, 15 to 20 minutes, switching and rotating sheets halfway through baking. Transfer pretzels to wire rack and let cool for 10 minutes. Serve. (Pretzels will keep at room temperature in an airtight container for up to 2 days. Freeze pretzels, wrapped well in plastic wrap, for up to 1 month. To reheat room-temperature pretzels, brush tops lightly with water, sprinkle with salt, and toast on baking sheet at 300 degrees for 5 minutes. Let frozen pretzels thaw before reheating.)

BIALYS

✓ WHY THIS RECIPE WORKS: A New York City classic, these savory yeasted rolls (a distant cousin to the bagel) are filled with a mixture of softened onions and poppy seeds. Allowing the dough to rise and rest three times (once after mixing, once after forming into balls, and a third time after shaping) made for more tender dough, with a pleasantly chewy texture. Adding 1 tablespoon of sugar to the dough helped balance the saltiness of the golden-brown exterior of the bialys.

Kissing cousin to the bagel, the bialy was first brought to the United States by Jewish immigrants from Poland (specifically the city of Bialystok, in the northeast of the country) who settled in the lower part of Manhattan in the early 20th century. Downtown bakeries producing the golden, chewy, onion-and-poppy-seed-filled rolls eventually became so prevalent that the Lower East Side was once referred to as Bialy-town.

I searched our cookbook library for recipes, finding plenty that claimed to produce authentic New York bialys. But once I had mixed, kneaded, filled, and baked a few versions, I was left scratching my head. How could such disparate rolls all be "authentic"? I'd produced dense and chewy bialys, light and tender bialys, and a few in-betweens. And the onion fillings ran the gamut from dark to golden, from sweet to savory. With so many recipes leading me down such different paths, I decided a little legwork was in order to find out just what an authentic New York bialy should be.

Kossar's, the oldest bialy bakery in the United States, opened for business on the Lower East Side in 1934, and the bialys made there are considered the best and most authentic in the city. I got my hands on a batch and tried them for myself. The edges were puffed and lightly brown, with a generous dimple in the middle to hold the sweet onion filling. I was taken by the salty flavor and soft but chewy texture of the roll.

Back in the kitchen, the onion filling proved to be the easy part. Simply sautéing the finely chopped onions in olive oil with kosher salt until they were golden and sweet and then stirring in the poppy seeds created a perfect onion filling. I could turn my attention to the more complicated conundrum: the roll.

I started with a simple dough of bread flour, water, yeast, and salt. I allowed it to double in size and then shaped it into flat rounds, dimpled the rounds, and

BIALYS

filled them with cooked onions before baking. The rolls were denser and chewier than those I had found in New York and lacked the distinctive salty flavor. So I upped the salt amount to a generous 2 tablespoons of kosher salt, and to address the discrepancy in the texture, I tried all-purpose flour rather than bread flour, thinking that its lower gluten content would help tenderize the dough. The end product was two steps closer to my goal, but the rolls were still too tough.

The recipe I was using required an initial proof before portioning and shaping the rolls, but once shaped and filled, the rolls were immediately baked. Previous baking experience suggested that letting the dough rest after portioning it might give the gluten a chance to relax and the yeast an opportunity to create bigger air pockets within the dough, ultimately producing more-tender bialys.

This time, after the initial rise, I shaped the dough into 12 equal-size balls and allowed them to rest at room temperature for an additional 30 minutes. After this second rise, I shaped the rested balls into 5-inch flat disks and gave them one more chance to rest before filling and baking. The texture was improved, but the bialys were pale. I wanted a crusty exterior with golden-brown spots, so I turned to an obvious but often overlooked browning agent: sugar. The addition of just 1 tablespoon of sugar to the entire batch did wonders to improve the browning on the crust.

Finally, I had bialys that were golden brown, were tender yet chewy, and held just enough sweet onion filling to balance the salty flavor of the roll.

—CRISTIN WALSH, *Cook's Country*

Bialys

MAKES 12 BIALYS

If you substitute table salt for kosher, cut the salt amounts in half.

DOUGH

- 2 cups warm water (110 degrees)
- 1 tablespoon sugar
- 2 teaspoons instant or rapid-rise yeast
- 4¾ cups (23¾ ounces) all-purpose flour
- 2 tablespoons kosher salt

FILLING

- 3 tablespoons olive oil
- 3 onions, chopped fine
- 1 teaspoon kosher salt
- 1 tablespoon poppy seeds

1. FOR THE DOUGH: In bowl of stand mixer, combine warm water, sugar, and yeast and let sit until foamy, about 3 minutes. Add flour and salt to yeast mixture. Fit stand mixer with dough hook and knead on low speed until dough comes together, about 3 minutes.

2. Turn out dough onto lightly floured counter and knead by hand until smooth, about 1 minute. Transfer dough to greased bowl and cover tightly with plastic wrap. Let dough rise at room temperature until almost doubled in size, about 1 hour.

3. Line 2 rimmed baking sheets with parchment paper and lightly flour parchment. Gently press center of dough to deflate. Transfer dough to lightly floured counter and divide into 12 equal pieces. Form each piece into rough ball by pulling dough edges underneath so top is smooth. Arrange 6 balls on each prepared sheet and cover loosely with plastic. Let dough rise at room temperature for 30 minutes.

4. FOR THE FILLING: Heat oil in 12-inch nonstick skillet over medium heat until shimmering. Add onions and salt and cook until golden brown, about 10 minutes. Off heat, stir in poppy seeds.

5. Adjust oven racks to upper-middle and lower-middle positions and heat oven to 475 degrees. On lightly floured counter, use your hands to gently press each dough ball into 5-inch round. Return to sheets and cover loosely with plastic. Let dough rise at room temperature until puffy, 15 to 20 minutes.

6. Grease and flour bottom of round 1-cup dry measuring cup (or 3-inch-diameter drinking glass). Press cup firmly into center of each dough round until cup touches sheet to make indentation for filling. (Reflour cup as needed to prevent sticking.)

7. Divide filling evenly among bialys (about 1 heaping tablespoon each) and smooth with back of spoon. Bake until spotty golden brown, 15 to 20 minutes, rotating and switching sheets halfway through baking. Transfer bialys to wire rack and let cool for 10 minutes. Serve.

CHOCOLATE CRINKLE COOKIES

CHOCOLATE CRINKLE COOKIES

✓ **WHY THIS RECIPE WORKS:** For cookies that live up to the name, we used a combination of unsweetened chocolate and cocoa powder (plus a boost from espresso powder) for a deep, rich chocolate flavor. Using brown sugar instead of granulated lent a more complex, tempered sweetness with a bitter molasses edge that complemented the chocolate. A combination of both baking powder and baking soda gave us cookies with the right amount of lift and spread, helping produce good fissures on the outside. But the real key was rolling the cookies in granulated sugar before the powdered sugar. It helped produce the perfect crackly exterior and kept the powdered sugar coating in place.

Rolled in powdered sugar before going into the oven, chocolate crinkle cookies feature dark chocolaty fissures that break through the bright white surface during baking. They have a striking appearance, with an irresistible chocolaty richness to back it up.

Or at least that's how I think they should be. Most versions of this cookie are too sweet, the chocolate flavor is underwhelming, the cracks are sparse and more like gaping chasms than fissures, and the confectioners' sugar coating all but vanishes in the oven. I wanted a cookie with deep chocolate flavor and only enough sweetness to balance the chocolate's bitterness, a moist and tender—but not gooey—interior, and plenty of small irregular crinkly fissures breaking through a bright-white surface.

I started by trying a handful of published recipes, limiting myself to those that called for preparing the dough by hand—no stand mixer required. To my surprise, no matter what type of chocolate a recipe called for (and these were all over the map, from unsweetened, bittersweet, and semisweet bar chocolate to cocoa powder) or how much sugar was used, the results were all strikingly similar: The cookies were too sweet, with muted chocolate flavor. Furthermore, they all had cracks that were too wide yet few in number.

The most promising recipe of the bunch achieved decent chocolate flavor from cocoa powder and equal amounts of unsweetened chocolate and bittersweet bar chocolate. Since these cookies were too sweet, my first decision was to drop the bittersweet chocolate because it contains added sugar. In its place, I upped the unsweetened chocolate and cocoa powder. Using less sugar substituting brown sugar for granulated helped bring the chocolate flavor to the fore and put the sweetness in an acceptable range. After I added some espresso powder, which helps heighten chocolate flavor, my cookies really hit the mark for bold chocolate taste. It was time to move on to issues of appearance.

Just as I'd seen in the initial recipe tests, the cracks on my cookies were too few and too wide, and the cookies weren't spreading enough—they looked a bit humped. In the past, we've found that leaveners not only contribute to rise and spread in cookies but also help create a more crackly, fissured surface. Before a cookie sets in the oven, bubbles produced by the leavener rise to the surface and burst, leaving fissures.

Cookies with baking soda alone weren't impressive. Using ¼ teaspoon didn't provide enough leavening power, and ½ teaspoon gave the cookies a metallic aftertaste. Baking powder, as I already knew, did a decent job by itself, but a combination of baking powder and baking soda proved to be the winner. However, the cracks still gaped and were fewer in number than I had hoped for.

I wondered if the temperature of the dough was playing a role. I had been refrigerating the dough overnight before portioning the cookies and baking them. This is a common crinkle cookie step, but maybe it was doing more harm than good. To find out, I baked another batch—letting the dough sit at room temperature until the melted chocolate and butter cooled just enough to make the dough workable, which took only 10 minutes—and compared it with my current recipe that had the refrigerated overnight rest. My hunch was right. The cookies made after the 10-minute rest were the better of the two, with finer and more numerous cracks than the original batch (and it didn't hurt that I didn't have to wait as long to enjoy them, either).

What was happening? The cookies made with refrigerated dough were cold in the center and thus hadn't spread much by the time the heat of the oven had dried out their exteriors. This meant that these cookies did almost all their spreading after that dried exterior had formed, forcing the cracks to open wide as the cookies spread. Meanwhile, the room-temperature dough had already spread somewhat by the time the exterior dried in the oven. Minimal spreading once the exterior had dried meant smaller, more numerous cracks. The cookies were looking pretty good—certainly the best yet—so I decided to turn my attention to the signature sugar coating.

I recalled that some of the recipes in my early tests called for rolling the cookies in granulated sugar before the powdered sugar, producing cookies with a picture-perfect bright-white exterior. When I added this step to my recipe, not only did the powdered sugar stay put, but the cracking improved significantly. These cookies had my ideal fine cracks all over the surface.

The heavy coating of granulated sugar created a barrier that kept the fine-grained confectioners' sugar from dissolving and disappearing into the dough. As for the increase in fine cracks, our science editor explained that the crystalline structure of granulated sugar was key. Because granulated sugar is effectively hygroscopic, a layer on the outside of the cookie pulled moisture from the inside, drying out the cookie surface so it is more prone to cracking. The crystals in granulated sugar dissolve as they draw out moisture but then rapidly recrystallize as that moisture burns off in the heat of the oven. And once recrystallized, the sugar continues to pull more water from the cookie, creating a very dry top surface that breaks into numerous fine cracks as the cookie spreads.

Finally I had the cookie I'd always pictured. Combined with their deep chocolate flavor, these chocolate crinkle cookies were all they were cracked up to be.

—SARAH MULLINS, *Cook's Illustrated*

Chocolate Crinkle Cookies

MAKES 22 COOKIES

Both natural and Dutch-processed cocoa will work in this recipe. Our favorite natural cocoa is Hershey's Natural Cocoa Unsweetened; our favorite Dutch-processed cocoa is Droste Cocoa. Our preferred unsweetened chocolate is Hershey's Unsweetened Baking Bar.

- 1 **cup (5 ounces) all-purpose flour**
- ½ **cup (1½ ounces) unsweetened cocoa powder**
- 1 **teaspoon baking powder**
- ¼ **teaspoon baking soda**
- ½ **teaspoon salt**
- 1½ **cups packed (10½ ounces) brown sugar**
- 3 **large eggs**
- 4 **teaspoons instant espresso powder (optional)**
- 1 **teaspoon vanilla extract**
- 4 **ounces unsweetened chocolate, chopped**
- 4 **tablespoons unsalted butter**
- ½ **cup (3½ ounces) granulated sugar**
- ½ **cup (2 ounces) confectioners' sugar**

1. Adjust oven rack to middle position and heat oven to 325 degrees. Line 2 baking sheets with parchment paper. Whisk flour, cocoa, baking powder, baking soda, and salt together in bowl.

2. Whisk brown sugar, eggs, espresso powder, if using, and vanilla together in large bowl. Combine chocolate and butter in bowl and microwave at 50 percent power, stirring occasionally, until melted, 2 to 3 minutes.

3. Whisk chocolate mixture into egg mixture until combined. Fold in flour mixture until no dry streaks remain. Let dough sit at room temperature for 10 minutes.

4. Place granulated sugar and confectioners' sugar in separate shallow dishes. Working with 2 tablespoons (or use #30 scoop) at a time, roll dough into balls. Drop dough balls directly into granulated sugar and roll to coat. Transfer dough balls to confectioners' sugar and roll to coat evenly. Evenly space dough balls on prepared sheets, 11 per sheet.

5. Bake cookies, 1 sheet at a time, until puffed and cracked and edges have begun to set but centers are still soft (cookies will look raw between cracks and seem underdone), about 12 minutes, rotating sheet halfway through baking. Let cool completely on sheet before serving.

NOTES FROM THE TEST KITCHEN

ARRANGING THE COOKIES

Our recipe makes 22 cookies, not the usual two dozen. Here's how to space 11 cookies on each baking sheet.

TOFFEE SQUARES

✔ **WHY THIS RECIPE WORKS:** How do you replicate the buttery-sweet flavor of toffee without making it from scratch? With a few tricks and some smart shopping. We used a combination of brown sugar and confectioners' sugar to build a crunchy but tender shortbread base, which we covered with convenient store-bought toffee bits. Sprinkling milk chocolate chips over the still-hot base and then allowing them to soften before swiping a spatula across the top created a thin, even layer of chocolate—just enough to hold on to toasted almonds and even more toffee bits.

Here's the thing about toffee: While its buttery flavor and crunchy texture are incredibly appealing, it can be a pain in the neck to make. Most recipes require the cook to carefully and constantly stir a bubbling-hot mixture of sugar and butter while using a candy thermometer to keep tabs on its temperature. Minor issues like a 5-degree difference in temperature, insufficient stirring, or a too-humid kitchen can ruin it. So it comes as no surprise that most home recipes for toffee treats rely on the flavor of brown sugar and/or store-bought toffee bits. No shame in this game: Commercial toffee bits can be great.

But I quickly discovered that they typically lack not just toffee flavor but also a solid balance of the sweet, salty, and crunchy elements that should define them. I set out to make toffee squares that would bridge these gaps.

The recipes I'd tried were all very different. Some crusts had crushed graham crackers, while others were closer to shortbread. The toppings ranged from a buttery syrup to caramel, melted chocolate, and melted toffee bits. I combined our favorite elements of these recipes to put together a baseline working recipe that I could then break down into components to perfect.

I started by baking a simple brown sugar–shortbread crust (made with flour, granulated and brown sugars, salt, and butter) to provide a toffee-like base flavor. When the crust was hot out of the oven, I sprinkled chocolate chips and chopped almonds on top. Not bad, but it was a little tough and short on toffee. Switching the granulated sugar for confectioners' sugar (which contains a little cornstarch) was an easy fix for a more-tender crust. Adding store-bought toffee bits to the crust upped the toffee flavor considerably.

Crust settled, I focused on chocolate. I did several side-by-side tests with different types of chocolate (semisweet, milk, and white) melted over the base. Tasters preferred the sweet and mild milk chocolate chips. I increased the amount to a full cup so the thicker layer of melted chocolate would better anchor the almonds to the top of the squares.

I was almost there, but my tasters wanted more crunch. For my next test, I toasted the almonds to simultaneously amplify their flavor and their crunch. And since I was already using toffee bits in the crust, I tried adding ¼ cup on top of the bars for added impact. Sweet victory: I'd achieved deep buttery, salty, sweet toffee flavor without having to pull out a saucepan or candy thermometer.

—MORGAN BOLLING, *Cook's Country*

Toffee Squares
MAKES 24 BARS

There are two kinds of toffee bits sold at the market; be sure to buy the ones without chocolate. Note that the squares need to cool for about 3 hours after baking in order to set the chocolate; if you're in a hurry, you can put the bars in the refrigerator for 1 hour. But don't store them in the fridge much longer than that because the crust can become too hard. Take care when toasting the nuts; if you overheat them, they'll turn bitter.

- 1½ cups (7½ ounces) all-purpose flour
- ½ teaspoon salt
- 10 tablespoons unsalted butter, softened
- ⅓ cup packed (2⅓ ounces) dark brown sugar
- ⅓ cup (1⅓ ounces) confectioners' sugar
- ½ cup plain toffee bits
- 1 cup (6 ounces) milk chocolate chips
- ¾ cup whole almonds, toasted and chopped coarse

1. Adjust oven rack to middle position and heat oven to 350 degrees. Make foil sling for 13 by 9-inch baking pan by folding 2 long sheets of aluminum foil; first sheet should be 13 inches wide and second sheet should be 9 inches wide. Lay sheets of foil in pan perpendicular to each other, with extra foil hanging over edges of pan. Push foil into corners and up sides of pan, smoothing foil flush to pan. Spray lightly with vegetable oil spray.

2. Combine flour and salt in bowl. Using stand mixer fitted with paddle, beat butter, brown sugar, and confectioners' sugar on medium-high speed until light and fluffy, about 3 minutes. Reduce speed to low and add flour mixture in 3 additions, scraping down bowl

EASY CHOCOLATE LAYER

For chocolate layer, sprinkle chips onto hot baked crust. In just 5 minutes, chocolate is soft enough to spread.

as needed, until dough becomes sandy with large pea-size pieces, about 30 seconds. Add ¼ cup toffee bits and mix until combined.

3. Transfer dough to prepared pan and press into even layer using bottom of dry measuring cup. Bake until golden brown, about 20 minutes, rotating pan halfway through baking.

4. Remove crust from oven, sprinkle with chocolate chips, and let sit until softened, about 5 minutes. Spread softened chocolate into even layer over crust using small offset spatula. Sprinkle almonds and remaining ¼ cup toffee bits evenly over chocolate, then press gently to set into chocolate. Let bars sit at room temperature until chocolate is set, about 3 hours.

5. Using foil overhang, lift bars out of pan. Cut into 24 pieces, and serve. (Toffee squares can be stored in airtight container at room temperature for up to 2 days.)

CREAM CHEESE BROWNIES

✓ **WHY THIS RECIPE WORKS:** Cream cheese brownies are an American classic. However, to be done right, the two batters must complement each other rather than compete. We used unsweetened chocolate and a cakey brownie batter so that the added liquid from the cream cheese filling wouldn't make the brownies soggy or too dense. The addition of sour cream to the cream cheese swirl gave it a pleasing tang that complemented the brownies' sweetness. To ensure even baking and the right balance of cream cheese swirl and chocolate in every bite, we spread the cream cheese mixture evenly over the brownie batter and then dolloped reserved brownie batter on top before swirling.

Though I love the idea of cream cheese brownies, every one I've encountered has had serious flaws. Either the cream cheese swirl is chalky and flavorless, overwhelmed by the chocolate brownie, or the cream cheese is properly creamy and moist but the brownie portion is wet and dense. And often the swirl is so uneven, one bite is all cream cheese and the next is all chocolate.

For a cream cheese brownie that lived up to my ideal, I would need to develop a brownie and a cream cheese swirl that worked with, not against, each other.

For my ideal moist, chocolaty brownie component, I started with a test kitchen recipe that relies on a combination of 2 ounces of unsweetened chocolate and 4 ounces of bittersweet for deep and complex chocolate flavor, plus just ¾ cup of flour and 1 cup of sugar—enough to tame any bitterness without making the dessert candy-like. As for the cream cheese portion, I mixed 12 ounces of softened cream cheese with ¼ cup of granulated sugar and an egg (for both moisture and structure). I spread the brownie batter in the pan, dropped spoonfuls of the cream cheese mixture on top, and then swirled them together with a knife.

Once cooled and cut, my brownies revealed a problem common to so many of the bad versions I'd tried: They were too wet. The cream cheese swirl was leaching liquid into the brownie portion. I switched to another test kitchen recipe, one that delivers cakier brownies by using proportionally more flour and less chocolate (just 3 ounces of unsweetened), as well as a little baking powder for lift. I also dropped the cream cheese down to 8 ounces to help with the moisture issue and move the chocolate flavor more to the front—but the chocolate was still a bit muted. When I upped the unsweetened chocolate from 3 to 4 ounces, the brownies were more chocolaty, but they also turned overly bitter.

I wondered if another variety of chocolate would be a better choice. I made three pans of brownies, comparing batches made with cocoa powder and bittersweet chocolate with my working recipe. The two made with bittersweet chocolate definitely weren't bitter but they lacked the assertive chocolate punch that my brownies needed for contrast with the cream cheese swirl. Cocoa powder produced a flat chocolate flavor and also went too far texturally, making the brownies way too dry. My best approach turned out to be simple: I stuck with the 4 ounces of unsweetened chocolate for depth of flavor and increased the sugar from 1 cup to 1¼ cups to tame the bitterness.

CREAM CHEESE BROWNIES

DOLLOP BROWNIE BATTER, NOT CREAM CHEESE

By rethinking the standard swirling process, we get a perfectly marbled brownie that bakes evenly from edge to center.

1. Spread cream cheese mixture over brownie base. Evenly spreading the cream cheese mixture prevents it from weighing down the brownie base.

2. Warm reserved brownie batter, and then dollop over cream cheese layer. Using knife, swirl brownie batter through cream cheese filling.

TASTING ARTISANAL CREAM CHEESE

To find out if a small-batch approach could take this supermarket staple to the next level, we mail-ordered three tubs of handmade cream cheese, from Vermont, Michigan, and Virginia. When tasted plain, all three won over tasters, who singled out strong notes of herbs, fresh milk, radishes, and butter. When it came to smearing the cream cheese on bagels, two of the small-batch samples were favored over the familiar tacky, dense texture of our supermarket favorite from Kraft Philadelphia Brand for their lighter consistency. In baked applications, the lack of stabilizers was problematic when the cream cheese was the primary ingredient. Excess moisture sank to the bottom of cheesecake, while cream cheese frosting looked curdled. However, as a secondary ingredient in our Cream Cheese Brownies, all three artisanal cream cheeses excelled, even beating out our favorite supermarket brand.

CREAM OF CREAM CHEESE CROP
Zingerman's Creamery Fresh Cream Cheese
Price: $15 for 1-lb tub
Comments: This cheese won top marks for being super creamy and smooth, with "impressive depth of flavor."

With the brownie portion where I wanted it, I moved on to the cream cheese swirl. Its texture was spot-on, but the flavor was wan and it got lost in the rich chocolate. Cutting the sugar in the swirl mixture in half, down from ¼ cup to just 2 tablespoons, allowed the swirl's dairy profile to come out a bit more, but it needed more tang. Adding lemon juice made it more tart than tangy, so I tried substituting increasing amounts of sour cream for a portion of the cream cheese. This gave the swirl enough refreshing tanginess to stand out against the chocolate (any more and it tasted sour). Of course, adding sour cream had reintroduced an old enemy: moisture. So I took out the egg and added 1 tablespoon of flour to return the body that the mixture had just lost.

Finally, I was getting really close to my ideal—the two batters had the right texture and flavor—but the cream cheese swirl wasn't evenly distributed. And beyond the aesthetics, this was causing structural problems. The brownies were sinking in the center because of the heavier, moister cream cheese batter, while the edges where the brownie batter dominated were puffed and overly dry. The cause, I realized, was my swirling approach—spreading the brownie batter in the pan, dolloping the cream cheese mixture on top, and then swirling them together.

For my next test, I spread most of the brownie batter evenly in the pan and then topped it with the cream cheese mixture, this time spreading it into an even layer all the way to the pan's edges. Then I dolloped the small amount of remaining brownie batter (microwaved briefly to loosen it up) on top and swirled it together with a knife. These brownies not only had a more evenly distributed layer of the cream cheese filling but also baked more evenly.

Finally I had a moist, chocolaty brownie with a rich, tangy cheesecake swirl—and now, old-fashioned brownies seemed a bit boring.

—SARAH MULLINS, *Cook's Illustrated*

Cream Cheese Brownies

MAKES SIXTEEN 2-INCH BROWNIES

To accurately test the doneness of the brownies, be sure to stick the toothpick into the brownie portion, not the cream cheese. Leftover brownies should be stored in the refrigerator. Let leftovers stand at room temperature for 1 hour before serving.

CREAM CHEESE FILLING

- 4 ounces cream cheese, cut into 8 pieces
- ½ cup sour cream
- 2 tablespoons sugar
- 1 tablespoon all-purpose flour

BROWNIE BATTER

- ⅔ cup (3⅓ ounces) all-purpose flour
- ½ teaspoon baking powder
- ½ teaspoon salt
- 4 ounces unsweetened chocolate, chopped fine
- 8 tablespoons unsalted butter
- 1¼ cups (8¾ ounces) sugar
- 2 large eggs
- 1 teaspoon vanilla extract

1. FOR THE CREAM CHEESE FILLING: Microwave cream cheese until soft, 20 to 30 seconds. Add sour cream, sugar, and flour and whisk to combine. Set aside.

2. Adjust oven rack to middle position and heat oven to 325 degrees. Make foil sling for 8-inch square baking pan by folding 2 long sheets of aluminum foil so each is 8 inches wide. Lay sheets of foil in pan perpendicular to each other, with extra foil hanging over edges of pan. Push foil into corners and up sides of pan, smoothing foil flush to pan. Grease foil.

3. FOR THE BROWNIE BATTER: Whisk flour, baking powder, and salt together in bowl and set aside. Microwave chocolate and butter in bowl at 50 percent power, stirring occasionally, until melted, 1 to 2 minutes.

4. Whisk sugar, eggs, and vanilla together in medium bowl. Add melted chocolate mixture (do not clean bowl) and whisk until incorporated. Add flour mixture and fold to combine.

5. Transfer ½ cup batter to bowl used to melt chocolate. Spread remaining batter in prepared pan. Spread cream cheese filling evenly over batter.

6. Microwave bowl of reserved batter until warm and pourable, 10 to 20 seconds. Using spoon, dollop softened batter over cream cheese filling, 6 to 8 dollops. Using knife, swirl batter through cream cheese filling, making marbled pattern, 10 to 12 strokes, leaving ½-inch border around edges.

7. Bake until toothpick inserted in center comes out with few moist crumbs attached, 35 to 40 minutes,

rotating pan halfway through baking. Let cool in pan on wire rack for 1 hour.

8. Using foil overhang, lift brownies out of pan. Place brownies to wire rack and let cool completely, about 1 hour. Cut into 2-inch squares and serve.

MILK CHOCOLATE CHEESECAKE

✔ **WHY THIS RECIPE WORKS:** Unlike traditional cheesecake that is baked in a water bath for gentle, moderate cooking, we simplified our rich and creamy chocolate cheesecake by baking it at a low temperature (225 degrees). To temper the heat even more, we covered the cheesecake with foil for the first hour and then uncovered it to finish cooking. Decorated with a chocolate drizzle and boasting an Oreo-cookie crust, this is an impressive dessert that comes together easily.

Chocolate makes everything better, right? This misguided thinking has caused me to repeatedly order chocolate cheesecake at restaurants and cafés in expectation of something akin to a flourless chocolate tart, only fluffier, creamier, and even richer. Instead, too often I bite into a disappointingly dense or sour wedge. Chocolate's bitter side, usually considered a good thing, can really clash with, rather than complement, the tangy flavor of cream cheese.

Call me an optimist, but something that sounds so good shouldn't have to be bad. To prove it, I loaded myself up with cream cheese, chocolate bars, and a few promising recipes and headed into the kitchen.

While none of the recipes I had collected produced the chocolate cheesecake of my dreams, each held a glimmer of promise. Some showed restraint in the amount of chocolate to keep its bitterness to a minimum, while others had the foresight to call for first melting the chocolate with heavy cream to mute its bite and produce a creamier texture. Good ideas, but none struck the perfect balance.

Crusts were all over the map, varying from crushed graham crackers to pie dough pastry. One inspired recipe used crushed Oreo cookies. My tasters were especially enthusiastic about this one, so I stuck with it.

The most interesting thing I observed was that many of the recipes didn't bother with a water bath when baking the cake. I'd always thought that the steady, gentle heat produced by placing a foil-wrapped springform pan into a roasting pan half-full of water was essential for a smooth, evenly baked cheesecake. But I was intrigued by the freedom of baking without a water bath, if I could only make it work.

Using four eggs, 1½ pounds of cream cheese, and 4 ounces of bittersweet chocolate, I made three cheesecakes and baked them at 225, 250, and 275 degrees, respectively. At 225 degrees the cheesecake emerged with no cracks, but it took longer than 2 hours to bake (too long for me). At 275 degrees my cheesecake looked like a relief map of the American Southwest. But at 250 degrees, while I still had to exercise some patience, the cake came out with no cracks at all.

But my work was nowhere near done. There were flavor challenges—most notably a subtle, lingering bitterness from the bittersweet chocolate. Adding cream helped soften the sharpness, but only slightly. I tried semisweet chocolate in place of bittersweet; this was an improvement, but only a modest one. I needed a dramatic change.

So I got to thinking—what if I used mild-mannered milk chocolate? Milk chocolate gets its gentle, milky character from the milk powder added to the basic ingredients of chocolate liquor and cocoa butter, and it delivers almost no bitterness. Could this often-maligned ingredient be my salvation for chocolate cheesecake?

I made my next cake with 6 ounces of milk chocolate. Its sweet milky flavor was an ideal counterpoint to the tangy cream cheese, and with one taste I knew I had the makings of a winner. But switching to milk chocolate created an obvious problem. The cake now needed more complex, deep, and round chocolate flavor.

Luckily, the fix was relatively easy: Adding cocoa powder provided chocolate nuance—just 2 tablespoons was enough to add some complexity without compromising the texture or welcoming back the bitterness.

I was almost there—no cracks, a light consistency, a fully realized chocolate flavor—but a tough, dry skin was forming on top of my cheesecake. So I did what I usually do to keep things from drying out in the oven: I covered the pan tightly with a piece of aluminum foil. This kept the top moist while also reducing the baking time by about 15 minutes, to about an hour and a half. The only downside was that the cheesecake's top was too moist from its own steam when I took it out of the oven. I solved this issue by removing the foil after an hour in the oven to give the top some time to dry out and set up.

The result? Spectacular. The key to a successful chocolate cheesecake turned out to be an exercise in matchmaking—finding the right kind of chocolate to pair with the tangy cream cheese. Not only had the switch to milk chocolate helped solve my chocolate cheesecake conundrum, but it had transformed the dessert. I had a showstopper of a cheesecake, fluffy

NOTES FROM THE TEST KITCHEN

KEY STEPS FOR THE BEST CHOCOLATE CHEESECAKE

1. TAP: After pouring batter into prebaked crust, gently tap pan on counter to release air bubbles.

2. TEMP: Use instant-read thermometer to determine when cheesecake is perfectly baked; it should register 150 degrees.

3. SLICE: For neatest pieces, heat knife by running it under hot water, quickly dry with a cloth, and slice cheesecake.

MELT MILK CHOCOLATE CAREFULLY

Because milk chocolate contains milk solids, its protein content is generally higher than that of dark chocolate. The extra protein means that milk chocolate melts at a slightly lower temperature than dark; what's more, when you add heat to protein and sugar, new molecules may form, introducing unwelcome scorched or burned flavors. Microwaves are generally gentle, but notoriously inconsistent, so choose 50 percent power, keep a close eye on the chocolate, and give it a stir every 15 seconds.

and creamy, with a soothing milk chocolate flavor (one taster described it as a giant, creamy, slightly tangy malted milk ball) and no cracks.

And with such a straightforward, no-water-bath baking method, who needs disappointing restaurant versions? I'll be making this milk chocolate cheesecake at home from now on.

—ERIKA BRUCE, *Cook's Country*

Milk Chocolate Cheesecake

SERVES 12

Our favorite milk chocolate is Dove Silky Smooth Milk Chocolate. For the crust, use the entire Oreo cookie, filling and all. The cheesecake needs to be refrigerated for at least 8 hours before serving.

16	Oreo sandwich cookies, broken into rough pieces
1	tablespoon sugar plus ½ cup (3½ ounces)
2	tablespoons unsalted butter, melted
8	ounces milk chocolate, chopped
⅓	cup heavy cream
2	tablespoons unsweetened cocoa powder
¼	teaspoon salt
1½	pounds cream cheese, softened
4	large eggs, room temperature
2	teaspoons vanilla extract

1. Adjust oven rack to middle position and heat oven to 350 degrees. Grease bottom and sides of 9-inch non-stick springform pan.

2. Process cookies and 1 tablespoon sugar in food processor until finely ground, about 30 seconds. Add melted butter and pulse until combined, about 6 pulses. Transfer crumb mixture to prepared pan and press firmly with bottom of dry measuring cup into even layer in bottom of pan. Bake until fragrant and set, about 10 minutes. Let cool completely on wire rack.

3. Reduce oven temperature to 250 degrees. Combine 6 ounces chocolate and cream in medium bowl and microwave at 50 percent power, stirring occasionally, until melted and smooth, 60 to 90 seconds. Let cool for 10 minutes. In small bowl, whisk cocoa, salt, and remaining ½ cup sugar until no lumps remain.

4. Using stand mixer fitted with paddle, beat cream cheese and cocoa mixture on medium speed until creamy and smooth, about 3 minutes, scraping down bowl as needed. Reduce speed to medium-low, add

chocolate mixture, and beat until combined. Gradually add eggs, one at a time, until incorporated, scraping down bowl as needed. Add vanilla and give batter final stir by hand until no streaks of chocolate remain.

5. Pour cheesecake mixture into cooled crust and smooth top with spatula. Tap cheesecake gently on counter to release air bubbles. Cover pan tightly with aluminum foil (taking care not to touch surface of cheesecake with foil) and place on rimmed baking sheet. Bake for 1 hour, then remove foil. Continue to bake until edges are set and center registers 150 degrees and jiggles slightly when shaken, 30 to 45 minutes. Let cool completely on wire rack, then cover with plastic wrap and refrigerate in pan until cold, about 8 hours. (Cake can be refrigerated for up to 4 days.)

6. To unmold cheesecake, remove sides of pan, slide thin metal spatula between crust and pan bottom to loosen, and slide cake onto serving platter. Microwave remaining 2 ounces chocolate in small bowl at 50 percent power, stirring occasionally, until melted, 60 to 90 seconds. Let cool for 5 minutes. Transfer to small zipper-lock bag, cut small hole in corner, and pipe chocolate in thin zigzag pattern across top of cheesecake. Let cheesecake stand at room temperature for 30 minutes. Using warm, dry knife, cut into wedges and serve.

PERFECT LATIN FLAN

✓ **WHY THIS RECIPE WORKS:** Latin American flan should be a dense and creamy custard, but the high-protein canned milks that recipes call for can make it rubbery. It can also bake unevenly, and the caramel tends to stick to the pan rather than pour out when you unmold the custard. To ensure even baking, we baked our flan at a low temperature, covered to keep any skin from forming. We also used a combination of canned milk and a little fresh milk to produce a custard with a creamy but sturdy texture. Finally, an overnight rest and adding extra water to the finished caramel allowed the easy release of plenty of caramel sauce.

Spain is known for flan that is creamy and lightly set, but I've always been partial to the versions served in Mexican and Cuban restaurants. Though they share the same layer of caramelized sugar glistening on top

PERFECT LATIN FLAN

and pooling at the bottom, the Latin style of this baked custard isn't light and quivering like its European counterparts. It is far richer and more densely creamy, with a texture somewhere between pudding and cheesecake.

I made a few recipes, cooking sugar with a little water on the stove to create a caramel that I poured into a mold (typically a round cake pan), adding eggs whisked together with evaporated and sweetened condensed milk, baking the custard in a water bath, and inverting it onto a platter when chilled. The first things I noticed: Too often the custard was so dense that it was borderline stiff, with even thicker skin where the flan had been exposed to the direct heat of the oven.

I homed in on the best-tasting recipe: three whole eggs and five yolks whisked together with one can each of evaporated and sweetened condensed milk baked in a water bath at 350 degrees for about an hour. The texture was not only stiff but also uneven; while the exterior was rubbery, the core was pudding-like.

A review of how custards work seemed in order. When the proteins in the eggs are heated, they link up and form a matrix that traps the dairy's water, giving the custard structure. The exact texture of a custard mainly depends on the ratio of eggs to dairy: The more the proteins are diluted with water, the looser the custard's consistency will be.

But in Latin flan, the dairy plays a different role. Since canned milks contain less water than fresh milk, they contribute to the custard. Not only that, but these concentrated forms of milk contribute at least twice as much protein per ounce than fresh milk.

Knowing that an overload of protein was making my flan too stiff, I tried removing one egg. I knew I was on the right track when the next batch of flan turned out noticeably creamier, though still uneven from edge to center and a tad too firm.

Cutting back on dairy was one option, but I quickly dismissed it, realizing that this would not only reduce the volume of the custard but also leave me with a small amount of canned milk I would surely waste.

The other option would be to add some liquid to the mixture, and fresh milk was the obvious choice. I went with what I hoped was a judicious ½ cup of fresh milk, whisking it into the egg-and-canned-milk mixture and proceeding with the recipe as before.

This was the texture I had in mind: dense, but not stiff, and luxuriously creamy, and I wrapped the cake pan in aluminum foil before baking to prevent a pesky skin.

Now my flan tasted great—but unfortunately, it wasn't looking so hot. When I unmolded the more-fragile custard, a crack inevitably developed on the surface, and the caramel remained stuck to the bottom of the pan.

It occurred to me that the cake pan I'd been using was not helping the problem, as it produced a wide, shallow flan that was clearly inclined to crack. I wondered if the deeper walls and narrower surface area of a loaf pan might produce a sturdier flan. That it did. Even better, this taller flan was more statuesque—a presentation bonus.

Now to that caramel-sticking problem. I suspected that the lack of water in this style of flan was partly to blame, since the caramel relies on moisture from the custard to keep it fluid. Up until now, I'd been resting the flan for about 4 hours but resting it longer would surely allow more of the custard's moisture to seep into the caramel. I let the next batch sit overnight; the longer rest was worth it, as the liquid did indeed dilute the caramel, so that more caramel traveled with the custard this time.

And yet I wanted even more of the caramel to release with the custard. After cooking one more batch of caramel, I swirled 2 tablespoons of warm water into the sugar just as it turned reddish-amber and then poured it into the pan and proceeded as before. When I turned out the next flan and saw that it was covered with a substantial layer of runny caramel, I knew I'd hit the mark. Plus, the small amount of caramel left in the pan was soft enough to scrape out with a spatula.

I created a few easy flavor variations by infusing the custard with orange and cardamom, as well as with typically Latin flavors: coffee and almond extract. That made four rich, densely creamy desserts—a profile that may have permanently stolen my allegiance from French custards.

—SARAH MULLINS, *Cook's Illustrated*

Perfect Latin Flan

SERVES 8 TO 10

This recipe should be made at least 1 day before serving. We recommend an 8½ by 4½-inch loaf pan for this recipe. If your pan is 9 by 5 inches, begin checking for doneness at 1 hour. You may substitute 2 percent milk for the whole milk, but do not use skim milk. Serve the flan on a platter with a raised rim to contain the liquid caramel.

⅔ cup (4⅔ ounces) sugar

2 large eggs plus 5 large yolks

1 (14-ounce) can sweetened condensed milk

1 (12-ounce) can evaporated milk

½ cup whole milk

1½ tablespoons vanilla extract

½ teaspoon salt

1. Stir together sugar and ¼ cup water in medium heavy saucepan until sugar is completely moistened. Bring to boil over medium-high heat, 3 to 5 minutes, and cook, without stirring, until mixture begins to turn golden, another 1 to 2 minutes. Gently swirling pan, continue to cook until sugar is color of peanut butter, 1 to 2 minutes. Remove from heat and swirl pan until sugar is reddish-amber and fragrant, 15 to 20 seconds. Carefully swirl in 2 tablespoons warm tap water until incorporated; mixture will bubble and steam. Pour caramel into 8½ by 4½-inch loaf pan; do not scrape out saucepan. Set loaf pan aside.

2. Adjust oven rack to middle position and heat oven to 300 degrees. Line bottom of 13 by 9-inch baking pan with dish towel, folding towel to fit smoothly, and set aside. Bring 2 quarts water to boil.

3. Whisk eggs and yolks in large bowl until combined. Add sweetened condensed milk, evaporated milk, whole milk, vanilla, and salt and whisk until incorporated. Strain mixture through fine-mesh strainer into prepared loaf pan.

4. Cover loaf pan tightly with aluminum foil and place in prepared baking pan. Place baking pan in oven and carefully pour all of boiling water into pan. Bake until center of custard jiggles slightly when shaken and custard registers 180 degrees, 1¼ to 1½ hours. Remove foil and leave custard in water bath until loaf pan has cooled completely. Remove loaf pan from water bath, wrap tightly with plastic wrap, and chill overnight or up to 4 days.

5. To unmold, slide paring knife around edges of pan. Invert serving platter on top of pan and turn pan and platter over. When flan is released, remove loaf pan. Using rubber spatula, scrape residual caramel onto flan. Slice and serve. (Leftover flan may be covered loosely with plastic wrap and refrigerated for up to 4 days.)

WHEN GOODNESS COMES (MAINLY) FROM A CAN

The advent of canned milk in Latin America in the late 1800s helped make flan, which was introduced by Spanish conquistadores 300 years earlier, even more popular. When refrigeration became widespread and shelf-stable milk was no longer as necessary, the practice of using the canned stuff stuck. And with good reason: Evaporated and sweetened condensed milks give flan a distinctively thick, luxurious texture and caramelized notes. (In some Latin American countries, this texture has given rise to the alternate name quesillo, or little cheesecake.) But these milks can also have a negative effect, contributing to a stiff, almost rubbery consistency. This is because they have about twice as much protein as an equivalent amount of fresh dairy, which, when combined with egg proteins in the custard, can create an overly tight structure. Our solution? Add ½ cup of fresh milk, which loosens the texture without adding much protein of its own or diluting dairy flavor.

EVAPORATED

This canned milk is made by heating pasteurized fresh milk in two stages to drive off nearly half of its water, which also triggers some Maillard browning. Once sealed in a can, the milk is sterilized to become shelf-stable, a process that triggers more browning and the creation of subtle caramel flavors.

SWEETENED CONDENSED

Adding sucrose or glucose syrups to milk that's been evaporated (and undergone Maillard browning) results in this canned milk. In combination with the lactose naturally present in the milk, these added sugars make up more than 50 percent of its weight, rendering sterilization unnecessary.

VARIATIONS

Almond Latin Flan

Reduce vanilla to 1 tablespoon and whisk 1 teaspoon almond extract into the egg-milk mixture.

Coffee Latin Flan

Whisk 4 teaspoons of instant espresso powder into the egg-milk mixture until dissolved.

Orange-Cardamom Latin Flan

Whisk 2 tablespoons orange zest and ¼ teaspoon ground cardamom into the egg-milk mixture before straining.

ZEPPOLES

✓ **WHY THIS RECIPE WORKS:** To create a light and airy version of these Italian fritters, we switched from a simple *choux* batter to a batter that used two leaveners: baking powder and yeast. We fried the sticky dough at 350 degrees, which yielded a crispy exterior that didn't get too dark by the time the interior finished cooking. A dusting of powdered sugar lent a good deal of sweetness and made the zeppoles worthy of any street fair.

Go to an Italian American festival, and you'll likely pass multiple booths selling fresh *zeppoles*. These deep-fried Italian confections are golden brown and crispy on the outside and soft and airy inside, with a light sprinkle of powdered sugar on top. They usually aren't eccentric or fancy in their flavorings, nor are they meant to be; their charm is their simplicity.

I was reminded of this on my fifth day of testing as I pulled the 18th batch out of the frying oil and sampled a disappointing, stodgy zeppole, overworked and overthought—so far from the simple fried dough ball I'd set out to create.

I'd started my testing according to our usual methods in the test kitchen: frying a variety of zeppoles from existing recipes using the two standard options of yeasted and *choux* batters. Unfortunately, none matched what I had devoured at street fairs.

I quickly ditched the choux batter. Choux is a simple batter of flour, eggs, butter, and water that's used for cream puffs and éclairs. Without a leavening agent like yeast or soda, choux relies on its moisture for leavening: When heated, the water inside the batter turns to steam, creating pockets of air and puffing the pastry. In my testing I'd found the choux-dough zeppoles lacking in flavor and the dough itself fussy to work with.

Instead, I focused on yeasted dough, which proved both easier and more flavorful in those early tests. Stirring together flour, sugar, water, and yeast and letting it rest for 15 minutes before dropping spoonfuls into the hot oil gave me flavorful little nuggets, but not the light, fluffy zeppoles I was aiming for. Taking a cue from earlier test kitchen experimentation, I decided to double up on leavening and use both yeast and baking powder. Though usually used independently, in tandem they can make a lighter, fluffier end product—and did just that in this case. My zeppoles were noticeably lighter and still maintained a mild, yeasted flavor.

I loved these simple zeppoles—they were so easy to make, beautiful and delicious and satisfying—but despite warnings about inquisitive cats, I couldn't help being curious: Could I improve on them even more?

I continued experimenting, adjusting the amounts of vanilla, sugar, and salt. I went further into untraditional territory, adding ingredients from milk to ricotta to see if they improved the texture or added appealing flavors. I even diverted from the traditional coating of confectioners' sugar, trying sprinkles of cocoa, cinnamon, and salt. But as I continued to test these tweaks against my straightforward two-leavener zeppoles tossed with powdery confectioners' sugar, none matched up.

When I ran out of detours to take, I traced my steps back to that simple 15-minute recipe. I tinkered just a bit, adjusting proportions to make the perfect amount for a small group to share. I fried off that final batch, and when my tasters quickly devoured them, I realized, as with many things in life, sometimes the simplest path is the best.

—MORGAN BOLLING, *Cook's Country*

Zeppoles

MAKES 15 TO 18 ZEPPOLES

This dough is very wet and sticky. If you own a 4-cup liquid measuring cup, you can combine the batter in it to make it easier to tell when it has doubled in volume in step 1. Zeppoles are best served warm.

- 1⅓ cups (6⅔ ounces) all-purpose flour
- 1 tablespoon granulated sugar
- 2 teaspoons instant or rapid-rise yeast
- 1 teaspoon baking powder
- ½ teaspoon salt
- 1 cup warm water (110 degrees)
- ½ teaspoon vanilla extract
- 2 quarts peanut or vegetable oil
  Confectioners' sugar

1. Combine flour, granulated sugar, yeast, baking powder, and salt in large bowl. Whisk water and vanilla into flour mixture until fully combined. Cover tightly with plastic wrap and let rise at room temperature until doubled in size, 15 to 25 minutes.

2. Set wire rack in rimmed baking sheet and line rack with triple layer of paper towels. Adjust oven rack to middle position and heat oven to 200 degrees. Add oil to large Dutch oven until it measures about 1½ inches deep and heat over medium-high heat to 350 degrees.

3. Using greased tablespoon measure, add 6 heaping tablespoonfuls of batter to oil. (Use dinner spoon to help scrape batter from tablespoon if necessary.) Fry until golden brown and toothpick inserted in center of zeppole comes out clean, 2 to 3 minutes, flipping once halfway through frying. Adjust burner, if necessary, to maintain oil temperature between 325 and 350 degrees.

4. Using slotted spoon, transfer zeppoles to prepared wire rack; roll briefly so paper towels absorb grease. Transfer sheet to oven to keep warm. Return oil to 350 degrees and repeat twice more with remaining batter. Dust zeppoles with confectioners' sugar and serve.

SLOW-COOKER RICE PUDDING WITH CHERRIES

✔ **WHY THIS RECIPE WORKS:** The long simmering time and creamy texture of rice pudding suggests that converting the recipe from the stovetop to the slow cooker would be a breeze, but we had to develop some new tricks to get the dessert we wanted. Rather than milk, which curdled while cooking, we used a combination of water and half-and-half for a smooth custard. For evenly cooked rice, we boiled the liquids before mixing them into the slow cooker with the rice. Brown rice gave the pudding a slightly nutty taste and a more healthy character. Dried cherries and cinnamon, added at the end, complemented the nutty rice and gave us a straightforward, fuss-free recipe with sumptuous results.

When it comes to simple yet sublime desserts, it doesn't get much better than rice pudding. At its best, rice pudding is simple, lightly sweetened, and tastes of its primary component: rice. And the typically long simmering time means it should be perfectly suited to the slow cooker, right?

But my early tests showed that simply throwing the standard stovetop recipe into the slow cooker wouldn't work. Both the texture and the flavor of these batches were far from my ideal of tender grains bound loosely in a subtly sweet, milky custard. The rice flavor was lost to cloying sweetness and the consistency was either pasty and leaden or watery and loose.

My initial cooking strategy was to mix everything into the slow cooker and wait while the dessert cooked on low, hoping to mimic the slow simmer of the stovetop. But this resulted in rice that was gummy and unevenly cooked. In my other slow-cooker recipes, I'd found that pasta and grains are sometimes better when the liquid is boiled ahead of time. I applied this trick here and boiled the liquids first before combining them with the rice and turned the slow cooker up to high while the dessert cooked. Success. The rice was perfectly cooked, although the texture and flavor of the custard still needed work.

My next challenge was determining how much and what types of liquid to use. Milk (often used in traditional recipes) did not fare well, leaving unappealing flecks of curdled milk throughout the pudding. Cream, on the other hand, was too rich and obscured the flavor of the rice. But I wasn't ready to give up on the rich potential of cream. For the next round, I combined equal parts of half-and-half and water. I was hoping that the cream in the half and half would help to solidify the custard while the water would help to lighten the consistency and prevent curdling. The resulting pudding was a bit too thin and the consistency wasn't ideal, but I was definitely on the right track. I moved to 2¼ cups of half-and-half and 3 cups of water. This did the trick, providing a satisfying but not-too-rich custard. And with the slight sweetness from the half-and-half, I could reduce the sugar from ¾ to ½ cup and avoid the overly sweet taste from earlier tests.

Looking to boost the nutrition of this comfort classic, I reached for brown rice as my starting point, forgoing the usual white rice. Brown rice is less processed than white rice and is considered a whole grain. Each individual grain of rice is made up of an endosperm, germ, bran, and a husk or hull. After the husk is removed, brown rice is sold with the bran and germ intact, while white rice is stripped of all but the endosperm. Brown rice has more fiber than white rice, as well as a subtle, nutty flavor. And because the bran and germ contain oils, brown rice requires longer cooking to allow water to penetrate the bran, making it better suited for the slow cooker. To ensure an even better texture, I went with short-grain brown rice, which is starchier than long-grain—a plus when making this pudding.

With a classic version mastered, I turned to a variation that played off the subtly nutty flavor of the rice—rice pudding with sweet dried cherries and warm cinnamon. I stirred these final ingredients into the slow cooker near the end of cooking time, allowing them to warm through and meld with the creamy pudding.

Finally I had a simple, satisfying dessert that required almost no hands-on time.

—MEAGHEN WALSH, *America's Test Kitchen Books*

Slow-Cooker Rice Pudding with Dried Cherries

- 3 cups water
- 2¼ cups half-and-half
- ½ cup (3½ ounces) sugar
- ¼ teaspoon salt
- 1 cup short-grain brown rice
- ½ cup dried cherries
- 2 teaspoons vanilla extract
- 1 teaspoon ground cinnamon

1. Lightly spray inside of slow cooker with vegetable oil spray. Bring water, half-and-half, sugar, and salt to boil in saucepan over medium heat, stirring occasionally; transfer to slow cooker. Stir in rice, cover, and cook until tender, 3 to 4 hours on high.

2. Stir cherries, vanilla, and cinnamon into pudding. Turn slow cooker off and let pudding rest, uncovered, until fully set, about 20 minutes. Adjust pudding consistency as desired before serving; if too loose, gently stir pudding until excess liquid is absorbed or, if too dry, stir in hot water as needed to loosen.

RASPBERRY CHARLOTTE

⚓ **WHY THIS RECIPE WORKS:** Cake surrounding creamy fruit mousse promises the best of old-world elegance. But it doesn't matter how gorgeous it looks if the filling is rubbery and the cake is tough. We found that traditional lady fingers left the cake soggy and structurally fickle—sturdy but moist chiffon cake gave the filling, a creamy raspberry curd, a reliable frame. Rather than topping the charlotte with whipped cream, we topped it off with a jam swirl for maximum fruit flavor.

When I first read about charlotte russe, a classic and stately 19th-century French dessert composed of a creamy fruit filling encased in cake (usually in the form of sponge cake piped into lady fingers), I thought it might be just the thing to infuse my repertoire of homey desserts with a bit of old-world elegance. But after I made some, I understood why so few cooks today make it. First, there were a lot of steps: I had to make the sponge cake, let it cool, and line the mold with it. Next I had to make a Bavarian cream for the filling—a multistep procedure involving a fruit puree, crème anglaise (a stovetop custard sauce), gelatin, and whipped cream. Then the dessert needed assembling, chilling, and unmolding. After all that, the fillings were downright bouncy and didn't have much fruit flavor, while the sponge cake came off as lean with filling seeping between the gaps.

I knew that this dessert had a lot of showstopper potential, but I didn't want to sacrifice texture for presentation. To bring back charlotte russe, I'd have to make the filling and the cake tender enough to be pleasant to eat but sturdy enough for the dessert to hold its shape. I also wanted bright fruit flavor that stood up to the cream and cake.

I made my first charlotte with the simplest option, store-bought ladyfingers, but they turned soggy and fell apart. I then tried making my own; these were more structurally sound, even though the edges were not perfectly straight, the filling seeped between the gaps. They were also fussy to make, a bit chewy, and prone to drying out around the edges. I realized that the key to the sponge cake's structural integrity was also the reason for its troublingly resilient texture. Without the tenderizing influence of fat, the whipped egg whites had formed a sturdy protein network—excellent for keeping the sides of the charlotte in place but not for producing the tender cake my tasters and I preferred.

Then I had a brainstorm. I knew I needed a cake that contained egg whites for structure, but some fat for tenderness. What has those qualities? Chiffon cake. It uses an egg white foam for strength, but it also contains some egg yolks and fat for tenderness. And since the fat is vegetable oil, which doesn't solidify at cool temperatures, the cake would stay soft even when refrigerated.

For my charlotte, I halved my standard chiffon cake recipe and baked 1 cup of batter in an 8-inch round cake pan and the rest in an 8-inch square pan. Putting the

RASPBERRY CHARLOTTE

cake pans on a baking sheet insulated them as they baked and prevented browning on the bottom. These shallow cakes took about 10 minutes to bake, and they cooled quickly.

I placed the cooled round cake in the bottom of my 9-inch springform pan, which left a ½-inch space between the cake and the sides of the pan. I then cut the square cake into four equal strips, trimmed the browned edges, and tucked them, standing each on a narrow edge, between the round cake and the loosened pan's sides. A perfect fit.

Next, I started on the filling. My placeholder filling of sweetened raspberry puree, gelatin, and whipped cream was a good start, but without eggs, it lacked richness and depth. Why not make a fruit curd instead? Most people are familiar with lemon curd, but a curd can be made with almost any fruit, and it has a thicker, more set consistency that would allow me to use less gelatin.

I whisked three egg yolks with 2 teaspoons of cornstarch in a bowl (the cornstarch would prevent the egg yolks from curdling when cooked) and set it aside. Then I cooked 1 pound of thawed frozen raspberries (they were just going to be mashed anyway, so this was a good place to economize) with sugar, butter, and a pinch of salt in a saucepan until the raspberries broke down. I added the egg yolk mixture to the saucepan, cooking it until it was simmering and thickened. After passing everything through a sieve to remove the raspberry seeds, I stirred my curd with unflavored gelatin that I had softened in water until the gelatin dissolved and set it aside to cool.

All that remained was to fold heavy cream that I had whipped to soft peaks into the gelatin-curd mixture. I poured the filling into my charlotte shell, smoothed the top, and placed it in the refrigerator to set.

This was a huge improvement. The springform ring came away easily from the base (though it was tricky to transfer the charlotte from the pan base to the platter). The cake and filling were tender, the dessert was sliceable but not overly gelled, and it had loads of raspberry flavor. Still, the overall visual effect was a bit austere.

But first, a strategic improvement: For my next charlotte, I skipped the base of the springform pan altogether and put the ring directly on my serving platter. Why move the dessert if I didn't have to? Next, I mixed ½ cup of warm seedless raspberry jam with ½ teaspoon of gelatin that I had softened in lemon juice for extra brightness. I spread some of this jam

onto the cakes before assembling the charlotte, and I swirled the remainder into the top of the filling. As a crowning touch, I arranged some fresh raspberries on the top of the charlotte before placing it in the fridge.

This charlotte's impressive appearance made it suitable for the most sophisticated of dessert tables, and its bright raspberry flavor, tender cake, and soft yet sliceable filling was sure to meet the demands of any 21st-century cook.

—ANDREA GEARY, *Cook's Illustrated*

NOTES FROM THE TEST KITCHEN

ASSEMBLING RASPBERRY CHARLOTTE

Our charlotte requires 2 cakes—one round cake as the base and a square cake, cut into strips to line the sides. We construct our charlotte inside the ring of a springform pan, right on the serving platter.

1. Place round cake in center of serving platter. Spread with 2 tablespoons jam mixture. Place ring from 9-inch springform pan around cake, leaving equal space on all sides. Leave clasp of ring slightly loose.

2. Spread 2 tablespoons jam on square cake, cut into strips, and place cake strips vertically around round cake, jam side in, taking care to nestle ends together neatly. Fasten clasp of springform ring.

3. Pour prepared filling into cake ring and spread evenly to edge. (Surface of filling will be above edge of cake.)

4. Drizzle remaining jam mixture over surface of filling. Using knife, swirl jam through surface of filling, making marbled pattern.

Raspberry Charlotte

SERVES 12 TO 16

It is fine to use frozen raspberries in the filling. Thaw frozen berries completely before using and use any collected juices, too. It is important to measure the berries for the filling by weight. If you wish to garnish the top of the charlotte with berries, arrange 1 to 1½ cups fresh berries (depending on size) around the edge of the assembled charlotte before refrigerating. For clean, neat slices, dip your knife in hot water and wipe it dry before each slice.

FILLING

1¼ teaspoons unflavored gelatin
2 tablespoons water
3 large egg yolks (reserve whites for cake)
2 teaspoons cornstarch
1 pound (3¼ cups) fresh or thawed
 frozen raspberries
⅔ cup (4⅔ ounces) sugar
2 tablespoons unsalted butter
 Pinch salt
1¾ cups heavy cream

JAM MIXTURE

½ teaspoon unflavored gelatin
1 tablespoon lemon juice
½ cup seedless raspberry jam

CAKE

⅔ cup (2⅔ ounces) cake flour
6 tablespoons (2⅔ ounces) sugar
¾ teaspoon baking powder
⅛ teaspoon salt
¼ cup vegetable oil
1 large egg plus 3 large egg whites
 (reserved from filling)
2 tablespoons water
1 teaspoon vanilla extract
¼ teaspoon cream of tartar

1. FOR THE FILLING: Sprinkle gelatin over water in large bowl and set aside. Whisk egg yolks and cornstarch together in medium bowl until combined. Combine raspberries, sugar, butter, and salt in medium saucepan. Mash lightly with whisk and stir until no dry sugar remains. Cook over medium heat, whisking frequently, until mixture is simmering and raspberries are almost completely broken down, 4 to 6 minutes.

2. Remove raspberry mixture from heat and, whisking constantly, slowly add ½ cup raspberry mixture to yolk mixture to temper. Whisking constantly, return tempered yolk mixture to mixture in saucepan. Return saucepan to medium heat and cook, whisking constantly, until mixture thickens and bubbles, about 1 minute. Pour through fine-mesh strainer set over gelatin mixture and press on solids with back of ladle or rubber spatula until only seeds remain. Discard seeds and stir raspberry mixture until gelatin is dissolved. Set aside, stirring occasionally, until curd is slightly thickened and reaches room temperature, at least 30 minutes or up to 1 hour 15 minutes.

3. FOR THE JAM MIXTURE: Sprinkle gelatin over lemon juice in small bowl and let sit until gelatin softens, about 5 minutes. Heat jam in microwave, whisking occasionally, until hot and fluid, 30 to 60 seconds. Add softened gelatin to jam and whisk until dissolved. Set aside.

4. FOR THE CAKE: Adjust oven rack to upper-middle position and heat oven to 350 degrees. Lightly grease 8-inch round cake pan and 8-inch square baking pan, line with parchment paper, and lightly grease parchment. Whisk flour, sugar, baking powder, and salt together in medium bowl. Whisk oil, whole egg, water, and vanilla into flour mixture until smooth batter forms.

5. Using stand mixer fitted with whisk, whip egg whites and cream of tartar on medium-low speed until foamy, about 1 minute. Increase speed to medium-high and whip until soft peaks form, 2 to 3 minutes. Transfer one-third of egg whites to batter; whisk gently until mixture is lightened. Using rubber spatula, gently fold remaining egg whites into batter.

6. Pour 1 cup batter into round pan and spread evenly. Pour remaining batter into square pan and spread evenly. Place pans on rimmed baking sheet and bake until cakes spring back when pressed lightly in center and surface is no longer sticky, 8 to 11 minutes (round cake, which is shallower, will be done before square cake). Cakes should not brown.

7. Let cakes cool in pans on wire rack for 5 minutes. Invert round cake onto wire rack. Carefully remove parchment, then reinvert onto second wire rack. Repeat with square cake. Let cool completely, at least 15 minutes.

8. Place round cake in center of serving platter. Spread with 2 tablespoons jam mixture. Place ring from 9-inch springform pan around cake, leaving equal space on all sides. Leave clasp of ring slightly loose. Using sharp chef's knife, trim ⅛ inch off all edges of square cake. Spread square cake with 2 tablespoons jam mixture. Cut cake in half. Cut each half lengthwise into two pieces to make four equal-size long strips. Place cake strips vertically around round cake, jam side in, taking care to nestle ends together neatly. Fasten clasp of springform ring.

9. Using stand mixer fitted with whisk, whip cream on medium-low speed until foamy, about 1 minute. Increase speed to high and whip until soft peaks form, 1 to 2 minutes. Transfer one-third of whipped cream to chilled filling; whisk gently until mixture is lightened. Using rubber spatula, gently fold in remaining cream until mixture is homogenous.

10. Pour filling into cake ring and spread evenly to edge. (Surface of filling will be above edge of cake.) Drizzle remaining jam mixture over surface of filling. Using knife, swirl jam through surface of filling, making marbled pattern. Refrigerate for at least 5 hours or up to 24 hours.

11. To unmold, run thin knife around edge of ring (just ½ inch down). Release ring and lift to remove. Let stand at room temperature for 20 minutes before slicing and serving.

STRAWBERRY CHIFFON PIE

✅ **WHY THIS RECIPE WORKS:** For a pie that was as light as chiffon but actually tasted like fresh berries, we started with our own strawberry puree, which we strained for a silky-smooth texture. We thickened it with both gelatin and whipped egg whites for a firm and sliceable but not bouncy texture. Folding in whipped cream right before chilling added welcome richness to this fruit pie. Finally, a crunchy, buttery crumb crust made from store-bought shortbread cookies was the perfect foil for the cool, creamy filling.

When chiffon pies first showed up in the early 20th century (at which point they were called, among other names, fairy tarts and soufflé pies), they were made by mixing pudding with egg whites and baking the resulting mixture. Later, gelatin became the favored thickening agent. But whatever the technique, the defining characteristic of these pies (which were usually flavored with some type of fruit) has always been their superlight, almost fluffy texture. Strawberry is my favorite flavor for this type of pie, so after searching out recipes old and new, I made five of the most promising and called my tasters to sample them. Overall, the fillings were stiff and rubbery, and most lacked strawberry flavor, as they had just a bit of fruit stirred in at the end. Plus, many of the pies tasted too lean, almost as if they were trying to be healthful.

The crusts, on the other hand, were mostly successful. We particularly liked one made from shortbread cookies and toasted almonds; its nutty flavor and crunchy texture were well suited to the fluffy fruit pie.

Now back to those unsatisfying fillings. For flavor, I knew that simply stirring in sliced strawberries wasn't going to cut it, but the versions that had achieved better flavor by pureeing the fruit had an unpleasant texture. To solve this, I made my own strawberry juice by pureeing fresh berries and forcing them through a fine-mesh strainer until I had a full cup of smooth, deeply flavorful ruby liquid to add to the filling.

The pie with the best texture in the initial round supplemented the traditional gelatin with cornstarch for firm setting and sliceability without the bounce factor, a tactic that seemed worth borrowing. The pie I made using this approach had a good texture, but again, it felt lean. Fat seemed the obvious antidote, and when I looked back at some of the old recipes, I found the solution: While most relied solely on whipped egg whites for lift, some used whipped cream as well. For my next test, I whipped the egg whites as before and then poured chilled cream into the empty mixer bowl. After folding the whipped cream into the berry–egg white mixture, I poured my enriched filling into the crust, chilled it, and waited.

I had finally made headway; the filling was as fluffy as ever but now had a velvety texture from the added fat and almost tasted like strawberry ice cream—in pie form. To strengthen the berry flavor a bit more while also adding visual appeal, I folded sliced strawberries into the finished filling right before pouring it into the crust. Finally, a generous splash of lemon juice enhanced the sweet-tart berries.

—REBECCAH MARSTERS, *Cook's Country*

Strawberry Chiffon Pie

SERVES 8

You will need about 3 pints of fresh strawberries for this recipe.

CRUST

- 1 (5.3-ounce) box shortbread cookies, broken into 1-inch pieces
- 2 tablespoons sugar
- ¼ teaspoon salt
- ½ cup slivered almonds, toasted
- 2 tablespoons unsalted butter, melted

FILLING

- 2 teaspoons unflavored gelatin
- 2 tablespoons water
- 12 ounces strawberries, hulled (2½ cups), plus 8 ounces strawberries, hulled, halved, and sliced thin (1⅓ cups)
- ¾ cup (5¼ ounces) plus 2 tablespoons sugar
- 2 tablespoons cornstarch
- ¼ teaspoon salt
- 2 tablespoons lemon juice
- 2 large egg whites
- ⅛ teaspoon cream of tartar
- ½ cup heavy cream, chilled

1. FOR THE CRUST: Adjust oven rack to middle position and heat oven to 325 degrees. Grease 9-inch pie plate. Process cookies, sugar, and salt in food processor until finely ground, about 1 minute. Add almonds and pulse until coarsely chopped, about 8 pulses. Add melted butter and pulse until combined, about 10 pulses. Transfer crumb mixture to pie plate. Using bottom of dry measuring cup, press crumbs evenly into bottom and up sides of plate. Bake until crust is golden brown, 18 to 20 minutes, rotating halfway through baking. Let crust cool completely on wire rack, about 30 minutes. (Crust can be wrapped in plastic and stored at room temperature for up to 24 hours.)

2. FOR THE FILLING: Sprinkle gelatin over water in small bowl and let sit until gelatin softens, about 5 minutes. Process hulled whole strawberries in food processor until completely smooth, about 1 minute. Transfer to fine-mesh strainer set over medium bowl and press on solids to extract 1 cup of juice; discard solids. Whisk ¾ cup sugar, cornstarch, salt, and strawberry juice together in small saucepan.

3. Bring juice mixture to simmer over medium heat, stirring constantly. Cook until slightly thickened, about 1 minute. Off heat, whisk in gelatin mixture until dissolved. Transfer to large bowl, stir in lemon juice, and let cool completely, about 30 minutes, stirring occasionally.

4. Using stand mixer fitted with whisk, whip egg whites and cream of tartar on medium-low speed until foamy, about 1 minute. Increase speed to medium-high and whip whites to soft, billowy mounds, about 1 minute. Gradually add remaining 2 tablespoons sugar and whip until glossy, stiff peaks form, 2 to 3 minutes. Whisk one-third of meringue into cooled strawberry mixture until smooth. Fold remaining meringue into strawberry mixture until only few white streaks remain.

5. In now-empty mixer bowl, whip cream on medium-low speed until foamy, about 1 minute. Increase speed to high and whip until stiff peaks form, 1 to 3 minutes. Gently fold whipped cream into strawberry mixture until no white streaks remain. Fold in sliced strawberries. Spoon filling into crust and spread into even layer using back of spoon. Refrigerate pie for at least 3 hours or up to 24 hours. Serve.

MAPLE SYRUP PIE

✓ **WHY THIS RECIPE WORKS:** For a pie that truly tasted of maple, we found that a hefty dose of syrup was in order—a full 1¾ cups of dark amber syrup, in fact. But with maple flavor comes maple sweetness, so we added just a touch of cider vinegar, balancing the sweetness and introducing welcome tang. Cornstarch thickened the pie without tasting starchy. Eggs and cream produced a rich custard, while an extra yolk helped the pie set up for neater slicing.

Every year, the holiday feast includes the obligatory parade of pies: apple, pumpkin, pecan . . . Nothing against these heavy hitters, but I was on the prowl for a new pie for my holiday table. When a coworker suggested maple syrup pie, I jumped.

Maple syrup pie was once common in the syrup-producing northern regions of the United States and in Canada. What was a mystery, though, was why so many of the recipes I found used brown sugar, white sugar, or even sweetened condensed milk in addition to the syrup, which ought to be sweet enough.

MAPLE SYRUP PIE

I did find a few recipes that relied solely on syrup as a sweetener. I baked a couple of these alongside a few of the sugar-supplemented recipes and called my tasters. Some pies had so much dairy and egg that they were essentially custard pies with a whiff of maple flavor, while others used so much brown sugar that they were dense and chewy, like a pecan pie without the nuts—but light on maple flavor. The pie with the most maple flavor had syrup as its only sweetener—a full 2 cups. The flavor was there, but the pie was granular and much too sweet—like the leaf-shaped maple sugar candies I ate as a kid. Fine for candy, but too much for a slice of pie.

Far from wasted experiments, these early tests helped me home in on what I wanted: a sweet but balanced pie with major maple flavor.

I started with the proportions from our favorite pie in the initial test, using 2 cups of maple syrup, three eggs, 4 tablespoons of butter, and ½ cup of cream, along with 1 tablespoon of flour for thickening. (I also added salt, which none of the recipes called for.) The procedure involved cooking the syrup and cream on the stovetop, whisking in the butter and flour and then stirring in the eggs after the mixture cooled a bit.

The process wasn't too cumbersome, but other recipes simply called for whisking all the ingredients together and pouring them into the pie shell. I hoped this easier method would work, so using the test kitchen's favorite single-crust pie dough, I baked two pies: one with a cooked filling and one simply stirred together. Both pies emerged from the oven bronzed and beautiful, but after they cooled and we tasted them, it was clear that the cooked filling was more consistent, its maple flavor was more concentrated, and it sliced much more neatly. The good news was that since the filling was still warm when it went into the oven, it cooked faster than the stir-and-bake version, so time-wise it was nearly a draw.

With the technique settled, I moved on to the pie's other issues. Besides the overbearing sweetness, a few tasters also noticed a slight starchiness in the filling. I tried a side-by-side test of flour versus cornstarch for thickening. All the recipes I'd found called for flour, which is more traditional, but I discovered that cornstarch produced a creamier pie.

Moving on to the sweetness surfeit: Since maple syrup equals maple flavor, I was hesitant to decrease the amount. Luckily, I found that if I backed down by just ¼ cup of syrup, the sweetness ebbed slightly with no noticeable difference in flavor. I couldn't decrease the sweetness any more, but maybe I could balance it. I wondered if additional richness would help, providing a foil for the sugar and coaxing the maple flavor to the fore—fat carries flavor, after all. Increasing the cream and butter helped balance the sweetness, as did adding two egg yolks for even more richness.

I was making headway. My pie was still sweet, but tasters were polishing off whole slices now. To add the final note to this pie, I turned to a trick that we use for fruit desserts here in the test kitchen: adding acid. Citrus didn't seem right for this nonfruit pie, so I tried vinegar. I stirred 2 teaspoons of vinegar into the filling before baking (I chose cider vinegar for its mellow tang), and when we tasted the vinegar-spiced next to a plain pie, the verdict was unanimous. Without guessing my secret ingredient, tasters noted that the pie with the vinegar had more pronounced maple flavor and was brighter and more balanced overall. That sounded like a mission accomplished to me.

—REBECCAH MARSTERS, *Cook's Country*

Maple Syrup Pie

SERVES 8

Serve with unsweetened whipped cream or Crème Fraîche (recipe follows).

- 1 recipe Classic Single-Crust Pie Dough (recipe follows)
- 1¾ cups pure maple syrup
- ⅔ cup heavy cream
- ¼ teaspoon salt
- 5 tablespoons unsalted butter
- 2 tablespoons cornstarch
- 3 large eggs plus 2 large yolks
- 2 teaspoons cider vinegar

1. Adjust oven rack to middle position and heat oven to 375 degrees. Line chilled pie shell with parchment paper or double layer of aluminum foil, covering edges to prevent burning, and fill with pie weights. Bake until edges are light golden brown, 18 to 25 minutes, rotating pie plate halfway through baking. Remove parchment and weights and continue to bake until center begins to look opaque and slightly drier, 3 to 6 minutes. Remove from oven and let cool for at least 30 minutes. (Baked, cooled crust can be wrapped in plastic and stored at room temperature for up to 24 hours.)

2. Reduce oven temperature to 350 degrees. Bring maple syrup, cream, and salt to boil in medium saucepan. Add butter and whisk until melted. Reduce heat to medium-low and whisk in cornstarch. Bring to simmer and cook for 1 minute, whisking frequently. Transfer to large bowl and let cool at least 30 minutes. Whisk in eggs and yolks and vinegar until smooth. (Cooled filling can be refrigerated for up to 24 hours. Whisk to recombine and proceed with step 3, increasing baking time to 55 to 65 minutes.)

3. Place cooled crust on rimmed baking sheet, and pour filling into crust. Bake until just set, 35 to 45 minutes. Let pie cool completely on wire rack, about 2 hours. Transfer to refrigerator and chill until fully set, at least 2 hours or up to 24 hours. Serve cold or at room temperature.

Classic Single-Crust Pie Dough

MAKES ENOUGH FOR ONE 9-INCH PIE

- 1¼ cups (6¼ ounces) all-purpose flour
- 1 tablespoon sugar
- ½ teaspoon salt
- 4 tablespoons vegetable shortening, cut into ¼-inch pieces and chilled
- 6 tablespoons unsalted butter, cut into ¼-inch pieces and chilled
- 3–4 tablespoons ice water

1. Process flour, sugar, and salt in food processor until combined, about 5 seconds. Scatter shortening over top and process until mixture resembles coarse cornmeal, about 10 seconds. Scatter butter over top and pulse until mixture resembles coarse crumbs, about 10 pulses. Transfer to bowl.

2. Sprinkle 3 tablespoons water over flour mixture. Using rubber spatula, stir and press dough until it sticks together. If dough does not come together, add remaining 1 tablespoon water. Flatten dough into 4-inch disk, wrap tightly in plastic wrap, and refrigerate for 1 hour.

3. Let chilled dough soften slightly. Lightly flour counter, then roll dough into 12-inch circle and fit it into 9-inch pie plate. Trim, fold, and crimp edges of dough. Wrap dough-lined pie plate in plastic and place in freezer until dough is fully chilled and firm, about 30 minutes, before using.

Crème Fraîche

MAKES 1 CUP

Don't use ultrapasteurized or UHT cream for this recipe—organic pasteurized cream works best. The ideal temperature for the crème fraîche to culture is 75 degrees. It will work at lower temperatures but may take up to 36 hours.

- 1 cup pasteurized heavy cream, room temperature
- 2 tablespoons buttermilk, room temperature

Combine cream and buttermilk in 1-pint jar. Cover jar with triple layer of cheesecloth and secure with a rubber band. Let sit in warm place (about 75 degrees) until thickened but still pourable, 12 to 24 hours. Stir to recombine. Serve. (Crème Fraîche can be refrigerated for up to 1 month.)

NOTES FROM THE TEST KITCHEN

MAKING THE GRADE

Maple syrup labels have confounded consumers for years: Why are some syrups marked Grade A and others Grade B when both products are high quality? The system, based on syrup color, made sense for early 20th-century cooks who often turned to maple syrup as a substitute for expensive cane sugar. Lighter syrup, the easiest swap, was given the highest grade.

Matthew Gordon, of the Vermont Maple Sugar Makers Association acknowledges that contemporary consumers "understandably thought that Grade B was somehow inferior." He's joined the International Maple Syrup Institute in a push for more descriptive labels like "Grade A: Golden Color with Delicate Taste," or "Grade A: Amber with Rich Taste."

CHOCOLATE CHESS PIE

✓ **WHY THIS RECIPE WORKS:** A catch-all term for a kind of one-crust custard pie, chess pie was brought by English settlers to the New World as early as the 17th century. For our chocolate version, we used melted unsweetened chocolate and cream for richness, while four eggs plus two additional yolks created a silky, creamy texture. Three tablespoons of flour helped bind the ingredients for neat slicing. We baked this pie in a 325-degree oven to yield a soft but fully cooked custard with deep chocolate flavor and a golden crust. An even coat of granulated sugar over the pie provided a crunchy textural contrast.

What's the point of chess pie? Simplicity, of course, coupled with plenty of sweetness. Chess pies—creamy custards baked in pie shells—are country-kitchen staples, delivering a soothing dose of comfort with accessible ingredients and a minimum of effort. They are everyday pies, easy to make, easy to love, charming, and, dare I say, humble—in the very best sense of the word.

The test kitchen has visited this territory before with recipes for lemon chess pie and buttermilk pie. But I wanted to take chess pie in a more luxurious direction with chocolate. I found several existing recipes for chocolate chess pie in my initial research, but none agreed on exactly what this pie should be: Some described the pie as "rich" and "fudgy," while others claimed to produce pies that were "buttery" or "creamy." I knew I wanted something sweet, soft, soothing, and with big chocolate flavor that was nowhere near bitter. It was time to get to work.

Per our usual process, I started by preparing and tasting pies made using the recipes I'd found. They mostly followed the same procedure: Stir together melted butter and chocolate (either cocoa powder or melted baking chocolate) with granulated sugar; beat in a few eggs; add vanilla and sometimes cream, milk, buttermilk, or evaporated milk; and bake in a partially baked pie shell. A few of the pies also called for a bit of cornmeal—a typical ingredient in chess pie—to help create the textural contrast of the thin top layer.

My panel of tasters and I were surprised at how varied these first pies were. Some were dense and fudgy, while others were light, thin, and almost runny. I decided I'd aim for a pie that was big on chocolate flavor, but light on texture—a soft custard with a delicate, sugary crust on top.

I took various elements from these recipes to create a rough working recipe. We preferred the richness of pies made with melted unsweetened chocolate to those made with cocoa. We favored a little cream over tangy buttermilk or cloying evaporated milk. And after two or three tries, I settled on four eggs, plus two additional yolks, for the silkiest, creamiest texture. Three tablespoons of flour helped everything cohere enough to slice neatly.

The biggest bugaboo in my testing proved to be the baking temperature: Custards are notoriously fussy in the oven. Most of my initial recipes called for pies to be cooked at anywhere from 325 degrees to 375 degrees. After testing several pies, I found that baking at 350 degrees and higher caused the eggs to puff too much, cooking the outside of the filling faster than the inside and resulting in a collapsed, sunken pie. I found that a 325-degree oven and a 35- to 40-minute baking time gave me the most consistent pie, with a softly textured but fully cooked custard, a satisfying chocolate flavor, and a golden-brown shell.

Now for the final touch: The delicate crackly crust atop the custard. My tasters weren't fond of cornmeal's flavor in this chocolate pie. Instead, I sprinkled an even coat of granulated sugar over the pie just as I was putting it in the oven. The resulting crisp, delicate sugar crust provided that extra textural contrast I wanted.

It took many experiments—and plenty of failed pies—to get there, but finally I had a handsome chocolate chess pie that was simple to prepare, as promised, but thanks to the chocolate, full of complex luxury, too.

—AARON FURMANEK, *Cook's Country*

Chocolate Chess Pie

SERVES 8 TO 12

Our preferred unsweetened chocolate is Hershey's Unsweetened Baking Bar. Take care when melting the chocolate in the microwave, using only 50 percent power and stopping to stir every 30 seconds or so. This pie needs to sit for 4 hours after baking to set up. Serve with our Tangy Whipped Cream (recipe follows), if desired.

- 1 recipe Classic Single-Crust Pie Dough (see page 255)
- 12 tablespoons unsalted butter, cut into 12 pieces
- 3 ounces unsweetened chocolate, chopped
- 1½ cups (10½ ounces) plus 1 teaspoon sugar
- 3 tablespoons all-purpose flour
- ½ teaspoon salt
- 4 large eggs plus 2 large yolks
- ¼ cup heavy cream
- 1½ teaspoons vanilla extract

1. Adjust oven rack to middle position and heat oven to 375 degrees. Line chilled pie shell with 2 (12-inch) squares parchment paper, letting parchment lie over edges of dough, and fill with pie weights. Bake until lightly golden around edges, 18 to 25 minutes. Carefully remove parchment and weights, rotate crust, and continue to bake until center begins to look opaque and slightly drier, 3 to 6 minutes. Remove from oven

CHOCOLATE CHESS PIE

and let cool completely. Reduce oven temperature to 325 degrees.

2. Microwave butter and chocolate in bowl at 50 percent power, stirring occasionally, until melted, about 2 minutes. In separate bowl, whisk 1½ cups sugar, flour, and salt together until combined. Whisk eggs and yolks, cream, and vanilla into sugar mixture until combined. Whisk chocolate mixture into sugar-egg mixture until fully incorporated and no streaks remain.

3. Pour filling into cooled pie shell. Sprinkle top of pie with remaining 1 teaspoon sugar. Bake until center of pie is just set and registers 180 degrees, 35 to 40 minutes. (Slight crust will form on top.) Transfer to wire rack and let cool completely, about 4 hours. Serve. (Pie can be refrigerated for up to 4 days. Bring to room temperature before serving.)

NOTES FROM THE TEST KITCHEN

COMMON PITFALLS FOR CUSTARD PIES

SLUMPED CRUST
Our method calls for filling a chilled pie shell filled with pie weights (set on parchment paper in the shell) before prebaking. If you don't use pie weights when prebaking, your crust may shrink and pull away from the edges of the pie plate, and its compromised structure may leave your pie with a soggy bottom.

RUNNY SLICES
It's not easy to wait for dessert, but it's important to allow custard pies to cool and set up for at least 4 hours for clean, even slices. Slicing and serving the pie before it's completely cooled and set will result in pudding on a plate. Still delicious, but not exactly the look you want.

Tangy Whipped Cream
MAKES 1½ CUPS

Be sure that the heavy cream and sour cream are cold before whipping.

- 1   **cup heavy cream, chilled**
- ¼   **cup sour cream, chilled**
- ¼   **cup packed (1¾ ounces) light brown sugar**
- ⅛   **teaspoon vanilla extract**

Using stand mixer fitted with whisk, whip all ingredients together on medium-low speed until foamy, about 1 minute. Increase speed to high and whip until soft peaks form, 1 to 3 minutes.

FRENCH COCONUT PIE

✓ **WHY THIS RECIPE WORKS:** Balancing the flavor in this Southern custard pie was all about using the right coconut. The first tests using sweetened shredded coconut made the custard cloyingly sweet. Reducing the amount of sugar wasn't an option because it affected the custard's texture and volume. Instead, we used unsweetened coconut to keep the sweetness subdued. And because there was less sugar to mask its natural flavor, the coconut flavor came through even stronger. The custard was too eggy, so we used only two whole eggs and one extra yolk. The additional yolk gave the pie just the right amount of richness and a clean, sweet flavor without the "eggy" flavor from the egg whites. To keep the coconut from floating to the top of the custard, we soaked it in buttermilk and vanilla for 15 minutes. The moistened coconut was well distributed in the custard and was significantly softer. We parbaked the crust before pouring in the custard, which kept the crust crisp.

French coconut pie is a custard pie similar to chess pie that has been popular across the American South for three generations. Bryan Roof, *Cook's Country*'s executive food editor, encountered the pie at Papa KayJoe's BBQ in Centerville, Tennessee, on a recent road trip, and the sweet, coconut-filled custard pie left a powerful impression on him. "We need to make this pie," he immediately said upon his return. And so I, in turn, found myself in our cookbook library researching recipes for it.

I discovered that most recipes for this pie use the same basic ingredients: coconut, eggs, sugar, melted butter, dairy, vanilla, and vinegar or buttermilk. Although sweetened shredded coconut seemed to be the default, one or two called for fresh or canned coconut. None, however, called for unsweetened coconut. The method was simple: Whisk the ingredients together, pour into a prepared (usually unbaked) pie crust, and bake for up to an hour. The pies I made were uniformly sweet (some toothachingly so) and had a dense, custardy texture. The major complaints voiced by tasters were that the pies were too sweet, too eggy, or that they lacked coconut flavor.

First, I focused on the custard. Most pies called for two to four eggs to give the custard the proper set and richness. Based on the pie that my tasters liked best, I started with three eggs, 1 cup of sugar, 8 tablespoons of butter, ½ cup of buttermilk, 1 cup of sweetened shredded coconut, and 2 tablespoons of flour to thicken the custard. The resulting custard was nicely dense but had an "eggy" flavor that detracted from the flavor of the coconut. Reducing the number of eggs affected the texture and volume of the pie; the diminished filling looked more appropriate for a tart than a pie. Since the egg whites contain the sulfur that contributes the "eggy" flavor, I tried another pie using two whole eggs and one extra yolk. This pie had just the right amount of richness and a clean, sweet (albeit too sweet) custard flavor.

Correcting for the sweetness was a little more difficult, since both the sugar and sweetened coconut were factors. The recipes I tried required anywhere from ¾ cup to a whopping 2 cups of sugar in the custard. Since sugar contributes to the texture of the custard as well as the sweetness level, adding or removing it wasn't just about flavor. Our preferred pie used 1 cup of sugar, but it also contained sweetened coconut. The combination was too sweet, for sure, but I didn't know which variable to change. Since I didn't think substituting the same amount of unsweetened coconut for sweetened coconut would affect the texture as much as changing the sugar level would, I started with the coconut. What a surprise. Not only did the unsweetened coconut bring the sweetness in check, but without the extra sweetness to mask it, the unsweetened coconut also packed a wallop of coconut flavor. Since I could now add more coconut without making the pie too sweet, I went up to 1¼ cups of the flaky stuff.

The only problem was the texture of the coconut on top of the pie; since the custard was so dense, the coconut rose and created a dry, chewy crust on top. I tried soaking the coconut in water and draining it before adding it to the pie, but that method drained away flavor. What if I soaked it in the liquid I was using in the pie? I tossed the coconut in the buttermilk and vanilla, covered it, and let it soak for 15 minutes while I assembled the rest of the ingredients. The extra step paid off; the moistened coconut was more evenly distributed throughout the custard and had a markedly softer texture.

Most recipes for this pie don't call for prebaking the crust, but I found that both premade and homemade crusts benefited from some alone time in the oven. Blind-baking the pie with pie weights for 18 to 25 minutes helped dry out the crust and set the bottom and sides (eliminating slumping). Keeping the temperature lower (at 325 degrees instead of the usual 375 degrees) ensured that the crust wouldn't overcook after I added the filling and continued to bake the pie for another 40 minutes or so.

The finished pie was golden brown from edge to edge—from the pie crust to the lovely sugar crust that formed on top of the custard. I let it cool to room temperature (a lesson in patience) before digging in for a bite. One taster described it as a little like biting into a macaroon. Bryan thought that it tasted like a very pleasant memory.

—CHRISTIE MORRISON, *Cook's Country*

French Coconut Pie

SERVES 8 TO 10

Look for shredded unsweetened coconut, about ¼ inch in length, in the natural foods section of the supermarket. It sometimes goes by the name "coconut flakes." Do not use large flaked coconut in this recipe.

1	recipe Classic Single-Crust Pie Dough (see page 255), chilled
1¼	cups (3¾ ounces) unsweetened shredded coconut
½	cup buttermilk
1	teaspoon vanilla extract
1	cup (7 ounces) sugar
8	tablespoons unsalted butter, melted and cooled
2	large eggs plus 1 large yolk
2	tablespoons all-purpose flour
¼	teaspoon salt

1. Adjust oven rack to lower-middle position and heat oven to 325 degrees. Line chilled pie shell with 2 (12-inch) squares of parchment paper, letting parchment lie over edges of dough, and fill with pie weights. Bake until lightly golden around edges, 18 to 25 minutes. Transfer to wire rack and carefully remove parchment and weights. (Pie shell needn't cool completely before proceeding.)

2. Meanwhile, combine coconut, buttermilk, and vanilla in bowl. Cover with plastic and let sit for 15 minutes.

3. Whisk sugar, butter, eggs and yolk, flour, and salt together in large bowl. Stir in coconut mixture until

fully incorporated. Pour coconut-custard mixture into warm pie shell. Bake until custard is set and golden-brown crust forms on top of pie, 40 to 55 minutes.

4. Transfer pie to wire rack and let cool completely, about 4 hours. Serve at room temperature. (Cooled pie can be covered with plastic and refrigerated for up to 2 days. Let come to room temperature before serving.)

STRAWBERRY-RHUBARB PIE

✓ **WHY THIS RECIPE WORKS:** Sweet strawberries and tart rhubarb are a winning flavor combination, but they can turn into a soupy mess when baked unless you take steps to manage their high water content. For our recipe, we macerated the rhubarb and some of the strawberries with sugar to draw out their excess liquid; then we cooked the resulting syrup down with the remaining strawberries to make a jam-like mixture that we folded back into the rhubarb. Because we removed the excess water, we were able to use less thickener and more fruit than most strawberry-rhubarb pies, which created an intensely flavored filling that was chunky and softly gelled. To complement the tartness of the fruit, we gave our double-crust pie a crackly sugar top, which we achieved by thoroughly brushing the crust with water before sprinkling on the sugar.

It's hard to pin down exactly when American cooks began adding strawberries to rhubarb pie, but the two have been paired together for so long that we think of them as a great match. Except that they're not. The trouble lies not in their differences—fruit and vegetable, sweet and sour—but their similarity: Both are loaded with water. When the two are enclosed in pastry and baked, that water heats up and causes both to soften dramatically, albeit differently: Rhubarb often blows out completely, releasing all that moisture into the filling and collapsing into mush, while strawberries remain intact but become unappealingly bloated.

Rhubarb blows out because its rigid cell walls can't accommodate the expansion that occurs when heat converts its abundant moisture to steam—a fact that I confirmed early on when I tried precooking the rhubarb, both on the stove and in the oven. I had to remove water, but high heat was out of the question, so I tried the most obvious no-heat method I could think of: macerating the stalks in sugar. Sugar is hygroscopic—that

is, it has an affinity for water molecules and draws moisture out of plant cells via osmosis, which leaves the flesh compact but intact.

I tossed 1½ pounds of the trimmed stalks with a generous 1¼ cups sugar and let the mixture sit. And sit. In fact, 90 minutes passed before a full cup of liquid had been drawn out. That was far too long to wait, but the macerating step was definitely worth it.

It occurred to me that the microwave might help speed up the macerating process since it would provide more energy to drive osmosis, thus helping the sugar to dissolve and pull moisture from the cells faster. Encouragingly, when I nuked the sugared rhubarb pieces for a couple of minutes, some of the sugar dissolved, but the rhubarb got only slightly warm and was therefore not in danger of blowing out. When I found that the microwaved rhubarb exuded even more juice—10 ounces—after just 30 minutes than it had in 90 minutes at room temperature, I knew the microwave method was a keeper.

I decided to see how the drained rhubarb would function in the finished dessert, so I threw together a basic pie. I combined the drained pieces with 1 pound of cut-up strawberries and 1 tablespoon of instant tapioca. I poured the mixture into our Foolproof Pie Dough—it contains vodka, which makes the pastry moist enough to roll out easily but doesn't encourage gluten development the way water does, and thus doesn't toughen the crust. I brushed the top crust with egg wash and sprinkled it with a teaspoon of sugar before baking it in a hot oven to ensure a nicely browned crust.

But as I might have expected, discarding the syrupy rhubarb liquid robbed the filling of sweetness and left the pie unpalatably tart. Moving forward, I simmered the rhubarb syrup in a saucepan to reduce it and concentrate its flavor. But adding even some of this concentrated syrup back to the filling made it loose, not softly gelled. Part of the problem was that I hadn't yet addressed what to do about all the excess moisture in the strawberries.

That's when I realized I might be able to take care of both the runny rhubarb syrup and the berry liquid at the same time if I just cooked down the strawberries in the rhubarb syrup. I gave it a shot, simmering the berries with the syrup until it had reduced and the berries were starting to break down. I combined the berry mixture with the microwaved rhubarb, poured the filling into the pastry, and baked another pie.

Now I was getting somewhere. The filling comprised tender yet intact chunks of rhubarb that were lightly coated with perfectly thickened, jammy gel—not too stiff and not too runny. My tasters' only comment: Now that they were being cooked down and mashed, there was very little strawberry presence. The fix was as simple as macerating 1 cup of the cut-up berries with the microwaved rhubarb so that the final filling contained intact rhubarb and strawberry pieces glossed with the soft, jammy, gelled liquid.

The filling tasted bright and pleasantly tart, so I thought that an extra burst of sugar on the top crust would be a subtle way to add contrasting sweetness. But when I sprinkled any more than a couple of teaspoons of sugar onto the pastry, most of the granules didn't stick. When I mentioned the problem to a colleague, he suggested a trick of his mother's that, quite frankly, sounded bizarre: Instead of brushing on an egg wash, she runs her pies under a faucet to flood the surface with water so that it can grip more sugar.

I was at once intrigued and skeptical. Wouldn't running the pie under the faucet potentially sog out the crust? Still, I had to try it—and was startled by the impressive results. Not only did the wetter pastry hold a whopping 3 tablespoons of sugar, but that heavy coat of sugar absorbed the liquid and transformed into a candy-like layer as the pie baked. The result: Visual appeal, crunch, and just the right amount of sweetness to balance the tart filling. My only change was to brush on the water, lest the pressure of water direct from the faucet tear the crust.

With chunks of fruit clearly visible in the perfectly gelled filling and all of it encased in a sweet, crunchy crust, there was no doubt as to what kind of pie this was: strawberry, rhubarb, and perfect.

—ANDREA GEARY, *Cook's Illustrated*

Strawberry-Rhubarb Pie
SERVES 8

This dough is unusually moist and requires full ¼ cup of flour when rolling it out to prevent it from sticking. Rhubarb varies in the amount of trimming required. Buy 2 pounds to ensure that you end up with 7 cups of rhubarb pieces. If desired, serve the pie with whipped cream or ice cream.

STRAWBERRY-RHUBARB PIE

CRUST

2½ cups (12½ ounces) unbleached all-purpose flour

2 tablespoons sugar, plus 3 tablespoons for sprinkling

1 teaspoon salt

12 tablespoons unsalted butter, cut into ¼-inch slices and chilled

½ cup vegetable shortening, cut into 4 pieces and chilled

¼ cup vodka, chilled

¼ cup cold water

FILLING

2 pounds rhubarb, trimmed and cut into ½-inch pieces (7 cups)

1¼ cups (8¾ ounces) sugar

1 pound strawberries, hulled, halved if less than 1 inch, quartered if more than 1 inch (3 to 4 cups)

3 tablespoons instant tapioca

1. FOR THE CRUST: Process 1½ cups flour, 2 tablespoons sugar, and salt in food processor until combined, about 5 seconds. Scatter butter and shortening over top and process until incorporated and mixture begins to form uneven clumps with no remaining floury bits, about 15 seconds.

2. Scrape down bowl and redistribute dough around processor blade. Sprinkle remaining 1 cup flour over top and pulse until mixture has broken up into pieces and is evenly distributed around bowl, 4 to 6 pulses.

3. Transfer mixture to large bowl. Sprinkle vodka and cold water over mixture. Using rubber spatula, stir and press dough until it sticks together.

4. Divide dough in half. Turn each half onto sheet of plastic wrap and form into 4-inch disk. Wrap disks tightly in plastic and refrigerate for 1 hour. Let chilled dough sit on counter to soften slightly, about 10 minutes, before rolling. (Wrapped dough can be refrigerated for up to 2 days or frozen for up to 1 month. If frozen, let dough thaw completely on counter before rolling.)

5. FOR THE FILLING: While dough chills, combine rhubarb and sugar in bowl and microwave for 1½ minutes. Stir and continue to microwave until sugar is mostly dissolved, about 1 minute longer. Stir in 1 cup strawberries and set aside for 30 minutes, stirring once halfway through.

6. Drain rhubarb mixture through fine-mesh sieve set over large saucepan. Return drained rhubarb mixture to bowl and set aside. Add remaining strawberries to rhubarb liquid and cook over medium-high heat until

VENTING GUIDES

Cutting vents in a pie's top crust allows steam to escape—important for juicy fruit pies. By cutting eight evenly spaced slits in a spoke-like pattern, we create slicing guidelines that help produce even portions.

strawberries are very soft and mixture is reduced to 1½ cups, about 10 to 15 minutes. Mash berries with fork (mixture does not have to be smooth). Add strawberry mixture and tapioca to drained rhubarb mixture and stir to combine. Set aside.

7. Roll 1 disk of dough into 12-inch circle on well-floured counter. Loosely roll dough around rolling pin and gently unroll onto 9-inch pie plate, letting excess dough hang over edge. Ease dough into plate by gently lifting edge of dough with your hand while pressing into plate bottom with your other hand. Wrap dough-lined pie plate loosely in plastic and refrigerate until dough is firm, about 30 minutes.

8. Roll remaining disk of dough into 12-inch circle on well-floured counter, then transfer to parchment paper–lined baking sheet; cover with plastic and refrigerate for 30 minutes. Adjust rack to middle position and heat oven to 425 degrees.

9. Transfer filling to chilled dough–lined pie plate and spread into even layer. Loosely roll remaining dough round around rolling pin and gently unroll onto filling. Trim overhang to ½ inch beyond lip of pie plate. Pinch edges of top and bottom crusts firmly together. Tuck overhang under itself; folded edge should be flush with edge of pie plate. Crimp dough evenly around edge of pie plate. Brush surface thoroughly with water and sprinkle with 3 tablespoons sugar. Cut eight 2-inch slits in top crust.

10. Place pie on parchment-lined rimmed baking sheet and bake until crust is set and begins to brown, about 25 minutes. Rotate pie and reduce oven temperature to 375 degrees; continue to bake until crust is deep golden brown and filling is bubbling, 30 to 40 minutes longer. If edges of pie begin to get too brown before pie is done, cover loosely with foil. Let cool on wire rack for 2½ hours before serving.

TEST KITCHEN RESOURCES

* Every product tested may not be listed in these pages. Please visit CooksIllustrated.com to find complete listings and information on all products tested and reviewed.

BEST KITCHEN QUICK TIPS

STEADYING TIPPY TACOS

The rounded base of a hard taco shell usually requires one hand to steady it while the other stuffs. Olivia Tipton of Carlisle, Ohio, frees up both hands by cleverly wedging the shell between the tines of a fork to keep it upright.

CORN KERNEL CATCHER

Corn kernels have a tendency to ricochet across the kitchen as they are cut from the cob. Elise Bayard-Franklin of Belmont, Mass., devised this setup to contain them.

1. Place a small bowl upside down inside a larger bowl.

2. Steady the wide end of a corn cob on top of the overturned bowl and slice downward to remove kernels. The smaller bowl elevates the cob so you can get a clean slice, and the larger bowl catches the kernels.

KEEPING 'SHROOMS SUBMERGED

When Linda Miller of Stowe, Pa., rehydrates dried mushrooms in hot liquid, they tend to bob on the surface of the broth instead of staying submerged, leaving some parts tough or even crunchy. She now anchors them by nesting a 1-cup liquid measuring cup inside a 2-cup vessel. The 2-cup measure holds the liquid and mushrooms, while the 1-cup measure (a small bowl would work, too) ensures that the mushrooms stay below the surface while they soak.

PINEAPPLE (PREP) EXPRESS

Michelle Emond of Worthington, Ohio, makes double use of her strawberry huller to remove the spiny eyes from a pineapple. The tool's prongs pluck out the fruit's tough spots with minimal waste.

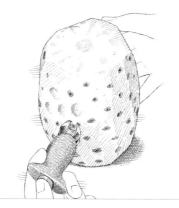

IMPROVISED EGG CUPS

Betsy Wise of Lubbock, Texas, a fan of soft-cooked eggs, invested in an egg topper to easily remove the tops of the shells—only to realize that she lacked egg cups to steady them as she sliced. Instead, she places the cooked egg in an empty shot glass, which keep the top of the egg propped above the rim of the glass.

MAKESHIFT BREAD SLICING GUIDE

Amanda Fuerst of Los Angeles, Calif., had trouble cutting evenly thick slices of homemade sandwich bread until she arrived at this tip: Let the loaf cool on its side on an oven rack. The rack's bars leave subtle vertical indentations that act as a template for evenly spaced slices.

DUTCH OVEN STORAGE

Due to limited cabinet space, Martha Butterfield of Raritan, N.J., had to find an alternative option for storing her large Dutch oven. She discovered that affixing two sturdy coat hooks, spaced 3 inches apart, to the side of her cabinet allowed her to hang the pot by its handle on the lower hook and prop the lid on the top hooks.

HANDY WEIGHT CHART

Greg Manning of Portland, Ore., sometimes forgets to tare his digital scale (i.e., zeroing out the weight of the empty container before adding ingredients). Instead of removing the ingredients from the container and reweighing, he references a bowl-weight chart he made and taped to the inside of a cabinet door. Determining the accurate weight is as easy as subtracting the recorded bowl weight from the total.

MAKING MORE COUNTER SPACE

Stephanie Rouse of San Francisco, Calif., has limited counter space, which is problematic when she's portioning cookie dough onto multiple baking sheets. She creates extra room by pulling out a cabinet drawer and resting a sheet on top.

A TWIST ON TYING BAGS

Heather Tuttle of Watertown, Mass., had always secured open bags of frozen vegetables with a twist tie or rubber band until she realized the answer was already in the bag—she simply cuts a strip of plastic from the top and then uses that strip to tie the bag closed.

A MEASURING STICK FOR WATER

Dina MacDonald of Arcata, Calif., who often makes soft-cooked eggs, devised a quick way to measure the ½ inch of water for the saucepan: Mark the level on a chopstick, hold it upright in the pan, and fill the water to the marked line.

KEEPING A RECORD OF RISES

To keep track of which step he's on when making a bread recipe that calls for several folds and rises, William Lundy of Belleville, Ontario, jots notes with a marker on the plastic wrap covering the bowl of rising dough.

WHIPPED CREAM ON THE GO

When Paige Hill of Acton, Mass., brings a pie to someone's house for dessert, she likes to serve it with fresh whipped cream. Since this accompaniment doesn't travel well, she came up with an efficient way to transport cream and "whip" it all in one container.

1. Place ½ cup of heavy cream and 1½ teaspoons of sugar in a pint jar and secure the lid. Keep cool until ready to use.

2. Shake the jar until the contents double in volume, about 4 minutes. Serve immediately. (The volume will be a bit less than cream that's been whipped in a stand mixer.)

USING A POUNDER FOR PRESSING

To evenly press dough into his tart pan, Philip Gordon of Mashpee, Mass., uses his meat pounder. Its flat, curved shape aligns nicely with the sides of the round vessel. (Just be sure to press lightly to avoid thinning out the dough too much.)

BEST KITCHEN QUICK TIPS

LID GRIPPER

When simmering a long-cooking sauce or stew partially covered, Kathleen Monaghan of Walnut Creek, Calif., found a way to give a slightly ajar lid more purchase: Nick a slit in a wine cork and insert it on the pot's rim. The prop creates enough space for the steam to escape, while ensuring that the lid stays in place.

A DELICATE WAY TO TEST FOR FISH DONENESS

A quick way to tell if fish is cooked is to see if it flakes easily with a fork, but the pronged utensil can leave unsightly gaps in the fillet, ruining the presentation. Wayne Drady of Little Compton, R.I., uses a gentler approach: a cake tester. Its thin point allows him to separate just a few flakes to check for doneness without marring the fillet's appearance.

TOASTER OVEN BAKING STONE

Azim Mazagonwalla of Lincoln, R.I., likes the convenience of heating up slices of leftover pizza or panini in the toaster oven but wishes the results were as crisp as those heated on a baking stone. So he made a mini stone for the toaster oven with unglazed quarry tiles (like those sold at home improvement stores) covered with parchment paper. For the crispest results, preheat the tiles for at least 15 minutes at 425 degrees before baking.

MESS-FREE CHOCOLATE CHOPPING

Chopping baking chocolate usually leaves bits of the bar strewn all over the work surface, so Anna Henriquez of New York City, N.Y., came up with a neater solution: In lieu of chopping, she whacks the unwrapped bar against the edge of the counter to break it up into pieces while the wrapper keeps the pieces contained. (The uneven pieces will work fine in any recipe that calls for melted chocolate, such as brownies or ganache.)

STAND-IN STRAINER

We found that a key step to boosting the nutty flavor of sesame seeds was brining them. When Trip DuBard of Florence, S.C., was trying this for the first time, he realized that he didn't have a strainer fine enough to drain the small seeds. Instead, he grabbed a coffee filter (paper or mesh is fine), which worked just as well, so long as he poured slowly enough to let the water drain through the filter.

AN EFFICIENT WAY TO STUFF SHELLS

To quickly stuff cooked pasta shells with cheese filling, Yvonne Pannucci of Pawleys Island, S.C., uses her ice cream scoop. Not only does the scoop portion the filling evenly, but its release lever helps deposit the filling neatly in the cooked pasta.

EASIER SLICED BREAD

It can be difficult to saw through the tough exterior of a crusty loaf of bread. To make the task easier, Jessica Nare of San Diego, Calif., turns the bread on its side, where the crust is not only thinner but also slightly softer and thus easier to cut through.

TOTING TOTES

Susy Sedano of Los Angeles, Calif., offers this tip to keep reusable grocery bags organized: Roll them up and stick them in a wine-bottle tote.

A CAP THAT MAKES THE CUT

When Mike D'Angelo of New York, N.Y., misplaced his cookie cutter, he quickly improvised with the cap of his nonstick cooking spray. Its thin edges easily cut through the dough (it works for biscuits and homemade ravioli, too). It's smaller than a drinking glass—the usual stand-in—and has a finer edge.

TRULY INSTANT OATMEAL

Rachael Theresa of Eagan, M.N., didn't always have time in the morning to prepare a hot breakfast—until she started freezing prepared oatmeal, complete with all the toppings. Here's how:

1. Portion prepared oatmeal into lightly greased muffin tins and top with desired toppings, pressing them in slightly to adhere.

ANOTHER WAY TO KEEP BROWN SUGAR SOFT

To prevent brown sugar from turning rock hard, Pam Danely of Raleigh, N.C., drops a large marshmallow into the package. Its moisture prevents the sugar from drying out.

CLEANING CREVICES

Cookware with tight crevices, like panini presses and grill pans, can be hard to clean. Karen Pizzuto-Sharp of Seattle, Wash., has found a solution in a compressed air duster. Designed to clean in between the keys on a keyboard, the can's fine blast of air also lifts off crumbs in narrow cooking spaces.

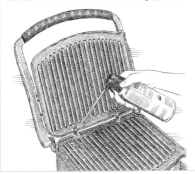

2. Place tin in freezer. When oatmeal is frozen, remove and store portions in zipper-lock freezer bag. To serve, place portion(s) in bowl and microwave until warm, 1 to 2 minutes.

A MORE EFFICIENT WAY TO TENDERIZE KALE

We've found that kneading and squeezing chopped raw kale tenderizes the hearty green, but since you can work only so much kale in your hands at one time, Joni McGary of Bloomington, Ind., came up with a more efficient approach: She places a few cups of leaves in a partially open zipper-lock bag and presses on them with a rolling pin for about 2½ minutes.

DISPOSABLE "GLOVES" FOR SEEDING CHILES

When Dan Siegel of Philadelphia, Pa., needs to seed chiles but doesn't have any latex gloves to protect against the burn of capsaicin, he covers his hands with a pair of plastic zipper-lock bags. Use sandwich bags if your hands are smaller, quart-size if they're larger.

ICE WATER, HOLD THE ICE

When a recipe calls for ice water, Peter Spinner of Middletown, Conn., has a nifty trick: He puts the ice and water in a fat separator. When he pours the water, the ice stays in the pitcher while the cold water pours from the spout.

ERASING COFFEE CUP STAINS

To remove dingy tea and coffee stains left inside mugs, Quinton Carlson of Lake Oswego, Ore., scrubs the stains with a mixture of 1 tablespoon of baking soda and 1½ teaspoons of water. This alkaline solution removes dark acidic stains like brewed tea and coffee more effectively than soap and water.

HOW TO COOK PERFECT EGGS

The two-part nature of eggs makes it maddeningly difficult to cook them just right. Understanding how heat affects each part is the key to better results.

THE EGG CHALLENGE: ONE INGREDIENT, TWO PARTS

The fundamental challenge in most egg cookery is that an egg is essentially not just one ingredient but two: the white and the yolk. Each has different types and ratios of proteins, fats, and water, which means that each reacts differently to heat, coagulating (or solidifying) at different temperatures. Furthermore, the white, being on the outside and in direct contact with the heat source, cooks much faster than the yolk. The goal of most basic forms of egg cookery (hard-cooking, soft-cooking, poaching, and frying) is to prevent the white from turning rubbery before the yolk has a chance to reach the desired consistency.

WHITE
88 percent water

11 percent protein

1 percent minerals and carbohydrates

Fully set at 180 degrees

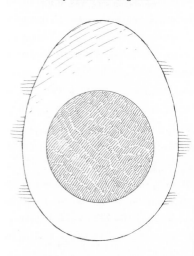

YOLK
50 percent water

34 percent lipids

16 percent protein

Fully set at 158 degrees

IDEAL HARD-COOKED

COMMON PROBLEMS
Rubbery whites; dry, chalky yolks

OUR SOLUTIONS

START IN COLD WATER: Goal is to get whites and yolks to fully cook at same rates; starting in cold water ensures minimal temperature differential between outside of egg and inside.

USE ENOUGH WATER: Covering eggs with 1 inch water ensures water has enough thermal capacity to cook them through.

BRING TO BOIL; REST OFF HEAT: Taking pan off heat causes water temperature to quickly drop below boiling point.

COVER POT: A tight-fitting lid locks in enough heat to ensure that eggs are fully (and perfectly) cooked in 10 minutes.

Hard-Cooked Eggs

6 large eggs

1. Place eggs in medium saucepan, cover with 1 inch water, and bring to rolling boil over high heat. Remove pan from heat, cover, and let rest for 10 minutes. Fill medium bowl with 1 quart water and 1 tray ice cubes.

2. Transfer eggs to ice bath with slotted spoon; let sit for 5 minutes. Serve.

ADJUSTING THE YIELD: Works with any number of eggs, so long as they fit in a single layer covered by 1 inch of water.

TIP: PEELING MADE EASIER

Very fresh eggs are hard to peel because the relatively low pH of the white causes it to adhere strongly to the inner shell membrane. If you have fresh eggs, wait a few days to hard-cook them, or try one of the following tricks.

- **ADD** ½ teaspoon of baking soda for every quart of cooking water to raise its pH, which raises the pH of the egg white.

- **CRACK** the eggs on the broad end where there is an air pocket, and then roll them on their sides to fracture the shells all over before peeling.

FOOLPROOF SOFT-COOKED

COMMON PROBLEMS
Inconsistently set whites and overdone yolks

OUR SOLUTIONS

USE COLD EGGS AND HIGH HEAT: Temperature extremes deliver steepest temperature gradient, ensuring that yolk stays fluid while white cooks through. Using refrigerator-cold eggs and boiling water—consistent temperatures—also makes recipe more foolproof.

STEAM; DON'T BOIL: Steaming isn't just faster than boiling; it's more flexible. With only ½ inch water in pan, you can cook anywhere from 1 to 6 eggs without altering timing. That's because curved eggs make very little contact with (and therefore don't lower temperature of) water.

SHOCK WITH COLD WATER: Transferring pot of eggs to sink and placing under cold running water halts carryover cooking, so yolks stay runny and whites stay tender.

Soft-Cooked Eggs

6 large eggs, cold

1. Bring ½ inch water to boil in medium saucepan over medium-high heat. Place eggs in water. Cover and cook for 6½ minutes.

2. Remove cover, transfer saucepan to sink, and place under cold running water for 30 seconds. Serve.

ADJUSTING THE YIELD: Works with 1 to 6 eggs.

GET UP A HEAD OF STEAM
With steam, the water temperature doesn't change when you add the eggs, allowing you to cook up to six.

FLAWLESS FRIED

COMMON PROBLEMS

Overcooked bottoms and raw tops; different cooking rates

OUR SOLUTIONS

PREHEAT PAN GENTLY: Preheating skillet over low heat for 5 minutes eliminates hot spots and produces consistent temperature over surface.

INCLUDE TWO FATS: Oil can preheat without smoking. Butter delivers great flavor, contains milk proteins that encourage browning, and offers visual cue for pan's temperature: It should take about 1 minute to stop foaming; if it browns in that time, pan is too hot and you should start over.

START MEDIUM-HIGH; FINISH OFF HEAT: Briefly frying eggs, covered to trap heat, starts to set whites and brown edges. Finishing them off heat allows whites to cook through without overcooking yolks.

Fried Eggs

- 2 teaspoons vegetable oil
- 4 large eggs
  Salt and pepper
- 2 teaspoons unsalted butter,
  cut into 4 pieces and chilled

1. Heat oil in 12-inch nonstick skillet over low heat for 5 minutes. Crack 2 eggs into bowl and season with salt and pepper. Repeat with remaining 2 eggs and second bowl.

2. Increase heat to medium-high and heat until oil is shimmering. Add butter and swirl to coat pan. Simultaneously pour both bowls of eggs into pan.

3. Cover and cook for 1 minute. Remove skillet from burner and let stand, covered, 15 to 45 seconds, depending on preferred doneness. Serve.

PUT A LID ON IT
Covering the pan ensures that the eggs cook from both the bottom and the top.

PERFECT POACHED

COMMON PROBLEMS

Under- or overcooked yolks; raggedy-looking whites

OUR SOLUTIONS

USE SKILLET: Shallow-sided skillet (nonstick eliminates risk of sticking) allows easier access than deep pot for sliding eggs into and retrieving them from water but holds enough water to keep eggs submerged.

ADD SALT AND VINEGAR: Salt seasons eggs, and vinegar (white distilled, white wine, rice, and cider all work) helps egg white proteins set quickly, reducing risk of fraying.

CRACK EGGS INTO TEACUPS: Portioning eggs into teacups (2 per cup) allows you to add as many as 8 eggs to skillet simultaneously so they cook at same rate.

POACH OFF HEAT: Since bubbles cause eggs to jostle and whites to fray, bring water to rolling boil, add eggs, cover skillet (to trap heat), and poach them gently off heat.

Poached eggs

- 1 teaspoon salt
- 2 tablespoons vinegar
- 4 large eggs, cracked into small
  handled cups (2 per cup)

1. Fill 12-inch nonstick skillet nearly to rim with water, add salt and vinegar, and bring mixture to boil over high heat.

2. Tip eggs into boiling water all at once, cover, and remove from heat. Let stand until yolks are medium-firm, 4 minutes. Drain eggs on paper towel–lined plate. Serve.

ADJUSTING THE YIELD: For 8 large eggs, poach 5 minutes; for 12, 6 minutes.

SYNCHRONIZE THE START
Use teacups to pour all the eggs in at once.

SOFT, TENDER SCRAMBLED

COMMON PROBLEMS

Dry, tough curds

OUR SOLUTIONS

ADD FAT: Half-and-half and extra egg yolks raise coagulation temperature of egg proteins by keeping them from bonding together too tightly. Water in dairy turns to steam and helps eggs puff.

SEASON BEFORE COOKING: Salt tenderizes by preventing egg proteins from bonding too tightly.

USE SMALL(ER) SKILLET: Relatively small 10-inch pan keeps eggs in thicker layer that traps more steam, producing billowy curds.

START HIGH; FINISH LOW: Starting over medium-high heat creates puffy curds; lowering once eggs coagulate ensures that they won't overcook.

Scrambled Eggs

- 8 large eggs plus 2 large yolks
- ¼ cup half-and-half
- ⅜ teaspoon salt
- ¼ teaspoon pepper
- 1 tablespoon unsalted butter,
  chilled

1. Beat eggs and yolks, half-and-half, salt, and pepper together in bowl.

2. Heat butter in 10-inch nonstick skillet over medium-high heat until foaming subsides. Add egg mixture and, using rubber spatula, scrape along bottom and sides of skillet until eggs begin to clump, 1½ to 2½ minutes. Reduce heat to low and fold eggs until clumped and just slightly wet, 30 to 60 seconds. Serve.

TIP: ELECTRIC STOVE? USE TWO BURNERS

Because electric stoves don't respond quickly to heat changes, it's best to heat one burner on low heat and the second on medium-high and to move the skillet between the burners for temperature adjustment.

THE SCIENCE OF ONIONS

Though flavor starts with the type of onion you buy at the supermarket, how you cut and cook it can have a dramatic impact on how it tastes.

TWO BASIC ONION TYPES

There are at least several hundred onion varieties, but all fall into two broad flavor categories: pungent and mild. Pungent onions contain more of the sulfur molecules that impart characteristic oniony flavor and—somewhat surprisingly—lots of sugars. The abundance of both kinds of flavor molecules translates into more complexity in cooking, making pungent onions the best choice for heated applications. Though mild onions have even more of the sugars glucose, fructose, and sucrose than pungent onions, they also have more water and far fewer sulfur molecules, for an overall weaker taste that makes them more suitable for raw applications.

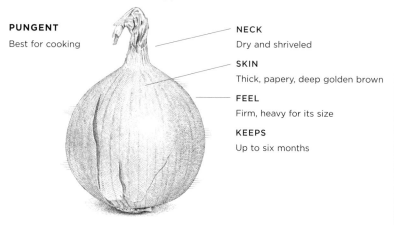

PUNGENT
Best for cooking

NECK
Dry and shriveled

SKIN
Thick, papery, deep golden brown

FEEL
Firm, heavy for its size

KEEPS
Up to six months

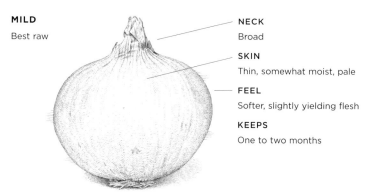

MILD
Best raw

NECK
Broad

SKIN
Thin, somewhat moist, pale

FEEL
Softer, slightly yielding flesh

KEEPS
One to two months

ONION DO'S AND DON'TS

DO: Keep them dry

Moisture encourages rot, so keep onions in a dry, well-aerated place. We found that a colander in a pantry is ideal. Also keep them away from light, which can cause the onions to sprout.

DON'T: Store with potatoes

Storing onions with produce that gives off a lot of moisture, such as potatoes or apples, will cause them to spoil faster. Onions can also pick up the flavor of other produce, and vice versa.

DON'T: Eat the sprout

We found that the sprout not only tastes bitter but pulls sugar and moisture from the bulb, making the onion itself taste harsh and dull. Consider tossing a sprouted bulb—or if you decide to cook with it, be sure to remove the sprout.

DO: Cover your eyes

Cutting an onion releases a tear-inducing compound called propanethial S-oxide. Of the 20-plus methods we tested to stave off tears, we found that wearing ski, swim, or specialty onion goggles, or contacts, will help protect your eyes.

DO: Light a flame

Cutting an onion near a candle or a lit gas burner isn't as effective as covering your eyes, but we found that it does help. The flame completely oxidizes the sulfuric propanethial S-oxide that comes near the flame.

SHOPPING TIPS

The only way to know for sure that you're getting a mild onion is to buy a trademarked mild variety, such as Vidalia or Walla Walla. That said, the following tips can still help you predict onion flavor.

DON'T RELY ON COLOR
Though the yellow onions in most supermarkets tend to be pungent, color is generally not a good indicator of pungency: Yellow, white, or red onions can be pungent as well as mild. To single out a pungent onion, inspect the shape of the neck, skin thickness, and firmness.

GIVE IT A SQUEEZE
Because they generally have less water, pungent onions will feel quite firm compared with mild varieties. The bulb of a pungent onion should feel smooth, rock-hard, and heavy for its size. Onions that give a little when pressed are more likely to be mild. Either way, avoid onions that are soft only in spots, which indicates bruised, rotting flesh.

CHECK THE NECK (AND SKIN)
Most pungent onions will have drier, tighter necks and thicker skins. That's because pungent onions undergo a curing process that dries their outer scales and causes their necks to shrivel, sealing off the bulb to moisture and allowing it to keep longer. Mild onions tend to have broader necks and thinner skins, both of which make them more perishable.

HOW ONION FLAVOR WORKS—AND HOW YOU CAN CONTROL IT

As soon as you cut an onion, you start its flavor in motion. The ruptured cell walls of both pungent and mild onions release odorless sulfur-containing molecules that react with an enzyme known as alliinase. The interaction transforms them into new compounds called thiosulfinates and thiosulfonates that are responsible for a raw onion's characteristic harsh flavor and odor. At that point, there are three factors that can further influence flavor: how finely the onion is cut; how long it is exposed to air when raw; and, most significant, how it's cooked.

PREPPING AND CUTTING

- **AVOID USING AN ONION'S CORE IN RAW APPLICATIONS.** We've found that the outer layers of an onion taste noticeably milder than the inner layers. When we consulted onion experts, they confirmed that the inner layers contain a higher concentration of flavor precursors than the outer layers do, and therefore have stronger flavor.

- **FOR FULLER, MORE COMPLEX FLAVOR IN COOKED APPLICATIONS, CUT ONIONS FINELY.** The more you process an onion, the more thiosulfinates and thiosulfonates will develop, and the more potential there will be for the development of complex flavor during cooking.

- **FOR MILDER FLAVOR IN RAW APPLICATIONS, SLICE ONIONS WITH THE GRAIN.** We sniffed and tasted eight onions sliced pole to pole (with the grain) and parallel to the equator (against the grain). Because slicing pole to pole ruptures fewer cell walls, thus leading to the creation of fewer sulfur molecules, we weren't surprised that these onions were clearly less pungent in taste and odor than those cut along the equator.

- **FOR EVEN MILDER FLAVOR, GIVE THEM A SOAK.** Many sources recommend soaking chopped raw onions in milk or vinegar to remove sulfur compounds from their surface; we found that a 15-minute soak in plain water was just as effective. That said, if you like the flavor of lightly pickled onions, go ahead and soak them in vinegar instead.

- **BEWARE OF CUTTING ONIONS IN ADVANCE.** Whether you're cutting pungent or mild onions, their flavor will degrade as they sit. We found that pungent onions can turn "sour," while mild onions can taste harsh. If you must cut onions in advance, store them in a zipper-lock bag, give them a quick rinse before using, and use them only in cooked applications.

COOKING

- **FOR TENDERNESS AND EVEN SEASONING, SALT ONIONS DURING, NOT AFTER, COOKING.** Since salting onions draws moisture out of their cells and softens them, we wondered if salting onions at the outset of cooking—rather than after—would produce more tender onions. Sure enough, when we sautéed two batches of chopped onions for the same amount of time, the ones salted from the start were meltingly tender compared with the almost-crunchy batch that was salted postcooking. Not only that, but onions salted earlier were more deeply seasoned.

- **TO BOOST MEATY TASTE, COOK ONIONS IN WATER.** When chopped, onions slowly form a water-soluble compound called 3-mercapto-2-methylpentan-1-ol, or MMP for short, that tastes meaty when a cut onion is heated in water. For meatless preparations that need a savory boost, such as vegetable stock, process the onions finely to release as much MMP as possible and use enough water so that the onion's cut surfaces are fully submerged.

- **FOR SWEETER—AND MORE COMPLEX—FLAVOR, COOK YOUR ONIONS LOW AND SLOW.** High heat makes onions taste flat by deactivating the enzyme alliinase, thereby putting a halt to the formation of sulfur molecules. Low heat has the opposite effect. It not only encourages the creation of thiosulfinates and thiosulfonates but encourages these harsh-tasting molecules to transform into sweeter, mellower substances called disulfides and trisulfides.

TEST: To verify this bit of culinary science, we made two batches of tomato sauce, cooking one batch of the onions for 10 minutes over low heat and the other onions for 8 minutes over high heat. The low-and-slow-cooked-onion sauce, which tasters praised as rich, round, and sweet, was the overwhelming favorite.

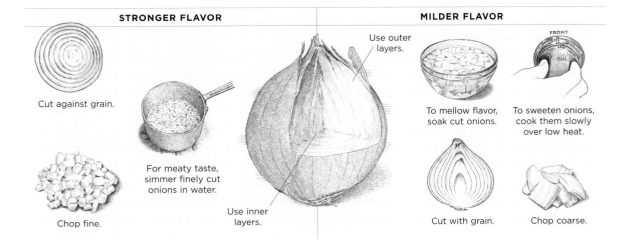

| STRONGER FLAVOR | MILDER FLAVOR |

Cut against grain.

For meaty taste, simmer finely cut onions in water.

Chop fine.

Use outer layers.

Use inner layers.

To mellow flavor, soak cut onions.

To sweeten onions, cook them slowly over low heat.

Cut with grain.

Chop coarse.

FRONT

HOLIDAY BAKING 911

The holidays are when you bake the most but also when time is short and do-overs are not an option. Here's our fix-it list for common baking emergencies.

SOFTEN COLD BUTTER IN A HURRY

Either of these tricks will quickly soften cold butter—which can typically take 30 minutes at room temperature—without oversoftening it. Both methods can also be applied to cream cheese.

POUND IT

Place the butter in a plastic zipper-lock bag and use a rolling pin to pound it until soft.

CUT IT

Slice the butter into tablespoon-size pieces and let it sit at room temperature while you measure the other ingredients.

FILLING A SLUMPED PIE SHELL

There's no reshaping slumped pie pastry, but holding back on some of the filling will prevent it from overflowing during baking. For shells that will be baked again after you fill them, such as pumpkin, leave ¼ inch of space at the top of the crust for the filling to expand. (No-bake fillings, such as those for cream pies, can be filled to the top of the crust.)

PARCHMENT PAPER SHORTAGE?

If you run out of parchment paper when making cookies, don't grease the baking sheet or spray it with vegetable spray; the extra fat will cause the cookies to spread and bake unevenly. Waxed paper isn't a good option either, as heat can melt the wax coating. Ungreased aluminum foil is the best substitute. The cookies might stick a little, but you'll be able to gently lift them off the foil.

NOT ENOUGH COOLING RACKS?

Improvise with a pair of inverted empty egg cartons. Simply set them side by side to support the baking sheet.

MEND A CRACKED CHEESECAKE

Loosening the sides of a baked cheesecake from the springform pan while it is still warm will prevent it from fusing to the pan and creating tension that causes cracking during cooling. But if the cake cracks during baking, you can seal up the fissure with this trick.

1. Remove sides from springform pan while cheesecake is warm. Wrap cloth ribbon snugly around cake, preferably one that covers sides completely.

2. Secure ribbon with binder clip; leave in place until cake is completely cooled.

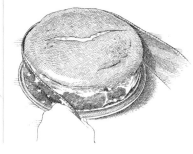

MUFFIN TIN MIA?

Foil muffin tin liners are sturdy enough to hold muffin (and cupcake) batters. Simply arrange the liners on a rimmed baking sheet and fill with batter.

NOTE: Unlike muffins baked in a muffin tin, only the bottoms will brown.

WRONG SIZE PAN?

To switch between different sizes of cake, loaf, pie, and tart pans, you'll need to scale the recipe up or down or adjust the baking time. Here are some guidelines.

CAKES AND QUICK BREADS: Since standard-size cake and loaf pans usually measure within an inch of one another, and dividing leaveners and eggs can be tricky, it's better to adjust the baking time instead of the batter's yield. Add or subtract about 5 minutes from the baking time, and check the cake regularly for doneness. Note: In a larger vessel, the cake will be more squat.

PIES: Any of our pie doughs meant to be rolled to 12 inches for a 9-inch pan can be rolled to 13½ inches to fit a 9½-inch (often labeled "deep dish") pan. To do the reverse, roll the dough to 12 inches.

TARTS: The 2-inch difference between 9- and 11-inch pans is surprisingly substantial. We found that when using a 9-inch pan in a recipe that calls for an 11-inch one, or vice versa, it's necessary to scale the recipe down or up by 50 percent, respectively, to ensure that the pastry and filling are flush with the vessel's edge.

PORTION WITHOUT A SCOOP

You can portion cookie dough with a measuring cup just as accurately as you would with a portion scoop. Fill a ¼-cup dry measuring cup (equal to 4 tablespoons) with dough and then divide it according to the desired sizes.

TUBE PAN TROUBLESHOOTING

If your pan lacks feet, simply invert it over a bottle to cool the cake. And if it doesn't have a removable bottom, it's easy to prevent sticking by lining it with parchment paper as follows:

1. Place pan right side up on sheet of parchment paper and trace outside perimeter. Turn pan upside down and place parchment on top of pan bottom.

2. Place measuring cup that fits opening of center hole in middle of traced circle, where hole is. Use it as guide to trace center hole.

3. Fold parchment into quarters and cut out hole. Finally, cut out circle and line pan. When baked cake has cooled, gently peel away parchment.

"UNWHIP" OVERWHIPPED CREAM

There's no going back on cream you've whipped into butter, but here's our fix for loosening up whipped cream that's just a bit too stiff.

1. Add unwhipped heavy cream into overwhipped cream 1 tablespoon at a time.

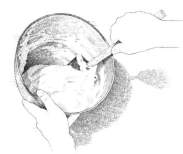

2. Gently fold mixture, adding more unwhipped cream until the desired consistency is reached.

PREVENT OVERBAKED COOKIES

Rather than allow just-baked cookies to rest briefly on the baking sheet, which helps them set, immediately transfer them to a wire rack where there will be less carryover cooking.

FIRM UP TOO-SOFT BUTTER

Butter that yields completely to pressure or is starting to melt can't support the air bubbles generated during creaming. To re-establish butter's structure, mix it with a few ice cubes and stir constantly until it firms up, about 1 minute. (The amount of water that leaks into the butter will be negligible.) We found that sugar cookies and buttercream frosting made with rehabbed butter were comparable to those made with butter that had been softened properly.

SAVE AN UNDERDONE PIE

Baked custard pies, like pumpkin or sweet potato, should be baked to 175 and 165 degrees, respectively, when the edges of the filling are set but the center is still a bit loose. (The pie fully sets as it cools.) But if you don't have an instant-read thermometer and you pulled the pie too early, rebake it in a preheated 275-degree oven for about 30 to 45 minutes (the filling should be set but not firm). If the pie has been in the refrigerator, let it sit at room temperature for 1 hour before rebaking.

PIE PLATES IN A PINCH

If you don't own enough vessels for all the pies you want to bake during the holidays, these alternatives make good substitutes for the traditional 9-inch glass pie plate.

DISPOSABLE PIE PLATE

Disposable aluminum pie plates have relatively thin walls that don't hold or transfer heat as efficiently as our preferred glass pie plates do, so crusts don't brown or crisp as quickly. But we found that simply extending the baking time for pies baked in disposable pie plates can produce comparable results.

FOR EMPTY CRUSTS: Increase the time that the crust bakes with weights by up to 10 minutes, or until the crust turns golden brown and crisp.

FOR FILLED DOUBLE-CRUST PIES: Increase the baking time by up to 10 minutes, covering the top of the pie with aluminum foil if it starts to get too dark.

TIP: It's especially important to bake pies in aluminum pie plates on a baking sheet—both to ensure a well-browned bottom crust and for stability when transporting the pies.

CAST-IRON SKILLET

For double-crust pies, use a very well-seasoned cast-iron skillet that's 9 or 10 inches in diameter to keep the baking times consistent with the recipe. Because the pan is deeper than a pie plate, use 60 percent of the dough for the bottom crust so that it will reach up the sides. (Don't bake single-crust pies in a cast-iron skillet; the pan's relatively straight sides will cause the dough to slump.)

MAKING THE MOST OF LEMONS

Lemons are the key flavoring in countless recipes, but in the test kitchen, they are almost as indispensable as salt for seasoning and enhancing our cooking.

WHAT MAKES A LEMON LEMONY?

The juice and the zest of a lemon can be thought of as two different components, with each bringing a little something different to the table. Fresh juice gets its tart flavor primarily from citric acid and its distinctively lemony taste and scent from a mix of volatile aromatic compounds—chiefly limonene, pinene, and citral—contained in oil droplets in the juice sacs. The zest contains these compounds and many more (and likely in greater concentrations than in the juice), giving it a more intense and complex flavor and scent.

ZEST
is packed with oil glands containing volatile aromatic compounds.

JUICE
gets its tart flavor from citric acid, while oils within the juice sacs provide aroma.

PITH
contains bitter phenolic compounds as well as pectin.

WHEN TO COOK WITH JUICE VERSUS ZEST

Juice and zest behave very differently when exposed to heat, primarily due to the way the volatile aroma compounds are bound up in each. The volatile compounds in juice are suspended in water, where they readily evaporate, so juice that's been heated loses its aroma and tastes flat (though it still contributes a tartness from citric acid, which isn't affected by heat). To retain its bright, fresh taste, we typically wait to add lemon juice toward the end of cooking or as a finishing touch, or we use it in uncooked applications like icings and glazes. When we use lemon juice in baked goods, while it can contribute tartness, its main purpose is to activate the leavening. Because the aromatic compounds in the zest are trapped in oil glands within the peel's cell walls, which make it harder for them to escape, zest retains a more complex lemony flavor when heated. For this reason, we tend to use zest in baked goods and other recipes that involve long exposure to heat.

CHOOSING THE JUICIEST LEMONS

Most lemons at the supermarket come in just two varieties. Lisbon lemons are often characterized by slightly smoother skin, a rounder shape, and a flatter stem end, while Eureka lemons are frequently distinguished by a more elliptical shape and knobs at both ends. No matter the variety, the most important trait to look for is fruit that gives under pressure, which indicates a thin skin and pith. We found that thin-skinned specimens yielded an average of 8 percent more of their weight in juice (or about 2½ teaspoons per medium lemon) than those that felt rock hard. Green skin is also not a problem. In our tests, as long as they were thin-skinned, lemons with a greenish cast had as much juice as their more uniformly yellow counterparts, and they did not taste more tart.

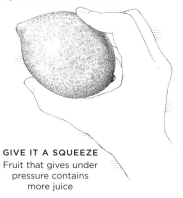

GIVE IT A SQUEEZE
Fruit that gives under pressure contains more juice

BEST STORAGE OPTIONS

Like all citrus, lemons are nonclimacteric. On the down side, this means that they don't continue to ripen after harvest. On the plus side, it means that they retain their quality longer than other fruits. But to keep lemons as juicy as possible, store them chilled—and protect them from air.

BAG WHOLE LEMONS

Unwrapped lemons will start to lose their moisture after about a week in the refrigerator. But we found that they'll stay in perfect condition for up to four weeks when sealed in a zipper-lock bag and chilled.

TIGHTLY WRAP ZESTED LEMONS

Since the oil in the zest protects the fruit from drying out, a lemon without its skin needs even more protection. Tightly wrap it in plastic wrap before refrigerating it.

FREEZE LEFTOVER JUICE AND ZEST

In tests, we found that freezing leftover juice led to a deterioration in flavor, but it was still acceptable in recipes that call for only a small quantity, such as for a pan sauce. Freeze leftover zest in a zipper-lock bag for up to three weeks. Its color will fade, but it will still be fine for baking and cooking.

JUICING

- **BEST TOOLS:** Our preferred way to extract juice is to insert tongs or even a fork into the lemon and twist over a bowl.

- **AVOID COLD LEMONS:** Room-temperature lemons are much easier to squeeze than cold lemons. To quickly take the chill off a cold lemon, microwave it until it is warm to the touch.

- **ROLL ON A HARD SURFACE FIRST:** We found that rolling a lemon makes it easier to juice because it softens the membrane and tears the juice sacs.

- **PANTRY ALTERNATIVES:** In a pinch, ReaLemon 100% Lemon Juice from Concentrate is an acceptable substitute in most cooking and baking applications. Lemon extract is an acceptable, though less sour, substitute for 1 tablespoon of juice or less in baking recipes only (substitute ¼ teaspoon of extract per tablespoon of juice).

ZESTING

- **BEST TOOLS:** Use a rasp-style grater for fine zest and a vegetable peeler for strips.

- **DON'T ZEST TOO SOON:** The volatile oils in the peel are strongest just after zesting; for maximum flavor, zest just before using.

- **AVOID THE PITH:** The oils in the zest are the key to its floral flavor; avoid the bitter white pith beneath the zest by grating over the same area only once or twice.

- **PANTRY ALTERNATIVE:** In baked goods where lemon is the main flavor, there is no substitute for fresh. But when lemon is only a background flavor, an equal amount of lemon extract is a fine stand-in. Lemon extract is derived from oils in the peel and shares the same flavor compounds as the fresh zest.

GREAT WAYS TO USE LEMONS

PROTECT POACHED FISH

Put slices under fish when poaching to lift it off the pan's bottom to ensure even cooking or around fish when steaming to infuse it with a delicate flavor.

PREVENT STICKY PASTA

Tap water is often slightly alkaline, which can weaken the protein network in pasta, allowing surface starches to absorb water and burst, leaving a sticky residue. Adding 2 teaspoons of lemon juice to 4 quarts of cooking water strengthens the pasta's protein mesh and helps keep starch granules intact.

DRESS MILD GREENS

Vinaigrette made with lemon is better suited for dressing milder greens, such as green leaf, Bibb, and Boston lettuces, than dressings made with sharper-tasting vinegar. Use a 3:1 ratio of oil to lemon juice.

PERK UP SOUPS AND STEWS

Add lemon juice to taste before serving to brighten chicken, fish, or vegetable soups and stews, or add a strip or two of zest at the start of cooking (discard before serving) for an infusion of floral lemon flavor.

GRILL AND SQUEEZE OVER PROTEINS

Grill halved lemons until charred and then squeeze over finished fish or poultry or add to a dressing. Grilling lemons caramelizes the sugars in the juice, creating more complex flavor. (You can also use lemons to cap the ends of skewers, so food at the ends won't overcook.)

KEEP PESTO GREEN

It's common knowledge that lemon juice prevents cut vegetables from browning. But we found that the citric and ascorbic acids it contains can also keep basil pesto from oxidizing and losing its bright color: Add 2 teaspoons lemon juice for every cup of the packed herb.

BRIGHTEN BASTING OIL

Add 1 teaspoon of grated zest, 1 tablespoon of juice, and 1 teaspoon of a minced herb such as rosemary to ½ cup of extra-virgin olive oil for a basting oil with a hint of citrus flavor.

SUBSTITUTE FOR WINE

To replace up to ½ cup of wine in soups and pan sauces, add ½ cup of chicken broth plus 1 teaspoon of lemon juice.

A REST MAKES LEMONADE BETTER

AGE JUICE

Letting lemon juice rest for up to 6 hours will allow the aromatic compounds in the fruit's oil to oxidize, making the lemon flavor more mellow and complex, a benefit most noticeable when juice is used in beverages. But don't let it sit too long—it will eventually lose potency and develop off-flavors.

STEEP ZEST

We've found that steeping zest in lemon juice for lemonade pulls out the zest's water-soluble flavor compounds, lending a deeper, more complex flavor (we discard the zest before serving). You can also use less sugar because compounds in the zest known as flavanones mask bitter flavors in the lemonade so it tastes sweeter.

THE GOOEY SECRETS OF MELTING CHEESE

After making countless grilled cheese sandwiches, cheeseburgers, casseroles, and pizzas, we've learned a few tricks about how to melt cheese perfectly.

Whether it's oozing from a grilled cheese or a quesadilla, stretching from a slice of pizza, or making a pasta casserole rich and gooey, melted cheese has universal appeal. Plus, melted cheese has an ultra-savory umami quality that makes its flavor as addictive as its texture.

But achieving that perfect stretch or creaminess is harder than it looks—and too often the result is a greasy, stringy, clumpy mess. By understanding the way a cheese melts and how to manipulate it, you can produce perfect results every time.

HOW CHEESE MELTS—OR DOESN'T

All cheeses can be categorized into two groups based on how they are coagulated: with acid (such as vinegar or lemon juice) or with an enzyme known as rennet (which can be animal- or plant-derived).

ACID-COAGULATED CHEESES (such as feta, ricotta, and fresh goat cheese) resist melting because the acid dissolves the calcium ions between the casein proteins and alters their electrical charge, both of which cause the proteins to link up tightly and clump. Heat then makes the proteins bond together even more tightly, which squeezes out the water and causes the cheese to dry out and stiffen.

RENNET-COAGULATED CHEESES (such as cheddar, Monterey Jack, and mozzarella) melt in two stages: First, their fat globules change from solid to liquid, which makes the cheese more supple. Then, as the temperature continues to rise, the tightly bonded casein proteins loosen their grip on one another and the cheese flows like a thick liquid.

THREE TYPES OF MELTERS

GREAT MELTERS

Younger, moister cheeses contribute relatively mild flavor but melt beautifully on pizza and burgers and in grilled cheese, macaroni and cheese, lasagna, and enchiladas.

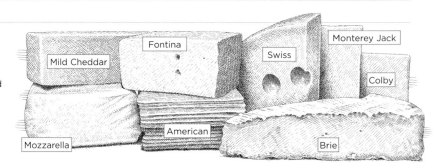

POOR MELTERS

Aged cheeses lend strong flavor to pasta casseroles, gratins, omelets, sandwiches, and sauces but must be paired with younger, moister cheeses or stabilizers like starch or fat to make them melt without "breaking."

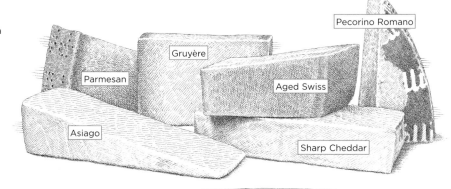

NONMELTERS

We use these acid-coagulated cheeses, which resist melting, as last-minute additions to pastas, salads, and crostini.

HOW TO MAKE FLAVORFUL CHEESES MELT WELL

We like to cook with aged cheeses because they offer stronger flavor, but they often melt poorly. This is because cheese loses moisture as it ages, so its proteins become more concentrated and cling together more tightly than those in younger cheeses. Heating makes the proteins loosen their grip on one another only slightly so they flow (i.e., melt) less readily and are more prone to recombining, leaving behind a gritty texture and pools of fat. To get the best flavor and texture, we turn to the following tricks.

ADD STARCH

We toss shredded cheese for fondue with cornstarch and purposely cook pasta in a reduced amount of water to make a starch-concentrated liquid base for a creamy and stable cheese sauce. The starch granules release threads of amylose, which bind to the cheese's casein proteins and prevent them from squeezing out fat and recombining into gritty curds.

ADD A MOIST CHEESE

When we're making grilled cheese, baked pasta casseroles like macaroni and cheese, and fondue, we supplement flavorful aged cheeses like sharp cheddar and Gruyère with moister varieties like Monterey Jack, fontina, and even Brie, which helps the mixture melt smoothly. For pasta casseroles, a 50/50 ratio of aged-to-moist cheeses works well; for grilled cheese, increase the amount of aged cheese to between 75 and 80 percent.

GRATE FINE

Smaller, finer shreds of hard cheeses like Parmesan will disperse more evenly throughout the dish than coarser shreds will and, thus, help stave off clumping. For thinner shreds, use a rasp-style grater or the fine holes of a box grater.

ADD DAIRY

Adding a couple of tablespoons of cream to a pasta sauce made with aged cheese, such as Pecorino Romano, can help keep it smooth. The cream contains molecules called lipoproteins that allow it to act as an emulsifier, keeping the fat and proteins together.

A SHRED OF ADVICE

Semifirm cheeses like cheddar, Monterey Jack, and mozzarella often smear, break apart, and clog the holes when shredding. Here's our three-part fix:

1. Freeze cheese for 30 minutes before grating to keep it firm while grating.

2. Use the large holes of a grater to prevent clumping.

3. Coat the face of the grater with vegetable oil spray to prevent sticking.

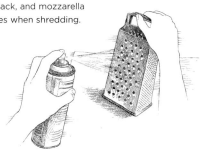

WHAT MAKES MOZZARELLA SO STRETCHY?

When melted, mozzarella has a distinctive elasticity, due to its pH during processing: Mozzarella has low acidity, which allows it to retain more calcium—the "glue" that holds proteins in cheese together. More calcium means a more stable protein structure that's less prone to breaking apart when heated. When milk curds are stretched and pulled to make mozzarella, this stability allows its proteins to line up in a straight, uniform fashion (if you look closely, you can see a fine ribbed pattern in the cheese). When enough heat is applied, the strands loosen and flow in the same direction. Because cheeses like cheddar and Monterey Jack are more acidic during processing, they have less calcium. Their proteins are thus held together more loosely, and when heated, they flow in all directions.

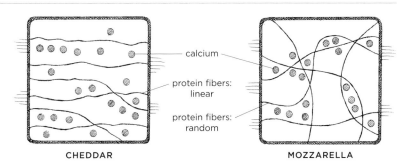

CHEDDAR — calcium — protein fibers: linear — protein fibers: random — MOZZARELLA

DON'T SUBSTITUTE FRESH FOR BLOCK

While mozzarella in general stretches better than other cheeses, block mozzarella stretches much better than the fresh kind. The acidity during processing plays a critical role: The pH of block mozzarella is basic enough that it doesn't lose calcium, so its proteins can flow and stretch. Meanwhile, fresh mozzarella is even less acidic, so its protein structure is even more stable. Another boon for block-style mozzarella: It bubbles and browns better than the fresh kind because it contains up to 15 percent less moisture.

SHELLFISH WITHOUT FEAR

It's not just about shrimp. Other shellfish also require little prep, cook quickly, and can fit any occasion. Our tips will inspire you to buy and cook them with the same confidence.

MUSSELS

IMPORTANT TIPS

- **TO DETERMINE FRESHNESS, USE YOUR NOSE.** Live mussels will smell pleasantly briny. Those that have died will smell sour or sulfurous and should be discarded. Also discard any with cracked or open shells that won't close when lightly tapped.

- **TO STORE, KEEP IN A WET, BREATHABLE ENVIRONMENT.** Mussels can come in contact with ice, but you don't want them sitting in water. Place them in a colander set in a bowl, surround them with ice in the colander and cover with wet paper towels (wet newspaper is even better as it retains moisture longer). They will keep in the fridge for up to three days.

- **DON'T CROWD THE POT.** Tightly packing mussels in a pot to steam them will overcook those at the bottom. For this reason, when cooking several pounds, we prefer to cook them spread out in a large roasting pan, covered, in the oven.

- **UNOPENED COOKED MUSSELS NEEDN'T BE DISCARDED.** Try microwaving any unopened mussel briefly (30 seconds or so) to see if the muscle that keeps the shell closed will relax with more heat. If the shell still won't open, then throw out the mussel.

Oven-Steamed Mussels
SERVES 4

1	tablespoon extra-virgin olive oil
3	garlic cloves, minced
	Pinch red pepper flakes
1	cup dry white wine
3	sprigs fresh thyme
2	bay leaves
4	pounds mussels, scrubbed and debearded
¼	teaspoon salt
2	tablespoons unsalted butter, cut into 4 pieces
2	tablespoons minced fresh parsley

1. Adjust oven rack to lowest position and heat oven to 500 degrees. Heat oil, garlic, and pepper flakes in large roasting pan over medium heat; cook, stirring constantly, until fragrant, about 30 seconds. Add wine, thyme sprigs, and bay leaves and bring to boil. Cook until wine is slightly reduced, about 1 minute. Add mussels and salt. Cover pan tightly with aluminum foil and transfer to oven. Cook until most mussels have opened (a few may remain closed), 15 to 18 minutes.

2. Remove pan from oven. Push mussels to sides of pan. Add butter to center and whisk until melted. Discard thyme sprigs and bay leaves, sprinkle parsley over mussels, and toss to combine. Serve immediately.

CLAMS

IMPORTANT TIPS

- **FRESH, LIVE CLAMS SHOULD SMELL CLEAN.** Discard any that have a bad odor as well as those that have cracked shells or won't close when lightly tapped.

- **FRESH WATER WILL KILL CLAMS, SO AVOID CONTACT WITH ICE WHEN STORING.** Place them in a bowl, cover with wet paper towels or newspaper, and set in another bowl filled with ice. They will keep in the fridge for up to one week.

- **CLEANING IS EASY.** Because farmed hard-shell clams are typically held on flats submerged in saltwater for several days after being dug up, they usually expel any grit that they have ingested prior to making it to market. You need only to scrub their shells before cooking.

- **UNOPENED COOKED CLAMS NEEDN'T BE DISCARDED.** As with mussels, unopened clams may just need more cooking. Microwave briefly to see if their shells open; discard clams if they don't.

Clams Steamed in White Wine
SERVES 4

How fast the clams cook depends on the pot and clam size; to prevent overcooking, start checking for doneness after 4 minutes.

1½	cups dry white wine
3	shallots, chopped fine
4	garlic cloves, minced
1	bay leaf
4	pounds littleneck clams, scrubbed
3	tablespoons unsalted butter
2	tablespoons minced fresh parsley
	Lemon wedges

1. Bring wine, shallots, garlic, and bay leaf to simmer in Dutch oven over medium heat; continue to simmer to blend flavors, 3 minutes. Increase heat to high. Add clams, cover, and cook, stirring twice, until clams open, 4 to 8 minutes.

2. Using slotted spoon, remove clams from liquid and transfer to large serving bowl. Once all clams have been removed from pot, whisk butter into liquid to make emulsified sauce. Pour sauce over clams, sprinkle with parsley, and serve immediately with lemon wedges.

Four pounds of clams will cook evenly on the stovetop.

SEA SCALLOPS

IMPORTANT TIPS

- **STORE SCALLOPS AS YOU WOULD FISH FILLETS OR STEAKS.** Keep scallops in the refrigerator in a bag or sealed container on a bed of ice. Dry scallops can be kept for up to five days; wet scallops for up to one week.

- **DON'T WORRY IF SCALLOPS SMELL MILDLY FISHY.** Scallops release gas as soon as they have been shucked, which you may smell when you first open the bag or container. The smell should dissipate after a few minutes. (However, if it doesn't, the scallops are past their prime.)

- **CHECK IF SCALLOPS ARE WET OR DRY.** Wet scallops (treated with a solution of water and sodium tripolyphosphate to preserve them) typically look more uniformly white than those that haven't been treated, but to find out for sure, microwave one scallop on a paper towel–lined plate for 15 seconds. A wet scallop will leave a sizable ring of moisture on the towel (the scallop can then be cooked as is).

- **SOAK WET SCALLOPS TO IMPROVE THEIR TASTE.** Combine 1 quart of cold water, ¼ cup of lemon juice, and 2 tablespoons of salt and soak scallops in mixture for 30 minutes.

- **REMOVE TOUGH MUSCLE.** Most scallops have a crescent-shaped muscle attached to their sides that cooks up tough. Use your fingers to peel it off before cooking.

Pan-Seared Scallops
SERVES 4

1½ pounds dry sea scallops, 10 to 20 per pound, tendons removed
    Salt and pepper
2   tablespoons vegetable oil
2   tablespoons unsalted butter
    Lemon wedges

1. Place scallops on rimmed baking sheet lined with clean dish towel. Place second clean dish towel on top of scallops and press gently on towel to blot liquid. Let scallops sit at room temperature for 10 minutes while towels absorb moisture.

2. Sprinkle scallops on both sides with salt and pepper. Heat 1 tablespoon oil in 12-inch nonstick skillet over high heat until just smoking. Add half of scallops in single layer, flat side down, and cook, without moving them, until well browned, 1½ to 2 minutes.

3. Add 1 tablespoon butter to skillet. Using tongs, flip scallops; continue to cook, using large spoon to baste scallops with melted butter (tilt skillet so butter runs to 1 side) until sides of scallops are firm and centers are opaque and register 115 degrees, 30 to 90 seconds longer (remove smaller scallops as they finish cooking). Transfer scallops to large plate and tent loosely with aluminum foil. Wipe out skillet with paper towels and repeat with remaining oil, scallops, and butter. Serve immediately with lemon wedges.

LOBSTERS

IMPORTANT TIPS

- **LIVE AND KICKING IS A GOOD THING.** While a lively lobster can be challenging to handle, its movement indicates good health and the best texture and flavor once the lobster is cooked.

- **HARD-SHELL VERSUS SOFT-SHELL.** Most of the year the lobsters you find are hard-shell, but due to their molting cycle, the lobsters available during the late summer into early fall are generally soft-shell. Consider buying extra when lobsters are soft-shell, since they haven't fully grown into their shells and yield less by weight—about 17 percent compared with the 25 percent yield from a hard-shell.

- **BOIL LOBSTERS SERVED SHELLED, STEAM LOBSTERS SERVED WHOLE.** Use salted water to boil lobsters that you're shelling ahead of time for well-seasoned meat. Shell them over the sink, since water trapped in the shells will make a mess. Steam lobsters that you plan to serve whole at the table. They're less waterlogged and messy than boiled lobsters.

- **USE A THERMOMETER TO CHECK DONENESS.** The only way to know for sure that the lobster is cooked just right is to go by temperature. We cook lobster to 175 degrees. Its muscle fibers are longer and require more heat to shrink to the length that delivers a tender, pleasantly resilient texture.

Steamed Whole Lobsters
SERVES 4

4   (1¼-pound) hard-shell lobsters
8   tablespoons butter, melted (optional)
    Lemon wedges

Bring about 1 inch water to boil over high heat in large pot set up with wire rack. Add lobsters, cover, and return to boil. Reduce heat to medium-high; steam until tails register 175 degrees, 13 to 14 minutes. Serve with melted butter, if using, and lemon wedges.

Freezing lobsters briefly puts them in a coma-like state that makes them easier to handle.

FROZEN YOGURT

These days, supermarket frozen yogurts are flying off the shelves. Is this because they're healthful and taste good—or because they simply sound that way? We wanted to judge for ourselves, so we scooped up eight of the best-selling national products, both low-fat and nonfat versions, in the most straightforward flavor: vanilla. With a few exceptions, the yogurts either tested our tolerance for sweetness or exhibited odd off-flavors. Even more damning were their textures—no surprise, since when you remove fat from a frozen dairy product, it becomes difficult to attain an ultrasmooth consistency. The better brands achieved creaminess thanks to a few key components. The first: corn syrup, which inhibits iciness by restricting the movement of the water molecules so that they are less likely to form large crystals. Stabilizers, like carrageenan, also help stave off ice crystal formation and boost the perception of creaminess. We rated the products on flavor, texture, and overall appeal. Frozen yogurts appear below in order of preference.

RECOMMENDED

TCBY Classic Vanilla Bean Frozen Yogurt

PRICE: $3.95 per 1.5-qt container ($0.08 per oz)   **FAT:** 2.5 g per ½ cup   **SUGAR:** 15 g per ½ cup

COMMENTS: Tasters praised the "balanced sweetness" of this product. (We tested its supermarket-only formulation.) Its combination of corn syrup, carrageenan, and cream gave it a smooth texture, though some tasters felt it bordered on "bouncy."

BEN & JERRY'S Vanilla Greek Frozen Yogurt

PRICE: $6.50 per 1-pt container ($0.41 per oz)   **FAT:** 4.5 g per ½ cup   **SUGAR:** 19 g per ½ cup

COMMENTS: With a "pleasant tang" that was "recognizably like yogurt" and a "natural vanilla flavor," this frozen yogurt (available in Ben & Jerry's shops) was "appealing" and reminded some of "cheesecake." Tasters also praised its "smooth," if "a bit runny," texture.

TURKEY HILL Dairy Vanilla Bean Frozen Yogurt

PRICE: $3.69 per 1.5-qt container ($0.08 per oz)   **FAT:** 0 g per ½ cup   **SUGAR:** 14 g per ½ cup

COMMENTS: Lots of stabilizers and emulsifiers (including carrageenan) created a "smooth" consistency in this nonfat yogurt, though some tasters found it "a little thin and icy," with "not enough milkfat." It was "not even vaguely tart"; rather, it tasted "clean," "appealing," and "sweet."

NOT RECOMMENDED

HÄAGEN-DAZS Vanilla Low Fat Frozen Yogurt

PRICE: $3.99 per 14-oz container ($0.29 per oz)   **FAT:** 2.5 g per ½ cup   **SUGAR:** 21 g per ½ cup

COMMENTS: We had high hopes for this product, which has the shortest ingredient list of the bunch. But without any stabilizers, tasters bemoaned its chalky texture and "syrupy," "cloying" flavor that one taster compared to "eating liquid marshmallows."

NOT RECOMMENDED *(continued)*

HEALTHY CHOICE Vanilla Bean Greek Frozen Yogurt

PRICE: $3.99 per package of three 4-oz containers ($0.33 per oz)   **FAT:** 2 g per ½ cup   **SUGAR:** 11 g per ½ cup

COMMENTS: Tasters found this Greek frozen yogurt "sludgy," perhaps due to a lack of corn syrup. That texture, paired with "buttermilk" tang (which may have been enhanced by the addition of citric acid), was more reminiscent of "frozen cheesecake" than yogurt.

BLUE BELL Country Vanilla Lowfat Frozen Yogurt

PRICE: $5.75 per ½-gal container ($0.09 per oz)   **FAT:** 1.5 g per ½ cup   **SUGAR:** 16 g per ½ cup

COMMENTS: This product's "really yellow" color suggested eggy richness, but it "doesn't taste as rich and creamy as it looks." In fact, tasters found it "foamy," noting that it "just slumps in the cup." Its "supersweet" flavor was "cloying"—like "fake sugar"—and there was "not enough vanilla" flavor.

STONYFIELD Gotta Have Vanilla Organic Nonfat Frozen Yogurt

PRICE: $3.99 per 1-pt container ($0.25 per oz)   **FAT:** 0 g per ½ cup   **SUGAR:** 19 g per ½ cup

COMMENTS: "Tastes like the worst qualities of low-cal dairy," said one taster. "Sweet, fake, lean." Without any fat, corn syrup, or carrageenan to aid smoothness, this product had a texture that was "more crystal-y than creamy."

STONYFIELD Greek Vanilla Organic Nonfat Frozen Yogurt

PRICE: $4.29 per 1-pt container ($0.27 per oz)   **FAT:** 0 g per ½ cup   **SUGAR:** 17 g per ½ cup

COMMENTS: This nonfat yogurt was plagued by a host of off-flavors that summoned comparisons to "spoiled milk" and "stinky tropical fruit." Like its sibling, this product lacked ingredients like corn syrup and carrageenan that promote smoothness, and its "gritty" texture helped secure its low rating.

PRESLICED PROSCIUTTO

Not too long ago, the only way to buy prosciutto was to find an Italian market and wait while someone sliced imported prosciutto di Parma or prosciutto di San Daniele by hand. Since American and Canadian producers have gotten into the game, prosciutto is easier to come by and available in grab 'n' go packages at local supermarkets. We tried them plain and also seared in chicken saltimbocca. The good news: We liked most of the samples. While our top six producers follow the Italians and use nothing but pork and salt, the makers of two of the losing products add nitrates—preservatives that turn the meat's color bright red and boost its savory flavor so that it tastes like "salami." The texture of the hams mattered at least as much as their flavor. Low-moisture hams that were sliced thinner delivered that ideal combination of complex flavor and supple texture. Prosciutti are listed in order of preference.

RECOMMENDED

VOLPI Traditional Prosciutto
PRICE: 3 oz for $5.75 ($1.92 per oz/$30.67 per pound)   **MADE IN:** Missouri
AGED: 9 months
SODIUM: 771 mg per 1-oz serving   **FAT:** 15.64%
MOISTURE: 45.91%   **SLICE THICKNESS:** 0.5 mm
COMMENTS: "Tender" and "buttery" with a "very nice porky complexity" and a "salty punch" that came from having one of the highest sodium levels in the lineup. Tasters were wowed by its "silky," "ultrasupple" texture that was highlighted by the meat being sliced thinly. Fried in chicken saltimbocca, it continued to win fans: "The prosciutto elevated the dish . . . with rich, meaty flavor."

DEL DUCA Prosciutto
PRICE: 3 oz for $3.59 ($1.20 per oz/$19.15 per pound)   **MADE IN:** Rhode Island
AGED: Just over 1 year
SODIUM: 522 mg per 1-oz serving   **FAT:** 12.58%
MOISTURE: 51.61%   **SLICE THICKNESS:** 0.9 mm
COMMENTS: With a "nice porky sweetness" and "clean" but "intense" flavor, this prosciutto was one of the most thickly sliced in the lineup, but its ample moisture also gave it a "supple" texture. In saltimbocca, it was lauded for its "rich pork belly flavor."

CITTERIO All Natural Prosciutto
PRICE: 4 oz for $6.99 ($1.75 per oz/$27.96 per pound)   **MADE IN:** Pennsylvania
AGED: 9 to 11 months
SODIUM: 857 mg per 1-oz serving   **FAT:** 9.90%
MOISTURE: 53.92%   **SLICE THICKNESS:** 0.58 mm
COMMENTS: Tasters described this prosciutto as "so tender it practically disintegrates on the way to your mouth." Its "salty, sweet, oaky" flavor was deemed "classic" and "very pleasant." Citterio's thin slices became extra-crispy and "crunchy," though mild, when fried in chicken saltimbocca.

BELLENTANI Prosciutto
PRICE: 3 oz for $6.49 ($2.16 per ounce/$34.61 per pound)   **MADE IN:** Pennsylvania
AGED: At least 200 days (6.6 months)
SODIUM: 363 mg per 1-oz serving   **FAT:** 9.43%
MOISTURE: 55.51%   **SLICE THICKNESS:** 0.66 mm
COMMENTS: These slices won fans for their "moist," "soft, easy to eat" texture that helped tasters forgive their "supermild," "not very complex" taste. In saltimbocca, tasters noted "simple flavor" but "lovely texture."

RECOMMENDED (continued)

LA QUERCIA Berkshire Prosciutto
PRICE: 4 oz for $8.99 plus shipping ($2.25 per ounce/$35.96 per pound)   **MADE IN:** Iowa
AGED: 9 to 12 months, depending on size of pig
SODIUM: 564 mg per 1-oz serving   **FAT:** 14.42%
MOISTURE: 42.56%   **SLICE THICKNESS:** 0.82 mm
COMMENTS: "Beautiful ruby color," raved tasters, giving this prosciutto "points for presentation." Tasters praised its "salty, gamy, nutty," "lush, full pork flavor" that boasted "real character." But its combination of low moisture and thick slices made it taste "chewy," or even "hard and stringy."

RECOMMENDED WITH RESERVATIONS

LA QUERCIA Prosciutto Americano
PRICE: 3 oz for $10.99 plus shipping ($3.66 per ounce/$58.61 per pound)   **MADE IN:** Iowa
AGED: 9 to 12 months
SODIUM: 384 mg per 1-oz serving   **FAT:** 17.36%
MOISTURE: 44.12%   **SLICE THICKNESS:** 0.75 mm
COMMENTS: There were near-unanimous raves for the complex flavor of this prosciutto, our former top pick: "so rich, with notes of toasty nuts, wine, and a lovely sweet finish," "meaty and quite sweet," and "an almost cheddar-y flavor." But as with its sibling, tasters found it "too dry—almost like a prosciutto jerky" as well as "tough" and "leathery"—whether plain or in saltimbocca.

NOT RECOMMENDED

APPLEGATE Naturals Prosciutto
PRICE: 4 oz for $6.99 ($1.75 per oz/$27.96 per pound)   **MADE IN:** Canada
AGED: 6 to 9 months
SODIUM: 729 mg per 1-oz serving   **FAT:** 15.62%
MOISTURE: 49.09%   **SLICE THICKNESS:** 1 mm
COMMENTS: "Chewy" was the repeated description of this ham. While some tasters liked its "sweet porkiness," others found it "supermild," not to mention "gummy," even "flabby." In saltimbocca, its inclusion of unspecified flavoring reminded one taster of "Domino's pepperoni."

COLUMBUS Prosciutto
PRICE: 3 oz for $5.89 ($1.96 per oz/$31.41 per pound)   **MADE IN:** California
AGED: Company would not disclose
SODIUM: 358 mg per 1-oz serving   **FAT:** 7.4%
MOISTURE: 58.49%   **SLICE THICKNESS:** 0.8 mm
COMMENTS: This prosciutto's "salami" flavor can likely be traced to its lactic acid starter culture. The other additives imparted flavor that tasted more like "hot dogs" or "bologna" than prosciutto. The texture was also too "lean," "wet," and "waxy."

HERITAGE TURKEYS

Eating turkey on Thanksgiving is an American tradition, but most turkey breeders today cater to consumer preferences for white meat, breeding turkeys to have big breasts and small legs. These birds can grow to full size on less feed and in half the time as the old-breed turkeys, but something has been lost. Near extinction not so long ago, old-breed heritage turkeys have had a renaissance in the past decade. We bought heritage turkeys from seven farms scattered across the United States; all featured startlingly long legs and wings, a more angular breast and high keel bone, almost bluish-purple dark meat, and traces of dark pinfeathers in the skin around the tail. Tasters raved about the "buttery," "nutty-sweet," "incredibly satisfying, rich flavor" of the meat. There's no denying that price is a big factor when considering heritage turkeys, which can cost upwards of $10 per pound, not including overnight or two-day shipping. A heritage bird is a centerpiece for a special occasion, like beef tenderloin or prime rib (which can cost $75 to $100 at the supermarket). We'll be happy to splurge on this bird for the holidays—not just to save them from extinction, but for the great taste they bring to our Thanksgiving table. Turkey are listed in order of preference.

HIGHLY RECOMMENDED

MARY'S Free-Range Heritage Turkey

PRICE: $166.72 for 7- to 14-lb bird, plus shipping
RAISED IN: California
BREED: Standard Bronze
FAT IN WHITE MEAT: 5.75%
FAT IN DARK MEAT: 7.25%
COMMENTS: Our top pick was "richly flavored," with "great texture and moisture," and exquisitely "crisp" skin. This big turkey (just over 14 pounds) was "quite fatty," with "remarkably tender, moist white meat that tastes like poultry, not just wet fiber. Dark meat is "dee-lish and also very tender." Tasters raved about its "good scent" and "nutty-sweet poultry flavor. Even the skin tastes meatier than [that of] most [other] turkey." One taster summed it up: "Amazing."

RECOMMENDED

ELMWOOD STOCK FARM Organic Heritage Turkey

PRICE: $149 for 9- to 10.9-lb bird, plus shipping
RAISED IN: Kentucky
BREED: Narragansett, Slate, or Bourbon Red (farm decides for you)
FAT IN WHITE MEAT: 8.03%
FAT IN DARK MEAT: 5.21%
COMMENTS: This turkey was "supertender and juicy," with white meat "so rich in flavor that it tastes like dark meat." The dark meat was even more tender and flavorful, prompting one taster to ask, "Is this turkey or pulled pork? So fall-apart tender that it's almost shredding itself."

GOOD SHEPHERD POULTRY RANCH Heritage Turkey

PRICE: $119 for 12- to 14-pound bird, plus shipping
RAISED IN: Kansas
BREED: Standard Bronze
FAT IN WHITE MEAT: 10.63%
FAT IN DARK MEAT: 6.34%
COMMENTS: Tasters praised the "very, very moist and intensely sweet breast meat," that was "moist but not wet," with "substantial turkey flavor," and dark meat that was "rich, almost fatty, in a good way, like duck," and "incredibly tender, quite fat-streaked." Indeed, lab results showed that it had one of the highest fat percentages of all the turkeys we tasted.

RECOMMENDED (continued)

HERITAGE TURKEY FARM Heritage Turkey BEST BUY

PRICE: $85 for 10- to 13-lb bird, plus shipping
RAISED IN: Wisconsin
BREED: American Bronze
FAT IN WHITE MEAT: 5.10%
FAT IN DARK MEAT: 3.82%
COMMENTS: "A fine specimen of turkey here," one taster wrote, and others agreed: "plenty moist and tender" "but not mushy," "fantastic," "perfectly juicy," and "full of turkey taste." The "lovely" dark meat was praised for being "packed with meaty flavor," "supple," and "richly flavored." A taster concluded: "Overall, unique enough that I'd spend money for this."

RECOMMENDED WITH RESERVATIONS

EBERLY Heritage Turkey

PRICE: $84 for 8- to 9-lb bird, plus shipping
RAISED IN: Pennsylvania
BREED: Bourbon Red
FAT IN WHITE MEAT: 8.25%
FAT IN DARK MEAT: 9.15%
COMMENTS: This smaller bird's "white meat is moist, with a nice, unexpected sweetness." Tasters praised its "crispy" skin and "tender, savory" meat. But they were divided on their opinion of the dark meat: While some rated it "excellent—smooth and flavorful," "rich," and "acorn-y"—several others found it "a bit liver-y." "This one's an acquired taste," wrote one taster.

BN RANCH Heritage Turkey

PRICE: $138.98 for 10- to 12-lb bird, plus shipping
RAISED IN: California
BREED: Mixed, with "parent stock from five heritage breeds"
FAT IN WHITE MEAT: 5.34%
FAT IN DARK MEAT: 6.99%
COMMENTS: While this turkey, raised in a new venture by Bill Niman, founder of Niman Ranch, was "wildly moist," some tasters found it "lighter on turkey flavor, with the dark meat tasting almost of white." "One of the less impressive white meat samples," wrote one taster. "Quite moist but bland," agreed others, like "typical turkey breast." While there was nothing wrong with this bird, a turkey that costs this much should be perfect.

VEGETARIAN BROTH

The last time we tasted vegetable broth, we found that the vast majority were awful—sour, cloyingly sweet, or bitter. Since then, however, dozens more vegetable broth products have popped up on supermarket shelves. Of the ten we tested, the product we liked most in recipes contained only a smattering of vegetables, and many of the broths we had serious reservations about had lots of vegetables positioned high on their ingredient lists. Could it actually be that more vegetables make bad commercial broth? Turns out, vegetable broth sold in liquid form can oxidize, creating sour, musty off-flavors. Broths are listed in order of preference.

RECOMMENDED

ORRINGTON FARMS Vegan Chicken Flavored Broth Base & Seasoning
PRICE: $3.50 for 6 oz ($0.02 per fl oz)
STYLE: Powder (2 tsp per cup of water, makes 28 cups)
SODIUM: 750 mg   SUGAR: 0 g

COMMENTS: With barely any vegetables, this powder didn't suffer from some of the off-flavors that plagued more vegetable-heavy products. In risotto, numerous tasters commented on its saltiness, but it also made the dish "very flavorful." In soup, it lent "great savory depth." Another bonus: It's cheap and easy to store.

SWANSON Certified Organic Vegetable Broth

PRICE: $3.69 for 32 oz ($0.12 per fl oz)
STYLE: Liquid
SODIUM: 530 mg   SUGAR: 2 g
COMMENTS: Pear and cane juices and three forms of carrot made this liquid broth notably sweet, particularly when reduced in risotto. While some found that it contributed "nice vegetal flavor" to soup, overall it was "neutral" and "inoffensive."

BETTER THAN BOUILLON Vegetable Base, Reduced Sodium
PRICE: $5.69 for 8 oz ($0.02 per fl oz)
STYLE: Paste (1 tsp per cup of water, makes 38 cups)
SODIUM: 500 mg   SUGAR: 0 g

COMMENTS: Tasters described soup and risotto made with this reconstituted paste as "earthy," "mushroomy," and "carroty." While some tasters found it too salty (the "reduced sodium" label refers to its sodium content in relation to its regular vegetable base), most thought it provided a savory base that let "other flavors come through."

RECOMMENDED WITH RESERVATIONS

IMAGINE Organic Vegetarian No-Chicken Broth

PRICE: $3.79 for 32 oz ($0.12 per fl oz)
STYLE: Liquid
SODIUM: 520 mg   SUGAR: less than 1 g
COMMENTS: Some tasters picked up on the onions and carrots in this liquid broth, finding it sweet, while others noted slightly "sour" or "bitter" aftertastes. Most agreed with the taster who called it "nothing offensive; nothing stellar."

SEITENBACHER Vegetarian Vegetable Broth and Seasoning
PRICE: $6.99 for 5 oz ($0.02 per fl oz)
STYLE: Powder (1 tsp per cup of water, makes 40 cups)
SODIUM: 420 mg   SUGAR: 0 g

COMMENTS: With yeast extract as its first ingredient, this powder gave soup a "funky packaged soup taste," but some found it "nicely neutral" when reduced in risotto.

RECOMMENDED WITH RESERVATIONS (continued)

PACIFIC FOODS Organic Vegetable Broth

PRICE: $3.99 for 32 oz ($0.12 per fl oz)
STYLE: Liquid
SODIUM: 540 mg   SUGAR: 2 g
INGREDIENTS: Water, carrots, onion, celery, tomatoes, leeks, sea salt, mushrooms, garlic, savory leaf, ground bay leaf (organic)
COMMENTS: This broth made risotto taste "too carroty"; in soup it was mainly "boring," though a few found that it contributed a "very vegetal taste."

RACHAEL RAY Stock-in-a-Box All-Natural Veggie Stock

PRICE: $2.99 for 32 oz ($0.09 per fl oz)
STYLE: Liquid
SODIUM: 480 mg   SUGAR: 0 g
COMMENTS: While a few deemed this broth "savory" and "complex" in recipes, the majority felt that its "roasted vegetable flavor" was out of place. "It feels heavy and tastes oniony," one taster said. Others picked up on "bitter celery notes."

KNORR Homestyle Stock—Vegetable
PRICE: $3.99 for 4.66 oz ($0.04 per fl oz)
STYLE: Paste (1 tub per 3½ cups of water; 4-tub package makes 14 cups)
SODIUM: 750 mg   SUGAR: less than 1 g
COMMENTS: Like the Orrington Farms powder, this paste was loaded with salt and yeast extract that gave it "depth" in recipes—

but it lacked the winner's balance. It's "a salt bomb," tasters said, comparing it to "Lipton Cup-a-Soup." Each tub makes 3½ cups of broth, an amount that doesn't match most recipes.

KITCHEN ACCOMPLICE Veggie Broth Concentrate, Reduced Sodium
PRICE: $8.75 for 12 oz ($0.04 per fl oz)

STYLE: Liquid concentrate (2 tsp per cup of water, makes 28 cups)
SODIUM: 440 mg   SUGAR: less than 1 g
COMMENTS: Some found this liquid concentrate "pretty decent" for adding "herbal" notes to food. Most agreed that it was "too sweet"; others picked up a "canned soup flavor." The thick, bouncy texture of this concentrate made it difficult to squeeze a small amount into a measuring spoon.

NOT RECOMMENDED

KITCHEN BASICS Unsalted Vegetable Stock

PRICE: $3.49 for 32 oz ($0.11 per fl oz)
STYLE: Liquid
SODIUM: 240 mg   SUGAR: 3 g
COMMENTS: With no added salt and the most sugar, this broth made soup taste like "cheap marinara sauce." In risotto, it had a "weird onion flavor" and an "unpleasant, bitter finish." (Note: The company slightly reformulated its broth just after our tasting. We tried it and still do not recommend this broth.)

SUPERMARKET BRIE

Most Americans have never tasted authentic French Brie, which is a regional product made with raw milk and aged for only a few weeks—the FDA bans raw milk cheeses unless they've been aged 60 days. The Brie found in American supermarkets is made with pasteurized milk, and, in the case of double or triple crème Bries, can contain added cream. We found that factors such as origin, price, and butterfat had no bearing on our preferences, so we dug deep into the Brie-making process and uncovered the key factor explaining what gives a Brie the lush texture and earthy flavor we liked best: the culturing process. The cultures fall under two main categories: mesophilic or thermophilic. Mesophilic cultures lead to a cheese that more closely mimics the traditional French raw-milk variety, with fuller flavor, gooier texture, and a thinner, spottier rind. Thermophilic cultures create milder, firmer cheese with a thicker, more uniform rind. Thermophilic cheeses are referred to as "stabilized" in the industry; although the cheeses are more consistently firm and mild, many tasters found them bland. Bries are listed in order of preference.

HIGHLY RECOMMENDED

FROMAGER D'AFFINOIS
MADE IN: France
FORMAT AND PRICE: Wedges, $17.99 per lb
STYLE AND AGE: Not disclosed, 14 days
BUTTERFAT CLASSIFICATION: Double crème
COMMENTS: The runaway favorite in both tastings, this Brie boasts "nutty richness," "ultracreamy" body, and a pillowy rind—all characteristics associated with traditional versions (though the manufacturer wouldn't confirm the culturing process). As one taster put it, eating this cheese was "sheer pleasure."

RECOMMENDED

MARIN Triple Crème Brie
MADE IN: USA
FORMAT AND PRICE: 8-oz wheels, $9.99 each ($19.98 per lb)
STYLE AND AGE: Traditional, 10 to 14 days
BUTTERFAT CLASSIFICATION: Triple crème
COMMENTS: The lone triple crème, this traditional Brie was "complex but not too pungent," "tangy," and "pleasantly earthy," but moderately so, with a "slight funk" that tasters found pleasant. Even more appealing was its "silky," "unctuous" texture that "almost melts in your mouth."

FROMAGE DE MEAUX
MADE IN: France
FORMAT AND PRICE: Wedges, $17.99 per lb
STYLE AND AGE: Traditional, 4 to 8 weeks
BUTTERFAT CLASSIFICATION: Standard fat
COMMENTS: This traditional Brie was aged up to twice as long as our other top scorers and offered "mushroomy" depth. Its texture was "beautifully runny," "creamy," and "so velvety." But don't mistake this for Brie de Meaux, one of just two name-protected Bries that are made in the Seine-et-Marne region of France according to strict laws.

RENY PICOT Brie
MADE IN: USA
FORMAT AND PRICE: 7-oz wedges, $2.59 each ($5.92 per lb)
STYLE AND AGE: Stabilized, 15 to 20 days
BUTTERFAT CLASSIFICATION: Double crème
COMMENTS: Tasters praised this Brie's "hint of ooze" and "good balance" of "tang" and "buttery flavor." But what made it really stand out was its bargain price—one-third the cost of other recommended products.

RECOMMENDED WITH RESERVATIONS

ALOUETTE Double Crème Brie
MADE IN: USA
FORMAT AND PRICE: 8-oz wheels, $6.49 each ($12.98 per lb)
STYLE AND AGE: Stabilized, not disclosed
BUTTERFAT CLASSIFICATION: Double crème
COMMENTS: Though this stabilized Brie, with a "thick, dry rind," was "pleasant" enough, the general consensus was that it was "unremarkable," "bland," and "boring." As one taster said, "This could almost be American cheese."

BRIE D'ISIGNY
MADE IN: France
FORMAT AND PRICE: Wedges, $11.99 per lb
STYLE AND AGE: Not disclosed, up to 4 weeks
BUTTERFAT CLASSIFICATION: Double crème
COMMENTS: Some tasters loved the texture of this "plush," "silky-smooth" Brie—traits that made us think it was a traditional version (the manufacturer wouldn't confirm the style), but most found its flavor "sharp" and "almost sour."

PRÉSIDENT Brie
MADE IN: USA
FORMAT AND PRICE: 8-oz wheels, $7.69 each ($15.38 per lb)
STYLE AND AGE: Not disclosed, 6 to 11 days
BUTTERFAT CLASSIFICATION: Double crème
COMMENTS: Tasters weren't offended by this well-known Brie, but they weren't impressed either. Most offered complaints about its "stiff," "plasticky" texture; "chalky rind"; and flavor that was "nothing special" (features that made us assume it was a stabilized Brie). In other words, "it's kind of boring" and "generic."

JOAN OF ARC Double Crème Brie
MADE IN: USA
FORMAT AND PRICE: Wedges, $13.99 per lb
STYLE AND AGE: Not disclosed, 7 to 10 days
BUTTERFAT CLASSIFICATION: Double crème
COMMENTS: "Mild" and "unremarkable," this Brie (which we assumed was stabilized) "verged on bland." As a result of its "bouncy" texture, the cheese remained "in firm little cubes" when we baked it in phyllo cups; tasters found this texture off-putting.

DIJON MUSTARD

In the test kitchen, we understand the appeal of good Dijon mustard: It is creamy, with more body than conventional yellow mustard, and packs a wallop of clean, nose-tingling heat. After testing different mustards, we discovered that the three best indicators of a strong, spicy Dijon are right on the label: Fat content—even a small amount indicates more mustard seeds and stronger flavor; sell-by date—fresher mustards are spicier, so buy jars as far from their dates as possible; and choice of preservative—sulfur dioxide is more effective than tartaric acid at staving off oxidation and, thus, preserving heat. Clean flavor, intense heat, and creamy body were exactly the qualities we liked in a Dijon. Those that were "sweet," "too mild," or seasoned with ingredients beyond the standard formula simply didn't meet our expectations for what Dijon should be. Dijons are listed in order of preference.

RECOMMENDED

TROIS PETITS COCHONS Moutarde de Dijon
PRICE: $6.99 for a 7-oz jar ($1.00 per oz)
INGREDIENTS: Mustard seeds, vinegar, water, sea salt (may contain naturally occurring sulfites)
FAT: 0.5 g   SODIUM: 115 mg per teaspoon
COMMENTS: Thanks to a high ratio of mustard seeds (it's the only product we tasted to list them as the first ingredient), this pricey Dijon impressed tasters with "nasal-clearing" heat that "kicks in gradually" and "builds." It was balanced, too, delivering just enough salt and "tangy," "bright" flavor to even out its spiciness.

MAILLE Dijon Originale
PRICE: $4.49 for a 7.5-oz jar ($0.60 per oz)
INGREDIENTS: Water, mustard seeds, vinegar, salt, citric acid, sulphur dioxide (preservative)
FAT: 0.5 g   SODIUM: 125 mg per teaspoon
COMMENTS: A good choice for those who prefer a more moderate heat level, this "well-rounded" Dijon was "fairly spicy but not too sharp" and boasted "bright flavor typical of Dijon."

ROLAND Extra Strong Dijon Mustard
PRICE: $5.16 for 10.1-oz jar ($0.51 per oz)
INGREDIENTS: Water, mustard seeds, vinegar, salt, citric acid, sodium metabisulfate (as a preservative)
FAT: 0.5 g   SODIUM: 125 mg per teaspoon
COMMENTS: With "big, nasal-clearing heat" that reminded tasters of "wasabi" and "horseradish," this mustard was rated the hottest in our lineup. The heat made it an especially appealing condiment on hot dogs, where it "cut through the saltiness" of the meat.

FRENCH'S Dijon Mustard
PRICE: $2.99 for 12-oz jar ($0.25 per oz)
INGREDIENTS: Distilled vinegar, water, #1 grade mustard seed, salt, chardonnay wine, citric acid, tartaric acid, spices and turmeric
FAT: 0 g   SODIUM: 130 mg per teaspoon
COMMENTS: This mustard was fairly spicy, but some tasters lamented that its heat "doesn't linger" as long as other products'. What they did pick up on was tanginess, noting its "kick from acid."

KOOPS' Dijon Mustard
PRICE: $4.98 for 12-oz jar ($0.42 per oz)
INGREDIENTS: Water, mustard seed, vinegar, salt, white wine, citric acid, turmeric, tartaric acid, spices
FAT: 0 g   SODIUM: 120 mg per teaspoon
COMMENTS: Heat-seekers wanted more zip, depth, and bite from this "mellow" Dijon. But despite that, tasters found it "bright" and "pleasant" enough to recommend it. In sum: "It would do a grilled frank justice."

RECOMMENDED *(continued)*

GREY POUPON Dijon Mustard
PRICE: $3.29 for 8-oz jar ($0.41 per oz)
INGREDIENTS: Water, vinegar, mustard seed, salt, white wine, fruit pectin, citric acid, and tartaric acid, sugar, spices
FAT: 0 g   SODIUM: 120 mg per teaspoon
COMMENTS: The "familiar" flavor of our former winner combined "sharp vinegar tang" with a "creamy" texture, which one taster deemed "mustard heaven." But the consensus among most tasters was that this Dijon "could use more heat."

RECOMMENDED WITH RESERVATIONS

EMERIL'S Dijon Mustard
PRICE: $2.25 for 12-oz jar ($0.19 per jar)
INGREDIENTS: Distilled vinegar, water, mustard seed, salt, white wine, citric acid, tartaric acid, spices, oleoresin turmeric
FAT: 0 g   SODIUM: 135 mg per teaspoon
COMMENTS: With "more vinegar than heat" and spices, this Dijon reminded tasters of "yellow mustard." Some also noticed a "slightly sweet" and "perfumey" flavor. As one taster summed up: "It's not a bad mustard, but it's not Dijon."

WOEBER'S Supreme Dijon Mustard
PRICE: $6.00 for 10-oz jar ($0.60 per oz)
INGREDIENTS: Distilled vinegar, water, #1 mustard seed, salt, white wine, citric acid, tartaric acid, spices
FAT: 0 g   SODIUM: 120 mg per teaspoon
COMMENTS: Heavy on the vinegar and wine flavors and light on the spiciness, this Dijon was "tart" and "tangy"—a "middle-of-the-road" mustard, tasters said. But its bright flavor was overwhelmed by the hot dog, and it had a "slightly bitter" aftertaste.

SILVER SPRING Dijon Mustard
PRICE: $4.83 for 9.5-oz jar ($0.51 per oz)
INGREDIENTS: Vinegar, water, mustard seed, salt, white wine, citric acid, tartaric acid, turmeric, spices
FAT: 0 g   SODIUM: 45 mg per teaspoon
COMMENTS: Most tasters found this mustard "mellow." On its own, it offered only a "mild" burn; on a hot dog, it tasted "a little weak." Some even detected off-flavors in the form of a "weirdly fruity," "slightly sweet aftertaste," and even distracting hints of "garlic" and "clove."

FROZEN PEPPERONI PIZZA

Frozen pizza has a bad rep, but a slew of new "artisanal" options promise pizzeria quality from the freezer aisle. We focused on pepperoni and assembled a lineup of seven pizzas—three artisanal-style pies and four national best sellers. Every product had sufficiently plentiful and flavorful pepperoni. Cheese, though, was a bit more contentious. Tasters liked clean, traditional, milky mozzarellas, and four of the seven products delivered. When we got to the sauce, the gap between good and bad was even wider. Our tasters preferred herby sauces with strong tomato flavor and balanced tang, rejecting sweeter sauces that tasted more "processed." It all came down to the crust, and newer artisanal-style crusts won by a landslide: They had a thick base with an "airy" chew and a solid rim to hold on to. Thin crusts were veritable crackers—"dried out" and "cardboardy." When we examined the underside of each pizza straight from the freezer, we found a clue about artisanal pies. Top-ranked products showed visible char marks and browning on their crusts, while lower-scoring pies had pale undersides that hardly looked baked at all. Pizzas are listed in order of preference.

RECOMMENDED

PIZZERIA! BY DIGIORNO Primo Pepperoni
PRICE: $8.49 for 18.7 oz ($0.45 per oz)
CRUST THICKNESS: 20.9 mm
COMMENTS: With a "thick," "crisp and airy" crust, this product delivered its promise of a "classic," "pizzeria-like" pie. Tasters praised DiGiorno's "very meaty" pepperoni and "herby," "zesty" sauce, which "balanced sweet and tangy," resulting in an all-around "vibrant" pizza.

FRESCHETTA Brick Oven Crust Pepperoni and Italian Style Cheese
PRICE: $7.99 for 22.7 oz ($0.35 per oz)
CRUST THICKNESS: 14.8 mm
COMMENTS: Tasters enjoyed the "smoky" taste of this product's "really porky," "spicier" pepperoni and compared its "crispy" crust to "fresh delivery pizza." Many noticed the "heft" to this pizza's crust, which didn't wilt under its "earthy," "fruity" sauce.

RED BARON Fire Baked Pepperoni Pizza
PRICE: $6.49 for 19.86 oz ($0.33 per oz)
CRUST THICKNESS: 14.2 mm
COMMENTS: This pizza's "rich," "very saucy" topping held up nicely on its "crispy," "tender" crust. A few tasters found this product's sauce "overly sweet," but most were pleased with its "nice spicy flavor."

RECOMMENDED WITH RESERVATIONS

TOMBSTONE Original Pepperoni Pizza
PRICE: $3.67 for 21.6 oz ($0.17 per oz)
CRUST THICKNESS: 8.1 mm
COMMENTS: While many tasters were won over by this pizza's "very cheesy" topping and "meaty" sauce (which was speckled with extra crumbles of pepperoni), others compared its crust to "bad elementary school" pizza: "soggy and bready" in some parts and "dry and stale" in others.

NOT RECOMMENDED

TOTINO'S Party Pizza Classic Pepperoni
PRICE: $1.36 for 9.8 oz ($0.14 per oz)
CRUST THICKNESS: 9.6 mm
COMMENTS: "Grease bomb!" Tasters were put off by the "gross" amount of oil on this pizza, which turned its crust "soggy," "mushy," and "bland." Worse, this pizza uses a cheese substitute that tasters found "pale," "anemic," and "grainy."

JACK'S Original Pepperoni Pizza
PRICE: $3.99 for 16.5 oz ($0.24 per oz)
CRUST THICKNESS: 5.4 mm
COMMENTS: This pizza's cheese had an "off, funky, sour" flavor, and its "sweet," "superwet" sauce was closer to "ketchup" than tomato sauce. Tasters were equally put off by the "limp" crust, which was "floppy and gummy" like a "cracker that is getting soggy."

CALIFORNIA PIZZA KITCHEN Crispy Thin Crust Signature Pepperoni
PRICE: $7.69 for 17 oz ($0.45 per oz)
CRUST THICKNESS: 10.0 mm
COMMENTS: One taster unfavorably compared this product to bottled Italian dressing: "too herby," "overly seasoned," and dotted with "watery" unripe tomato chunks. Gouda cheese added a "weird smoky flavor," and the crust was "thin and dry" like "stale bread."

SALTED BUTTER

Though we prefer unsalted butter for most recipes because it allows finer control over flavor and texture, we use salted butter when butter flavor needs to be front and center as for slathering on corn on the cob, biscuits, or toast. We tested six nationally available products and one top-selling regional product. Although we liked all the butters we tried, it was clear that some products were in a league of their own. The most critical factor was the packaging, which can have a huge impact on butter's flavor potential. Butters wrapped in plain parchment landed at the bottom of our ranking. Tasters detected a number of off, "fridge-y" flavors in these butters even though they were well within their expiration dates. Parchment-wrapped butters also had a harder, cheese-like consistency that contrasted with the airy, almost whipped texture that the foil-wrapped butters had. In the end, we couldn't find a bad butter in the bunch and recommended all seven products in our lineup, but one was clearly cream of the crop. Our winner is the only butter in the lineup to undergo a process called "culturing." The result: a complex, rich butter with tangy, yogurt-y notes. Butters are listed in order of preference.

HIGHLY RECOMMENDED

LURPAK Lightly Salted Butter
PRICE: $3.59 for 8 oz ($0.45 per oz)
WRAPPER: Foil   **CULTURED:** Yes
GRASS-FED: No   **SALT:** 1.14%
COMMENTS: This Danish import was "creamy" and "rich," with "intense butter flavor" and "spot-on salt." The only product in our lineup made with cultured cream, this "complex," "flowery" butter had a "sharp," "crème fraîche" tanginess that our tasters loved.

RECOMMENDED

KATE'S Homemade Butter
PRICE: $4.99 for 1 lb ($0.31 per oz)
WRAPPER: Foil   **CULTURED:** No
GRASS-FED: No   **SALT:** 1.72%
COMMENTS: This "soft and velvety," "fresh-tasting" butter from Maine was praised for its "simple, classic" creaminess and "great dairy flavor." Tasters loved the "markedly salty," "ocean" notes in this sea-salted butter, which contains the highest percentage of salt in our lineup.

PLUGRÁ European-Style Butter
PRICE: $4.99 for 8 oz ($0.62 per oz)
WRAPPER: Foil   **CULTURED:** No
GRASS-FED: No   **SALT:** 1.50%
COMMENTS: American-made with a European name, this butter (from the brand that makes our favorite unsalted butter) was praised for its "sweet caramel notes," "silky-smooth" texture, and "almost spicy" aftertaste. Said one taster: "I'd love this on bread . . . or scones . . . or anything!"

LAND O'LAKES Salted Butter
PRICE: $4.49 for 1 lb ($0.28 per oz)
WRAPPER: FlavorProtect Parchment   **CULTURED:** No
GRASS-FED: No   **SALT:** 1.24%
COMMENTS: This best-selling butter had a "remarkably airy," almost "whipped" texture and a "mild," "milky richness" with lots of "dairy flavor." Wrapped in a special protective parchment that kept out any fridge-y aftertastes, this butter was markedly "clean," "fresh," and "bright."

RECOMMENDED *(continued)*

KERRYGOLD Pure Irish Butter
PRICE: $4.99 for 8 oz ($0.62 per oz)
WRAPPER: Foil   **CULTURED:** No
GRASS-FED: Yes   **SALT:** 1.25%
COMMENTS: "Tangy," "custardy," and "very rich," this Irish import (made from the milk of all pasture-raised cows) had a pronounced "grassy" earthiness. While too "barnyard-y" for some tasters, most loved its "melt-in-your-mouth," "silky" texture.

CHALLENGE Butter
PRICE: $3.15 for 1 lb ($0.20 per oz)
WRAPPER: Parchment   **CULTURED:** No
GRASS-FED: No   **SALT:** 1.58%
COMMENTS: Tasters found this California-made butter "sweet," "nutty," and "almost floral," with a "silky," "cheesy texture." Some detected a "slightly sour," "off-flavor" from this parchment-wrapped butter, though most liked its "rich," "rounded" creaminess.

ORGANIC VALLEY Salted Butter
PRICE: $5.99 for 1 lb ($0.37 per oz)
WRAPPER: Parchment   **CULTURED:** No
GRASS-FED: Yes   **SALT:** 1.05%
COMMENTS: "Grassy, herbaceous, complex, and a little funky," this organic butter had a "vivid" yellow color and "farm-fresh" tang. "You can really taste the pasture," said one taster. Some noted "papery," "refrigerator" flavors from its parchment wrapper.

FROZEN BREAKFAST SAUSAGE LINKS

Plump and juicy with hints of sweetness and spice, sausage links are a staple of a hearty breakfast. When we found out our winning breakfast links were reformulated, we focused on frozen in our search for a new favorite. We gathered six top-selling sausage products and included one raw frozen sausage to see how it compared. It immediately stood out: Bright white and oddly chunky, the sole raw frozen offering cooked up rubbery and pasty. But even juicy, fully cooked products were rife with texture differences: Some were "tender" and "juicy," while others were "tough" or "mushy." While most products had comparable percentages of protein, our favorite "moist" sausages were more than 39 percent fat, while bottom-ranked "gristly" and "rubbery" links contained anywhere from 17 percent to 34 percent fat. Fat not only adds flavor but is also the key to tender, juicy texture, as it helps keep meat fragments from sticking together and becoming tough during cooking. Our top manufacturers also combat moisture loss by adding two special salts to their sausage, phosphates and monosodium glutamate (MSG), which keep sausages moist and heighten the perception of savory flavors in foods. Sausage links are listed in order of preference.

RECOMMENDED

JIMMY DEAN Fully Cooked Original Pork Sausage Links
PRICE: $4.99 for 9.6 oz ($0.52 per oz)
FAT: 39.1%
COMMENTS: This sausage was "fatty but not too greasy," with a "meaty chew" and a "crisp," "golden" crust. "Nice and plump," with hints of "maple," this "very juicy" sausage balanced "sweet" and "spicy" for a "rich pork taste."

ODOM'S Tennessee Pride Fully Cooked Original Sausage Links
PRICE: $4.78 for 9 oz ($0.53 per oz)
FAT: 39.3%
COMMENTS: With just a "hint of heat" and a "strong herby flavor," these "porky" links were favored for their "loose" texture and "rich," "mild" sweetness. "Nice balance of seasoning and pork," summarized one taster.

BOB EVANS Fully Cooked Original Pork Sausage Links
PRICE: $3.29 for 8 oz ($0.41 per oz)
FAT: 25.0%
COMMENTS: Though it's lower in fat than other products, tasters enjoyed the "snappy," "chewy" texture of this sausage—the only product with a casing, which helps keep in moisture. "Meaty" and "mild," this sausage's "traditional" flavors were "completely familiar and quite satisfying."

RECOMMENDED WITH RESERVATIONS

JONES All Natural Golden Brown Mild Pork Sausage Links
PRICE: $3.39 for 7 oz ($0.48 per oz)
FAT: 41.9%
COMMENTS: While some tasters felt that these "mushy" links were "more greasy than porky," most enjoyed the "balanced" sweetness and "maple-y" notes in this preservative-free sausage.

NOT RECOMMENDED

FARMLAND Fully Cooked Sausage Links
PRICE: $4.91 for 9.6 oz ($0.51 per oz)
FAT: 17.4%
COMMENTS: The reformulated version of our previous winning sausage links, this product adds turkey and a whole lot of extra water. The result is a "soggy," "mushy interior" and "bland," "unremarkable" flavor. "Tastes and feels like it's been microwaved straight from the freezer," said one taster.

BANQUET Brown 'N Serve Original Sausage Links
PRICE: $2.49 for 6.4 oz ($0.39 per oz)
FAT: 33.2%
COMMENTS: The mix of turkey and soy protein in this sausage perplexed tasters, who compared its "rubbery," "spongy" texture to "hot dogs" and vegetarian "tofurkey." Equally off-putting was its "aggressive" spiciness and "really processed," "sour" flavor.

HORMEL Little Sizzlers Pork Sausage
PRICE: $2.39 for 12 oz ($0.20 per oz)
FAT: 34.3%
COMMENTS: This raw frozen sausage was "rubbery," like "Styrofoam," and "weird" and "pale" in color. "I know pork is the other white meat, but this is creepily white," said one taster. Summarized another: "I would skip breakfast rather than eat this."

BROWN RICE

Brown rice—whole grain, gluten-free, cheap, and healthy—is booming in popularity. To find the best product, we selected four top-selling dried products and three prepared products. After we cooked enough brown rice to feed a commune, only one of the quick products turned out consistently decent; the other two were either clumpy and mealy or soft and mushy. As for the dry rice, when cooked according to our own recipes, all performed admirably, with similar scores for flavor and texture. But when we cooked each product according to its instructions, one was great, one was decent, and two were utter mush. The mushy products don't sell bad rice; they're just telling you to add too much water. We cooked the two mushy products with the water ratio called for in our best rice, 1¾ cups per cup of rice, and they vastly improved. Our winning rice covered all the bases and is the only company in our tasting that grows its own rice, and that level of control, coupled with smart directions, turns out consistently superior, firm, nutty grains. Rice are listed in order of preference.

RECOMMENDED

LUNDBERG Organic Brown Long Grain Rice
PRICE: $3.79 for 32 oz ($0.25 per cup cooked)
STYLE: Dry
FAT: 2 g per cup cooked
SODIUM: 0 mg per cup cooked
COMMENTS: This dry rice has the best instructions and works with a range of other cooking methods. Tasters said its kernels were "plump" and "almost springy," as well as "distinct and pleasantly chewy." They were the most flavorful, too: "buttery," "nutty," and "earthy."

RICELAND Extra Long Grain Natural Brown Rice
PRICE: $1.88 for 32 oz ($0.11 per cup cooked)
STYLE: Dry
FAT: 1.3 g per cup cooked
SODIUM: 0 mg per cup cooked
COMMENTS: This rice's directions were slightly more successful because they called for less water, but the rice was still a bit "soft." Cooked with alternative instructions, it was very good, with "firm, intact grains" that were "chewy, yet distinct," "nutty," "rich," and "toasted."

CAROLINA Whole Grain Brown Rice (sold as Carolina in the Northeast, Mahatma everywhere else)
PRICE: $4.19 for 32 oz ($0.25 per cup cooked)
STYLE: Dry
FAT: 1.3 g per cup cooked
SODIUM: 0 mg per cup cooked
COMMENTS: This rice is good—if you ignore its package instructions. Prepared correctly, it can be "pleasantly chewy," with "distinct individual grains." Neutral in flavor and softer than other products we tried, some tasters compared it with white rice.

GOYA Brown Rice
PRICE: $2 for 16 oz ($0.25 per cup cooked)
STYLE: Dry
FAT: 0 g per cup cooked
SODIUM: 0 mg per cup cooked
COMMENTS: This rice turned to mush when prepared according to its package instructions. But adjust the cooking method and you get "nicely chewy," "tender yet toothsome" kernels. It was milder in flavor, "kind of white rice-y."

RECOMMENDED (continued)

MINUTE Ready to Serve Brown Rice
PRICE: $2.39 for 8.8 oz ($1.20 per cup cooked)
STYLE: Shelf-stable microwavable
FAT: 3.5 g per cup cooked
SODIUM: 150 mg per cup cooked
COMMENTS: This fully cooked microwavable rice isn't perfect, but it consistently turned out decent rice in 60 seconds. The grains were "bouncy," "almost like wheat berries." They also come lightly oiled and salted, which tasters thought added nice flavor but which does limit control.

NOT RECOMMENDED

BIRDS EYE Steamfresh Whole Grain Brown Rice
PRICE: $2.59 for 10 oz ($1.30 per cup cooked)
STYLE: Frozen
FAT: 1 g per cup cooked
SODIUM: 5 mg per cup cooked
COMMENTS: The sole frozen product was OK dressed with vinaigrette in a salad, but otherwise tasters found it "dry" and "mushy." The process of cooking, freezing, and reheating the rice is harsh on the grains and leaves them dry on the inside and "pasty" outside. It was also bland, with notes of "dust" and "metal."

UNCLE BEN'S Ready Rice Whole Grain Brown
PRICE: $2.39 for 8.8 oz ($1.20 per cup cooked)
STYLE: Shelf-stable microwavable
FAT: 3 g per cup cooked
SODIUM: 15 mg per cup cooked
COMMENTS: "Arid like the Sahara!" declared one taster of this "dry," "crumbly" parboiled rice, with intermittently "chewy," "hard," straw-like kernels. At best it was bland and underseasoned; at worst, tasters said it was "oddly fragrant," and "floral," like "chemicals" or "wet newspaper."

AMERICAN CHEESE

American cheese is polarizing. A good American cheese is mild, but not bland, and melts like a dream in grilled cheese sandwiches and atop burgers. But in this age of slow food, plastic-wrapped cheese slices have become a symbol of hyperprocessing. We sampled seven nationally available American cheeses plain and in grilled cheese sandwiches and noticed a pattern: The shorter the ingredient list, the better-tasting the cheese. Some food experts explained that some manufacturers cut costs by using less actual cheese in their products and more comparatively cheap dairy ingredients. Since cheese is higher in fat and protein than other dairy products, products with more natural cheese will also usually have significantly more fat and protein than products that use whey or milk concentrates. Cheeses are listed in order of preference.

HIGHLY RECOMMENDED

BOAR'S HEAD American Cheese
PRICE: $5.49 for 8 oz ($0.69 per oz)
CLASSIFICATION: Process cheese
PROTEIN: 19.1%
FAT: 30.7%
MOISTURE: 40.1%
COMMENTS: Our winning cheese, which is made from a blend of cheddar cheeses, had "nutty," "sharp" tanginess and a "slightly soft," "tender" texture. These "superthin" slices melted perfectly.

RECOMMENDED

KRAFT Deli Deluxe American Cheese
PRICE: $5.99 for 12 oz ($0.50 per oz)
CLASSIFICATION: Process cheese
PROTEIN: 19.1%
FAT: 31.2%
MOISTURE: 39.3%
COMMENTS: These "crumbly" slices made "molten" and "melty" grilled cheese that was "rich," "sharp," and "cheddary," with "balanced" notes of "cream" and "butter."

LAND O'LAKES Deli American Cheese Product
PRICE: $4.49 for 8 oz ($0.56 per oz)
CLASSIFICATION: Cheese product
PROTEIN: 19.6%
FAT: 27.8%
MOISTURE: 39.7%
COMMENTS: Though this "cheese product" contains added whey and milk protein concentrates, a lower moisture level made these "thicker" slices "crumbly" like "aged" cheese, with "cheddar-like sharpness" to match. This product's "tangy" acidity made for "rich" and "assertive" grilled cheese.

RECOMMENDED WITH RESERVATIONS

KRAFT Singles
PRICE: $3.49 for 12 oz ($0.29 per oz)
CLASSIFICATION: Cheese product
PROTEIN: 18.7%
FAT: 22.1%
MOISTURE: 41.9%
COMMENTS: Most tasters agreed that this product had "classic" flavor, though a few found it too bland: "good for kids, but boring for adults." It melted well, but was "plasticky" and "rubbery" when tasted plain.

NOT RECOMMENDED

BORDEN American Cheese Singles
PRICE: $3.49 for 12 oz ($0.29 per oz)
CLASSIFICATION: Cheese product
PROTEIN: 16.9%
FAT: 21.4%
MOISTURE: 44.6%
COMMENTS: "Bland," "greasy," and "waxy," these high-moisture slices melted into a "slimy," "wet" mass that coated tasters' mouths and teeth. Many also thought that this cheese had a "funky," "artificial" sourness.

CRYSTAL FARMS American Cheese
PRICE: $3.40 for 12 oz ($0.28 per oz)
CLASSIFICATION: Cheese product
PROTEIN: 18.7%
FAT: 23.2%
MOISTURE: 45.2%
COMMENTS: Another "mouth-coating" cheese, this product was "rubbery" and "gummy" when melted and had a "super-processed," "plastic wrapper" flavor. Sampled plain, this cheese was "really bland," "boring," and "oily."

VELVEETA Slices
PRICE: $2.99 for 12 oz ($0.25 per oz)
CLASSIFICATION: Cheese product
PROTEIN: 13.6%
FAT: 8.1%
MOISTURE: 51.8%
COMMENTS: One of the few products without any natural cheese, these "vibrant yellow" slices were "thick," "tacky," and "gluey" from added gelatin. Tasters were turned off by their "sickening" sweetness and "microwave popcorn flavor."

SUPERMARKET SHARP CHEDDAR CHEESE

In recent years, inexpensive supermarket cheddars have taken top honors in international cheese competitions, beating out much-pricier artisan brands. We selected seven nationally available products to test plain and in grilled cheese. While we liked most of the cheddars, a few fell to the bottom of the pack for "funky," "sweet" flavors that were unexpected. We preferred products with the familiar "bright" and "buttery" flavor of "classic" cheddar. The longer-aged cheddars at the bottom of our rankings had higher pH values (meaning they were less acidic) than top-ranked cheddars: A high pH is a good indication that the product didn't age well. High moisture content, like high pH, can also prevent the development of flavor and cause the cheese to age poorly. Ultimately, we ended up recommending six of the seven cheddars we tried. Cheeses are listed in order of preference.

RECOMMENDED

CABOT Vermont Sharp Cheddar
PRICE: $3.78 for 8 oz ($0.47 per oz)
COLOR: White   PH: 5.4
MOISTURE: 35.8%   AGED FOR: 9 months
COMMENTS: This white cheddar took top honors for its "nutty," "almost smoky" "caramel" notes and "complex" sharpness. Tasters loved its "buttery," "creamy" texture that "completely satisfied comfort food cravings" when it was melted for grilled cheese.

TILLAMOOK Sharp Cheddar Cheese
PRICE: $5.48 for 8 oz ($0.69 per oz)
COLOR: Orange   PH: 5.2
MOISTURE: 34.6%   AGED FOR: 9 months
COMMENTS: This faintly orange cheddar was deemed "bright" and "almost citrusy" for its "zesty" tang and "bold" sharpness. When melted, its "gooey," "buttery" texture earned this cheddar recognition as "a perfect cheese for grilled cheese."

CRACKER BARREL Sharp Cheddar Cheese
PRICE: $3.89 for 8 oz ($0.49 per oz)
COLOR: Orange   PH: 5.2
MOISTURE: 35.2%
AGED FOR: Proprietary
COMMENTS: This popular block cheese was "salty," "acidic," "balanced," and "punchy," with a "quintessential sharp cheddar" flavor that made it "great for snacking." In grilled cheese, tasters found this cheddar "friendly" and "tame."

KRAFT Natural Sharp Cheddar Cheese
PRICE: $4.79 for 8 oz ($0.60 per oz)
COLOR: Orange   PH: 5.2
MOISTURE: 35.2%
AGED FOR: Not disclosed
COMMENTS: "Mild," "bright," and "waxy," this orange cheddar had a "rich," "elegant sharpness" and "smooth" texture that made for "gooey," "melty" grilled cheese. "Tastes like childhood," said one taster, who thought this product's "classic" flavor would be popular with kids.

RECOMMENDED (continued)

KERRYGOLD Aged Cheddar
PRICE: $5 for 7 oz ($0.71 per oz)
COLOR: White   PH: 5.6
MOISTURE: 36.6%
AGED FOR: 12 months
COMMENTS: With a "mild" sharpness, this Irish import earned comparisons with Swiss cheese for its "slightly funky," "tangy" flavor. Its subtle "grassy," "onion" notes added "complexity" to grilled cheese, though a few tasters felt that it had "too many unexpected flavors" for cheddar.

SARGENTO Tastings Aged Wisconsin Cheddar Cheese
PRICE: $2.79 for 3.95 oz ($0.71 per oz)
COLOR: Orange   PH: 5.7
MOISTURE: 35.3%
AGED FOR: 12 months
COMMENTS: This petite orange wedge was "thick" and "chewy," with "toasty" "butterscotch" notes that became "sweet" and "slightly nutty" when the cheese was melted. A few tasters thought that this cheddar had an unusual "tannic," "tart flavor," "like port wine cheese."

RECOMMENDED WITH RESERVATIONS

BOAR'S HEAD Sharp Wisconsin Cheddar Cheese
PRICE: $4.50 for 10 oz ($0.45 per oz)
COLOR: White   PH: 5.2
MOISTURE: 37.1%   AGED FOR: 9 months
COMMENTS: Tasters enjoyed this product's "mild," "creamy" flavor and "smooth" texture for snacking, but a higher moisture content caused this white cheddar to become "bland" and "boring" when melted into grilled cheese. Summarized one taster: "more reminiscent of Monterey Jack than cheddar."

FOOD STORAGE BAGS

Crummy plastic food storage bags leak, rip, and are tricky to seal. We wanted a strong, leakproof bag that would close securely without a fuss and keep food fresher longer. We focused on gallon-size freezer bags. To see how well bags stood up to abuse, we poured ¾ gallon of tomato sauce into each bag, sealed the bags, and pushed them off the counter. Our top bags didn't leak even a dribble. In the abuse tests, all the failures but one happened at the site of the seal. We concluded that while thick plastic helps, strong seals are more important. Products appear below in order of preference.

HIGHLY RECOMMENDED	PERFORMANCE	TESTERS' COMMENTS
ZIPLOC Brand Double Zipper Gallon Freezer Bags with the Smart Zip Seal MODEL: UPC #0-25700-00382-3 PRICE: $3.99 for 30 bags ($0.13 per bag) STYLE: Zipper-lock THICKNESS: 2.4 mil	FREEZER PROTECTION ★★★ DURABILITY ★★★ LEAKPROOF ★★★ EASE OF USE ★★★	Frozen food stayed fresh in this bag even after two months. Its band of thicker plastic extending 2 inches below the zipper provided structure that made for easier filling and offered an extra barrier of protection. Its double zipper helped it remain leakproof and stand up to abuse.
ELKAY PLASTICS Ziplock Heavy Weight Freezer Bag MODEL: UPC #6-54866-01303-4 PRICE: $9.69 for 100 bags ($0.10 per bag), plus shipping STYLE: Zipper-lock THICKNESS: 3.7 mil 	FREEZER PROTECTION ★★★ DURABILITY ★★ LEAKPROOF ★★½ EASE OF USE ★★★	With the thickest plastic in the lineup and a tight seal, this bag provided excellent protection. Frozen cookie dough and pork chops had virtually no ice crystals and were fresh-looking after two months. A side seam split when we dropped this bag (full of tomato sauce), and the bag let in a little moisture when we submerged it.

RECOMMENDED

	PERFORMANCE	TESTERS' COMMENTS
GREEN'N'PACK Food Storage Freezer Gallon Bags MODEL: UPC #8-54347-00303-9 PRICE: $11.90 for 30 bags ($0.40 per bag) STYLE: Zipper-lock THICKNESS: 2.7 mil 	FREEZER PROTECTION ★★½ DURABILITY ★★ LEAKPROOF ★★½ EASE OF USE ★★½	This eco-friendly bag, designed to biodegrade, performed well, though it didn't quite match our top bags. Frozen food stayed in excellent shape for a month but began to show a few signs of ice crystals after two months. Its seal could be a little bigger and stronger.
DIVERSEY, INC. Ziploc Commercial Resealable Gallon Freezer Bags MODEL: 94604 PRICE: $34.99 for 250 bags ($0.14 per bag), plus shipping STYLE: Zipper-lock THICKNESS: 2.5 mil	FREEZER PROTECTION ★★ DURABILITY ★★ LEAKPROOF ★★★ EASE OF USE ★★½	This food-service version of our winner just wasn't as good. Frozen foods stayed in very good condition for the first two weeks but then began showing moderate amounts of ice crystals. While it has dual zippers like our winner, it lacks that bag's collar of thicker plastic, which meant it was not as easy to handle and delivered less freezer protection.
HEFTY Slider Bag, Gallon Freezer MODEL: UPC #0-13700-82413-5 PRICE: $3.29 for 13 bags ($0.25 per bag) STYLE: Slider THICKNESS: 2.5 mil 	FREEZER PROTECTION ★★ DURABILITY ★★★ LEAKPROOF ★★½ EASE OF USE ★★	Frozen food quickly acquired a moderate amount of "snow" around the edges. This bag claims to have "a stronger seal than Ziploc bags when shaken, dropped, or stacked," and it tied our top-ranked Ziploc when dropped and shaken, but its zipper leaked. It was also a bit too floppy.

RECOMMENDED WITH RESERVATIONS

	PERFORMANCE	TESTERS' COMMENTS
ZIPLOC Brand Gallon Freezer Slider Bags MODEL: UPC #0-25700-02313-5 PRICE: $2.49 for 10 bags ($0.25 per bag) STYLE: Slider THICKNESS: 2.8 mil 	FREEZER PROTECTION ★★★ DURABILITY ★ LEAKPROOF ★★ EASE OF USE ★★★	We really liked this bag's gusseted, expandable bottom, and foods stayed in good condition in the freezer. We only wish its sliding seal were stronger: It failed during abuse testing, dripped when full, and let in some moisture when submerged.

NOT RECOMMENDED

	PERFORMANCE	TESTERS' COMMENTS
ZIPLOC Brand Double Guard Double Layer Gallon Freezer Bags MODEL: UPC #0-25700-01261-0 PRICE: $6.37 for 13 bags ($0.49 per bag) STYLE: Zipper-lock THICKNESS: 3.0 mil 	FREEZER PROTECTION ★★ DURABILITY ★ LEAKPROOF ★ EASE OF USE ★	This pricey double-layer bag claims to provide a better barrier against freezer burn; we found it only middling. Floppy and flimsy, this bag was also hard to fill and its weak seal burst during abuse tests. The side seams above the zipper ripped as we filled bags and leaked steadily when filled with liquids.

MIXING BOWLS

They may not be as sexy as chef's knives or *sous vide* circulators, but when it comes to basic cooking tasks, mixing bowls can't be beat. A good bowl should be so steady, durable, and comfortable to handle that it goes almost unnoticed while you work. We find it useful to have small, medium, and large bowls in both stainless steel and glass: The lightness of metal makes it easy to use, but only glass can go in the microwave. In each of the small bowls, we whisked oil into vinegar to make dressing. In the medium and large bowls we mixed up muffin and pancake batters and bread doughs, and used the medium bowls to melt chocolate in a jury-rigged double boiler. Our winning metal and glass bowls both have a rim for gripping and a wide, gently curved basin. Products appear below in order of preference.

Stainless-Steel Bowls

HIGHLY RECOMMENDED | PERFORMANCE | TESTERS' COMMENTS

VOLLRATH Economy Stainless Steel Mixing Bowls
MATERIAL: Stainless steel
SOLD AS: Open stock
SIZES TESTED: 1½ qt ($2.90, model 47932); 3 qt ($4.50, model 47933); 5 qt ($6.90, model 47935)
WEIGHTS: 4⅝ oz (1½ qt); 6⅛ oz (3 qt); 8⅞ oz (5 qt)

PERFORMANCE ★★★
EASE OF USE ★★★
DURABILITY ★★★

The broad, shallow shape of these inexpensive bowls put food within easy reach and allowed for wide turns of a spatula. These were also the lightest bowls in the lineup—the combined weight of all three that we tested was less than 1½ pounds—allowing us to comfortably lift, scrape, and pour.

RECOMMENDED

CUISINART Set of 3 Stainless Steel Mixing Bowls with Lids
MATERIAL: Stainless steel with plastic lids
SOLD AS: Three-bowl set ($29.99, model CTG-00-SMB)
SIZES TESTED: 1½ qt; 3 qt; 5 qt
WEIGHTS: 9¾ oz (1½ qt); 13¾ oz (3 qt); 1 lb, 3⅝ oz (5 qt)

PERFORMANCE ★★★
EASE OF USE ★★
DURABILITY ★★★

Though their relatively tall and narrow build made it a little challenging for shorter testers to access their contents, these bowls were lightweight and sported a generous rim—features that made them easy to grasp and hold while we scraped them clean.

NOT RECOMMENDED

OXO Good Grips Stainless Steel Mixing Bowl Set
MATERIAL: Stainless steel interior, white plastic exterior with nonskid Santoprene base
SOLD AS: Three-bowl set ($59.99, model 1107600V1)
SIZES TESTED: 1½ qt; 3 qt; 5 qt
WEIGHTS: 11½ oz (1½ qt); 1 lb, 3 oz (3 qt); 1 lb, 10¾ oz (5 qt)

PERFORMANCE ★
EASE OF USE ★½
DURABILITY ★★★

Apart from having wide rims, these bowls were not user-friendly—and certainly not worth the high price. Their small, Santoprene-coated bases caused them to spin and almost tip over as we mixed. Plus, the company does not recommend using them in a double boiler, lest the exterior plastic coating come in contact with the pot and overheat.

Glass Bowls

HIGHLY RECOMMENDED

PYREX Smart Essentials Mixing Bowl Set with Colored Lids
MATERIAL: Tempered glass with plastic lids
SOLD AS: Four-bowl set ($13.19, model 1086053)
SIZES TESTED: 1 qt; 2½ qt; 4 qt
WEIGHTS: 1 lb, 3½ oz (1 qt); 2 lb, 4¼ oz (2½ qt); 3 lb, 7⅜ oz (4 qt)

PERFORMANCE ★★★
EASE OF USE ★★★
DURABILITY ★★★

Even though these bowls were heavy, they never felt cumbersome to handle, thanks to their shallow, gently curved walls and easy-to-grip rims. Notably, they did not break when we dropped them. A bonus: Tight-fitting lids kept food well protected.

RECOMMENDED

ARC INTERNATIONAL Luminarc 10 Piece Stackable Bowl Set
MATERIAL: Tempered glass
SOLD AS: Ten-bowl set ($29.75, model E4371)
SIZES TESTED: 1 qt; 3 qt; 4½ qt
WEIGHTS: 15⅛ oz (1 qt); 2 lb, 1⅛ oz (3 qt); 3 lb, ⅜ oz (4½ qt)

PERFORMANCE ★★½
EASE OF USE ★★
DURABILITY ★★★

These shallow, wide bowls were easy to navigate with a whisk or a spatula. They were also one of the lighter glass sets, although they would have been easier to grip if they'd had rims instead of food-trapping collars. They survived the drop tests with minor scratches.

CARBON-STEEL CHEF'S KNIVES

We've always been intrigued by knives made from carbon steel. This alloy is considered superior to stainless steel by many chefs and knife enthusiasts because it is belived to be harder and stronger and able to take on and retain a keener edge. But were skeptical. Carbon steel is a high-maintenance metal that rusts if not kept dry. We singled out eight carbon-steel chef's knives and put them through our standard cutting tests: mincing parsley, dicing onions, quartering squash, and butchering whole raw chickens. Before and after each round of tests, we tested the sharpness of the blades. Our top-ranking knives, which were sharpened to between 10 and 15 degrees, slid through food, while we had to use more force with wider blades and higher scores on the Rockwell scale—a measurement of the metal's strength. Our winner's equal performance to our stainless steel favorite made us suspect that how the metal is manufactured is more important than whether it's carbon or stainless. Products appear below in order of preference.

RECOMMENDED	PERFORMANCE		TESTERS' COMMENTS
BOB KRAMER 8" Carbon Steel Chef's Knife by Zwilling J.A. Henckels PRICE: $299.95 MODEL: 789693 ROCKWELL: 61 HRC BLADE ANGLE: 10° to 15°	CUTTING COMFORT EDGE RETENTION	★★★ ★★★ ★★★	With this knife's "precise" tip and "samurai-sharp," ultrathin blade, whole chickens seemed to butcher themselves. More impressively, it maintained that edge throughout testing. Its ultracomfortable handle was also a gorgeous piece of craftsmanship.
TSUKIJI Masamoto Gyuto, 8¼" PRICE: $258 MODEL: N/A ROCKWELL: 62 to 63 HRC BLADE ANGLE: 12° to 15°	CUTTING COMFORT EDGE RETENTION	★★★ ★★½ ★★★	This "razor-sharp" knife—crafted in a seventh-generation shop at Tokyo's famous Tsukiji Fish Market—sliced through food "like butter." Its handle was smooth and comfortable, though a few testers wished it had a bit more heft.
TOGIHARU Virgin Carbon Steel Gyutou, 8.2" PRICE: $98.50 MODEL: HTO-HCGY ROCKWELL: 62 HRC BLADE ANGLE: 12° to 15°	CUTTING COMFORT EDGE RETENTION	★★½ ★★★ ★★★	An impressive knife for the price, this Japanese model was just as strong and almost as narrow as our winner but felt a shade less sharp. Testers praised its "agile," "precise," and "clean" handling and balanced, medium-size blade.
MISONO Swedish Carbon Steel Gyutou, 8.2" PRICE: $119 MODEL: 112 ROCKWELL: 60 HRC BLADE ANGLE: 12° to 15°	CUTTING COMFORT EDGE RETENTION	★★½ ★★½ ★★★	This "light," "maneuverable" Japanese blade "springs through" food with ease, testers said. Where it fell short was its narrow handle; some testers complained that the grip felt "unsubstantial" compared with that of other knives.
MASAMOTO SOHONTEN Virgin Carbon Steel Gyutou, 8.2" PRICE: $195 MODEL: HMA-VSGY ROCKWELL: 61 to 62 HRC BLADE ANGLE: 12° to 15°	CUTTING COMFORT EDGE RETENTION	★★ ★★★ ★★	Though this knife boasted "solid," "balanced" weight and a comfortable handle with enough girth to grip, the business end—the blade—just wasn't as sharp as those of higher-ranking knives. As a result, testers complained that it made them work harder.

RECOMMENDED WITH RESERVATIONS

MESSERMEISTER Park Plaza Carbon 8" Chef's Knife PRICE: $75 MODEL: 8107-8 ROCKWELL: 57 HRC BLADE ANGLE: 20°	CUTTING COMFORT EDGE RETENTION	★½ ★★★ ★★	The best part of this knife was its smooth, rounded handle. The blade, on the other hand, was not as sharp as others, probably due to its 20-degree edge and lower Rockwell rating, so testers had to use more force when cutting.

NOT RECOMMENDED

R. MURPHY Chef's Select 8" Carbon Steel Chef's Knife PRICE: $90 MODEL: CH8CIIHO ROCKWELL: 58 to 60 HRC BLADE ANGLE: 12° to 15°	CUTTING COMFORT EDGE RETENTION	★½ ★½ ★★★	Despite this blade's strong steel and narrow edge, its bevel was short, making it feel dull; testers reported needing to exert "three times the force" as they did with other knives. Its handle had "boxy," "sharp angles" that caused hand fatigue.
SABATIER Mexeur et Cie 8" Chef PRICE: $72.99 MODEL: 23688 ROCKWELL: 52 to 54 HRC BLADE ANGLE: 20° to 25°	CUTTING COMFORT EDGE RETENTION	★ ★ ★	This knife's low Rockwell rating and wide-angle blade explained why it was the softest and dullest knife we tested. The blade's sharp spine dug into hands, and because it was short (from spine to edge), testers' knuckles hit the cutting board.

CARVING BOARDS

Eight years ago we selected the J.K. Adams Maple Reversible Carving Board as our favorite. But when we noticed some new boards with features like pour spouts, clever liquid channeling designs, and innovative ways to anchor the meat, we decided an update was in order. We knew from our previous testing that we should consider only boards at least 18 inches long—boards rated highest if they were roomy enough for large roasts and steady on the counter. We expect a carving board to trap at least ½ cup of liquid, roughly the amount released by a midsize turkey as it rests. Finally, we rated each board on how easy and comfortable it was to lift, carry, carve on, and clean. We preferred boards that fit in our kitchen sink and didn't develop deep or unsightly knife marks. Products appear below in order of preference.

HIGHLY RECOMMENDED	PERFORMANCE	TESTERS' COMMENTS

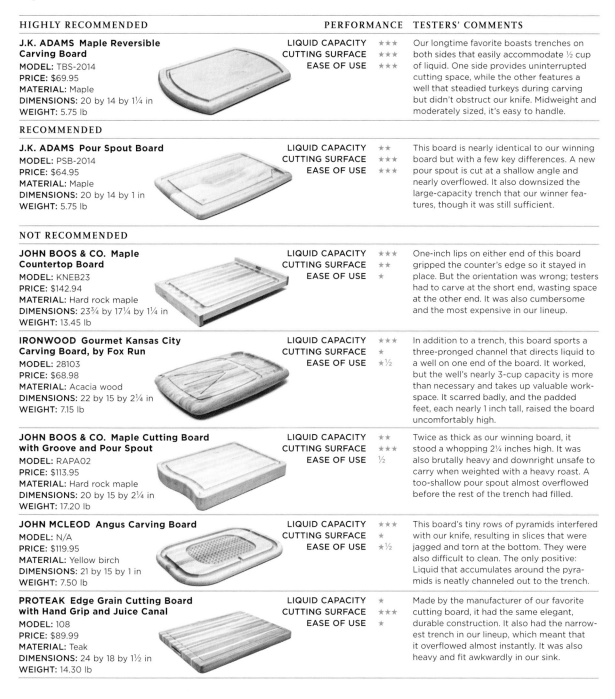

J.K. ADAMS Maple Reversible Carving Board
MODEL: TBS-2014
PRICE: $69.95
MATERIAL: Maple
DIMENSIONS: 20 by 14 by 1¼ in
WEIGHT: 5.75 lb

LIQUID CAPACITY ★★★
CUTTING SURFACE ★★★
EASE OF USE ★★★

Our longtime favorite boasts trenches on both sides that easily accommodate ½ cup of liquid. One side provides uninterrupted cutting space, while the other features a well that steadied turkeys during carving but didn't obstruct our knife. Midweight and moderately sized, it's easy to handle.

RECOMMENDED

J.K. ADAMS Pour Spout Board
MODEL: PSB-2014
PRICE: $64.95
MATERIAL: Maple
DIMENSIONS: 20 by 14 by 1 in
WEIGHT: 5.75 lb

LIQUID CAPACITY ★★
CUTTING SURFACE ★★★
EASE OF USE ★★★

This board is nearly identical to our winning board but with a few key differences. A new pour spout is cut at a shallow angle and nearly overflowed. It also downsized the large-capacity trench that our winner features, though it was still sufficient.

NOT RECOMMENDED

JOHN BOOS & CO. Maple Countertop Board
MODEL: KNEB23
PRICE: $142.94
MATERIAL: Hard rock maple
DIMENSIONS: 23¾ by 17¼ by 1¼ in
WEIGHT: 13.45 lb

LIQUID CAPACITY ★★★
CUTTING SURFACE ★★
EASE OF USE ★

One-inch lips on either end of this board gripped the counter's edge so it stayed in place. But the orientation was wrong; testers had to carve at the short end, wasting space at the other end. It was also cumbersome and the most expensive in our lineup.

IRONWOOD Gourmet Kansas City Carving Board, by Fox Run
MODEL: 28103
PRICE: $68.98
MATERIAL: Acacia wood
DIMENSIONS: 22 by 15 by 2¼ in
WEIGHT: 7.15 lb

LIQUID CAPACITY ★★★
CUTTING SURFACE ★
EASE OF USE ★½

In addition to a trench, this board sports a three-pronged channel that directs liquid to a well on one end of the board. It worked, but the well's nearly 3-cup capacity is more than necessary and takes up valuable workspace. It scarred badly, and the padded feet, each nearly 1 inch tall, raised the board uncomfortably high.

JOHN BOOS & CO. Maple Cutting Board with Groove and Pour Spout
MODEL: RAPA02
PRICE: $113.95
MATERIAL: Hard rock maple
DIMENSIONS: 20 by 15 by 2¼ in
WEIGHT: 17.20 lb

LIQUID CAPACITY ★★
CUTTING SURFACE ★★★
EASE OF USE ½

Twice as thick as our winning board, it stood a whopping 2¼ inches high. It was also brutally heavy and downright unsafe to carry when weighted with a heavy roast. A too-shallow pour spout almost overflowed before the rest of the trench had filled.

JOHN MCLEOD Angus Carving Board
MODEL: N/A
PRICE: $119.95
MATERIAL: Yellow birch
DIMENSIONS: 21 by 15 by 1 in
WEIGHT: 7.50 lb

LIQUID CAPACITY ★★★
CUTTING SURFACE ★
EASE OF USE ★½

This board's tiny rows of pyramids interfered with our knife, resulting in slices that were jagged and torn at the bottom. They were also difficult to clean. The only positive: Liquid that accumulates around the pyramids is neatly channeled out to the trench.

PROTEAK Edge Grain Cutting Board with Hand Grip and Juice Canal
MODEL: 108
PRICE: $89.99
MATERIAL: Teak
DIMENSIONS: 24 by 18 by 1½ in
WEIGHT: 14.30 lb

LIQUID CAPACITY ★
CUTTING SURFACE ★★★
EASE OF USE ★

Made by the manufacturer of our favorite cutting board, it had the same elegant, durable construction. It also had the narrowest trench in our lineup, which meant that it overflowed almost instantly. It was also heavy and fit awkwardly in our sink.

LAUNDRY STAIN REMOVERS

Stain removers all guarantee spotless results. But when it comes to removing stubborn food stains, almost none of them work. We tested seven laundry stain removers to find a reliable weapon against cooking-related stains. We used white cotton T-shirts and yards of blue cotton fabric and stained them with the toughest food stains we could find: melted dark chocolate, bacon grease, yellow mustard, black tea, a puree of chipotle chiles in adobo sauce, and pureed blueberries. We applied the stain removers and washed the clothing in separate wash loads. Even when treating the maximum amount of time recommended, most of the fabric was still stained. The notable exception was our winner, which was the only product to require a pre-soak. Products appear below in order of preference.

HIGHLY RECOMMENDED	PERFORMANCE		TESTERS' COMMENTS

OXICLEAN Versatile Stain Remover

PRICE: $8.59 for 3-lb tub
METHOD: Dissolve powder in water, soak garment for 1 to 6 hours, launder
CLEANING AGENTS: Sodium percarbonate (oxygen-based bleach), surfactants

FRESH STAINS	★★½
LAUNDERED STAINS	★★★
OLD STAINS	★★½
EASE OF USE	★★½

Though it required more time to dissolve this powder in water and presoak stained clothes for hours, the stellar results made it worthwhile. Only a ghost of adobo sauce remained on the shirt when we left stains untouched for 72 hours before treating, but even that virtually disappeared with another treatment.

RECOMMENDED WITH RESERVATIONS

TIDE Ultra Stain Release

PRICE: $5.85 for 25-oz bottle
METHOD: Pour on, scrub with cap, launder
CLEANING AGENTS: Surfactants, four enzymes, fabric brightener

FRESH STAINS	★★
LAUNDERED STAINS	★★
OLD STAINS	★
EASE OF USE	★★★

The nubbly Zap! Cap, designed to rub the product onto the garment, was easy to use and did help this stain remover penetrate. It did a better job at removing more stains than most of the rest of the lineup and left fabrics looking brighter. That said, it wasn't effective on chocolate or mustard, and on stains that sat for 72 hours before treating, it left all but the grease stain clearly visible on our T-shirt.

NOT RECOMMENDED

RESOLVE Spray & Wash Laundry Stain Remover

PRICE: $3.79 for 22-oz spray
METHOD: Spray, wait 5 minutes maximum, rub into stain, launder
CLEANING AGENTS: Surfactant, solvent, one enzyme

FRESH STAINS	★½
LAUNDERED STAINS	★½
OLD STAINS	★
EASE OF USE	★★½

This poorly focused spray is hard to keep off surrounding surfaces, and it instructs the user never to leave it on fabric for longer than 5 minutes or risk permanent damage (the label even warns that it could damage plastic and paint). It did remove bacon grease, but too many other spots were still clearly visible.

ZOUT Laundry Stain Remover

PRICE: $4.45 for 22-oz spray
METHOD: Spray, rub in, wait 1 to 5 minutes, launder
CLEANING AGENTS: Surfactant, three enzymes

FRESH STAINS	★
LAUNDERED STAINS	★½
OLD STAINS	★
EASE OF USE	★★★

Spraying on this "action foam" felt satisfying because it bubbled up, making it look like it was working right away. But the results were a huge letdown: The only stain it removed was grease (though it faded chocolate stains significantly, an especially tough stain for other products).

SHOUT Trigger Triple-Acting Formula

PRICE: $3.59 for 22-oz spray
METHOD: Spray, rub in, wait 1 to 5 minutes, launder
CLEANING AGENTS: Surfactant, one enzyme

FRESH STAINS	★
LAUNDERED STAINS	★
OLD STAINS	★
EASE OF USE	★★★

This spray was especially easy to pump, with good coverage where we wanted it. But the good news stopped there. While it lightened most stains, it removed only fresh grease stains.

CLOROX 2 Stain Remover & Color Booster Liquid

PRICE: $7.19 for 33-oz bottle
METHOD: Pour on, rub in gently, wait 5 to 10 minutes, launder (suggests adding capful to wash)
CLEANING AGENTS: Hydrogen peroxide, surfactant, fabric brightener

FRESH STAINS	★
LAUNDERED STAINS	★
OLD STAINS	★
EASE OF USE	★★

The only stain this product completely removed was grease; it especially failed on bright orange chipotles in adobo sauce. Leftover stains lightened up slightly when treated a second time but were still clearly present. It was also hard to control how much product poured out of the wide opening onto the stain.

RESOLVE Max Power Gel with Scrubnubs

PRICE: $3.49 for 6.7-oz bottle
METHOD: Squeeze onto stains, scrub with top of bottle, wait 1 to 5 minutes, wash
CLEANING AGENTS: Surfactant, solvent, three enzymes

FRESH STAINS	½
LAUNDERED STAINS	★
OLD STAINS	★
EASE OF USE	★

This "power gel" made stains worse, creating one giant blot. And it was a pain to use: The scrubnubs, which surround a hole that dispenses the gel, scooped up food residue and redeposited it on the clothes as we scrubbed. (We tried to rinse food out of the hole, but this was difficult.)

CAST IRON SKILLETS

Cheap and tough, a cast-iron skillet is a kitchen workhorse, but the upkeep makes some cooks balk. Could enameled cast-iron pans, which need no special care, top the classic? We gathered both traditional and enameled pans and began our tests. We first seared steaks and made an acidic sauce, looking for good crust and flavor without off-notes. We tested browning and sticking with skillet-roasted fish fillets, shallow-fried breaded chicken cutlets, and cornbread. Durability is important, so we heated pans to 400 degrees and then plunged them into ice water, made cuts inside, scraped with a metal spatula, and whacked a metal spoon on the rims and sides of pans. In the final analysis, neither traditional nor enamel pans was "best." The choice between them is up to you. Pans appear in order of preference. Oven-safe temperature ratings are from manufacturers.

Traditional Cast Iron

HIGHLY RECOMMENDED

	PERFORMANCE	TESTERS' COMMENTS

LODGE Classic Cast Iron Skillet, 12"
MODEL: L10SK3
PRICE: $33.31
WEIGHT: 7 lb, 10⅛ oz
COOKING SURFACE: 10 in
OVENSAFE TO: At least 1,000°

BROWNING ★★★
STICKING ★★★
EASE OF USE ★★★
DURABILITY ★★★

Our old winner arrived with the slickest preseasoned interior, and it only got better. It browned foods deeply, and its thorough seasoning ensured that our acidic pan sauce picked up no off-flavors. Though its handle is short, the pan has a helper handle that made lifting easy. It survived abuse testing without a scratch.

CALPHALON 12-in. Pre-Seasoned Cast Iron Skillet
MODEL: 1873975
PRICE: $34.95
WEIGHT: 6 lb, 12 oz
COOKING SURFACE: 10¼ in
OVENSAFE TO: "Well above broiler level"

BROWNING ★★★
STICKING ★★½
EASE OF USE ★★★
DURABILITY ★★★

Even browning made this pan stand out; we also liked the unusual helper handle and curved sides, which added to its cooking area. However, its pebbly surface stuck to food a bit more than our smoother top-rated pan and took a little more effort to scrub clean.

RECOMMENDED

CAMP CHEF 12" Seasoned Cast Iron Skillet
MODEL: SK12
PRICE: $21.99
WEIGHT: 7 lb, ¾ oz
COOKING SURFACE: 9¾ in
OVENSAFE TO: 600°

BROWNING ★★★
STICKING ★★
EASE OF USE ★★½
DURABILITY ★★★

This inexpensive choice browned steak, chicken, and cornbread beautifully and made a pan sauce with no off-flavors. Nevertheless, its preseasoning seemed thin, looking patchy after washing; fish and eggs stuck at first, but the pan acquired good seasoning in time and endured abuse well.

Enameled Cast Iron

HIGHLY RECOMMENDED

	PERFORMANCE	TESTERS' COMMENTS

LE CREUSET Signature 11¾" Iron Handle Skillet
MODEL: LS2024-30
PRICE: $179.95
WEIGHT: 6 lb, 8⅝ oz
COOKING SURFACE: 10 in
OVENSAFE TO: No maximum set by company

BROWNING ★★★
STICKING ★★½
EASE OF USE ★★★
DURABILITY ★★★

With flaring sides, an oversize helper handle, wide pour spouts, a satiny interior, and balanced weight, this expensive but beautifully made pan is a pleasure to cook in. Our only quibbles: A small piece of cornbread stuck, and scrambled eggs stuck a little (but scrubbed out easily). After abuse testing, the pan still looked nearly new.

RECOMMENDED

MARIO BATALI by Dansk 12" Open Sauté Pan
MODEL: 826782
(cobalt color)
PRICE: $59.95
WEIGHT: 8 lb, 10½ oz
COOKING SURFACE: 10¼ in
OVENSAFE TO: 475°

BROWNING ★★★
STICKING ★★★
EASE OF USE ★★½
DURABILITY ★★

This pan felt well-balanced, and its ample size and great heat capacity rendered deep browning on every food we cooked. Its surface resisted sticking, releasing cornbread perfectly. It's a bit less durable than others: Half-inch areas of enamel chipped off both of the handles' tips, and the pan bottom looked blotchy.

LODGE Enamel Coated Cast Iron Skillet, 11"
MODEL: EC11S43
PRICE: $48.90
WEIGHT: 6 lb, 13⅜ oz
COOKING SURFACE: 9¼ in
OVENSAFE TO: 400°

BROWNING ★★★
STICKING ★★½
EASE OF USE ★★½
DURABILITY ★★

The long handle on this small pan made it comfortable to lift, and its curved sides were easy to swipe with a spatula. It released cornbread perfectly but performed slightly less well with fish and eggs. Foods browned evenly. But two big steaks barely fit and steamed rather than seared. Good for small households.

VACUUM SEALERS

Vacuum sealers are great for storing food, but in the past their cost and size made them impractical for most home cooks. Fortunately, a new wave of sealers offers less expensive options, so we set ourselves a price cap of $200 and bought seven models to test. Eventually, a pattern emerged. Sealers come in two basic styles—heat seal or valve seal—and the latter lost their seals faster. Another important factor was the vacuum strength, which is measured in inches of mercury (inHg); a higher number means a stronger suction. Also important: a manual pulse. Manual mode allows control over the vacuum, so you can stop it before it crunches your food. Our winning sealer had a responsive pulse mode, a large motor, and a powerful vacuum. It kept frozen food looking fresh and pantry items crisp for three months and counting. Products appear below in order of preference.

HIGHLY RECOMMENDED	PERFORMANCE	TESTERS' COMMENTS

WESTON Professional Advantage Vacuum Sealer
MODEL: 65-0501-W
PRICE: $189.99
VACUUM STRENGTH: 23 inHg
STYLE: Heat

PERFORMANCE ★★★
EASE OF USE ★★★

This compact, powerful heat-sealing model kept food fresh for three months and counting. Its intuitive interface has a responsive pulse mode and bright blue lights that indicate its progress. It works with a wide variety of bags, canisters, and rolls that were the cheapest of any sealer in our lineup.

RECOMMENDED

WARING PRO Pistol Vac Professional Vacuum Sealer System BEST BUY
MODEL: PVS1000
PRICE: $69.95
VACUUM STRENGTH: 18 inHg
STYLE: Valve

PERFORMANCE ★★½
EASE OF USE ★★★

This compact handheld model was the only valve sealer we liked. The key to its success is a 2-inch plastic clamp that you run over the zipper to make sure it's closed. Most of its food looked great at three months, and while you have to charge the sealer, you don't have to rest 15 seconds between seals as you do with heat sealers.

RECOMMENDED WITH RESERVATIONS

FOODSAVER 2-in-1 Vacuum Sealer System
MODEL: V4865
PRICE: $199
VACUUM STRENGTH: Proprietary
STYLE: Heat

PERFORMANCE ★★
EASE OF USE ★★½

This heat sealer has two unique features: first, a sensor that automatically grabs, vacuums, and seals bags and, second, a roll storage compartment with a built-in plastic slicer that tidily cuts bags to size. Both are handy, but we found this sealer to be bulky, and some of its seals had loosened by month three.

FOODSAVER Vacuum Sealing System
MODEL: V2244
PRICE: $79.99
VACUUM STRENGTH: Proprietary
STYLE: Heat

PERFORMANCE ★★½
EASE OF USE ★★

This entry-level heat sealer is light, small, and quiet and, more important, held its own against pricier models, keeping food freezer-burn-free for three months and counting. While we didn't have any issues, the light plastic frame had us concerned about its durability.

SEAL-A-MEAL Vacuum Food Sealer
MODEL: FSSMSL0160-000
PRICE: $49.99
VACUUM STRENGTH: 11 inHg
STYLE: Heat

PERFORMANCE ★★
EASE OF USE ★½

This small, basic heat sealer is the only model you still have to press on while it initiates the seal, but it's a gentle push. It has no manual pulse mode, so it crunched pretzels and cereal into crumbs. That said, it kept frozen food ice-free just as long as models that cost four times its price, three months and counting.

NOT RECOMMENDED

OLISO Frisper PRO-1000 Vacuum Sealer Starter Kit
MODEL: PRO-1000
PRICE: $179.99
VACUUM STRENGTH: 18 inHg
STYLE: Heat

PERFORMANCE ★½
EASE OF USE ★

This heat sealer punctures a small hole in its zippered bags to extract the air and then seals off a circle around the pin prick–size vent. Its zippers were thick and hard to close, and only half of its frozen food looked good at three months. The pantry items were stale. The company makes a plastic clamp to help close the bags, but it's sold separately; at this price, it should be standard.

SOUSVIDE Supreme Zip Sealer
MODEL: VS0500
PRICE: $74.99
VACUUM STRENGTH: 17 inHg
STYLE: Valve

PERFORMANCE ½
EASE OF USE ★

The size of a computer mouse, this valve sealer was easy to use but it was near impossible to tell if its bags were sealed. Testers fiddled with the zippers until they were certain they were closed, only to find the bags drawing air when they vacuumed them. After two weeks food was stale or covered in frost.

SLOW COOKERS

Today's slow cookers come in a wide array of sizes with lots of different features. We wondered whether the new generation of slow cookers, many with jazzy new features promising easier, better food, could really deliver. To find out which models performed best and which features really mattered, we chose seven slow cookers, all digital, 6 to 6½ quarts. We used these models to prepare finicky pasta, meaty chili, and delicate boneless, skinless chicken breasts. None of the new technology impressed us, but we did find a model that improved slow cooking at its core, with more even cooking and a few perks like satisfyingly clickable buttons, brighter lights, helpful beeps, and cool-to-the-touch handles. Products appear below in order of preference.

HIGHLY RECOMMENDED		PERFORMANCE	TESTERS' COMMENTS
KITCHENAID 6-Quart Slow Cooker with Solid Glass Lid MODEL: KSC6223SS PRICE: $99.99 CAPACITY: 6 qt SPECIAL FEATURES: N/A		COOKING ★★★ DESIGN ★★★	This model made juicy and tender chicken, turkey, pork, and chili, and caramelized onions were evenly cooked. Testers liked its bright, intuitive control panel, with tactile buttons and beeps that alert you to changes. Cool-to-the-touch handles were a bonus.
RECOMMENDED			
CROCK-POT Countdown Touchscreen Digital Slow Cooker MODEL: SCVT650-PS PRICE: $89.99 CAPACITY: 6½ qt SPECIAL FEATURES: Touch screen control panel		COOKING ★★½ DESIGN ★★★	Our previous winner performed admirably again with an easily understood and attractive control panel. It made food well, but it runs slightly hot; in a runoff against our new winner, it scorched caramelized onions and made acceptable, but drier, chicken breasts.
RECOMMENDED WITH RESERVATIONS			
HAMILTON BEACH Set 'n Forget 6 Qt. Programmable Slow Cooker with Spoon/Lid MODEL: 33967 PRICE: $59.99 CAPACITY: 6 qt SPECIAL FEATURES: Programmable thermometer		COOKING ★★½ DESIGN ★★	This model's thermometer sticks through the lid and into meat. Once the meat reaches a safe temperature, the cooker switches to warming mode. But because it checks the temperature in only one spot and slow cookers often cook unevenly, it frequently shut off before the meat was fully cooked. It had a nice control panel and cooked well without the probe.
CROCK-POT Digital Slow Cooker with iStir Stirring System MODEL: SCCPVC600AS-P PRICE: $69.99 CAPACITY: 6 qt SPECIAL FEATURES: Stirring mechanism		COOKING ★★ DESIGN ★★	This cooker has a removable stirring system that made rich chili but didn't prevent scorching in a thick pasta dish because it stirs food in only the middle, not at the edges near the heat. It was hard to tell whether the machine was on if we weren't using the brightly lit timer.
CROCK-POT Slow Cooker featuring Smart Cook Technology MODEL: SCCPVM650-PS PRICE: $99.99 CAPACITY: 6½ qt SPECIAL FEATURES: Lengthens or shortens recipe cooking time		COOKING ★½ DESIGN ★★	This slow cooker had a user-friendly control panel and was the more intuitive of the two time-altering machines, but we still had mixed results. Ribs that we stretched the cooking time for were so tender that they limply fell apart. When we set the time and temperature, this cooker ran slightly hot and testers noted minor scorching.
HAMILTON BEACH IntelliTime 6 Quart Slow Cooker MODEL: 33564 PRICE: $59.99 CAPACITY: 6 qt SPECIAL FEATURES: Lengthens or shortens recipe cooking time		COOKING ★★ DESIGN ★½	This slow cooker's controls are on one round dial that you spin to set, which testers found counterintuitive because you had to flip through it like a Rolodex searching for the right setting. It cooked food well when we set the time and temperature, but the IntelliTime settings were hit or miss.
NOT RECOMMENDED			
WEST BEND Versatility Cooker MODEL: 84966 PRICE: $79.99 CAPACITY: 6 qt SPECIAL FEATURES: Removable crock, works in oven and on stovetop; griddle/warming tray base		COOKING ★ DESIGN ★½	This slow cooker's crock is a metal pot that is stove- and ovensafe; its heating base doubles as a griddle and warming tray (though it's too small to do much good). Versatile but unsuccessful, it consistently scorched its contents thanks to a paper-thin pot and a piping-hot heating element.

HANDHELD ELECTRIC MIXERS

While we use stand mixers for heavy- duty tasks like kneading bread, a good handheld mixer helps if you don't want to lug out the stand mixer every time you need to whip ½ cup of cream. We chose a lineup of seven mixers with a range of speeds. We ran them through a series of tests that covered light, medium, and heavy mixing tasks: We timed how long it took them to whip heavy cream and to cream softened butter and sugar. We incorporated flour, oats, and raisins into the creamed mixture to make heavy oatmeal cookie dough. So what makes a great basic hand-held mixer? Testing confirmed our strong preference for open beaters, light mixers, and user-friendly speed settings. Our winner was comfortable to use, with five logical, calibrated speeds that covered all our recipe needs. Products appear below in order of preference.

	PERFORMANCE	TESTERS' COMMENTS

HIGHLY RECOMMENDED

KITCHENAID 5-Speed Ultra Power Hand Mixer
MODEL: KHM512
PRICE: $69.99
SPEEDS: 5
WEIGHT: 1 lb, 15½ oz

DESIGN ★★★
HEAVY MIXING ★★★
MODERATE MIXING ★★★
LIGHT WHIPPING ★★★

This felt like the sports car of the group: light, maneuverable, and efficient. Its five speeds were powerful and well calibrated, nicely covering the range called for in recipes.

RECOMMENDED

CUISINART PowerSelect 3-Speed Hand Mixer
MODEL: CHM-3
PRICE: $26.77
SPEEDS: 3
WEIGHT: 2 lb, 2 oz

DESIGN ★★
HEAVY MIXING ★★★
MODERATE MIXING ★★★
LIGHT WHIPPING ★★★

Comfortable to hold and plenty power-ful, this unit had three fast speeds. It made quick work of all the tests but doesn't have medium-low or medium-high settings; a good simple mixer for basic tasks like whipping cream.

CUISINART Power Advantage 7-Speed Hand Mixer
MODEL: HM-70
PRICE: $59.00
SPEEDS: 7
WEIGHT: 2 lb, 6 oz

DESIGN ★★
HEAVY MIXING ★★★
MODERATE MIXING ★★
LIGHT WHIPPING ★★★

This unit was powerful, with well-calibrated speeds that covered all the bases with a few to spare. Our previous winner, this mixer was edged out of the top spot in favor of lighter, more pared-down models.

BODUM Bistro Electric Hand Mixer
MODEL: 11532
PRICE: $72.00
SPEEDS: 5
WEIGHT: 2 lb, 1⅛ oz

DESIGN ★
HEAVY MIXING ★★★
MODERATE MIXING ★★★
LIGHT WHIPPING ★★★

This mixer started fast, causing a light flour spray; otherwise, its power levels were sufficient. The power cord faces downward from the mixer's body, which causes it to catch on the edge of the bowl and collect food while you work.

RECOMMENDED WITH RESERVATIONS

KITCHENAID 9-Speed Hand Mixer
MODEL: KHM926
PRICE: $99.99
SPEEDS: 9
WEIGHT: 2 lb, 2¼ oz

DESIGN ★★★
HEAVY MIXING ★★
MODERATE MIXING ★★
LIGHT WHIPPING ★★

This machine felt light and balanced and the digital controls responded quickly. Testers found themselves wanting a bit more oomph; we had to scroll through too many similar middle speeds to get enough power.

NOT RECOMMENDED

BREVILLE Handy Mix Digital
MODEL: BHM500X
PRICE: $79.95
SPEEDS: 16
WEIGHT: 2 lb, 4 oz

DESIGN ★
HEAVY MIXING ★½
MODERATE MIXING ★★★
LIGHT WHIPPING ★★★

This model's 16 speeds were unnecessary and often redundant. Its center-posted beaters clogged with dough, its digital controls were slow, and its power boost button was easily hit by mistake. The timer was hard to see.

HAMILTON BEACH SoftScrape 6 Speed Mixer with Case
MODEL: 62637
PRICE: $32.20
SPEEDS: 6
WEIGHT: 2 lb, 11½ oz

DESIGN ★
HEAVY MIXING ★★★
MODERATE MIXING ★★★
LIGHT WHIPPING ★

This mixer was very beater-heavy, which caused testers to move their hands closer to the front of the mixer to main-tain balance. That, in turn, accidentally engaged the power boost button. The self-scraping beaters produced no benefit and, in fact, caused excessive whipped cream splatter.

NONSTICK SPRAY

Recently, manufacturers have tried to address consumer concerns about health and environmental safety by creating nonstick cooking sprays that omit the chemicals (antifoaming agents and propellants) used to force oil out of the can. We tested four top-selling traditional aerosol sprays and three new, innovative sprays. The innovative products make a "cleaner" aerosol either by switching the propellant to a naturally occurring gas or using a system in which the gas and oil never mix in the can. Throughout the testing we compared each product to plain canola oil sprayed from our winning refillable oil mister. Plain canola oil doesn't contain lecithin, which is an addition that helps oil adhere evenly to a pan's surface. Products with lecithin released foods more readily, but there's a tradeoff—lecithin causes oil to darken at a lower temperature, which can impart off flavors. Our winning spray contains palm oil, which counteracts this by discouraging unwanted browning. It also contains chemical antifoaming agents and propellants; currently none of the innovative products can outperform the traditional aerosol spray. Products appear below in order of preference.

RECOMMENDED

	PERFORMANCE		TESTERS' COMMENTS
PAM Original No-Stick Spray PRICE: $2.99 for 6 oz ($0.50 per oz) INGREDIENTS: Canola oil, palm oil, coconut oil, lecithin from soybeans (nonstick agent), dimethyl silicone (for antifoaming), rosemary extract (preservative), propellant	TASTE SPRAYING NONSTICK BROWNING	★★½ ★★★ ★★★ ★★	This best-selling brand corners the market on cooking spray and for good reason: This product sprayed in a fine, broad mist without pooling or foaming and effortlessly released eggs, chicken, waffles, and cakes. In addition to canola oil, PAM Original also contains palm oil—a highly saturated oil—which makes this spray less prone to unwanted browning and funky flavors.
WINONA Pure 100% Canola Oil PRICE: $4.65 for 5 oz ($0.93 per oz) INGREDIENTS: Canola oil	TASTE SPRAYING NONSTICK BROWNING	★★★ ★½ ★★ ★★★	This innovative product combines the purity of an oil mister with the convenience of a supermarket spray. It performed identically to plain canola oil, maintaining its clear color and neutral flavor well past 400 degrees. The absence of lecithin makes this spray slightly less effective.
CRISCO Original No-Stick Cooking Spray PRICE: $3.53 for 6 oz ($0.59 per oz) INGREDIENTS: Canola oil, soy lecithin, dimethyl silicone (for antifoaming), propellant	TASTE SPRAYING NONSTICK BROWNING	★★ ★★★ ★★★ ★½	This spray breezed through all our tests, and its broad mist adhered well to the crevices of waffle irons and Bundt pans. Our one gripe: its low browning point, which changed its normally "neutral" taste from "slightly buttery" to "burnt popcorn" when cooking at temperatures higher than 400 degrees.
SMART BALANCE Non-Stick Cooking Spray, Original PRICE: $3.19 for 6 oz ($0.53 per oz) INGREDIENTS: Vegetable oil blend (canola, soy, and olive oils), soy lecithin, grain alcohol (preservative), dimethyl-polysiloxane, and propellant	TASTE SPRAYING NONSTICK BROWNING	★★ ★½ ★★★ ★½	This product was perfectly adept at preventing sticking but sprayed quickly and directly, making it hard to control the amount of oil on the pan. It does contain an antifoaming agent, so this is likely the result of a bad nozzle. When sampled plain, this spray tasted "neutral," but it took on a "spoiled margarine" flavor when heated until smoking.
MAZOLA Original Cooking Spray PRICE: $4.41 for 5 oz ($0.88 per oz) INGREDIENTS: Canola oil, soy lecithin, dimethylpolysiloxane, propellant	TASTE SPRAYING NONSTICK BROWNING	★★ ★½ ★★★ ★½	While this product had a superfine mist that evenly coated pans and efficiently released sticky foods, it required constant shaking to form a steady stream and stopped spraying with plenty of oil left in the can. Still, it didn't bog down food with grease, and tasters liked its "clean" flavor.

NOT RECOMMENDED

	PERFORMANCE		TESTERS' COMMENTS
PAM Organic Canola Oil PRICE: $4.39 for 5 oz ($0.88 per oz) INGREDIENTS: Organic canola oil, organic grain alcohol (added for clarity), organic lecithin from soybeans (prevents sticking), propellant	TASTE SPRAYING NONSTICK BROWNING	★ ★ ★★★ ★	This spray was less appealing than its nonorganic counterpart, taking on an unappetizing dark brown color 100 degrees before its smoke point (because it lacks an antifoaming agent) and making waffles and cakes greasy from excessive oil pooling. Tasters didn't like the flavor either, calling it "chemical" and "sour."
SPECTRUM NATURALS Canola Spray Oil PRICE: $8.09 for 16 oz ($0.51 per oz) INGREDIENTS: Mechanically (expeller) pressed canola oil, soy lecithin, propellant	TASTE SPRAYING NONSTICK BROWNING	★ ★ ★★★ ★	With no antifoaming agent, this spray coated the pan in thick, unappealing froth and turned black when heated to 400 degrees. While perfectly adept at preventing sticking, this product had a "fishy" flavor and charred color when heated that were intolerable to most testers.

CAN OPENERS

Our past winning can openers have been discontinued or redesigned, so we decided to take a fresh look. We included both safety and traditional models in our lineup of seven openers. Our goal: to find one that attached and detached easily, was comfortable to operate, and dealt safely and easily with the severed lid. We opened hundreds of cans: squat cans of tuna, small cans of tomato paste, medium cans of chickpeas, and large cans of whole tomatoes. We evaluated each model during every step. All traditional openers attached the same way—their two straight arms opened and clamped the gears onto the can. As for safety openers, we prefer side-style openers—blades were visible for easy alignment, and a thin metal railing propped the opener at the correct height. We preferred straight, oval handles and longer driving handles for better leverage and easier turning, with ergonomic grooves. Finally, we evaluated detaching, safety, and lid disposal. Products appear below in order of preference.

HIGHLY RECOMMENDED

	PERFORMANCE		TESTERS' COMMENTS
FISSLER Magic Smooth-Edge Can Opener MODEL: FIS7570 PRICE: $29 STYLE: Safety DISHWASHER-SAFE: Yes LID DISPOSAL: Automatic	ATTACHING EASE OF OPERATION LID DISPOSAL	★★★ ★★★ ★★★	Sleek, smart, and comfortable, this opener's visible gears were easy to attach. The straight, textured handle fit comfortably and securely in hand, and the ergonomic driving handle was longer for better leverage and easier turning. It pulled off the lid when it was finished for safe and easy disposal.

RECOMMENDED WITH RESERVATIONS

	PERFORMANCE		TESTERS' COMMENTS
ZYLISS Lock 'N Lift Can Opener MODEL: 20362 PRICE: $15.99 STYLE: Traditional DISHWASHER-SAFE: No LID DISPOSAL: Magnet	ATTACHING EASE OF OPERATION LID DISPOSAL	★★★ ★★★ ★	This opener attached readily with an obvious click and turned easily, with grippy plastic handles. While it did have a lid-lifting magnet, it was often too strong to readily release the lid; also, it was located on the front, so testers had to dip the head of the opener into the can's contents to retrieve the lid.
J.A. HENCKELS Twin Pure Can Opener MODEL: 12914-000 PRICE: $19.99 STYLE: Safety DISHWASHER-SAFE: Yes LID DISPOSAL: Automatic	ATTACHING EASE OF OPERATION LID DISPOSAL	★★★ ★ ★★★	This opener had an intuitive and visible attaching mechanism and seamless lid disposal, just like our winner. But it was heavier, with uncomfortable handles that were round, short, and without any ergonomic grooves, which made it physically much harder to turn.

NOT RECOMMENDED

	PERFORMANCE		TESTERS' COMMENTS
KUHN RIKON Auto Safety Master Opener MODEL: 2266 (black) PRICE: $18 STYLE: Safety DISHWASHER-SAFE: No LID DISPOSAL: Pincers	ATTACHING EASE OF OPERATION LID DISPOSAL	★★ ★★ ★	This opener was hard to attach because its head blocked its gears. It had pincers for lid disposal, but they were finicky. Designed to be a five-purpose opener—cans, jars, tabs, and two kinds of bottle caps, its other uses hindered basic can opening—namely the large spike at the end of the handle for opening tabs that poked testers in the belly with each rotation.
SAVORA Can Opener MODEL: 5099588 (crimson) PRICE: $19.03 STYLE: Traditional DISHWASHER-SAFE: No LID DISPOSAL: None	ATTACHING EASE OF OPERATION LID DISPOSAL	★ ★★★ ★	This opener was easy to turn, but its smooth, hard, plastic handles were slippery to use with damp hands. Thanks to a stiff latch, it was also hard to clip on and off. It doesn't have a lid disposal device, and while the company said that it was dishwasher-safe, ours rusted in the machine overnight.
OXO Smooth Edge Can Opener MODEL: 1049953V1 PRICE: $21.99 STYLE: Safety DISHWASHER-SAFE: No LID DISPOSAL: Pincers	ATTACHING EASE OF OPERATION LID DISPOSAL	★ ★★ ★	This opener had grippy handles but also a bulky head that blocked our view and made it hard to latch onto the can. It was difficult to tell when the lid was severed, and you have to use the pincers on the side of the opener to pry off the lid, an annoying additional step worsened by the bulky head's blocking our view of the tiny pincers.
CHEF'N EZ Squeeze Can Opener MODEL: 102-150-001 PRICE: $15.88 STYLE: Traditional DISHWASHER-SAFE: No LID DISPOSAL: Magnet	ATTACHING EASE OF OPERATION LID DISPOSAL	★ ★ ★	There was nothing "EZ" about this can opener. Intended to be operated using just one hand, it was hard even using two. Its lid-lifting magnet was weak and only worked half the time, and you had to dip the whole front of the opener into the can to retrieve the top—messy and inconvenient.

INNOVATIVE POTHOLDERS

Every home kitchen should have a few good potholders. We saw several new designs trying to improve on the classic cotton square, and wondered: Could any raise the bar for protection and dexterity? To find out, we pitted five new potholders against our old winner, a classic terry-cloth square. To assess our six potholders, testers moved hot oven racks and loaded, rotated, and unloaded full baking sheets, cake pans, and pie plates. We also maneuvered 6.5-quart Dutch ovens filled with hot water in and out of 500-degree ovens and did the same with screaming-hot stainless-steel skillets, first empty and then loaded with sizzling whole chickens. We stained each potholder with tomato soup, left it overnight, and then washed and dried each five times (per manufacturer specifications), after which we assessed staining, wear, and shrinkage. Products appear below in order of preference.

HIGHLY RECOMMENDED	PERFORMANCE	TESTERS' COMMENTS

OXO Good Grips Silicone Pot Holder with Magnet
MODEL: 1148607 (licorice)
PRICE: $9.99 each
INNOVATION: Silicone/cotton combo
DIMENSIONS: 10 by 8 in
MATERIAL: Silicone and cotton
CLEANUP: Machine wash/dry

PROTECTION ★★★
DEXTERITY ★★★
CLEANUP ★★★

Whether maneuvering a screaming-hot stainless-steel skillet or a Dutch oven filled with boiling water, we always felt safe and confident using this potholder. It had cotton for flexibility and comfort and grippy, high-heat silicone for protection. At 10 by 8 inches, it was big enough for full coverage but also nimble, thanks to a pocket that allowed testers to precisely pinch thin baking sheet rims and to rotate cake pans with ease.

RECOMMENDED

LE CREUSET Fingertip Potholders
MODEL: TH5004
PRICE: $15 for two (sold as set)
INNOVATION: Small size
DIMENSIONS: 7 by 5 in
MATERIAL: Cotton
CLEANUP: Machine wash/air dry

PROTECTION ★★½
DEXTERITY ★★★
CLEANUP ★★★

These trim potholders wowed testers with their dexterity, comfort, and protection. Small but precise, they made rotating baking sheets, cake pans, and pie plates a cinch, and they still protected testers wielding 500-degree stainless-steel skillets. Like a folded dish towel, they required a smidge more mindfulness because their trim design left more hand exposed.

RECOMMENDED WITH RESERVATIONS

RITZ Basic Potholder
MODEL: 30024 (federal blue)
PRICE: $9.99 for two (sold as set)
INNOVATION: N/A
DIMENSIONS: 9 by 8 in
MATERIAL: Cotton
CLEANUP: Machine wash/dry

PROTECTION ★★
DEXTERITY ★★
CLEANUP ★★★

Our old favorite, a simple cotton square, was protective enough for handling baking sheets, cake pans, and pie plates—at 400 degrees or less. But any higher and it was too thin and left testers challenging the boundaries of work-appropriate language. It was cumbersome, too. Testers were constantly tucking away the excess fabric to avoid mashing cookies and denting cakes.

NOT RECOMMENDED

CALPHALON 6 x 10-in Pot Holder
MODEL: 32178 (biscotti)
PRICE: $9.99 each
INNOVATION: Silicone/cotton combo, smaller size
DIMENSIONS: 10 by 5 in
MATERIAL: Cotton and silicone
CLEANUP: Machine wash/air dry

PROTECTION ★½
DEXTERITY ★½
CLEANUP ★★★

This potholder slimmed down the classic square, but the shape didn't work. It was narrower in the middle, left the lower palm exposed where it was natural to grip, and testers burnt themselves more than once. Lengthwise, it was floppy and unwieldy; it got pinned under a hot skillet and keeled over, smashing cookies and dunking into cake batter.

SILICONEZONE Soft Cell Grid Potholders
MODEL: SZ11-KA-11426
PRICE: $9.99 each
INNOVATION: Silicone grid design
DIMENSIONS: 7¼ by 7¼ in
MATERIAL: Silicone
CLEANUP: Dishwasher-safe

PROTECTION ★★
DEXTERITY ★
CLEANUP ★★★

Even with a new grid design, an all-silicone potholder still proved too stiff. It couldn't fold away like fabric, so it smashed into cookies, crumbled pie crusts, and dove into cake batter. It was so stiff that it even thwacked a crater into a fully baked cake. It also wasn't protective enough to safely remove a skillet or a Dutch oven from a 500-degree oven.

TRUDEAU Stay Cool Silicone Pinch Grips
MODEL: 998500
PRICE: $7.99 for two (sold as set)
INNOVATION: Small size
DIMENSIONS: 2½ by 2½ in
MATERIAL: Silicone
CLEANUP: Dishwasher-safe

PROTECTION ★
DEXTERITY ★
CLEANUP ★★★

These small pinch grips excelled at rotating hot pans, but that was it. They only held three fingertips, which made handling anything heavy impossible, hot or cold. Protection-wise, they were useless, too. Testers didn't trust them near hot oven racks, skillets, baking sheets, cake pans, pie plates, or Dutch ovens. "I value my hands too much," said one.

INDEX

Note: Page references in *italics* indicate photographs.

Chile(s)
  Ancho-Orange Pork Burritos, 121–23, *122*
  Carne Guisada, 41–43, *42*
  Coffee-Chipotle Top Sirloin Roast, 136
  Crispy Salt and Pepper Shrimp, 189–91
  dried, toasting, 43
  Drunken Beans, 51–54, *52*
  Huevos Rancheros, *198*, 199–200
  Pumpkin Seed Dip, 4–5
  Red, Salsa, 133
  seeding, without gloves, 269
  Shrimp a la Diabla, 194–95
  Tomatillo Salsa, 6–8, *7*
Chilled Marinated Tofu, 55–58, *57*
Chives, Potato Biscuits with, 211–12, *213*
Chocolate
  Chess Pie, 255–58, *257*
  chopping, tip for, 268
  Cream Cheese Brownies, 236–39, *237*
  Crinkle Cookies, *232*, 233–34
  Milk, Cheesecake, 239–41
  milk, melting, 240
  Toffee Squares, 235–36
Chorizo and Manchego Breakfast Pizza, 205
Chutney, Cilantro-Mint, 55
Cilantro
  Drunken Beans, 51–54, *52*
  -Mint Chutney, 55
  Tomatillo Salsa, 6–8, *7*
Clams
  about, 280
  Steamed in White Wine, 280
Classic Single-Crust Pie Dough, 255
Cocoa Zucchini Bread with Dried Cherries, 209
Coconut
  Pie, French, 258–60
  unsweetened shredded, taste tests on, 260
Cod Fillets, Make-Ahead Crispy Breaded, 184–86
Coffee
  -Chipotle Top Sirloin Roast, 136
  cup stains, removing, 269
  filter, straining foods with, 268
  Latin Flan, 244
Collard greens, preparing, 32
Cookie cutter, stand-in for, 269
Cookie dough, portioning out, 274
Cookies and bars
  Chocolate Crinkle Cookies, *232*, 233–34

Cookies and bars *(cont.)*
  Cream Cheese Brownies, 236–39, *237*
  overbaked, preventing, 275
  Toffee Squares, 235–36
Cooling racks, improvising, 274
Coq au Riesling, 167–70, *168*
Corn kernels, removing from cob, 266
Cornmeal
  Savory Corn Muffins, 210–11
  Savory Corn Muffins with Cheddar and Scallions, 211
Cottage cheese
  Breakfast Pizza, 202–4, *203*
  Chorizo and Manchego Breakfast Pizza, 205
  Sausage and Red Bell Pepper Breakfast Pizza, 205
Counter space, extending, 267
Cream, whipped
  See Whipped Cream
Cream Cheese
  artisanal, taste tests on, 238
  Brownies, 236–39, *237*
  Milk Chocolate Cheesecake, 239–41
Crème Fraîche, 255
Crispy Onions, 49
Crispy Salt and Pepper Shrimp, 189–91
Croutons
  for Kale Caesar Salad, *14*, 15
  Spiced, 28
Cucumbers
  Tzatziki Sauce, 161
  Vegetable Bibimbap, 60–63, *61*
Curried dishes
  Make-Ahead Curried Chicken and Brown Rice with Red Peppers, 172–74
  Singapore Noodles, 103–6, *105*

D

Desserts
  Chocolate Chess Pie, 255–58, *257*
  Chocolate Crinkle Cookies, *232*, 233–34
  Cream Cheese Brownies, 236–39, *237*
  French Coconut Pie, 258–60
  Latin Flan
    Almond, 244
    Coffee, 244
    Orange-Cardamom, 244
    Perfect, 241–44, *242*
  Maple Syrup Pie, 252–55, *253*